PENGUIN BOOKS

THE PENGUIN COMPLETE LONGER NON-FICTION OF GEORGE ORWELL

Eric Arthur Blair (George Orwell) was born in 1903 in India, where his father worked for the Civil Service. The family moved to England in 1907 and in 1917 Orwell entered Eton, where he contributed regularly to the various college magazines. He left in 1921 and joined the Indian Imperial Police in Burma the following year. He resigned in 1928 having come to hate imperialism, as *Burmese Days* (1934), his first novel, shows.

After this he lived for several years in poverty, at times among tramps, experiences which he relates in *Down and Out in Paris and London* (1933). For a time he worked as a schoolteacher but due to poor health he gave this up and worked as a part-time assistant in a Hampstead bookshop; later he was able to earn his living reviewing novels for the *New English Weekly*, a post he kept until 1940. In 1936 he visited areas of mass unemployment in Lancashire and Yorkshire and *The Road to Wigan Pier* (1937) is a powerful description of the poverty he saw there. At the end of 1936 Orwell went to Spain to fight for the Republicans and was wounded; his account of the civil war, *Homage to Catalonia*, is considered by many to be his greatest achievement. During the Second World War he was a member of the Home Guard and worked for the BBC Eastern Service from 1940 to 1943. As literary editor of *Tribune* he contributed a regular page of political and literary commentary. From 1945 Orwell was the *Observer*'s war correspondent and later became a regular contributor to the *Manchester Evening News*. His unique political allegory, *Animal Farm*, was published in 1945, and it was this novel, together with *Nineteen Eighty-Four* (1949), which brought Orwell world-wide fame.

Orwell suffered from tuberculosis and was in and out of hospital from 1947 until his death in 1950 at the age of forty-six.

All Orwell's works have been published in Penguins.

THE
PENGUIN
COMPLETE LONGER
NON-FICTION
OF
GEORGE ORWELL

George Orwell

PENGUIN BOOKS
in association with Martin Secker & Warburg

Penguin Books Ltd, Harmondsworth, Middlesex, England
Penguin Books, 40 West 23rd Street, New York, New York 10010, U.S.A.
Penguin Books Australia Ltd, Ringwood, Victoria, Australia
Penguin Books Canada Ltd, 2801 John Street, Markham, Ontario, Canada L3R 1B4
Penguin Books (N.Z.) Ltd, 182-190 Wairau Road, Auckland 10, New Zealand

Down and Out in Paris and London first published by Victor Gollancz 1933
Published in Penguin Books 1940
Published in a new uniform edition by Martin Secker & Warburg 1949
Copyright © the Estate of Eric Blair, 1933

The Road to Wigan Pier first published by Victor Gollancz 1937
Published in Penguin Books 1962
Copyright © the Estate of Eric Blair, 1937

Homage to Catalonia first published by Martin Secker & Warburg 1938
Published in Penguin Books 1962
'Looking Back on the Spanish War' first published in *England Your
England* by Martin Secker & Warburg 1953
Published in one volume in Penguin Books 1966
Copyright © the Estate of Eric Blair, 1938, 1953

This collection published as *The Penguin Complete Longer Non-Fiction
of George Orwell* 1983
Copyright © the Estate of Eric Blair, 1983
All rights reserved

Scanned and phototypeset by
Comprehensive Text Processing, London
Reproduced, printed and bound in Great Britain by
Hazell Watson & Viney Limited,
Member of the BPCC Group,
Aylesbury, Bucks
Set in Times

CONTENTS

DOWN AND OUT
IN
PARIS AND LONDON

O scathful harm, condition of poverte!
CHAUCER

1

THE rue du Coq d'Or, Paris, seven in the morning. A succession of furious, choking yells from the street. Madame Monce, who kept the little hotel opposite mine, had come out on to the pavement to address a lodger on the third floor. Her bare feet were stuck into sabots and her grey hair was streaming down.

MADAME MONCE: '*Salope! Salope!* How many times have I told you not to squash bugs on the wallpaper? Do you think you've bought the hotel, eh? Why can't you throw them out of the window like everyone else? *Putain! Salope!*'

THE WOMAN ON THE THIRD FLOOR: '*Vache!*'

Thereupon a whole variegated chorus of yells, as windows were flung open on every side and half the street joined in the quarrel. They shut up abruptly ten minutes later, when a squadron of cavalry rode past and people stopped shouting to look at them.

I sketch this scene, just to convey something of the spirit of the rue du Coq d'Or. Not that quarrels were the only thing that happened there – but still, we seldom got through the morning without at least one outburst of this description. Quarrels, and the desolate cries of street hawkers, and the shouts of children chasing orange-peel over the cobbles, and at night loud singing and the sour reek of the refuse-carts, made up the atmosphere of the street.

It was a very narrow street – a ravine of tall, leprous houses, lurching towards one another in queer attitudes, as though they had all been frozen in the act of collapse. All the houses were hotels and packed to the tiles with lodgers, mostly Poles, Arabs and Italians. At the foot of the hotels were tiny *bistros*, where you could be drunk for the equivalent of a shilling. On Saturday nights about a third of the male population of the quarter was drunk. There was fighting over women, and the Arab navvies who lived in the cheapest hotels used to conduct mysterious feuds, and fight them out with chairs and occasionally revolvers. At night the policemen would only come through the street two together. It was a fairly rackety place. And yet amid the noise and dirt lived the usual respectable French shopkeepers, bakers and laundresses and the like, keeping themselves to themselves and quietly piling up small fortunes. It was quite a representative Paris slum.

My hotel was called the Hôtel des Trois Moineaux. It was a dark, rickety warren of five storeys, cut up by wooden partitions into forty rooms. The rooms were small and inveterately dirty, for there was no maid, and Madame F., the *patronne*, had no time to do any sweeping. The walls were as thin as matchwood, and to hide the cracks they had been covered with layer after layer of pink paper, which had come loose and housed innumerable bugs. Near the ceiling long lines of bugs marched all day like columns of soldiers, and at night came down ravenously hungry, so that one had to get up every few hours and kill them in hecatombs. Sometimes when the bugs got too bad one used to burn sulphur and drive them into the next room; whereupon the lodger next door would retort by having *his* room sulphured, and drive the bugs back. It was a dirty place, but homelike, for Madame F. and her husband were good sorts. The rent of the rooms varied between thirty and fifty francs a week.

The lodgers were a floating population, largely foreigners, who used to turn up without luggage, stay a week and then disappear again. They were of every trade – cobblers, bricklayers, stonemasons, navvies, students, prostitutes, rag-pickers. Some of them were fantastically poor. In one of the attics there was a Bulgarian student who made fancy shoes for the American market. From six to twelve he sat on his bed, making a dozen pairs of shoes and earning thirty-five francs; the rest of the day he attended lectures at the Sorbonne. He was studying for the Church, and books of theology lay face-down on his leather-strewn floor. In another room lived a Russian woman and her son, who called himself an artist. The mother worked sixteen hours a day, darning socks at twenty-five centimes a sock, while the son, decently dressed, loafed in the Montparnasse cafés. One room was let to two different lodgers, one a day worker and the other a night worker. In another room a widower shared the same bed with his two grown-up daughters, both consumptive.

There were eccentric characters in the hotel. The Paris slums are a gathering-place for eccentric people – people who have fallen into solitary, half-mad grooves of life and given up trying to be normal or decent. Poverty frees them from ordinary standards of behaviour, just as money frees people from work. Some of the lodgers in our hotel lived lives that were curious beyond words.

There were the Rougiers, for instance, an old, ragged, dwarfish couple who plied an extraordinary trade. They used to sell postcards on the Boulevard St Michel. The curious thing was that the postcards were sold in sealed packets as pornographic ones, but were actually photographs of châteaux on the Loire; the buyers did not discover this till too late, and of course never complained. The Rougiers earned about a hundred francs a week, and by strict economy managed to be always half starved and half drunk. The filth of their room was such that one could smell it on the floor below. According to Madame F., neither of the Rougiers had taken off their clothes for four years.

Or there was Henri, who worked in the sewers. He was a tall, melancholy man with curly hair, rather romantic-looking in his long, sewer-man's boots. Henri's peculiarity was that he did not speak, except for the purposes of work, literally for days together. Only a year before he had been a chauffeur in good employ and saving money. One day he fell in love, and when the girl refused him he lost his temper and kicked her. On being kicked the girl fell desperately in love with Henri, and for a fortnight they lived together and spent a thousand francs of Henri's money. Then the girl was unfaithful; Henri planted a knife in her upper arm and was sent to prison for six months. As soon as she had been stabbed the girl fell more in love with Henri than ever, and the two made up their quarrel and agreed that when Henri came out of jail he should buy a taxi and they would marry and settle down. But a fortnight later the girl was unfaithful again, and when Henri came out she was with child. Henri did not stab her again. He drew out all his savings and went on a drinking-bout that ended in another month's imprisonment; after that he went to work in the sewers. Nothing would induce Henri to talk. If you asked him why he worked in the sewers he never answered, but simply crossed his wrists to signify handcuffs, and jerked his head southward, towards the prison. Bad luck seemed to have turned him half-witted in a single day.

Or there was R., an Englishman, who lived six months of the year in Putney with his parents and six months in France. During his time in France he drank four litres of wine a day, and six litres on Saturdays; he had once travelled as far as the Azores, because the wine there is cheaper than anywhere in Europe. He was a gentle, domesticated creature, never rowdy or quarrelsome, and never sober. He would lie in bed till midday, and from then till midnight he was in his corner of the *bistro*, quietly and methodically soaking. While he soaked he talked, in a refined, womanish voice, about antique furniture. Except myself, R. was the only Englishman in the quarter.

There were plenty of other people who lived lives just as eccentric as these: Monsieur Jules, the Roumanian, who had a glass eye and would not admit it, Furex the Limousin stonemason, Roucolle the miser – he died before my time, though – old Laurent the rag-merchant, who used to copy his signature from a slip of paper he carried in his pocket. It would be fun to write some of their biographies, if one had time. I am trying to describe the people in our quarter, not for the mere curiosity, but because they are all part of the story. Poverty is what I am writing about, and I had my first contact with poverty in this slum. The slum, with its dirt and its queer lives, was first an object-lesson in poverty, and then the background of my own experiences. It is for that reason that I try to give some idea of what life was like there.

2

LIFE in the quarter. Our *bistro*, for instance, at the foot of the Hôtel des Trois Moineaux. A tiny brick-floored room, half underground, with wine-sodden tables, and a photograph of a funeral inscribed '*Crédit est mort*'; and red-sashed workmen carving sausage with big jack-knives; and Madame F., a splendid Auvergnat peasant woman with the face of a strong-minded cow, drinking Malaga all day 'for her stomach'; and games of dice for *apéritifs*; and songs about '*Les Fraises et Les Framboises*', and about Madelon, who said, '*Comment épouser un soldat, moi qui aime tout le régiment?*'; and extraordinarily public love-making. Half the hotel used to meet in the *bistro* in the evenings. I wish one could find a pub in London a quarter as cheery.

One heard queer conversations in the *bistro*. As a sample I give you Charlie, one of the local curiosities, talking.

Charlie was a youth of family and education who had run away from home and lived on occasional remittances. Picture him very pink and young, with the fresh cheeks and soft brown hair of a nice little boy, and lips excessively red and wet, like cherries. His feet are tiny, his arms abnormally short, his hands dimpled like a baby's. He has a way of dancing and capering while he talks, as though he were too happy and too full of life to keep still for an instant. It is three in the afternoon, and there is no one in the *bistro* except Madame F. and one or two men who are out of work; but it is all the same to Charlie whom he talks to, so long as he can talk about himself. He declaims like an orator on a barricade, rolling the words on his tongue and gesticulating with his short arms. His small, rather piggy eyes glitter with enthusiasm. He is, somehow, profoundly disgusting to see.

He is talking of love, his favourite subject.

'*Ah, l'amour, l'amour! Ah, que les femmes m'ont tué!* Alas, *messieurs et dames*, women have been my ruin, beyond all hope my ruin. At twenty-two I am utterly worn out and finished. But what things I have learned, what abysses of wisdom have I not plumbed! How great a thing it is to have acquired the true wisdom, to have become in the highest sense of the word a civilized man, to have become *raffiné, vicieux,*' etc. etc.

'*Messieurs et dames*, I perceive that you are sad. *Ah, mais la vie est belle* – you must not be sad. Be more gay, I beseech you!

> 'Fill high ze bowl vid Samian vine,
> Ve vill not sink of semes like zese!

'*Ah, que la vie est belle!* Listen, *messieurs et dames*, out of the fullness of my experience I will discourse to you of love. I will explain to you what is the true meaning of love – what is the true sensibility, the higher, more refined pleasure which is known to civilized men alone. I will tell you of the happiest day of my life. Alas, but I am past the time when I could know such happiness as that. It is gone for ever – the very possibility, even the desire for it, are gone.

'Listen, then. It was two years ago; my brother was in Paris – he is a lawyer – and my parents had told him to find me and take me out to dinner. We hate each other, my brother and I, but we preferred not to disobey my parents. We dined, and at dinner he grew very drunk upon three bottles of Bordeaux. I took him back to his hotel, and on the way I bought a bottle of brandy, and when we had arrived I made my brother drink a tumblerful of it – I told him it was something to make him sober. He drank it, and immediately he fell down like somebody in a fit, dead drunk. I lifted him up and propped his back against the bed; then I went through his pockets. I found eleven hundred francs, and with that I hurried down the stairs, jumped into a taxi, and escaped. My brother did not know my address – I was safe.

'Where does a man go when he has money? To the *bordels*, naturally. But you do not suppose that I was going to waste my time on some vulgar debauchery fit only for navvies? Confound it, one is a civilized man! I was fastidious, *exigeant*, you understand, with a thousand francs in my pocket. It was midnight before I found what I was looking for. I had fallen in with a very smart youth of eighteen, dressed *en smoking* and with his hair cut *à l'américaine*, and we were talking in a quiet *bistro* away from the boulevards. We understood one another well, that youth and I. We talked of this and that, and discussed ways of diverting oneself. Presently we took a taxi together and were driven away.

'The taxi stopped in a narrow, solitary street with a single gas-lamp flaring at the end. There were dark puddles among the stones. Down one side ran the high, blank wall of a convent. My guide led me to a tall, ruinous house with shuttered windows, and knocked several times at the door. Presently there was a sound of footsteps and a shooting of bolts, and the door opened a little. A hand came round the edge of it; it was a large, crooked hand, that held itself palm upwards under our noses, demanding money.

'My guide put his foot between the door and the step. "How much do you want?" he said.

'"A thousand francs," said a woman's voice. "Pay up at once or you don't come in."

'I put a thousand francs into the hand and gave the remaining hundred to my guide: he said good night and left me. I could hear the voice inside counting the notes, and then a thin old crow of a woman in a black dress put her nose out and regarded me suspiciously before letting me in. It was very dark inside: I could see nothing except a flaring gas-jet that illuminated a patch of plaster wall, throwing everything else into deeper shadow. There was a smell of rats and dust. Without speaking, the old woman lighted a candle at the gas-jet, then hobbled in front of me down a stone passage to the top of a flight of stone steps.

'"*Voilà!*" she said; "go down into the cellar there and do what you like. I shall see nothing, hear nothing, know nothing. You are free, you understand – perfectly free."

'Ha, *messieurs*, need I describe to you – *forcément*, you know it yourselves – that shiver, half of terror and half of joy, that goes through one at these moments? I crept down, feeling my way; I could hear my breathing and the scraping of my shoes on the stones, otherwise all was silence. At the bottom of the stairs my hand met an electric switch. I turned it, and a great electrolier of twelve red globes flooded the cellar with a red light. And behold, I was not in a cellar, but in a bedroom, a great, rich, garish bedroom, coloured blood red from top to bottom. Figure it to yourselves, *messieurs et dames*! Red carpet on the floor, red paper on the walls, red plush on the chairs, even the ceiling red; everywhere red, burning into the eyes. It was a heavy, stifling red, as though the light were shining through bowls of blood. At the far end stood a huge, square bed, with quilts red like the rest, and on it a girl was lying, dressed in a frock

of red velvet. At the sight of me she shrank away and tried to hide her
knees under the short dress.

'I had halted by the door. "Come here, my chicken," I called to her.

'She gave a whimper of fright. With a bound I was beside the bed; she
tried to elude me, but I seized her by the throat – like this, do you see?
– tight! She struggled, she began to cry out for mercy, but I held her fast,
forcing back her head and staring down into her face. She was twenty
years old, perhaps; her face was the broad, dull face of a stupid child, but
it was coated with paint and powder, and her blue, stupid eyes, shining in
the red light, wore that shocked, distorted look that one sees nowhere save
in the eyes of these women. She was some peasant girl, doubtless, whom
her parents had sold into slavery.

'Without another word I pulled her off the bed and threw her on to the
floor. And then I fell upon her like a tiger! Ah, the joy, the incomparable
rapture of that time! There, *messieurs et dames*, is what I would expound
to you; *voilà l'amour*! There is the true love, there is the only thing in the
world worth striving for; there is the thing beside which all your arts and
ideals, all your philosophies and creeds, all your fine words and high
attitudes, are as pale and profitless as ashes. When one has experienced
love – the true love – what is there in the world that seems more than a
mere ghost of joy?

'More and more savagely I renewed the attack. Again and again the
girl tried to escape; she cried out for mercy anew, but I laughed at her.

' "Mercy!" I said, "do you suppose I have come here to show mercy?
Do you suppose I have paid a thousand francs for that?" I swear to you,
messieurs et dames, that if it were not for that accursed law that robs us
of our liberty, I would have murdered her at that moment.

'Ah, how she screamed, with what bitter cries of agony. But there was
no one to hear them; down there under the streets of Paris we were as
secure as at the heart of a pyramid. Tears streamed down the girl's face,
washing away the powder in long, dirty smears. Ah, that irrecoverable
time! You, *messieurs et dames*, you who have not cultivated the finer
sensibilities of love, for you such pleasure is almost beyond conception.
And I too, now that my youth is gone – ah, youth! – shall never again see
life so beautiful as that. It is finished.

'Ah yes, it is gone – gone for ever. Ah, the poverty, the shortness, the
disappointment of human joy! For in reality – *car en réalité*, what is the
duration of the supreme moment of love? It is nothing, an instant, a second
perhaps. A second of ecstasy, and after that – dust, ashes, nothingness.

'And so, just for one instant, I captured the supreme happiness, the highest and most refined emotion to which human beings can attain. And in the same moment it was finished, and I was left – to what? All my savagery, my passion, were scattered like the petals of a rose. I was left cold and languid, full of vain regrets; in my revulsion I even felt a kind of pity for the weeping girl on the floor. Is it not nauseous, that we should be the prey of such mean emotions? I did not look at the girl again; my sole thought was to get away. I hastened up the steps of the vault and out into the street. It was dark and bitterly cold, the streets were empty, the stones echoed under my heels with a hollow, lonely ring. All my money was gone, I had not even the price of a taxi fare. I walked back alone to my cold, solitary room.

'But there, *messieurs et dames*, that is what I promised to expound to you. That is Love. That was the happiest day of my life.'

He was a curious specimen, Charlie. I describe him, just to show what diverse characters could be found flourishing in the Coq d'Or quarter.

3

I LIVED in the Coq d'Or quarter for about a year and a half. One day, in summer, I found that I had just four hundred and fifty francs left, and beyond this nothing but thirty-six francs a week, which I earned by giving English lessons. Hitherto I had not thought about the future, but I now realized that I must do something at once. I decided to start looking for a job, and – very luckily, as it turned out – I took the precaution of paying two hundred francs for a month's rent in advance. With the other two hundred and fifty francs, besides the English lessons, I could live a month, and in a month I should probably find work. I aimed at becoming a guide to one of the tourist companies, or perhaps an interpreter. However, a piece of bad luck prevented this.

One day there turned up at the hotel a young Italian who called himself a compositor. He was rather an ambiguous person, for he wore side whiskers, which are the mark either of an apache or an intellectual, and nobody was quite certain in which class to put him. Madame F. did not like the look of him, and made him pay a week's rent in advance. The Italian paid the rent and stayed six nights at the hotel. During this time he managed to prepare some duplicate keys, and on the last night he robbed a dozen rooms, including mine. Luckily, he did not find the money that was in my pockets, so I was not left penniless. I was left with just forty-seven francs – that is, seven and tenpence.

This put an end to my plans of looking for work. I had now got to live at the rate of about six francs a day, and from the start it was too difficult to leave much thought for anything else. It was now that my experiences of poverty began – for six francs a day, if not actual poverty, is on the fringe of it. Six francs is a shilling, and you can live on a shilling a day in Paris if you know how. But it is a complicated business.

It is altogether curious, your first contact with poverty. You have thought so much about poverty – it is the thing you have feared all your life, the thing you knew would happen to you sooner or later; and it is all so utterly and prosaically different. You thought it would be quite simple; it is extraordinarily complicated. You thought it would be terrible; it is merely squalid and boring. It is the peculiar *lowness* of poverty that you discover first; the shifts that it puts you to, the complicated meanness, the crust-wiping.

You discover, for instance, the secrecy attaching to poverty. At a sudden stroke you have been reduced to an income of six francs a day. But of course you dare not admit it – you have got to pretend that you are living quite as usual. From the start it tangles you in a net of lies, and even with the lies you can hardly manage it. You stop sending clothes to the laundry, and the laundress catches you in the street and asks you why; you mumble something, and she, thinking you are sending the clothes elsewhere, is your enemy for life. The tobacconist keeps asking why you have cut down your smoking. There are letters you want to answer, and cannot, because stamps are too expensive. And then there are your meals – meals are the worst difficulty of all. Every day at meal-times you go out, ostensibly to a restaurant, and loaf an hour in the Luxembourg Gardens, watching the pigeons. Afterwards you smuggle your food home in your pockets. Your food is bread and margarine, or bread and wine, and even the nature of the food is governed by lies. You have to buy rye bread instead of household bread, because the rye loaves, though dearer, are round and can be smuggled in your pockets. This wastes you a franc a day. Sometimes, to keep up appearances, you have to spend sixty centimes on a drink, and go correspondingly short of food. Your linen gets filthy, and you run out of soap and razor-blades. Your hair wants cutting, and you try to cut it yourself, with such fearful results that you have to go to the barber after all, and spend the equivalent of a day's food. All day you are telling lies, and expensive lies.

You discover the extreme precariousness of your six francs a day. Mean disasters happen and rob you of food. You have spent your last eighty centimes on half a litre of milk, and are boiling it over the spirit lamp. While it boils a bug runs down your forearm; you give the bug a flick with your nail, and it falls, plop! straight into the milk. There is nothing for it but to throw the milk away and go foodless.

You go to the baker's to buy a pound of bread, and you wait while the girl cuts a pound for another customer. She is clumsy, and cuts more than a pound. '*Pardon, monsieur*,' she says, 'I suppose you don't mind paying two sous extra?' Bread is a franc a pound, and you have exactly a franc. When you think that you too might be asked to pay two sous extra, and would have to confess that you could not, you bolt in panic. It is hours before you dare venture into a baker's shop again.

You go to the greengrocer's to spend a franc on a kilogram of potatoes. But one of the pieces that make up the franc is a Belgian piece, and the shopman refuses it. You slink out of the shop, and can never go there again.

You have strayed into a respectable quarter, and you see a prosperous friend coming. To avoid him you dodge into the nearest café. Once in the café you must buy something, so you spend your last fifty centimes on a glass of black coffee with a dead fly in it. One could multiply these disasters by the hundred. They are part of the process of being hard up.

You discover what it is like to be hungry. With bread and margarine in your belly, you go out and look into the shop windows. Everywhere there is food insulting you in huge, wasteful piles; whole dead pigs, baskets of hot loaves, great yellow blocks of butter, strings of sausages, mountains of potatoes, vast Gruyère cheeses like grindstones. A snivelling self-pity comes over you at the sight of so much food. You plan to grab a loaf and run, swallowing it before they catch you; and you refrain, from pure funk.

You discover the boredom which is inseparable from poverty; the times when you have nothing to do and, being underfed, can interest yourself in nothing. For half a day at a time you lie on your bed, feeling like the *jeune squelette* in Baudelaire's poem. Only food could rouse you. You discover that a man who has gone even a week on bread and margarine is not a man any longer, only a belly with a few accessory organs.

This – one could describe it further, but it is all in the same style – is life on six francs a day. Thousands of people in Paris live it – struggling artists and students, prostitutes when their luck is out, out-of-work people of all kinds. It is the suburbs, as it were, of poverty.

I continued in this style for about three weeks. The forty-seven francs were soon gone, and I had to do what I could on thirty-six francs a week from the English lessons. Being inexperienced, I handled the money badly, and sometimes I was a day without food. When this happened I used to sell a few of my clothes, smuggling them out of the hotel in small packets and taking them to a second-hand shop in the rue de la Montagne St Geneviève. The shopman was a red-haired Jew, an extraordinary disagreeable man, who used to fall into furious rages at the sight of a client. From his manner one would have supposed that we had done him some injury by coming to him. '*Merde!*' he used to shout, '*you* here again? What do you think this is? A soup kitchen?' And he paid incredibly low prices. For a hat which I had bought for twenty-five shillings and scarcely worn he gave five francs; for a good pair of shoes, five francs; for shirts, a franc each. He always preferred to exchange rather than buy, and he had a trick of thrusting some useless article into one's hand and then pretending that one had accepted it. Once I saw him take a good overcoat from an old woman, put two white billiard-balls into her hand, and then push her rapidly out of the shop before she could protest. It would have been a pleasure to flatten the Jew's nose, if only one could have afforded it.

These three weeks were squalid and uncomfortable, and evidently there was worse coming, for my rent would be due before long. Nevertheless, things were not a quarter as bad as I had expected. For, when you are approaching poverty, you make one discovery which outweighs some of the others. You discover boredom and mean complications and the beginnings of hunger, but you also discover the great redeeming feature of poverty: the fact that it annihilates the future. Within certain limits, it is actually true that the less money you have, the less you worry. When you have a hundred francs in the world you are liable to the most craven panics. When you have only three francs you are quite indifferent; for three francs will feed you till tomorrow, and you cannot think further than that. You are bored, but you are not afraid. You think vaguely, 'I shall be starving in a day or two – shocking, isn't it?' And then the mind wanders to other topics. A bread and margarine diet does, to some extent, provide its own anodyne.

And there is another feeling that is a great consolation in poverty. I believe everyone who has been hard up has experienced it. It is a feeling of relief, almost of pleasure, at knowing yourself at last genuinely down and out. You have talked so often of going to the dogs – and well, here are the dogs, and you have reached them, and you can stand it. It takes off a lot of anxiety.

4

ONE day my English lessons ceased abruptly. The weather was getting hot and one of my pupils, feeling too lazy to go on with his lessons, dismissed me. The other disappeared from his lodgings without notice, owing me twelve francs. I was left with only thirty centimes and no tobacco. For a day and a half I had nothing to eat or smoke, and then, too hungry to put it off any longer, I packed my remaining clothes into my suitcase and took them to the pawnshop. This put an end to all pretence of being in funds, for I could not take my clothes out of the hotel without asking Madame F.'s leave. I remember, however, how surprised she was at my asking her instead of removing the clothes on the sly, shooting the moon being a common trick in our quarter.

It was the first time that I had been in a French pawnshop. One went through grandiose stone portals (marked, of course, '*Liberté, Égalité, Fraternité*' – they write that even over the police stations in France) into a large, bare room like a school classroom, with a counter and rows of benches. Forty or fifty people were waiting. One handed one's pledge over the counter and sat down. Presently, when the clerk had assessed its value he would call out, '*Numéro* such and such, will you take fifty francs?' Sometimes it was only fifteen francs, or ten, or five – whatever it was, the whole room knew it. As I came in the clerk called with an air of offence, '*Numéro* 83 – here!' and gave a little whistle and a beckon, as though calling a dog. *Numéro* 83 stepped to the counter; he was an old bearded man, with an overcoat buttoned up at the neck and frayed trouser-ends. Without a word the clerk shot the bundle across the counter – evidently it was worth nothing. It fell to the ground and came open, displaying four pairs of men's woollen pants. No one could help laughing. Poor *Numéro* 83 gathered up his pants and shambled out, muttering to himself.

The clothes I was pawning, together with the suitcase, had cost over twenty pounds, and were in good condition. I thought they must be worth ten pounds, and a quarter of this (one expects quarter value at a pawnshop) was two hundred and fifty or three hundred francs. I waited without anxiety, expecting two hundred francs at the worst.

At last the clerk called my number: '*Numéro* 97!'

'Yes,' I said, standing up.

'Seventy francs?'

Seventy francs for ten pounds' worth of clothes! But it was no use arguing; I had seen someone else attempt to argue, and the clerk had instantly refused the pledge. I took the money and the pawnticket and walked out. I had now no clothes except what I stood up in – the coat badly out at the elbow – an overcoat, moderately pawnable, and one spare shirt. Afterwards, when it was too late, I learned that it was wiser to go to a pawnshop in the afternoon. The clerks are French, and, like most French people, are in a bad temper till they have eaten their lunch.

When I got home, Madame F. was sweeping the *bistro* floor. She came up the steps to meet me. I could see in her eye that she was uneasy about my rent.

'Well,' she said, 'what did you get for your clothes? Not much, eh?'

'Two hundred francs,' I said promptly.

'*Tiens!*' she said, surprised; 'well, *that's* not bad. How expensive those English clothes must be!'

The lie saved a lot of trouble, and, strangely enough, it came true. A few days later I did receive exactly two hundred francs due to me for a newspaper article, and, though it hurt to do it, I at once paid every penny of it in rent. So, though I came near to starving in the following weeks, I was hardly ever without a roof.

It was now absolutely necessary to find work, and I remembered a friend of mine, a Russian waiter named Boris, who might be able to help me. I had first met him in the public ward of a hospital, where he was being treated for arthritis in the left leg. He had told me to come to him if I were ever in difficulties.

I must say something about Boris, for he was a curious character and my close friend for a long time. He was a big, soldierly man of about thirty-five, and had been good-looking, but since his illness he had grown immensely fat from lying in bed. Like most Russian refugees, he had had an adventurous life. His parents, killed in the Revolution, had been rich people, and he had served through the war in the Second Siberian Rifles, which, according to him, was the best regiment in the Russian Army. After the war he had first worked in a brush factory, then as a porter at Les Halles, then had become a dishwasher, and had finally worked his way up to be a waiter. When he fell ill he was at the Hôtel Scribe, and taking a hundred francs a day in tips. His ambition was to become a *maître d'hôtel*, save fifty thousand francs, and set up a small, select restaurant on the Right Bank.

Boris always talked of the war as the happiest time of his life. War and soldiering were his passion; he had read innumerable books of strategy and military history, and could tell you all about the theories of Napoleon, Kutuzof, Clausewitz, Moltke and Foch. Anything to do with soldiers pleased him. His favourite café was the Closerie des Lilas in Montparnasse, simply because the statue of Marshal Ney stands outside it. Later on, Boris and I sometimes went to the rue du Commerce together. If we went by Métro, Boris always got out at Cambronne station instead of Commerce, though Commerce was nearer; he liked the association with General Cambronne, who was called on to surrender at Waterloo, and answered simply, 'Merde!'

The only things left to Boris by the Revolution were his medals and some photographs of his old regiment; he had kept these when everything else went to the pawnshop. Almost every day he would spread the photographs out on the bed and talk about them:

'Voilà, mon ami. There you see me at the head of my company. Fine big men, eh? Not like these little rats of Frenchmen. A captain at twenty – not bad, eh? Yes, a captain in the Second Siberian Rifles; and my father was a colonel.

'Ah, mais, mon ami, the ups and downs of life! A captain in the Russian Army, and then, piff! the Revolution – every penny gone. In 1916 I stayed a week at the Hôtel Édouard Sept; in 1920 I was trying for a job as night watchman. I have been night watchman, cellarman, floor scrubber, dishwasher, porter, lavatory attendant. I have tipped waiters, and I have been tipped by waiters.

'Ah, but I have known what it is to live like a gentleman, mon ami. I do not say it to boast, but the other day I was trying to compute how many mistresses I have had in my life, and I made it out to be over two hundred. Yes, at least two hundred . . . Ah, well, ça reviendra. Victory is to him who fights the longest. Courage!' etc. etc.

Boris had a queer, changeable nature. He always wished himself back in the army, but he had also been a waiter long enough to acquire the waiter's outlook. Though he had never saved more than a few thousand francs, he took it for granted that in the end he would be able to set up his own restaurant and grow rich. All waiters, I afterwards found, talk and think of this; it is what reconciles them to being waiters. Boris used to talk interestingly about hotel life:

'Waiting is a gamble,' he used to say; 'you may die poor, you may make your fortune in a year. You are not paid wages, you depend on tips – ten per cent of the bill, and a commission from the wine companies on champagne corks. Sometimes the tips are enormous. The barman at Maxim's, for instance, makes five hundred francs a day. More than five hundred, in the season . . . I have made two hundred francs a day myself. It was at a hotel in Biarritz, in the season. The whole staff, from the manager down to the *plongeurs*, was working twenty-one hours a day. Twenty-one hours' work and two and a half hours in bed, for a month on end. Still, it was worth it, at two hundred francs a day.

'You never know when a stroke of luck is coming. Once when I was at the Hôtel Royal an American customer sent for me before dinner and ordered twenty-four brandy cocktails. I brought them all together on a tray, in twenty-four glasses. "Now, *garçon*," said the customer (he was drunk), "I'll drink twelve and you'll drink twelve, and if you can walk to the door afterwards you get a hundred francs." I walked to the door, and he gave me a hundred francs. And every night for six days he did the same thing; twelve brandy cocktails, then a hundred francs. A few months later I heard he had been extradited by the American Government – embezzlement. There is something fine, do you not think, about these Americans?'

I liked Boris, and we had interesting times together, playing chess and talking about war and hotels. Boris used often to suggest that I should become a waiter. 'The life would suit you,' he used to say; 'when you are in work, with a hundred francs a day and a nice mistress, it's not bad. You say you go in for writing. Writing is bosh. There is only one way to make money at writing, and that is to marry a publisher's daughter. But you would make a good waiter if you shaved that moustache off. You are tall and you speak English – those are the chief things a waiter needs. Wait till I can bend this accursed leg, *mon ami*. And then, if you are ever out of a job, come to me.'

Now that I was short of my rent, and getting hungry, I remembered Boris's promise, and decided to look him up at once. I did not hope to become a waiter so easily as he had promised, but of course I knew how to scrub dishes, and no doubt he could get me a job in the kitchen. He had said that dishwashing jobs were to be had for the asking during the summer. It was a great relief to remember that I had after all one influential friend to fall back on.

5

A SHORT time before, Boris had given me an address in the rue du Marché des Blancs Manteaux. All he had said in his letter was that 'things were not marching too badly', and I assumed that he was back at the Hôtel Scribe, touching his hundred francs a day. I was full of hope, and wondered why I had been fool enough not to go to Boris before. I saw myself in a cosy restaurant, with jolly cooks singing love-songs as they broke eggs into the pan, and five solid meals a day. I even squandered two francs fifty on a packet of Gaulois Bleu, in anticipation of my wages.

In the morning I walked down to the rue du Marché des Blancs Manteaux; with a shock, I found it a slummy back street as bad as my own. Boris's hotel was the dirtiest hotel in the street. From its dark doorway there came out a vile, sour odour, a mixture of slops and synthetic soup – it was Bouillon Zip, twenty-five centimes a packet. A misgiving came over me. People who drink Bouillon Zip are starving, or near it. Could Boris possibly be earning a hundred francs a day? A surly *patron*, sitting in the office, said to me, Yes, the Russian was at home – in the attic. I went up six flights of narrow, winding stairs, the Bouillon Zip growing stronger as one got higher. Boris did not answer when I knocked at his door, so I opened it and went in.

The room was an attic, ten feet square, lighted only by a skylight, its sole furniture a narrow iron bedstead, a chair, and a washhand-stand with one game leg. A long S-shaped chain of bugs marched slowly across the wall above the bed. Boris was lying asleep, naked, his large belly making a mound under the grimy sheet. His chest was spotted with insect bites. As I came in he woke up, rubbed his eyes, and groaned deeply.

'Name of Jesus Christ!' he exclaimed, 'oh, name of Jesus Christ, my back! Curse it, I believe my back is broken!'

'What's the matter?' I exclaimed.

'My back is broken, that is all. I have spent the night on the floor. Oh, name of Jesus Christ! If you knew what my back feels like!'

'My dear Boris, are you ill?'

'Not ill, only starving – yes, starving to death if this goes on much longer. Besides sleeping on the floor, I have lived on two francs a day for weeks past. It is fearful. You have come at a bad moment, *mon ami*.'

It did not seem much use to ask whether Boris still had his job at the Hôtel Scribe. I hurried downstairs and bought a loaf of bread. Boris threw himself on the bread and ate half of it, after which he felt better, sat up in bed, and told me what was the matter with him. He had failed to get a job after leaving the hospital, because he was still very lame, and he had spent all his money and pawned everything, and finally starved for several days. He had slept a week on the quay under the Pont d'Austerlitz, among some empty wine barrels. For the past fortnight he had been living in this room, together with a Jew, a mechanic. It appeared (there was some complicated explanation) that the Jew owed Boris three hundred francs, and was repaying this by letting him sleep on the floor and allowing him two francs a day for food. Two francs would buy a bowl of coffee and three rolls. The Jew went to work at seven in the mornings, and after that Boris would leave his sleeping-place (it was beneath the skylight, which let in the rain) and get into the bed. He could not sleep much even there owing to the bugs, but it rested his back after the floor.

It was a great disappointment, when I had come to Boris for help, to find him even worse off than myself. I explained that I had only about sixty francs left and must get a job immediately. By this time, however, Boris had eaten the rest of the bread and was feeling cheerful and talkative. He said carelessly:

'Good heavens, what are you worrying about? Sixty francs – why, it's a fortune! Please hand me that shoe, *mon ami*. I'm going to smash some of those bugs if they come within reach.'

'But do you think there's any chance of getting a job?'

'Chance? It's a certainty. In fact, I have got something already. There is a new Russian restaurant which is to open in a few days in the rue du Commerce. It is *une chose entendue* that I am to be *maître d'hôtel*. I can easily get you a job in the kitchen. Five hundred francs a month and your food – tips, too, if you are lucky.'

'But in the meantime? I've got to pay my rent before long.'

'Oh, we shall find something. I have got a few cards up my sleeve. There are people who owe me money, for instance – Paris is full of them. One of them is bound to pay up before long. Then think of all the women who have been my mistress! A woman never forgets, you know – I have only to ask and they will help me. Besides, the Jew tells me he is going to steal some magnetos from the garage where he works, and he will pay us five francs a day to clean them before he sells them. That alone would keep us. Never worry, *mon ami*. Nothing is easier to get than money.'

'Well, let's go out now and look for a job.'

'Presently, *mon ami*. We shan't starve, don't you fear. This is only the fortune of war – I've been in a worse hole scores of times. It's only a question of persisting. Remember Foch's maxim: "*Attaquez! Attaquez! Attaquez!*" '

It was midday before Boris decided to get up. All the clothes he now had left were one suit, with one shirt, collar and tie, a pair of shoes almost worn out, and a pair of socks all holes. He had also an overcoat which was to be pawned in the last extremity. He had a suitcase, a wretched twenty-franc cardboard thing, but very important, because the *patron* of the hotel believed that it was full of clothes – without that, he would probably have turned Boris out of doors. What it actually contained were the medals and photographs, various odds and ends, and huge bundles of love-letters. In spite of all this Boris managed to keep a fairly smart appearance. He shaved without soap and with a razor-blade two months old, tied his tie so that the holes did not show, and carefully stuffed the soles of his shoes with newspaper. Finally, when he was dressed, he produced an ink-bottle and inked the skin of his ankles where it showed through his socks. You would never have thought, when it was finished, that he had recently been sleeping under the Seine bridges.

We went to a small café off the rue de Rivoli, a well-known rendezvous of hotel managers and employees. At the back was a dark, cave-like room where all kinds of hotel workers were sitting – smart young waiters, others not so smart and clearly hungry, fat pink cooks, greasy dishwashers, battered old scrubbing-women. Everyone had an untouched glass of black coffee in front of him. The place was, in effect, an employment bureau, and the money spent on drinks was the *patron*'s commission. Sometimes a stout, important-looking man, obviously a restaurateur, would come in and speak to the barman, and the barman would call to one of the people at the back of the café. But he never called to Boris or me, and we left after two hours, as the etiquette was that you could only stay two hours for one drink. We learned afterwards, when it was too late, that the dodge was to bribe the barman; if you could afford twenty francs he would generally get you a job.

We went to the Hôtel Scribe and waited an hour on the pavement, hoping that the manager would come out, but he never did. Then we dragged ourselves down to the rue du Commerce, only to find that the new restaurant, which was being redecorated, was shut up and the *patron* away. It was now night. We had walked fourteen kilometres over pavement, and we were so tired that we had to waste one franc fifty on going home by Métro. Walking was agony to Boris with his game leg, and his optimism wore thinner and thinner as the day went on. When he got out of the Métro at the Place d'Italie he was in despair. He began to say that it was no use looking for work – there was nothing for it but to try crime.

'Sooner rob than starve, *mon ami*. I have often planned it. A fat, rich American – some dark corner down Montparnasse way – a cobblestone in a stocking – bang! And then go through his pockets and bolt. It is feasible, do you not think? I would not flinch – I have been a soldier, remember.'

He decided against the plan in the end, because we were both foreigners and easily recognized.

When we had got back to my room we spent another one franc fifty on bread and chocolate. Boris devoured his share, and at once cheered up like magic; food seemed to act on his system as rapidly as a cocktail. He took out a pencil and began making a list of the people who would probably give us jobs. There were dozens of them, he said.

'Tomorrow we shall find something, *mon ami*, I know it in my bones. The luck always changes. Besides, we both have brains – a man with brains can't starve.

'What things a man can do with brains! Brains will make money out of anything. I had a friend once, a Pole, a real man of genius; and what do you think he used to do? He would buy a gold ring and pawn it for fifteen francs. Then – you know how carelessly the clerks fill up the tickets – where the clerk had written "*en or*" he would add "*et diamants*" and he would change "fifteen francs" to "fifteen thousand". Neat, eh? Then, you see, he could borrow a thousand francs on the security of the ticket. That is what I mean by brains . . .'

For the rest of the evening Boris was in a hopeful mood, talking of the times we should have together when we were waiters together at Nice or Biarritz, with smart rooms and enough money to set up mistresses. He was too tired to walk the three kilometres back to his hotel, and slept the night on the floor of my room, with his coat rolled round his shoes for a pillow.

6

WE again failed to find work the next day, and it was three weeks before the luck changed. My two hundred francs saved me from trouble about the rent, but everything else went as badly as possible. Day after day Boris and I went up and down Paris, drifting at two miles an hour through the crowds, bored and hungry, and finding nothing. One day, I remember, we crossed the Seine eleven times. We loitered for hours outside service doorways, and when the manager came out we would go up to him ingratiatingly, cap in hand. We always got the same answer: they did not want a lame man, nor a man without experience. Once we were very nearly engaged. While we spoke to the manager Boris stood straight upright, not supporting himself with his stick, and the manager did not see that he was lame. 'Yes,' he said, 'we want two men in the cellars. Perhaps you would do. Come inside.' Then Boris moved, the game was up. 'Ah,' said the manager, 'you limp. *Malheureusement –*'

We enrolled our names at agencies and answered advertisements, but walking everywhere made us slow, and we seemed to miss every job by half an hour. Once we very nearly got a job swabbing out railway trucks, but at the last moment they rejected us in favour of Frenchmen. Once we answered an advertisement calling for hands at a circus. You had to shift benches and clean up litter, and, during the performance, stand on two tubs and let a lion jump through your legs. When we got to the place, an hour before the time named, we found a queue of fifty men already waiting. There is some attraction in lions, evidently.

Once an agency to which I had applied months earlier sent me a *petit bleu*, telling me of an Italian gentleman who wanted English lessons. The *petit bleu* said 'Come at once' and promised twenty francs an hour. Boris and I were in despair. Here was a splendid chance, and I could not take it, for it was impossible to go to the agency with my coat out at the elbow. Then it occurred to us that I could wear Boris's coat – it did not match my trousers, but the trousers were grey and might pass for flannel at a short distance. The coat was so much too big for me that I had to wear it unbuttoned and keep one hand in my pocket. I hurried out, and wasted seventy-five centimes on a bus fare to get to the agency. When I got there I found that the Italian had changed his mind and left Paris.

Once Boris suggested that I should go to Les Halles and try for a job as a porter. I arrived at half-past four in the morning, when the work was getting into its swing. Seeing a short, fat man in a bowler hat directing some porters, I went up to him and asked for work. Before answering he seized my right hand and felt the palm.

'You are strong, eh?' he said.

'Very strong,' I said untruly.

'*Bien.* Let me see you lift that crate.'

It was a huge wicker basket full of potatoes. I took hold of it, and found that, so far from lifting it, I could not even move it. The man in the bowler hat watched me, then shrugged his shoulders and turned away. I made off. When I had gone some distance I looked back and saw *four* men lifting the basket on to a cart. It weighed three hundred-weight, possibly. The man had seen that I was no use, and taken this way of getting rid of me.

Sometimes in his hopeful moments Boris spent fifty centimes on a stamp and wrote to one of his ex-mistresses, asking for money. Only one of them ever replied. It was a woman who, besides having been his mistress, owed him two hundred francs. When Boris saw the letter waiting and recognized the handwriting, he was wild with hope. We seized the letter and rushed up to Boris's room to read it, like a child with stolen sweets. Boris read the letter, then handed it silently to me. It ran:

My Little Cherished Wolf,

With what delight did I open thy charming letter, reminding me of the days of our perfect love, and of the so dear kisses which I have received from thy lips. Such memories linger for ever in the heart, like the perfume of a flower that is dead.

As to thy request for two hundred francs, alas! it is impossible. Thou dost not know, my dear one, how I am desolated to hear of thy embarrassments. But what wouldst thou? In this life which is so sad, trouble comes to everyone. I too have had my share. My little sister has been ill (ah, the poor little one, how she suffered!) and we are obliged to pay I know not what to the doctor. All our money is gone and we are passing, I assure thee, very difficult days.

Courage, my little wolf, always the courage! Remember that the bad days are not for ever, and the trouble which seems so terrible will disappear at last.

Rest assured, my dear one, that I will remember thee always. And receive the most sincere embraces of her who has never ceased to love thee, thy

Yvonne

This letter disappointed Boris so much that he went straight to bed and would not look for work again that day.

My sixty francs lasted about a fortnight. I had given up the pretence of going out to restaurants, and we used to eat in my room, one of us sitting on the bed and the other on the chair. Boris would contribute his two francs and I three or four francs, and we would buy bread, potatoes, milk and cheese, and make soup over my spirit lamp. We had a saucepan and a coffee-bowl and one spoon; every day there was a polite squabble as to who should eat out of the saucepan and who out of the coffee-bowl (the saucepan held more), and every day, to my secret anger, Boris gave in first and had the saucepan. Sometimes we had more bread in the evening, sometimes not. Our linen was getting filthy, and it was three weeks since I had had a bath; Boris, so he said, had not had a bath for months. It was tobacco that made everything tolerable. We had plenty of tobacco, for some time before Boris had met a soldier (the soldiers are given their tobacco free) and bought twenty or thirty packets at fifty centimes each.

All this was far worse for Boris than for me. The walking and sleeping on the floor kept his leg and back in constant pain, and with his vast Russian appetite he suffered torments of hunger, though he never seemed to grow thinner. On the whole he was surprisingly gay, and he had vast capacities for hope. He used to say seriously that he had a patron saint who watched over him, and when things were very bad he would search the gutter for money, saying that the saint often dropped a two-franc piece there. One day we were waiting in the rue Royale; there was a Russian restaurant near by, and we were going to ask for a job there. Suddenly, Boris made up his mind to go into the Madeleine and burn a fifty-centime candle to his patron saint. Then, coming out, he said that he would be on the safe side, and solemnly put a match to a fifty-centime stamp, as a sacrifice to the immortal gods. Perhaps the gods and the saints did not get on together; at any rate, we missed the job.

On some mornings Boris collapsed in the most utter despair. He would lie in bed almost weeping, cursing the Jew with whom he lived. Of late the Jew had become restive about paying the daily two francs, and, what was worse, had begun putting on intolerable airs of patronage. Boris said that I, as an Englishman, could not conceive what torture it was to a Russian of family to be at the mercy of a Jew.

'A Jew, *mon ami*, a veritable Jew! And he hasn't even the decency to be ashamed of it. To think that I, a captain in the Russian Army – have I ever told you, *mon ami*, that I was a captain in the Second Siberian

Rifles? Yes, a captain, and my father was a colonel. And here I am, eating the bread of a Jew. A Jew . . .

'I will tell you what Jews are like. Once, in the early months of the war, we were on the march, and we had halted at a village for the night. A horrible old Jew, with a red beard like Judas Iscariot, came sneaking up to my billet. I asked him what he wanted. "Your honour," he said, "I have brought a girl for you, a beautiful young girl only seventeen. It will only be fifty francs." "Thank you," I said, "you can take her away again. I don't want to catch any diseases." "Diseases!" cried the Jew, "*mais, monsieur le capitaine*, there's no fear of that. It's my own daughter!" That is the Jewish national character for you.

'Have I ever told you, *mon ami*, that in the old Russian Army it was considered bad form to spit on a Jew? Yes, we thought a Russian officer's spittle was too precious to be wasted on Jews . . .' etc. etc.

On these days Boris usually declared himself too ill to go out and look for work. He would lie till evening in the greyish, verminous sheets, smoking and reading old newspapers. Sometimes we played chess. We had no board, but we wrote down the moves on a piece of paper, and afterwards we made a board from the side of a packing-case, and a set of men from buttons, Belgian coins and the like. Boris, like many Russians, had a passion for chess. It was a saying of his that the rules of chess are the same as the rules of love and war, and that if you can win at one you can win at the others. But he also said that if you have a chessboard you do not mind being hungry, which was certainly not true in my case.

7

MY money oozed away – to eight francs, to four francs, to one franc, to twenty-five centimes; and twenty-five centimes is useless, for it will buy nothing except a newspaper. We went several days on dry bread, and then I was two and a half days with nothing to eat whatever. This was an ugly experience. There are people who do fasting cures of three weeks or more, and they say that fasting is quite pleasant after the fourth day; I do not know, never having gone beyond the third day. Probably it seems different when one is doing it voluntarily and is not underfed at the start.

The first day, too inert to look for work, I borrowed a rod and went fishing in the Seine, baiting with bluebottles. I hoped to catch enough for a meal, but of course I did not. The Seine is full of dace, but they grew cunning during the siege of Paris, and none of them has been caught since, except in nets. On the second day I thought of pawning my overcoat, but it seemed too far to walk to the pawnshop, and I spent the day in bed, reading the *Memoirs of Sherlock Holmes*. It was all that I felt equal to, without food. Hunger reduces one to an utterly spineless, brainless condition, more like the after-effects of influenza than anything else. It is as though one had been turned into a jellyfish, or as though all one's blood had been pumped out and luke-warm water substituted. Complete inertia is my chief memory of hunger; that, and being obliged to spit very frequently, and the spittle being curiously white and flocculent, like cuckoo-spit. I do not know the reason for this, but everyone who has gone hungry several days has noticed it.

On the third morning I felt very much better. I realized that I must do something at once, and I decided to go and ask Boris to let me share his two francs, at any rate for a day or two. When I arrived I found Boris in bed, and furiously angry. As soon as I came in he burst out, almost choking:

'He has taken it back, the dirty thief! He has taken it back!'

'Who's taken what?' I said.

'The Jew! Taken my two francs, the dog, the thief! He robbed me in my sleep!'

It appeared that on the previous night the Jew had flatly refused to pay the daily two francs. They had argued and argued, and at last the Jew had consented to hand over the money; he had done it, Boris said, in the most offensive manner, making a little speech about how kind he was, and extorting abject gratitude. And then in the morning he had stolen the money back before Boris was awake.

This was a blow. I was horribly disappointed, for I had allowed my belly to expect food, a great mistake when one is hungry. However, rather to my surprise, Boris was far from despairing. He sat up in bed, lighted his pipe and reviewed the situation.

'Now listen, *mon ami*, this is a tight corner. We have only twenty-five centimes between us, and I don't suppose the Jew will ever pay my two francs again. In any case his behaviour is becoming intolerable. Will you believe it, the other night he had the indecency to bring a woman in here, while I was there on the floor. The low animal! And I have a worse thing to tell you. The Jew intends clearing out of here. He owes a week's rent, and his idea is to avoid paying that and give me the slip at the same time.

If the Jew shoots the moon I shall be left without a roof, and the *patron* will take my suitcase in lieu of rent, curse him! We have got to make a vigorous move.'

'All right. But what can we do? It seems to me that the only thing is to pawn our overcoats and get some food.'

'We'll do that, of course, but I must get my possessions out of this house first. To think of my photographs being seized! Well, my plan is ready. I'm going to forestall the Jew and shoot the moon myself. *F— le camp* – retreat, you understand. I think that is the correct move, eh?'

'But, my dear Boris, how can you, in daytime? You're bound to be caught.'

'Ah well, it will need strategy, of course. Our *patron* is on the watch for people slipping out without paying their rent; he's been had that way before. He and his wife take it in turns all day to sit in the office – what misers, these Frenchmen! But I have thought of a way to do it, if you will help.'

I did not feel in a very helpful mood, but I asked Boris what his plan was. He explained it carefully.

'Now listen. We must start by pawning our overcoats. First go back to your room and fetch your overcoat, then come back here and fetch mine, and smuggle it out under cover of yours. Take them to the pawnshop in the rue des Francs Bourgeois. You ought to get twenty francs for the two, with luck. Then go down to the Seine bank and fill your pockets with stones, and bring them back and put them in my suitcase. You see the idea? I shall wrap as many of my things as I can carry in a newspaper, and go down and ask the *patron* the way to the nearest laundry. I shall be very brazen and casual, you understand, and of course the *patron* will think the bundle is nothing but dirty linen. Or, if he does suspect anything, he will do what he always does, the mean sneak; he will go up to my room and feel the weight of my suitcase. And when he feels the weight of stones he will think it is still full. Strategy, eh? Then afterwards I can come back and carry my other things out in my pockets.'

'But what about the suitcase?'

'Oh, that? We shall have to abandon it. The miserable thing only cost about twenty francs. Besides, one always abandons something in a retreat. Look at Napoleon at the Beresina! He abandoned his whole army.'

Boris was so pleased with this scheme (he called it *une ruse de guerre*) that he almost forgot being hungry. Its main weakness – that he would have nowhere to sleep after shooting the moon – he ignored.

At first the *ruse de guerre* worked well. I went home and fetched my overcoat (that made already nine kilometres, on an empty belly) and smuggled Boris's coat out successfully. Then a hitch occurred. The receiver at the pawnshop, a nasty, sour-faced, interfering, little man – a typical French official – refused the coats on the ground that they were not wrapped up in anything. He said that they must be put either in a valise or a cardboard box. This spoiled everything, for we had no box of any kind, and with only twenty-five centimes between us we could not buy one.

I went back and told Boris the bad news. '*Merde!*' he said, 'that makes it awkward. Well, no matter, there is always a way. We'll put the overcoats in my suitcase.'

'But how are we to get the suitcase past the *patron*? He's sitting almost in the door of the office. It's impossible!'

'How easily you despair, *mon ami*! Where is that English obstinacy that I have read of? Courage! We'll manage it.'

Boris thought for a little while, and then produced another cunning plan. The essential difficulty was to hold the *patron*'s attention for perhaps five seconds, while we could slip past with the suitcase. But, as it happened, the *patron* had just one weak spot – that he was interested in *Le Sport*, and was ready to talk if you approached him on this subject. Boris read an article about bicycle races in an old copy of the *Petit Parisien*, and then, when he had reconnoitred the stairs, went down and managed to set the *patron* talking. Meanwhile, I waited at the foot of the stairs, with the overcoats under one arm and the suitcase under the other. Boris was to give a cough when he thought the moment favourable. I waited trembling, for at any moment the *patron*'s wife might come out of the door opposite the office, and then the game was up. However, presently Boris coughed. I sneaked rapidly past the office and out into the street, rejoicing that my shoes did not creak. The plan might have failed if Boris had been thinner, for his big shoulders blocked the doorway of the office. His nerve was splendid, too; he went on laughing and talking in the most casual way, and so loud that he quite covered any noise I made. When I was well away he came and joined me round the corner, and we bolted.

And then, after all our trouble, the receiver at the pawnshop again refused the overcoats. He told me (one could see his French soul revelling in the pedantry of it) that I had not sufficient papers of identification; my *carte d'identité* was not enough, and I must show a passport or addressed envelopes. Boris had addressed envelopes by the score, but his *carte d'identité* was out of order (he never renewed it, so as to avoid the tax), so we could not pawn the overcoats in his name. All we could do was to trudge up to my room, get the necessary papers, and take the coats to the pawnshop in the Boulevard Port Royal.

I left Boris at my room and went down to the pawnshop. When I got there I found that it was shut and would not open till four in the afternoon. It was now about half-past one, and I had walked twelve kilometres and had no food for sixty hours. Fate seemed to be playing a series of extraordinarily unamusing jokes.

Then the luck changed as though by a miracle. I was walking home through the Rue Broca when suddenly, glittering on the cobbles, I saw a five-sou piece. I pounced on it, hurried home, got our other five-sou piece and bought a pound of potatoes. There was only enough alcohol in the stove to parboil them, and we had no salt, but we wolfed them, skins and all. After that we felt like new men, and sat playing chess till the pawnshop opened.

At four o'clock I went back to the pawnshop. I was not hopeful, for if I had only got seventy francs before, what could I expect for two shabby overcoats in a cardboard suitcase? Boris had said twenty francs, but I thought it would be ten francs, or even five. Worse yet, I might be refused altogether, like poor *Numéro* 83 on the previous occasion. I sat on the front bench, so as not to see people laughing when the clerk said five francs.

At last the clerk called my number: '*Numéro* 117!'

'Yes,' I said, standing up.

'Fifty francs?'

It was almost as great a shock as the seventy francs had been the time before. I believe now that the clerk had mixed my number up with someone else's, for one could not have sold the coats outright for fifty francs. I hurried home and walked into my room with my hands behind my back, saying nothing. Boris was playing with the chessboard. He looked up eagerly.

'What did you get?' he exclaimed. 'What, not twenty francs? Surely you got ten francs, anyway? *Nom de Dieu*, five francs – that is a bit too thick. *Mon ami, don't* say it was five francs. If you say it was five francs I shall really begin to think of suicide.'

I threw the fifty-franc note on to the table. Boris turned white as chalk, and then, springing up, seized my hand and gave it a grip that almost broke the bones. We ran out, bought bread and wine, a piece of meat and alcohol for the stove, and gorged.

After eating, Boris became more optimistic than I had ever known him. 'What did I tell you?' he said. 'The fortune of war! This morning with five sous, and now look at us. I have always said it, there is nothing easier to get than money. And that reminds me, I have a friend in the rue Fondary whom we might go and see. He has cheated me of four thousand francs, the thief. He is the greatest thief alive when he is sober, but it is a curious thing, he is quite honest when he is drunk. I should think he would be drunk by six in the evening. Let's go and find him. Very likely he will pay up a hundred on account. *Merde!* He might pay two hundred. *Allons-y!*'

We went to the rue Fondary and found the man, and he was drunk, but we did not get our hundred francs. As soon as he and Boris met there was a terrible altercation on the pavement. The other man declared that he did not owe Boris a penny, but that on the contrary Boris owed *him* four thousand francs, and both of them kept appealing to me for my opinion. I never understood the rights of the matter. The two argued and argued, first in the street, then in a *bistro*, then in a *prix fixe* restaurant where we went for dinner, then in another *bistro*. Finally, having called one another thieves for two hours, they went off together on a drinking bout that finished up the last sou of Boris's money.

Boris slept the night at the house of a cobbler, another Russian refugee, in the Commerce quarter. Meanwhile, I had eight francs left, and plenty of cigarettes, and was stuffed to the eyes with food and drink. It was a marvellous change for the better after two bad days.

8

WE had now twenty-eight francs in hand, and could start looking for work once more. Boris was still sleeping, on some mysterious terms, at the house of the cobbler, and he had managed to borrow another twenty francs from a Russian friend. He had friends, mostly ex-officers like himself, here and there all over Paris. Some were waiters or dishwashers, some drove taxis, a few lived on women, some had managed to bring money away from Russia and owned garages or dancing-halls. In general, the Russian refugees in Paris are hard-working people, and have put up with their bad luck far better than one can imagine Englishmen of the same class doing. There are exceptions, of course. Boris told me of an exiled Russian duke whom he had once met, who frequented expensive restaurants. The duke

would find out if there was a Russian officer among the waiters, and, after
he had dined, call him in a friendly way to his table.

'Ah,' the duke would say, 'so you are an old soldier, like myself? These
are bad days, eh? Well, well, the Russian soldier fears nothing. And what
was your regiment?'

'The so-and-so, sir,' the waiter would answer.

'A very gallant regiment! I inspected them in 1912. By the way, I have
unfortunately left my notecase at home. A Russian officer will, I know,
oblige me with three hundred francs.'

If the waiter had three hundred francs he would hand it over, and, of
course, never see it again. The duke made quite a lot in this way. Probably
the waiters did not mind being swindled. A duke is a duke, even in exile.

It was through one of these Russian refugees that Boris heard of
something which seemed to promise money. Two days after we had pawned
the overcoats, Boris said to me rather mysteriously:

'Tell me, *mon ami*, have you any political opinions?'

'No,' I said.

'Neither have I. Of course, one is always a patriot; but still – Did not
Moses say something about spoiling the Egyptians? As an Englishman
you will have read the Bible. What I mean is, would you object to earning
money from Communists?'

'No, of course not.'

'Well, it appears that there is a Russian secret society in Paris who
might do something for us. They are Communists; in fact they are agents
for the Bolsheviks. They act as a friendly society, get in touch with exiled
Russians, and try to get them to turn Bolshevik. My friend has joined
their society, and he thinks they would help us if we went to them.'

'But what can they do for us? In any case they won't help me, as I'm
not a Russian.'

'That is just the point. It seems that they are correspondents for a
Moscow paper, and they want some articles on English politics. If we got
to them at once they may commission you to write the articles.'

'Me? But I don't know anything about politics.'

'*Merde!* Neither do they. Who *does* know anything about politics? It's
easy. All you have to do is to copy it out of the English papers. Isn't there
a Paris *Daily Mail*? Copy it from that.'

'But the *Daily Mail* is a Conservative paper. They loathe the Communists.'

'Well, say the opposite of what the *Daily Mail* says, then you *can't* be wrong. We mustn't throw this chance away, *mon ami*. It might mean hundreds of francs.'

I did not like the idea, for the Paris police are very hard on Communists, especially if they are foreigners, and I was already under suspicion. Some months before, a detective had seen me come out of the office of a Communist weekly paper, and I had had a great deal of trouble with the police. If they caught me going to this secret society, it might mean deportation. However, the chance seemed too good to be missed. That afternoon Boris's friend, another waiter, came to take us to the rendezvous. I cannot remember the name of the street – it was a shabby street running south from the Seine bank, somewhere near the Chamber of Deputies. Boris's friend insisted on great caution. We loitered casually down the street, marked the doorway we were to enter – it was a laundry – and then strolled back again, keeping an eye on all the windows and cafés. If the place were known as a haunt of Communists it was probably watched, and we intended to go home if we saw anyone at all like a detective. I was frightened, but Boris enjoyed these conspiratorial proceedings, and quite forgot that he was about to trade with the slayers of his parents.

When we were certain that the coast was clear we dived quickly into the doorway. In the laundry was a Frenchwoman ironing clothes, who told us that 'the Russian gentlemen' lived up a staircase across the courtyard. We went up several flights of dark stairs and emerged on to a landing. A strong, surly-looking young man, with hair growing low on his head, was standing at the top of the stairs. As I came up he looked at me suspiciously, barred the way with his arm and said something in Russian.

'*Mot d'ordre!*' he said sharply when I did not answer.

I stopped, startled. I had not expected passwords.

'*Mot d'ordre!*' repeated the Russian.

Boris's friend, who was walking behind, now came forward and said something in Russian, either the password or an explanation. At this, the surly young man seemed satisfied, and led us into a small, shabby room with frosted windows. It was like a very poverty-stricken office, with propaganda posters in Russian lettering and a huge, crude picture of Lenin tacked on the walls. At the table sat an unshaven Russian in shirt sleeves, addressing newspaper wrappers from a pile in front of him. As I came in he spoke to me in French, with a bad accent.

'This is very careless!' he exclaimed fussily. 'Why have you come here without a parcel of washing?'

'Washing?'

'Everybody who comes here brings washing. It looks as though they were going to the laundry downstairs. Bring a good, large bundle next time. We don't want the police on our tracks.'

This was even more conspiratorial than I had expected. Boris sat down in the only vacant chair, and there was a great deal of talking in Russian. Only the unshaven man talked; the surly one leaned against the wall with his eyes on me, as though he still suspected me. It was queer, standing in the little secret room with its revolutionary posters, listening to a conversation of which I did not understand a word. The Russians talked quickly and eagerly, with smiles and shrugs of the shoulders. I wondered what it was all about. They would be calling each other 'little father', I thought, and 'little dove', and 'Ivan Alexandrovitch', like the characters in Russian novels. And the talk would be of revolutions. The unshaven man would be saying firmly, 'We never argue. Controversy is a bourgeois pastime. Deeds are our arguments.' Then I gathered that it was not this exactly. Twenty francs was being demanded, for an entrance fee apparently, and Boris was promising to pay it (we had just seventeen francs in the world). Finally Boris produced our precious store of money and paid five francs on account.

At this the surly man looked less suspicious, and sat down on the edge of the table. The unshaven one began to question me in French, making notes on a slip of paper. Was I a Communist? he asked. By sympathy, I answered; I had never joined any organization. Did I understand the political situation in England? Oh, of course, of course. I mentioned the names of various Ministers, and made some contemptuous remarks about the Labour Party. And what about *Le Sport*? Could I do articles on *Le Sport*? (Football and Socialism have some mysterious connexion on the Continent.) Oh, of course, again. Both men nodded gravely. The unshaven one said:

'*Évidemment*, you have a thorough knowledge of conditions in England. Could you undertake to write a series of articles for a Moscow weekly paper? We will give you the particulars.'

'Certainly.'

'Then, comrade, you will hear from us by the first post tomorrow. Or possibly the second post. Our rate of pay is a hundred and fifty francs an article. Remember to bring a parcel of washing next time you come. *Au revoir*, comrade.'

We went downstairs, looked carefully out of the laundry to see if there was anyone in the street, and slipped out. Boris was wild with joy. In a sort of sacrificial ecstasy he rushed into the nearest tobacconist's and spent fifty centimes on a cigar. He came out thumping his stick on the pavement and beaming.

'At last! At last! Now, *mon ami*, our fortune really *is* made. You took them in finely. Did you hear him call you comrade? A hundred and fifty francs an article – *nom de Dieu*, what luck!'

Next morning when I heard the postman I rushed down to the *bistro* for my letter; to my disappointment, it had not come. I stayed at home for the second post; still no letter. When three days had gone by and I had not heard from the secret society, we gave up hope, deciding that they must have found somebody else to do their articles.

Ten days later we made another visit to the office of the secret society, taking care to bring a parcel that looked like washing. And the secret society had vanished! The woman in the laundry knew nothing – she simply said that '*ces messieurs*' had left some days ago, after trouble about the rent. What fools we looked, standing there with our parcel! But it was a consolation that we had paid only five francs instead of twenty.

And that was the last we ever heard of the secret society. Who or what they really were, nobody knew. Personally I do not think they had anything to do with the Communist Party; I think they were simply swindlers, who preyed upon Russian refugees by extracting entrance fees to an imaginary society. It was quite safe, and no doubt they are still doing it in some other city. They were clever fellows, and played their part admirably. Their office looked exactly as a secret Communist office should look, and as for that touch about bringing a parcel of washing, it was genius.

9

FOR three more days we continued traipsing about looking for work, coming home for diminishing meals of soup and bread in my bedroom. There were now two gleams of hope. In the first place, Boris had heard of a possible job at the Hôtel X, near the Place de la Concorde, and in the second, the *patron* of the new restaurant in the rue du Commerce had at last come back. We went down in the afternoon and saw him. On the way Boris talked of the vast fortunes we should make if we got this job, and on the importance of making a good impression on the *patron*.

'Appearance – appearance is everything, *mon ami*. Give me a new suit and I will borrow a thousand francs by dinner-time. What a pity I did not buy a collar when we had money. I turned my collar inside out this morning; but what is the use, one side is as dirty as the other. Do you think I look hungry, *mon ami*?'

'You look pale.'

'Curse it, what can one do on bread and potatoes? It is fatal to look hungry. It makes people want to kick you. Wait.'

He stopped at a jeweller's window and smacked his cheeks sharply to bring the blood into them. Then, before the flush had faded, we hurried into the restaurant and introduced ourselves to the *patron*.

The *patron* was a short, fattish, very dignified man with wavy grey hair, dressed in a smart, double-breasted flannel suit and smelling of scent. Boris told me that he too was an ex-colonel of the Russian Army. His wife was there too, a horrid, fat Frenchwoman with a dead-white face and scarlet lips, reminding me of cold veal and tomatoes. The *patron* greeted Boris genially, and they talked together in Russian for a few minutes. I stood in the background, preparing to tell some big lies about my experience as a dishwasher.

Then the *patron* came over towards me. I shuffled uneasily, trying to look servile. Boris had rubbed it into me that a *plongeur* is a slave's slave, and I expected the *patron* to treat me like dirt. To my astonishment, he seized me warmly by the hand.

'So you are an Englishman!' he exclaimed. 'But how charming! I need not ask, then, whether you are a golfer?'

'*Mais certainement*,' I said, seeing that this was expected of me.

'All my life I have wanted to play golf. Will you, my dear *monsieur*, be so kind as to show me a few of the principal strokes?'

Apparently this was the Russian way of doing business. The *patron* listened attentively while I explained the difference between a driver and an iron, and then suddenly informed me that it was all *entendu*; Boris was to be *maître d'hôtel* when the restaurant opened, and I *plongeur*, with a chance of rising to lavatory attendant if trade was good. When would the restaurant open? I asked. 'Exactly a fortnight from today,' the *patron* answered grandly (he had a manner of waving his hand and flicking off his cigarette ash at the same time, which looked very grand), 'exactly a fortnight from today, in time for lunch.' Then, with obvious pride, he showed us over the restaurant.

It was a smallish place, consisting of a bar, a dining-room, and a kitchen no bigger than the average bathroom. The *patron* was decorating it in a trumpery 'picturesque' style (he called it '*le Normand*'; it was a matter of sham beams stuck on the plaster, and the like) and proposed to call it the Auberge de Jehan Cottard, to give a medieval effect. He had a leaflet printed, full of lies about the historical associations of the quarter, and this leaflet actually claimed, among other things, that there had once been an inn on the site of the restaurant which was frequented by Charlemagne. The *patron* was very pleased with this touch. He was also having the bar decorated with indecent pictures by an artist from the Salon. Finally he gave us each an expensive cigarette, and after some more talk we went home.

I felt strongly that we should never get any good from this restaurant. The *patron* had looked to me like a cheat, and, what was worse, an incompetent cheat, and I had seen two unmistakable duns hanging about the back door. But Boris, seeing himself a *maître d'hôtel* once more, would not be discouraged.

'We've brought it off – only a fortnight to hold out. What is a fortnight? *Je m'en f—.* To think that in only three weeks I shall have my mistress! Will she be dark or fair, I wonder? I don't mind, so long as she is not too thin.'

Two bad days followed. We had only sixty centimes left, and we spent it on half a pound of bread, with a piece of garlic to rub it with. The point of rubbing garlic on bread is that the taste lingers and gives one the illusion of having fed recently. We sat most of that day in the Jardin des Plantes. Boris had shots with stones at the tame pigeons, but always missed them, and after that we wrote dinner menus on the backs of envelopes. We were too hungry even to try and think of anything except food. I remember the dinner Boris finally selected for himself. It was: a dozen oysters, bortsch soup (the red, sweet, beetroot soup with cream on top), crayfishes, a young chicken *en casserole*, beef with stewed plums, new potatoes, a salad, suet pudding and Roquefort cheese, with a litre of Burgundy and some old brandy. Boris had international tastes in food. Later on, when we were prosperous, I occasionally saw him eat meals almost as large without difficulty.

When our money came to an end I stopped looking for work, and was another day without food. I did not believe that the Auberge de Jehan Cottard was really going to open, and I could see no other prospect, but I was too lazy to do anything but lie in bed. Then the luck changed abruptly. At night, at about ten o'clock, I heard an eager shout from the street. I got up and went to the window. Boris was there, waving his stick and beaming. Before speaking he dragged a bent loaf from his pocket and threw it up to me.

'*Mon ami, mon cher ami*, we're saved! What do you think?'

'Surely you haven't got a job!'

'At the Hôtel X, near the Place de la Concorde – five hundred francs a month, and food. I have been working there today. Name of Jesus Christ, how I have eaten!'

After ten or twelve hours' work, and with his game leg, his first thought had been to walk three kilometres to my hotel and tell me the good news! What was more, he told me to meet him in the Tuileries the next day during his afternoon interval, in case he should be able to steal some food for me. At the appointed time I met Boris on a public bench. He undid his waistcoat and produced a large, crushed, newspaper packet; in it were some minced veal, a wedge of Camembert cheese, bread and an éclair, all jumbled together.

'*Voilà!*' said Boris, 'that's all I could smuggle out for you. The door-keeper is a cunning swine.'

It is disagreeable to eat out of a newspaper on a public seat, especially in the Tuileries, which are generally full of pretty girls, but I was too hungry to care. While I ate, Boris explained that he was working in the cafeterie of the hotel – that is, in English, the stillroom. It appeared that the cafeterie was the very lowest post in the hotel, and a dreadful come-down for a waiter, but it would do until the Auberge de Jehan Cottard opened. Meanwhile I was to meet Boris every day in the Tuileries, and he would smuggle out as much food as he dared. For three days we continued with this arrangement, and I lived entirely on the stolen food. Then all our troubles came to an end, for one of the *plongeurs* left the Hôtel X, and on Boris's recommendation I was given a job there myself.

10

THE Hôtel X was a vast, grandiose place with a classical façade, and at one side a little, dark doorway like a rat-hole, which was the service entrance. I arrived at a quarter to seven in the morning. A stream of men with greasy trousers were hurrying in and being checked by a doorkeeper who sat in a tiny office. I waited, and presently the *chef du personnel*, a sort of assistant manager, arrived and began to question me. He was an Italian, with a round, pale face, haggard from overwork. He asked whether I was an experienced dishwasher, and I said that I was; he glanced at my hands and saw that I was lying, but on hearing that I was an Englishman he changed his tone and engaged me.

'We have been looking for someone to practise our English on,' he said. 'Our clients are all Americans, and the only English we know is – ' He repeated something that little boys write on the walls in London. 'You may be useful. Come downstairs.'

He led me down a winding staircase into a narrow passage, deep underground, and so low that I had to stoop in places. It was stiflingly hot and very dark, with only dim, yellow bulbs several yards apart. There seemed to be miles of dark labyrinthine passages – actually, I suppose, a few hundred yards in all – that reminded one queerly of the lower decks of a liner; there were the same heat and cramped space and warm reek of food, and a humming, whirring noise (it came from the kitchen furnaces) just like the whir of engines. We passed doorways which let out sometimes a shouting of oaths, sometimes the red glare of a fire, once a shuddering draught from an ice chamber. As we went along, something struck me violently in the back. It was a hundred-pound block of ice, carried by a blue-aproned porter. After him came a boy with a great slab of veal on his shoulder, his cheek pressed into the damp, spongy flesh. They shoved me aside with a cry of '*Sauve-toi, idiot!*' and rushed on. On the wall, under one of the lights, someone had written in a very neat hand: 'Sooner will you find a cloudless sky in winter, than a woman at the Hôtel X who has her maidenhead.' It seemed a queer sort of place.

One of the passages branched off into a laundry, where an old, skull-faced woman gave me a blue apron and a pile of dishcloths. Then the *chef du personnel* took me to a tiny underground den – a cellar below a cellar, as it were – where there were a sink and some gas-ovens. It was too low for me to stand quite upright, and the temperature was perhaps 110 degrees Fahrenheit. The *chef du personnel* explained that my job was to fetch meals for the higher hotel employees, who fed in a small dining-room above, clean their room and wash their crockery. When he had gone, a waiter, another Italian, thrust a fierce, fuzzy head into the doorway and looked down at me.

'English, eh?' he said. 'Well, I'm in charge here. If you work well' – he made the motion of up-ending a bottle and sucked noisily. 'If you don't' – he gave the doorpost several vigorous kicks. 'To me, twisting your neck would be no more than spitting on the floor. And if there's any trouble, they'll believe me, not you. So be careful.'

After this I set to work rather hurriedly. Except for about an hour, I was at work from seven in the morning till a quarter past nine at night;

first at washing crockery, then at scrubbing the tables and floors of the employees' dining-room, then at polishing glasses and knives, then at fetching meals, then at washing crockery again, then at fetching more meals and washing more crockery. It was easy work, and I got on well with it except when I went to the kitchen to fetch meals. The kitchen was like nothing I had ever seen or imagined – a stifling, low-ceilinged inferno of a cellar, red-lit from the fires, and deafening with oaths and the clanging of pots and pans. It was so hot that all the metal-work except the stoves had to be covered with cloth. In the middle were furnaces, where twelve cooks skipped to and fro, their faces dripping sweat in spite of their white caps. Round that were counters where a mob of waiters and *plongeurs* clamoured with trays. Scullions, naked to the waist, were stoking the fires and scouring huge copper saucepans with sand. Everyone seemed to be in a hurry and a rage. The head cook, a fine, scarlet man with big moustachios, stood in the middle booming continuously, '*Ça marche deux œufs brouillés! Ça marche un Chateaubriand aux pommes sautées!*' except when he broke off to curse at a *plongeur*. There were three counters, and the first time I went to the kitchen I took my tray unknowingly to the wrong one. The head cook walked up to me, twisted his moustaches, and looked me up and down. Then he beckoned to the breakfast cook and pointed at me.

'Do you see *that*? That is the type of *plongeur* they send us nowadays. Where do you come from, idiot? From Charenton, I suppose?' (There is a large lunatic asylum at Charenton.)

'From England,' I said.

'I might have known it. Well, *mon cher monsieur l'Anglais*, may I inform you that you are the son of a whore? And now f— the camp to the other counter, where you belong.'

I got this kind of reception every time I went to the kitchen, for I always made some mistake; I was expected to know the work, and was cursed accordingly. From curiosity I counted the number of times I was called *maquereau* during the day, and it was thirty-nine.

At half past four the Italian told me that I could stop working, but that it was not worth going out, as we began at five. I went to the lavatory for a smoke; smoking was strictly forbidden, and Boris had warned me that the lavatory was the only safe place. After that I worked again till a quarter past nine, when the waiter put his head into the doorway and told me to leave the rest of the crockery. To my astonishment, after calling me pig, mackerel, etc., all day, he had suddenly grown quite friendly. I realized that the curses I had met with were only a kind of probation.

'That'll do, *mon p'tit*,' said the waiter. '*Tu n'es pas débrouillard*, but you work all right. Come up and have your dinner. The hotel allows us two litres of wine each, and I've stolen another bottle. We'll have a fine booze.'

We had an excellent dinner from the leavings of the higher employees. The waiter, grown mellow, told me stories about his love-affairs, and about two men whom he had stabbed in Italy, and about how he had dodged his military service. He was a good fellow when one got to know him; he reminded me of Benvenuto Cellini, somehow. I was tired and drenched with sweat, but I felt a new man after a day's solid food. The work did not seem difficult, and I felt that this job would suit me. It was not certain, however, that it would continue, for I had been engaged as an 'extra' for the day only, at twenty-five francs. The sour-faced doorkeeper counted out the money, less fifty centimes which he said was for insurance (a lie, I discovered afterwards). Then he stepped out into the passage, made me take off my coat, and carefully prodded me all over, searching for stolen food. After this the *chef du personnel* appeared and spoke to me. Like the waiter, he had grown more genial on seeing that I was willing to work.

'We will give you a permanent job if you like,' he said. 'The head waiter says he would enjoy calling an Englishman names. Will you sign on for a month?'

Here was a job at last, and I was ready to jump at it. Then I remembered the Russian restaurant, due to open in a fortnight. It seemed hardly fair to promise working a month, and then leave in the middle. I said that I had other work in prospect – could I be engaged for a fortnight? But at that the *chef du personnel* shrugged his shoulders and said that the hotel only engaged men by the month. Evidently I had lost my chance of a job.

Boris, by arrangement, was waiting for me in the Arcade of the Rue de Rivoli. When I told him what had happened, he was furious. For the first time since I had known him he forgot his manners and called me a fool.

'Idiot! Species of idiot! What's the good of my finding you a job when you go and chuck it up the next moment? How could you be such a fool as to mention the other restaurant? You'd only to promise you would work for a month.'

'It seemed more honest to say I might have to leave,' I objected.

'Honest! Honest! Who ever heard of a *plongeur* being honest? *Mon ami*' – suddenly he seized my lapel and spoke very earnestly – '*mon ami*, you have worked here all day. You see what hotel work is like. Do you think a *plongeur* can afford a sense of honour?'

'No, perhaps not.'

'Well, then, go back quickly and tell the *chef du personnel* you are quite ready to work for a month. Say you will throw the other job over. Then, when our restaurant opens, we have only to walk out.'

'But what about my wages if I break my contract?'

Boris banged his stick on the pavement and cried out at such stupidity. 'Ask to be paid by the day, then you won't lose a sou. Do you suppose they would prosecute a *plongeur* for breaking his contract? A *plongeur* is too low to be prosecuted.'

I hurried back, found the *chef du personnel*, and told him that I would work for a month, whereat he signed me on. This was my first lesson in *plongeur* morality. Later I realized how foolish it had been to have any scruples, for the big hotels are quite merciless towards their employees. They engage or discharge men as the work demands, and they all sack ten per cent or more of their staff when the season is over. Nor have they any difficulty in replacing a man who leaves at short notice, for Paris is thronged by hotel employees out of work.

11

As it turned out, I did not break my contract, for it was six weeks before the Auberge de Jehan Cottard even showed signs of opening. In the meantime I worked at the Hôtel X, four days a week in the cafeterie, one day helping the waiter on the fourth floor, and one day replacing the woman who washed up for the dining-room. My day off, luckily, was Sunday, but sometimes another man was ill and I had to work that day as well. The hours were from seven in the morning till two in the afternoon, and from five in the evening till nine – eleven hours; but it was a fourteen-hour day when I washed up for the dining-room. By the ordinary standards of a Paris *plongeur*, these are exceptionally short hours. The only hardship of life was the fearful heat and stuffiness of these labyrinthine cellars. Apart from this the hotel, which was large and well organized, was considered a comfortable one.

Our cafeterie was a murky cellar measuring twenty feet by seven by eight high, and so crowded with coffee-urns, breadcutters and the like that one could hardly move without banging against something. It was lighted by one dim electric bulb, and four or five gas-fires that sent out a fierce red breath. There was a thermometer there, and the temperature never fell below 110 degrees Fahrenheit – it neared 130 at some times of the day. At one end were five service lifts, and at the other an ice cupboard where we stored milk and butter. When you went into the ice cupboard you dropped a hundred degrees of temperature at a single step; it used to remind me of the hymn about Greenland's icy mountains and India's coral strand. Two men worked in the cafeterie besides Boris and myself. One was Mario, a huge, excitable Italian – he was like a city policeman with operatic gestures – and the other, a hairy, uncouth animal whom we called the Magyar; I think he was a Transylvanian, or something even more remote. Except the Magyar we were all big men, and at the rush hours we collided incessantly.

The work in the cafeterie was spasmodic. We were never idle, but the real work only came in bursts of two hours at a time – we called each burst '*un coup de feu*'. The first *coup de feu* came at eight, when the guests upstairs began to wake up and demand breakfast. At eight a sudden banging and yelling would break out all through the basement; bells rang on all sides, blue-aproned men rushed through the passages, our service lifts came down with a simultaneous crash, and the waiters on all five floors began shouting Italian oaths down the shafts. I don't remember all our duties, but they included making tea, coffee and chocolate, fetching meals from the kitchen, wines from the cellar and fruit and so forth from the dining-room, slicing bread, making toast, rolling pats of butter, measuring jam, opening milk-cans, counting lumps of sugar, boiling eggs, cooking porridge, pounding ice, grinding coffee – all this for from a hundred to two hundred customers. The kitchen was thirty yards away, and the dining-room sixty or seventy yards. Everything we sent up in the service lifts had to be covered by a voucher, and the vouchers had to be carefully filed, and there was trouble if even a lump of sugar was lost. Besides this, we had to supply the staff with bread and coffee, and fetch the meals for the waiters upstairs. All in all, it was a complicated job.

I calculated that one had to walk and run about fifteen miles during the day, and yet the strain of the work was more mental than physical. Nothing could be easier, on the face of it, than this stupid scullion work, but it is astonishingly hard when one is in a hurry. One has to leap to and fro between a multitude of jobs – it is like sorting a pack of cards against the clock. You are, for example, making toast, when bang! down comes a service lift with an order for tea, rolls and three different kinds of jam, and simultaneously bang! down comes another demanding scrambled eggs, coffee and grapefruit; you run to the kitchen for the eggs and to the dining-room for the fruit, going like lightning so as to be back before your toast burns, and having to remember about the tea and coffee, besides half a dozen other orders that are still pending; and at the same time some waiter is following you and making trouble about a lost bottle of soda-water, and you are arguing with him. It needs more brains than one might think. Mario said, no doubt truly, that it took a year to make a reliable cafetier.

The time between eight and half past ten was a sort of delirium. Sometimes we were going as though we had only five minutes to live; sometimes there were sudden lulls when the orders stopped and everything seemed quiet for a moment. Then we swept up the litter from the floor, threw down fresh sawdust, and swallowed gallipots of wine or coffee or water – anything, so long as it was wet. Very often we used to break off chunks of ice and suck them while we worked. The heat among the gas-fires was nauseating; we swallowed quarts of drink during the day, and after a few hours even our aprons were drenched with sweat. At times we were hopelessly behind with the work, and some of the customers would have gone without their breakfast, but Mario always pulled us through. He had worked fourteen years in the cafeterie, and he had the skill that never wastes a second between jobs. The Magyar was very stupid and I was inexperienced, and Boris was inclined to shirk, partly because of his lame leg, partly because he was ashamed of working in the cafeterie after being a waiter; but Mario was wonderful. The way he would stretch his great arms right across the cafeterie to fill a coffee-pot with one hand and boil an egg with the other, at the same time watching toast and shouting directions to the Magyar, and between whiles singing snatches from *Rigoletto*, was beyond all praise. The *patron* knew his value, and he was paid a thousand francs a month, instead of five hundred like the rest of us.

The breakfast pandemonium stopped at half past ten. Then we scrubbed the cafeterie tables, swept the floor and polished the brasswork, and, on good mornings, went one at a time to the lavatory for a smoke. This was our slack time – only relatively slack, however, for we had only ten minutes for lunch, and we never got through it uninterrupted. The customers' luncheon hour, between twelve and two, was another period of turmoil like the breakfast hour. Most of our work was fetching meals from the kitchen, which meant constant *engueulades* from the cooks. By this time the cooks had sweated in front of their furnaces for four or five hours, and their tempers were all warmed up.

At two we were suddenly free men. We threw off our aprons and put on our coats, hurried out of doors, and, when we had money, dived into the nearest *bistro*. It was strange, coming up into the street from those firelit cellars. The air seemed blindingly clear and cold, like arctic summer; and how sweet the petrol did smell, after the stenches of sweat and food! Sometimes we met some of our cooks and waiters in the *bistros*, and they were friendly and stood us drinks. Indoors we were their slaves, but it is an etiquette in hotel life that between hours everyone is equal, and the *engueulades* do not count.

At a quarter to five we went back to the hotel. Till half-past six there were no orders, and we used this time to polish silver, clean out the coffee-urns, and do other odd jobs. Then the grand turmoil of the day started – the dinner hour. I wish I could be Zola for a little while, just to describe that dinner hour. The essence of the situation was that a hundred or two hundred people were demanding individually different meals of five or six courses, and that fifty or sixty people had to cook and serve them and clean up the mess afterwards; anyone with experience of catering will know what that means. And at this time when the work was doubled, the whole staff was tired out, and a number of them were drunk. I could write pages about the scene without giving a true idea of it. The chargings to and fro in the narrow passages, the collisions, the yells, the struggling with crates and trays and blocks of ice, the heat, the darkness, the furious festering quarrels which there was no time to fight out – they pass description. Anyone coming into the basement for the first time would have thought himself in a den of maniacs. It was only later, when I understood the working of a hotel, that I saw order in all this chaos.

At half past eight the work stopped very suddenly. We were not free till nine, but we used to throw ourselves full length on the floor, and lie there resting our legs, too lazy even to go to the ice cupboard for a drink. Sometimes the *chef du personnel* would come in with bottles of beer, for the hotel stood us an extra beer when we had had a hard day. The food we were given was no more than eatable, but the *patron* was not mean about drink; he allowed us two litres of wine a day each, knowing that if a *plongeur* is not given two litres he will steal three. We had the heeltaps of bottles as well, so that we often drank too much – a good thing, for one seemed to work faster when partially drunk.

Four days of the week passed like this; of the other two working days, one was better and one worse. After a week of this life I felt in need of a holiday. It was Saturday night, so the people in our *bistro* were busy getting drunk, and with a free day ahead of me I was ready to join them. We all went to bed, drunk, at two in the morning, meaning to sleep till noon. At half past five I was suddenly awakened. A night-watchman, sent from the hotel, was standing at my bedside. He stripped the clothes back and shook me roughly.

'Get up!' he said. '*Tu t'es bien saoulé la gueule, eh*? Well, never mind that, the hotel's a man short. You've got to work today.'

'Why should I work?' I protested. 'This is my day off.'

'Day off, nothing! The work's got to be done. Get up!'

I got up and went out, feeling as though my back were broken and my skull filled with hot cinders. I did not think that I could possibly do a day's work. And yet, after only an hour in the basement, I found that I was perfectly well. It seemed that in the heat of those cellars, as in a turkish bath, one could sweat out almost any quantity of drink. *Plongeurs* know this, and count on it. The power of swallowing quarts of wine, and then sweating it out before it can do much damage, is one of the compensations of their life.

12

BY far my best time at the hotel was when I went to help the waiter on the fourth floor. We worked in a small pantry which communicated with the cafeterie by service lifts. It was delightfully cool after the cellars, and the work was chiefly polishing silver and glasses, which is a humane job. Valenti, the waiter, was a decent sort, and treated me almost as an equal when we were alone, though he had to speak roughly when there was anyone else present, for it does not do for a waiter to be friendly with *plongeurs*. He used sometimes to tip me five francs when he had had a good day. He was a comely youth, aged twenty-four but looking eighteen, and, like most waiters, he carried himself well and knew how to wear his clothes. With his black tail-coat and white tie, fresh face and sleek brown hair, he looked just like an Eton boy; yet he had earned his living since he was twelve, and worked his way up literally from the gutter. Crossing the Italian frontier without a passport, and selling chestnuts from a barrow on the northern boulevards, and being given fifty days' imprisonment in London for working without a permit, and being made love to by a rich old woman in a hotel, who gave him a diamond ring and afterwards accused him of stealing it, were among his experiences. I used to enjoy talking to him, at slack times when we sat smoking down the lift shaft.

My bad day was when I washed up for the dining-room. I had not to wash the plates, which were done in the kitchen, but only the other crockery, silver, knives and glasses; yet, even so, it meant thirteen hours' work, and I used between thirty and forty dishcloths during the day. The antiquated methods used in France double the work of washing up. Plate-racks are unheard-of, and there are no soap-flakes, only the treacly soft soap, which refuses to lather in the hard, Paris water. I worked in a dirty, crowded little den, a pantry and scullery combined, which gave straight on the dining-room. Besides washing up, I had to fetch the waiters' food and serve them at table; most of them were intolerably insolent, and I had to use my fists more than once to get common civility. The person who normally washed up was a woman, and they made her life a misery.

It was amusing to look round the filthy little scullery and think that only a double door was between us and the dining-room. There sat the customers in all their splendour – spotless table-cloths, bowls of flowers, mirrors and gilt cornices and painted cherubim; and here, just a few feet away, we in our disgusting filth. For it really was disgusting filth. There was no time to sweep the floor till evening, and we slithered about in a compound of soapy water, lettuce-leaves, torn paper and trampled food. A dozen waiters with their coats off, showing their sweaty armpits, sat at the table mixing salads and sticking their thumbs into the cream pots. The room had a dirty, mixed smell of food and sweat. Everywhere in the cupboards, behind the piles of crockery, were squalid stores of food that the waiters had stolen. There were only two sinks, and no washing basin, and it was nothing unusual for a waiter to wash his face in the water in which clean crockery was rinsing. But the customers saw nothing of this. There were a coco-nut mat and a mirror outside the dining-room door, and the waiters used to preen themselves up and go in looking the picture of cleanliness.

It is an instructive sight to see a waiter going into a hotel dining-room. As he passes the door a sudden change comes over him. The set of his shoulders alters; all the dirt and hurry and irritation have dropped off in an instant. He glides over the carpet, with a solemn priest-like air. I remember our assistant *maître d'hôtel*, a fiery Italian, pausing at the dining-room door to address an apprentice who had broken a bottle of wine. Shaking his fist above his head he yelled (luckily the door was more or less soundproof):

'*Tu me fais* – Do you call yourself a waiter, you young bastard? You a waiter! You're not fit to scrub floors in the brothel your mother came from. *Maquereau!*'

Words failing him, he turned to the door; and as he opened it he farted loudly, a favourite Italian insult.

Then he entered the dining-room and sailed across it dish in hand, graceful as a swan. Ten seconds later he was bowing reverently to a customer. And you could not help thinking, as you saw him bow and smile, with that benign smile of the trained waiter, that the customer was put to shame by having such an aristocrat to serve him.

This washing up was a thoroughly odious job – not hard, but boring and silly beyond words. It is dreadful to think that some people spend their whole decades at such occupations. The woman whom I replaced was quite sixty years old, and she stood at the sink thirteen hours a day, six days a week, the year round; she was, in addition, horribly bullied by the waiters. She gave out that she had once been an actress – actually, I imagine, a prostitute; most prostitutes end as charwomen. It was strange to see that in spite of her age and her life she still wore a bright blonde wig, and darkened her eyes and painted her face like a girl of twenty. So apparently even a seventy-eight-hour week can leave one with some vitality.

13

ON my third day at the hotel the *chef du personnel*, who had generally spoken to me in quite a pleasant tone, called me up and said sharply:

'Here, you, shave that moustache off at once! *Nom de Dieu*, who ever heard of a *plongeur* with a moustache?'

I began to protest, but he cut me short. 'A *plongeur* with a moustache – nonsense! Take care I don't see you with it tomorrow.'

On the way home I asked Boris what this meant. He shrugged his shoulders. 'You must do what he says, *mon ami*. No one in the hotel wears a moustache, except the cooks. I should have thought you would have noticed it. Reason? There is no reason. It is the custom.'

I saw that it was an etiquette, like not wearing a white tie with a dinner-jacket, and shaved off my moustache. Afterwards I found out the explanation of the custom, which is this: waiters in good hotels do not wear moustaches, and to show their superiority they decree that *plongeurs* shall not wear them either; and the cooks wear their moustaches to show their contempt for the waiters.

This gives some idea of the elaborate caste system existing in a hotel. Our staff, amounting to about a hundred and ten, had their prestige graded as accurately as that of soldiers, and a cook or waiter was as much above a *plongeur* as a captain above a private. Highest of all came the manager, who could sack anybody, even the cooks. We never saw the *patron*, and all we knew of him was that his meals had to be prepared more carefully than those of the customers; all the discipline of the hotel depended on the manager. He was a conscientious man, and always on the lookout for slackness, but we were too clever for him. A system of service bells ran through the hotel, and the whole staff used these for signalling to one another. A long ring and a short ring, followed by two more long rings, meant that the manager was coming, and when we heard it we took care to look busy.

Below the manager came the *maître d'hôtel*. He did not serve at table, unless to a lord or someone of that kind, but directed the other waiters and helped with the catering. His tips, and his bonus from the champagne companies (it was two francs for each cork he returned to them), came to two hundred francs a day. He was in a position quite apart from the rest of the staff, and took his meals in a private room, with silver on the table and two apprentices in clean white jackets to serve him. A little below the head waiter came the head cook, drawing about five thousand francs a month; he dined in the kitchen, but at a separate table, and one of the apprentice cooks waited on him. Then came the *chef du personnel*; he drew only fifteen hundred francs a month, but he wore a black coat and did no manual work, and he could sack *plongeurs* and fine waiters. Then came the other cooks, drawing anything between three thousand and seven hundred and fifty francs a month; then the waiters, making about seventy francs a day in tips, besides a small retaining fee; then the laundresses and sewing women; then the apprentice waiters, who received no tips, but were paid seven hundred and fifty francs a month; then the *plongeurs*, also at seven hundred and fifty francs; then the chambermaids, at five or six hundred francs a month; and lastly the cafetiers, at five hundred a month. We of the cafeterie were the very dregs of the hotel, despised and *tutoied* by everyone.

There were various others – the office employees, called generally couriers, the storekeeper, the cellarman, some porters and pages, the ice man, the bakers, the night-watchman, the doorkeeper. Different jobs were done by different races. The office employees and the cooks and sewing-women were French, the waiters Italians and Germans (there is hardly such a thing as a French waiter in Paris), the *plongeurs* of every race in

Europe, beside Arabs and Negroes. French was the lingua franca, even the Italians speaking it to one another.

All the departments had their special perquisites. In all Paris hotels it is the custom to sell the broken bread to bakers for eight sous a pound, and the kitchen scraps to pigkeepers for a trifle, and to divide the proceeds of this among the *plongeurs*. There was much pilfering, too. The waiters all stole food – in fact, I seldom saw a waiter trouble to eat the rations provided for him by the hotel – and the cooks did it on a larger scale in the kitchen, and we in the cafeterie swilled illicit tea and coffee. The cellarman stole brandy. By a rule of the hotel the waiters were not allowed to keep stores of spirits, but had to go to the cellarman for each drink as it was ordered. As the cellarman poured out the drinks he would set aside perhaps a teaspoonful from each glass, and he amassed quantities in this way. He would sell you the stolen brandy for five sous a swig if he thought he could trust you.

There were thieves among the staff, and if you left money in your coat pockets it was generally taken. The doorkeeper, who paid our wages and searched us for stolen food, was the greatest thief in the hotel. Out of my five hundred francs a month, this man actually managed to cheat me of a hundred and fourteen francs in six weeks. I had asked to be paid daily, so the doorkeeper paid me sixteen francs each evening, and, by not paying for Sundays (for which of course payment was due), pocketed sixty-four francs. Also, I sometimes worked on a Sunday, for which, though I did not know it, I was entitled to an extra twenty-five francs. The doorkeeper never paid me this either, and so made away with another seventy-five francs. I only realized during my last week that I was being cheated, and, as I could prove nothing, only twenty-five francs were refunded. The doorkeeper played similar tricks on any employee who was fool enough to be taken in. He called himself a Greek, but in reality he was an Armenian. After knowing him I saw the force of the proverb 'Trust a snake before a Jew and a Jew before a Greek, but don't trust an Armenian.'

There were queer characters among the waiters. One was a gentleman – a youth who had been educated at a university, and had had a well-paid job in a business office. He had caught a venereal disease, lost his job, drifted, and now considered himself lucky to be a waiter. Many of the waiters had slipped into France without passports, and one or two of them were spies – it is a common profession for a spy to adopt. One day there was a fearful row in the waiters' dining-room between Morandi, a dangerous-looking man with eyes set too far apart, and another Italian. It appeared that Morandi had taken the other man's mistress. The other man, a weakling and obviously frightened of Morandi, was threatening vaguely.

Morandi jeered at him. 'Well, what are you going to do about it? I've slept with your girl, slept with her three times. It was fine. What can you do, eh?'

'I can denounce you to the secret police. You are an Italian spy.'

Morandi did not deny it. He simply produced a razor from his tail pocket and made two swift strokes in the air, as though slashing a man's cheeks open. Whereat the other waiter took it back.

The queerest type I ever saw in the hotel was an 'extra'. He had been engaged at twenty-five francs for the day to replace the Magyar, who was ill. He was a Serbian, a thick-set nimble fellow of about twenty-five, speaking six languages, including English. He seemed to know all about hotel work, and up till midday he worked like a slave. Then, as soon as it had struck twelve, he turned sulky, shirked his work, stole wine, and finally crowned all by loafing about openly with a pipe in his mouth. Smoking, of course, was forbidden under severe penalties. The manager himself heard of it and came down to interview the Serbian, fuming with rage.

'What the devil do you mean by smoking here?' he cried.

'What the devil do you mean by having a face like that?' answered the Serbian, calmly.

I cannot convey the blasphemy of such a remark. The head cook, if a *plongeur* had spoken to him like that, would have thrown a saucepan of hot soup in his face. The manager said instantly, 'You're sacked!' and at two o'clock the Serbian was given his twenty-five francs and duly sacked. Before he went out Boris asked him in Russian what game he was playing. He said the Serbian answered:

'Look here, *mon vieux*, they've got to pay me a day's wages if I work up to midday, haven't they? That's the law. And where's the sense of working after I get my wages? So I'll tell you what I do. I go to a hotel and get a job as an extra, and up to midday I work hard. Then, the moment it's struck twelve, I start raising such hell that they've no choice but to sack me. Neat, eh? Most days I'm sacked by half past twelve; today it was two o'clock; but I don't care, I've saved four hours' work. The only trouble is, one can't do it at the same hotel twice.'

It appeared that he had played this game at half the hotels and restaurants in Paris. It is probably quite an easy game to play during the summer, though the hotels protect themselves against it as well as they can by means of a black list.

14

IN a few days I had grasped the main principles on which the hotel was run. The thing that would astonish anyone coming for the first time into the service quarters of a hotel would be the fearful noise and disorder during the rush hours. It is something so different from the steady work in a shop or a factory that it looks at first sight like mere bad management. But it is really quite unavoidable, and for this reason. Hotel work is not particularly hard, but by its nature it comes in rushes and cannot be economized. You cannot, for instance, grill a steak two hours before it is wanted; you have to wait till the last moment, by which time a mass of other work has accumulated, and then do it all together, in frantic haste. The result is that at meal-times everyone is doing two men's work, which is impossible without noise and quarrelling. Indeed the quarrels are a necessary part of the process, for the pace would never be kept up if everyone did not accuse everyone else of idling. It was for this reason that during the rush hours the whole staff raged and cursed like demons. At those times there was scarcely a verb in the hotel except *foutre*. A girl in the bakery, aged sixteen, used oaths that would have defeated a cabman. (Did not Hamlet say 'cursing like a scullion'? No doubt Shakespeare had watched scullions at work.) But we were not losing our heads and wasting time; we were just stimulating one another for the effort of packing four hours' work into two hours.

What keeps a hotel going is the fact that the employees take a genuine pride in their work, beastly and silly though it is. If a man idles, the others soon find him out, and conspire against him to get him sacked. Cooks, waiters and *plongeurs* differ greatly in outlook, but they are all alike in being proud of their efficiency.

Undoubtedly the most workmanlike class, and the least servile, are the cooks. They do not earn quite so much as waiters, but their prestige is higher and their employment steadier. The cook does not look upon himself as a servant, but as a skilled workman; he is generally called '*un ouvrier*', which a waiter never is. He knows his power – knows that he alone makes or mars a restaurant, and that if he is five minutes late everything is out of gear. He despises the whole non-cooking staff, and makes it a point of

honour to insult everyone below the head waiter. And he takes a genuine
artistic pride in his work, which demands very great skill. It is not the
cooking that is so difficult, but the doing everything to time. Between
breakfast and luncheon the head cook at the Hôtel X would receive orders
for several hundred dishes, all to be served at different times; he cooked
few of them himself, but he gave instructions about all of them and
inspected them before they were sent up. His memory was wonderful. The
vouchers were pinned on a board, but the head cook seldom looked at
them; everything was stored in his mind, and exactly to the minute, as
each dish fell due, he would call out, '*Faites marcher une côtelette de
veau*' (or whatever it was) unfailingly. He was an insufferable bully, but
he was also an artist. It is for their punctuality, and not for any superiority
in technique, that men cooks are preferred to women.

The waiter's outlook is quite different. He too is proud in a way of his
skill, but his skill is chiefly in being servile. His work gives him the
mentality, not of a workman, but of a snob. He lives perpetually in sight
of rich people, stands at their tables, listens to their conversation, sucks
up to them with smiles and discreet little jokes. He has the pleasure of
spending money by proxy. Moreover, there is always the chance that he
may become rich himself, for, though most waiters die poor, they have
long runs of luck occasionally. At some cafés on the Grand Boulevard
there is so much money to be made that the waiters actually pay the
patron for their employment. The result is that between constantly seeing
money, and hoping to get it, the waiter comes to identify himself to some
extent with his employers. He will take pains to serve a meal in style,
because he feels that he is participating in the meal himself.

I remember Valenti telling me of some banquet at Nice at which he
had once served, and of how it cost two hundred thousand francs and
was talked of for months afterwards. 'It was splendid, *mon p'tit, mais
magnifique*! Jesus Christ! The champagne, the silver, the orchids – I have
never seen anything like them, and I have seen some things. Ah, it was
glorious!'

'But,' I said, 'you were only there to wait?'

'Oh, of course. But still, it was splendid.'

The moral is, never be sorry for a waiter. Sometimes when you sit in a
restaurant, still stuffing yourself half an hour after closing time, you feel
that the tired waiter at your side must surely be despising you. But he is
not. He is not thinking as he looks at you, 'What an overfed lout'; he is
thinking, 'One day, when I have saved enough money, I shall be able to
imitate that man.' He is ministering to a kind of pleasure he thoroughly

understands and admires. And that is why waiters are seldom Socialists, have no effective trade union, and will work twelve hours a day – they work fifteen hours, seven days a week, in many cafés. They are snobs, and they find the servile nature of their work rather congenial.

The *plongeurs*, again, have a different outlook. Theirs is a job which offers no prospects, is intensely exhausting, and at the same time has not a trace of skill or interest; the sort of job that would always be done by women if women were strong enough. All that is required of them is to be constantly on the run, and to put up with long hours and a stuffy atmosphere. They have no way of escaping from this life, for they cannot save a penny from their wages, and working from sixty to a hundred hours a week leaves them no time to train for anything else. The best they can hope for is to find a slightly softer job as night-watchman or lavatory attendant.

And yet the *plongeurs*, low as they are, also have a kind of pride. It is the pride of the drudge – the man who is equal to no matter what quantity of work. At that level, the mere power to go on working like an ox is about the only virtue attainable. *Débrouillard* is what every *plongeur* wants to be called. A *débrouillard* is a man who, even when he is told to do the impossible, will *se débrouiller* – get it done somehow. One of the kitchen *plongeurs* at the Hôtel X, a German, was well known as a *débrouillard*. One night an English lord came to the hotel, and the waiters were in despair, for the lord had asked for peaches, and there were none in stock; it was late at night, and the shops would be shut. 'Leave it to me,' said the German. He went out, and in ten minutes he was back with four peaches. He had gone into a neighbouring restaurant and stolen them. That is what is meant by a *débrouillard*. The English lord paid for the peaches at twenty francs each.

Mario, who was in charge of the cafeterie, had the typical drudge mentality. All he thought of was getting through the '*boulot*', and he defied you to give him too much of it. Fourteen years underground had left him with about as much natural laziness as a piston rod. '*Faut être dur*,' he used to say when anyone complained. You will often hear *plongeurs* boast, '*Je suis dur*' – as though they were soldiers, not male charwomen.

Thus everyone in the hotel had his sense of honour, and when the press of work came we were all ready for a grand concerted effort to get through it. The constant war between the different departments also made for efficiency, for everyone clung to his own privileges and tried to stop the others idling and pilfering.

This is the good side of hotel work. In a hotel a huge and complicated machine is kept running by an inadequate staff, because every man has a well-defined job and does it scrupulously. But there is a weak point, and it is this – that the job the staff are doing is not necessarily what the customer pays for. The customer pays, as he sees it, for good service; the employee is paid, as he sees it, for the *boulot* – meaning, as a rule, an imitation of good service. The result is that, though hotels are miracles of punctuality, they are worse than the worst private houses in the things that matter.

Take cleanliness, for example. The dirt in the Hôtel X, as soon as one penetrated into the service quarters, was revolting. Our cafeterie had year-old filth in all the dark corners, and the bread-bin was infested with cockroaches. Once I suggested killing these beasts to Mario. 'Why kill the poor animals?' he said reproachfully. The others laughed when I wanted to wash my hands before touching the butter. Yet we were clean where we recognized cleanliness as part of the *boulot*. We scrubbed the tables and polished the brasswork regularly, because we had orders to do that; but we had no orders to be genuinely clean, and in any case we had no time for it. We were simply carrying out our duties; and as our first duty was punctuality, we saved time by being dirty.

In the kitchen the dirt was worse. It is not a figure of speech, it is a mere statement of fact to say that a French cook will spit in the soup – that is, if he is not going to drink it himself. He is an artist, but his art is not cleanliness. To a certain extent he is even dirty because he is an artist, for food, to look smart, needs dirty treatment. When a steak, for instance, is brought up for the head cook's inspection, he does not handle it with a fork. He picks it up in his fingers and slaps it down, runs his thumb round the dish and licks it to taste the gravy, runs it round and licks again, then steps back and contemplates the piece of meat like an artist judging a picture, then presses it lovingly into place with his fat, pink fingers, every one of which he has licked a hundred times that morning. When he is satisfied, he takes a cloth and wipes his fingerprints from the dish, and hands it to the waiter. And the waiter, of course, dips *his* fingers into the gravy – his nasty, greasy fingers which he is for ever running through his brilliantined hair. Whenever one pays more than, say, ten francs for a dish of meat in Paris, one may be certain that it has been fingered in this manner. In very cheap restaurants it is different; there, the same trouble is not taken over the food, and it is just forked out of the pan and flung on to a plate, without handling. Roughly speaking, the more one pays for food, the more sweat and spittle one is obliged to eat with it.

Dirtiness is inherent in hotels and restaurants, because sound food is sacrificed to punctuality and smartness. The hotel employee is too busy getting food ready to remember that it is meant to be eaten. A meal is simply 'une commande' to him, just as a man dying of cancer is simply 'a case' to the doctor. A customer orders, for example, a piece of toast. Somebody, pressed with work in a cellar deep underground, has to prepare it. How can he stop and say to himself, 'This toast is to be eaten – I must make it eatable'? All he knows is that it must look right and must be ready in three minutes. Some large drops of sweat fall from his forehead on to the toast. Why should he worry? Presently the toast falls among the filthy sawdust on the floor. Why trouble to make a new piece? It is much quicker to wipe the sawdust off. On the way upstairs the toast falls again, butter side down. Another wipe is all it needs. And so with everything. The only food at the Hôtel X which was ever prepared cleanly was the staff's, and the patron's. The maxim, repeated by everyone, was: 'Look out for the patron, and as for the clients, s'en f— pas mal!' Everywhere in the service quarters dirt festered – a secret vein of dirt, running through the great garish hotel like the intestines through a man's body.

Apart from the dirt, the patron swindled the customers wholeheartedly. For the most part the materials of the food were very bad, though the cooks knew how to serve it up in style. The meat was at best ordinary, and as to the vegetables, no good housekeeper would have looked at them in the market. The cream, by a standing order, was diluted with milk. The tea and coffee were of inferior sorts, and the jam was synthetic stuff out of vast, unlabelled tins. All the cheaper wines, according to Boris, were corked vin ordinaire. There was a rule that employees must pay for anything they spoiled, and in consequence damaged things were seldom thrown away. Once the waiter on the third floor dropped a roast chicken down the shaft of our service lift, where it fell into a litter of broken bread, torn paper and so forth at the bottom. We simply wiped it with a cloth and sent it up again. Upstairs there were dirty tales of once-used sheets not being washed, but simply damped, ironed and put back on the beds. The patron was as mean to us as to the customers. Throughout the vast hotel there was not, for instance, such a thing as a brush and pan; one had to manage with a broom and a piece of cardboard. And the staff lavatory was worthy of Central Asia, and there was no place to wash one's hands, except the sinks used for washing crockery.

In spite of all this the Hôtel X was one of the dozen most expensive hotels in Paris, and the customers paid startling prices. The ordinary charge for a night's lodging, not including breakfast, was two hundred francs. All wine and tobacco were sold at exactly double shop prices, though of course the *patron* bought at the wholesale price. If a customer had a title, or was reputed to be a millionaire, all his charges went up automatically. One morning on the fourth floor an American who was on a diet wanted only salt and hot water for his breakfast. Valenti was furious. 'Jesus Christ!' he said, 'what about my ten per cent? Ten per cent of salt and water!' And he charged twenty-five francs for the breakfast. The customer paid without a murmur.

According to Boris, the same kind of thing went on in all Paris hotels, or at least in all the big, expensive ones. But I imagine that the customers at the Hôtel X were especially easy to swindle, for they were mostly Americans, with a sprinkling of English – no French – and seemed to know nothing whatever about good food. They would stuff themselves with disgusting American 'cereals', and eat marmalade at tea, and drink vermouth after dinner, and order a *poulet à la reine* at a hundred francs and then souse it in Worcester sauce. One customer, from Pittsburg, dined every night in his bedroom on grape-nuts, scrambled eggs and cocoa. Perhaps it hardly matters whether such people are swindled or not.

15

I HEARD queer tales in the hotel. There were tales of dope fiends, of old debauchees who frequented hotels in search of pretty page boys, of thefts and blackmail. Mario told me of a hotel in which he had been, where a chambermaid stole a priceless diamond ring from an American lady. For days the staff were searched as they left work, and two detectives searched the hotel from top to bottom, but the ring was never found. The chamber-maid had a lover in the bakery, and he had baked the ring into a roll, where it lay unsuspected until the search was over.

Once Valenti, at a slack time, told me a story about himself.

'You know, *mon p'tit*, this hotel life is all very well, but it's the devil when you're out of work. I expect you know what it is to go without eating, eh? *Forcément*, otherwise you wouldn't be scrubbing dishes. Well, I'm not a poor devil of a *plongeur*; I'm a waiter, and I went five days without eating, once. Five days without even a crust of bread – Jesus Christ!

'I tell you, those five days were the devil. The only good thing was, I had my rent paid in advance, I was living in a dirty, cheap little hotel in the Rue Sainte Éloise up in the Latin quarter. It was called the Hôtel Suzanne May, after some famous prostitute of the time of the Empire. I was starving, and there was nothing I could do; I couldn't even go to the cafés where the hotel proprietors come to engage waiters, because I hadn't the price of a drink. All I could do was to lie in bed getting weaker and weaker, and watching the bugs running about the ceiling. I don't want to go through that again, I can tell you.

'In the afternoon of the fifth day I went half mad; at least, that's how it seems to me now. There was an old faded print of a woman's head hanging on the wall of my room, and I took to wondering who it could be; and after about an hour I realized that it must be Sainte Éloise, who was the patron saint of the quarter. I had never taken any notice of the thing before, but now, as I lay staring at it, a most extraordinary idea came into my head.

' "*Écoute, mon cher*," I said to myself, "you'll be starving to death if this goes on much longer. You've got to do something. Why not try a prayer to Sainte Éloise? Go down on your knees and ask her to send you some money. After all, it can't do any harm. Try it!"

'Mad, eh? Still, a man will do anything when he's hungry. Besides, as I said, it couldn't do any harm. I got out of bed and began praying. I said:

' "Dear Sainte Éloise, if you exist, please send me some money. I don't ask for much – just enough to buy some bread and a bottle of wine and get my strength back. Three or four francs would do. You don't know how grateful I'll be, Sainte Éloise, if you help me this once. And be sure, if you send me anything, the first thing I'll do will be to go and burn a candle for you, at your church down the street. Amen."

'I put in that about the candle, because I had heard that saints like having candles burnt in their honour. I meant to keep my promise, of course. But I am an atheist and I didn't really believe that anything would come of it.

'Well, I got into bed again, and five minutes later there came a bang at the door. It was a girl called Maria, a big fat peasant girl who lived at our hotel. She was a very stupid girl, but a good sort, and I didn't much care for her to see me in the state I was in.

'She cried out at the sight of me. "*Nom de Dieu!*" she said, "what's the matter with you? What are you doing in bed at this time of day? *Quelle mine que tu as!* You look more like a corpse than a man."

'Probably I did look a sight. I had been five days without food, most of the time in bed, and it was three days since I had had a wash or a shave. The room was a regular pigsty, too.

' "What's the matter?" said Maria again.

' "The matter!" I said; "Jesus Christ! I'm starving. I haven't eaten for five days. That's what's the matter."

'Maria was horrified. "Not eaten for five days?" she said. "But why? Haven't you any money, then?"

' "Money!" I said. "Do you suppose I should be starving if I had money? I've got just five sous in the world, and I've pawned everything. Look round the room and see if there's anything more I can sell or pawn. If you can find anything that will fetch fifty centimes, you're cleverer than I am."

'Maria began looking round the room. She poked here and there among a lot of rubbish that was lying about, and then suddenly she got quite excited. Her great thick mouth fell open with astonishment.

' "You idiot!" she cried out. "Imbecile! What's *this*, then?"

'I saw that she had picked up an empty oil *bidon* that had been lying in the corner. I had bought it weeks before, for an oil lamp I had before I sold my things.

' "That?" I said. "That's an oil *bidon*. What about it?"

' "Imbecile! Didn't you pay three francs fifty deposit on it?"

'Now, of course I had paid the three francs fifty. They always make you pay a deposit on the *bidon*, and you get it back when the *bidon* is returned. But I'd forgotten all about it.

' "Yes – " I began.

' "Idiot!" shouted Maria again. She got so excited that she began to dance about until I thought her sabots would go through the floor, "Idiot! *T'es fou! T'es fou!* What have you got to do but take it back to the shop and get your deposit back? Starving, with three francs fifty staring you in the face! Imbecile!"

'I can hardly believe now that in all those five days I had never once thought of taking the *bidon* back to the shop. As good as three francs fifty in hard cash, and it had never occurred to me! I sat up in bed. "Quick!" I shouted to Maria, "you take it for me. Take it to the grocer's at the corner – run like the devil. And bring back food!"

'Maria didn't need to be told. She grabbed the *bidon* and went clattering down the stairs like a herd of elephants and in three minutes she was back with two pounds of bread under one arm and a half-litre bottle of wine under the other. I didn't stop to thank her; I just seized the bread and sank my teeth in it. Have you noticed how bread tastes when you have been hungry for a long time? Cold, wet, doughy – like putty almost. But,

Jesus Christ, how good it was! As for the wine, I sucked it all down in one draught, and it seemed to go straight into my veins and flow round my body like new blood. Ah, that made a difference!

'I wolfed the whole two pounds of bread without stopping to take breath. Maria stood with her hands on her hips, watching me eat. "Well, you feel better, eh?" she said when I had finished.

' "Better!" I said. "I feel perfect! I'm not the same man as I was five minutes ago. There's only one thing in the world I need now – a cigarette."

'Maria put her hand in her apron pocket. "You can't have it," she said. "I've no money. This is all I had left out of your three francs fifty – seven sous. It's no good; the cheapest cigarettes are twelve sous a packet."

' "Then I can have them!" I said. "Jesus Christ, what a piece of luck! I've got five sous – it's just enough."

'Maria took the twelve sous and was starting out to the tobacconist's. And then something I had forgotten all this time came into my head. There was that cursed Sainte Éloise! I had promised her a candle if she sent me money; and really, who could say that the prayer hadn't come true? "Three or four francs," I had said; and the next moment along came three francs fifty. There was no getting away from it. I should have to spend my twelve sous on a candle.

'I called Maria back. "It's no use," I said; "there is Sainte Éloise – I have promised her a candle. The twelve sous will have to go on that. Silly, isn't it? I can't have my cigarettes after all."

' "Sainte Éloise?" said Maria. "What about Sainte Éloise?"

' "I prayed to her for money and promised her a candle," I said. "She answered the prayer – at any rate, the money turned up. I shall have to buy that candle. It's a nuisance, but it seems to me I must keep my promise."

' "But what put Sainte Éloise into your head?" said Maria.

' "It was her picture," I said, and I explained the whole thing. "There she is, you see," I said, and I pointed to the picture on the wall.

'Maria looked at the picture, and then to my surprise she burst into shouts of laughter. She laughed more and more, stamping about the room and holding her fat sides as though they would burst. I thought she had gone mad. It was two minutes before she could speak.

' "Idiot!" she cried at last. "*T'es fou! T'es fou!* Do you mean to tell me you really knelt down and prayed to that picture? Who told you it was Sainte Éloise?"

' "But I made sure it was Sainte Éloise!" I said.

' "Imbecile! It isn't Sainte Éloise at all. Who do you think it is?"

' "Who?" I said.

' "It is Suzanne May, the woman this hotel is called after."

'I had been praying to Suzanne May, the famous prostitute of the Empire . . .

'But, after all, I wasn't sorry. Maria and I had a good laugh, and then we talked it over, and we made out that I didn't owe Sainte Éloise anything. Clearly it wasn't she who had answered the prayer, and there was no need to buy her a candle. So I had my packet of cigarettes after all.'

16

TIME went on and the Auberge de Jehan Cottard showed no signs of opening. Boris and I went down there one day during our afternoon interval and found that none of the alterations had been done, except the indecent pictures, and there were three duns instead of two. The *patron* greeted us with his usual blandness, and the next instant turned to me (his prospective dishwasher) and borrowed five francs. After that I felt certain that the restaurant would never get beyond talk. The *patron*, however, again named the opening for 'exactly a fortnight from today', and introduced us to the woman who was to do the cooking, a Baltic Russian five feet tall and a yard across the hips. She told us that she had been a singer before she came down to cooking, and that she was very artistic and adored English literature, especially *La Case de l'Oncle Tom*.

In a fortnight I had got so used to the routine of a *plongeur*'s life that I could hardly imagine anything different. It was a life without much variation. At a quarter to six one woke with a sudden start, tumbled into grease-stiffened clothes, and hurried out with dirty face and protesting muscles. It was dawn, and the windows were dark except for the workmen's cafés. The sky was like a vast flat wall of cobalt, with roofs and spires of black paper pasted upon it. Drowsy men were sweeping the pavements with ten-foot besoms, and ragged families picking over the dustbins. Workmen, and girls with a piece of chocolate in one hand and a *croissant* in the other, were pouring into the Métro stations. Trams, filled with more workmen, boomed gloomily past. One hastened down to the station, fought for a place – one does literally have to fight on the Paris Métro at six in the morning – and stood jammed in the swaying mass of passengers, nose to nose with some hideous French face, breathing sour wine and garlic. And then one descended into the labyrinth of the hotel basement, and forgot daylight till two o'clock, when the sun was hot and the town black with people and cars.

After my first week at the hotel I always spent the afternoon interval in sleeping, or, when I had money, in a *bistro*. Except for a few ambitious waiters who went to English classes, the whole staff wasted their leisure in this way; one seemed too lazy after the morning's work to do anything better. Sometimes half a dozen *plongeurs* would make up a party and go to an abominable brothel in the Rue de Sieyès, where the charge was only five francs twenty-five centimes – tenpence half-penny. It was nicknamed '*le prix fixe*', and they used to describe their experiences there as a great joke. It was a favourite rendezvous of hotel workers. The *plongeurs'* wages did not allow them to marry, and no doubt work in the basement does not encourage fastidious feelings.

For another four hours one was in the cellars, and then one emerged, sweating, into the cool street. It was lamp-light – that strange purplish gleam of the Paris lamps – and beyond the river the Eiffel Tower flashed from top to bottom with zigzag skysigns, like enormous snakes of fire. Streams of cars glided silently to and fro, and women, exquisite-looking in the dim light, strolled up and down the arcade. Sometimes a woman would glance at Boris or me, and then, noticing our greasy clothes, look hastily away again. One fought another battle in the Métro and was home by ten. Generally from ten to midnight I went to a little *bistro* in our street, an underground place frequented by Arab navvies. It was a bad place for fights, and I sometimes saw bottles thrown, once with fearful effect, but as a rule the Arabs fought among themselves and let Christians alone. Raki, the Arab drink, was very cheap, and the *bistro* was open at all hours, for the Arabs – lucky men – had the power of working all day and drinking all night.

It was the typical life of a *plongeur*, and it did not seem a bad life at the time. I had no sensation of poverty, for even after paying my rent and setting aside enough for tobacco and journeys and my food on Sundays, I still had four francs a day for drinks, and four francs was wealth. There was – it is hard to express it – a sort of heavy contentment, the contentment a well-fed beast might feel, in a life which had become so simple. For nothing could be simpler than the life of a *plongeur*. He lives in a rhythm between work and sleep, without time to think, hardly conscious of the exterior world; his Paris has shrunk to the hotel, the Métro, a few *bistros* and his bed. If he goes afield, it is only a few streets away, on a trip with some servant-girl who sits on his knee swallowing oysters and beer. On his free day he lies in bed till noon, puts on a clean shirt, throws dice for drinks, and after lunch goes back to bed again. Nothing is quite real to him but the *boulot*, drinks and sleep; and of these sleep is the most important.

One night, in the small hours, there was a murder just beneath my window. I was woken by a fearful uproar, and, going to the window, saw a man lying flat on the stones below; I could see the murderers, three of them, flitting away at the end of the street. Some of us went down and found that the man was quite dead, his skull cracked with a piece of lead piping. I remember the colour of his blood, curiously purple, like wine; it was still on the cobbles when I came home that evening, and they said the school-children had come from miles round to see it. But the thing that strikes me in looking back is that I was in bed and asleep within three minutes of the murder. So were most of the people in the street; we just made sure that the man was done for, and went straight back to bed. We were working people, and where was the sense of wasting sleep over a murder?

Work in the hotel taught me the true value of sleep, just as being hungry had taught me the true value of food. Sleep had ceased to be a mere physical necessity; it was something voluptuous, a debauch more than a relief. I had no more trouble with the bugs. Mario had told me of a sure remedy for them, namely pepper, strewed thick over the bedclothes. It made me sneeze, but the bugs all hated it, and emigrated to other rooms.

17

WITH thirty francs a week to spend on drinks I could take part in the social life of the quarter. We had some jolly evenings, on Saturdays, in the little *bistro* at the foot of the Hôtel des Trois Moineaux.

The brick-floored room, fifteen feet square, was packed with twenty people, and the air dim with smoke. The noise was deafening, for everyone was either talking at the top of his voice or singing. Sometimes it was just a confused din of voices; sometimes everyone would burst out together in the same song – the 'Marseillaise', or the 'Internationale', or 'Madelon', or 'Les Fraises et les Framboises'. Azaya, a great clumping peasant girl who worked fourteen hours a day in a glass factory, sang a song about, '*Il a per*du *ses pantalons, tout en dans*ant *le Charleston*.' Her friend Marinette, a thin, dark Corsican girl of obstinate virtue, tied her knees together and danced the *danse du ventre*. The old Rougiers wandered in and out, cadging drinks and trying to tell a long, involved story about someone who had once cheated them over a bedstead. R., cadaverous and silent, sat in his corner quietly boozing. Charlie, drunk, half danced, half staggered to and fro with a glass of sham absinthe balanced in one fat hand, pinching the women's breasts and declaiming poetry. People played darts and diced for drinks. Manuel, a Spaniard, dragged the girls to the bar and shook the dice-box against their bellies, for luck. Madame F. stood at the bar rapidly pouring *chopines* of wine through the pewter funnel, with a wet dishcloth always handy, because every man in the room tried to make love to her. Two children, bastards of big Louis the bricklayer, sat in a corner sharing a glass of *sirop*. Everyone was very happy, overwhelmingly certain that the world was a good place and we a notable set of people.

For an hour the noise scarcely slackened. Then about midnight there was a piercing shout of '*Citoyens!*' and the sound of a chair falling over. A blond, red-faced workman had risen to his feet and was banging a bottle on the table. Everyone stopped singing; the word went round, 'Sh! Furex is starting!' Furex was a strange creature, a Limousin stonemason who worked steadily all the week and drank himself into a kind of paroxysm on Saturdays. He had lost his memory and could not remember anything before the war, and he would have gone to pieces through drink if Madame F. had not taken care of him. On Saturday evenings at about five o'clock she would say to someone, 'Catch Furex before he spends his wages,' and when he had been caught she would take away his money, leaving him enough for one good drink. One week he escaped, and, rolling blind drunk in the Place Monge, was run over by a car and badly hurt.

The queer thing about Furex was that, though he was a Communist when sober, he turned violently patriotic when drunk. He started the evening with good Communist principles, but after four or five litres he was a rampant Chauvinist, denouncing spies, challenging all foreigners to fight, and, if he was not prevented, throwing bottles. It was at this stage that he made his speech – for he made a patriotic speech every Saturday night. The speech was always the same, word for word. It ran:

'Citizens of the Republic, are there any Frenchmen here? If there are any Frenchmen here, I rise to remind them – to remind them in effect, of the glorious days of the war. When one looks back upon that time of comradeship and heroism – one looks back, in effect, upon that time of comradeship and heroism. When one remembers the heroes who are dead – one remembers, in effect, the heroes who are dead. Citizens of the Republic, I was wounded at Verdun –'

Here he partially undressed and showed the wound he had received at Verdun. There were shouts of applause. We thought nothing in the world could be funnier than this speech of Furex's. He was a well-known spectacle in the quarter; people used to come in from other *bistros* to watch him when his fit started.

The word was passed round to bait Furex. With a wink to the others someone called for silence, and asked him to sing the 'Marseillaise'. He sang it well, in a fine bass voice, with patriotic gurgling noises deep down in his chest when he came to *'Aux arrmes, citoyens! Forrmez vos bataillons!'* Veritable tears rolled down his cheeks; he was too drunk to see that everyone was laughing at him. Then, before he had finished, two strong workmen seized him by either arm and held him down, while Azaya shouted, *'Vive l'Allemagne!'* just out of his reach. Furex's face went purple at such infamy. Everyone in the *bistro* began shouting together, *'Vive l'Allemagne! À bas la France!'* while Furex struggled to get at them. But suddenly he spoiled the fun. His face turned pale and doleful, his limbs went limp, and before anyone could stop him he was sick on the table. Then Madame F. hoisted him like a sack and carried him up to bed. In the morning he reappeared quiet and civil, and bought a copy of *L'Humanité*.

The table was wiped with a cloth, Madame F. brought more litre bottles and loaves of bread, and we settled down to serious drinking. There were more songs. An itinerant singer came in with his banjo and performed for five-sou pieces. An Arab and a girl from the *bistro* down the street did a dance, the man wielding a painted wooden phallus the size of a rolling-pin. There were gaps in the noise now. People had begun to talk about their love-affairs, and the war, and the barbel-fishing in the Seine, and the best way to *faire la révolution*, and to tell stories. Charlie, grown sober again, captured the conversation and talked about his soul for five minutes. The doors and windows were opened to cool the room. The street was emptying, and in the distance one could hear the lonely milk train thundering down the Boulevard St Michel. The air blew cold on our foreheads, and the coarse African wine still tasted good: we were still happy, but meditatively, with the shouting and hilarious mood finished.

By one o'clock we were not happy any longer. We felt the joy of the evening wearing thin, and called hastily for more bottles, but Madame F.

was watering the wine now, and it did not taste the same. Men grew quarrelsome. The girls were violently kissed and hands thrust into their bosoms and they made off lest worse should happen. Big Louis, the bricklayer, was drunk, and crawled about the floor barking and pretending to be a dog. The others grew tired of him and kicked at him as he went past. People seized each other by the arm and began long rambling confessions, and were angry when these were not listened to. The crowd thinned. Manuel and another man, both gamblers, went across to the Arab *bistro*, where card-playing went on till daylight. Charlie suddenly borrowed thirty francs from Madame F. and disappeared, probably to a brothel. Men began to empty their glasses, call briefly, ' *'Sieurs, dames!'* and go off to bed.

By half past one the last drop of pleasure had evaporated, leaving nothing but headaches. We perceived that we were not splendid inhabitants of a splendid world, but a crew of underpaid workmen grown squalidly and dismally drunk. We went on swallowing the wine, but it was only from habit, and the stuff seemed suddenly nauseating. One's head had swollen up like a balloon, the floor rocked, one's tongue and lips were stained purple. At last it was no use keeping it up any longer. Several men went out into the yard behind the *bistro* and were sick. We crawled up to bed, tumbled down half dressed, and stayed there ten hours.

Most of my Saturday nights went in this way. On the whole, the two hours when one was perfectly and wildly happy seemed worth the subsequent headache. For many men in the quarter, unmarried and with no future to think of, the weekly drinking-bout was the one thing that made life worth living.

18

CHARLIE told us a good story one Saturday night in the *bistro*. Try and picture him – drunk, but sober enough to talk consecutively. He bangs on the zinc bar and yells for silence:

'Silence, *messieurs et dames* – silence, I implore you! Listen to this story, that I am about to tell you. A memorable story, an instructive story, one of the souvenirs of a refined and civilized life. Silence, *messieurs et dames*!

'It happened at a time when I was hard up. You know what that is like – how damnable, that a man of refinement should ever be in such a condition. My money had not come from home; I had pawned everything, and there was nothing open to me except to work, which is a thing I will not do. I was living with a girl at the time – Yvonne her name was – a great half-witted peasant girl like Azaya there, with yellow hair and fat legs. The two of us had eaten nothing in three days. *Mon Dieu*, what sufferings! The girl used to walk up and down the room with her hands on her belly, howling like a dog that she was dying of starvation. It was terrible.

'But to a man of intelligence nothing is impossible. I propounded to myself the question, "What is the easiest way to get money without working?" And immediately the answer came: "To get money easily one must be a woman. Has not every woman something to sell?" And then, as I lay reflecting upon the things I should do if I were a woman, an idea came into my head. I remembered the Government maternity hospitals – you know the Government maternity hospitals? They are places where women who are *enceinte* are given meals free and no questions are asked. It is done to encourage childbearing. Any woman can go there and demand a meal, and she is given it immediately.

' "*Mon Dieu!*" I thought, "if only I were a woman! I would eat at one of those places every day. Who can tell whether a woman is *enceinte* or not, without an examination?"

'I turned to Yvonne. "Stop that insufferable bawling." I said, "I have thought of a way to get food."

' "How?" she said.

' "It is simple," I said. "Go to the Government maternity hospital. Tell them you are *enceinte* and ask for food. They will give you a good meal and ask no questions."

'Yvonne was appalled. "*Mais, mon Dieu*," she cried, "I am not *enceinte*!"

' "Who cares?" I said. "That is easily remedied. What do you need except a cushion – two cushions if necessary? It is an inspiration from heaven, *ma chère*. Don't waste it."

'Well, in the end I persuaded her, and then we borrowed a cushion and I got her ready and took her to the maternity hospital. They received her with open arms. They gave her cabbage soup, a ragoût of beef, a purée of potatoes, bread and cheese and beer, and all kinds of advice about her baby. Yvonne gorged till she almost burst her skin, and managed to slip some of the bread and cheese into her pocket for me. I took her there every day until I had money again. My intelligence had saved us.

'Everything went well until a year later. I was with Yvonne again, and one day we were walking down the Boulevard Port Royal, near the barracks. Suddenly Yvonne's mouth fell open, and she began turning red and white, and red again.

' "*Mon Dieu!*" she cried, "look at that who is coming! It is the nurse who was in charge at the maternity hospital. I am ruined!"

' "Quick!" I said, "run!" But it was too late. The nurse had recognized Yvonne, and she came straight up to us, smiling. She was a big fat woman with a gold pince-nez and red cheeks like the cheeks of an apple. A motherly, interfering kind of woman.

' "I hope you are well, *ma petite*?" she said kindly. "And your baby, is he well too? Was it a boy, as you were hoping?"

'Yvonne had begun trembling so hard that I had to grip her arm. "No," she said at last.

' "Ah, then, *évidemment*, it was a girl?"

'Thereupon Yvonne, the idiot, lost her head completely. "No," she actually said again!

'The nurse was taken aback. "*Comment!*" she exclaimed, "neither a boy nor a girl! But how can that be?"

'Figure to yourselves, *messieurs et dames*, it was a dangerous moment. Yvonne had turned the colour of a beetroot and she looked ready to burst into tears; another second and she would have confessed everything. Heaven knows what might have happened. But as for me, I had kept my head; I stepped in and saved the situation.

' "It was twins," I said calmly.

' "Twins!" exclaimed the nurse. And she was so pleased that she took Yvonne by the shoulders and embraced her on both cheeks, publicly.

'Yes, twins . . .'

19

ONE day, when we had been at the Hôtel X five or six weeks, Boris disappeared without notice. In the evening I found him waiting for me in the Rue de Rivoli. He slapped me gaily on the shoulder.

'Free at last, *mon ami*! You can give notice in the morning. The Auberge opens tomorrow.'

'Tomorrow?'

'Well, possibly we shall need a day or two to arrange things. But, at any rate, no more cafeteria! *Nous sommes lancés, mon ami!* My tail coat is out of pawn already.'

His manner was so hearty that I felt sure there was something wrong, and I did not at all want to leave my safe and comfortable job at the hotel. However, I had promised Boris, so I gave notice, and the next morning at seven went down to the Auberge de Jehan Cottard. It was locked, and I went in search of Boris, who had once more bolted from his lodgings and taken a room in the rue de la Croix Nivert. I found him asleep, together with a girl whom he had picked up the night before, and who he told me was 'of a very sympathetic temperament'. As to the restaurant, he said that it was all arranged; there were only a few little things to be seen to before we opened.

At ten I managed to get Boris out of bed, and we unlocked the restaurant. At a glance I saw what the 'few little things' amounted to. It was briefly this: that the alterations had not been touched since our last visit. The stoves for the kitchen had not arrived, the water and electricity had not been laid on, and there was all manner of painting, polishing and carpentering to be done. Nothing short of a miracle could open the restaurant within ten days, and by the look of things it might collapse without even opening. It was obvious what had happened. The *patron* was short of money, and he had engaged the staff (there were four of us) in order to use us instead of workmen. He would be getting our services almost free, for waiters are paid no wages, and though he would have to pay me, he would not be feeding me till the restaurant opened. In effect, he had swindled us of several hundred francs by sending for us before the restaurant was open. We had thrown up a good job for nothing.

Boris, however, was full of hope. He had only one idea in his head, namely, that here at last was a chance of being a waiter and wearing a tail coat once more. For this he was quite willing to do ten days' work unpaid, with the chance of being left jobless in the end. 'Patience!' he kept saying. 'That will arrange itself. Wait till the restaurant opens, and we'll get it all back. Patience, *mon ami!*'

We needed patience, for days passed and the restaurant did not even progress towards opening. We cleaned out the cellars, fixed the shelves, distempered the walls, polished the woodwork, whitewashed the ceiling, stained the floor; but the main work, the plumbing and gas-fitting and electricity, was still not done, because the *patron* could not pay the bills. Evidently he was almost penniless, for he refused the smallest charges, and he had a trick of swiftly disappearing when asked for money. His blend of shiftiness and aristocratic manners made him very hard to deal with. Melancholy duns came looking for him at all hours, and by instruction we always told them that he was at Fontainebleau, or Saint Cloud, or some other place that was safely distant. Meanwhile, I was getting hungrier and hungrier. I had left the hotel with thirty francs, and I had to go back immediately to a diet of dry bread. Boris had managed in the beginning to extract an advance of sixty francs from the *patron*, but he had spent half of it, in redeeming his waiter's clothes, and half on the girl of sympathetic temperament. He borrowed three francs a day from Jules, the second waiter, and spent it on bread. Some days we had not even money for tobacco.

Sometimes the cook came to see how things were getting on, and when she saw that the kitchen was still bare of pots and pans she usually wept. Jules, the second waiter, refused steadily to help with the work. He was a Magyar, a little dark, sharp-featured fellow in spectacles, and very talkative; he had been a medical student, but had abandoned his training for lack of money. He had a taste for talking while other people were working, and he told me all about himself and his ideas. It appeared that he was a Communist, and had various strange theories (he could prove to you by figures that it was wrong to work), and he was also, like most Magyars, passionately proud. Proud and lazy men do not make good waiters. It was Jules's dearest boast that once when a customer in a restaurant had insulted him, he had poured a plate of hot soup down the customer's neck, and then walked straight out without even waiting to be sacked.

As each day went by Jules grew more and more enraged at the trick the *patron* had played on us. He had a spluttering, oratorical way of talking. He used to walk up and down shaking his fist, and trying to incite me not to work:

'Put that brush down, you fool! You and I belong to proud races; we don't work for nothing, like these damned Russian serfs. I tell you, to be cheated like this is torture to me. There have been times in my life, when someone has cheated me even of five sous, when I have vomited – yes, vomited with rage.

'Besides, *mon vieux*, don't forget that I'm a Communist. *À bas la bourgeoisie!* Did any man alive ever see me working when I could avoid it? No. And not only I don't wear myself out working, like you other fools, but I steal, just to show my independence. Once I was in a restaurant where the *patron* thought he could treat me like a dog. Well, in revenge I found out a way to steal milk from the milk-cans and seal them up again so that no one should know. I tell you I just swilled that milk down night and morning. Every day I drank four litres of milk, besides half a litre of cream. The *patron* was at his wits' end to know where the milk was going. It wasn't that I wanted milk, you understand, because I hate the stuff; it was principle, just principle.

'Well, after three days I began to get dreadful pains in my belly, and I went to the doctor. "What have you been eating?" he said. I said: "I drink four litres of milk a day, and half a litre of cream." "Four litres!" he said. "Then stop it at once. You'll burst if you go on." "What do I care?" I said. "With me principle is everything. I shall go on drinking that milk, even if I do burst."

'Well, the next day the *patron* caught me stealing milk. "You're sacked," he said; "you leave at the end of the week." "*Pardon, monsieur,*" I said, "I shall leave this morning." "No, you won't," he said, "I can't spare you till Saturday." "Very well, *mon patron,*" I thought to myself, "we'll see who gets tired of it first." And then I set to work to smash the crockery. I broke nine plates the first day and thirteen the second; after that the *patron* was glad to see the last of me.

'Ah, I'm not one of your Russian *moujiks* . . .'

Ten days passed. It was a bad time. I was absolutely at the end of my money, and my rent was several days overdue. We loafed about the dismal empty restaurant, too hungry even to get on with the work that remained. Only Boris now believed that the restaurant would open. He had set his heart on being *maître d'hôtel*, and he invented a theory that the *patron*'s money was tied up in shares and he was waiting a favourable moment for selling. On the tenth day I had nothing to eat or smoke, and I told the *patron* that I could not continue working without an advance on my wages.

As blandly as usual, the *patron* promised the advance, and then, according to his custom, vanished. I walked part of the way home, but I did not feel equal to a scene with Madame F. over the rent, so I passed the night on a bench on the boulevard. It was very uncomfortable – the arm of the seat cuts into your back – and much colder than I had expected. There was plenty of time, in the long boring hours between dawn and work, to think what a fool I had been to deliver myself into the hands of these Russians.

Then, in the morning, the luck changed. Evidently the *patron* had come to an understanding with his creditors, for he arrived with money in his pockets, set the alterations going, and gave me my advance. Boris and I bought macaroni and a piece of horse's liver, and had our first hot meal in ten days.

The workmen were brought in and the alterations made, hastily and with incredible shoddiness. The tables, for instance, were to be covered with baize, but when the *patron* found that baize was expensive he bought instead disused army blankets, smelling incorrigibly of sweat. The table cloths (they were check, to go with the 'Norman' decorations) would cover them, of course. On the last night we were at work till two in the morning, getting things ready. The crockery did not arrive till eight, and, being new, had all to be washed. The cutlery did not arrive till the next morning, nor the linen either, so that we had to dry the crockery with a shirt of the *patron*'s and an old pillowslip belonging to the concierge. Boris and I did all the work. Jules was skulking, and the *patron* and his wife sat in the bar with a dun and some Russian friends, drinking success to the restaurant. The cook was in the kitchen with her head on the table, crying, because she was expected to cook for fifty people, and there were not pots and pans enough for ten. About midnight there was a fearful interview with some duns, who came intending to seize eight copper saucepans which the *patron* had obtained on credit. They were bought off with half a bottle of brandy.

Jules and I missed the last Métro home and had to sleep on the floor of the restaurant. The first thing we saw in the morning were two large rats sitting on the kitchen table, eating from a ham that stood there. It seemed a bad omen, and I was surer than ever that the Auberge de Jehan Cottard would turn out a failure.

20

THE *patron* had engaged me as kitchen *plongeur*; that is, my job was to wash up, keep the kitchen clean, prepare vegetables, make tea, coffee and sandwiches, do the simpler cooking, and run errands. The terms were, as usual, five hundred francs a month and food, but I had no free day and no fixed working hours. At the Hôtel X I had seen catering at its best, with unlimited money and good organization. Now, at the Auberge, I learned how things are done in a thoroughly bad restaurant. It is worth describing, for there are hundreds of similar restaurants in Paris, and every visitor feeds in one of them occasionally.

I should add, by the way, that the Auberge was not the ordinary cheap eating-house frequented by students and workmen. We did not provide an adequate meal at less than twenty-five francs, and we were picturesque and artistic, which sent up our social standing. There were the indecent pictures in the bar, and the Norman decorations – sham beams on the walls, electric lights done up as candlesticks, 'peasant' pottery, even a mounting-block at the door – and the *patron* and the head waiter were Russian officers, and many of the customers titled Russian refugees. In short, we were decidedly chic.

Nevertheless, the conditions behind the kitchen door were suitable for a pigsty. For this is what our service arrangements were like.

The kitchen measured fifteen feet long by eight broad, and half this space was taken up by the stoves and tables. All the pots had to be kept on shelves out of reach, and there was only room for one dustbin. This dustbin used to be crammed full by midday, and the floor was normally an inch deep in a compost of trampled food.

For firing we had nothing but three gas-stoves, without ovens, and all joints had to be sent out to the bakery.

There was no larder. Our substitute for one was a half-roofed shed in the yard, with a tree growing in the middle of it. The meat, vegetables and so forth lay there on the bare earth, raided by rats and cats.

There was no hot water laid on. Water for washing up had to be heated in pans, and, as there was no room for these on the stoves when meals were cooking, most of the plates had to be washed in cold water. This,

with soft soap and the hard Paris water, meant scraping the grease off
with bits of newspaper.

We were so short of saucepans that I had to wash each one as soon as
it was done with, instead of leaving them till the evening. This alone
wasted probably an hour a day.

Owing to some scamping of expense in the installation, the electric light
usually fused at eight in the evening. The *patron* would only allow us three
candles in the kitchen, and the cook said three were unlucky, so we had
only two.

Our coffee-grinder was borrowed from a *bistro* near by, and our dustbin
and brooms from the concierge. After the first week a quantity of linen
did not come back from the wash, as the bill was not paid. We were in
trouble with the inspector of labour, who had discovered that the staff
included no Frenchmen; he had several private interviews with the *patron*,
who, I believe, was obliged to bribe him. The electric company was still
dunning us, and when the duns found that we would buy them off with
apéritifs, they came every morning. We were in debt at the grocery, and
credit would have been stopped, only the grocer's wife (a moustachio'd
woman of sixty) had taken a fancy to Jules, who was sent every morning
to cajole her. Similarly I had to waste an hour every day haggling over
vegetables in the rue du Commerce, to save a few centimes.

These are the results of starting a restaurant on insufficient capital. And
in these conditions the cook and I were expected to serve thirty or forty
meals a day, and would later on be serving a hundred. From the first day
it was too much for us. The cook's working hours were from eight in the
morning till midnight, and mine from seven in the morning till half past
twelve the next morning – seventeen and a half hours, almost without a
break. We never had time to sit down till five in the afternoon, and even
then there was no seat except the top of the dustbin. Boris, who lived near
by and had not to catch the last Métro home, worked from eight in the
morning till two the next morning – eighteen hours a day, seven days a
week. Such hours, though not usual, are nothing extraordinary in Paris.

Life settled at once into a routine that made the Hôtel X seem like a
holiday. Every morning at six I drove myself out of bed, did not shave,
sometimes washed, hurried up to the Place d'Italie and fought for a place
on the Métro. By seven I was in the desolation of the cold, filthy kitchen,
with the potato skins and bones and fishtails littered on the floor, and a
pile of plates, stuck together in their grease, waiting from overnight. I
could not start on the plates yet, because the water was cold, and I had
to fetch milk and make coffee, for the others arrived at eight and expected

to find coffee ready. Also, there were always several copper saucepans to clean. Those copper saucepans are the bane of a *plongeur*'s life. They have to be scoured with sand and bunches of chain, ten minutes to each one, and then polished on the outside with Brasso. Fortunately, the art of making them has been lost and they are gradually vanishing from French kitchens, though one can still buy them second-hand.

When I had begun on the plates the cook would take me away from the plates to begin skinning onions, and when I had begun on the onions the *patron* would arrive and send me out to buy cabbages. When I came back with the cabbages the *patron*'s wife would tell me to go to some shop half a mile away and buy a pot of rouge; by the time I came back there would be more vegetables waiting, and the plates were still not done. In this way our incompetence piled one job on another throughout the day, everything in arrears.

Till ten, things went comparatively easily, though we were working fast, and no one lost his temper. The cook would find time to talk about her artistic nature, and say did I not think Tolstoy was *épatant*, and sing in a fine soprano voice as she minced beef on the board. But at ten the waiters began clamouring for their lunch, which they had early, and at eleven the first customers would be arriving. Suddenly everything became hurry and bad temper. There was not the same furious rushing and yelling as at the Hôtel X, but an atmosphere of muddle, petty spite and exasperation. Discomfort was at the bottom of it. It was unbearably cramped in the kitchen, and dishes had to be put on the floor, and one had to be thinking constantly about not stepping on them. The cook's vast buttocks banged against me as she moved to and fro. A ceaseless, nagging chorus of orders streamed from her:

'Unspeakable idiot! How many times have I told you not to bleed the beetroots? Quick, let me get to the sink! Put those knives away; get on with the potatoes. What have you done with my strainer? Oh, leave those potatoes alone. Didn't I tell you to skim the *bouillon*? Take that can of water off the stove. Never mind the washing up, chop this celery. No, not like that, you fool, like this. There! Look at you letting those peas boil over! Now get to work and scale these herrings. Look, do you call this plate clean? Wipe it on your apron. Put that salad on the floor. That's right, put it where I'm bound to step in it! Look out, that pot's boiling over! Get me down that saucepan. No, the other one. Put this on the grill. Throw those potatoes away. Don't waste time, throw them on the floor. Tread them in. Now throw down some sawdust; this floor's like a skating-rink. Look, you fool, that steak's burning! *Mon Dieu*, why did they send me an idiot for a *plongeur*? Who are you talking to? Do you realize that my aunt was a Russian countess?' etc. etc. etc.

This went on till three o'clock without much variation, except that about eleven the cook usually had a *crise de nerfs* and a flood of tears. From three to five was a fairly slack time for the waiters, but the cook was still busy, and I was working my fastest, for there was a pile of dirty plates waiting, and it was a race to get them done, or partly done, before dinner began. The washing up was doubled by the primitive conditions – a cramped draining-board, tepid water, sodden cloths, and a sink that got blocked once in an hour. By five the cook and I were feeling unsteady on our feet, not having eaten or sat down since seven. We used to collapse, she on the dustbin and I on the floor, drink a bottle of beer, and apologize for some of the things we had said in the morning. Tea was what kept us going. We took care to have a pot always stewing, and drank pints during the day.

At half past five the hurry and quarrelling began again, and now worse than before, because everyone was tired out. The cook had a *crise de nerfs* at six and another at nine; they came on so regularly that one could have told the time by them. She would flop down on the dustbin, begin weeping hysterically, and cry out that never, no, never had she thought to come to such a life as this; her nerves would not stand it; she had studied music at Vienna; she had a bedridden husband to support, etc. etc. At another time one would have been sorry for her, but, tired as we all were, her whimpering voice merely infuriated us. Jules used to stand in the doorway and mimic her weeping. The *patron*'s wife nagged, and Boris and Jules quarrelled all day, because Jules shirked his work, and Boris, as head waiter, claimed the larger share of the tips. Only the second day after the restaurant opened, they came to blows in the kitchen over a two-franc tip, and the cook and I had to separate them. The only person who never forgot his manners was the *patron*. He kept the same hours as the rest of us, but he had no work to do, for it was his wife who really managed things. His sole job, besides ordering the supplies, was to stand in the bar smoking cigarettes and looking gentlemanly, and he did that to perfection.

The cook and I generally found time to eat our dinner between ten and eleven o'clock. At midnight the cook would steal a packet of food for her husband, stow it under her clothes, and make off, whimpering that these hours would kill her and she would give notice in the morning. Jules also left at midnight, usually after a dispute with Boris, who had to look after the bar till two. Between twelve and half past I did what I could to finish the washing up. There was no time to attempt doing the work properly,

and I used simply to rub the grease off the plates with table-napkins. As
for the dirt on the floor, I let it lie, or swept the worst of it out of sight
under the stoves.

At half past twelve I would put on my coat and hurry out. The *patron*,
bland as ever, would stop me as I went down the alley-way past the bar.
'*Mais, mon cher monsieur*, how tired you look! Please do me the favour
of accepting this glass of brandy.'

He would hand me the glass of brandy as courteously as though I had
been a Russian duke instead of a *plongeur*. He treated all of us like this.
It was our compensation for working seventeen hours a day.

As a rule the last Métro was almost empty – a great advantage, for one
could sit down and sleep for a quarter of an hour. Generally I was in bed
by half past one. Sometimes I missed the train and had to sleep on the
floor of the restaurant, but it hardly mattered, for I could have slept on
cobblestones at that time.

21

THIS life went on for about a fortnight, with a slight increase of work as
more customers came to the restaurant. I could have saved an hour a day
by taking a room near the restaurant, but it seemed impossible to find
time to change lodgings – or, for that matter, to get my hair cut, look at
a newspaper, or even undress completely. After ten days I managed to
find a free quarter of an hour, and wrote to my friend B. in London asking
him if he could get me a job of some sort – anything, so long as it allowed
more than five hours sleep. I was simply not equal to going on with a
seventeen-hour day, though there are plenty of people who think nothing
of it. When one is overworked, it is a good cure for self-pity to think of
the thousands of people in Paris restaurants who work such hours, and
will go on doing it, not for a few weeks, but for years. There was a girl in
a *bistro* near my hotel who worked from seven in the morning till midnight
for a whole year, only sitting down to her meals. I remember once asking
her to come to a dance, and she laughed and said that she had not been
farther than the street corner for several months. She was consumptive,
and died about the time I left Paris.

After only a week we were all neurasthenic with fatigue, except Jules, who skulked persistently. The quarrels, intermittent at first, had now become continuous. For hours one would keep up a drizzle of useless nagging, rising into storms of abuse every few minutes. 'Get me down that saucepan, idiot!' the cook would cry (she was not tall enough to reach the shelves where the saucepans were kept). 'Get it down yourself, you old whore,' I would answer. Such remarks seemed to be generated spontaneously from the air of the kitchen.

We quarrelled over things of inconceivable pettiness. The dustbin, for instance, was an unending source of quarrels – whether it should be put where I wanted it, which was in the cook's way, or where she wanted it, which was between me and the sink. Once she nagged and nagged until at last, in pure spite, I lifted the dustbin up and put it out in the middle of the floor, where she was bound to trip over it.

'Now, you cow,' I said, 'move it yourself.'

Poor old woman, it was too heavy for her to lift, and she sat down, put her head on the table and burst out crying. And I jeered at her. This is the kind of effect that fatigue has upon one's manners.

After a few days the cook had ceased talking about Tolstoy and her artistic nature, and she and I were not on speaking terms, except for the purposes of work, and Boris and Jules were not on speaking terms, and neither of them was on speaking terms with the cook. Even Boris and I were barely on speaking terms. We had agreed beforehand that the *engueulades* of working hours did not count between times; but we had called each other things too bad to be forgotten – and besides, there were no between times. Jules grew lazier and lazier, and he stole food constantly – from a sense of duty, he said. He called the rest of us *jaune* – blackleg – when we would not join with him in stealing. He had a curious, malignant spirit. He told me, as a matter of pride, that he had sometimes wrung a dirty dishcloth into a customer's soup before taking it in, just to be revenged upon a member of the bourgeoisie.

The kitchen grew dirtier and the rats bolder, though we trapped a few of them. Looking round that filthy room, with raw meat lying among refuse on the floor, and cold, clotted saucepans sprawling everywhere, and the sink blocked and coated with grease, I used to wonder whether there could be a restaurant in the world as bad as ours. But the other three all said that they had been in dirtier places. Jules took a positive pleasure in seeings things dirty. In the afternoon, when he had not much to do, he used to stand in the kitchen doorway jeering at us for working too hard:

'Fool! Why do you wash that plate? Wipe it on your trousers. Who cares about the customers? *They* don't know what's going on. What is restaurant work? You are carving a chicken and it falls on the floor. You apologize, you bow, you go out; and in five minutes you come back by another door – with the same chicken. That is restaurant work,' etc.

And, strange to say, in spite of all this filth and incompetence, the Auberge de Jehan Cottard was actually a success. For the first few days all our customers were Russians, friends of the *patron*, and these were followed by Americans and other foreigners – no Frenchmen. Then one night there was tremendous excitement, because our first Frenchman had arrived. For a moment our quarrels were forgotten and we all united in the effort to serve a good dinner. Boris tiptoed into the kitchen, jerked his thumb over his shoulder and whispered conspiratorially:

'*Sh! Attention, un Français!*'

A moment later the *patron*'s wife came and whispered:

'*Attention, un Français!* See that he gets a double portion of all vegetables.'

While the Frenchman ate, the *patron*'s wife stood behind the grille of the kitchen door and watched the expression of his face. Next night the Frenchman came back with two other Frenchmen. This meant that we were earning a good name; the surest sign of a bad restaurant is to be frequented only by foreigners. Probably part of the reason for our success was that the *patron*, with the sole gleam of sense he had shown in fitting out the restaurant, had bought very sharp table-knives. Sharp knives, of course, are *the* secret of a successful restaurant. I am glad that this happened, for it destroyed one of my illusions, namely, the idea that Frenchmen know good food when they see it. Or perhaps we *were* a fairly good restaurant by Paris standards; in which case the bad ones must be past imagining.

In a very few days after I had written to B. he replied to say that there was a job he could get for me. It was to look after a congenital imbecile, which sounded a splendid rest cure after the Auberge de Jehan Cottard. I pictured myself loafing in the country lanes, knocking thistle-heads off with my stick, feeding on roast lamb and treacle tart, and sleeping ten hours a night in sheets smelling of lavender. B. sent me a fiver to pay my passage and get my clothes out of the pawn, and as soon as the money arrived I gave one day's notice and left the restaurant. My leaving so suddenly embarrassed the *patron*, for as usual he was penniless, and he had to pay my wages thirty francs short. However he stood me a glass of Courvoisier '48 brandy, and I think he felt that this made up the difference. They engaged a Czech, a thoroughly competent *plongeur*, in my place, and the poor old cook was sacked a few weeks later. Afterwards I heard that, with two first-rate people in the kitchen, the *plongeur*'s work had been cut down to fifteen hours a day. Below that no one could have cut it, short of modernizing the kitchen.

22

FOR what they are worth I want to give my opinions about the life of a Paris *plongeur*. When one comes to think of it, it is strange that thousands of people in a great modern city should spend their waking hours swabbing dishes in hot dens underground. The question I am raising is why this life goes on – what purpose it serves, and who wants it to continue, and why I am not taking the merely rebellious, *fainéant* attitude. I am trying to consider the social significance of a *plongeur*'s life.

I think one should start by saying that a *plongeur* is one of the slaves of the modern world. Not that there is any need to whine over him, for he is better off than many manual workers, but still, he is no freer than if he were bought and sold. His work is servile and without art; he is paid just enough to keep him alive; his only holiday is the sack. He is cut off from marriage, or, if he marries, his wife must work too. Except by a lucky chance, he has no escape from this life, save into prison. At this moment there are men with university degrees scrubbing dishes in Paris for ten or fifteen hours a day. One cannot say that it is mere idleness on their part, for an idle man cannot be a *plongeur*; they have simply been trapped by a routine which makes thought impossible. If *plongeurs* thought at all, they would long ago have formed a union and gone on strike for better treatment. But they do not think, because they have no leisure for it; their life has made slaves of them.

The question is, why does this slavery continue? People have a way of taking it for granted that all work is done for a sound purpose. They see somebody else doing a disagreeable job, and think that they have solved things by saying that the job is necessary. Coal-mining, for example, is hard work, but it is necessary – we must have coal. Working in the sewers is unpleasant, but somebody must work in the sewers. And similarly with a *plongeur*'s work. Some people must feed in restaurants, and so other people must swab dishes for eighty hours a week. It is the work of civilization, therefore unquestionable. This point is worth considering.

Is a *plongeur*'s work really necessary to civilization? We have a feeling that it must be 'honest' work, because it is hard and disagreeable, and we have made a sort of fetish of manual work. We see a man cutting down a tree, and we make sure that he is filling a social need, just because he uses his muscles; it does not occur to us that he may only be cutting down a beautiful tree to make room for a hideous statue. I believe it is the same with a *plongeur*. He earns his bread in the sweat of his brow, but it does not follow that he is doing anything useful; he may be only supplying a luxury which, very often, is not a luxury.

As an example of what I mean by luxuries which are not luxuries, take an extreme case, such as one hardly sees in Europe. Take an Indian rickshaw puller, or a gharry pony. In any Far Eastern town there are rickshaw pullers by the hundred, black wretches weighing eight stone, clad in loin-cloths. Some of them are diseased; some of them are fifty years old. For miles on end they trot in the sun or rain, head down, dragging at the shafts, with the sweat dripping from their grey moustaches. When they go too slowly the passenger calls them *bahinchut*. They earn thirty or forty rupees a month, and cough their lungs out after a few years. The gharry ponies are gaunt, vicious things that have been sold cheap as having a few years' work left in them. Their master looks on the whip as a substitute for food. Their work expresses itself in a sort of equation – whip plus food equals energy; generally it is about sixty per cent whip and forty per cent food. Sometimes their necks are encircled by one vast sore, so that they drag all day on raw flesh. It is still possible to make them work, however; it is just a question of thrashing them so hard that the pain behind outweighs the pain in front. After a few years even the whip loses its virtue, and the pony goes to the knacker. These are instances of unnecessary work, for there is no real need for gharries and rickshaws; they only exist because Orientals consider it vulgar to walk. They are luxuries, and, as anyone who has ridden in them knows, very poor luxuries. They afford a small amount of convenience, which cannot possibly balance the suffering of the men and animals.

Similarly with the *plongeur*. He is a king compared with a rickshaw puller or a gharry pony, but his case is analogous. He is the slave of a hotel or a restaurant, and his slavery is more or less useless. For, after all, where is the *real* need of big hotels and smart restaurants? They are supposed to provide luxury, but in reality they provide only a cheap, shoddy imitation of it. Nearly everyone hates hotels. Some restaurants are better than others, but it is impossible to get as good a meal in a restaurant as one can get, for the same expense, in a private house. No doubt hotels and restaurants must exist, but there is no need that they should enslave hundreds of people. What makes the work in them is not the essentials; it is the shams that are supposed to represent luxury. Smartness, as it is called, means, in effect, merely that the staff work more and the customers pay more; no one benefits except the proprietor, who will presently buy himself a striped villa at Deauville. Essentially, a 'smart' hotel is a place where a hundred people toil like devils in order that two hundred may pay through the nose for things they do not really want. If the nonsense were cut out of hotels and restaurants, and the work done with simple efficiency, *plongeurs* might work six or eight hours a day instead of ten or fifteen.

Suppose it is granted that a *plongeur*'s work is more or less useless. Then the question follows, Why does anyone want him to go on working? I am trying to go beyond the immediate economic cause, and to consider what pleasure it can give anyone to think of men swabbing dishes for life. For there is no doubt that people – comfortably situated people – do find a pleasure in such thoughts. A slave, Marcus Cato said, should be working when he is not sleeping. It does not matter whether his work is needed or not, he must work, because work in itself is good – for slaves, at least. This sentiment still survives, and it has piled up mountains of useless drudgery.

I believe that this instinct to perpetuate useless work is, at bottom, simply fear of the mob. The mob (the thought runs) are such low animals that they would be dangerous if they had leisure; it is safer to keep them too busy to think. A rich man who happens to be intellectually honest, if he is questioned about the improvement of working conditions, usually says something like this:

'We know that poverty is unpleasant; in fact, since it is so remote, we rather enjoy harrowing ourselves with the thought of its unpleasantness. But don't expect us to do anything about it. We are sorry for you lower classes, just as we are sorry for a cat with the mange, but we will fight like devils against any improvement of your condition. We feel that you are much safer as you are. The present state of affairs suits us, and we are not going to take the risk of setting you free, even by an extra hour a day. So, dear brothers, since evidently you must sweat to pay for our trips to Italy, sweat and be damned to you.'

This is particularly the attitude of intelligent, cultivated people; one can read the substance of it in a hundred essays. Very few cultivated people have less than (say) four hundred pounds a year, and naturally they side with the rich, because they imagine that any liberty conceded to the poor is a threat to their own liberty. Foreseeing some dismal Marxian Utopia as the alternative, the educated man prefers to keep things as they are. Possibly he does not like his fellow-rich very much, but he supposes that even the vulgarest of them are less inimical to his pleasures, more his kind of people, than the poor, and that he had better stand by them. It is this fear of a supposedly dangerous mob that makes nearly all intelligent people conservative in their opinions.

Fear of the mob is a superstitious fear. It is based on the idea that there is some mysterious, fundamental difference between rich and poor, as though they were two different races, like Negroes and white men. But in reality there is no such difference. The mass of the rich and the poor are differentiated by their incomes and nothing else, and the average millionaire is only the average dishwasher dressed in a new suit. Change places, and handy dandy, which is the justice, which is the thief? Everyone who has mixed on equal terms with the poor knows this quite well. But the trouble is that intelligent, cultivated people, the very people who might be expected to have liberal opinions, never do mix with the poor. For what do the majority of educated people know about poverty? In my copy of Villon's poems the editor has actually thought it necessary to explain the line '*Ne pain ne voyent qu'aux fenestres*' by a footnote; so remote is even hunger from the educated man's experience. From this ignorance a superstitious fear of the mob results quite naturally. The educated man pictures a horde of submen, wanting only a day's liberty to loot his house, burn his books, and set him to work minding a machine or sweeping out a lavatory. 'Anything,' he thinks, 'any injustice, sooner than let that mob loose.' He does not see that since there is no difference between the mass of rich and poor, there is no question of setting the mob loose. The mob is in fact loose now, and – in the shape of rich men – is using its power to set up enormous treadmills of boredom, such as 'smart' hotels.

To sum up. A *plongeur* is a slave, and a wasted slave, doing stupid and largely unnecessary work. He is kept at work, ultimately, because of a vague feeling that he would be dangerous if he had leisure. And educated people, who should be on his side, acquiesce in the process, because they know nothing about him and consequently are afraid of him. I say this of the *plongeur* because it is his case I have been considering; it would apply equally to numberless other types of worker. These are only my own ideas about the basic facts of a *plongeur*'s life, made without reference to immediate economic questions, and no doubt largely platitudes. I present them as a sample of the thoughts that are put into one's head by working in an hotel.

23

As soon as I left the Auberge de Jehan Cottard I went to bed and slept the clock round, all but one hour. Then I washed my teeth for the first time in a fortnight, bathed and had my hair cut, and got my clothes out of pawn. I had two glorious days of loafing. I even went in my best suit to the Auberge, leant against the bar and spent five francs on a bottle of English beer. It is a curious sensation, being a customer where you have been a slave's slave. Boris was sorry that I had left the restaurant just at the moment when we were *lancés* and there was a chance of making money. I have heard from him since, and he tells me that he is making a hundred francs a day and has set up a girl who is *très sérieuse* and never smells of garlic.

I spent a day wandering about our quarter, saying good-bye to everyone. It was on this day that Charlie told me about the death of old Roucolle the miser, who had once lived in the quarter. Very likely Charlie was lying as usual, but it was a good story.

Roucolle died, aged seventy-four, a year or two before I went to Paris, but the people in the quarter still talked of him while I was there. He never equalled Daniel Dancer or anyone of that kind, but he was an interesting character. He went to Les Halles every morning to pick up damaged vegetables, and ate cat's meat, and wore newspaper instead of underclothes, and used the wainscoting of his room for firewood, and made himself a pair of trousers out of a sack – all this with half a million francs invested. I should like very much to have known him.

Like many misers, Roucolle came to a bad end through putting his money into a wildcat scheme. One day a Jew appeared in the quarter, an alert, business-like young chap who had a first-rate plan for smuggling cocaine into England. It is easy enough, of course, to buy cocaine in Paris, and the smuggling would be quite simple in itself, only there is always some spy who betrays the plan to the customs or the police. It is said that this is often done by the very people who sell the cocaine, because the smuggling trade is in the hands of a large combine, who do not want competition. The Jew, however, swore that there was no danger. He knew a way of getting cocaine direct from Vienna, not through the usual channels, and there would be no blackmail to pay. He had got into touch with Roucolle through a young Pole, a student at the Sorbonne, who was going to put four thousand francs into the scheme if Roucolle would put six thousand. For this they could buy ten pounds of cocaine, which would be worth a small fortune in England.

The Pole and the Jew had a tremendous struggle to get the money from between old Roucolle's claws. Six thousand francs was not much – he had more than that sewn into the mattress in his room – but it was agony for him to part with a sou. The Pole and the Jew were at him for weeks on end, explaining, bullying, coaxing, arguing, going down on their knees and imploring him to produce the money. The old man was half frantic between greed and fear. His bowels yearned at the thought of getting, perhaps, fifty thousand francs' profit, and yet he could not bring himself to risk the money. He used to sit in a corner with his head in his hands, groaning and sometimes yelling out in agony, and often he would kneel down (he was very pious) and pray for strength, but still he couldn't do it. But at last, more from exhaustion than anything else, he gave in quite suddenly; he slit open the mattress where his money was concealed and handed over six thousand francs to the Jew.

The Jew delivered the cocaine the same day, and promptly vanished. And meanwhile, as was not surprising after the fuss Roucolle had made, the affair had been noised all over the quarter. The very next morning the hotel was raided and searched by the police.

Roucolle and the Pole were in agonies. The police were downstairs, working their way up and searching every room in turn, and there was the great packet of cocaine on the table, with no place to hide it and no chance of escaping down the stairs. The Pole was for throwing the stuff out of the window, but Roucolle would not hear of it. Charlie told me that he had been present at the scene. He said that when they tried to take the packet from Roucolle he clasped it to his breast and struggled like a madman, although he was seventy-four years old. He was wild with fright, but he would go to prison rather than throw his money away.

At last, when the police were searching only one floor below, somebody had an idea. A man on Roucolle's floor had a dozen tins of face-powder which he was selling on commission; it was suggested that the cocaine could be put into the tins and passed off as face-powder. The powder was hastily thrown out of the window and the cocaine substituted, and the tins were put openly on Roucolle's table, as though there there were nothing to conceal. A few minutes later the police came to search Roucolle's room. They tapped the walls and looked up the chimney and turned out the drawers and examined the floorboards, and then, just as they were about to give it up, having found nothing, the inspector noticed the tins on the table.

'*Tiens,*' he said, 'have a look at those tins. I hadn't noticed them. What's in them, eh?'

'Face-powder,' said the Pole as calmly as he could manage. But at the same instant Roucolle let out a loud groaning noise, from alarm, and the police became suspicious immediately. They opened one of the tins and tipped out the contents, and after smelling it, the inspector said that he believed it was cocaine. Roucolle and the Pole began swearing on the names of the saints that it was only face-powder; but it was no use, the more they protested the more suspicious the police became. The two men were arrested and led off to the police station, followed by half the quarter.

At the station, Roucolle and the Pole were interrogated by the Commissaire while a tin of the cocaine was sent away to be analysed. Charlie said that the scene Roucolle made was beyond description. He wept, prayed, made contradictory statements and denounced the Pole all at once, so loud that he could be heard half a street away. The policemen almost burst with laughing at him.

After an hour a policeman came back with the tin of cocaine and a note from the analyst. He was laughing.

'This is not cocaine, *monsieur,*' he said.

'What, not cocaine?' said the Commissaire. '*Mais, alors* – what is it, then?'

'It is face-powder.'

Roucolle and the Pole were released at once, entirely exonerated but very angry. The Jew had double-crossed them. Afterwards, when the excitement was over, it turned out that he had played the same trick on two other people in the quarter.

The Pole was glad enough to escape, even though he had lost his four thousand francs, but poor old Roucolle was utterly broken down. He took to his bed at once, and all that day and half the night they could hear him thrashing about, mumbling, and sometimes yelling out at the top of his voice:

'Six thousand francs! *Nom de Jésus-Christ!* Six thousand francs!'

Three days later he had some kind of stroke, and in a fortnight he was dead – of a broken heart, Charlie said.

24

I TRAVELLED to England third class via Dunkirk and Tilbury, which is the cheapest and not the worst way of crossing the Channel. You had to pay extra for a cabin, so I slept in the saloon, together with most of the third-class passengers. I find this entry in my diary for that day:

'Sleeping in the saloon, twenty-seven men, sixteen women. Of the women, not a single one has washed her face this morning. The men mostly went to the bathroom; the women merely produced vanity cases and covered the dirt with powder. *Q.* A secondary sexual difference?'

On the journey I fell in with a couple of Roumanians, mere children, who were going to England on their honeymoon trip. They asked innumerable questions about England, and I told them some startling lies. I was so pleased to be getting home, after being hard up for months in a foreign city, that England seemed to me a sort of Paradise. There are, indeed, many things in England that make you glad to get home; bathrooms, armchairs, mint sauce, new potatoes properly cooked, brown bread, marmalade, beer made with veritable hops – they are all splendid, if you can pay for them. England is a very good country when you are not poor; and, of course, with a tame imbecile to look after, I was not going to be poor. The thought of not being poor made me very patriotic. The more questions the Roumanians asked, the more I praised England; the climate, the scenery, the art, the literature, the laws – everything in England was perfect.

Was the architecture in England good? the Roumanians asked. 'Splendid!' I said. 'And you should just see the London statues! Paris is vulgar – half grandiosity and half slums. But London –'

Then the boat drew alongside Tilbury pier. The first building we saw on the waterside was one of those huge hotels, all stucco and pinnacles, which stare from the English coast like idiots staring over an asylum wall. I saw the Roumanians, too polite to say anything, cocking their eyes at the hotel. 'Built by French architects,' I assured them; and even later, when the train was crawling into London through the eastern slums, I still kept it up about the beauties of English architecture. Nothing seemed too good to say about England, now that I was coming home and was not hard up any more.

I went to B.'s office, and his first words knocked everything to ruins. 'I'm sorry,' he said; 'your employers have gone abroad, patient and all. However, they'll be back in a month. I suppose you can hang on till then?'

I was outside in the street before it even occurred to me to borrow some more money. There was a month to wait, and I had exactly nineteen and sixpence in hand. The news had taken my breath away. For a long time I could not make up my mind what to do. I loafed the day in the streets, and at night, not having the slightest notion of how to get a cheap bed in London, I went to a 'family' hotel, where the charge was seven and sixpence. After paying the bill I had ten and twopence in hand.

By the morning I had made my plans. Sooner or later I should have to go to B. for more money, but it seemed hardly decent to do so yet, and in the meantime I must exist in some hole-and-corner way. Past experience set me against pawning my best suit. I would leave all my things at the station cloakroom, except my second-best suit, which I could exchange for some cheap clothes and perhaps a pound. If I was going to live a month on thirty shillings I must have bad clothes – indeed, the worse the better. Whether thirty shillings could be made to last a month I had no idea, not knowing London as I knew Paris. Perhaps I could beg, or sell bootlaces, and I remembered articles I had read in the Sunday papers about beggars who have two thousand pounds sewn into their trousers. It was, at any rate, notoriously impossible to starve in London, so there was nothing to be anxious about.

To sell my clothes I went down into Lambeth, where the people are poor and there are a lot of rag shops. At the first shop I tried the proprietor was polite but unhelpful; at the second he was rude; at the third he was stone deaf, or pretended to be so. The fourth shopman was a large blond young man, very pink all over, like a slice of ham. He looked at the clothes I was wearing and felt them disparagingly between thumb and finger.

'Poor stuff,' he said, 'very poor stuff, that is.' (It was quite a good suit.) 'What yer want for 'em?'

I explained that I wanted some older clothes and as much money as he could spare. He thought for a moment, then collected some dirty-looking rags and threw them on to the counter. 'What about the money?' I said, hoping for a pound. He pursed his lips, then produced *a shilling* and laid it beside the clothes. I did not argue – I was going to argue, but as I opened my mouth he reached out as though to take up the shilling again;

I saw that I was helpless. He let me change in a small room behind the shop.

The clothes were a coat, once dark brown, a pair of black dungaree trousers, a scarf and a cloth cap; I had kept my own shirt, socks and boots, and I had a comb and razor in my pocket. It gives one a very strange feeling to be wearing such clothes. I had worn bad enough things before, but nothing at all like these; they were not merely dirty and shapeless, they had – how is one to express it? – a gracelessness, a patina of antique filth, quite different from mere shabbiness. They were the sort of clothes you see on a bootlace seller, or a tramp. An hour later, in Lambeth, I saw a hang-dog man, obviously a tramp, coming towards me, and when I looked again it was myself, reflected in a shop window. The dirt was plastering my face already. Dirt is a great respecter of persons; it lets you alone when you are well dressed, but as soon as your collar is gone it flies towards you from all directions.

I stayed in the streets till late at night, keeping on the move all the time. Dressed as I was, I was half afraid that the police might arrest me as a vagabond, and I dared not speak to anyone, imagining that they must notice a disparity between my accent and my clothes. (Later I discovered that this never happened.) My new clothes had put me instantly into a new world. Everyone's demeanour seemed to have changed abruptly. I helped a hawker pick up a barrow that he had upset. 'Thanks, mate,' he said with a grin. No one had called me mate before in my life – it was the clothes that had done it. For the first time I noticed, too, how the attitude of women varies with a man's clothes. When a badly dressed man passes them they shudder away from him with a quite frank movement of disgust, as though he were a dead cat. Clothes are powerful things. Dressed in a tramp's clothes it is very difficult, at any rate for the first day, not to feel that you are genuinely degraded. You might feel the same shame, irrational but very real, your first night in prison.

At about eleven I began looking for a bed. I had read about doss-houses (they are never called doss-houses, by the way), and I supposed that one could get a bed for fourpence or thereabouts. Seeing a man, a navvy or something of the kind, standing on the kerb in the Waterloo Road, I stopped and questioned him. I said that I was stony broke and wanted the cheapest bed I could get.

'Oh,' said he, 'you go to that 'ouse across the street there, with the sign "Good Beds for Single Men". That's a good kip [sleeping place], that is. I bin there myself on and off. You'll find it cheap *and* clean.'

It was a tall, battered-looking house, with dim lights in all the windows, some of which were patched with brown paper. I entered a stone passage-way, and a little etiolated boy with sleepy eyes appeared from a door leading to a cellar. Murmurous sounds came from the cellar, and a wave of hot air and cheese. The boy yawned and held out his hand.

'Want a kip? That'll be a 'og, guv'nor.'

I paid the shilling, and the boy led me up a rickety unlighted staircase to a bedroom. It had a sweetish reek of paregoric and foul linen; the windows seemed to be tight shut, and the air was almost suffocating at first. There was a candle burning, and I saw that the room measured fifteen feet square by eight high, and had eight beds in it. Already six lodgers were in bed, queer lumpy shapes with all their own clothes, even their boots, piled on top of them. Someone was coughing in a loathsome manner in one corner.

When I got into the bed I found that it was as hard as a board, and as for the pillow, it was a mere hard cylinder like a block of wood. It was rather worse than sleeping on a table, because the bed was not six feet long, and very narrow, and the mattress was convex, so that one had to hold on to avoid falling out. The sheets stank so horribly of sweat that I could not bear them near my nose. Also, the bedclothes only consisted of the sheets and a cotton counterpane, so that though stuffy it was none too warm. Several noises recurred throughout the night. About once in an hour the man on my left – a sailor, I think – woke up, swore vilely, and lighted a cigarette. Another man, victim of a bladder disease, got up and noisily used his chamber-pot half a dozen times during the night. The man in the corner had a coughing fit once in every twenty minutes, so regularly that one came to listen for it as one listens for the next yap when a dog is baying the moon. It was an unspeakably repellent sound; a foul bubbling and retching, as though the man's bowels were being churned up within him. Once when he struck a match I saw that he was a very old man, with a grey, sunken face like that of a corpse, and he was wearing his trousers wrapped round his head as a nightcap, a thing which for some reason disgusted me very much. Every time he coughed or the other man swore, a sleepy voice from one of the other beds cried out:

'Shut up! Oh, for Christ's – *sake* shut up!'

I had about an hour's sleep in all. In the morning I was woken by a dim impression of some large brown thing coming towards me. I opened my eyes and saw that it was one of the sailor's feet, sticking out of bed close to my face. It was dark brown, quite dark brown like an Indian's, with dirt. The walls were leprous, and the sheets, three weeks from the wash, were almost raw umber colour. I got up, dressed and went downstairs. In the cellar were a row of basins and two slippery roller towels. I had a piece of soap in my pocket, and I was going to wash, when I noticed that every basin was streaked with grime – solid, sticky filth as black as boot-blacking. I went out unwashed. Altogether, the lodging-house had not come up to its description as cheap *and* clean. It was however, as I found later, a fairly representative lodging-house.

I crossed the river and walked a long way eastward, finally going into a coffee-shop on Tower Hill. An ordinary London coffee-shop, like a thousand others, it seemed queer and foreign after Paris. It was a little stuffy room with the high-backed pews that were fashionable in the forties, the day's menu written on a mirror with a piece of soap, and a girl of fourteen handling the dishes. Navvies were eating out of newspaper parcels, and drinking tea in vast saucerless mugs like china tumblers. In a corner by himself a Jew, muzzle down in the plate, was guiltily wolfing bacon.

'Could I have some tea and bread and butter?' I said to the girl.

She stared. 'No butter, only marg,' she said, surprised. And she repeated the order in the phrase that is to London what the eternal *coup de rouge* is to Paris: 'Large tea and two slices!'

On the wall beside my pew there was a notice saying 'Pocketing the sugar not allowed', and beneath it some poetic customer had written:

> He that takes away the sugar,
> Shall be called a dirty —

but someone else had been at pains to scratch out the last word. This was England. The tea-and-two-slices cost threepence halfpenny, leaving me with eight and twopence.

25

THE eight shillings lasted three days and four nights. After my bad experience in the Waterloo Road* I moved eastward, and spent the next night in a lodging-house in Pennyfields. This was a typical lodging-house, like scores of others in London. It had accommodation for between fifty and a hundred men, and was managed by a 'deputy' – a deputy for the

* It is a curious but well-known fact that bugs are much commoner in south than north London. For some reason they have not yet crossed the river in any great numbers.

owner, that is, for these lodging-houses are profitable concerns and are owned by rich men. We slept fifteen or twenty in a dormitory; the beds were again cold and hard, but the sheets were not more than a week from the wash, which was an improvement. The charge was ninepence or a shilling (in the shilling dormitory the beds were six feet apart instead of four) and the terms were cash down by seven in the evening or out you went.

Downstairs there was a kitchen common to all lodgers, with free firing and a supply of cooking-pots, tea-basins, and toasting-forks. There were two great clinker fires, which were kept burning day and night the year through. The work of tending the fires, sweeping the kitchen and making the beds was done by the lodgers in rotation. One senior lodger, a fine Norman-looking stevedore named Steve, was known as 'head of the house', and was arbiter of disputes and unpaid chucker-out.

I liked the kitchen. It was a low-ceiled cellar deep underground, very hot and drowsy with coke fumes, and lighted only by the fires, which cast black velvet shadows in the corners. Ragged washing hung on strings from the ceiling. Red-lit men, stevedores mostly, moved about the fires with cooking-pots; some of them were quite naked, for they had been laundering and were waiting for their clothes to dry. At night there were games of nap and draughts, and songs – 'I'm a chap what's done wrong by my parents' was a favourite, and so was another popular song about a shipwreck. Sometimes late at night men would come in with a pail of winkles they had bought cheap, and share them out. There was a general sharing of food, and it was taken for granted to feed men who were out of work. A little pale, wizened creature, obviously dying, referred to as 'pore Brown, bin under the doctor and cut open three times', was regularly fed by the others.

Two or three of the lodgers were old-age pensioners. Till meeting them I had never realized that there are people in England who live on nothing but the old-age pension of ten shillings a week. None of these old men had any other resource whatever. One of them was talkative, and I asked him how he managed to exist. He said:

'Well, there's ninepence a night for yer kip – that's five an' threepence a week. Then there's threepence on Saturday for a shave – that's five an' six. Then say you 'as a 'aircut once a month for sixpence – that's another three'apence a week. So you 'as about four an' fourpence for food an' bacca.'

He could imagine no other expenses. His food was bread and margarine and tea – towards the end of the week dry bread and tea without milk –

and perhaps he got his clothes from charity. He seemed contented, valuing his bed and fire more than food. But, with an income of ten shillings a week, to spend money on a shave – it is awe-inspiring.

All day I loafed in the streets, east as far as Wapping, west as far as Whitechapel. It was queer after Paris; everything was so much cleaner and quieter and drearier. One missed the scream of the trams, and the noisy, festering life of the back streets, and the armed men clattering through the squares. The crowds were better dressed and the faces comelier and milder and more alike, without that fierce individuality and malice of the French. There was less drunkenness, and less dirt, and less quarrelling, and more idling. Knots of men stood at all the corners, slightly underfed, but kept going by the tea-and-two-slices which the Londoner swallows every two hours. One seemed to breathe a less feverish air than in Paris. It was the land of the tea urn and the Labour Exchange, as Paris is the land of the *bistro* and the sweatshop.

It was interesting to watch the crowds. The East London women are pretty (it is the mixture of blood, perhaps), and Limehouse was sprinkled with Orientals – Chinamen, Chittagonian lascars, Dravidians selling silk scarves, even a few Sikhs, come goodness knows how. Here and there were street meetings. In Whitechapel somebody called The Singing Evangel undertook to save you from hell for the charge of sixpence. In the East India Dock Road the Salvation Army were holding a service. They were singing 'Anybody here like sneaking Judas?' to the tune of 'What's to be done with a drunken sailor?' On Tower Hill two Mormons were trying to address a meeting. Round their platform struggled a mob of men, shouting and interrupting. Someone was denouncing them for polygamists. A lame, bearded man, evidently an atheist, had heard the word God and was heckling angrily. There was a confused uproar of voices.

'My dear friends, if you would only let us finish what we were saying – ! – That's right, give 'em a say. Don't get on the argue! – No, no, you answer me. Can you *show* me God? You *show* 'im me, then I'll believe in 'im. – Oh, shut up, don't keep interrupting of 'em! – Interrupt yourself! F— polygamists! – Well, there's a lot to be said for polygamy. Take the f— women out of industry, anyway. – My dear friends, if you would just – No, no, don't you slip out of it. 'Ave you *seen* God? 'Ave you *touched* 'im? 'Ave you shook *'ands* with 'im? – Oh, don't get on the argue, for Christ's sake don't get on the *argue*!' etc. etc. I listened for twenty minutes, anxious to learn something about Mormonism, but the meeting never got beyond shouts. It is the general fate of street meetings.

In Middlesex Street, among the crowds at the market, a draggled, down-at-heel woman was hauling a brat of five by the arm. She brandished a tin trumpet in its face. The brat was squalling.

'Enjoy yourself!' yelled the mother. 'What yer think I brought yer out 'ere for an' bought y' a trumpet an' all? D'ya want to go across my knee? You little bastard, you *shall* enjoy yerself!'

Some drops of spittle fell from the trumpet. The mother and the child disappeared, both bawling. It was all very queer after Paris.

The last night that I was in the Pennyfields lodging-house there was a quarrel between two of the lodgers, a vile scene. One of the old-age pensioners, a man of about seventy, naked to the waist (he had been laundering), was violently abusing a short, thick-set stevedore, who stood with his back to the fire. I could see the old man's face in the light of the fire, and he was almost crying with grief and rage. Evidently something very serious had happened.

The old-age pensioner: 'You —!'

The stevedore: 'Shut yer mouth, you ole —, afore I set about yer!'

The old-age pensioner: 'Jest you try it on, you —! I'm thirty year older'n you, but it wouldn't take much to make me give you one as'd knock you into a bucketful of piss!'

The stevedore: 'Ah, an' then p'raps I wouldn't smash you up after, you ole —!'

Thus for five minutes. The lodgers sat round, unhappy, trying to disregard the quarrel. The stevedore looked sullen, but the old man was growing more and more furious. He kept making little rushes at the other, sticking out his face and screaming from a few inches distant like a cat on a wall, and spitting. He was trying to nerve himself to strike a blow, and not quite succeeding. Finally he burst out:

'A —, that's what you are, a — —! Take that in your dirty gob and suck it, you —! By —, I'll smash you afore I've done with you. A —, that's what you are, a son of a — whore. Lick that, you —! That's what I think of you, you —, you —, you — you BLACK BASTARD!'

Whereat he suddenly collapsed on a bench, took his face in his hands, and began crying. The other man, seeing that public feeling was against him, went out.

Afterwards I heard Steve explaining the cause of the quarrel. It appeared that it was all about a shilling's worth of food. In some way the old man had lost his store of bread and margarine, and so would have nothing to eat for the next three days, except what the others gave him in charity. The stevedore, who was in work and well fed, had taunted him; hence the quarrel.

When my money was down to one and fourpence I went for a night to a lodging-house in Bow, where the charge was only eightpence. One went down an area and through an alley-way into a deep, stifling cellar, ten feet square. Ten men, navvies mostly, were sitting in the fierce glare of the fire. It was midnight, but the deputy's son, a pale, sticky child of five, was there playing on the navvies' knees. An old Irishman was whistling to a blind bullfinch in a tiny cage. There were other songbirds there – tiny, faded things, that had lived all their lives underground. The lodgers habitually made water in the fire, to save going across a yard to the lavatory. As I sat at the table I felt something stir near my feet, and, looking down, saw a wave of black things moving slowly across the floor; they were black-beetles.

There were six beds in the dormitory, and the sheets, marked in huge letters 'Stolen from No. — Bow Road', smelt loathsome. In the next bed to me lay a very old man, a pavement artist, with some extraordinary curvature of the spine that made him stick right out of bed, with his back a foot or two from my face. It was bare, and marked with curious swirls of dirt, like a marble table-top. During the night a man came in drunk and was sick on the floor, close to my bed. There were bugs too – not so bad as in Paris, but enough to keep one awake. It was a filthy place. Yet the deputy and his wife were friendly people, and ready to make one a cup of tea at any hour of the day or night.

26

IN the morning after paying for the usual tea-and-two-slices and buying half an ounce of tobacco, I had a halfpenny left. I did not care to ask B. for more money yet, so there was nothing for it but to go to a casual ward. I had very little idea how to set about this, but I knew that there was a casual ward at Romton, so I walked out there, arriving at three or four in the afternoon. Leaning against the pigpens in Romton market-place was a wizened old Irishman, obviously a tramp. I went and leaned beside him, and presently offered him my tobacco-box. He opened the box and looked at the tobacco in astonishment:

'By God,' he said, 'dere's sixpennorth o' good baccy here! Where de hell d'you get hold o' dat? *You* ain't been on de road long.'

'What, don't you have tobacco on the road?' I said.

'Oh, we *has* it. Look.'

He produced a rusty tin which had once held Oxo Cubes. In it were twenty or thirty cigarette ends, picked up from the pavement. The Irishman said that he rarely got any other tobacco; he added that, with care, one could collect two ounces of tobacco a day on the London pavements.

'D'you come out o' one o' de London spikes [casual wards], eh?' he asked me.

I said yes, thinking this would make him accept me as a fellow tramp, and asked him what the spike at Romton was like. He said:

'Well, 'tis a cocoa spike. Dere's tay spikes, and cocoa spikes, and skilly spikes. Dey don't give you skilly in Romton, t'ank God — leastways, dey didn't de last time I was here. I been up to York and round Wales since.'

'What is skilly?' I said.

'Skilly? A can o' hot water wid some bloody oatmeal at de bottom; dat's skilly. De skilly spikes is always de worst.'

We stayed talking for an hour or two. The Irishman was a friendly old man, but he smelt very unpleasant, which was not surprising when one learned how many diseases he suffered from. It appeared (he described his symptoms fully) that taking him from top to bottom he had the following things wrong with him: on his crown, which was bald, he had eczema; he was shortsighted, and had no glasses; he had chronic bronchitis; he had some undiagnosed pain in the back; he had dyspepsia; he had urethritis; he had varicose veins, bunions and flat feet. With this assemblage of diseases he had tramped the roads for fifteen years.

At about five the Irishman said, 'Could you do wid a cup o' tay? De spike don't open till six.'

'I should think I could.'

'Well, dere's a place here where dey gives you a free cup o' tay and a bun. *Good* tay it is. Dey makes you say a lot o' bloody prayers after; but hell! It all passes de time away. You come wid me.'

He led the way to a small tin-roofed shed in a side-street, rather like a village cricket pavilion. About twenty-five other tramps were waiting. A few of them were dirty old habitual vagabonds, the majority decent-looking lads from the north, probably miners or cotton operatives out of work. Presently the door opened and a lady in a blue silk dress, wearing gold spectacles and a crucifix, welcomed us in. Inside were thirty or forty hard chairs, a harmonium, and a very gory lithograph of the Crucifixion.

Uncomfortably we took off our caps and sat down. The lady handed out the tea, and while we ate and drank she moved to and fro, talking benignly. She talked upon religious subjects – about Jesus Christ always having a soft spot for poor rough men like us, and about how quickly the time passed when you were in church, and what a difference it made to a man on the road if he said his prayers regularly. We hated it. We sat against the wall fingering our caps (a tramp feels indecently exposed with his cap off), and turning pink and trying to mumble something when the lady addressed us. There was no doubt that she meant it all kindly. As she came up to one of the north country lads with the plate of buns, she said to him:

'And you, my boy, how long is it since you knelt down and spoke with your Father in Heaven?'

Poor lad, not a word could he utter; but his belly answered for him, with a disgraceful rumbling which it set up at sight of the food. Thereafter he was so overcome with shame that he could scarcely swallow his bun. Only one man managed to answer the lady in her own style, and he was a spry, red-nosed fellow looking like a corporal who had lost his stripe for drunkenness. He could pronounce the words 'the dear Lord Jesus' with less shame than anyone I ever saw. No doubt he had learned the knack in prison.

Tea ended, and I saw the tramps looking furtively at one another. An unspoken thought was running from man to man – could we possibly make off before the prayers started? Someone stirred in his chair – not getting up actually, but with just a glance at the door, as though half-suggesting the idea of departure. The lady quelled him with one look. She said in a more benign tone than ever:

'I don't think you need go *quite* yet. The casual ward doesn't open till six, and we have time to kneel down and say a few words to our Father first. I think we should all feel better after that, shouldn't we?'

The red-nosed man was very helpful, pulling the harmonium into place and handing out the prayerbooks. His back was to the lady as he did this, and it was his idea of a joke to deal the books like a pack of cards, whispering to each man as he did so, 'There y'are, mate, there's a f— nap 'and for yer! Four aces and a king!' etc.

Bareheaded, we knelt down among the dirty teacups and began to mumble that we had left undone those things that we ought to have done, and done those things that we ought not to have done, and there was no health in us. The lady prayed very fervently, but her eyes roved over us all the time, making sure that we were attending. When she was not looking we grinned and winked at one another, and whispered bawdy jokes, just to show that we did not care; but it stuck in our throats a little. No one except the red-nosed man was self-possessed enough to speak the responses above a whisper. We got on better with the singing, except that one old tramp knew no tune but 'Onward, Christian soldiers', and reverted to it sometimes, spoiling the harmony.

The prayers lasted half an hour, and then, after a handshake at the door, we made off. 'Well,' said somebody as soon as we were out of hearing, 'the trouble's over. I thought them f— prayers was never goin' to end.'

'You 'ad your bun,' said another; 'you got to pay for it.'

'Pray for it, you mean. Ah, you don't get much for nothing. They can't even give you a twopenny cup of tea without you go down on your f— knees for it.'

There were murmurs of agreement. Evidently the tramps were not grateful for their tea. And yet it was excellent tea, as different from coffee-shop tea as good Bordeaux is from the muck called colonial claret, and we were all glad of it. I am sure too that it was given in a good spirit, without any intention of humiliating us; so in fairness we ought to have been grateful – still, we were not.

27

AT about a quarter to six the Irishman led me to the spike. It was a grim, smoky yellow cube of brick, standing in a corner of the workhouse grounds. With its rows of tiny, barred windows, and a high wall and iron gates separating it from the road, it looked much like a prison. Already a long queue of ragged men had formed up, waiting for the gates to open. They were of all kinds and ages, the youngest a fresh-faced boy of sixteen, the oldest a doubled-up, toothless mummy of seventy-five. Some were hardened tramps, recognizable by their sticks and billies and dust-darkened faces; some were factory hands out of work, some agricultural labourers, one a clerk in collar and tie, two certainly imbeciles. Seen in the mass, lounging there, they were a disgusting sight; nothing villainous or dangerous, but a graceless, mangy crew, nearly all ragged and palpably underfed. They

were friendly, however, and asked no questions. Many offered me tobacco
– cigarette ends, that is.

We leaned against the wall, smoking, and the tramps began to talk
about the spikes they had been in recently. It appeared from what they
said that all spikes are different, each with its peculiar merits and demerits,
and it is important to know these when you are on the road. An old hand
will tell you the peculiarities of every spike in England, as: at A you are
allowed to smoke but there are bugs in the cells; at B the beds are
comfortable but the porter is a bully; at C they let you out early in the
morning but the tea is undrinkable; at D the officials steal your money if
you have any – and so on interminably. There are regular beaten tracks
where the spikes are within a day's march of one another. I was told that
the Barnet–St Albans route is the best, and they warned me to steer clear
of Billericay and Chelmsford, also Ide Hill in Kent. Chelsea was said to
be the most luxurious spike in England; someone, praising it, said that the
blankets there were more like prison than the spike. Tramps go far afield
in summer, and in winter they circle as much as possible round the large
towns, where it is warmer and there is more charity. But they have to
keep moving, for you may not enter any one spike, or any two London
spikes, more than once in a month, on pain of being confined for a week.

Some time after six the gates opened and we began to file in one at a
time. In the yard was an office where an official entered in a ledger our
names and trades and ages, also the places we were coming from and
going to – this last is intended to keep a check on the movements of
tramps. I gave my trade as 'painter'; I had painted water-colours – who
has not? The official also asked us whether we had any money, and every
man said no. It is against the law to enter the spike with more than
eightpence, and any sum less than this one is supposed to hand over at
the gate. But as a rule the tramps prefer to smuggle their money in, tying
it tight in a piece of cloth so that it will not chink. Generally they put it
in the bag of tea and sugar that every tramp carries, or among their
'papers'. The 'papers' are considered sacred and are never searched.

After registering at the office we were led into the spike by an official
known as the Tramp Major (his job is to supervise casuals, and he is
generally a workhouse pauper) and a great bawling ruffian of a porter in
a blue uniform, who treated us like cattle. The spike consisted simply of
a bathroom and lavatory, and, for the rest, long double rows of stone cells,
perhaps a hundred cells in all. It was a bare, gloomy place of stone and
whitewash, unwillingly clean, with a smell which, somehow, I had foreseen

from its appearance; a smell of soft soap, Jeyes' fluid and latrines – a cold, discouraging, prisonish smell.

The porter herded us all into the passage, and then told us to come into the bathroom six at a time, to be searched before bathing. The search was for money and tobacco, Romton being one of those spikes where you can smoke once you have smuggled your tobacco in, but it will be confiscated if it is found on you. The old hands had told us that the porter never searched below the knee, so before going in we had all hidden our tobacco in the ankles of our boots. Afterwards, while undressing, we slipped it into our coats, which we were allowed to keep, to serve as pillows.

The scene in the bathroom was extraordinarily repulsive. Fifty dirty, stark-naked men elbowing each other in a room twenty feet square, with only two bathtubs and two slimy roller towels between them all. I shall never forget the reek of dirty feet. Less than half the tramps actually bathed (I heard them saying that hot water is 'weakening' to the system), but they all washed their faces and feet, and the horrid greasy little clouts known as toe-rags which they bind round their toes. Fresh water was only allowed for men who were having a complete bath, so many men had to bathe in water where others had washed their feet. The porter shoved us to and fro, giving the rough side of his tongue when anyone wasted time. When my turn came for the bath, I asked if I might swill out the tub, which was streaked with dirt, before using it. He answered simply, 'Shut yer — mouth and get on with yer bath!' That set the social tone of the place, and I did not speak again.

When we had finished bathing, the porter tied our clothes in bundles and gave us workhouse shirts – grey cotton things of doubtful cleanliness, like abbreviated nightgowns. We were sent along to the cells at once, and presently the porter and the Tramp Major brought our supper across from the workhouse. Each man's ration was a half-pound wedge of bread smeared with margarine, and a pint of bitter sugarless cocoa in a tin billy. Sitting on the floor we wolfed this in five minutes, and at about seven o'clock the cell doors were locked on the outside, to remain locked till eight in the morning.

Each man was allowed to sleep with his mate, the cells being intended to hold two men apiece. I had no mate, and was put in with another solitary man, a thin scrubby-faced fellow with a slight squint. The cell measured eight feet by five by eight high, was made of stone, and had a tiny barred window high up in the wall and a spyhole in the door, just like a cell in a prison. In it were six blankets, a chamber-pot, a hot-water pipe, and nothing else whatever. I looked round the cell with a vague feeling that there was something missing. Then, with a shock of surprise, I realized what it was, and exclaimed:

'But I say, damn it, where are the beds?'

'*Beds?*' said the other man, surprised. 'There aren't no beds! What yer expect? This is one of them spikes where you sleeps on the floor. Christ! Ain't you got used to that yet?'

It appeared that no beds was quite a normal condition in the spike. We rolled up our coats and put them against the hot-water pipe, and made ourselves as comfortable as we could. It grew foully stuffy, but it was not warm enough to allow of our putting all the blankets underneath, so that we could only use one to soften the floor. We lay a foot apart, breathing into one another's face, with our naked limbs constantly touching, and rolling against one another whenever we fell asleep. One fidgeted from side to side, but it did not do much good; whichever way one turned there would be first a dull numb feeling, then a sharp ache as the hardness of the floor wore through the blanket. One could sleep, but not for more than ten minutes on end.

About midnight the other man began making homosexual attempts upon me – a nasty experience in a locked, pitch-dark cell. He was a feeble creature and I could manage him easily, but of course it was impossible to go to sleep again. For the rest of the night we stayed awake, smoking and talking. The man told me the story of his life – he was a fitter, out of work for three years. He said that his wife had promptly deserted him when he lost his job, and he had been so long away from women that he had almost forgotten what they were like. Homosexuality is general among tramps of long standing, he said.

At eight the porter came along the passage unlocking the doors and shouting 'All out!' The doors opened, letting out a stale, fetid stink. At once the passage was full of squalid, grey-shirted figures, each chamber-pot in hand, scrambling for the bathroom. It appeared that in the morning only one tub of water was allowed for the lot of us, and when I arrived twenty tramps had already washed their faces; I took one glance at the black scum floating on the water, and went unwashed. After this we were given a breakfast identical with the previous night's supper, our clothes were returned to us, and we were ordered out into the yard to work. The work was peeling potatoes for the paupers' dinner, but it was a mere formality, to keep us occupied until the doctor came to inspect us. Most of the tramps frankly idled. The doctor turned up at about ten o'clock and we were told to go back to our cells, strip and wait in the passage for the inspection.

Naked and shivering, we lined up in the passage. You cannot conceive what ruinous, degenerate curs we looked, standing there in the merciless morning light. A tramp's clothes are bad, but they conceal far worse things; to see him as he really is, unmitigated, you must see him naked. Flat feet, pot bellies, hollow chests, sagging muscles – every kind of physical rottenness was there. Nearly everyone was under-nourished, and some clearly diseased; two men were wearing trusses, and as for the old mummy-like creature of seventy-five, one wondered how he could possibly make his daily march. Looking at our faces, unshaven and creased from the sleepless night, you would have thought that all of us were recovering from a week on the drink.

The inspection was designed merely to detect smallpox, and took no notice of our general condition. A young medical student, smoking a cigarette, walked rapidly along the line glancing us up and down, and not inquiring whether any man was well or ill. When my cell companion stripped I saw that his chest was covered with a red rash, and, having spent the night a few inches away from him, I fell into a panic about smallpox. The doctor, however, examined the rash and said that it was due merely to under-nourishment.

After the inspection we dressed and were sent into the yard, where the porter called our names over, gave us back any possessions we had left at the office, and distributed meal tickets. These were worth sixpence each, and were directed to coffee-shops on the route we had named the night before. It was interesting to see that quite a number of the tramps could not read, and had to apply to myself and other 'scholards' to decipher their tickets.

The gates were opened, and we dispersed immediately. How sweet the air does smell – even the air of a back street in the suburbs – after the shut-in, subfaecal stench of the spike! I had a mate now, for while we were peeling potatoes I had made friends with an Irish tramp named Paddy Jaques, a melancholy pale man who seemed clean and decent. He was going to Edbury spike, and suggested that we should go together. We set out, getting there at three in the afternoon. It was a twelve-mile walk, but we made it fourteen by getting lost among the desolate north London slums. Our meal tickets were directed to a coffee-shop in Ilford. When we got there, the little chit of a serving-maid, having seen our tickets and grasped that we were tramps, tossed her head in contempt and for a long time would not serve us. Finally she slapped on the table two 'large teas' and four slices of bread and dripping – that is, eightpennyworth of food. It appeared that the shop habitually cheated the tramps of twopence or so on each ticket; having tickets instead of money, the tramps could not protest or go elsewhere.

28

PADDY was my mate for about the next fortnight, and, as he was the first tramp I had known at all well, I want to give an account of him. I believe that he was a typical tramp and there are tens of thousands in England like him.

He was a tallish man, aged about thirty-five, with fair hair going grizzled and watery blue eyes. His features were good, but his cheeks had lanked and had that greyish, dirty-in-the-grain look that comes of a bread and margarine diet. He was dressed, rather better than most tramps, in a tweed shooting-jacket and a pair of old evening trousers with the braid still on them. Evidently the braid figured in his mind as a lingering scrap of respectability, and he took care to sew it on again when it came loose. He was careful of his appearance altogether, and carried a razor and bootbrush that he would not sell, though he had sold his 'papers' and even his pocket-knife long since. Nevertheless, one would have known him for a tramp a hundred yards away. There was something in his drifting style of walk, and the way he had of hunching his shoulders forward, essentially abject. Seeing him walk, you felt instinctively that he would sooner take a blow than give one.

He had been brought up in Ireland, served two years in the war, and then worked in a metal polish factory, where he had lost his job two years earlier. He was horribly ashamed of being a tramp, but he had picked up all a tramp's ways. He browsed the pavements unceasingly, never missing a cigarette end, or even an empty cigarette packet, as he used the tissue paper for rolling cigarettes. On our way into Edbury he saw a newspaper parcel on the pavement, pounced on it, and found that it contained two mutton sandwiches, rather frayed at the edges; these he insisted on my sharing. He never passed an automatic machine without giving a tug at the handle, for he said that sometimes they are out of order and will eject pennies if you tug at them. He had no stomach for crime, however. When we were in the outskirts of Romton, Paddy noticed a bottle of milk on a doorstep, evidently left there by mistake. He stopped, eyeing the bottle hungrily.

'Christ!' he said, 'dere's good food goin' to waste. Somebody could knock dat bottle off, eh? Knock it off easy.'

I saw that he was thinking of 'knocking it off' himself. He looked up and down the street; it was a quiet residential street and there was nobody in sight. Paddy's sickly, chap-fallen face yearned over the milk. Then he turned away, saying gloomily:

'Best leave it. It don't do a man no good to steal. T'ank God, I ain't never stolen nothin' yet.'

It was funk, bred of hunger, that kept him virtuous. With only two or three sound meals in his belly, he would have found courage to steal the milk.

He had two subjects of conversation, the shame and come-down of being a tramp, and the best way of getting a free meal. As we drifted through the streets he would keep up a monologue in this style, in a whimpering, self-pitying Irish voice:

'It's hell bein' on de road, eh? It breaks yer heart goin' into dem bloody spikes. But what's a man to do else, eh? I ain't had a good meat meal for about two months, an' me boots is getting bad, an' – Christ! How'd it be if we was to try for a cup o' tay at one o' dem convents on de way to Edbury? Most times dey're good for a cup o' tay. Ah, what'd a man do widout religion, eh? I've took cups o' tay from de convents, an' de Baptists, an' de Church of England, an' all sorts. I'm a Catholic meself. Dat's to say, I ain't been to confession for about seventeen year, but still I got me religious feelin's, y'understand. An' dem convents is always good for a cup o' tay . . .' etc. etc. He would keep this up all day, almost without stopping.

His ignorance was limitless and appalling. He once asked me, for instance, whether Napoleon lived before Jesus Christ or after. Another time, when I was looking into a bookshop window, he grew very perturbed because one of the books was called *Of the Imitation of Christ*. He took this for blasphemy. 'What de hell do dey want to go imitatin' of *Him* for?' he demanded angrily. He could read, but he had a kind of loathing for books. On our way from Romton to Edbury I went into a public library, and, though Paddy did not want to read, I suggested that he should come in and rest his legs. But he preferred to wait on the pavement. 'No,' he said, 'de sight of all dat bloody print makes me sick.'

Like most tramps, he was passionately mean about matches. He had a box of matches when I met him, but I never saw him strike one, and he used to lecture me for extravagance when I struck mine. His method was to cadge a light from strangers, sometimes going without a smoke for half an hour rather than strike a match.

Self-pity was the clue to his character. The thought of his bad luck never seemed to leave him for an instant. He would break long silences to exclaim, apropos of nothing, 'It's hell when yer clo'es begin to go up de spout, eh?' or 'Dat tay in de spike ain't tay, it's piss,' as though there was nothing else in the world to think about. And he had a low, worm-like envy of anyone who was better off – not of the rich, for they were beyond his social horizon, but of men in work. He pined for work as an artist pines to be famous. If he saw an old man working he would say bitterly, 'Look at dat old — keepin' able-bodied men out o' work'; or if it was a boy, 'It's dem young devils what's takin' de bread out of our mouths.' And all foreigners to him were 'dem bloody dagoes' – for, according to his theory, foreigners were responsible for unemployment.

He looked at women with a mixture of longing and hatred. Young, pretty women were too much above him to enter into his ideas, but his mouth watered at prostitutes. A couple of scarlet-lipped old creatures would go past; Paddy's face would flush pale pink, and he would turn and stare hungrily after the women. 'Tarts!' he would murmur, like a boy at a sweetshop window. He told me once that he had not had to do with a woman for two years – since he had lost his job, that is – and he had forgotten that one could aim higher than prostitutes. He had the regular character of a tramp – abject, envious, a jackal's character.

Nevertheless, he was a good fellow, generous by nature and capable of sharing his last crust with a friend; indeed he did literally share his last crust with me more than once. He was probably capable of work too, if he had been well fed for a few months. But two years of bread and margarine had lowered his standards hopelessly. He had lived on this filthy imitation of food till his own mind and body were compounded of inferior stuff. It was malnutrition and not any native vice that had destroyed his manhood.

29

ON the way to Edbury I told Paddy that I had a friend from whom I could be sure of getting money, and suggested going straight into London rather than face another night in the spike. But Paddy had not been in Edbury spike recently, and, tramp-like, he would not waste a night's free lodging. We arranged to go into London the next morning. I had only a halfpenny, but Paddy had two shillings, which would get us a bed each and a few cups of tea.

The Edbury spike did not differ much from the one at Romton. The worst feature was that all tobacco was confiscated at the gate, and we were warned that any man caught smoking would be turned out at once. Under the Vagrancy Act tramps can be prosecuted for smoking in the spike – in fact, they can be prosecuted for almost anything; but the authorities generally save the trouble of a prosecution by turning disobedient men out of doors. There was no work to do, and the cells were fairly comfortable. We slept two in a cell, 'one up, one down' – that is, one on a wooden shelf and one on the floor, with straw palliasses and plenty of blankets, dirty but not verminous. The food was the same as at Romton, except that we had tea instead of cocoa. One could get extra tea in the morning, as the Tramp Major was selling it at a halfpenny a mug, illicitly no doubt. We were each given a hunk of bread and cheese to take away for our midday meal.

When we got into London we had eight hours to kill before the lodging-houses opened. It is curious how one does not notice things. I had been in London innumerable times, and yet till that day I had never noticed one of the worst things about London – the fact that it costs money even to sit down. In Paris, if you had no money and could not find a public bench, you would sit on the pavement. Heaven knows what sitting on the pavement would lead to in London – prison, probably. By four we had stood five hours, and our feet seemed red-hot from the hardness of the stones. We were hungry, having eaten our ration as soon as we left the spike, and I was out of tobacco – it mattered less to Paddy, who picked up cigarette ends. We tried two churches and found them locked. Then we tried a public library, but there were no seats in it. As a last hope Paddy suggested trying a Rowton House; by the rules they would not let us in before seven, but we might slip in unnoticed. We walked up to the magnificent doorway (the Rowton Houses really are magnificent) and very casually, trying to look like regular lodgers, began to stroll in. Instantly a man lounging in the doorway, a sharp-faced fellow, evidently in some position of authority, barred the way.

'You men sleep 'ere last night?'

'No.'

'Then — off.'

We obeyed, and stood two more hours on the street corner. It was unpleasant, but it taught me not to use the expression 'street-corner loafer', so I gained something from it.

At six we went to a Salvation Army shelter. We could not book beds till eight and it was not certain that there would be any vacant, but an official, who called us 'Brother', let us in on the condition that we paid for two cups of tea. The main hall of the shelter was a great white-washed barn of a place, oppressively clean and bare, with no fires. Two hundred decentish, rather subdued-looking people were sitting packed on long wooden benches. One or two officers in uniform prowled up and down. On the wall were pictures of General Booth, and notices prohibiting cooking, drinking, spitting, swearing, quarrelling, and gambling. As a specimen of these notices, here is one that I copied word for word:

Any man found gambling or playing cards will be expelled and will not be admitted under any circumstances.

A reward will be given for information leading to the discovery of such persons.

The officers in charge appeal to all lodgers to assist them in keeping this hostel free from the DETESTABLE EVIL OF GAMBLING.

'Gambling or playing cards' is a delightful phrase.

To my eye these Salvation Army shelters, though clean, are far drearier than the worst of the common lodging-houses. There is such a hopelessness about some of the people there – decent, broken-down types who have pawned their collars but are still trying for office jobs. Coming to a Salvation Army shelter, where it is at least clean, is their last clutch at respectability. At the next table to me were two foreigners, dressed in rags but manifestly gentlemen. They were playing chess verbally, not even writing down the moves. One of them was blind, and I heard them say that they had been saving up for a long time to buy a board, price half a crown, but could never manage it. Here and there were clerks out of work, pallid and moody. Among a group of them a tall, thin, deadly pale young man was talking excitedly. He thumped his fist on the table and boasted in a strange, feverish style. When the officers were out of hearing he broke out into startling blasphemies:

'I tell you what, boys, I'm going to get that job tomorrow. I'm not one of your bloody down-on-the-knee brigade; I can look after myself. Look at that — notice there! "The Lord will provide!" A bloody lot He's ever provided me with. You don't catch me trusting to the — Lord. You leave it to me, boys. *I'm going a get that job,*' etc. etc.

I watched him, struck by the wild, agitated way in which he talked; he seemed hysterical, or perhaps a little drunk. An hour later I went into a small room, apart from the main hall, which was intended for reading. It had no books or papers in it, so few of the lodgers went there. As I opened the door I saw the young clerk in there all alone; he was on his knees, *praying.* Before I shut the door again I had time to see his face, and it looked agonized. Quite suddenly I realized, from the expression of his face, that he was starving.

The charge for beds was eightpence. Paddy and I had fivepence left, and we spent it at the 'bar', where food was cheap, though not so cheap as in some common lodging-houses. The tea appeared to be made with tea *dust*, which I fancy had been given to the Salvation Army in charity, though they sold it at threehalfpence a cup. It was foul stuff. At ten o'clock an officer marched round the hall blowing a whistle. Immediately everyone stood up.

'What's this for?' I said to Paddy, astonished.

'Dat means you has to go off to bed. An' you has to look sharp about it, too.'

Obediently as sheep, the whole two hundred men trooped off to bed, under the command of the officers.

The dormitory was a great attic like a barrack room, with sixty or seventy beds in it. They were clean and tolerably comfortable, but very narrow and very close together, so that one breathed straight into one's neighbour's face. Two officers slept in the room, to see that there was no smoking and no talking after lights-out. Paddy and I had scarcely a wink of sleep, for there was a man near us who had some nervous trouble, shellshock perhaps, which made him cry out 'Pip!' at irregular intervals. It was a loud, startling noise, something like the toot of a small motor-horn. You never knew when it was coming, and it was a sure preventer of sleep. It appeared that Pip, as the others called him, slept regularly in the shelter, and he must have kept ten or twenty people awake every night.

He was an example of the kind of thing that prevents one from ever getting enough sleep when men are herded as they are in these lodging-houses.

At seven another whistle blew, and the officers went round shaking those who did not get up at once. Since then I have slept in a number of Salvation Army shelters, and found that, though the different houses vary a little, this semi-military discipline is the same in all of them. They are certainly cheap, but they are too like workhouses for my taste. In some of them there is even a compulsory religious service once or twice a week, which the lodgers must attend or leave the house. The fact is that the Salvation Army are so in the habit of thinking themselves a charitable body that they cannot even run a lodging-house without making it stink of charity.

At ten I went to B.'s office and asked him to lend me a pound. He gave me two pounds and told me to come again when necessary, so that Paddy and I were free of money troubles for a week at least. We loitered the day in Trafalgar Square, looking for a friend of Paddy's who never turned up, and at night went to a lodging-house in a back alley near the Strand. The charge was elevenpence, but it was a dark, evil-smelling place, and a notorious haunt of the 'nancy boys'. Downstairs, in the murky kitchen, three ambiguous-looking youths in smartish blue suits were sitting on a bench apart, ignored by the other lodgers. I suppose they were 'nancy boys'. They looked the same type as the apache boys one sees in Paris, except that they wore no side-whiskers. In front of the fire a fully dressed man and a stark-naked man were bargaining. They were newspaper sellers. The dressed man was selling his clothes to the naked man. He said:

' 'Ere y'are, the best rig-out you ever 'ad. A tosheroon [half a crown] for the coat, two 'ogs for the trousers, one and a tanner for the boots, and a 'og for the cap and scarf. That's seven bob.'

'You got a 'ope! I'll give yer one and a tanner for the coat, a 'og for the trousers, and two 'ogs for the rest. That's four and a tanner.'

'Take the 'ole lot for five and a tanner, chum.'

'Right y'are, off with 'em. I got to get out to sell my late edition.'

The clothed man stripped, and in three minutes their positions were reversed; the naked man dressed, and the other kilted with a sheet of the *Daily Mail*.

The dormitory was dark and close, with fifteen beds in it. There was a horrible hot reek of urine, so beastly that at first one tried to breathe in small, shallow puffs, not filling one's lungs to the bottom. As I lay down in bed a man loomed out of the darkness, leant over me and began babbling in an educated, half-drunken voice:

'An old public schoolboy, what? [He had heard me say something to

Paddy.] Don't meet many of the old school here. I am an old Etonian.
You know – twenty years hence this weather and all that.' He began to
quaver out the Eton boating-song, not untunefully:

> Jolly boating weather,
> And a hay harvest –

'Stop that — noise!' shouted several lodgers.

'Low types,' said the old Etonian, 'very low types. Funny sort of place
for you and me, eh? Do you know what my friends say to me? They say,
"M—, you are past redemption." Quite true, I *am* past redemption. I've
come down in the world; not like these —s here, who couldn't come down
if they tried. We chaps who have come down ought to hang together a
bit. Youth will be still in our faces – you know. May I offer you a drink?'

He produced a bottle of cherry brandy, and at the same moment lost
his balance and fell heavily across my legs. Paddy, who was undressing,
pulled him upright.

'Get back to yer bed, you silly ole —!'

The old Etonian walked unsteadily to his bed and crawled under the
sheets with all his clothes on, even his boots. Several times in the night I
heard him murmuring, 'M—, you are past redemption,' as though the
phrase appealed to him. In the morning he was lying asleep fully dressed,
with the bottle clasped in his arms. He was a man of about fifty, with a
refined, worn face, and, curiously enough, quite fashionably dressed. It
was queer to see his good patent-leather shoes sticking out of that filthy
bed. It occurred to me, too, that the cherry brandy must have cost the
equivalent of a fortnight's lodging, so he could not have been seriously
hard up. Perhaps he frequented common lodging-houses in search of the
'nancy boys'.

The beds were not more than two feet apart. About midnight I woke
up to find that the man next to me was trying to steal the money from
beneath my pillow. He was pretending to be asleep while he did it, sliding
his hand under the pillow as gently as a rat. In the morning I saw that he
was a hunchback, with long, apelike arms. I told Paddy about the attempted
theft. He laughed and said:

'Christ! You got to get used to dat. Dese lodgin'-houses is full o' thieves.
In some houses dere's nothin' safe but to sleep wid all yer clo'es on. I seen
'em steal a wooden leg off a cripple before now. Once I see a man –
fourteen-stone man he was – come into a lodgin'-house wid four pound
ten. He puts it under his mattress. "Now," he says, "any — dat touches
dat money does it over my body," he says. But dey done him all de same.

In de mornin' he woke up on de floor. Four fellers had took his mattress by de corners an' lifted him off as light as a feather. He never saw his four pound ten again.'

30

THE next morning we began looking once more for Paddy's friend, who was called Bozo, and was a screever – that is, a pavement artist. Addresses did not exist in Paddy's world, but he had a vague idea that Bozo might be found in Lambeth, and in the end we ran across him on the Embankment, where he had established himself not far from Waterloo Bridge. He was kneeling on the pavement with a box of chalks, copying a sketch of Winston Churchill from a penny note-book. The likeness was not at all bad. Bozo was a small, dark, hook-nosed man, with curly hair growing low on his head. His right leg was dreadfully deformed, the foot being twisted heel forward in a way horrible to see. From his appearance one could have taken him for a Jew, but he used to deny this vigorously. He spoke of his hook-nose as 'Roman', and was proud of his resemblance to some Roman Emperor – it was Vespasian, I think.

Bozo had a strange way of talking, Cockneyfied and yet very lucid and expressive. It was as though he had read good books but had never troubled to correct his grammar. For a while Paddy and I stayed on the Embankment, talking, and Bozo gave us an account of the screeving trade. I repeat what he said more or less in his own words.

'I'm what they call a serious screever. I don't draw in blackboard chalks like these others, I use proper colours the same as what painters use; bloody expensive they are, especially the reds. I use five bobs' worth of colours in a long day, and never less than two bobs' worth.* Cartoons is my line – you know, politics and cricket and that. Look here' – he showed me his notebook – 'here's likenesses of all the political blokes, what I've copied from the papers. I have a different cartoon every day. For instance, when the Budget was on I had one of Winston trying to push an elephant marked "Debt", and underneath I wrote, "Will he budge it?" See? You can have cartoons about any of the parties, but you mustn't put anything

---

* Pavement artists buy their colours in the form of powder, and work them into cakes with condensed milk.

in favour of Socialism, because the police won't stand it. Once I did a cartoon of a boa constrictor marked Capital swallowing a rabbit marked Labour. The copper came along and saw it, and he says, "You rub that out, and look sharp about it," he says. I had to rub it out. The copper's got the right to move you on for loitering, and it's no good giving them a back answer.'

I asked Bozo what one could earn at screeving. He said:

'This time of year, when it don't rain, I take about three quid between Friday and Sunday – people get their wages Fridays, you see. I can't work when it rains; the colours get washed off straight away. Take the year round, I make about a pound a week, because you can't do much in the winter. Boat Race day, and Cup Final day, I've took as much as four pounds. But you have to *cut* it out of them, you know; you don't take a bob if you just sit and look at them. A halfpenny's the usual drop [gift], and you don't get even that unless you give them a bit of backchat. Once they've answered you they feel ashamed not to give you a drop. The best thing's to keep changing your picture, because when they see you drawing they'll stop and watch you. The trouble is, the beggars scatter as soon as you turn round with the hat. You really want a nobber [assistant] at this game. You keep at work and get a crowd watching you, and the nobber comes casual-like round the back of them. They don't know he's the nobber. Then suddenly he pulls his cap off, and you got them between two fires like. You'll never get a drop off real toffs. It's shabby sort of blokes you get most off, and foreigners. I've had even sixpences off Japs, and blackies, and that. They're not so bloody mean as what an Englishman is. Another thing to remember is to keep your money covered up, except perhaps a penny in the hat. People won't give you anything if they see you got a bob or two already.'

Bozo had the deepest contempt for the other screevers on the Embankment. He called them 'the salmon platers'. At that time there was a screever almost every twenty-five yards along the Embankment – twenty-five yards being the recognized minimum between pitches. Bozo contemptuously pointed out an old white-bearded screever fifty yards away.

'You see that silly old fool? He's bin doing the same picture every day for ten years. "A faithful friend" he calls it. It's of a dog pulling a child out of the water. The silly old bastard can't draw any better than a child of ten. He's learned just that one picture by rule of thumb, like you learn to put a puzzle together. There's a lot of that sort about here. They come pinching my ideas sometimes; but I don't care; the silly —s can't think of anything for themselves, so I'm always ahead of them. The whole thing with cartoons is being up to date. Once a child got its head stuck in the railings of Chelsea Bridge. Well, I heard about it, and my cartoon was on the pavement before they'd got the child's head out of the railings. Prompt, I am.'

Bozo seemed an interesting man, and I was anxious to see more of him. That evening I went down to the Embankment to meet him, as he had arranged to take Paddy and myself to a lodging-house south of the river. Bozo washed his pictures off the pavement and counted his takings – it was about sixteen shillings, of which he said twelve or thirteen would be profit. We walked down into Lambeth. Bozo limped slowly, with a queer crablike gait, half sideways, dragging his smashed foot behind him. He carried a stick in each hand and slung his box of colours over his shoulder. As we were crossing the bridge he stopped in one of the alcoves to rest. He fell silent for a minute or two, and to my surprise I saw that he was looking at the stars. He touched my arm and pointed to the sky with his stick.

'Say, will you look at Aldebaran! Look at the colour. Like a — great blood orange!'

From the way he spoke he might have been an art critic in a picture gallery. I was astonished. I confessed that I did not know which Aldebaran was – indeed, I had never even noticed that the stars were of different colours. Bozo began to give me some elementary hints on astronomy, pointing out the chief constellations. He seemed concerned at my ignorance. I said to him, surprised:

'You seem to know a lot about stars.'

'Not a great lot. I know a bit, though. I got two letters from the Astronomer Royal thanking me for writing about meteors. Now and again I go out at night and watch for meteors. The stars are a free show; it don't cost anything to use your eyes.'

'What a good idea! I should never have thought of it.'

'Well, you got to take an interest in something. It don't follow that because a man's on the road he can't think of anything but tea-and-two-slices.'

'But isn't it very hard to take an interest in things – things like stars – living this life?'

'Screeving, you mean? Not necessarily. It don't need turn you into a bloody rabbit – that is, not if you set your mind to it.'

'It seems to have that effect on most people.'

'Of course. Look at Paddy – a tea-swilling old moocher, only fit to scrounge for fag-ends. That's the way most of them go. I despise them.

But you don't *need* to get like that. If you've got any education, it don't matter to you if you're on the road for the rest of your life.'

'Well, I've found just the contrary,' I said. 'It seems to me that when you take a man's money away he's fit for nothing from that moment.'

'No, not necessarily. If you set yourself to it, you can live the same life, rich or poor. You can still keep on with your books and your ideas. You just got to say to yourself, "I'm a free man in *here*" ' – he tapped his forehead – 'and you're all right.'

Bozo talked further in the same strain, and I listened with attention. He seemed a very unusual screever, and he was, moreover, the first person I had heard maintain that poverty did not matter. I saw a good deal of him during the next few days, for several times it rained and he could not work. He told me the history of his life, and it was a curious one.

The son of a bankrupt bookseller, he had gone to work as a house-painter at eighteen, and then served three years in France and India during the war. After the war he had found a house-painting job in Paris, and had stayed there several years. France suited him better than England (he despised the English), and he had been doing well in Paris, saving money, and engaged to a French girl. One day the girl was crushed to death under the wheels of an omnibus. Bozo went on the drink for a week, and then returned to work, rather shaky; the same morning he fell from a stage on which he was working, forty feet on to the pavement, and smashed his right foot to pulp. For some reason he received only sixty pounds compensation. He returned to England, spent his money in looking for jobs, tried hawking books in Middlesex Street market, then tried selling toys from a tray, and finally settled down as a screever. He had lived hand to mouth ever since; half starved throughout the winter, and often sleeping in the spike or on the Embankment. When I knew him he owned nothing but the clothes he stood up in, and his drawing materials and a few books. The clothes were the usual beggar's rags, but he wore a collar and tie, of which he was rather proud. The collar, a year or more old, was constantly 'going' round the neck, and Bozo used to patch it with bits cut from the tail of his shirt so that the shirt had scarcely any tail left. His damaged leg was getting worse and would probably have to be amputated, and his knees, from kneeling on the stones, had pads of skin on them as thick as boot-soles. There was, clearly, no future for him but beggary and a death in the workhouse.

With all this, he had neither fear, nor regret, nor shame, nor self-pity. He had faced his position, and made a philosophy for himself. Being a beggar, he said, was not his fault, and he refused either to have any compunction about it or to let it trouble him. He was the enemy of society, and quite ready to take to crime if he saw a good opportunity. He refused on principle to be thrifty. In the summer he saved nothing, spending his surplus earnings on drink, as he did not care about women. If he was penniless when winter came on, then society must look after him. He was ready to extract every penny he could from charity, provided that he was not expected to say thank you for it. He avoided religious charities, however, for he said it stuck in his throat to sing hymns for buns. He had various other points of honour; for instance, it was his boast that never in his life, even when starving, had he picked up a cigarette end. He considered himself in a class above the ordinary run of beggars, who, he said, were an abject lot, without even the decency to be ungrateful.

He spoke French passably, and had read some of Zola's novels, all Shakespeare's plays, *Gulliver's Travels*, and a number of essays. He could describe his adventures in words that one remembered. For instance, speaking of funerals, he said to me:

'Have you ever seen a corpse burned? I have, in India. They put the old chap on the fire, and the next moment I almost jumped out of my skin, because he'd started kicking. It was only his muscles contracting in the heat – still, it give me a turn. Well, he wriggled about for a bit like a kipper on hot coals, and then his belly blew up and went off with a bang you could have heard fifty yards away. It fair put me against cremation.'

Or, again, apropos of his accident:

'The doctor says to me, "You fell on one foot, my man. And bloody lucky for you you didn't fall on both feet," he says. "Because if you had of fallen on both feet you'd have shut up like a bloody concertina, and your thigh bones'd be sticking out of your ears!" '

Clearly the phrase was not the doctor's but Bozo's own. He had a gift for phrases. He had managed to keep his brain intact and alert, and so nothing could make him succumb to poverty. He might be ragged and cold, or even starving, but so long as he could read, think, and watch for meteors, he was, as he said, free in his own mind.

He was an embittered atheist (the sort of atheist who does not so much disbelieve in God as personally dislike Him), and took a sort of pleasure in thinking that human affairs would never improve. Sometimes, he said, when sleeping on the Embankment, it had consoled him to look up at Mars or Jupiter and think that there were probably Embankment sleepers there. He had a curious theory about this. Life on earth, he said, is harsh because the planet is poor in the necessities of existence. Mars, with its cold climate and scanty water, must be far poorer, and life correspondingly harsher. Whereas on earth you are merely imprisoned for stealing sixpence, on Mars you are probably boiled alive. This thought cheered Bozo, I do not know why. He was a very exceptional man.

31

THE charge at Bozo's lodging-house was ninepence a night. It was a large, crowded place, with accommodation for five hundred men, and a well-known rendezvous of tramps, beggars, and petty criminals. All races, even black and white, mixed in it on terms of equality. There were Indians there, and when I spoke to one of them in bad Urdu he addressed me as 'tum' – a thing to make one shudder, if it had been in India. We had got below the range of colour prejudice. One had glimpses of curious lives. Old 'Grandpa', a tramp of seventy who made his living, or a great part of it, by collecting cigarette ends and selling the tobacco at threepence an ounce. 'The Doctor' – he was a real doctor, who had been struck off the register for some offence, and besides selling newspapers gave medical advice at a few pence a time. A little Chittagonian lascar, barefoot and starving, who had deserted his ship and wandered for days through London, so vague and helpless that he did not even know the name of the city he was in – he thought it was Liverpool, until I told him. A begging-letter writer, a friend of Bozo's, who wrote pathetic appeals for aid to pay for his wife's funeral, and, when a letter had taken effect, blew himself out with huge solitary gorges of bread and margarine. He was a nasty, hyena-like creature. I talked to him and found that, like most swindlers, he believed a great part of his own lies. The lodging-house was an Alsatia for types like these.

While I was with Bozo he taught me something about the technique of London begging. There is more in it than one might suppose. Beggars vary greatly, and there is a sharp social line between those who merely cadge and those who attempt to give some value for money. The amounts that one can earn by the different 'gags' also vary. The stories in the Sunday papers about beggars who die with two thousand pounds sewn into their trousers are, of course, lies; but the better-class beggars do have runs of luck, when they earn a living wage for weeks at a time. The most prosperous beggars are street acrobats and street photographers. On a good pitch – a theatre queue, for instance – a street acrobat will often earn five pounds a week. Street photographers can earn about the same, but they are dependent on fine weather. They have a cunning dodge to stimulate trade. When they see a likely victim approaching one of them runs behind the camera and pretends to take a photograph. Then as the victim reaches them, they exclaim:

'There y'are, sir, took yer photo lovely. That'll be a bob.'

'But I never asked you to take it,' protests the victim.

'What, you didn't want it took? Why, we thought you signalled with your 'and. Well, there's a plate wasted! That's cost us sixpence, that 'as.'

At this the victim usually takes pity and says he will have the photo after all. The photographers examine the plate and say that it is spoiled, and that they will take a fresh one free of charge. Of course, they have not really taken the first photo; and so, if the victim refuses, they waste nothing.

Organ-grinders, like acrobats, are considered artists rather than beggars. An organ-grinder named Shorty, a friend of Bozo's, told me all about his trade. He and his mate 'worked' the coffee-shops and public-houses round Whitechapel and the Commercial Road. It is a mistake to think that organ-grinders earn their living in the street; nine-tenths of their money is taken in coffee-shops and pubs – only the cheap pubs, for they are not allowed into the good-class ones. Shorty's procedure was to stop outside a pub and play one tune, after which his mate, who had a wooden leg and could excite compassion, went in and passed round the hat. It was a point of honour with Shorty always to play another tune after receiving the 'drop' – an encore, as it were; the idea being that he was a genuine entertainer and not merely paid to go away. He and his mate took two or three pounds a week between them, but, as they had to pay fifteen shillings a week for the hire of the organ, they only averaged a pound a week each. They were on the streets from eight in the morning till ten at night, and later on Saturdays.

Screevers can sometimes be called artists, sometimes not. Bozo introduced me to one who was a 'real' artist – that is, he had studied art in Paris and submitted pictures to the Salon in his day. His line was copies of Old Masters, which he did marvellously, considering that he was drawing on stone. He told me how he began as a screever:

'My wife and kids were starving. I was walking home late at night, with a lot of drawings I'd been taking round the dealers, and wondering how the devil to raise a bob or two. Then, in the Strand, I saw a fellow kneeling on the pavement drawing, and people giving him pennies. As I came past he got up and went into a pub. "Damn it," I thought, "if he can make money at that, so can I." So on the impulse I knelt down and began drawing with his chalks. Heaven knows how I came to do it; I must have been lightheaded with hunger. The curious thing was that I'd never used pastels before; I had to learn the technique as I went along. Well, people began to stop and say that my drawing wasn't bad, and they gave me ninepence between them. At this moment the other fellow came out of the pub. "What in — are you doing on my pitch?" he said. I explained that I was hungry and had to earn something. "Oh," said he, "come and have a pint with me." So I had a pint, and since that day I've been a screever. I make a pound a week. You can't keep six kids on a pound a week, but luckily my wife earns a bit taking in sewing.

'The worst thing in this life is the cold, and the next worst is the interference you have to put up with. At first, not knowing any better, I used sometimes to copy a nude on the pavement. The first I did was outside St Martin's-in-the-Fields church. A fellow in black – I suppose he was a churchwarden or something – came out in a tearing rage. "Do you think we can have that obscenity outside God's holy house?" he cried. So I had to wash it out. It was a copy of Botticelli's Venus. Another time I copied the same picture on the Embankment. A policeman passing looked at it, and then, without a word, walked on to it and rubbed it out with his great flat feet.'

Bozo told the same tale of police interference. At the time when I was with him there had been a case of 'immoral conduct' in Hyde Park, in which the police had behaved rather badly. Bozo produced a cartoon of Hyde Park with policemen concealed in the trees, and the legend, 'Puzzle, find the policemen.' I pointed out to him how much more telling it would be to put, 'Puzzle, find the immoral conduct,' but Bozo would not hear of it. He said that any policeman who saw it would move him on, and he would lose his pitch for good.

Below screevers come the people who sing hymns, or sell matches, or bootlaces, or envelopes containing a few grains of lavender – called, euphemistically, perfume. All these people are frankly beggars, exploiting an appearance of misery, and none of them takes on an average more than half a crown a day. The reason why they have to pretend to sell matches and so forth instead of begging outright is that this is demanded by the absurd English laws about begging. As the law now stands, if you approach a stranger and ask him for twopence, he can call a policeman and get you seven days for begging. But if you make the air hideous by droning

'Nearer, my God, to Thee,' or scrawl some chalk daubs on the pavement, or stand about with a tray of matches – in short, if you make a nuisance of yourself – you are held to be following a legitimate trade and not begging. Match-selling and street-singing are simply legalized crimes. Not profitable crimes, however; there is not a singer or match-seller in London who can be sure of £50 a year – a poor return for standing eighty-four hours a week on the kerb, with the cars grazing your backside.

It is worth saying something about the social position of beggars, for when one has consorted with them, and found that they are ordinary human beings, one cannot help being struck by the curious attitude that society takes towards them. People seem to feel that there is some essential difference between beggars and ordinary 'working' men. They are a race apart – outcasts, like criminals and prostitutes. Working men 'work', beggars do not 'work'; they are parasites, worthless in their very nature. It is taken for granted that a beggar does not 'earn' his living, as a bricklayer or a literary critic 'earns' his. He is a mere social excrescence, tolerated because we live in a humane age, but essentially despicable.

Yet if one looks closely one sees that there is no *essential* difference between a beggar's livelihood and that of numberless respectable people. Beggars do not work, it is said; but, then, what is *work*? A navvy works by swinging a pick. An accountant works by adding up figures. A beggar works by standing out of doors in all weathers and getting varicose veins, chronic bronchitis, etc. It is a trade like any other; quite useless, of course – but, then, many reputable trades are quite useless. And as a social type a beggar compares well with scores of others. He is honest compared with the sellers of most patent medicines, high-minded compared with a Sunday newspaper proprietor, amiable compared with a hire-purchase tout – in short, a parasite, but a fairly harmless parasite. He seldom extracts more than a bare living from the community, and, what should justify him according to our ethical ideas, he pays for it over and over in suffering. I do not think there is anything about a beggar that sets him in a different class from other people, or gives most modern men the right to despise him.

Then the question arises, Why are beggars despised? – for they are despised, universally. I believe it is for the simple reason that they fail to earn a decent living. In practice nobody cares whether work is useful or useless, productive or parasitic; the sole thing demanded is that it shall be profitable. In all the modern talk about energy, efficiency, social service and the rest of it, what meaning is there except 'Get money, get it legally, and get a lot of it'? Money has become the grand test of virtue. By this test beggars fail, and for this they are despised. If one could earn even ten pounds a week at begging, it would become a respectable profession immediately. A beggar, looked at realistically, is simply a businessman, getting his living, like other businessmen, in the way that comes to hand. He has not, more than most modern people, sold his honour; he has merely made the mistake of choosing a trade at which it is impossible to grow rich.

32

I WANT to put in some notes, as short as possible, on London slang and swearing. These (omitting the ones that everyone knows) are some of the cant words now used in London:

A gagger – beggar or street performer of any kind. A moocher – one who begs outright, without pretence of doing a trade. A nobbler – one who collects pennies for a beggar. A chanter – a street singer. A clodhopper – a street dancer. A mugfaker – a street photographer. A glimmer – one who watches vacant motor-cars. A gee (or jee – it is pronounced jee) – the accomplice of a cheapjack, who stimulates trade by pretending to buy something. A split – a detective. A flattie – a policeman. A dideki – a gypsy. A toby – a tramp.

A drop – money given to a beggar. Funkum – lavender or other perfume sold in envelopes. A boozer – a public-house. A slang – a hawker's licence. A kip – a place to sleep in, or a night's lodging. Smoke – London. A judy – a woman. The spike – the casual ward. The lump – the casual ward. A tosheroon – a half-crown. A deaner – a shilling. A hog – a shilling. A sprowsie – a sixpence. Clods – coppers. A drum – a billy can. Shackles – soup. A chat – a louse. Hard-up – tobacco made from cigarette ends. A stick or cane – a burglar's jemmy. A peter – a safe. A bly – a burglar's oxy-acetylene blow-lamp.

To bawl – to suck or swallow. To knock off – to steal. To skipper – to sleep in the open.

About half of these words are in the larger dictionaries. It is interesting to guess at the derivation of some of them, though one or two – for instance, 'funkum' and 'tosheroon' – are beyond guessing. 'Deaner' presumably comes from 'denier'. 'Glimmer' (with the verb 'to glim') may have something to do with the old word 'glim', meaning a light, or another old word 'glim', meaning a glimpse; but it is an instance of the formation of new words, for in its present sense it can hardly be older than motor-cars. 'Gee' is a curious word; conceivably it has arisen out of 'gee', meaning horse, in the sense of stalking horse. The derivation of 'screever' is mysterious. It must come ultimately from *scribo*, but there has been no similar word in English for the past hundred and fifty years; nor can it have come directly from the French, for pavement artists are unknown in France. 'Judy' and 'bawl' are East End words, not found west of Tower Bridge. 'Smoke' is a word used only by tramps. 'Kip' is Danish. Till quite recently the word 'doss' was used in this sense, but it is now quite obsolete.

London slang and dialect seem to change very rapidly. The old London accent described by Dickens and Surtees, with v for w and w for v and so forth, has now vanished utterly. The Cockney accent as we know it seems to have come up in the forties (it is first mentioned in an American book, Herman Melville's *White Jacket*), and Cockney is already changing; there are few people now who say 'fice' for 'face', 'nawce' for 'nice' and so forth as consistently as they did twenty years ago. The slang changes together with the accent. Twenty-five or thirty years ago, for instance, the 'rhyming slang' was all the rage in London. In the 'rhyming slang' everything was named by something rhyming with it – a 'hit or miss' for a kiss, 'plates of meat' for feet, etc. It was so common that it was even reproduced in novels; now it is almost extinct.* Perhaps all the words I have mentioned above will have vanished in another twenty years.

The swear words also change – or, at any rate, they are subject to fashions. For example, twenty years ago the London working classes habitually used the word 'bloody'. Now they have abandoned it utterly, though novelists still represent them as using it. No born Londoner (it is different with people of Scotch or Irish origin) now says 'bloody', unless he is a man of some education. The word has, in fact, moved up in the social scale and ceased to be a swear word for the purposes of the working classes. The current London adjective, now tacked on to every noun, is — .† No doubt in time —, like 'bloody', will find its way into the drawing-room and be replaced by some other word.

The whole business of swearing, especially English swearing, is mysterious. Of its very nature swearing is as irrational as magic – indeed, it is a species of magic. But there is also a paradox about it, namely this:

* It survives in certain abbreviations, such as 'use your twopenny' or 'use your head'. 'Twopenny' is arrived at like this: head – loaf of bread – twopenny loaf – twopenny.

† See note on page 153.

Our intention in swearing is to shock and wound, which we do by mentioning something that should be kept secret – usually something to do with the sexual functions. But the strange thing is that when a word is well established as a swear word, it seems to lose its original meaning; that is, it loses the thing that made it into a swear word. A word becomes an oath because it means a certain thing, and, because it has become an oath, it ceases to mean that thing. For example ——. The Londoners do not now use, or very seldom use, this word in its original meaning; it is on their lips from morning till night, but it is a mere expletive and means nothing. Similarly with ——, which is rapidly losing its original sense. One can think of similar instances in French – for example ——, which is now a quite meaningless expletive. The word ——, also, is still used occasionally in Paris, but the people who use it, or most of them, have no idea of what it once meant. The rule seems to be that words accepted as swear words have some magical character, which sets them apart and makes them useless for ordinary conversation.

Words used as insults seem to be governed by the same paradox as swear words. A word becomes an insult, one would suppose, because it means something bad; but in practice its insult-value has little to do with its actual meaning. For example, the most bitter insult one can offer to a Londoner is 'bastard' – which, taken for what it means, is hardly an insult at all. And the worst insult to a woman, either in London or Paris, is 'cow'; a name which might even be a compliment, for cows are among the most likeable of animals. Evidently a word is an insult simply because it is meant as an insult, without reference to its dictionary meaning; words, especially swear words, being what public opinion chooses to make them. In this connexion it is interesting to see how a swear word can change character by crossing a frontier. In England you can print 'Je m'en fous' without protest from anybody. In France you have to print it 'Je m'en f—'. Or, as another example, take the word 'barnshoot' – a corruption of the Hindustani word *bahinchut*. A vile and unforgivable insult in India, this word is a piece of gentle badinage in England. I have even seen it in a school text-book; it was in one of Aristophanes' plays, and the annotator suggested it as a rendering of some gibberish spoken by a Persian ambassador. Presumably the annotator knew what *bahinchut* meant. But, because it was a foreign word, it had lost its magical swear-word quality and could be printed.

One other thing is noticeable about swearing in London, and that is that the men do not usually swear in front of the women. In Paris it is quite different. A Parisian workman may prefer to suppress an oath in front of a woman, but he is not at all scrupulous about it, and the women themselves swear freely. The Londoners are more polite, or more squeamish, in this matter.

These are a few notes that I have set down more or less at random. It is a pity that someone capable of dealing with the subject does not keep a year-book of London slang and swearing, registering the changes accurately. It might throw useful light upon the formation, development, and obsolescence of words.

33

THE two pounds that B. had given me lasted about ten days. That it lasted so long was due to Paddy, who had learned parsimony on the road and considered even one sound meal a day a wild extravagance. Food, to him, had come to mean simply bread and margarine – the eternal tea-and-two-slices, which will cheat hunger for an hour or two. He taught me how to live, food, bed, tobacco, and all, at the rate of half a crown a day. And he managed to earn a few extra shillings by 'glimming' in the evenings. It was a precarious job, because illegal, but it brought in a little and eked out our money.

One morning we tried for a job as sandwich men. We went at five to an alley-way behind some offices, but there was already a queue of thirty or forty men waiting, and after two hours we were told that there was no work for us. We had not missed much, for sandwich men have an unenviable job. They are paid about three shillings a day for ten hours' work – it is hard work, especially in windy weather, and there is no skulking, for an inspector comes round frequently to see that the men are on their beat. To add to their troubles, they are only engaged by the day, or sometimes for three days, never weekly, so that they have to wait hours for their job every morning. The number of unemployed men who are ready to do the work makes them powerless to fight for better treatment. The job all sandwich men covet is distributing handbills, which is paid for at the same rate. When you see a man distributing handbills you can do him a good turn by taking one, for he goes off duty when he has distributed all his bills.

Meanwhile we went on with the lodging-house life – a squalid, eventless life of crushing boredom. For days together there was nothing to do but sit in the underground kitchen, reading yesterday's newspaper, or, when one could get hold of it, a back number of the *Union Jack*. It rained a great deal at this time, and everyone who came in steamed, so that the kitchen stank horribly. One's only excitement was the periodical tea-and-two-slices. I do not know how many men are living this life in London – it must be thousands at the least. As to Paddy, it was actually the best life he had known for two years past. His interludes from tramping, the times when he had somehow laid hands on a few shillings, had all been like this; the tramping itself had been slightly worse. Listening to his whimpering voice – he was always whimpering when he was not eating – one realized what torture unemployment must be to him. People are wrong when they think that an unemployed man only worries about losing his wages; on the contrary, an illiterate man, with the work habit in his bones, needs work even more than he needs money. An educated man can put up with enforced idleness, which is one of the worst evils of poverty. But a man like Paddy, with no means of filling up time, is as miserable out of work as a dog on the chain. That is why it is such nonsense to pretend that those who have 'come down in the world' are to be pitied above all others. The man who really merits pity is the man who has been down from the start, and faces poverty with a blank, resourceless mind.

It was a dull time, and little of it stays in my mind, except for talks with Bozo. Once the lodging-house was invaded by a slumming-party. Paddy and I had been out, and, coming back in the afternoon, we heard sounds of music downstairs. We went down to find three gentle-people, sleekly dressed, holding a religious service in our kitchen. They were a grave and reverend seignior in a frock coat, a lady sitting at a portable harmonium, and a chinless youth toying with a crucifix. It appeared that they had marched in and started to hold the service, without any kind of invitation whatever.

It was a pleasure to see how the lodgers met this intrusion. They did not offer the smallest rudeness to the slummers; they just ignored them. By common consent everyone in the kitchen – a hundred men, perhaps – behaved as though the slummers had not existed. There they stood patiently singing and exhorting, and no more notice was taken of them than if they had been earwigs. The gentleman in the frock coat preached a sermon, but not a word of it was audible; it was drowned in the usual din of songs, oaths, and the clattering of pans. Men sat at their meals and card games three feet away from the harmonium, peaceably ignoring it. Presently the slummers gave it up and cleared out, not insulted in any way, but merely disregarded. No doubt they consoled themselves by thinking how brave they had been, 'freely venturing into the lowest dens,' etc. etc.

Bozo said that these people came to the lodging-house several times a month. They had influence with the police, and the 'deputy' could not exclude them. It is curious how people take it for granted that they have a right to preach at you and pray over you as soon as your income falls below a certain level.

After nine days B.'s two pounds was reduced to one and ninepence. Paddy and I set aside eighteenpence for our beds, and spent threepence on the usual tea-and-two-slices, which we shared – an appetizer rather than a meal. By the afternoon we were damnably hungry and Paddy remembered a church near King's Cross Station where a free tea was given once a week to tramps. This was the day, and we decided to go there. Bozo, though it was rainy weather and he was almost penniless, would not come, saying that churches were not his style.

Outside the church quite a hundred men were waiting, dirty types who had gathered from far and wide at the news of a free tea, like kites round a dead buffalo. Presently the doors opened and a clergyman and some girls shepherded us into a gallery at the top of the church. It was an evangelical church, gaunt and wilfully ugly, with texts about blood and fire blazoned on the walls, and a hymn-book containing twelve hundred and fifty-one hymns; reading some of the hymns, I concluded that the book would do as it stood for an anthology of bad verse. There was to be a service after the tea, and the regular congregation were sitting in the well of the church below. It was a week-day, and there were only a few dozen of them, mostly stringy old women who reminded one of boiling-fowls. We ranged ourselves in the gallery pews and were given our tea; it was a one-pound jam-jar of tea each, with six slices of bread and margarine. As soon as tea was over, a dozen tramps who had stationed themselves near the door bolted to avoid the service; the rest stayed, less from gratitude than lacking the cheek to go.

The organ let out a few preliminary hoots and the service began. And instantly, as though at a signal, the tramps began to misbehave in the most outrageous way. One would not have thought such scenes possible in a church. All round the gallery men lolled in their pews, laughed, chattered, leaned over and flicked pellets of bread among the congregation; I had to restrain the man next to me, more or less by force, from lighting a cigarette. The tramps treated the service as a purely comic spectacle. It was, indeed, a sufficiently ludicrous service – the kind where there are sudden yells of 'Hallelujah!' and endless extempore prayers – but their behaviour passed all bounds. There was one old fellow in the congregation – Brother Bootle or some such name – who was often called on to lead us in prayer, and whenever he stood up the tramps would begin stamping as though in a theatre; they said that on a previous occasion he had kept up an extempore prayer for twenty-five minutes, until the minister had interrupted him. Once when Brother Bootle stood up a tramp called out, 'Two to one 'e don't beat seven minutes!' so loud that the whole church must hear. It was not long before we were making far more noise than the minister. Sometimes somebody below would send up an indignant 'Hush!' but it made no impression. We had set ourselves to guy the service, and there was no stopping us.

It was a queer, rather disgusting scene. Below were the handful of simple, well-meaning people, trying hard to worship; and above were the hundred men whom they had fed, deliberately making worship impossible. A ring of dirty, hairy faces grinned down from the gallery, openly jeering. What could a few women and old men do against a hundred hostile tramps? They were afraid of us, and we were frankly bullying them. It was our revenge upon them for having humiliated us by feeding us.

The minister was a brave man. He thundered steadily through a long sermon on Joshua, and managed almost to ignore the sniggers and chattering from above. But in the end, perhaps goaded beyond endurance, he announced loudly:

'I shall address the last five minutes of my sermon to the *unsaved* sinners!'

Having said which, he turned his face to the gallery and kept it so for five minutes, lest there should be any doubt about who were saved and who unsaved. But much we cared! Even while the minister was threatening hell fire, we were rolling cigarettes, and at the last amen we clattered down the stairs with a yell, many agreeing to come back for another free tea next week.

The scene had interested me. It was so different from the ordinary demeanour of tramps – from the abject worm-like gratitude with which they normally accept charity. The explanation, of course, was that we outnumbered the congregation and so were not afraid of them. A man receiving charity practically always hates his benefactor – it is a fixed characteristic of human nature; and, when he has fifty or a hundred others to back him, he will show it.

In the evening, after the free tea, Paddy unexpectedly earned another eighteenpence at 'glimming'. It was exactly enough for another night's lodging, and we put it aside and went hungry till nine the next evening. Bozo, who might have given us some food, was away all day. The pavements were wet, and he had gone to the Elephant and Castle, where he knew of a pitch under shelter. Luckily I still had some tobacco, so that the day might have been worse.

At half past eight Paddy took me to the Embankment, where a clergyman was known to distribute meal tickets once a week. Under Charing Cross Bridge fifty men were waiting, mirrored in the shivering puddles. Some of them were truly appalling specimens – they were Embankment sleepers, and the Embankment dredges up worse types than the spike. One of them, I remember, was dressed in an overcoat without buttons, laced up with rope, a pair of ragged trousers, and boots exposing his toes – not a rag else. He was bearded like a fakir, and he had managed to streak his chest and shoulders with some horrible black filth resembling train oil. What one could see of his face under the dirt and hair was bleached white as paper by some malignant disease. I heard him speak, and he had a goodish accent, as of a clerk or shopwalker.

Presently the clergyman appeared and the men ranged themselves in a queue in the order in which they had arrived. The clergyman was a nice, chubby, youngish man, and, curiously enough, very like Charlie, my friend in Paris. He was shy and embarrassed, and did not speak except for a brief good evening; he simply hurried down the line of men, thrusting a ticket upon each, and not waiting to be thanked. The consequence was that, for once, there was genuine gratitude, and everyone said that the clergyman was a — good feller. Someone (in his hearing, I believe) called out: 'Well, *he'll* never be a — bishop!' – this, of course, intended as a warm compliment.

The tickets were worth sixpence each, and were directed to an eating-house not far away. When we got there we found that the proprietor, knowing that the tramps could not go elsewhere, was cheating by only giving four pennyworth of food for each ticket. Paddy and I pooled our tickets, and received food which we could have got for sevenpence or eightpence at most coffee-shops. The clergyman had distributed well over a pound in tickets, so that the proprietor was evidently swindling the tramps to the tune of seven shillings or more a week. This kind of victimization is a regular part of a tramp's life, and it will go on as long as people continue to give meal tickets instead of money.

Paddy and I went back to the lodging-house and, still hungry, loafed in the kitchen, making the warmth of the fire a substitute for food. At half-past ten Bozo arrived, tired out and haggard, for his mangled leg made walking an agony. He had not earned a penny at screeving, all the pitches under shelter being taken, and for several hours he had begged outright, with one eye on the policemen. He had amassed eightpence – a penny short of his kip. It was long past the hour for paying, and he had only managed to slip indoors when the deputy was not looking; at any moment he might be caught and turned out, to sleep on the Embankment. Bozo took the things out of his pockets and looked them over, debating what to sell. He decided on his razor, took it round the kitchen, and in a few minutes he had sold it for threepence – enough to pay his kip, buy a basin of tea, and leave a halfpenny over.

Bozo got his basin of tea and sat down by the fire to dry his clothes. As he drank the tea I saw that he was laughing to himself as though at some good joke. Surprised, I asked him what he had to laugh at.

'It's bloody funny!' he said. 'It's funny enough for *Punch*. What do you think I been and done?'

'What?'

'Sold my razor without having a shave first: Of all the — fools!'

He had not eaten since the morning, had walked several miles with a twisted leg, his clothes were drenched, and he had a halfpenny between himself and starvation. With all this, he could laugh over the loss of his razor. One could not help admiring him.

34

THE next morning, our money being at an end, Paddy and I set out for the spike. We went southward by the Old Kent Road, making for Cromley; we could not go to a London spike, for Paddy had been in one recently and did not care to risk going again. It was a sixteen-mile walk over asphalt, blistering to the heels, and we were acutely hungry. Paddy browsed the pavement, laying up a store of cigarette ends against his time in the spike. In the end his perseverance was rewarded, for he picked up a penny. We bought a large piece of stale bread, and devoured it as we walked.

When we got to Cromley, it was too early to go to the spike, and we walked several miles farther, to a plantation beside a meadow, where one could sit down. It was a regular caravanserai of tramps – one could tell it by the worn grass and the sodden newspaper and rusty cans that they had left behind. Other tramps were arriving by ones and twos. It was jolly autumn weather. Near by, a deep bed of tansies was growing; it seems to me that even now I can smell the sharp reek of those tansies, warring with the reek of tramps. In the meadow two carthorse colts, raw sienna colour with white manes and tails, were nibbling at a gate. We sprawled about on the ground, sweaty and exhausted. Someone managed to find dry sticks and get a fire going, and we all had milkless tea out of a tin 'drum' which was passed round.

Some of the tramps began telling stories. One of them, Bill, was an interesting type, a genuine sturdy beggar of the old breed, strong as Hercules and a frank foe of work. He boasted that with his great strength he could get a navvying job any time he liked, but as soon as he drew his first week's wages he went on a terrific drunk and was sacked. Between whiles he 'mooched', chiefly from shopkeepers. He talked like this:

'I ain't goin' far in — Kent. Kent's a tight county, Kent is. There's too many bin' moochin' about 'ere. The — bakers get so as they'll throw their bread away sooner'n give it you. Now Oxford, that's the place for moochin', Oxford is. When I was in Oxford I mooched bread, and I mooched bacon, and I mooched beef, and every night I mooched tanners for my kip off of the students. The last night I was twopence short of my kip, so I goes up to a parson and mooches 'im for threepence. He give me threepence, and the next moment he turns round and gives me in charge for beggin'. "You bin beggin'," the copper says. "No I ain't," I says, "I was askin' the gentleman the time," I says. The copper starts feelin' inside my coat, and he pulls out a pound of meat and two loaves of bread. "Well, what's all this, then?" he says. "You better come 'long to the station," he says. The beak give me seven days. I don't mooch from no more — parsons. But Christ! what do I care for a lay-up of seven days?' etc. etc.

It seemed that his whole life was this – a round of mooching, drunks, and lay-ups. He laughed as he talked of it, taking it all for a tremendous joke. He looked as though he made a poor thing out of begging, for he wore only a corduroy suit, scarf, and cap – no socks or linen. Still, he was fat and jolly, and he even smelt of beer, a most unusual smell in a tramp nowadays.

Two of the tramps had been in Cromley spike recently, and they told a ghost story connected with it. Years earlier, they said, there had been a suicide there. A tramp had managed to smuggle a razor into his cell, and there cut his throat. In the morning, when the Tramp Major came round, the body was jammed against the door, and to open it they had to break the dead man's arm. In revenge for this, the dead man haunted his cell, and anyone who slept there was certain to die within the year; there were copious instances, of course. If a cell door stuck when you tried to open it, you should avoid that cell like the plague, for it was the haunted one.

Two tramps, ex-sailors, told another grisly story. A man (they swore they had known him) had planned to stow away on a boat bound for Chile. It was laden with manufactured goods packed in big wooden crates, and with the help of a docker the stowaway had managed to hide himself in one of these. But the docker had made a mistake about the order in which the crates were to be loaded. The crane gripped the stowaway, swung him aloft, and deposited him – at the very bottom of the hold, beneath hundreds of crates. No one discovered what had happened until the end of the voyage, when they found the stowaway rotting, dead of suffocation.

Another tramp told the story of Gilderoy, the Scottish robber. Gilderoy was the man who was condemned to be hanged, escaped, captured the judge who had sentenced him, and (splendid fellow!) hanged him. The tramps liked the story, of course, but the interesting thing was to see that they had got it all wrong. Their version was that Gilderoy escaped to America, whereas in reality he was recaptured and put to death. The story had been amended, no doubt deliberately; just as children amend the stories of Samson and Robin Hood, giving them happy endings which are quite imaginary.

This set the tramps talking about history, and a very old man declared that the 'one bite law' was a survival from days when the nobles hunted men instead of deer. Some of the others laughed at him, but he had the idea firm in his head. He had heard, too, of the Corn Laws, and the *jus primae noctis* (he believed it had really existed); also of the Great Rebellion, which he thought was a rebellion of poor against rich – perhaps he had got it mixed up with the peasant rebellions. I doubt whether the old man could read, and certainly he was not repeating newspaper articles. His scraps of history had been passed from generation to generation of tramps, perhaps for centuries in some cases. It was oral tradition lingering on, like a faint echo from the Middle Ages.

Paddy and I went to the spike at six in the evening, getting out at ten in the morning. It was much like Romton and Edbury, and we saw nothing of the ghost. Among the casuals were two young men named William and Fred, ex-fishermen from Norfolk, a lively pair and fond of singing. They had a song called 'Unhappy Bella' that is worth writing down. I heard them sing it half a dozen times during the next two days, and I

managed to get it by heart, except a line or two which I have guessed. It
ran:

> Bella was young and Bella was fair
> With bright blue eyes and golden hair,
> O unhappy Bella!
> Her step was light and her heart was gay,
> But she had no sense, and one fine day
> She got herself put in the family way
> By a wicked, heartless, cruel deceiver.
>
> Poor Bella was young, she didn't believe
> That the world is hard and men deceive,
> O unhappy Bella!
> She said, 'My man will do what's just,
> He'll marry me now, because he must';
> Her heart was full of loving trust
> In a wicked, heartless, cruel deceiver.
>
> She went to his house; that dirty skunk
> Had packed his bags and done a bunk,
> O unhappy Bella!
> Her landlady said, 'Get out, you whore,
> I won't have your sort a-darkening my door.'
> Poor Bella was put to affliction sore
> By a wicked heartless, cruel deceiver.
>
> All night she tramped the cruel snows,
> What she must have suffered nobody knows,
> O unhappy Bella!
> And when the morning dawned so red,
> Alas, alas, poor Bella was dead,
> Sent so young to her lonely bed
> By a wicked, heartless, cruel deceiver.
>
> So thus, you see, do what you will,
> The fruits of sin are suffering still,
> O unhappy Bella!
> As into the grave they laid her low,
> The men said, 'Alas, but life is so,'
> But the women chanted, sweet and low,
> 'It's all the men, the dirty bastards!'

Written by a woman, perhaps.

William and Fred, the singers of this song, were thorough scallywags,
the sort of men who get tramps a bad name. They happened to know that

the Tramp Major at Cromley had a stock of old clothes, which were to be given at need to casuals. Before going in William and Fred took off their boots, ripped the seams and cut pieces off the soles, more or less ruining them. Then they applied for two pairs of boots, and the Tramp Major, seeing how bad their boots were, gave them almost new pairs. William and Fred were scarcely outside the spike in the morning before they had sold these boots for one and ninepence. It seemed to them quite worth while, for one and ninepence, to make their own boots practically unwearable.

Leaving the spike, we all started southward, a long slouching procession, for Lower Binfield and Ide Hill. On the way there was a fight between two of the tramps. They had quarrelled overnight (there was some silly *casus belli* about one saying to the other, 'Bull shit', which was taken for Bolshevik – a deadly insult), and they fought it out in a field. A dozen of us stayed to watch them. The scene sticks in my mind for one thing – the man who was beaten going down, and his cap falling off and showing that his hair was quite white. After that some of us intervened and stopped the fight. Paddy had meanwhile been making inquiries, and found that the real cause of the quarrel was, as usual, a few pennyworth of food.

We got to Lower Binfield quite early, and Paddy filled in the time by asking for work at back doors. At one house he was given some boxes to chop up for firewood, and, saying he had a mate outside, he brought me in and we did the work together. When it was done the householder told the maid to take us out a cup of tea. I remember the terrified way in which she brought it out, and then, losing her courage, set the cups down on the path and bolted back to the house, shutting herself in the kitchen. So dreadful is the name of 'tramp'. They paid us sixpence each, and we bought a threepenny loaf and half an ounce of tobacco, leaving fivepence.

Paddy thought it wiser to bury our fivepence, for the Tramp Major at Lower Binfield was renowned as a tyrant and might refuse to admit us if we had any money at all. It is quite a common practice of tramps to bury their money. If they intend to smuggle at all a large sum into the spike they generally sew it into their clothes, which may mean prison if they are caught, of course. Paddy and Bozo used to tell a good story about this. An Irishman (Bozo said it was an Irishman; Paddy said an Englishman), not a tramp, and in possession of thirty pounds, was stranded in a small village where he could not get a bed. He consulted a tramp, who advised him to go to the workhouse. It is quite a regular proceeding, if one cannot get a bed elsewhere, to get one at the workhouse, paying a reasonable sum for it. The Irishman, however, thought he would be clever and get a bed for nothing, so he presented himself at the workhouse as an ordinary casual. He had sewn the thirty pounds into his clothes. Meanwhile the tramp who had advised him had seen his chance, and that night he privately asked the Tramp Major for permission to leave the spike early in the morning, as he had to see about a job. At six in the morning he was released and went out – in the Irishman's clothes. The Irishman complained of the theft, and was given thirty days for going into a casual ward under false pretences.

35

ARRIVED at Lower Binfield, we sprawled for a long time on the green, watched by cottagers from their front gates. A clergyman and his daughter came and stared silently at us for a while, as though we had been aquarium fishes, and then went away again. There were several dozen of us waiting. William and Fred were there, still singing, and the men who had fought, and Bill the moocher. He had been mooching from bakers, and had quantities of stale bread tucked away between his coat and his bare body. He shared it out, and we were all glad of it. There was a woman among us, the first woman tramp I had ever seen. She was a fattish, battered, very dirty woman of sixty, in a long, trailing black skirt. She put on great airs of dignity, and if anyone sat down near her she sniffed and moved farther off.

'Where you bound for, missis?' one of the tramps called to her.

The woman sniffed and looked into the distance.

'Come on, missis,' he said, 'cheer up. Be chummy. We're all in the same boat 'ere.'

'Thank you,' said the woman bitterly, 'when I want to get mixed up with a set of *tramps*, I'll let you know.'

I enjoyed the way she said *tramps*. It seemed to show you in a flash the whole of her soul; a small, blinkered, feminine soul, that had learned absolutely nothing from years on the road. She was, no doubt, a respectable widow woman, become a tramp through some grotesque accident.

The spike opened at six. This was Saturday, and we were to be confined over the week-end, which is the usual practice; why, I do not know, unless it is from a vague feeling that Sunday merits something disagreeable.

When we registered I gave my trade as 'journalist'. It was truer than 'painter', for I had sometimes earned money from newspaper articles, but it was a silly thing to say, being bound to lead to questions. As soon as we were inside the spike and had been lined up for the search, the Tramp Major called my name. He was a stiff, soldierly man of forty, not looking the bully he had been represented, but with an old soldier's gruffness. He said sharply:

'Which of you is Blank?' (I forget what name I had given.)

'Me, sir.'

'So you are a journalist?'

'Yes, sir,' I said, quaking. A few questions would betray the fact that I had been lying, which might mean prison. But the Tramp Major only looked me up and down and said:

'Then you are a gentleman?'

'I suppose so.'

He gave me another long look. 'Well, that's bloody bad luck, guv'nor,' he said; 'bloody bad luck that is.' And thereafter he treated me with unfair favouritism, and even with a kind of deference. He did not search me, and in the bathroom he actually gave me a clean towel to myself – an unheard-of luxury. So powerful is the word 'gentleman' in an old soldier's ear.

By seven we had wolfed our bread and tea and were in our cells. We slept one in a cell, and there were bedsteads and straw palliasses, so that one ought to have had a good night's sleep. But no spike is perfect, and the peculiar shortcoming at Lower Binfield was the cold. The hot pipes were not working, and the two blankets we had been given were thin cotton things and almost useless. It was only autumn, but the cold was bitter. One spent the long twelve-hour night in turning from side to side, falling asleep for a few minutes and waking up shivering. We could not smoke, for our tobacco, which we had managed to smuggle in, was in our clothes and we should not get these back till the morning. All down the passage one could hear groaning noises, and sometimes a shouted oath. No one, I imagine, got more than an hour or two of sleep.

In the morning, after breakfast and the doctor's inspection, the Tramp Major herded us all into the dining-room and locked the door upon us. It was a limewashed, stone-floored room, unutterably dreary, with its furniture of deal boards and benches, and its prison smell. The barred windows were too high to look out of, and there were no ornaments save a clock and a copy of the workhouse rules. Packed elbow to elbow on the benches, we were bored already, though it was barely eight in the morning. There was nothing to do, nothing to talk about, not even room to move. The sole consolation was that one could smoke, for smoking was connived at so long as one was not caught in the act. Scotty, a little hairy tramp with a bastard accent sired by Cockney out of Glasgow, was tobaccoless, his tin of cigarette ends having fallen out of his boot during the search and been impounded. I stood him the makings of a cigarette. We smoked furtively, thrusting our cigarettes into our pockets, like schoolboys, when we heard the Tramp Major coming.

Most of the tramps spent ten continuous hours in this comfortless, soulless room. Heaven knows how they put up with it. I was luckier than the others, for at ten o'clock the Tramp Major told off a few men for odd jobs, and he picked me out to help in the workhouse kitchen, the most coveted job of all. This, like the clean towel, was a charm worked by the word 'gentleman'.

There was no work to do in the kitchen, and I sneaked off into a small shed used for storing potatoes, where some workhouse paupers were skulking to avoid the Sunday morning service. There were comfortable packing-cases to sit on, and some back numbers of the *Family Herald*, and even a copy of *Raffles* from the workhouse library. The paupers talked interestingly about workhouse life. They told me, among other things, that the thing really hated in the workhouse, as a stigma of charity, is the uniform; if the men could wear their own clothes, or even their own caps and scarves, they would not mind being paupers. I had my dinner from the workhouse table, and it was a meal fit for a boa-constrictor – the largest meal I had eaten since my first day at the Hôtel X. The paupers said that they habitually gorged to the bursting-point on Sunday and were underfed the rest of the week. After dinner the cook set me to do the washing up, and told me to throw away the food that remained. The wastage was astonishing and, in the circumstances, appalling. Half-eaten joints of meat, and bucketfuls of broken bread and vegetables, were pitched away like so much rubbish and then defiled with tea-leaves. I filled five dustbins to overflowing with quite eatable food. And while I did so fifty tramps were sitting in the spike with their bellies half filled by the spike dinner of bread and cheese, and perhaps two cold boiled potatoes each in honour of Sunday. According to the paupers, the food was thrown away from deliberate policy, rather than that it should be given to the tramps.

At three I went back to the spike. The tramps had been sitting there since eight, with hardly room to move an elbow, and they were now half mad with boredom. Even smoking was at an end, for a tramp's tobacco is picked-up cigarette ends, and he starves if he is more than a few hours away from the pavement. Most of the men were too bored even to talk;

they just sat packed on the benches, staring at nothing, their scrubby faces split in two by enormous yawns. The room stank of *ennui*.

Paddy, his backside aching from the hard bench, was in a whimpering mood, and to pass the time away I talked with a rather superior tramp, a young carpenter who wore a collar and tie and was on the road, he said, for lack of a set of tools. He kept a little aloof from the other tramps, and held himself more like a free man than a casual. He had literary tastes, too, and carried a copy of *Quentin Durward* in his pocket. He told me that he never went into a spike unless driven there by hunger, sleeping under hedges and behind ricks in preference. Along the south coast he had begged by day and slept in bathing-huts for weeks at a time.

We talked of life on the road. He criticized the system that makes a tramp spend fourteen hours a day in the spike, and the other ten in walking and dodging the police. He spoke of his own case – six months at the public charge for want of a few pounds' worth of tools. It was idiotic, he said.

Then I told him about the wastage of food in the workhouse kitchen, and what I thought of it. And at that he changed his tone instantly. I saw that I had awakened the pew-renter who sleeps in every English workman. Though he had been famished along with the others, he at once saw reasons why the food should have been thrown away rather than given to the tramps. He admonished me quite severely.

'They have to do it,' he said. 'If they made these places too comfortable, you'd have all the scum of the country flocking into them. It's only the bad food as keeps all that scum away. These here tramps are too lazy to work, that's all that's wrong with them. You don't want to go encouraging of them. They're scum.'

I produced arguments to prove him wrong, but he would not listen. He kept repeating:

'You don't want to have any pity on these here tramps – scum, they are. You don't want to judge them by the same standards as men like you and me. They're scum, just scum.'

It was interesting to see the subtle way in which he disassociated himself from 'these here tramps'. He had been on the road six months, but in the sight of God, he seemed to imply, he was not a tramp. I imagine there are quite a lot of tramps who thank God they are not tramps. They are like the trippers who say such cutting things about trippers.

Three hours dragged by. At six supper arrived, and turned out to be quite uneatable; the bread, tough enough in the morning (it had been cut into slices on Saturday night), was now as hard as ship's biscuit. Luckily it was spread with dripping, and we scraped the dripping off and ate that alone, which was better than nothing. At a quarter past six we were sent to bed. New tramps were arriving, and in order not to mix the tramps of different days (for fear of infectious diseases) the new men were put in the cells and we in dormitories. Our dormitory was a barn-like room with thirty beds close together, and a tub to serve as a common chamber-pot. It stank abominably, and the older men coughed and got up all night. But being so many together kept the room warm, and we had some sleep.

We dispersed at ten in the morning, after a fresh medical inspection, with a hunk of bread and cheese for our midday dinner. William and Fred, strong in the possession of a shilling, impaled their bread on the spike railings – as a protest, they said. This was the second spike in Kent that they had made too hot to hold them, and they thought it a great joke. They were cheerful souls, for tramps. The imbecile (there is an imbecile in every collection of tramps) said that he was too tired to walk and clung to the railings, until the Tramp Major had to dislodge him and start him with a kick. Paddy and I turned north, for London. Most of the others were going on to Ide Hill, said to be about the worst spike in England.*

Once again it was jolly autumn weather, and the road was quiet, with few cars passing. The air was like sweet-briar after the spike's mingled stenches of sweat, soap, and drains. We two seemed the only tramps on the road. Then I heard a hurried step behind us, and someone calling. It was little Scotty, the Glasgow tramp, who had run after us panting. He produced a rusty tin from his pocket. He wore a friendly smile, like someone repaying an obligation.

'Here y'are, mate,' he said cordially. 'I owe you some fag ends. You stood me a smoke yesterday. The Tramp Major give me back my box of fag ends when we come out this morning. One good turn deserves another – here y'are.'

And he put four sodden, debauched, loathly cigarette ends into my hand.

* I have been in it since, and it is not so bad.

36

I WANT to set down some general remarks about tramps. When one comes to think of it, tramps are a queer product and worth thinking over. It is queer that a tribe of men, tens of thousands in number, should be marching up and down England like so many Wandering Jews. But though the case obviously wants considering, one cannot even start to consider it until one has got rid of certain prejudices. These prejudices are rooted in the idea that every tramp, *ipso facto*, is a blackguard. In childhood we have been taught that tramps are blackguards, and consequently there exists in our minds a sort of ideal or typical tramp – a repulsive, rather dangerous creature, who would die rather than work or wash, and wants nothing but to beg, drink, and rob hen-houses. This tramp-monster is no truer to life than the sinister Chinaman of the magazine stories, but he is very hard to get rid of. The very word 'tramp' evokes his image. And the belief in him obscures the real questions of vagrancy.

To take a fundamental question about vagrancy: Why do tramps exist at all? It is a curious thing, but very few people know what makes a tramp take to the road. And, because of the belief in the tramp-monster, the most fantastic reasons are suggested. It is said, for instance, that tramps tramp to avoid work, to beg more easily, to seek opportunities for crime, even – least probable of reasons – because they like tramping. I have even read in a book of criminology that the tramp is an atavism, a throw-back to the nomadic stage of humanity. And meanwhile the quite obvious cause of vagrancy is staring one in the face. Of course a tramp is not a nomadic atavism – one might as well say that a commercial traveller is an atavism. A tramp tramps, not because he likes it, but for the same reason as a car keeps to the left; because there happens to be a law compelling him to do so. A destitute man, if he is not supported by the parish, can only get relief at the casual wards, and as each casual ward will only admit him for one night, he is automatically kept moving. He is a vagrant because, in the state of the law, it is that or starve. But people have been brought up to believe in the tramp-monster, and so they prefer to think that there must be some more or less villainous motive for tramping.

As a matter of fact, very little of the tramp-monster will survive inquiry.

Take the generally accepted idea that tramps are dangerous characters. Quite apart from experience, one can say *a priori* that very few tramps are dangerous, because if they were dangerous they would be treated accordingly. A casual ward will often admit a hundred tramps in one night, and these are handled by a staff of at most three porters. A hundred ruffians could not be controlled by three unarmed men. Indeed, when one sees how tramps let themselves be bullied by the workhouse officials, it is obvious that they are the most docile, broken-spirited creatures imaginable. Or take the idea that all tramps are drunkards – an idea ridiculous on the face of it. No doubt many tramps would drink if they got the chance, but in the nature of things they cannot get the chance. At this moment a pale watery stuff called beer is sevenpence a pint in England. To be drunk on it would cost at least half a crown, and a man who can command half a crown at all often is not a tramp. The idea that tramps are impudent social parasites ('sturdy beggars') is not absolutely unfounded, but it is only true in a few per cent of the cases. Deliberate, cynical parasitism, such as one reads of in Jack London's books on American tramping, is not in the English character. The English are a conscience-ridden race, with a strong sense of the sinfulness of poverty. One cannot imagine the average Englishman deliberately turning parasite, and this national character does not necessarily change because a man is thrown out of work. Indeed, if one remembers that a tramp is only an Englishman out of work, forced by law to live as a vagabond, then the tramp-monster vanishes. I am not saying, of course, that most tramps are ideal characters; I am only saying that they are ordinary human beings, and that if they are worse than other people it is the result and not the cause of their way of life.

It follows that the 'Serve them damned well right' attitude that is normally taken towards tramps is no fairer than it would be towards cripples or invalids. When one has realized that, one begins to put oneself in a tramp's place and understand what his life is like. It is an extraordinarily futile, acutely unpleasant life. I have described the casual ward – the routine of a tramp's day – but there are three especial evils that need insisting upon. The first is hunger, which is the almost general fate of tramps. The casual ward gives them a ration which is probably not even meant to be sufficient, and anything beyond this must be got by begging – that is, by breaking the law. The result is that nearly every tramp is rotted by malnutrition; for proof of which one need only look at the men lining up outside any casual ward. The second great evil of a tramp's life – it seems much smaller at first sight, but it is a good second

– is that he is entirely cut off from contact with women. This point needs elaborating.

Tramps are cut off from women, in the first place, because there are very few women at their level of society. One might imagine that among destitute people the sexes would be as equally balanced as elsewhere. But it is not so; in fact, one can almost say that below a certain level society is entirely male. The following figures, published by the L.C.C. from a night census taken on February 13th, 1931, will show the relative numbers of destitute men and destitute women:

Spending the night in the streets, 60 men, 18 women.*
In shelters and homes not licensed as common lodging-houses, 1,057 men, 137 women.
In the crypt of St Martin's-in-the-Fields Church, 88 men, 12 women.
In L.C.C. casual wards and hostels, 674 men, 15 women.

It will be seen from these figures that at the charity level men outnumber women by something like ten to one. The cause is presumably that unemployment affects women less than men; also that any presentable woman can, in the last resort, attach herself to some man. The result, for a tramp, is that he is condemned to perpetual celibacy. For of course it goes without saying that if a tramp finds no women at his own level, those above – even a very little above – are as far out of his reach as the moon. The reasons are not worth discussing, but there is no doubt that women never, or hardly ever, condescend to men who are much poorer than themselves. A tramp, therefore, is a celibate from the moment when he takes to the road. He is absolutely without hope of getting a wife, a mistress, or any kind of woman except – very rarely, when he can raise a few shillings – a prostitute.

It is obvious what the results of this must be: homosexuality, for instance, and occasional rape cases. But deeper than these there is the degradation worked in a man who knows that he is not even considered fit for marriage. The sexual impulse, not to put it any higher, is a fundamental impulse, and starvation of it can be almost as demoralizing as physical hunger. The evil of poverty is not so much that it makes a man suffer as that it rots him physically and spiritually. And there can be no doubt that sexual starvation contributes to this rotting process. Cut off from the whole race of women, a tramp feels himself degraded to the rank of a cripple or a lunatic. No humiliation could do more damage to a man's self-respect.

The other great evil of a tramp's life is enforced idleness. By our

* This must be an underestimate. Still, the proportions probably hold good.

vagrancy laws things are so arranged that when he is not walking the road he is sitting in a cell; or, in the intervals, lying on the ground waiting for the casual ward to open. It is obvious that this is a dismal, demoralizing way of life, especially for an uneducated man.

Besides these one could enumerate scores of minor evils – to name only one, discomfort, which is inseparable from life on the road; it is worth remembering that the average tramp has no clothes but what he stands up in, wears boots that are ill-fitting, and does not sit in a chair for months together. But the important point is that a tramp's sufferings are entirely useless. He lives a fantastically disagreeable life, and lives it to no purpose whatever. One could not, in fact, invent a more futile routine than walking from prison to prison, spending perhaps eighteen hours a day in the cell and on the road. There must be at the least several tens of thousands of tramps in England. Each day they expend innumerable foot-pounds of energy – enough to plough thousands of acres, build miles of road, put up dozens of houses – in mere, useless walking. Each day they waste between them possibly ten years of time in staring at cell walls. They cost the country at least a pound a week a man, and give nothing in return for it. They go round and round, on an endless boring game of general post, which is of no use, and is not even meant to be of any use to any person whatever. The law keeps this process going, and we have got so accustomed to it that we are not surprised. But it is very silly.

Granting the futility of a tramp's life, the question is whether anything could be done to improve it. Obviously it would be possible, for instance, to make the casual wards a little more habitable, and this is actually being done in some cases. During the last year some of the casual wards have been improved – beyond recognition, if the accounts are true – and there is talk of doing the same to all of them. But this does not go to the heart of the problem. The problem is how to turn the tramp from a bored, half-alive vagrant into a self-respecting human being. A mere increase of comfort cannot do this. Even if the casual wards became positively luxurious (they never will)* a tramp's life would still be wasted. He would still be a pauper, cut off from marriage and home life, and a dead loss to the community. What is needed is to depauperize him, and this can only be done by finding him work – not work for the sake of working, but work of which he can enjoy the benefit. At present, in the great majority of casual wards, tramps do no work whatever. At one time they were made

* In fairness it must be added that a few of the casual wards have been improved recently, at least from the point of view of sleeping accommodation. But most of them are the same as ever, and there has been no real improvement in the food.

to break stones for their food, but this was stopped when they had broken enough stone for years ahead and put the stone-breakers out of work. Nowadays they are kept idle, because there is seemingly nothing for them to do. Yet there is a fairly obvious way of making them useful, namely this: Each workhouse could run a small farm, or at least a kitchen garden, and every able-bodied tramp who presented himself could be made to do a sound day's work. The produce of the farm or garden could be used for feeding the tramps, and at the worst it would be better than the filthy diet of bread and margarine and tea. Of course, the casual wards could never be quite self-supporting, but they could go a long way towards it, and the rates would probably benefit in the long run. It must be remembered that under the present system tramps are as dead a loss to the country as they could possibly be, for they do not only do no work, but they live on a diet that is bound to undermine their health; the system, therefore, loses lives as well as money. A scheme which fed them decently, and made them produce at least a part of their own food, would be worth trying.

It may be objected that a farm or even a garden could not be run with casual labour. But there is no real reason why tramps should only stay a day at each casual ward; they might stay a month or even a year, if there were work for them to do. The constant circulation of tramps is something quite artificial. At present a tramp is an expense to the rates, and the object of each workhouse is therefore to push him on to the next; hence the rule that he can stay only one night. If he returns within a month he is penalized by being confined for a week, and, as this is much the same as being in prison, naturally he keeps moving. But if he represented labour to the workhouse, and the workhouse represented sound food to him, it would be another matter. The workhouses would develop into partially self-supporting institutions, and the tramps, settling down here or there according as they were needed, would cease to be tramps. They would be doing something comparatively useful, getting decent food, and living a settled life. By degrees, if the scheme worked well, they might even cease to be regarded as paupers, and be able to marry and take a respectable place in society.

This is only a rough idea, and there are some obvious objections to it. Nevertheless, it does suggest a way of improving the status of tramps without piling new burdens on the rates. And the solution must, in any case, be something of this kind. For the question is, what to do with men who are underfed and idle; and the answer – to make them grow their own food – imposes itself automatically.

37

A WORD about the sleeping accommodation open to a homeless person in London. At present it is impossible to get a *bed* in any non-charitable institution in London for less than sevenpence a night. If you cannot afford sevenpence for a bed, you must put up with one of the following substitutes:

1. The Embankment. Here is the account that Paddy gave me of sleeping on the embankment:

'De whole t'ing wid de Embankment is gettin' to sleep early. You got to be on your bench by eight o'clock, because dere ain't too many benches and sometimes dey're all taken. And you got to try to get to sleep at once. 'Tis too cold to sleep much after twelve o'clock, an' de police turns you off at four in de mornin'. It ain't easy to sleep, dough, wid dem bloody trams flyin' past your head all de time, an' dem sky-signs across de river flickin' on an' off in your eyes. De cold's cruel. Dem as sleeps dere generally wraps demselves up in newspaper, but it don't do much good. You'd be bloody lucky if you got t'ree hours' sleep.'

I have slept on the Embankment and found that it corresponded to Paddy's description. It is, however, much better than not sleeping at all, which is the alternative if you spend the night in the streets, elsewhere than on the Embankment. According to the law in London, you may sit down for the night, but the police must move you on if they see you asleep; the Embankment and one or two odd corners (there is one behind the Lyceum Theatre) are special exceptions. This law is evidently a piece of wilful offensiveness. Its object, so it is said, is to prevent people from dying of exposure; but clearly if a man has no home and is going to die of exposure, die he will, asleep or awake. In Paris there is no such law. There, people sleep by the score under the Seine bridges, and in doorways, and on benches in the squares, and round the ventilating shafts of the Métro, and even inside the Métro stations. It does no apparent harm. No one will spend a night in the street if he can possibly help it, and if he is going to stay out of doors he might as well be allowed to sleep, if he can.

2. The Twopenny Hangover. This comes a little higher than the Embankment. At the Twopenny Hangover, the lodgers sit in a row on a bench; there is a rope in front of them, and they lean on this as though leaning

over a fence. A man, humorously called the valet, cuts the rope at five in the morning. I have never been there myself, but Bozo had been there often. I asked him whether anyone could possibly sleep in such an attitude, and he said that it was more comfortable than it sounded – at any rate, better than bare floor. There are similar shelters in Paris, but the charge there is only twenty-five centimes (a halfpenny) instead of twopence.

3. The Coffin, at fourpence a night. At the Coffin you sleep in a wooden box, with a tarpaulin for covering. It is cold, and the worst thing about it are the bugs, which, being enclosed in a box, you cannot escape.

Above this come the common lodging-houses, with charges varying between sevenpence and one and a penny a night. The best are the Rowton Houses, where the charge is a shilling, for which you get a cubicle to yourself, and the use of excellent bathrooms. You can also pay half a crown for a 'special', which is practically hotel accommodation. The Rowton Houses are splendid buildings, and the only objection to them is the strict discipline, with rules against cooking, card-playing, etc. Perhaps the best advertisement for the Rowton Houses is the fact that they are always full to overflowing. The Bruce Houses, at one and a penny, are also excellent.

Next best, in point of cleanliness, are the Salvation Army hostels, at sevenpence or eightpence. They vary (I have been in one or two that were as dirty as common lodging-houses), but most of them are clean, and they have good bathrooms; you have to pay extra for a bath, however. You can get a cubicle for a shilling. In the eightpenny dormitories the beds are comfortable, but there are so many of them (as a rule at least forty to a room), and so close together, that it is impossible to get a quiet night. The numerous restrictions stink of prison and charity. The Salvation Army hostels would only appeal to people who put cleanliness before anything else.

Beyond this there are the ordinary common lodging-houses. Whether you pay sevenpence or a shilling, they are all stuffy and noisy, and the beds are uniformly dirty and uncomfortable. What redeems them are their *laissez-faire* atmosphere and the warm home-like kitchens where one can lounge at all hours of the day or night. They are squalid dens, but some kind of social life is possible in them. The women's lodging-houses are said to be generally worse than the men's, and there are very few houses with accommodation for married couples. In fact, it is nothing out of the common for a homeless man to sleep in one lodging-house and his wife in another.

At this moment at least fifteen thousand people in London are living in common lodging-houses. For an unattached man earning two pounds a week, or less, a lodging-house is a great convenience. He could hardly get a furnished room so cheaply, and the lodging-house gives him free firing, a bathroom of sorts, and plenty of society. As for the dirt, it is a minor evil. The really bad fault of lodging-houses is that they are places in which one pays to sleep, and in which sound sleep is impossible. All one gets for one's money is a bed measuring five feet six by two feet six, with a hard convex mattress and a pillow like a block of wood, covered by one cotton counterpane and two grey, stinking sheets. In winter there are blankets, but never enough. And this bed is in a room where there are never less than five, and sometimes fifty or sixty beds, a yard or two apart. Of course, no one can sleep soundly in such circumstances. The only other places where people are herded like this are barracks and hospitals. In the public wards of a hospital no one even hopes to sleep well. In barracks the soldiers are crowded, but they have good beds, and they are healthy; in a common lodging-house nearly all the lodgers have chronic coughs, and a large number have bladder diseases which make them get up at all the hours of the night. The result is a perpetual racket, making sleep impossible. So far as my observation goes, no one in a lodging-house sleeps more than five hours a night – a damnable swindle when one has paid sevenpence or more.

Here legislation could accomplish something. At present there is all manner of legislation by the L.C.C. about lodging-houses, but it is not done in the interests of the lodgers. The L.C.C. only exert themselves to forbid drinking, gambling, fighting, etc. etc. There is no law to say that the beds in a lodging-house must be comfortable. This would be quite an easy thing to enforce – much easier, for instance, than restrictions upon gambling. The lodging-house keepers should be compelled to provide adequate bedclothes and better mattresses, and above all to divide their dormitories into cubicles. It does not matter how small a cubicle is, the important thing is that a man should be alone when he sleeps. These few changes, strictly enforced, would make an enormous difference. It is not impossible to make a lodging-house reasonably comfortable at the usual rates of payment. In the Croydon municipal lodging-house, where the charge is only ninepence, there are cubicles, good beds, chairs (a very rare luxury in lodging-houses), and kitchens above ground instead of in a cellar. There is no reason why every ninepenny lodging-house should not come up to this standard.

Of course, the owners of lodging-houses would be opposed *en bloc* to any improvement, for their present business is an immensely profitable one. The average house takes five or ten pounds a night, with no bad debts (credit being strictly forbidden), and except for rent the expenses are small. Any improvement would mean less crowding, and hence less profit. Still, the excellent municipal lodging-house at Croydon shows how well one *can* be served for ninepence. A few well-directed laws could make these conditions general. If the authorities are going to concern themselves with lodging-houses at all, they ought to start by making them more comfortable, not by silly restrictions that would never be tolerated in a hotel.

38

AFTER we left the spike at Lower Binfield, Paddy and I earned half a crown at weeding and sweeping in somebody's garden, stayed the night at Cromley, and walked back to London. I parted from Paddy a day or two later. B. lent me a final two pounds, and, as I had only another eight days to hold out, that was the end of my troubles. My tame imbecile turned out worse than I had expected, but not bad enough to make me wish myself back in the spike or the Auberge de Jehan Cottard.

Paddy set out for Portsmouth, where he had a friend who might conceivably find work for him, and I have never seen him since. A short time ago I was told that he had been run over and killed, but perhaps my informant was mixing him up with someone else. I had news of Bozo only three days ago. He is in Wandsworth – fourteen days for begging. I do not suppose prison worries him very much.

My story ends here. It is a fairly trivial story, and I can only hope that it has been interesting in the same way as a travel diary is interesting. I can at least say, Here is the world that awaits you if you are ever penniless. Some days I want to explore that world more thoroughly. I should like to know people like Mario and Paddy and Bill the moocher, not from casual encounters, but intimately; I should like to understand what really goes on in the souls of *plongeurs* and tramps and Embankment sleepers. At present I do not feel that I have seen more than the fringe of poverty.

Still I can point to one or two things I have definitely learned by being hard up. I shall never again think that all tramps are drunken scoundrels, nor expect a beggar to be grateful when I give him a penny, nor be surprised if men out of work lack energy, nor subscribe to the Salvation Army, nor pawn my clothes, nor refuse a handbill, nor enjoy a meal at a smart restaurant. That is a beginning.

Victor Gollancz writes: 'The blanks in this passage appeared in the original edition, which I had the pleasure of publishing. The text cannot now be debowdlerized, for the manuscript and original proofs have disappeared. The words written by George Orwell were doubtless of a kind that no publisher could have printed at that time without risking gaol; and even if he had decided to risk it, no printer would have abetted him. The code was very rigid: Gerald Gould circulated a poem (apropos of a current obscenity trial) with the following refrain:

> ... Once aboard the lugger
> Straight from the quarter-deck the fiat falls:
> You may say bloody but not say bugger,
> You may say bottom but may not say balls.

THE ROAD
TO
WIGAN PIER

PART ONE

1

THE first sound in the mornings was the clumping of the mill-girls' clogs down the cobbled street. Earlier than that, I suppose, there were factory whistles which I was never awake to hear.

There were generally four of us in the bedroom, and a beastly place it was, with that defiled impermanent look of rooms that are not serving their rightful purpose. Years earlier the house had been an ordinary dwelling-house, and when the Brookers had taken it and fitted it out as a tripe-shop and lodging-house, they had inherited some of the more useless pieces of furniture and had never had the energy to remove them. We were therefore sleeping in what was still recognizably a drawing-room. Hanging from the ceiling there was a heavy glass chandelier on which the dust was so thick that it was like fur. And covering most of one wall there was a huge hideous piece of junk, something between a sideboard and a hall-stand, with lots of carving and little drawers and strips of looking-glass, and there was a once-gaudy carpet ringed by the slop-pails of years, and two gilt chairs with burst seats, and one of those old-fashioned horsehair armchairs which you slide off when you try to sit on them. The room had been turned into a bedroom by thrusting four squalid beds in among this other wreckage.

My bed was in the right-hand corner on the side nearest the door. There was another bed across the foot of it and jammed hard against it (it had to be in that position to allow the door to open) so that I had to sleep with my legs doubled up; if I straightened them out I kicked the occupant of the other bed in the small of the back. He was an elderly man named Mr Reilly, a mechanic of sorts and employed 'on top' at one of the coal pits. Luckily he had to go to work at five in the morning, so I could uncoil my legs and have a couple of hours' proper sleep after he was gone. In the bed opposite there was a Scotch miner who had been injured in a pit accident (a huge chunk of stone pinned him to the ground and it was a couple of hours before they could lever it off), and had received five hundred pounds compensation. He was a big handsome man of forty, with grizzled hair and a clipped moustache, more like a sergeant-major than a miner, and he would lie in bed till late in the day, smoking a short pipe.

The other bed was occupied by a succession of commercial travellers, newspaper-canvassers, and hire-purchase touts who generally stayed for a couple of nights. It was a double bed and much the best in the room. I had slept in it myself my first night there, but had been manoeuvred out of it to make room for another lodger. I believe all newcomers spent their first night in the double bed, which was used, so to speak, as bait. All the windows were kept tight shut, with a red sand-bag jammed in the bottom, and in the morning the room stank like a ferret's cage. You did not notice it when you got up, but if you went out of the room and came back, the smell hit you in the face with a smack.

I never discovered how many bedrooms the house contained, but strange to say there was a bathroom, dating from before the Brookers' time. Downstairs there was the usual kitchen living-room with its huge open range burning night and day. It was lighted only by a skylight, for on one side of it was the shop and on the other the larder, which opened into some dark subterranean place where the tripe was stored. Partly blocking the door of the larder there was a shapeless sofa upon which Mrs Brooker, our landlady, lay permanently ill, festooned in grimy blankets. She had a big, pale yellow, anxious face. No one knew for certain what was the matter with her; I suspect that her only real trouble was over-eating. In front of the fire there was almost always a line of damp washing, and in the middle of the room was the big kitchen table at which the family and all the lodgers ate. I never saw this table completely uncovered, but I saw its various wrappings at different times. At the bottom there was a layer of old newspaper stained by Worcester Sauce; above that a sheet of sticky white oil-cloth; above that a green serge cloth; above that a coarse linen cloth, never changed and seldom taken off. Generally the crumbs from breakfast were still on the table at supper. I used to get to know individual crumbs by sight and watch their progress up and down the table from day to day.

The shop was a narrow, cold sort of room. On the outside of the window a few white letters, relics of ancient chocolate advertisements, were scattered like stars. Inside there was a slab upon which lay the great white folds of tripe, and the grey flocculent stuff known as 'black tripe', and the ghostly translucent feet of pigs, ready boiled. It was the ordinary 'tripe and pea' shop, and not much else was stocked except bread, cigarettes, and tinned stuff. 'Teas' were advertised in the window, but if a customer demanded a cup of tea he was usually put off with excuses. Mr Brooker, though out of work for two years, was a miner by trade, but he and his wife had been keeping shops of various kinds as a side-line all their lives.

At one time they had had a pub, but they had lost their licence for allowing gambling on the premises. I doubt whether any of their businesses had ever paid; they were the kind of people who run a business chiefly in order to have something to grumble about. Mr Brooker was a dark, small-boned, sour, Irish-looking man, and astonishingly dirty. I don't think I ever once saw his hands clean. As Mrs Brooker was now an invalid he prepared most of the food, and like all people with permanently dirty hands he had a peculiarly intimate, lingering manner of handling things. If he gave you a slice of bread-and-butter there was always a black thumb-print on it. Even in the early morning when he descended into the mysterious den behind Mrs Brooker's sofa and fished out the tripe, his hands were already black. I heard dreadful stories from the other lodgers about the place where the tripe was kept. Blackbeetles were said to swarm there. I do not know how often fresh consignments of tripe were ordered, but it was at long intervals, for Mrs Brooker used to date events by it. 'Let me see now, I've had in three lots of froze (frozen tripe) since that happened,' etc. We lodgers were never given tripe to eat. At the time I imagined that this was because tripe was too expensive; I have since thought that it was merely because we knew too much about it. The Brookers never ate tripe themselves, I noticed.

The only permanent lodgers were the Scotch miner, Mr Reilly, two old-age pensioners, and an unemployed man on the P.A.C. named Joe – he was the kind of person who has no surname. The Scotch miner was a bore when you got to know him. Like so many unemployed men he spent too much time reading newspapers, and if you did not head him off he would discourse for hours about such things as the Yellow Peril, trunk murders, astrology, and the conflict between religion and science. The old-age pensioners had, as usual, been driven from their homes by the Means Test. They handed their weekly ten shillings over to the Brookers and in return got the kind of accommodation you would expect for ten shillings; that is, a bed in the attic and meals chiefly of bread-and-butter. One of them was of 'superior' type and was dying of some malignant disease – cancer, I believe. He only got out of bed on the days when he went to draw his pension. The other, called by everyone Old Jack, was an ex-miner aged seventy-eight who had worked well over fifty years in the pits. He was alert and intelligent, but curiously enough he seemed only to remember his boyhood experiences and to have forgotten all about the modern mining machinery and improvements. He used to tell me tales of fights with savage horses in the narrow galleries underground. When he heard that I was arranging to go down several coal mines he was contemptuous and declared that a man of my size (six feet two and a half) would never manage the 'travelling'; it was no use telling him that the 'travelling' was better than it used to be. But he was friendly to everyone and used to give us all a fine shout of 'Good night, boys!' as he crawled up the stairs to his bed somewhere under the rafters. What I most admired about Old Jack was that he never cadged; he was generally out of tobacco towards the end of the week, but he always refused to smoke anyone else's. The Brookers had insured the lives of both old-age pensioners with one of the tanner-a-week companies. It was said that they were overheard anxiously asking the insurance-tout 'how long people lives when they've got cancer'.

Joe, like the Scotchman, was a great reader of newspapers and spent almost his entire day in the public library. He was the typical unmarried unemployed man, a derelict-looking, frankly ragged creature with a round, almost childish face on which there was a naively naughty expression. He looked more like a neglected little boy than a grown-up man. I suppose it is the complete lack of responsibility that makes so many of these men look younger than their ages. From Joe's appearance I took him to be about twenty-eight, and was amazed to learn that he was forty-three. He had a love of resounding phrases and was very proud of the astuteness with which he had avoided getting married. He often said to me, 'Matrimonial chains is a big item,' evidently feeling this to be a very subtle and portentous remark. His total income was fifteen shillings a week, and he paid out six or seven to the Brookers for his bed. I sometimes used to see him making himself a cup of tea over the kitchen fire, but for the rest he got his meals somewhere out of doors; it was mostly slices of bread-and-marg and packets of fish and chips, I suppose.

Besides these there was a floating clientele of commercial travellers of the poorer sort, travelling actors – always common in the North because most of the larger pubs hire variety artists at the week-ends – and newspaper-canvassers. The newspaper-canvassers were a type I had never met before. Their job seemed to me so hopeless, so appalling that I wondered how anyone could put up with such a thing when prison was a possible alternative. They were employed mostly by weekly or Sunday papers, and they were sent from town to town, provided with maps and given a list of streets which they had to 'work' each day. If they failed to secure a minimum of twenty orders a day, they got the sack. So long as they kept up their twenty orders a day they received a small salary – two pounds a week, I think; on any order over the twenty they drew a tiny commission. The thing is not so impossible as it sounds, because in working-class districts every family takes in a twopenny weekly paper and changes it every few weeks; but I doubt whether anyone keeps a job of that kind long. The newspapers engage poor desperate wretches, out-of-work clerks and commercial travellers and the like, who for a while make frantic efforts and keep their sales up to the minimum; then as the deadly work wears them down they are sacked and fresh men are taken on. I got to know two who were employed by one of the more notorious weeklies. Both of them were middle-aged men with families to support, and one of them was a grandfather. They were on their feet ten hours a day, 'working' their appointed streets, and then busy late into the night filling in blank forms for some swindle their paper was running – one of those schemes by which you are 'given' a set of crockery if you take out a six-weeks' subscription and send a two-shilling postal order as well. The fat one, the grandfather, used to fall asleep with his head on a pile of forms. Neither of them could afford the pound a week which the Brookers charged for full board. They used to pay a small sum for their beds and make shamefaced meals in a corner of the kitchen off bacon and bread-and-margarine which they stored in their suit-cases.

The Brookers had large numbers of sons and daughters, most of whom had long since fled from home. Some were in Canada 'at Canada', as Mrs Brooker used to put it. There was only one son living near by, a large pig-like young man employed in a garage, who frequently came to the house for his meals. His wife was there all day with the two children, and most of the cooking and laundering was done by her and by Emmie, the fiancée of another son who was in London. Emmie was a fair-haired, sharp-nosed, unhappy-looking girl who worked at one of the mills for some starvation wage, but nevertheless spent all her evenings in bondage at the Brookers' house. I gathered that the marriage was constantly being postponed and would probably never take place, but Mrs Brooker had already appropriated Emmie as a daughter-in-law, and nagged her in that peculiar watchful, loving way that invalids have. The rest of the housework was done, or not done, by Mr Brooker. Mrs Brooker seldom rose from her sofa in the kitchen (she spent the night there as well as the day) and was too ill to do anything except eat stupendous meals. It was Mr Brooker who attended to the shop, gave the lodgers their food, and 'did out' the bedrooms. He was always moving with incredible slowness from one hated job to another. Often the beds were still unmade at six in the evening, and at any hour of the day you were liable to meet Mr Brooker on the stairs, carrying a full chamber-pot which he gripped with his thumb well over the rim. In the mornings he sat by the fire with a tub of filthy water, peeling potatoes at the speed of a slow-motion picture. I never saw anyone

who could peel potatoes with quite such an air of brooding resentment.
You could see the hatred of this 'bloody woman's work', as he called it,
fermenting inside him, a kind of bitter juice. He was one of those people
who can chew their grievances like a cud.

Of course, as I was indoors a good deal, I heard all about the Brookers'
woes, and how everyone swindled them and was ungrateful to them, and
how the shop did not pay and the lodging-house hardly paid. By local
standards they were not so badly off, for, in some way I did not understand,
Mr Brooker was dodging the Means Test and drawing an allowance from
the P.A.C., but their chief pleasure was talking about their grievances to
anyone who would listen. Mrs Brooker used to lament by the hour, lying
on her sofa, a soft mound of fat and self-pity, saying the same things over
and over again. 'We don't seem to get no customers nowadays. I don't
know 'ow it is. The tripe's just a-laying there day after day – such beautiful
tripe it is, too! It does seem 'ard, don't it now?' etc., etc., etc. All Mrs
Brooker's laments ended with 'It does seem 'ard, don't it now?' like the
refrain of a ballade. Certainly it was true that the shop did not pay. The
whole place had the unmistakable dusty, flyblown air of a business that is
going down. But it would have been quite useless to explain to them *why*
nobody came to the shop, even if one had had the face to do it; neither
was capable of understanding that last year's dead bluebottles supine in
the shop window are not good for trade.

But the thing that really tormented them was the thought of those two
old-age pensioners living in their house, usurping floor-space, devouring
food, and paying only ten shillings a week. I doubt whether they were
really losing money over the old-age pensioners, though certainly the profit
on ten shillings a week must have been very small. But in their eyes the
two old men were a kind of dreadful parasite who had fastened on them
and were living on their charity. Old Jack they could just tolerate, because
he kept out-of-doors most of the day, but they really hated the bedridden
one, Hooker by name. Mr Brooker had a queer way of pronouncing his
name, without the H and with a long U – 'Uker'. What tales I heard
about old Hooker and his fractiousness, the nuisance of making his bed,
the way he 'wouldn't eat' this and 'wouldn't eat' that, his endless ingratitude and, above all, the selfish obstinacy with which he refused to die!
The Brookers were quite openly pining for him to die. When that happened
they could at least draw the insurance money. They seemed to feel him
there, eating their substance day after day, as though he had been a living
worm in their bowels. Sometimes Mr Brooker would look up from his
potato-peeling, catch my eye, and jerk his head with a look of inexpressible

bitterness towards the ceiling, towards old Hooker's room. 'It's a b—,
ain't it?' he would say. There was no need to say more; I had heard all
about old Hooker's ways already. But the Brookers had grievances of one
kind and another against all their lodgers, myself included, no doubt. Joe,
being on the P.A.C., was practically in the same category as the old-age
pensioners. The Scotchman paid a pound a week, but he was indoors most
of the day and they 'didn't like him always hanging round the place', as
they put it. The newspaper-canvassers were out all day, but the Brookers
bore them a grudge for bringing in their own food, and even Mr Reilly,
their best lodger, was in disgrace because Mrs Brooker said that he woke
her up when he came downstairs in the mornings. They couldn't, they
complained perpetually, get the kind of lodgers they wanted – good-class
'commercial gentlemen' who paid full board and were out all day. Their
ideal lodger would have been somebody who paid thirty shillings a week
and never came indoors except to sleep. I have noticed that people who
let lodgings nearly always hate their lodgers. They want their money but
they look on them as intruders and have a curiously watchful, jealous
attitude which at bottom is a determination not to let the lodger make
himself too much at home. It is an inevitable result of the bad system by
which the lodger has to live in somebody else's house without being one
of the family.

The meals at the Brookers' house were uniformly disgusting. For
breakfast you got two rashers of bacon and a pale fried egg, and bread-
and-butter which had often been cut overnight and always had thumb-
marks on it. However tactfully I tried, I could never induce Mr Brooker
to let me cut my own bread-and-butter; he *would* hand it to me slice by
slice, each slice gripped firmly under that broad black thumb. For dinner
there were generally those threepenny steak puddings which are sold
ready-made in tins – these were part of the stock of the shop, I think –
and boiled potatoes and rice pudding. For tea there was more bread-and-
butter and frayed-looking sweet cakes which were probably bought as
'stales' from the baker. For supper there was the pale flabby Lancashire
cheese and biscuits. The Brookers never called these biscuits biscuits. They
always referred to them reverently as 'cream crackers' – 'Have another
cream cracker, Mr Reilly. You'll like a cream cracker with your cheese'
– thus glozing over the fact that there was only cheese for supper.
Several bottles of Worcester Sauce and a half-full jar of marmalade lived
permanently on the table. It was usual to souse everything, even a piece
of cheese, with Worcester Sauce, but I never saw anyone brave the
marmalade jar, which was an unspeakable mass of stickiness and dust.

Mrs Brooker had her meals separately but also took snacks from any meal that happened to be going, and manoeuvred with great skill for what she called 'the bottom of the pot', meaning the strongest cup of tea. She had a habit of constantly wiping her mouth on one of her blankets. Towards the end of my stay she took to tearing off strips of newspaper for this purpose, and in the morning the floor was often littered with crumpled-up balls of slimy paper which lay there for hours. The smell of the kitchen was dreadful, but, as with that of the bedroom, you ceased to notice it after a while.

It struck me that this place must be fairly normal as lodging-houses in the industrial areas go, for on the whole the lodgers did not complain. The only one who ever did so to my knowledge was a little black-haired, sharp-nosed Cockney, a traveller for a cigarette firm. He had never been in the North before, and I think that till recently he had been in better employ and was used to staying in commercial hotels. This was his first glimpse of really low-class lodgings, the kind of place in which the poor tribe of touts and canvassers have to shelter upon their endless journeys. In the morning as we were dressing (he had slept in the double bed, of course) I saw him look round the desolate room with a sort of wondering aversion. He caught my eye and suddenly divined that I was a fellow-Southerner.

'The filthy bloody bastards!' he said feelingly.

After that he packed his suit-case, went downstairs and, with great strength of mind, told the Brookers that this was not the kind of house he was accustomed to and that he was leaving immediately. The Brookers could never understand why. They were astonished and hurt. The ingratitude of it! Leaving them like that for no reason after a single night! Afterwards they discussed it over and over again, in all its bearings. It was added to their store of grievances.

On the day when there was a full chamber-pot under the breakfast table I decided to leave. The place was beginning to depress me. It was not only the dirt, the smells, and the vile food, but the feeling of stagnant meaning-less decay, of having got down into some subterranean place where people go creeping round and round, just like blackbeetles, in an endless muddle of slovened jobs and mean grievances. The most dreadful thing about people like the Brookers is the way they say the same things over and over again. It gives you the feeling that they are not real people at all, but a kind of ghost for ever rehearsing the same futile rigmarole. In the end Mrs Brooker's self-pitying talk – always the same complaints, over and over, and always ending with the tremulous whine of 'It does seem 'ard, don't it now?' – revolted me even more than her habit of wiping her mouth with bits of newspaper. But it is no use saying that people like the Brookers are just disgusting and trying to put them out of mind. For they exist in tens and hundreds of thousands; they are one of the characteristic by-products of the modern world. You cannot disregard them if you accept the civilization that produced them. For this is part at least of what industrialism has done for us. Columbus sailed the Atlantic, the first steam engines tottered into motion, the British squares stood firm under the French guns at Waterloo, the one-eyed scoundrels of the nineteenth century praised God and filled their pockets; and this is where it all led – to labyrinthine slums and dark back kitchens with sickly, ageing people creeping round and round them like blackbeetles. It is a kind of duty to see and smell such places now and again, especially smell them, lest you should forget that they exist; though perhaps it is better not to stay there too long.

The train bore me away, through the monstrous scenery of slag-heaps, chimneys, piled scrap-iron, foul canals, paths of cindery mud criss-crossed by the prints of clogs. This was March, but the weather had been horribly cold and everywhere there were mounds of blackened snow. As we moved slowly through the outskirts of the town we passed row after row of little grey slum houses running at right angles to the embankment. At the back of one of the houses a young woman was kneeling on the stones, poking a stick up the leaden waste-pipe which ran from the sink inside and which I suppose was blocked. I had time to see everything about her – her sacking apron, her clumsy clogs, her arms reddened by the cold. She looked up as the train passed, and I was almost near enough to catch her eye. She had a round pale face, the usual exhausted face of the slum girl who is twenty-five and looks forty, thanks to miscarriages and drudgery; and it wore, for the second in which I saw it, the most desolate, hopeless expression I have ever seen. It struck me then that we are mistaken when we say that 'It isn't the same for them as it would be for us,' and that people bred in the slums can imagine nothing but the slums. For what I saw in her face was not the ignorant suffering of an animal. She knew well enough what was happening to her – understood as well as I did how dreadful a destiny it was to be kneeling there in the bitter cold, on the slimy stones of a slum backyard, poking a stick up a foul drain-pipe.

But quite soon the train drew away into open country, and that seemed strange, almost unnatural, as though the open country had been a kind of park; for in the industrial areas one always feels that the smoke and filth must go on for ever and that no part of the earth's surface can escape them. In a crowded, dirty little country like ours one takes defilement almost for granted. Slag-heaps and chimneys seem a more normal, probable landscape than grass and trees, and even in the depths of the country when you drive your fork into the ground you half expect to lever up a broken bottle or a rusty can. But out here the snow was untrodden and lay so deep that only the tops of the stone boundary-walls were showing, winding over the hills like black paths. I remembered that D. H. Lawrence, writing of this same landscape or another near by, said that the snow-covered hills rippled away into the distance 'like muscle'. It was not the simile that would have occurred to me. To my eye the snow and the black walls were more like a white dress with black piping running across it.

Although the snow was hardly broken the sun was shining brightly, and behind the shut windows of the carriage it seemed warm. According to the almanac this was spring, and a few of the birds seemed to believe it. For the first time in my life, in a bare patch beside the line, I saw rooks treading. They did it on the ground and not, as I should have expected, in a tree. The manner of courtship was curious. The female stood with her beak open and the male walked round her and appeared to be feeding her. I had hardly been in the train half an hour, but it seemed a very long way from the Brookers' back-kitchen to the empty slopes of snow, the bright sunshine, and the big gleaming birds.

The whole of the industrial districts are really one enormous town, of about the same population as Greater London but, fortunately, of much larger area; so that even in the middle of them there is still room for patches of cleanness and decency. That is an encouraging thought. In spite of hard trying, man has not yet succeeded in doing his dirt everywhere. The earth is so vast and still so empty that even in the filthy heart of civilization you find fields where the grass is green instead of grey; perhaps if you looked for them you might even find streams with live fish in them instead of salmon tins. For quite a long time, perhaps another twenty minutes, the train was rolling through open country before the villa-civilization began to close in upon us again, and then the outer slums, and then the slag-heaps, belching chimneys, blast-furnaces, canals, and gasometers of another industrial town.

2

OUR civilization, *pace* Chesterton, *is* founded on coal, more completely than one realizes until one stops to think about it. The machines that keep us alive, and the machines that make the machines, are all directly or indirectly dependent upon coal. In the metabolism of the Western world the coal-miner is second in importance only to the man who ploughs the soil. He is a sort of grimy caryatid upon whose shoulders nearly everything that is *not* grimy is supported. For this reason the actual process by which coal is extracted is well worth watching, if you get the chance and are willing to take the trouble.

When you go down a coal-mine it is important to try and get to the coal face when the 'fillers' are at work. This is not easy, because when the mine is working visitors are a nuisance and are not encouraged, but if you go at any other time, it is possible to come away with a totally wrong impression. On a Sunday, for instance, a mine seems almost peaceful. The time to go there is when the machines are roaring and the air is black with coal dust, and when you can actually see what the miners have to do. At those times the place is like hell, or at any rate like my own mental picture of hell. Most of the things one imagines in hell are there – heat, noise, confusion, darkness, foul air, and, above all, unbearably cramped space. Everything except the fire, for there is no fire down there except the feeble beams of Davy lamps and electric torches which scarcely penetrate the clouds of coal dust.

When you have finally got there – and getting there is a job in itself: I will explain that in a moment – you crawl through the last line of pit props and see opposite you a shiny black wall three or four feet high. This is the coal face. Overhead is the smooth ceiling made by the rock from which the coal has been cut; underneath is the rock again, so that the gallery you are in is only as high as the ledge of coal itself, probably not much more than a yard. The first impression of all, overmastering everything else for a while, is the frightful, deafening din from the conveyor belt which carries the coal away. You cannot see very far, because the fog of coal dust throws back the beam of your lamp, but you can see on either side of you the line of half-naked kneeling men, one to every four or five yards, driving their shovels under the fallen coal and flinging it swiftly over their left shoulders. They are feeding it on to the conveyor belt, a moving rubber belt a couple of feet wide which runs a yard or two behind them. Down this belt a glittering river of coal races constantly. In a big mine it is carrying away several tons of coal every minute. It bears it off to some place in the main roads where it is shot into tubs holding half a ton, and thence dragged to the cages and hoisted to the outer air.

It is impossible to watch the 'fillers' at work without feeling a pang of envy for their toughness. It is a dreadful job that they do, an almost superhuman job by the standards of an ordinary person. For they are not only shifting monstrous quantities of coal, they are also doing it in a position that doubles or trebles the work. They have got to remain kneeling all the while – they could hardly rise from their knees without hitting the ceiling – and you can easily see by trying it what a tremendous effort this means. Shovelling is comparatively easy when you are standing up, because you can use your knee and thigh to drive the shovel along; kneeling down, the whole of the strain is thrown upon your arm and belly muscles. And the other conditions do not exactly make things easier. There is the heat – it varies, but in some mines it is suffocating – and the coal dust that stuffs up your throat and nostrils and collects along your eyelids, and the unending rattle of the conveyor belt, which in that confined space is rather like the rattle of a machine-gun. But the fillers look and work as though they were made of iron. They really do look like iron – hammered iron statues – under the smooth coat of coal dust which clings to them from head to foot. It is only when you see miners down the mine and naked that you realize what splendid men they are. Most of them are small (big men are at a disadvantage in that job) but nearly all of them have the most noble bodies; wide shoulders tapering to slender supple waists, and small pronounced buttocks and sinewy thighs, with not an ounce of waste flesh anywhere. In the hotter mines they wear only a pair of thin drawers, clogs, and knee-pads; in the hottest mines of all, only the clogs and knee-pads. You can hardly tell by the look of them whether they are young or old. They may be any age up to sixty or even sixty-five, but when they are black and naked they all look alike. No one could do their work who had not a young man's body, and a figure fit for a guardsman at that; just a few pounds of extra flesh on the waist-line, and the constant bending would be impossible. You can never forget that spectacle once you have seen it – the line of bowed, kneeling figures, sooty black all over, driving their huge shovels under the coal with stupendous force and speed. They are on the job for seven and a half hours, theoretically without a break, for there is no time 'off'. Actually they snatch a quarter of an hour or so at some time during the shift to eat the food they have brought with them, usually a hunk of bread and dripping and a bottle of cold tea. The first time I was watching the 'fillers' at work I put my hand upon some dreadful slimy thing among the coal dust. It was a chewed quid of tobacco. Nearly all the miners chew tobacco, which is said to be good against thirst.

Probably you have to go down several coal-mines before you can get much grasp of the processes that are going on round you. This is chiefly because the mere effort of getting from place to place makes it difficult to notice anything else. In some ways it is even disappointing, or at least is unlike what you have expected. You get into the cage, which is a steel box about as wide as a telephone box and two or three times as long. It holds ten men, but they pack like pilchards in a tin, and a tall man cannot stand upright in it. The steel door shuts upon you, and somebody working the winding gear above drops you into the void. You have the usual momentary qualm in your belly and a bursting sensation in the ears, but not much sensation of movement till you get near the bottom, when the cage slows down so abruptly that you could swear it is going upwards again. In the middle of the run the cage probably touches sixty miles an hour; in some of the deeper mines it touches even more. When you crawl out at the bottom you are perhaps four hundred yards under ground. That is to say you have a tolerable-sized mountain on top of you; hundreds of yards of solid rock, bones of extinct beasts, subsoil, flints, roots of growing things, green grass, and cows grazing on it – all this suspended over your head and held back only by wooden props as thick as the calf of your leg. But because of the speed at which the cage has brought you down, and the complete blackness through which you have travelled, you hardly feel yourself deeper down than you would at the bottom of the Piccadilly Tube.

What *is* surprising, on the other hand, is the immense horizontal distances that have to be travelled underground. Before I had been down a mine I had vaguely imagined the miner stepping out of the cage and getting to work on a ledge of coal a few yards away. I had not realized that before he even gets to his work he may have to creep through passages as long as from London Bridge to Oxford Circus. In the beginning, of course, a mine shaft is sunk somewhere near a seam of coal. But as that seam is worked out and fresh seams are followed up, the workings get further and further from the pit bottom. If it is a mile from the pit bottom to the coal face, that is probably an average distance; three miles is a fairly normal one; there are even said to be a few mines where it is as much as five miles. But these distances bear no relation to distances above ground. For in all that mile or three miles as it may be, there is hardly anywhere outside the main road, and not many places even there, where a man can stand upright.

You do not notice the effect of this till you have gone a few hundred yards. You start off, stooping slightly, down the dim-lit gallery, eight or ten feet wide and about five high, with the walls built up with slabs of shale, like the stone walls in Derbyshire. Every yard or two there are wooden props holding up the beams and girders; some of the girders have buckled into fantastic curves under which you have to duck. Usually it is bad going underfoot – thick dust or jagged chunks of shale, and in some places where there is water it is mucky as a farmyard. Also there is the track for the coal tubs, like a miniature railway track with sleepers a foot to two apart, which is tiresome to walk on. Everything is grey with shale dust; there is a dusty fiery smell which seems to be the same in all mines. You see mysterious machines of which you never learn the purpose, and bundles of tools slung together on wires, and sometimes mice darting away from the beam of the lamps. They are surprisingly common, especially in mines where there are or have been horses. It would be interesting to know how they got there in the first place; possibly by falling down the shaft – for they say a mouse can fall any distance uninjured, owing to its surface area being so large relative to its weight. You press yourself against the wall to make way for lines of tubs jolting slowly towards the shaft, drawn by an endless steel cable operated from the surface. You creep through sacking curtains and thick wooden doors which, when they are opened, let out fierce blasts of air. These doors are an important part of the ventilation system. The exhausted air is sucked out of one shaft by means of fans, and the fresh air enters the other of its own accord. But if left to itself the air will take the shortest way round, leaving the deeper workings unventilated; so all short cuts have to be partitioned off.

At the start to walk stooping is rather a joke, but it is a joke that soon wears off. I am handicapped by being exceptionally tall, but when the roof falls to four feet or less it is a tough job for anybody except a dwarf or a child. You have not only got to bend double, you have also got to keep your head up all the while so as to see the beams and girders and dodge them when they come. You have, therefore, a constant crick in the neck, but this is nothing to the pain in your knees and thighs. After half a mile it becomes (I am not exaggerating) an unbeatable agony. You begin to wonder whether you will ever get to the end – still more, how on earth you are going to get back. Your pace grows slower and slower. You come to a stretch of a couple of hundred yards where it is all exceptionally low and you have to work yourself along in a squatting position. Then suddenly the roof opens out to a mysterious height – scene of an old fall of rock, probably – and for twenty whole yards you can stand upright. The relief is overwhelming. But after this there is another low stretch of a hundred yards and then a succession of beams which you have to crawl under. You go down on all fours; even this is a relief after the squatting business. But when you come to the end of the beams and try to get up again, you find that your knees have temporarily struck work and refuse to lift you. You call a halt, ignominiously, and say that you would like to rest for a minute or two. Your guide (a miner) is sympathetic. He knows that your muscles are not the same as his. 'Only another four hundred yards,' he says encouragingly; you feel that he might as well say another four hundred miles. But finally you do somehow creep as far as the coal face. You have gone a mile and taken the best part of an hour; a miner would do it in not much more than twenty minutes. Having got there, you have to sprawl in the coal dust and get your strength back for several minutes before you can even watch the work in progress with any kind of intelligence.

Coming back is worse than going, not only because you are already tired out but because the journey back to the shaft is probably slightly uphill. You get through the low places at the speed of a tortoise, and you have no shame now about calling a halt when your knees give way. Even the lamp you are carrying becomes a nuisance and probably when you stumble you drop it; whereupon, if it is a Davy lamp, it goes out. Ducking the beams becomes more and more of an effort, and sometimes you forget to duck. You try walking head down as the miners do, and then you bang your backbone. Even the miners bang their backbones fairly often. This is the reason why in very hot mines, where it is necessary to go about half naked, most of the miners have what they call 'buttons down the back' – that is, a permanent scab on each vertebra. When the track is downhill the miners sometimes fit their clogs, which are hollow underneath, on to the trolley rails and slide down. In mines where the 'travelling' is very bad all the miners carry sticks about two and a half feet long, hollowed out below the handle. In normal places you keep your hand on top of the stick and in the low places you slide your hand down into the hollow. These sticks are a great help, and the wooden crash-helmets – a comparatively recent invention – are a godsend. They look like a French or Italian steel helmet, but they are made of some kind of pith and very light, and so strong that you can take a violent blow on the head without feeling it. When finally you get back to the surface you have been perhaps three hours underground and travelled two miles, and you are more exhausted than you would be by a twenty-five-mile walk above ground. For a week afterwards your thighs are so stiff that coming downstairs is quite a difficult feat; you have to work your way down in a peculiar sidelong manner, without bending the knees. Your miner friends notice the stiffness of your walk and chaff you about it. ('How'd ta like to work down pit, eh?' etc.) Yet even a miner who has been long away from work – from illness, for instance – when he comes back to the pit, suffers badly for the first few days.

It may seem that I am exaggerating, though no one who has been down an old-fashioned pit (most of the pits in England are old-fashioned) and actually gone as far as the coal face, is likely to say so. But what I want to emphasize is this. Here is this frightful business of crawling to and fro, which to any normal person is a hard day's work in itself; and it is not part of the miner's work at all, it is merely an extra, like the City man's daily ride in the Tube. The miner does that journey to and fro, and sandwiched in between there are seven and a half hours of savage work. I have never travelled much more than a mile to the coal face; but often it is three miles, in which case I and most people other than coal-miners would never get there at all. This is the kind of point that one is always liable to miss. When you think of a coal-mine you think of depth, heat, darkness, blackened figures hacking at walls of coal; you don't think, necessarily, of those miles of creeping to and fro. There is the question of time, also. A miner's working shift of seven and a half hours does not sound very long, but one has got to add on to it at least an hour a day for 'travelling', more often two hours and sometimes three. Of course, the 'travelling' is not technically work and the miner is not paid for it; but it is as like work as makes no difference. It is easy to say that miners don't mind all this. Certainly, it is not the same for them as it would be for you or me. They have done it since childhood, they have the right muscles hardened, and they can move to and fro underground with a startling and rather horrible agility. A miner puts his head down and *runs*, with a long swinging stride, through places where I can only stagger. At the workings you see them on all fours, skipping round the pit props almost like dogs. But it is quite a mistake to think that they enjoy it. I have talked about this to scores of miners and they all admit that the 'travelling' is hard work; in any case when you hear them discussing a pit among themselves the 'travelling' is always one of the things they discuss. It is said that a shift always returns from work faster than it goes; nevertheless the miners all say that it is the coming away, after a hard day's work, that is especially irksome. It is part of their work and they are equal to it, but certainly it is an effort. It is comparable, perhaps, to climbing a smallish mountain before and after your day's work.

When you have been down two or three pits you begin to get some grasp of the processes that are going on underground. (I ought to say, by the way, that I know nothing whatever about the technical side of mining: I am merely describing what I have seen.) Coal lies in thin seams between enormous layers of rock, so that essentially the process of getting it out is like scooping the central layer from a Neapolitan ice. In the old days the miners used to cut straight into the coal with pick and crowbar – a very slow job because coal, when lying in its virgin state, is almost as hard as rock. Nowadays the preliminary work is done by an electrically-driven coal-cutter, which in principle is an immensely tough and powerful bandsaw, running horizontally instead of vertically, with teeth a couple of inches long and half an inch or an inch thick. It can move backwards or forwards on its own power, and the men operating it can rotate it this way and that. Incidentally it makes one of the most awful noises I have ever heard, and sends forth clouds of coal dust which make it impossible to see more than two or three feet and almost impossible to breathe. The machine travels along the coal face cutting into the base of the coal and undermining it to the depth of five feet or five feet and a half; after this it is comparatively easy to extract the coal to the depth to which it has been undermined. Where it is 'difficult getting', however, it has also to be loosened with explosives. A man with an electric drill, like a rather smaller version of the drills used in street-mending, bores holes at intervals in the coal, inserts blasting powder, plugs it with clay, goes round the corner if there is one handy (he is supposed to retire to twenty-five yards distance) and touches off the charge with an electric current. This is not intended to bring the coal out, only to loosen it. Occasionally, of course, the charge is too powerful, and then it not only brings the coal out but brings the roof down as well.

After the blasting has been done the 'fillers' can tumble the coal out, break it up, and shovel it on to the conveyor belt. It comes out at first in monstrous boulders which may weigh anything up to twenty tons. The conveyor belt shoots it on to tubs, and the tubs are shoved into the main road and hitched on to an endlessly revolving steel cable which drags them to the cage. Then they are hoisted, and at the surface the coal is sorted by being run over screens, and if necessary is washed as well. As far as possible the 'dirt' – the shale, that is – is used for making the roads below. All that cannot be used is sent to the surface and dumped; hence the monstrous 'dirt-heaps', like hideous grey mountains, which are the characteristic scenery of the coal areas. When the coal has been extracted to the depth to which the machine has cut, the coal face has advanced by five feet. Fresh props are put in to hold up the newly exposed roof, and during the next shift the conveyor belt is taken to pieces, moved five feet forward, and re-assembled. As far as possible the three operations of cutting, blasting, and extraction are done in three separate shifts, the cutting in the afternoon, the blasting at night (there is a law, not always kept, that forbids its being done when there are other men working near by), and the 'filling' in the morning shift, which lasts from six in the morning until half past one.

Even when you watch the process of coal-extraction you probably only watch it for a short time, and it is not until you begin making a few calculations that you realize what a stupendous task the 'fillers' are performing. Normally each man has to clear a space four or five yards wide. The cutter has undermined the coal to the depth of five feet, so that if the seam of coal is three or four feet high, each man has to cut out, break up, and load on to the belt something between seven and twelve cubic yards of coal. This is to say, taking a cubic yard as weighing twenty-seven hundredweight, that each man is shifting coal at a speed approaching two tons an hour. I have just enough experience of pick and shovel work to be able to grasp what this means. When I am digging trenches in my garden, if I shift two tons of earth during the afternoon, I feel that I have earned my tea. But earth is tractable stuff compared with coal, and I don't have to work kneeling down, a thousand feet underground, in suffocating heat and swallowing coal dust with every breath I take; nor do I have to walk a mile bent double before I begin. The miner's job would be as much beyond my power as it would be to perform on the flying trapeze or to win the Grand National. I am not a manual labourer and please God I never shall be one, but there are some kinds of manual work that I could do if I had to. At a pinch I could be a tolerable road-sweeper or an inefficient gardener or even a tenth-rate farm hand. But by no conceivable amount of effort or training could I become a coal-miner; the work would kill me in a few weeks.

Watching coal-miners at work, you realize momentarily what different universes different people inhabit. Down there where coal is dug it is a sort of world apart which one can quite easily go through life without ever hearing about. Probably a majority of people would even prefer not to hear about it. Yet it is the absolutely necessary counterpart of our world above. Practically everything we do, from eating an ice to crossing the Atlantic, and from baking a loaf to writing a novel, involves the use of coal, directly or indirectly. For all the arts of peace coal is needed; if war breaks out it is needed all the more. In time of revolution the miner must go on working or the revolution must stop, for revolution as much as reaction needs coal. Whatever may be happening on the surface, the hacking and shovelling have got to continue without a pause, or at any rate without pausing for more than a few weeks at the most. In order that Hitler may march the goosestep, that the Pope may denounce Bolshevism, that the cricket crowds may assemble at Lord's, that the Nancy poets may scratch one another's backs, coal has got to be forthcoming. But on the whole we are not aware of it; we all know that we 'must have coal', but we seldom or never remember what coal getting involves. Here am I, sitting writing in front of my comfortable coal fire. It is April but I still need a fire. Once a fortnight the coal cart drives up to the door and men in leather jerkins carry the coal indoors in stout sacks smelling of tar and shoot it clanking into the coal-hole under the stairs. It is only very rarely, when I make a definite mental effort, that I connect this coal with that far-off labour in the mines. It is just 'coal' – something that I have got to have; black stuff that arrives mysteriously from nowhere in particular, like manna except that you have to pay for it. You could quite easily drive a car right across the north of England and never once remember that hundreds of feet below the road you are on the miners are hacking at the coal. Yet in a sense it is the miners who are driving your car forward. Their lamp-lit world down there is as necessary to the daylight world above as the root is to the flower.

It is not long since conditions in the mines were worse than they are now. There are still living a few very old women who in their youth have worked underground, with a harness round their waists and a chain that passed between their legs, crawling on all fours and dragging tubs of coal. They used to go on doing this even when they were pregnant. And even now, if coal could not be produced without pregnant women dragging it to and fro, I fancy we should let them do it rather than deprive ourselves of coal. But most of the time, of course, we should prefer to forget that they were doing it. It is so with all types of manual work; it keeps us alive, and we are oblivious of its existence. More than anyone else, perhaps, the miner can stand as the type of the manual worker, not only because his work is so exaggeratedly awful, but also because it is so vitally necessary and yet so remote from our experience, so invisible, as it were, that we are capable of forgetting it as we forget the blood in our veins. In a way it is even humiliating to watch coal-miners working. It raises in you a momentary doubt about your own status as an 'intellectual' and a superior

person generally. For it is brought home to you, at least while you are
watching, that it is only because miners sweat their guts out that superior
persons can remain superior. You and I and the editor of the *Times Lit.
Supp.*, and the Nancy poets and the Archbishop of Canterbury and
Comrade X, author of *Marxism for Infants* – all of us *really* owe the
comparative decency of our lives to poor drudges underground, blackened
to the eyes, with their throats full of coal dust, driving their shovels forward
with arms and belly muscles of steel.

3

WHEN the miner comes up from the pit his face is so pale that it is
noticeable even through the mask of coal dust. This is due to the foul air
that he has been breathing, and will wear off presently. To a Southerner,
new to the mining districts, the spectacle of a shift of several hundred
miners streaming out of the pit is strange and slightly sinister. Their
exhausted faces, with the grime clinging in all the hollows, have a fierce,
wild look. At other times, when their faces are clean, there is not much
to distinguish them from the rest of the population. They have a very
upright square-shouldered walk, a reaction from the constant bending
underground, but most of them are shortish men and their thick ill-fitting
clothes hide the splendour of their bodies. The most definitely distinctive
thing about them is the blue scars on their noses. Every miner has blue
scars on his nose and forehead, and will carry them to his death. The coal
dust of which the air underground is full enters every cut, and then the
skin grows over it and forms a blue stain like tattooing, which in fact it
is. Some of the older men have their foreheads veined like Roquefort
cheeses from this cause.

As soon as the miner comes above ground he gargles a little water to
get the worst of the coal dust out of his throat and nostrils, and then goes
home and either washes or does not wash according to his temperament.
From what I have seen I should say that a majority of miners prefer to
eat their meal first and wash afterwards, as I should do in their circumstances. It is the normal thing to see a miner sitting down to his tea with
a Christy-minstrel face, completely black except for very red lips which
become clean by eating. After his meal he takes a largish basin of water

and washes very methodically, first his hands, then his chest, neck, and armpits, then his forearms, then his face and scalp (it is on the scalp that the grime clings thickest), and then his wife takes the flannel and washes his back. He has only washed the top half of his body and probably his navel is still a nest of coal dust, but even so it takes some skill to get passably clean in a single basin of water. For my own part I found I needed two complete baths after going down a coal-mine. Getting the dirt out of one's eyelids is a ten minutes' job in itself.

At some of the larger and better appointed collieries there are pithead baths. This is an enormous advantage, for not only can the miner wash himself all over every day, in comfort and even luxury, but at the baths he has two lockers where he can keep his pit clothes separate from his day clothes, so that within twenty minutes of emerging as black as a Negro he can be riding off to a football match dressed up to the nines. But it is only comparatively seldom because a seam of coal does not last for ever, so that it is not necessarily worth building a bath every time a shaft is sunk. I cannot get hold of exact figures, but it seems likely that rather less than one miner in three has access to a pithead bath. Probably a large majority of miners are completely black from the waist down for at least six days a week. It is almost impossible for them to wash all over in their own homes. Every drop of water has got to be heated up, and in a tiny living-room which contains, apart from the kitchen range and a quantity of furniture, a wife, some children, and probably a dog, there is simply not room to have a proper bath. Even with a basin one is bound to splash the furniture. Middle-class people are fond of saying that the miners would not wash themselves properly even if they could, but this is nonsense, as is shown by the fact that where pithead baths exist practically all the men use them. Only among the very old men does the belief still linger that washing one's legs 'causes lumbago'. Moreover the pithead baths, where they exist, are paid for wholly or partly by the miners themselves, out of the Miners' Welfare Fund. Sometimes the colliery company subscribes, sometimes the Fund bears the whole cost. But doubtless even at this late date the old ladies in Brighton boarding-houses are saying that 'if you give those miners baths they only use them to keep coal in'.

As a matter of fact it is surprising that miners wash as regularly as they do, seeing how little time they have between work and sleep. It is a great mistake to think of a miner's working day as being only seven and a half hours. Seven and a half hours is the time spent actually on the job, but, as I have already explained, one has got to add on to this time taken up in 'travelling', which is seldom less than an hour and may often be three hours. In addition most miners have to spend a considerable time in getting to and from the pit. Throughout the industrial districts there is an acute shortage of houses, and it is only in the small mining villages, where the village is grouped round the pit, that the men can be certain of living near their work. In the larger mining towns where I have stayed, nearly everyone went to work by bus; half a crown a week seemed to be the normal amount to spend on fares. One miner I stayed with was working on the morning shift, which was from six in the morning till half past one. He had to be out of bed at a quarter to four and got back somewhere after three in the afternoon. In another house where I stayed a boy of fifteen was working on the night shift. He left for work at nine at night and got back at eight in the morning, had his breakfast, and then promptly went to bed and slept till six in the evening; so that his leisure time amounted to about four hours a day – actually a good deal less, if you take off the time for washing, eating, and dressing.

The adjustments a miner's family have to make when he is changed from one shift to another must be tiresome in the extreme. If he is on the night shift he gets home in time for breakfast, on the morning shift he gets home in the middle of the afternoon, and on the afternoon shift he gets home in the middle of the night; and in each case, of course, he wants his principal meal of the day as soon as he returns. I notice that the Rev. W. R. Inge, in his book *England*, accuses the miners of gluttony. From my own observation I should say that they eat astonishingly little. Most of the miners I stayed with ate slightly less than I did. Many of them declare that they cannot do their day's work if they have had a heavy meal beforehand, and the food they take with them is only a snack, usually bread-and-dripping and cold tea. They carry it in a flat tin called a snap-can which they strap to their belts. When a miner gets back late at night his wife waits up for him, but when he is on the morning shift it seems to be the custom for him to get his breakfast for himself. Apparently the old superstition that it is bad luck to see a woman before going to work on the morning shift is not quite extinct. In the old days, it is said, a miner who happened to meet a woman in the early morning would often turn back and do no work that day.

Before I had been in the coal areas I shared the widespread illusion that miners are comparatively well paid. One hears it loosely stated that a miner is paid ten or eleven shillings a shift, and one does a small multiplication sum and concludes that every miner is earning round about £2 a week or £150 a year. But the statement that a miner receives ten or eleven shillings a shift is very misleading. To begin with, it is only the actual coal 'getter' who is paid at this rate; a 'dataller', for instance, who attends to the roofing, is paid at a lower rate, usually eight or nine shillings a shift. Again, when the coal 'getter' is paid piecework, so much per ton extracted, as is the case in many mines, he is dependent on the quality of the coal; a breakdown in the machinery or a 'fault' – that is, a streak of rock running through the coal seam – may rob him of his earnings for a day or two at a time. But in any case one ought not to think of the miner as working six days a week, fifty-two weeks a year. Almost certainly there will be a number of days when he is 'laid off'. The average earning per shift worked for every mine-worker, of all ages and both sexes, in Great Britain in 1934 was 9s. 1¾d.* If everyone were in work all the time, this would mean that the mine-worker was earning a little over £142 a year, or nearly £2 15s. a week. His real income, however, is far lower than this, for the 9s. 1¾d. is merely an average calculation on shifts actually worked and takes no account of blank days.

I have before me five pay-checks belonging to a Yorkshire miner, for five weeks (not consecutive) at the beginning of 1936. Averaging them up, the gross weekly wages they represent is £2 15s. 2d.; this is an average of nearly 9s. 2½d. a shift. But these pay-checks are for the winter, when nearly all mines are running full time. As spring advances the coal trade slacks off and more and more men are 'temporarily stopped', while others still technically in work are laid off for a day or two in every week. It is obvious therefore that £150 or even £142 is an immense over-estimate for the mine-worker's yearly income. As a matter of fact, for the year 1934 the average gross earnings of all miners throughout Great Britain was only £115 11s. 6d. It varied considerably from district to district, rising as high as £133 2s. 8d. in Scotland, while in Durham it was a little under £105 or barely more than £2 a week. I take these figures from *The Coal Scuttle*, by Mr Joseph Jones, Mayor of Barnsley, Yorkshire. Mr Jones adds:

These figures cover the earnings of youths as well as adults and of the higher-as well as the lower-paid grades . . . any particularly high earning would be included in these figures, as would theearnings of certain officials and other higher-paid men as well as the higher amounts paid for overtime work.

The figures, being averages, fail . . . to reveal the position of thousands of adult workers whose earnings were substantially below the average and who received only 30s. to 40s. or less per week.

Mr Jones's italics. But please notice that even these wretched earnings

* From the *Colliery Year Book and Coal Trades Directory* for 1935.

are *gross* earnings. On top of this there are all kinds of stoppages which are deducted from the miner's wages every week. Here is a list of weekly stoppages which was given me as typical in one Lancashire district:

	s.	d.
Insurance (unemployment and health)	1	5
Hire of lamp		6
For sharpening tools		6
Check-weighman		9
Infirmary		2
Hospital		1
Benevolent Fund		6
Union fees		6
Total	4	5

Some of these stoppages, such as the Benevolent Fund and the union fees, are, so to speak, the miner's own responsibility, others are imposed by the colliery company. They are not the same in all districts. For instance, the iniquitous swindle of making the miner pay for the hire of his lamp (at sixpence a week he buys the lamp several times over in a single year) does not obtain everywhere. But the stoppages always seem to total up to about the same amount. On the Yorkshire miner's five pay-checks, the average gross earning per week is £2 15s. 2d.; the average net earning, after the stoppages have come off, is only £2 11s. 4d. – a reduction of 3s. 10d. a week. But the pay-check, naturally, only mentions stoppages which are imposed or paid through the colliery company; one has got to add the union fees, bringing the total reduction up to something over four shillings. Probably it is safe to say that stoppages of one kind and another cut four shillings or thereabouts from *every* adult miner's weekly wage. So that the £115 11s. 6d. which was the mine-worker's average earning throughout Great Britain in 1934 should really be something nearer £105. As against this, most miners receive allowances in kind, being able to purchase coal for their own use at a reduced rate, usually eight or nine shillings a ton. But according to Mr Jones, quoted above, 'the average value of all allowances in kind for the country as a whole is only fourpence a day'. And this fourpence a day is offset, in many cases, by the amount the miner has to spend on fares in getting to and from the pit. So, taking the industry as a whole, the sum the miner can actually bring home and call his own does not average more, perhaps slightly less, than two pounds a week.

Meanwhile, how much coal is the average miner producing?

The tonnage of coal raised yearly per person employed in mining rises steadily though rather slowly. In 1914 every mine-worker produced, on average, 253 tons of coal; in 1934 he produced 280 tons.*This of course is an average figure for mine-workers of all kinds; those actually working at the coal face extract an enormously greater amount – in many cases, probably, well over a thousand tons each. But taking 280 tons as a representative figure, it is worth noticing what a vast achievement this is. One gets the best idea of it by comparing a miner's life with somebody else's. If I live to be sixty I shall probably have produced thirty novels, or enough to fill two medium-sized library shelves. In the same period the average miner produces 8400 tons of coal; enough coal to pave Trafalgar Square nearly two feet deep or to supply seven large families with fuel for over a hundred years.

Of the five pay-checks I mentioned above, no less than three are rubber-stamped with the words 'death stoppage'. When a miner is killed at work it is usual for the other miners to make up a subscription, generally of a shilling each, for his widow, and this is collected by the colliery company and automatically deducted from their wages. The significant detail here is the *rubber stamp*. The rate of accidents among miners is so high, compared with that in other trades, that casualties are taken for granted almost as they would be in a minor war. Every year one miner in about nine hundred is killed and one in about six is injured; most of these injuries, of course, are petty ones, but a fair number amount to total disablement. This means that if a miner's working life is forty years the chances are nearly seven to one against his escaping injury and not much more than twenty to one against his being killed outright. No other trade approaches this in dangerousness; the next most dangerous is the shipping trade, one sailor in a little under 1300 being killed every year. The figures I have given apply, of course, to mine-workers as a whole; for those actually working underground the proportion of injuries would be very much higher. Every miner of long standing that I have talked to had either been in a fairly serious accident himself or had seen some of his mates killed, and in every mining family they tell you tales of fathers, brothers, or uncles killed at work. ('And he fell seven hundred feet, and they wouldn't never have collected t'pieces only he were wearing a new suit of oil-skins,' etc., etc., etc.) Some of these tales are appalling in the extreme. One

---

* *The Coal Scuttle.* The *Colliery Year Book and Coal Trades Directory* gives a slightly higher figure.

miner, for instance, described to me how a mate of his, a 'dataller', was buried by a fall of rock. They rushed to him and managed to uncover his head and shoulders so that he could breathe, and he was alive and spoke to them. Then they saw that the roof was coming down again and had to run to save themselves; the 'dataller' was buried a second time. Once again they rushed to him and got his head and shoulders free, and again he was alive and spoke to them. Then the roof came down a third time, and this time they could not uncover him for several hours, after which, of course, he was dead. But the miner who told me the story (he had been buried himself on one occasion, but he was lucky enough to have his head jammed between his legs so that there was a small space in which he could breathe) did not think it was a particularly appalling one. Its significance, for him, was that the 'dataller' had known perfectly well that the place where he was working was unsafe, and had gone there in daily expectation of an accident. 'And it worked on his mind to that extent that he got to kissing his wife before he went to work. And she told me afterwards that it were over twenty years since he'd kissed her.'

The most obviously understandable cause of accidents is explosions of gas, which is always more or less present in the atmosphere of the pit. There is a special lamp which is used to test the air for gas, and when it is present in at all large quantities it can be detected by the flame of an ordinary Davy lamp burning blue. If the wick can be turned up to its full extent and the flame is still blue, the proportion of gas is dangerously high; it is, nevertheless, difficult to detect, because it does not distribute itself evenly throughout the atmosphere but hangs about in cracks and crevices. Before starting work a miner often tests for gas by poking his lamp into all the corners. The gas may be touched off by a spark during blasting operations, or by a pick striking a spark from a stone, or by a defective lamp, or by 'gob fires' – spontaneously generated fires which smoulder in the coal dust and are very hard to put out. The great mining disasters which happen from time to time, in which several hundred men are killed, are usually caused by explosions; hence one tends to think of explosions as the chief danger of mining. Actually, the great majority of accidents are due to the normal every-day dangers of the pit; in particular, to falls of roof. There are, for instance, 'pot-holes' – circular holes from which a lump of stone big enough to kill a man shoots out with the promptitude of a bullet. With, so far as I can remember, only one exception, all the miners I have talked to declared that the new machinery, and 'speeding up' generally, have made the work more dangerous. This may be partly due to conservatism, but they can give plenty of reasons. To begin with, the speed at which the coal is now extracted means that for hours at a time a dangerously large stretch of roof remains unpropped. Then there is the vibration, which tends to shake everything loose, and the noise, which makes it harder to detect signs of danger. One must remember that a miner's safety underground depend largely on his own care and skill. An experienced miner claims to know by a sort of instinct when the roof is unsafe; the way he puts it is that he 'can feel the weight on him'. He can, for instance, hear the faint creaking of the props. The reason why wooden props are still generally preferred to iron girders is that a wooden prop which is about to collapse gives warning by creaking, whereas a girder flies out unexpectedly. The devastating noise of the machines makes it impossible to hear anything else, and thus the danger is increased.

When a miner is hurt it is of course impossible to attend to him immediately. He lies crushed under several hundredweight of stone in some dreadful cranny underground, and even after he has been extricated it is necessary to drag his body a mile or more, perhaps, through galleries where nobody can stand upright. Usually when you talk to a man who has been injured you find that it was a couple of hours or so before they got him to the surface. Sometimes, of course, there are accidents to the cage. The cage is shooting several yards up or down at the speed of an express train, and it is operated by somebody on the surface who cannot see what is happening. He has very delicate indicators to tell him how far the cage has got, but it is possible for him to make a mistake, and there have been cases of the cage crashing into the pit-bottom at its very maximum speed. This seems to me a dreadful way to die. For as that tiny steel box whizzes through the blackness there must come a moment when the ten men who are locked inside it *know* that something has gone wrong; and the remaining seconds before they are smashed to pieces hardly bear thinking about. A miner told me he was once in a cage in which something went wrong. It did not slow up when it should have done, and they thought the cable must have snapped. As it happened they got to the bottom safely, but when he stepped out he found that he had broken a tooth; he had been clenching his teeth so hard in expectation of that frightful crash.

Apart from accidents miners seem to be healthy, as obviously they have got to be, considering the muscular efforts demanded of them. They are liable to rheumatism and a man with defective lungs does not last long in that dust-impregnated air, but the most characteristic industrial disease is nystagmus. This is a disease of the eyes which makes the eyeballs oscillate in a strange manner when they come near a light. It is due presumably to working in half-darkness, and sometimes results in total blindness. Miners who are disabled in this way or any other way are compensated by the colliery company, sometimes with a lump sum, sometimes with a weekly pension. This pension never amounts to more than twenty-nine shillings a week; if it falls below fifteen shillings the disabled man can also get something from the dole or the P.A.C. If I were a disabled miner I should very much prefer the lump sum, for then at any rate I should know that I had got my money. Disability pensions are not guaranteed by any centralized fund, so that if the colliery company goes bankrupt that is the end of the disabled miner's pension, though he does figure among the other creditors.

In Wigan I stayed for a while with a miner who was suffering from nystagmus. He could see across the room but not much further. He had been drawing compensation of twenty-nine shillings a week for the past nine months, but the colliery company were now talking of putting him on 'partial compensation' of fourteen shillings a week. It all depended on whether the doctor passed him as fit for light work 'on top'. Even if the doctor did pass him there would, needless to say, be no light work available, but he could draw the dole and the company would have saved itself fifteen shillings a week. Watching this man go to the colliery to draw his compensation, I was struck by the profound differences that are still made by *status*. Here was a man who had been half blinded in one of the most useful of all jobs and was drawing a pension to which he had a perfect right, if anybody has a right to anything. Yet he could not, so to speak, *demand* this pension – he could not, for instance, draw it when and how he wanted it. He had to go to the colliery once a week at a time named by the company, and when he got there he was kept waiting about for hours in the cold wind. For all I know he was also expected to touch his cap and show gratitude to whoever paid him; at any rate he had to waste an afternoon and spend sixpence in bus fares. It is very different for a member of the bourgeoisie, even such a down-at-heel member as I am. Even when I am on the verge of starvation I have certain rights attaching to my bourgeois status. I do not earn much more than a miner earns, but I do at least get it paid into my bank in a gentlemanly manner and can draw it out when I choose. And even when my account is exhausted the bank people are passably polite.

This business of petty inconvenience and indignity, of being kept waiting about, of having to do everything at other people's convenience, is inherent in working-class life. A thousand influences constantly press a working man down into a *passive* role. He does not act, he is acted upon. He feels himself the slave of mysterious authority and has a firm conviction that 'they' will never allow him to do this, that, and the other. Once when I was hop-picking I asked the sweated pickers (they earn something under sixpence an hour) why they did not form a union. I was told immediately that 'they' would never allow it. Who were 'they'? I asked. Nobody seemed to know; but evidently 'they' were omnipotent.

A person of bourgeois origin goes through life with some expectation of getting what he wants, within reasonable limits. Hence the fact that in times of stress 'educated' people tend to come to the front; they are no more gifted than the others and their 'education' is generally quite useless in itself, but they are accustomed to a certain amount of deference and consequently have the cheek necessary to a commander. That they *will* come to the front seems to be taken for granted, always and everywhere. In Lissagaray's *History of the Commune* there is an interesting passage describing the shootings that took place after the Commune had been suppressed. The authorities were shooting the ringleaders, and as they did not know who the ringleaders were, they were picking them out on the principle that those of better class would be the ringleaders. An officer walked down a line of prisoners, picking out likely-looking types. One man was shot because he was wearing a watch, another because he 'had an intelligent face'. I should not like to be shot for having an intelligent face, but I do agree that in almost any revolt the leaders would tend to be people who could pronounce their aitches.

4

AS you walk through the industrial towns you lose yourself in labyrinths of little brick houses blackened by smoke, festering in planless chaos round miry alleys and little cindered yards where there are stinking dust-bins and lines of grimy washing and half-ruinous W.C.s. The interiors of these houses are always very much the same, though the number of rooms varies between two or five. All have an almost exactly similar living-room, ten or fifteen feet square, with an open kitchen range; in the larger ones there is a scullery as well, in the smaller ones the sink and copper are in the living-room. At the back there is the yard, or part of a yard shared by a number of houses, just big enough for the dustbin and the W.C. Not a single one has hot water laid on. You might walk, I suppose, through literally hundreds of miles of streets inhabited by miners, every one of whom, when he is in work, gets black from head to foot every day, without ever passing a house in which one could have a bath. It would have been very simple to install a hot-water system working from the kitchen range, but the builder saved perhaps ten pounds on each house by not doing so, and at the time when these houses were built no one imagined that miners wanted baths.

For it is to be noted that the majority of these houses are old, fifty or sixty years old at least, and great numbers of them are by any ordinary standard not fit for human habitation. They go on being tenanted simply because there are no others to be had. And that is the central fact about housing in the industrial areas: not that the houses are poky and ugly, and insanitary and comfortless, or that they are distributed in incredibly filthy slums round belching foundries and stinking canals and slag-heaps that deluge them with sulphurous smoke – though all this is perfectly true – but simply that there are not enough houses to go round.

'Housing shortage' is a phrase that has been bandied about pretty freely since the war, but it means very little to anyone with an income of more than £10 a week, or even £5 a week for that matter. Where rents are high the difficulty is not to find houses but to find tenants. Walk down any street in Mayfair and you will see 'To Let' boards in half the windows. But in the industrial areas the mere difficulty of getting hold of a house is one of the worst aggravations of poverty. It means that people will put up with anything – any hole and corner slum, any misery of bugs and rotting floors and cracking walls, any extortion of skinflint landlords and blackmailing agents – simply to get a roof over their heads. I have been into appalling houses, houses in which I would not live a week if you paid me, and found that the tenants had been there twenty and thirty years and only hoped they might have the luck to die there. In general these conditions are taken as a matter of course, though not always. Some people hardly seem to realize that such things as decent houses exist and look on bugs and leaking roofs as acts of God; others rail bitterly against their landlords; but all cling desperately to their houses lest worse should befall. So long as the housing shortage continues the local authorities cannot do much to make existing houses more livable. They can 'condemn' a house, but they cannot order it to be pulled down till the tenant has another house to go to; and so the condemned houses remain standing and are all the worse for being condemned, because naturally the landlord will not spend more than he can help on a house which is going to be demolished sooner or later. In a town like Wigan, for instance, there are over two thousand houses standing which have been condemned for years, and whole sections of the town would be condemned *en bloc* if there were any hope of other houses being built to replace them. Towns like Leeds and Sheffield have scores of thousands of 'back to back' houses which are all of a condemned type but will remain standing for decades.

I have inspected great numbers of houses in various mining towns and villages and made notes on their essential points. I think I can best give an idea of what conditions are like by transcribing a few extracts from my notebook, taken more or less at random. They are only brief notes and they will need certain explanations which I will give afterwards. Here are a few from Wigan:

1. House in Wallgate quarter. Blind back type. One up, one down. Living-room measures 12 ft by 10 ft, room upstairs the same. Alcove under stairs measuring 5 ft by 5 ft and serving as larder, scullery, and coal-hole. Windows will open. Distance to lavatory 50 yards. Rent 4s. 9d., rates 2s. 6d., total 7s. 3d.

2. Another near by. Measurements as above, but no alcove under stairs, merely a recess two feet deep containing the sink – no room for larder, etc. Rent 3s. 2d., rates 2s., total 5s. 2d.

3. House in Scholes quarter. Condemned house. One up, one down. Rooms 15 ft by 15 ft. Sink and copper in living-room, coal-hole under stairs. Floor subsiding. No windows will open. House decently dry. Landlord good. Rent 3s. 8d., rates 2s. 6d., total 6s. 2d.

4. Another near by. Two up, two down, and coal-hole. Walls falling absolutely to pieces. Water comes into upstairs rooms in quantities. Floor lopsided. Downstairs windows will not open. Landlord bad. Rent 6s., rates 3s. 6d., total 9s. 6d.

5. House in Greenough's Row. One up, two down. Living-room 13 ft by 8 ft. Walls coming apart and water comes in. Back windows will not open, front ones will. Ten in family with eight children very near together in age. Corporations are trying to evict them for overcrowding but cannot find another house to send them to. Landlord bad. Rent 4s., rates 2s. 3d., total 6d. 3d.

So much for Wigan. I have pages more of the same type. Here is one from Sheffield – a typical specimen of Sheffield's several score thousand 'back to back' houses:

House in Thomas Street. Back to back, two up, one down (i.e. a three-storey house with one room on each storey). Cellar below. Living-room 14 ft by 10 ft, and rooms above corresponding. Sink in living-room. Top floor has no door but gives on open stairs. Walls in living-room slightly damp, walls in top rooms coming to pieces and oozing damp on all sides. House is so dark that light has to be kept burning all day. Electricity estimated at 6d. a day (probably an exaggeration). Six in family, parents and four children. Husband (on P.A.C.) is tuberculous. One child in hospital, the others appear healthy. Tenants have been seven years in this house. Would move, but no other house available. Rent 6s. 6d., rates included.

Here are one or two from Barnsley:

1. House in Wortley Street. Two up, one down. Living-room 12 ft by 10 ft. Sink and copper in living-room, coal-hole under stairs. Sink worn almost flat and constantly overflowing. Walls not too sound. Penny in slot gas-light. House very dark and gaslight estimated 4d. a day. Upstairs rooms are really one large room partitioned into two. Walls very bad – wall of back room cracked right through. Window-frames coming to pieces and have to be stuffed with wood. Rain comes through in several places. Sewer runs under house and stinks in summer but Corporation 'says they can't do nowt'. Six people in house, two adults and four children, the eldest aged fifteen. Youngest but one attending hospital – tuberculosis suspected. House infested by bugs. Rent 5s. 3d., including rates.

2. House in Peel Street. Back to back, two up, two down and large cellar. Living-room 10 ft square with copper and sink. The other downstairs room the same size, probably intended as parlour but used as bedroom. Upstairs rooms the same size as those below. Living-room very dark. Gas-light estimated at 4½d. a day. Distance to lavatory 70 yards. Four beds in house for eight people – two old parents, two adult girls (the eldest aged twenty-seven), one young man, and three children. Parents have one bed, eldest son another, and remaining five people share the other two. Bugs very bad – 'You can't keep 'em down when it's 'ot.' Indescribable squalor in downstairs room and smell upstairs almost unbearable. Rent 5s. 7½d., including rates.

3. House in Mapplewell (small mining village near Barnsley). Two up, one down. Living-room 14ft by 12 ft. Sink in living-room. Plaster cracking and coming off walls. No shelves in oven. Gas leaking slightly. The upstairs rooms each 10 ft by 8 ft. Four beds (for six persons, all adult), but 'one bed does nowt', presumably for lack of bedclothes. Room nearest stairs has no door and stairs have no banister, so that when you step out of bed your foot hangs in vacancy and you may fall ten feet on to stones. Dry rot so bad that one can see through the floor into the room below. Bugs, but 'I keeps 'em down with sheep dip'. Earth road past these cottages is like a muck-heap and said to be almost impassable in winter. Stone lavatories at ends of gardens in semi-ruinous condition. Tenants have been twenty-two years in this house. Are £11 in arrears with rent, and have been paying an extra 1s. a week to pay this off. Landlord now refuses this and has served orders to quit. Rent 5s., including rates.

And so on and so on and so on. I could multiply examples by the score – they could be multiplied by the hundred thousand if anyone chose to make a house-to-house inspection throughout the industrial districts. Meanwhile some of the expressions I have used need explaining. 'One up, one down' means one room on each storey – i.e. a two-roomed house. 'Back to back' houses are two houses built in one, each side of the house being somebody's front door, so that if you walk down a row of what is apparently twelve houses you are in reality seeing not twelve houses but twenty-four. The front houses give on the street and the back ones on the yard, and there is only one way out of each house. The effect of this is obvious. The lavatories are in the yard at the back, so that if you live on the side facing the street, to get to the lavatory or the dust-bin you have to go out of the front door and walk round the end of the block – a distance that may be as much as two hundred yards; if you live at the back, on the other hand, your outlook is on to a row of lavatories. There are also houses of what is called the 'blind back' type, which are single houses, but in which the builder has omitted to put in a back door – from pure spite, apparently. The windows which refuse to open are a peculiarity of old mining towns. Some of these towns are so undermined by ancient workings that the ground is constantly subsiding and the houses above slip sideways. In Wigan you pass whole rows of houses which have slid to startling angles, their windows being ten or twenty degrees out of the horizontal. Sometimes the front wall bellies outward till it looks as though the house were seven months gone in pregnancy. It can be refaced, but the new facing soon begins to bulge again. When a house sinks at all suddenly its windows are jammed for ever and the door has to be refitted. This excites no surprise locally. The story of the miner who comes home from work and finds that he can only get indoors by smashing down the front door with an axe is considered humorous. In some cases I have noted 'Landlord good' or 'Landlord bad', because there is great variation in what the slum-dwellers say about their landlords. I found – one might expect it, perhaps – that the small landlords are usually the worst. It goes against the grain to say this, but one can see why it should be so. Ideally, the worst type of slum landlord is a fat wicked man, preferably a bishop, who is drawing an immense income from extortionate rents. Actually, it is a poor old woman who has invested her life's savings in three slum houses, inhabits one of them, and tries to live on the rent of the other two – never, in consequence, having any money for repairs.

But mere notes like these are only valuable as reminders to myself. To me as I read them they bring back what I have seen, but they cannot in themselves give much idea of what conditions are like in those fearful northern slums. Words are such feeble things. What is the use of a brief phrase like 'roof leaks' or 'four beds for eight people'? It is the kind of thing your eye slides over, registering nothing. And yet what a wealth of misery it can cover! Take the question of overcrowding, for instance. Quite often you have eight or even ten people living in a three-roomed house. One of these rooms is a living-room, and as it probably measures about a dozen feet square and contains, besides the kitchen range and the sink, a table, some chairs, and a dresser, there is no room in it for a bed. So there are eight or ten people sleeping in two small rooms, probably in at most four beds. If some of these people are adults and have to go to work, so much the worse. In one house, I remember, three grown-up girls shared the same bed and all went to work at different hours, each disturbing the others when she got up or came in; in another house a young miner working on the night shift slept by day in a narrow bed in which another member of the family slept by night. There is an added difficulty when there are grown-up children, in that you cannot let adolescent youths and girls sleep in the same bed. In one family I visited there were a father and mother and a son and daughter aged round about seventeen, and only two beds for the lot of them. The father slept with the son and the mother with the daughter; it was the only arrangement that ruled out the danger of incest. Then there is the misery of leaking roofs and oozing walls, which in winter makes some rooms almost uninhabitable. Then there are bugs. Once bugs get into a house they are in it till the crack of doom; there is no sure way of exterminating them. Then there are the windows that will not open. I need not point out what this must mean, in summer, in a tiny stuffy living-room where the fire, on which all the cooking is done, has to be kept burning more or less constantly. And there are the special miseries attendant upon back to back houses. A fifty yards' walk to the lavatory or the dust-bin is not exactly an inducement to be clean. In the front houses – at any rate in a side-street where the Corporation don't interfere – the women get into the habit of throwing their refuse out of the front door, so that the gutter is always littered with tea-leaves and bread crusts. And it is worth considering what it is like for a child to grow up in one of the back alleys where its gaze is bounded by a row of lavatories and a wall.

In such places as these a woman is only a poor drudge muddling among an infinity of jobs. She may keep up her spirits, but she cannot keep up her standards of cleanliness and tidiness. There is always something to be done, and no conveniences and almost literally not room to turn round. No sooner have you washed one child's face than another's is dirty; before you have washed the crocks from one meal the next is due to be cooked. I found great variation in the houses I visited. Some were as decent as one could possibly expect in the circumstances, some were so appalling that I have no hope of describing them adequately. To begin with, the smell, the dominant and essential thing, is indescribable. But the squalor and the confusion! A tub full of filthy water here, a basin full of unwashed crocks there, more crocks piled in any odd corner, torn newspaper littered everywhere, and in the middle always the same dreadful table covered with sticky oilcloth and crowded with cooking pots and irons and half-darned stockings and pieces of stale bread and bits of cheese wrapped round with greasy newspaper! And the congestion in a tiny room where getting from one side to the other is a complicated voyage between pieces of furniture, with a line of damp washing getting you in the face every time you move and the children as thick underfoot as toadstools! There are scenes that stand out vividly in my memory. The almost bare living-room of a cottage in a little mining village, where the whole family was out of work and everyone seemed to be underfed; and the big family of grown-up sons and daughters sprawling aimlessly about, all strangely alike with red hair, splendid bones, and pinched faces ruined by malnutrition and idleness; and one tall son sitting by the fireplace, too listless even to notice the entry of a stranger, and slowly peeling a sticky sock from a bare foot. A dreadful room in Wigan where all the furniture seemed to be made of packing cases and barrel staves and was coming to pieces at that; and an old woman with a blackened neck and her hair coming down denouncing her landlord in a Lancashire-Irish accent; and her mother, aged well over ninety, sitting in the background on the barrel that served her as a commode and regarding us blankly with a yellow, cretinous face. I could fill up pages with memories of similar interiors.

Of course the squalor of these people's houses is sometimes their own fault. Even if you live in a back to back house and have four children and a total income of thirty-two and sixpence a week from the P.A.C., there is no *need* to have unemptied chamber-pots standing about in your living-room. But it is equally certain that their circumstances do not encourage self-respect. The determining factor is probably the number of children. The best-kept interiors I saw were always childless houses or houses where there were only one or two children; with, say, six children in a three-roomed house it is quite impossible to keep anything decent. One thing that is very noticeable is that the worst squalors are never downstairs. You might visit quite a number of houses, even among the poorest of the unemployed, and bring away a wrong impression. These people, you might reflect, cannot be so badly off if they still have a fair amount of furniture and crockery. But it is in the rooms upstairs that the gauntness of poverty really discloses itself. Whether this is because pride makes people cling to their living-room furniture to the last, or because bedding is more pawnable, I do not know, but certainly many of the bedrooms I saw were fearful places. Among people who have been unemployed for several years continuously I should say it is the exception to have anything like a full set of bedclothes. Often there is nothing that can be properly called bedclothes at all – just a heap of old overcoats and miscellaneous rags on a rusty iron bedstead. In this way overcrowding is aggravated. One family of four persons that I knew, a father and mother and two children, possessed two beds but could only use one of them because they had not enough bedding for the other.

Anyone who wants to see the effects of the housing shortage at their very worse should visit the dreadful caravan-dwellings that exist in numbers in many of the northern towns. Ever since the war, in the complete impossibility of getting houses, parts of the population have overflowed into supposedly temporary quarters in fixed caravans. Wigan, for instance, with a population of about 85,000, has round about 200 caravan-dwellings with a family in each – perhaps somewhere near 1000 people in all. How many of these caravan-colonies exist throughout the industrial areas it would be difficult to discover with any accuracy. The local authorities are reticent about them and the census report of 1931 seems to have decided to ignore them. But so far as I can discover by inquiry they are to be found in most of the larger towns in Lancashire and Yorkshire, and perhaps further north as well. The probability is that throughout the north of England there are some thousands, perhaps tens of thousands of *families* (not individuals) who have no home except a fixed caravan.

But the word 'caravan' is very misleading. It calls up a picture of a cosy gypsy-encampment (in fine weather, of course) with wood fires crackling and children picking blackberries and many-coloured washing fluttering on the lines. The caravan-colonies in Wigan and Sheffield are not like that. I had a look at several of them, I inspected those in Wigan with considerable care, and I have never seen comparable squalor except in the Far East. Indeed when I saw them I was immediately reminded of the filthy kennels in which I have seen Indian coolies living in Burma. But, as a matter of fact, nothing in the East could ever be quite as bad, for in the East you haven't our clammy, penetrating cold to contend with, and the sun is a disinfectant.

Along the banks of Wigan's miry canal are patches of waste ground on which the caravans have been dumped like rubbish shot out of a bucket. Some of them are actually gypsy caravans, but very old ones and in bad repair. The majority are old single-decker buses (the rather smaller buses of ten years ago) which have been taken off their wheels and propped up with struts of wood. Some are simply wagons with semi-circular slats on top, over which canvas is stretched, so that the people inside have nothing but canvas between them and the outer air. Inside, these places are usually about five feet wide by six high (I could not stand quite upright in any of them) and anything from six to fifteen feet long. Some, I suppose, are inhabited by only one person, but I did not see any that held less than two persons, and some of them contained large families. One, for instance, measuring fourteen feet long, had seven people in it – seven people in about 450 cubic feet of space; which is to say that each person had for his entire dwelling a space a *good deal* smaller than one compartment of a public lavatory. The dirt and congestion of these places is such that you cannot well imagine it unless you have tested it with your own eyes and more particularly your nose. Each contains a tiny cottage kitchener and such furniture as can be crammed in – sometimes two beds, more usually one, into which the whole family have to huddle as best they can. It is almost impossible to sleep on the floor, because the damp soaks up from below. I was shown mattresses which were still wringing wet at eleven in the morning. In winter it is so cold that the kitcheners have to be kept burning day and night, and the windows, needless to say, are never opened. Water is got from a hydrant common to the whole colony, some of the caravan-dwellers having to walk 150 or 200 yards for every bucket of water. There are no sanitary arrangements at all. Most of the people construct a little hut to serve as a lavatory on the tiny patch of ground surrounding their caravan, and once a week dig a deep hole in which to bury the refuse. All the people I saw in these places, especially the children, were unspeakably dirty, and I do not doubt that they were lousy as well. They could not possibly be otherwise. The thought that haunted me as I went from caravan to caravan was, What can happen in those cramped interiors when anybody dies? But that, of course, is the kind of question you hardly care to ask.

Some of the people have been in their caravans for many years. Theoretically the Corporation are doing away with the caravan-colonies and getting the inhabitants out into houses; but as the houses don't get built, the caravans remain standing. Most of the people I talked to had given up the idea of ever getting a decent habitation again. They were all out of work, and a job and a house seemed to them about equally remote and impossible. Some hardly seemed to care; others realized quite clearly in what misery they were living. One woman's face stays by me, a worn skull-like face on which was a look of intolerable misery and degradation.

I gathered that in that dreadful pigsty, struggling to keep her large brood of children clean, she felt as I should feel if I were coated all over with dung. One must remember that these people are not gypsies; they are decent English people who have all, except the children born there, had homes of their own in their day; besides, their caravans are greatly inferior to those of gypsies and they have not the great advantage of being on the move. No doubt there are still middle-class people who think that the Lower Orders don't mind that kind of thing and who, if they happened to pass a caravan-colony in the train, would immediately assume that the people lived there from choice. I never argue nowadays with that kind of person. But it is worth noticing that the caravan-dwellers don't even save money by living there, for they are paying about the same rents as they would for houses. I could not hear of any rent lower than five shillings a week (five shillings for 200 cubic feet of space!) and there are even cases where the rent is as high as ten shillings. Somebody must be making a good thing out of those caravans! But clearly their continued existence is due to the housing shortage and not directly to poverty.

Talking once with a miner I asked him when the housing shortage first became acute in his district; he answered, 'When we were told about it,' meaning that till recently people's standards were so low that they took almost any degree of overcrowding for granted. He added that when he was a child his family had slept eleven in a room and thought nothing of it, and that later, when he was grown-up, he and his wife had lived in one of the old-style back to back houses in which you not only had to walk a couple of hundred yards to the lavatory but often had to wait in a queue when you got there, the lavatory being shared by thirty-six people. And when his wife was sick with the illness that killed her, she still had to make that two hundred yards' journey to the lavatory. This, he said, was the kind of thing people would put up with 'till they were told about it'.

I do not know whether that is true. What is certain is that nobody *now* thinks it bearable to sleep eleven in a room, and that even people with comfortable incomes are vaguely troubled by the thought of 'the slums'. Hence the clatter about 'rehousing' and 'slum clearance' which we have had at intervals ever since the war. Bishops, politicians, philanthropists, and what not enjoy talking piously about 'slum clearance', because they can thus divert attention from more serious evils and pretend that if you abolish the slums you abolish poverty. But all this talk has led to surprisingly small results. So far as one can discover, the congestion is no better, perhaps slightly worse, than it was a dozen years ago. There is certainly great variation in the speed at which the different towns are attacking their housing problem. In some towns building seems to be almost at a standstill, in others it is proceeding rapidly and the private landlord is being driven out of business. Liverpool, for instance, has been very largely rebuilt, mainly by the efforts of the Corporation. Sheffield, too, is being torn down and rebuilt pretty fast, though perhaps, considering the unparalleled beastliness of its slums, not quite fast enough.*

Why rehousing has on the whole moved so slowly, and why some towns can borrow money for building purposes so much more easily than others, I do not know. Those questions would have to be answered by someone who knows more about the machinery of local government than I do. A Corporation house costs normally somewhere between three and four hundred pounds; it costs rather less when it is built by 'direct labour' than when built by contract. The rent of these houses would average something over twenty pounds a year not counting rates, so one would think that, even allowing for overhead expenses and interest on loans, it would pay any Corporation to build as many houses as could be tenanted. In many cases, of course, the houses would have to be inhabited by people on the P.A.C., so that the local bodies would merely be taking money out of one pocket and putting it into another – i.e. paying out money in the form of relief and taking it back in the form of rent. But they have got to pay the relief in any case, and at present a proportion of what they pay is being swallowed up by private landlords. The reasons given for the slow rate of building are lack of money and the difficulty of getting hold of sites – for Corporation houses are not erected piecemeal but in 'estates', sometimes of hundreds of houses at a time. One thing that always strikes me as mysterious is that so many of the northern towns see fit to build themselves immense and luxurious public buildings at the same time as they are in crying need of dwelling houses. The town of Barnsley, for instance, recently spent close on £150,000 on a new town hall, although admittedly needing at least 2000 new working-class houses, not to mention public baths. (The public baths in Barnsley contain *nineteen* men's slipper baths – this in a town of 70,000 inhabitants, largely miners, not one of whom has a bath in his house!) For £150,000 it could have built 350 Corporation houses and still had £10,000 to spend on a town hall. However, as I say, I do not pretend to understand the mysteries of local government. I merely record the fact that houses are desperately needed and are being built, on the whole, with paralytic slowness.

---

* The number of Corporation houses in process of construction in Sheffield at the beginning of 1936 was 1398. To replace the slum areas entirely Sheffield is said to need 100,000 houses.

Still, houses *are* being built, and the Corporation building estates, with
their row upon row of little red houses, all much liker than two peas
(where did that expression come from? Peas have great individuality) are
a regular feature of the outskirts of the industrial towns. As to what they
are like and how they compare with the slum houses, I can best give an
idea by transcribing two more extracts from my diary. The tenants'
opinions of their houses vary greatly, so I will give one favourable extract
and one unfavourable. Both of these are from Wigan and both are the
cheaper 'non-parlour type' houses:

1. House in Beech Hill Estate.
Downstairs. Large living-room with kitchener fireplace, cupboards, and fixed
dresser, composition floor. Small hallway, largish kitchen. Up to date electric
cooker hired from Corporation at much the same rate as a gas cooker.
Upstairs. Two largish bedrooms, one tiny one – suitable only for a boxroom or
temporary bedroom. Bathroom, W.C., with hot and cold water.
Smallish garden. These vary throughout the estate, but mostly rather smaller
than an allotment.
Four in family, parents and two children. Husband in good employ. Houses appear
well built and are quite agreeable to look at. Various restrictions, e.g. it is forbidden
to keep poultry or pigeons, take in lodgers, sub-let, or start any kind of business
without leave from the Corporation. (This is easily granted in the case of taking in
lodgers, but not in any of the others.) Tenant very well satisfied with house and proud
of it. Houses in this estate all well kept. Corporation are good about repairs, but keep
tenants up to the mark with regard to keeping the place tidy, etc.
Rent 11s. 3d. including rates. Bus fare into town 2d.

2. House in Welly Estate.
Downstairs. Living-room 14 ft by 10 ft, kitchen a good deal smaller, tiny larder
under stairs, small but fairly good bathroom. Gas cooker, electric lighting. Outdoor
W.C.
Upstairs. One bedroom 12 ft by 10 ft with tiny fireplace, another the same size
without fireplace, another 7 ft by 6 ft. Best bedroom has small wardrobe let into wall.
Garden about 20 yards by 10.
Six in family, parents and four children, eldest son nineteen, eldest daughter
twenty-two. None in work except eldest son. Tenants very discontented. Their
complaints are: 'House is cold, draughty, and damp. Fireplace in living-room gives
out no heat and makes room very dusty – attributed to its being set too low.
Fireplace in best bedroom too small to be of any use. Walls upstairs cracking.
Owing to uselessness of tiny bedroom, five are sleeping in one bedroom, one (the
eldest son) in the other.'
Gardens in this estate all neglected.
Rent 10s. 3d., inclusive. Distance to town a little over a mile – there is no bus
here.

I could multiply examples, but these two are enough, as the types of Corporation houses being built do not vary greatly from place to place. Two things are immediately obvious. The first is that at their very worst the Corporation houses are better than the slums they replace. The mere possession of a bathroom and a bit of garden would outweigh almost any disadvantage. The other is that they are much more expensive to live in. It is common enough for a man to be turned out of a condemned house where he is paying six or seven shillings a week and given a Corporation house where he has to pay ten. This only affects those who are in work or have recently been in work, because when a man is on the P.A.C. his rent is assessed at a quarter of his dole, and if it is more than this he gets an extra allowance; in any case, there are certain classes of Corporation houses to which people on the dole are not admitted. But there are other ways in which life in a Corporation estate is expensive, whether you are in work or out of it. To begin with, owing to the higher rents, the shops in the estate are much more expensive and there are not so many of them. Then again, in a comparatively large, detached house, away from the frowsy huddle of the slum, it is much colder and more fuel has to be burnt. And again there is the expense, especially for a man in work, of getting to and from town. This last is one of the more obvious problems of rehousing. Slum clearance means diffusion of the population. When you rebuild on a large scale, what you do in effect is to scoop out the centre of the town and redistribute it on the outskirts. This is all very well in a way; you have got the people out of fetid alleys into places where they have room to breathe; but from the point of view of the people themselves, what you have done is to pick them up and dump them down five miles from their work. The simplest solution is flats. If people are going to live in large towns at all they must learn to live on top of one another. But the northern working people do not take kindly to flats; even where flats exist they are contemptuously named 'tenements'. Almost everyone will tell you that he 'wants a house of his own', and apparently a house in the middle of an unbroken block of houses a hundred yards long seems to them more 'their own' than a flat situated in mid-air.

To revert to the second of the two Corporation houses I have just mentioned. The tenant complained that the house was cold, damp, and so forth. Perhaps the house was jerry-built, but equally probably he was exaggerating. He had come there from a filthy hovel in the middle of Wigan which I happened to have inspected previously; while there he had made every effort to get hold of a Corporation house, and he was no sooner in the Corporation house than he wanted to be back in the slum. This looks like mere captiousness but it covers a perfectly genuine grievance. In very many cases, perhaps in half the cases, I found that the people in Corporation houses don't really like them. They are glad to get out of the stink of the slum, they know that it is better for their children to have space to play about in, but they don't feel really at home. The exceptions are usually people in good employ who can afford to spend a little extra on fuel and furniture and journeys, and who in any case are of 'superior' type. The others, the typical slum-dwellers, miss the frowsy warmth of the slum. They complain that 'out in the country', i.e. on the edge of the town, they are 'starving' (freezing). Certainly mosi Corporation estates are pretty bleak in winter. Some I have been through, perched on treeless clayey hillsides and swept by icy winds, would be horrible places to live in. It is not that slum-dwellers want dirt and congestion for their own sakes, as the fat-bellied bourgeoisie love to believe. (See for instance the conversation about slum-clearance in Galsworthy's *Swan Song*, where the rentier's cherished belief that the slum-dweller makes the slum, and not vice versa, is put into the mouth of a philanthropic Jew.) Give people a decent house and they will soon learn to keep it decent. Moreover, with a smart-looking house to live up to they improve in self-respect and cleanliness, and their children start life with better chances. Nevertheless, in a Corporation estate there is an uncomfortable, almost prison-like atmosphere, and the people who live there are perfectly well aware of it.

And it is here that one comes on the central difficulty of the housing problem. When you walk through the smoke-dim slums of Manchester you think that nothing is needed except to tear down these abominations and build decent houses in their place. But the trouble is that in destroying the slum you destroy other things as well. Houses are desperately needed and are not being built fast enough; but in so far as rehousing is being done, it is being done – perhaps it is unavoidable – in a monstrously inhuman manner. I don't mean merely that the houses are new and ugly. All houses have got to be new at some time, and as a matter of fact the type of Corporation house now being built is not at all offensive to look at. On the outskirts of Liverpool there are what amount to whole towns consisting entirely of Corporation houses, and they are quite pleasing to the eye; the blocks of workers' flats in the centre of the town modelled, I believe, on the workers' flats in Vienna, are definitely fine buildings. But there is something ruthless and soulless about the whole business. Take, for instance, the restrictions with which you are burdened in a Corporation house. You are not allowed to keep your house and garden as you want them – in some estates there is even a regulation that every garden must have the same kind of hedge. You are not allowed to keep poultry or pigeons. The Yorkshire miners are fond of keeping homer pigeons; they keep them in the back yard and take them out and race them on Sundays. But pigeons are messy birds and the Corporation suppresses them as a matter of course. The restrictions about shops are more serious. The number of shops in a Corporation estate is rigidly limited, and it is said that preference is given to the Co-op and the chain stores; this may not be strictly true, but certainly those are the shops that one usually sees there. This is bad enough for the general public, but from the point of view of the independent shopkeeper it is a disaster. Many a small shopkeeper is utterly ruined by some rehousing scheme which takes no notice of his existence. A whole section of the town is condemned *en bloc*; presently the houses are pulled down and the people are transferred to some housing estate miles away. In this way all the small shopkeepers of the quarter have their whole clientele taken away from them at a single swoop and receive not a penny of compensation. They cannot transfer their business to the estate, because even if they can afford the move and the much higher rents, they would probably be refused a licence. As for pubs, they are banished from the housing estates almost completely, and the few that remain are dismal sham-Tudor places fitted out by the big brewery companies and very expensive. For a middle-class population this would be a nuisance – it might mean walking a mile to get a glass of beer; for a working-class population, which uses the pub as a kind of club, it is a serious blow at communal life. It is a great achievement to get slum-dwellers into decent houses, but it is unfortunate that, owing to the peculiar temper of our time, it is also considered necessary to rob them of the last vestiges of their liberty. The people themselves feel this, and it is this feeling that they are rationalizing when they complain that their new houses – so much better, *as* houses, than those they have come out of – are cold and uncomfortable and 'unhomelike'.

I sometimes think that the price of liberty is not so much eternal vigilance as eternal dirt. There are some Corporation estates in which new tenants are systematically de-loused before being allowed into their houses. All their possessions except what they stand up in are taken away from them, fumigated, and sent on to the new house. This procedure has its points, for it *is* a pity that people should take bugs into brand new houses (a bug will follow you about in your luggage if he gets half a chance), but it is the kind of thing that makes you wish that the word 'hygiene' could be dropped out of the dictionary. Bugs are bad, but a state of affairs in which men will allow themselves to be dipped like sheep is worse. Perhaps, however, when it is a case of slum clearance, one must take for granted a certain amount of restrictions and inhumanity. When all is said and done, the most important thing is that people shall live in decent houses and not in pigsties. I have seen too much of slums to go into Chestertonian raptures about them. A place where the children can breathe clean air, and women have a few conveniences to save them from drudgery, and a man has a bit of garden to dig in, *must* be better than the stinking back-streets of Leeds and Sheffield. On balance, the Corporation estates are better than the slums; but only by a small margin.

When I was looking into the housing question I visited and inspected numbers of houses, perhaps a hundred or two hundred houses altogether, in various mining towns and villages. I cannot end this chapter without remarking on the extraordinary courtesy and good nature with which I was received everywhere. I did not go alone – I always had some local friend among the unemployed to show me round – but even so, it is an impertinence to go poking into strangers' houses and asking to see the cracks in the bedroom wall. Yet everyone was astonishingly patient and seemed to understand almost without explanation why I was questioning them and what I wanted to see. If any unauthorized person walked into *my* house and began asking me whether the roof leaked and whether I was much troubled by bugs and what I thought of my landlord, I should probably tell him to go to hell. This only happened to me once, and in that case the woman was slightly deaf and took me for a Means Test nark; but even she relented after a while and gave me the information I wanted.

I am told that it is bad form for a writer to quote his own reviews, but I want here to contradict a reviewer in the *Manchester Guardian* who says apropos of one of my books:

Set down in Wigan or Whitechapel Mr Orwell would still exercise an unerring power of closing his vision to all that is good in order to proceed with his wholehearted vilification of humanity.

Wrong. Mr Orwell was 'set down' in Wigan for quite a while and it did not inspire him with any wish to vilify humanity. He liked Wigan very much – the people, not the scenery. Indeed, he has only one fault to find with it, and that is in respect of the celebrated Wigan Pier, which he had set his heart on seeing. Alas! Wigan Pier had been demolished, and even the spot where it used to stand is no longer certain.

5

WHEN you see the unemployment figures quoted at two millions, it is
fatally easy to take this as meaning that two million people are out of
work and the rest of the population is comparatively comfortable. I admit
that till recently I was in the habit of doing so myself. I used to calculate
that if you put the registered unemployed at round about two millions and
threw in the destitute and those who for one reason and another were not
registered, you might take the number of underfed people in England (for
everyone on the dole or thereabouts is underfed) as being, at the very
most, five millions.

This is an enormous under-estimate, because, in the first place, the only
people shown on unemployment figures are those actually drawing the
dole – that is, in general, heads of families. An unemployed man's
dependants do not figure on the list unless they too are drawing a separate
allowance. A Labour Exchange officer told me that to get at the real
number of people *living on* (not drawing) the dole, you have got to multiply
the official figures by something over three. This alone brings the number
of unemployed to round about six millions. But in addition there are great
numbers of people who are in work but who, from a financial point of
view, might equally well be unemployed, because they are not drawing
anything that can be described as a living wage.* Allow for these and
their dependants, throw in as before the old-age pensioners, the destitute,
and other nondescripts, and you get an *underfed* population of well over
ten millions. Sir John Orr puts it at twenty millions.

Take the figures for Wigan, which is typical enough of the industrial
and mining districts. The number of insured workers is round about 36,000
(26,000 men and 10,000 women). Of these, the number unemployed at
the beginning of 1936 was about 10,000. But this was in winter when the
mines are working full time; in summer it would probably be 12,000.

---

* For instance, a recent census of the Lancashire cotton mills revealed the fact that over
40,000 *full-time* employees receive less than thirty shillings a week each. In Preston, to take
only one town, the number receiving *over* thirty shillings a week was 640 and the number
receiving *under* thirty shillings was 3113.

Multiply by three, as above, and you get 30,000 or 36,000. The total
population of Wigan is a little under 87,000; so that at any moment more
than one person in three out of the whole population – not merely the
registered workers – is either drawing or living on the dole. Those ten or
twelve thousand unemployed contain a steady core of from four to five
thousand miners who have been continuously unemployed for the past
seven years. And Wigan is not especially badly off as industrial towns go.
Even in Sheffield, which has been doing well for the last year or so because
of wars and rumours of war, the proportion of unemployment is about the
same – one in three of registered workers unemployed.

When a man is first unemployed, until his insurance stamps are exhausted, he draws 'full benefit', of which the rates are as follows:

	per week
Single man	17s.
Wife	9s.
Each child below 14	3s.

Thus in a typical family of parents and three children of whom one was
over fourteen, the total income would be 32s. per week, plus anything that
might be earned by the eldest child. When a man's stamps are exhausted,
before being turned over to the P.A.C. (Public Assistance Committee), he
receives twenty-six weeks' 'transitional benefit' from the U.A.B. (Unemployment Assistance Board), the rates being as follows:

	per week
Single man	15s.
Man and wife	24s.
Children, 14–18	6s.
Children, 11–14	4s. 6d.
Children, 8–11	4s.
Children, 5–8	3s. 6d.
Children, 3–5	3s.

Thus on the U.A.B. the income of the typical family of five persons would
be 37s. 6d. a week if no child was in work. When a man is on the U.A.B. a
quarter of his dole is regarded as rent, with a minimum of 7s. 6d. a week.
If the rent he is paying is more than a quarter of his dole he receives an
extra allowance, but if it is less than 7s. 6d., a corresponding amount is
deducted. Payments on the P.A.C. theoretically come out of the local rates,
but are backed by a central fund. The rates of benefit are:

	per week
Single man	12s. 6d.
Man and wife	23s.
Eldest child	4s.
Any other child	3s.

Being at the discretion of the local bodies these rates vary slightly, and a single man may or may not get an extra 2s. 6d. weekly, bringing his benefit up to 15s. As on the U.A.B., a quarter of a married man's dole is regarded as rent. Thus in the typical family considered above the total income would be 33s. a week, a quarter of this being regarded as rent. In addition, in most districts a coal allowance of 1s. 6d. a week (1s. 6d. is equivalent to about a hundredweight of coal) is granted for six weeks before and six weeks after Christmas.

It will be seen that the income of a family on the dole normally averages round about thirty shillings a week. One can write at least a quarter of this off as rent, which is to say that the average person, child or adult, has got to be fed, clothed, warmed, and otherwise cared-for for six or seven shillings a week. Enormous groups of people, probably at least a third of the whole population of the industrial areas, are living at this level. The Means Test is very strictly enforced, and you are liable to be refused relief at the slightest hint that you are getting money from another source. Dock-labourers, for instance, who are generally hired by the half-day, have to sign on at a Labour Exchange twice daily; if they fail to do so it is assumed that they have been working and their dole is reduced correspondingly. I have seen cases of evasion of the Means Test, but I should say that in the industrial towns, where there is still a certain amount of communal life and everyone has neighbours who know him, it is much harder than it would be in London. The usual method is for a young man who is actually living with his parents to get an accommodation address, so that supposedly he has a separate establishment and draws a separate allowance. But there is much spying and tale-bearing. One man I knew, for instance, was seen feeding his neighbour's chickens while the neighbour was away. It was reported to the authorities that he 'had a job feeding chickens' and he had great difficulty in refuting this. The favourite joke in Wigan was about a man who was refused relief on the ground that he 'had a job carting firewood'. He had been seen, it was said, carting firewood at night. He had to explain that he was not carting firewood but doing a moonlight flit. The 'firewood' was his furniture.

The most cruel and evil effect of the Means Test is the way in which it breaks up families. Old people, sometimes bedridden, are driven out of their homes by it. An old age pensioner, for instance, if a widower, would normally live with one or other of his children; his weekly ten shillings goes towards the household expenses, and probably he is not badly cared for. Under the Means Test, however, he counts as a 'lodger' and if he stays at home his children's dole will be docked. So, perhaps at seventy or seventy-five years of age, he has to turn out into lodgings, handing his pension over to the lodging-house keeper and existing on the verge of starvation. I have seen several cases of this myself. It is happening all over England at this moment, thanks to the Means Test.

Nevertheless, in spite of the frightful extent of unemployment, it is a fact that poverty – extreme poverty – is less in evidence in the industrial North than it is in London. Everything is poorer and shabbier, there are fewer motorcars and fewer well-dressed people; but also there are fewer people who are obviously destitute. Even in a town the size of Liverpool or Manchester you are struck by the fewness of the beggars. London is a sort of whirlpool which draws derelict people towards it, and it is so vast that life there is solitary and anonymous. Until you break the law nobody will take any notice of you, and you can go to pieces as you could not possibly do in a place where you had neighbours who knew you. But in the industrial towns the old communal way of life has not yet broken up, tradition is still strong and almost everyone has a family – potentially, therefore, a home. In a town of 50,000 or 100,000 inhabitants there is no casual and as it were unaccounted-for population; nobody sleeping in the streets, for instance. Moreover, there is just this to be said for the unemployment regulations, that they do not discourage people from marrying. A man and wife on twenty-three shillings a week are not far from the starvation line, but they can make a home of sorts; they are vastly better off than a single man on fifteen shillings. The life of a single unemployed man is dreadful. He lives sometimes in a common lodging-house, more often in a 'furnished' room for which he usually pays six shillings a week, finding himself as best he can on the other nine (say six shillings a week for food and three for clothes, tobacco, and amusements). Of course he cannot feed or look after himself properly, and a man who pays six shillings a week for his room is not encouraged to be indoors more than is necessary. So he spends his days loafing in the public library or any other place where he can keep warm. That – keeping warm – is almost the sole preoccupation of a single unemployed man in winter. In Wigan a favourite refuge was the pictures, which are fantastically cheap there. You can always get a seat for fourpence, and at the matinée at some houses you can even get a seat for twopence. Even people on the verge of starvation will readily pay twopence to get out of the ghastly cold of a winter afternoon. In Sheffield I was taken to a public hall to listen to a lecture by a clergyman, and it was by a long way the silliest and worst-delivered lecture I have ever heard or ever expect to hear. I found it physically impossible to sit it out, indeed my feet carried me out, seemingly of their own accord, before it was half-way through. Yet the hall was thronged with unemployed men; they would have sat through far worse drivel for the sake of a warm place to shelter in.

At times I have seen unmarried men on the dole living in the extreme of misery. In one town I remember a whole colony of them who were squatting, more or less illicitly, in a derelict house which was practically falling down. They had collected a few scraps of furniture, presumably off refuse-tips, and I remember that their sole table was an old marble-topped wash-hand-stand. But this kind of thing is exceptional. A working-class bachelor is a rarity, and so long as a man is married unemployment makes comparatively little alteration in his way of life. His home is impoverished but it is still a home, and it is noticeable everywhere that the anomalous position created by unemployment – the man being out of work while the woman's work continues as before – has not altered the relative status of the sexes. In a working-class home it is the man who is the master and not, as in a middle-class home, the woman or the baby. Practically never, for instance, in a working-class home, will you see the man doing a stroke of the housework. Unemployment has not changed this convention, which on the face of it seems a little unfair. The man is idle from morning to night but the woman is as busy as ever – more so, indeed, because she has to manage with less money. Yet so far as my experience goes the women do not protest. I believe that they, as well as the men, feel that a man would lose his manhood if, merely because he was out of work, he developed into a 'Mary Ann'.

But there is no doubt about the deadening, debilitating effect of unemployment upon everybody, married or single, and upon men more than upon women. The best intellects will not stand up against it. Once or twice it has happened to me to meet unemployed men of genuine literary ability; there are others whom I haven't met but whose work I occasionally see in the magazines. Now and again, at long intervals, these men will produce an article or a short story which is quite obviously better than most of the stuff that gets whooped up by the blurb-reviewers. Why, then, do they make so little use of their talents? They have all the leisure in the world; why don't they sit down and write books? Because to write books you need not only comfort and solitude – and solitude is never easy to attain

in a working-class home – you also need peace of mind. You can't settle
to anything, you can't command the spirit of *hope* in which anything has
got to be created, with that dull evil cloud of unemployment hanging over
you. Still, an unemployed man who feels at home with books can at any
rate occupy himself by reading. But what about the man who cannot read
without discomfort? Take a miner, for instance, who has worked in the
pit since childhood and has been trained to be a miner and nothing else.
How the devil is he to fill up the empty days? It is absurd to say that he
ought to be looking for work. There is no work to look for, and everybody
knows it. You can't go on looking for work every day for seven years.
There are allotments, which occupy the time and help to feed a family,
but in a big town there are only allotments for a small proportion of the
people. Then there are the occupational centres which were started a few
years ago to help the unemployed. On the whole this movement has been
a failure, but some of the centres are still flourishing. I have visited one
or two of them. There are shelters where the men can keep warm and
there are periodical classes in carpentering, boot-making, leather-work,
handloom-weaving, basket-work, sea-grass work, etc., etc.; the idea being
that the men can make furniture and so forth, not for sale but for their
own homes, getting tools free and materials cheaply. Most of the Socialists
I have talked to denounce this movement as they denounce the project –
it is always being talked about but it never comes to anything – to give
the unemployed small-holdings. They say that the occupational centres
are simply a device to keep the unemployed quiet and give them the
illusion that something is being done for them. Undoubtedly that is the
underlying motive. Keep a man busy mending boots and he is less likely
to read the *Daily Worker*. Also there is a nasty Y.M.C.A. atmosphere about
these places which you can feel as soon as you go in. The unemployed
men who frequent them are mostly of the cap-touching type – the type
who tells you oilily that he is 'Temperance' and votes Conservative. Yet
even here you feel yourself torn both ways. For probably it is better that
a man should waste his time even with such rubbish as sea-grass work
than that for years upon end he should do absolutely *nothing*.

By far the best work for the unemployed is being done by the N.U.W.M.
– National Unemployed Workers' Movement. This is a revolutionary
organization intended to hold the unemployed together, stop them blackleg-
ging during strikes, and give them legal advice against the Means Test. It
is a movement that has been built out of nothing by the pennies and efforts
of the unemployed themselves. I have seen a good deal of the N.U.W.M.,
and I greatly admire the men, ragged and underfed like the others, who

keep the organization going. Still more I admire the tact and patience with which they do it; for it is not easy to coax even a penny-a-week subscription out of the pockets of people on the P.A.C. As I said earlier, the English working class do not show much capacity for leadership, but they have a wonderful talent for organization. The whole trade union movement testifies to this; so do the excellent working-men's clubs – really a sort of glorified cooperative pub, and splendidly organized – which are so common in Yorkshire. In many towns the N.U.W.M. have shelters and arrange speeches by Communist speakers. But even at these shelters the men who go there do nothing but sit round the stove and occasionally play a game of dominoes. If this movement could be combined with something along the lines of the occupational centres, it would be nearer what is needed. It is a deadly thing to see a skilled man running to seed, year after year, in utter, hopeless idleness. It ought not to be impossible to give him the chance of using his hands and making furniture and so forth for his own home, without turning him into a Y.M.C.A. cocoa-drunkard. We may as well face the fact that several million men in England will – unless another war breaks out – never have a real job this side of the grave. One thing that probably could be done and certainly ought to be done as a matter of course is to give every unemployed man a patch of ground and free tools if he chose to apply for them. It is disgraceful that men who are expected to keep alive on the P.A.C. should not even have the chance to grow vegetables for their families.

To study unemployment and its effects you have got to go to the industrial areas. In the South unemployment exists, but it is scattered and queerly unobtrusive. There are plenty of rural districts where a man out of work is almost unheard-of, and you don't anywhere see the spectacle of whole blocks of cities living on the dole and the P.A.C. It is only when you lodge in streets where nobody has a job, where getting a job seems about as probable as owning an aeroplane and much *less* probable than winning fifty pounds in the Football Pool, that you begin to grasp the changes that are being worked in our civilization. For a change *is* taking place, there is no doubt about that. The attitude of the submerged working class is profoundly different from what it was seven or eight years ago.

I first became aware of the unemployment problem in 1928. At that time I had just come back from Burma, where unemployment was only a word, and I had gone to Burma when I was still a boy and the post-war boom was not quite over. When I first saw unemployed men at close quarters, the thing that horrified and amazed me was to find that many of them were *ashamed* of being unemployed. I was very ignorant, but not so ignorant as to imagine that when the loss of foreign markets pushes two million men out of work, those two million are any more to blame than the people who draw blanks in the Calcutta Sweep. But at that time nobody cared to admit that unemployment was inevitable, because this meant admitting that it would probably continue. The middle classes were still talking about 'lazy idle loafers on the dole' and saying that 'these men could all find work if they wanted to', and naturally these opinions percolated to the working class themselves. I remember the shock of astonishment it gave me, when I first mingled with tramps and beggars, to find that a fair proportion, perhaps a quarter, of these beings whom I had been taught to regard as cynical parasites, were decent young miners and cotton-workers gazing at their destiny with the same sort of dumb amazement as an animal in a trap. They simply could not understand what was happening to them. They had been brought up to work, and behold! it seemed as if they were never going to have the chance of working again. In their circumstances it was inevitable, at first, that they should be haunted by a feeling of personal degradation. That was the attitude towards unemployment in those days: it was a disaster which happened to *you* as an individual and for which you were to blame.

When a quarter of a million miners are unemployed, it is part of the order of things that Alf Smith, a miner living in the back streets of Newcastle, should be out of work. Alf Smith is merely one of the quarter million, a statistical unit. But no human being finds it easy to regard himself as a statistical unit. So long as Bert Jones across the street is still at work, Alf Smith is bound to feel himself dishonoured and a failure. Hence that frightful feeling of impotence and despair which is almost the worst evil of unemployment – far worse than any hardship, worse than the demoralization of enforced idleness, and only less bad than the physical degeneracy of Alf Smith's children, born on the P.A.C. Everyone who saw Greenwood's play *Love on the Dole* must remember that dreadful moment when the poor, good, stupid working man beats on the table and cries out, 'O God, send me some work!' This was not dramatic exaggeration, it was a touch from life. That cry must have been uttered, in almost those words, in tens of thousands, perhaps hundreds of thousands of English homes, during the past fifteen years.

But, I think not again – or at least, not so often. That is the real point: people are ceasing to kick against the pricks. After all, even the middle classes – yes, even the bridge clubs in the country towns – are beginning to realize that there is such a thing as unemployment. The 'My dear, I don't *believe* in all this nonsense about unemployment. Why, only last week we wanted a man to weed the garden, and we simply couldn't get one. They don't *want* to work, that's all it is!' which you heard at every decent tea-table five years ago, is growing perceptibly less frequent. As for the working class themselves, they have gained immensely in economic knowledge. I believe that the *Daily Worker* has accomplished a great deal here: its influence is out of all proportion to its circulation. But in any case they have had their lesson well rubbed into them, not only because unemployment is so widespread but because it has lasted so long. When people live on the dole for years at a time they grow used to it, and drawing the dole, though it remains unpleasant, ceases to be shameful. Thus the old, independent, workhouse-fearing tradition is undermined, just as the ancient fear of debt is undermined by the hire-purchase system. In the back streets of Wigan and Barnsley I saw every kind of privation, but I probably saw much less *conscious* misery than I should have seen ten years ago. The people have at any rate grasped that unemployment is a thing they cannot help. It is not only Alf Smith who is out of work now; Bert Jones is out of work as well, and both of them have been 'out' for years. It makes a great deal of difference when things are the same for everybody.

So you have whole populations settling down, as it were, to a lifetime on the P.A.C. And what I think is admirable, perhaps even hopeful, is that they have managed to do it without going spiritually to pieces. A working man does not disintegrate under the strain of poverty as a middle-class person does. Take, for instance, the fact that the working class think nothing of getting married on the dole. It annoys the old ladies in Brighton, but it is a proof of their essential good sense; they realize that losing your job does not mean that you cease to be a human being. So that in one way things in the distressed areas are not as bad as they might be. Life is still fairly normal, more normal than one really has the right to expect. Families are impoverished, but the family-system has not broken up. The people are in effect living a reduced version of their former lives. Instead of raging against their destiny they have made things tolerable by lowering their standards.

But they don't necessarily lower their standards by cutting out luxuries and concentrating on necessities; more often it is the other way about – the more natural way, if you come to think of it. Hence the fact that in a decade of unparalleled depression the consumption of all cheap luxuries has increased. The two things that have probably made the greatest difference of all are the movies and the mass-production of cheap smart clothes since the war. The youth who leaves school at fourteen and gets a blind-alley job is out of work at twenty, probably for life; but for two pounds ten on the hire-purchase he can buy himself a suit which, for a little while and at a little distance, looks as though it had been tailored in Savile Row. The girl can look like a fashion plate at an even lower price. You may have three halfpence in your pocket and not a prospect in the world, and only the corner of a leaky bedroom to go home to; but in your new clothes you can stand on the street corner, indulging in a private daydream of yourself as Clark Gable or Greta Garbo, which compensates you for a great deal. And even at home there is generally a cup of tea going – a 'nice cup of tea' – and Father, who has been out of work since 1929, is temporarily happy because he has a sure tip for the Cesarewitch.

Trade since the war has had to adjust itself to meet the demands of underpaid, underfed people, with the result that a luxury is nowadays almost always cheaper than a necessity. One pair of plain solid shoes costs as much as two ultra-smart pairs. For the price of one square meal you can get two pounds of cheap sweets. You can't get much meat for threepence, but you can get a lot of fish-and-chips. Milk costs threepence a pint and even 'mild' beer costs fourpence, but aspirins are seven a penny and you can wring forty cups of tea out of a quarter-pound packet. And above all there is gambling, the cheapest of all luxuries. Even people on the verge of starvation can buy a few days' hope ('Something to live for', as they call it) by having a penny on a sweepstake. Organized gambling has now risen almost to the status of a major industry. Consider, for instance, a phenomenon like the Football Pools, with a turnover of about six million pounds a year, almost all of it from the pockets of working-class people. I happened to be in Yorkshire when Hitler re-occupied the Rhineland. Hitler, Locarno, Fascism, and the threat of war aroused hardly a flicker of interest locally, but the decision of the Football Association to stop publishing their fixtures in advance (this was an attempt to quell the Football Pools) flung all Yorkshire into a storm of fury. And then there is the queer spectacle of modern electrical science showering miracles upon people with empty bellies. You may shiver all night for lack of bedclothes, but in the morning you can go to the public library and read the news that has been telegraphed for your benefit from San Francisco and Singapore. Twenty million people are underfed but literally everyone in England has access to a radio. What we have lost in food we have gained in electricity. Whole sections of the working class who have been plundered of all they really need are being compensated, in part, by cheap luxuries which mitigate the surface of life.

Do you consider all this desirable? No, I don't. But it may be that the pyschological adjustment which the working class are visibly making is the best they could make in the circumstances. They have neither turned revolutionary nor lost their self-respect; merely they have kept their tempers and settled down to make the best of things on a fish-and-chip standard. The alternative would be God knows what continued agonies of despair; or it might be attempted insurrections which, in a strongly governed country like England, could only lead to futile massacres and a régime of savage repression.

Of course the post-war development of cheap luxuries has been a very fortunate thing for our rulers. It is quite likely that fish-and-chips, art-silk stockings, tinned salmon, cut-price chocolate (five two-ounce bars for sixpence), the movies, the radio, strong tea, and the Football Pools have between them averted revolution. Therefore we are sometimes told that the whole thing is an astute manoeuvre by the governing class – a sort of 'bread and circuses' business – to hold the unemployed down. What I have seen of our governing class does not convince me that they have that much intelligence. The thing has happened, but by an unconscious process – the quite natural interaction between the manufacturer's need for a market and the need of half-starved people for cheap palliatives.

6

WHEN I was a small boy at school a lecturer used to come once a term and deliver excellent lectures on famous battles of the past, such as Blenheim, Austerlitz, etc. He was fond of quoting Napoleon's maxim 'An army marches on its stomach', and at the end of his lecture he would suddenly turn to us and demand, 'What's the most important thing in the world?' We were expected to shout 'Food!' and if we did not do so he was disappointed.

Obviously he was right in a way. A human being is primarily a bag for putting food into; the other functions and faculties may be more godlike, but in point of time they come afterwards. A man dies and is buried, and all his words and actions are forgotten, but the food he has eaten lives after him in the sound or rotten bones of his children. I think it could be plausibly argued that changes of diet are more important than changes of dynasty or even of religion. The Great War, for instance, could never have happened if tinned food had not been invented. And the history of the past four hundred years in England would have been immensely different if it had not been for the introduction of root-crops and various other vegetables at the end of the Middle Ages, and a little later the introduction of non-alcoholic drinks (tea, coffee, cocoa) and also of distilled liquors to which the beer-drinking English were not accustomed. Yet it is curious how seldom the all-importance of food is recognized. You see statues everywhere to politicians, poets, bishops, but none to cooks or bacon-curers or market-gardeners. The Emperor Charles V is said to have erected a statue to the inventor of bloaters, but that is the only case I can think of at the moment.

So perhaps the really important thing about the unemployed, the really basic thing if you look to the future, is the diet they are living on. As I said earlier, the average unemployed family lives on an income of round about thirty shillings a week, of which at least a quarter goes in rent. It is worth considering in some detail how the remaining money is spent. I have here a budget which was made out for me by an unemployed miner and his wife. I asked them to make a list which represented as exactly as possible their expenditure in a typical week. This man's allowance was thirty-two shillings a week, and besides his wife he had two children, one aged two years and five months and the other ten months. Here is the list:

	s.	d.
Rent	9	0½
Clothing Club	3	0
Coal	2	0
Gas	1	3
Milk	0	10½
Union fees	0	3
Insurance (on the children)	0	2
Meat	2	6
Flour (2 stone)	3	4
Yeast	0	4
Potatoes	1	0
Dripping	0	10
Margarine	0	10
Bacon	1	2
Sugar	1	9
Tea	1	0
Jam	0	7½
Peas and cabbage	0	6

	s.	d.
Carrots and onions	0	4
Quaker oats	0	4½
Soap, powders, blue, etc.	0	10
Total	£1 12	0

In addition to this, three packets of dried milk were supplied weekly for the baby by the Infants' Welfare Clinic.

One or two comments are needed here. To begin with the list leaves out a great deal – blacking, pepper, salt, vinegar, matches, kindling-wood, razor blades, replacements of utensils, and wear and tear of furniture and bedding, to name the first few that come to mind. Any money spent on these would mean reduction on some other item. A more serious charge is tobacco. This man happened to be a small smoker, but even so his tobacco would hardly cost less than a shilling a week, meaning a further reduction on food. The 'clothing clubs' into which unemployed people pay so much a week are run by big drapers in all the industrial towns. Without them it would be impossible for unemployed people to buy new clothes at all. I don't know whether or not they buy bedding through these clubs. This particular family, as I happen to know, possessed next to no bedding.

In the above list, if you allow a shilling for tobacco and deduct this and the other non-food items, you are left with sixteen and fivepence halfpenny. Call it sixteen shillings and leave the baby out of account – for the baby was getting its weekly packets of milk from the Welfare Clinic. This sixteen shillings has got to provide the entire nourishment, *including fuel*, of three persons, two of them adult. The first question is whether it is even theoretically possible for three persons to be properly nourished on sixteen shillings a week. When the dispute over the Means Test was in progress there was a disgusting public wrangle about the minimum weekly sum on which a human being could keep alive. So far as I remember, one school of dieticians worked it out at five and ninepence, while another school, more generous, put it at five and ninepence halfpenny. After this there were letters to the papers from a number of people who claimed to be feeding themselves on four shillings a week. Here is a weekly budget (it was printed in the *New Statesman* and also in the *News of the World*) which I picked out from among a number of others:

	s.	d.
3 wholemeal loaves	1	0
½ lb. margarine	0	2½
½ lb. dripping	0	3

1 lb. cheese	0	7
1 lb. onions	0	1½
1 lb. carrots	0	1½
1 lb. broken biscuits	0	4
2 lb. dates	0	6
1 tin evaporated milk	0	5
10 oranges	0	5
Total	3	11½

Please notice that this budget contains *nothing for fuel*. In fact, the writer explicitly stated that he could not afford to buy fuel and ate all his food raw. Whether the letter was genuine or a hoax does not matter at the moment. What I think will be admitted is that this list represents about as wise an expenditure as could be contrived; if you *had* to live on three and elevenpence halfpenny a week, you could hardly extract more food-value from it than that. So perhaps it is possible to feed yourself adequately on the P.A.C. allowance if you concentrate on essential foodstuffs; but not otherwise.

Now compare this list with the unemployed miner's budget that I gave earlier. The miner's family spend only tenpence a week on green vegetables and tenpence halfpenny on milk (remember that one of them is a child less than three years old), and nothing on fruit; but they spend one and nine on sugar (about eight pounds of sugar, that is) and a shilling on tea. The half-crown spent on meat *might* represent a small joint and the materials for a stew; probably as often as not it would represent four or five tins of bully beef. The basis of their diet, therefore, is white bread and margarine, corned beef, sugared tea, and potatoes – an appalling diet. Would it not be better if they spent more money on wholesome things like oranges and wholemeal bread or if they even, like the writer of the letter to the *New Statesman*, saved on fuel and ate their carrots raw? Yes, it would, but the point is that no ordinary human being is ever going to do such a thing. The ordinary human being would sooner starve than live on brown bread and raw carrots. And the peculiar evil is this, that the less money you have, the less inclined you feel to spend it on wholesome food. A millionaire may enjoy breakfasting off orange juice and Ryvita biscuits; an unemployed man doesn't. Here the tendency of which I spoke at the end of the last chapter comes into play. When you are unemployed, which is to say when you are underfed, harassed, bored, and miserable, you don't *want* to eat dull wholesome food. You want something a little bit 'tasty'.

There is always some cheaply pleasant thing to tempt you. Let's have three pennorth of chips! Run out and buy us a twopenny ice-cream! Put the kettle on and we'll all have a nice cup of tea! *That* is how your mind works when you are at the P.A.C. level. White bread-and-marg and sugared tea don't nourish you to any extent, but they are *nicer* (at least most people think so) than brown bread-and-dripping and cold water. Unemployment is an endless misery that has got to be constantly palliated, and especially with tea, the Englishman's opium. A cup of tea or even an aspirin is much better as a temporary stimulant than a crust of brown bread.

The results of all this are visible in a physical degeneracy which you can study directly, by using your eyes, or inferentially, by having a look at the vital statistics. The physical average in the industrial towns is terribly low, lower even than in London. In Sheffield you have the feeling of walking among a population of troglodytes. The miners are splendid men, but they are usually small, and the mere fact that their muscles are toughened by constant work does not mean that their children start life with a better physique. In any case the miners are physically the pick of the population. The most obvious sign of under-nourishment is the badness of everybody's teeth. In Lancashire you would have to look for a long time before you saw a working-class person with good natural teeth. Indeed, you see very few people with natural teeth at all, apart from the children; and even the children's teeth have a frail bluish appearance which means, I suppose, calcium deficiency. Several dentists have told me that in industrial districts a person over thirty with any of his or her own teeth is coming to be an abnormality. In Wigan various people gave me their opinion that it is best to 'get shut of' your teeth as early in life as possible. 'Teeth is just a misery,' one woman said to me. In one house where I stayed there were, apart from myself, five people, the oldest being forty-three and the youngest a boy of fifteen. Of these the boy was the only one who possessed a single tooth of his own, and his teeth were obviously not going to last long. As for the vital statistics, the fact that in any large industrial town the death rate and infant mortality of the poorest quarters are always about double those of the well-to-do residential quarters – a good deal more than double in some cases – hardly needs commenting on.

Of course one ought not to imagine that the prevailing bad physique is due solely to unemployment, for it is probable that the physical average has been declining all over England for a long time past, and not merely among the unemployed in the industrial areas. This cannot be proved statistically, but it is a conclusion that is forced upon you if you use your eyes, even in rural places and even in a prosperous town like London. On the day when King George V's body passed through London on its way to Westminster, I happened to be caught for an hour or two in the crowd in Trafalgar Square. It was impossible, looking about one then, not to be struck by the physical degeneracy of modern England. The people surrounding me were *not* working-class people for the most part; they were the shopkeeper – commercial-traveller type, with a sprinkling of the well-to-do. But what a set they looked! Puny limbs, sickly faces, under the weeping London sky! Hardly a well-built man or a decent-looking woman, and not a fresh complexion anywhere. As the King's coffin went by, the men took off their hats, and a friend who was in the crowd at the other side of the Strand said to me afterwards, 'The only touch of colour anywhere was the bald heads.' Even the Guards, it seemed to me – there was a squad of guardsmen marching beside the coffin – were not what they used to be. Where are the monstrous men with chests like barrels and moustaches like the wings of eagles who strode across my childhood's gaze twenty or thirty years ago? Buried, I suppose, in the Flanders mud. In their place there are these pale-faced boys who have been picked for their height and consequently look like hop-poles in overcoats – the truth being that in modern England a man over six feet high is usually skin and bone and not much else. If the English physique has declined, this is no doubt partly due to the fact that the Great War carefully selected the million best men in England and slaughtered them, largely before they had had time to breed. But the process must have begun earlier than that, and it must be due ultimately to unhealthy ways of living, i.e. to industrialism. I don't mean the habit of living in towns – probably the town is healthier than the country, in many ways – but the modern industrial technique which provides you with cheap substitutes for everything. We may find in the long run that tinned food is a deadlier weapon than the machine gun.

It is unfortunate that the English working class – the English nation generally, for that matter – are exceptionally ignorant about and wasteful of food. I have pointed out elsewhere how civilized is a French navvy's idea of a meal compared with an Englishman's, and I cannot believe that you would ever see such wastage in a French house as you habitually see in English ones. Of course, in the very poorest homes, where everybody is unemployed, you don't see much actual waste, but those who can afford to waste food often do so. I could give startling instances of this. Even the Northern habit of baking one's own bread is slightly wasteful in itself, because an overworked woman cannot bake more than once or, at most, twice a week and it is impossible to tell beforehand how much bread will be wasted, so that a certain amount generally has to be thrown away. The usual thing is to bake six large loaves and twelve small ones at a time. All this is part of the old, generous English attitude to life, and it is an amiable quality, but a disastrous one at the present moment.

English working people everywhere, so far as I know, refuse brown bread; it is usually impossible to buy wholemeal bread in a working-class district. They sometimes give the reason that brown bread is 'dirty'. I suspect the real reason is that in the past brown bread has been confused with black bread, which is traditionally associated with Popery and wooden shoes. (They have plenty of Popery and wooden shoes in Lancashire. A pity they haven't the black bread as well!) But the English palate, especially the working-class palate, now rejects good food almost automatically. The number of people who *prefer* tinned peas and tinned fish to real peas and real fish must be increasing every year, and plenty of people who could afford real milk in their tea would much sooner have tinned milk – even that dreadful tinned milk which is made of sugar and cornflour and has UNFIT FOR BABIES on the tin in huge letters. In some districts efforts are now being made to teach the unemployed more about food-values and more about the intelligent spending of money. When you hear of a thing like this you feel yourself torn both ways. I have heard a Communist speaker on the platform grow very angry about it. In London, he said, parties of Society dames now have the cheek to walk into East End houses and give shopping-lessons to the wives of the unemployed. He gave this as an instance of the mentality of the English governing class. First you condemn a family to live on thirty shillings a week, and then you have the damned impertinence to tell them how they are to spend their money. He was quite right – I agree heartily. Yet all the same it is a pity that, merely for the lack of a proper tradition, people should pour muck like tinned milk down their throats and not even know that it is inferior to the product of the cow.

I doubt, however, whether the unemployed would ultimately benefit if they learned to spend their money more economically. For it is only the fact that they are *not* economical that keeps their allowances so high. An Englishman on the P.A.C. gets fifteen shillings a week because fifteen shillings is the smallest sum on which he can conceivably keep alive. If he were, say, an Indian or Japanese coolie, who can live on rice and onions, he wouldn't get fifteen shillings a week – he would be lucky if he got fifteen shillings a month. Our unemployment allowances, miserable though they are, are framed to suit a population with very high standards and not much notion of economy. If the unemployed learned to be better managers they would be visibly better off, and I fancy it would not be long before the dole was docked correspondingly.

There is one great mitigation of unemployment in the North, and that is the cheapness of fuel. Anywhere in the coal areas the retail price of coal is about one and sixpence a hundredweight; in the South of England it is about half a crown. Moreover, miners in work can usually buy coal direct from the pit at eight or nine shillings a ton, and those who have a cellar in their homes sometimes store a ton and sell it (illicitly, I suppose) to those who are out of work. But apart from this there is immense and systematic thieving of coal by the unemployed. I call it thieving because technically it is that, though it does no harm to anybody. In the 'dirt' that is sent up from the pits there is a certain amount of broken coal, and unemployed people spend a lot of time in picking it out of the slag-heaps. All day long over those strange grey mountains you see people wandering to and fro with sacks and baskets across the sulphurous smoke (many slag-heaps are on fire under the surface), prising out the tiny nuggets of coal which are buried here and there. You meet men coming away, wheeling strange and wonderful home-made bicycles – bicycles made of rusty parts picked off refuse-tips, without saddles, without chains and almost always without tyres – across which are slung bags containing perhaps half a hundredweight of coal, fruit of half a day's searching. In times of strikes, when everybody is short of fuel, the miners turn out with pick and shovel and burrow into the slag-heaps, whence the hummocky appearance which most slag-heaps have. During long strikes, in places where there are outcrops of coal, they have sunk surface mines and carried them scores of yards into the earth.

In Wigan the competition among unemployed people for the waste coal has become so fierce that it has led to an extraordinary custom called 'scrambling for the coal', which is well worth seeing. Indeed I rather wonder that it has never been filmed. An unemployed miner took me to see it one afternoon. We got to the place, a mountain range of ancient slag-heaps with a railway running through the valley below. A couple of hundred ragged men, each with a sack and coal-hammer strapped under his coat-tails, were waiting on the 'broo'. When the dirt comes up from the pit it is loaded on to trucks and an engine runs these to the top of another slag-heap a quarter of a mile away and there leaves them. The process of 'scrambling for the coal' consists in getting on to the train while it is moving; any truck which you have succeeded in boarding while it is in motion counts as 'your' truck. Presently the train hove in sight. With a wild yell a hundred men dashed down the slope to catch her as she rounded the bend. Even at the bend the train was making twenty miles an hour. The men hurled themselves upon it, caught hold of the rings at the rear of the trucks and hoisted themselves up by way of the bumpers, five or ten of them on each truck. The driver took no notice. He drove up to the top of the slag-heap, uncoupled the trucks, and ran the engine back to the pit, presently returning with a fresh string of trucks. There was the same wild rush of ragged figures as before. In the end only about fifty men had failed to get on to either train.

We walked up to the top of the slag-heap. The men were shovelling the dirt out of the trucks, while down below their wives and children were kneeling, swiftly scrabbling with their hands in the damp dirt and picking out lumps of coal the size of an egg or smaller. You would see a woman pounce on a tiny fragment of stuff, wipe it on her apron, scrutinize it to make sure it was coal, and pop it jealously into her sack. Of course, when you are boarding a truck you don't know beforehand what is in it; it may be actual 'dirt' from the roads or it may merely be shale from the roofing. If it is a shale truck there will be no coal in it, but there occurs among the shale another inflammable rock called cannel, which looks very like ordinary shale but is slightly darker and is known by splitting in parallel lines, like slate. It makes tolerable fuel, not good enough to be commercially valuable, but good enough to be eagerly sought after by the unemployed. The miners on the shale trucks were picking out the cannel and splitting it up with their hammers. Down at the bottom of the 'broo' the people who had failed to get on to either train were gleaning the tiny chips of coal that came rolling down from above – fragments no bigger than a hazel-nut, these, but the people were glad enough to get them.

We stayed there till the train was empty. In a couple of hours the people had picked the dirt over to the last grain. They slung their sacks over shoulder or bicycle, and started on the two-mile trudge back to Wigan. Most of the families had gathered about half a hundredweight of coal or cannel, so that between them they must have stolen five or ten tons of fuel. This business of robbing the dirt trains takes place every day in Wigan, at any rate in winter, and at more collieries than one. It is of course extremely dangerous. No one was hurt the afternoon I was there, but a man had had both his legs cut off a few weeks earlier, and another man lost several fingers a week later. Technically it is stealing but, as everybody knows, if the coal were not stolen it would simply be wasted. Now and again, for form's sake, the colliery companies prosecute somebody for coal-picking, and in that morning's issue of the local paper there was a paragraph saying that two men had been fined ten shillings. But no notice is taken of the prosecutions – in fact, one of the men named in the paper was there that afternoon – and the coal-pickers subscribe among themselves to pay the fines. The thing is taken for granted. Everyone knows that the unemployed have got to get fuel somehow. So every afternoon several hundred men risk their necks and several hundred women scrabble in the mud for hours – and all for half a hundredweight of inferior fuel, value ninepence.

That scene stays in my mind as one of my pictures of Lancashire: the dumpy, shawled women, with their sacking aprons and their heavy black clogs, kneeling in the cindery mud and the bitter wind, searching eagerly for tiny chips of coal. They are glad enough to do it. In winter they are desperate for fuel; it is more important almost than food. Meanwhile all round, as far as the eye can see, are the slag-heaps and hoisting gear of collieries, and not one of those collieries can sell all the coal it is capable of producing. This ought to appeal to Major Douglas.

7

As you travel northward your eye, accustomed to the South or East, does not notice much difference until you are beyond Birmingham. In Coventry you might as well be in Finsbury Park, and the Bull Ring in Birmingham is not unlike Norwich Market, and between all the towns of the Midlands there stretches a villa-civilization indistinguishable from that of the South. It is only when you get a little further north, to the pottery towns and beyond, that you begin to encounter the real ugliness of industrialism – an ugliness so frightful and so arresting that you are obliged, as it were, to come to terms with it.

A slag-heap is at best a hideous thing, because it is so planless and functionless. It is something just dumped on the earth, like the emptying of a giant's dust-bin. On the outskirts of the mining towns there are frightful landscapes where your horizon is ringed completely round by jagged grey mountains, and underfoot is mud and ashes and overhead the steel cables where tubs of dirt travel slowly across miles of country. Often the slag-heaps are on fire, and at night you can see the red rivulets of fire winding this way and that, and also the slow-moving blue flames of sulphur, which always seem on the point of expiring and always spring out again.

Even when a slag-heap sinks, as it does ultimately, only an evil brown grass grows on it, and it retains its hummocky surface. One in the slums of Wigan, used as a playground, looks like a choppy sea suddenly frozen; 'the flock mattress', it is called locally. Even centuries hence when the plough drives over the places where coal was once mined, the sites of ancient slag-heaps will still be distinguishable from an aeroplane.

I remember a winter afternoon in the dreadful environs of Wigan. All round was the lunar landscape of slag-heaps, and to the north, through the passes, as it were, between the mountains of slag, you could see the factory chimneys sending out their plumes of smoke. The canal path was a mixture of cinders and frozen mud, criss-crossed by the imprints of innumerable clogs, and all round, as far as the slag-heaps in the distance, stretched the 'flashes' – pools of stagnant water that had seeped into the hollows caused by the subsidence of ancient pits. It was horribly cold. The 'flashes' were covered with ice the colour of raw umber, the bargemen were muffled to the eyes in sacks, the lock gates wore beards of ice. It seemed a world from which vegetation had been banished; nothing existed except smoke, shale, ice, mud, ashes, and foul water. But even Wigan is beautiful compared with Sheffield. Sheffield, I suppose, could justly claim to be called the ugliest town in the Old World: its inhabitants, who want it to be pre-eminent in everything, very likely do make that claim for it. It has a population of half a million and it contains fewer decent buildings than the average East Anglian village of five hundred. And the stench! If at rare moments you stop smelling sulphur it is because you have begun smelling gas. Even the shallow river that runs through the town is usually bright yellow with some chemical or other. Once I halted in the street and counted the factory chimneys I could see; there were thirty-three of them, but there would have been far more if the air had not been obscured by smoke. One scene especially lingers in my mind. A frightful patch of waste ground (somehow, up there, a patch of waste ground attains a squalor that would be impossible even in London) trampled bare of grass and littered with newspapers and old saucepans. To the right an isolated row of gaunt four-roomed houses, dark red, blackened by smoke. To the left an interminable vista of factory chimneys, chimney beyond chimney, fading away into a dim blackish haze. Behind me a railway embankment made of the slag from furnaces. In front, across the patch of waste ground, a cubical building of red and yellow brick, with the sign 'Thomas Grocock, Haulage Contractor'.

At night, when you cannot see the hideous shapes of the houses and the blackness of everything, a town like Sheffield assumes a kind of sinister

magnificence. Sometimes the drifts of smoke are rosy with sulphur, and
serrated flames, like circular saws, squeeze themselves out from beneath
the cowls of the foundry chimneys. Through the open doors of foundries
you see fiery serpents of iron being hauled to and fro by redlit boys, and
you hear the whizz and thump of steam hammers and the scream of the
iron under the blow. The pottery towns are almost equally ugly in a pettier
way. Right in among the rows of tiny blackened houses, part of the street
as it were, are the 'pot banks' – conical brick chimneys like gigantic
burgundy bottles buried in the soil and belching their smoke almost in
your face. You come upon monstrous clay chasms hundreds of feet across
and almost as deep, with little rusty tubs creeping on chain railways up
one side, and on the other workmen clinging like samphire-gatherers and
cutting into the face of the cliff with their picks. I passed that way in
snowy weather, and even the snow was black. The best thing one can say
for the pottery towns is that they are fairly small and stop abruptly. Less
than ten miles away you can stand in undefiled country, on the almost
naked hills, and the pottery towns are only a smudge in the distance.

When you contemplate such ugliness as this, there are two questions
that strike you. First, is it inevitable? Secondly, does it matter?

I do not believe that there is anything inherently and unavoidably ugly
about industrialism. A factory or even a gasworks is not obliged of its own
nature to be ugly, any more than a palace or a dog-kennel or a cathedral.
It all depends on the architectural tradition of the period. The industrial
towns of the North are ugly because they happen to have been built at a
time when modern methods of steel-construction and smoke-abatement
were unknown, and when everyone was too busy making money to think
about anything else. They go on being ugly largely because the Northerners
have got used to that kind of thing and do not notice it. Many of the
people in Sheffield or Manchester, if they smelled the air along the Cornish
cliffs, would probably declare that it had no taste in it. But since the war,
industry has tended to shift southward and in doing so has grown almost
comely. The typical post-war factory is not a gaunt barrack or an awful
chaos of blackness and belching chimneys; it is a glittering white structure
of concrete, glass, and steel, surrounded by green lawns and beds of tulips.
Look at the factories you pass as you travel out of London on the G.W.R.;
they may not be aesthetic triumphs but certainly they are not ugly in the
same way as the Sheffield gasworks. But in any case, though the ugliness
of industrialism is the most obvious thing about it and the thing every
newcomer exclaims against, I doubt whether it is centrally important. And
perhaps it is not even desirable, industrialism being what it is, that it

should learn to disguise itself as something else. As Mr Aldous Huxley has truly remarked, a dark Satanic mill ought to look like a dark Satanic mill and not like the temple of mysterious and splendid gods. Moreover, even in the worst of the industrial towns one sees a great deal that is not ugly in the narrow aesthetic sense. A belching chimney or a stinking slum is repulsive chiefly because it implies warped lives and ailing children. Look at it from a purely aesthetic standpoint and it may have a certain macabre appeal. I find that anything outrageously strange generally ends by fascinating me even when I abominate it. The landscapes of Burma, which, when I was among them, so appalled me as to assume the qualities of nightmare, afterwards stayed so hauntingly in my mind that I was obliged to write a novel about them to get rid of them. (In all novels about the East the scenery is the real subject-matter.) It would probably be quite easy to extract a sort of beauty, as Arnold Bennett did, from the blackness of the industrial towns; one can easily imagine Baudelaire, for instance, writing a poem about a slag-heap. But the beauty or ugliness of industrialism hardly matters. Its real evil lies far deeper and is quite uneradicable. It is important to remember this, because there is always a temptation to think that industrialism is harmless so long as it is clean and orderly.

But when you go to the industrial North you are conscious, quite apart from the unfamiliar scenery, of entering a strange country. This is partly because of certain real differences which do exist, but still more because of the North – South antithesis which has been rubbed into us for such a long time past. There exists in England a curious cult of Northernness, sort of Northern snobbishness. A Yorkshireman in the South will always take care to let you know that he regards you as an inferior. If you ask him why, he will explain that it is only in the North that life is 'real' life, that the industrial work done in the North is the only 'real' work, that the North is inhabited by 'real' people, the South merely by rentiers and their parasites. The Northerner has 'grit', he is grim, 'dour', plucky, warm-hearted, and democratic; the Southerner is snobbish, effeminate, and lazy – that at any rate is the theory. Hence the Southerner goes north, at any rate for the first time, with the vague inferiority-complex of a civilized man venturing among savages, while the Yorkshireman, like the Scotchman, comes to London in the spirit of a barbarian out for loot. And feelings of this kind, which are the result of tradition, are not affected by visible facts. Just as an Englishman five feet four inches high and twenty-nine inches round the chest feels that as an Englishman he is the physical superior of Carnera (Carnera being a Dago), so also with the Northerner and the Southerner. I remember a weedy little Yorkshireman, who would

almost certainly have run away if a fox-terrier had snapped at him, telling
me that in the South of England he felt 'like a wild invader'. But the cult
is often adopted by people who are not by birth Northerners themselves.
A year or two ago a friend of mine, brought up in the South but now
living in the North, was driving me through Suffolk in a car. We passed
through a rather beautiful village. He glanced disapprovingly at the
cottages and said:

'Of course most of the villages in Yorkshire are hideous; but the Yorkshiremen
are splendid chaps. Down here it's just the other way about – beautiful villages
and rotten people. All the people in those cottages there are worthless, absolutely
worthless.'

I could not help inquiring whether he happened to know anybody in
that village. No, he did not know them; but because this was East Anglia
they were obviously worthless. Another friend of mine, again a Southerner
by birth, loses no opportunity of praising the North to the detriment of
the South. Here is an extract from one of his letters to me:

I am in Clitheroe, Lancs. . . . I think running water is much more attractive in
moor and mountain country than in the fat and sluggish South. 'The smug and
silver Trent,' Shakespeare says; and the South-er the smugger, I say.

Here you have an interesting example of the Northern cult. Not only
are you and I and everyone else in the South of England written off as
'fat and sluggish', but even water when it gets north of a certain latitude,
ceases to be H_2O and becomes something mystically superior. But the
interest of this passage is that its writer is an extremely intelligent
man of 'advanced' opinions who would have nothing but contempt for
nationalism in its ordinary form. Put to him some such proposition as
'One Britisher is worth three foreigners', and he would repudiate it with
horror. But when it is a question of North versus South, he is quite ready
to generalize. *All* nationalistic distinctions – all claims to be better than
somebody else because you have a different-shaped skull or speak a
different dialect – are entirely spurious, but they are important so long as
people believe in them. There is no doubt about the Englishman's inbred
conviction that those who live to the south of him are his inferiors; even
our foreign policy is governed by it to some extent. I think, therefore, that
it is worth pointing out when and why it came into being.
    When nationalism first became a religion, the English looked at the
map, and, noticing that their island lay very high in the Northern
Hemisphere, evolved the pleasing theory that the further north you live

the more virtuous you become. The histories I was given when I was a little boy generally started off by explaining in the naivest way that a cold climate made people energetic while a hot one made them lazy, and hence the defeat of the Spanish Armada. This nonsense about the superior energy of the English (actually the laziest people in Europe) has been current for at least a hundred years. 'Better is it for us', writes a Quarterly Reviewer of 1827, 'to be condemned to labour for our country's good than to luxuriate amid olives, vines, and vices.' 'Olives, vines, and vices' sums up the normal English attitude towards the Latin races. In the mythology of Carlyle, Creasey, etc., the Northerner ('Teutonic', later 'Nordic') is pictured as a hefty, vigorous chap with blond moustaches and pure morals, while the Southerner is sly, cowardly, and licentious. This theory was never pushed to its logical end, which would have meant assuming that the finest people in the world were the Eskimos, but it did involve admitting that the people who lived to the north of us were superior to ourselves. Hence, partly, the cult of Scotland and of Scotch things which has so deeply marked English life during the past fifty years. But it was the industrialization of the North that gave the North – South antithesis its peculiar slant. Until comparatively recently the northern part of England was the backward and feudal part, and such industry as existed was concentrated in London and the South-East. In the Civil War for instance, roughly speaking a war of money versus feudalism, the North and West were for the King and the South and East for the Parliament. But with the increasing use of coal industry passed to the North, and there grew up a new type of man, the self-made Northern business man – the Mr Rouncewell and Mr Bounderby of Dickens. The Northern business man, with his hateful 'get on or get out' philosophy, was the dominant figure of the nineteenth century, and as a sort of tyrannical corpse he rules us still. This is the type edified by Arnold Bennett – the type who starts off with half a crown and ends up with fifty thousand pounds, and whose chief pride is to be an even greater boor after he has made his money than before. On analysis his sole virtue turns out to be a talent for making money. We were bidden to admire him because though he might be narrow-minded, sordid, ignorant, grasping, and uncouth, he had 'grit', he 'got on'; in other words, he knew how to make money.

   This kind of cant is nowadays a pure anachronism, for the Northern business man is no longer prosperous. But traditions are not killed by facts, and the tradition of Northern 'grit' lingers. It is still dimly felt that a Northerner will 'get on', i.e. make money, where a Southerner will fail. At the back of the mind of every Yorkshireman and every Scotchman

who comes to London is a sort of Dick Whittington picture of himself as
the boy who starts off by selling newspapers and ends up as Lord Mayor.
And that, really, is at the bottom of his bumptiousness. But where one
can make a great mistake is in imagining that this feeling extends to the
genuine working class. When I first went to Yorkshire, some years ago, I
imagined that I was going to a country of boors. I was used to the London
Yorkshireman with his interminable harangues and his pride in the
supposed raciness of his dialect (' "A stitch in time saves nine", as we say
in the West Riding'), and I expected to meet with a good deal of rudeness.
But I met with nothing of the kind, and least of all among the miners.
Indeed the Lancashire and Yorkshire miners treated me with a kindness
and courtesy that were even embarrassing; for if there is one type of man
to whom I do feel myself inferior, it is a coal-miner. Certainly no one
showed any sign of despising me for coming from a different part of the
country. This has its importance when one remembers that the English
regional snobberies are nationalism in miniature; for it suggests that place-
snobbery is not a working-class characteristic.

There is nevertheless a real difference between North and South, and
there is at least a tinge of truth in that picture of Southern England as
one enormous Brighton inhabited by lounge-lizards. For climatic reasons
the parasitic dividend-drawing class tend to settle in the South. In a
Lancashire cotton-town you could probably go for months on end without
once hearing an 'educated' accent, whereas there can hardly be a town in
the South of England where you could throw a brick without hitting the
niece of a bishop. Consequently, with no petty gentry to set the pace, the
bourgeoisification of the working class, though it is taking place in the
North, is taking place more slowly. All the Northern accents, for instance,
persist strongly, while the Southern ones are collapsing before the movies
and the B.B.C. Hence your 'educated' accent stamps you rather as a
foreigner than as a chunk of the petty gentry; and this is an immense
advantage, for it makes it much easier to get into contact with the working
class.

But is it ever possible to be really intimate with the working class? I
shall have to discuss that later; I will only say here that I do not think it
is possible. But undoubtedly it is easier in the North than it would be in
the South to meet working-class people on approximately equal terms. It
is fairly easy to live in a miner's house and be accepted as one of the
family; with, say, a farm labourer in the Southern counties it probably
would be impossible. I have seen just enough of the working class to avoid
idealizing them, but I do know that you can learn a great deal in a

working-class home, if only you can get there. The essential point is that
your middle-class ideals and prejudices are tested by contact with others
which are not necessarily better but are certainly different.

Take for instance the different attitude towards the family. A working-
class family hangs together as a middle-class one does, but the relationship
is far less tyrannical. A working man has not that deadly weight of family
prestige hanging round his neck like a millstone. I have pointed out earlier
that a middle-class person goes utterly to pieces under the influence of
poverty; and this is generally due to the behaviour of his family – to the
fact that he has scores of relations nagging and badgering him night and
day for failing to 'get on'. The fact that the working class know how to
combine and the middle class don't is probably due to their different
conceptions of family loyalty. You cannot have an effective trade union
of middle-class workers, because in times of strikes almost every middle-
class wife would be egging her husband on to blackleg and get the other
fellow's job. Another working-class characteristic, disconcerting at first,
is their plain-spokenness towards anyone they regard as an equal. If you
offer a working man something he doesn't want, he tells you that he doesn't
want it; a middle-class person would accept it to avoid giving offence. And
again, take the working-class attitude towards 'education'. How different
it is from ours, and how immensely sounder! Working people often have
a vague reverence for learning in others, but where 'education' touches
their own lives they see through it and reject it by a healthy instinct. The
time was when I used to lament over quite imaginary pictures of lads of
fourteen dragged protesting from their lessons and set to work at dismal
jobs. It seemed to me dreadful that the doom of a 'job' should descend
upon anyone at fourteen. Of course I know now that there is not one
working-class boy in a thousand who does not pine for the day when he
will leave school. He wants to be doing real work, not wasting his time on
ridiculous rubbish like history and geography. To the working class, the
notion of staying at school till you are nearly grown-up seems merely
contemptible and unmanly. The idea of a great big boy of eighteen, who
ought to be bringing a pound a week home to his parents, going to school
in a ridiculous uniform and even being caned for not doing his lessons!
Just fancy a working-class boy of eighteen allowing himself to be caned!
He is a man when the other is still a baby. Ernest Pontifex, in Samuel
Butler's *Way of All Flesh*, after he had had a few glimpses of real life,
looked back on his public school and university education and found it a
'sickly, debilitating debauch'. There is much in middle-class life that looks
sickly and debilitating when you see it from a working-class angle.

In a working-class home – I am not thinking at the moment of the unemployed, but of comparatively prosperous homes – you breathe a warm, decent, deeply human atmosphere which it is not so easy to find elsewhere. I should say that a manual worker, if he is in steady work and drawing good wages – an 'if' which gets bigger and bigger – has a better chance of being happy than an 'educated' man. His home life seems to fall more naturally into a sane and comely shape. I have often been struck by the peculiar easy completeness, the perfect symmetry as it were, of a working-class interior at its best. Especially on winter evenings after tea, when the fire glows in the open range and dances mirrored in the steel fender, when Father, in shirt-sleeves, sits in the rocking chair at one side of the fire reading the racing finals, and Mother sits on the other with her sewing, and the children are happy with a pennorth of mint humbugs, and the dog lolls roasting himself on the rag mat – it is a good place to be in, provided that you can be not only in it but sufficiently *of* it to be taken for granted.

This scene is still reduplicated in a majority of English homes, though not in so many as before the war. Its happiness depends mainly upon one question – whether Father is in work. But notice that the picture I have called up, of a working-class family sitting round the coal fire after kippers and strong tea, belongs only to our own moment of time and could not belong either to the future or the past. Skip forward two hundred years into the Utopian future, and the scene is totally different. Hardly one of the things I have imagined will still be there. In that age when there is no manual labour and everyone is 'educated', it is hardly likely that Father will still be a rough man with enlarged hands who likes to sit in shirt-sleeves and says 'Ah wur coomin' oop street'. And there won't be a coal fire in the grate, only some kind of invisible heater. The furniture will be made of rubber, glass, and steel. If there are still such things as evening papers there will certainly be no racing news in them, for gambling will be meaningless in a world where there is no poverty and the horse will have vanished from the face of the earth. Dogs, too, will have been suppressed on grounds of hygiene. And there won't be so many children, either, if the birth-controllers have their way. But move backwards into the Middle Ages and you are in a world almost equally foreign. A windowless hut, a wood fire which smokes in your face because there is no chimney, mouldy bread, 'Poor John', lice, scurvy, a yearly child-birth and a yearly child-death, and the priest terrifying you with tales of Hell.

Curiously enough it is *not* the triumphs of modern engineering, nor the radio, nor the cinematograph, nor the five thousand novels which are published yearly, nor the crowds at Ascot and the Eton and Harrow match, but the memory of working-class interiors – especially as I sometimes saw them in my childhood before the war, when England was still prosperous – that reminds me that our age has not been altogether a bad one to live in.

PART TWO

8

THE road from Mandalay to Wigan is a long one and the reasons for taking it are not immediately clear.

In the earlier chapters of this book I have given a rather fragmentary account of various things I saw in the coal areas of Lancashire and Yorkshire. I went there partly because I wanted to see what mass-unemployment is like at its worst, partly in order to see the most typical section of the English working class at close quarters. This was necessary to me as part of my approach to Socialism, for before you can be sure whether you are genuinely in favour of Socialism, you have got to decide whether things at present are tolerable or not tolerable, and you have got to take up a definite attitude on the terribly difficult issue of class. Here I shall have to digress and explain how my own attitude towards the class question was developed. Obviously this involves writing a certain amount of autobiography, and I would not do it if I did not think that I am sufficiently typical of my class, or rather sub-caste, to have a certain symptomatic importance.

I was born into what you might describe as the lower-upper-middle class. The upper-middle class, which had its heyday in the eighties and nineties, with Kipling as its poet laureate, was a sort of mound of wreckage left behind when the tide of Victorian prosperity receded. Or perhaps it would be better to change the metaphor and describe it not as a mound but as a layer – the layer of society lying between £2000 and £300 a year: my own family was not far from the bottom. You notice that I define it in terms of money, because that is always the quickest way of making yourself understood. Nevertheless, the essential point about the English class-system is that it is *not* entirely explicable in terms of money. Roughly speaking it is a money-stratification, but it is also interpenetrated by a sort of shadowy caste-system; rather like a jerry-built modern bungalow haunted by medieval ghosts. Hence the fact that the upper-middle class extends or extended to incomes as low as £300 a year – to incomes, that is, much lower than those of merely middle-class people with no social pretensions. Probably there are countries where you can predict a man's opinions from his income, but it is never quite safe to do so in England;

you have always got to take his traditions into consideration as well. A naval officer and his grocer very likely have the same income, but they are not equivalent persons and they would only be on the same side in very large issues such as a war or a general strike – possibly not even then.

Of course it is obvious now that the upper-middle class is done for. In every country town in Southern England, not to mention the dreary wastes of Kensington and Earl's Court, those who knew it in the days of its glory are dying, vaguely embittered by a world which has not behaved as it ought. I never open one of Kipling's books or go into one of the huge dull shops which were once the favourite haunt of the upper-middle class, without thinking 'Change and decay in all around I see'. But before the war the upper-middle class, though already none too prosperous, still felt sure of itself. Before the war you were either a gentleman or not a gentleman, and if you were a gentleman you struggled to behave as such, whatever your income might be. Between those with £400 a year and those with £2000 or even £1000 a year there was a great gulf fixed, but it was a gulf which those with £400 a year did their best to ignore. Probably the distinguishing mark of the upper-middle class was that its traditions were not to any extent commercial, but mainly military, official, and professional. People in this class owned no land, but they felt that they were landowners in the sight of God and kept up a semi-aristocratic outlook by going into the professions and the fighting services rather than into trade. Small boys used to count the plum stones on their plates and foretell their destiny by chanting, 'Army, Navy, Church, Medicine, Law'; and even of these 'Medicine' was faintly inferior to the others and only put in for the sake of symmetry. To belong to this class when you were at the £400 a year level was a queer business, for it meant that your gentility was almost purely theoretical. You lived, so to speak, at two levels simultaneously. Theoretically you knew all about servants and how to tip them, although in practice you had one, at most, two resident servants. Theoretically you knew how to wear your clothes and how to order a dinner, although in practice you could never afford to go to a decent tailor or a decent restaurant. Theoretically you knew how to shoot and ride, although in practice you had no horses to ride and not an inch of ground to shoot over. It was this that explained the attraction of India (more recently Kenya, Nigeria, etc.) for the lower-upper-middle class. The people who went there as soldiers and officials did not go there to make money, for a soldier or an official does not want money; they went there because in India, with cheap horses, free shooting, and hordes of black servants, it was so easy to play at being a gentleman.

In the kind of shabby-genteel family that I am talking about there is far more *consciousness* of poverty than in any working-class family above the level of the dole. Rent and clothes and school-bills are an unending nightmare, and every luxury, even a glass of beer, is an unwarrantable extravagance. Practically the whole family income goes in keeping up appearances. It is obvious that people of this kind are in an anomalous position, and one might be tempted to write them off as mere exceptions and therefore unimportant. Actually, however, they are or were fairly numerous. Most clergymen and schoolmasters, for instance, nearly all Anglo-Indian officials, a sprinkling of soldiers and sailors, and a fair number of professional men and artists, fall into this category. But the real importance of this class is that they are the shock-absorbers of the bourgeoisie. The real bourgeoisie, those in the £2000 a year class and over, have their money as a thick layer of padding between themselves and the class they plunder; in so far as they are aware of the Lower Orders at all they are aware of them as employees, servants, and tradesmen. But it is quite different for the poor devils lower down who are struggling to live genteel lives on what are virtually working-class incomes. These last are forced into close and, in a sense, intimate contact with the working class, and I suspect it is from them that the traditional upper-class attitude towards 'common' people is derived.

And what is this attitude? An attitude of sniggering superiority punctuated by bursts of vicious hatred. Look at any number of *Punch* during the past thirty years. You will find it everywhere taken for granted that a working-class person, as such, is a figure of fun, except at odd moments when he shows signs of being too prosperous, whereupon he ceases to be a figure of fun and becomes a demon. It is no use wasting breath in denouncing this attitude. It is better to consider how it has arisen, and to do that one has got to realize what the working classes look like to those who live among them but have different habits and traditions.

A shabby genteel family is in much the same position as a family of 'poor whites' living in a street where everyone else is a Negro. In such circumstances you have got to cling to your gentility because it is the only thing you have; and meanwhile you are hated for your stuck-up-ness and for the accent and manners which stamp you as one of the boss class. I was very young, not much more than six, when I first became aware of class-distinctions. Before that age my chief heroes had generally been working-class people, because they always seemed to do such interesting things, such as being fishermen and blacksmiths and bricklayers. I remember the farm hands on a farm in Cornwall who used to let me ride on the drill when they were sowing turnips and would sometimes catch the ewes and milk them to give me a drink; and the workmen building the new house next door, who let me play with the wet mortar and from whom I first learned the word 'b—'; and the plumber up the road with whose children I used to go out bird-nesting. But it was not long before I was forbidden to play with the plumber's children; they were 'common' and I was told to keep away from them. This was snobbish, if you like, but it was also necessary, for middle-class people cannot afford to let their children grow up with vulgar accents. So, very early, the working class ceased to be a race of friendly and wonderful beings and became a race of enemies. We realized that they hated us, but we could never understand why, and naturally we set it down to pure, vicious malignity. To me in my early boyhood, to nearly all children of families like mine, 'common' people seemed almost sub-human. They had coarse faces, hideous accents, and gross manners, they hated everyone who was not like themselves, and if they got half a chance they would insult you in brutal ways. That was our view of them, and though it was false it was understandable. For one must remember that before the war there was much more *overt* class-hatred in England than there is now. In those days you were quite likely to be insulted simply for looking like a member of the upper classes; nowadays, on the other hand, you are more likely to be fawned upon. Anyone over thirty can remember the time when it was impossible for a well-dressed person to walk through a slum street without being hooted at. Whole quarters of big towns were considered unsafe because of 'hooligans' (now almost an extinct type), and the London gutter-boy everywhere, with his loud voice and lack of intellectual scruples, could make life a misery for people who considered it beneath their dignity to answer back. A recurrent terror of my holidays, when I was a small boy, was the gangs of 'cads' who were liable to set upon you five or ten to one. In term time, on the other hand, it was we who were in the majority and the 'cads' who were oppressed; I remember a couple of savage mass-battles in the cold winter of 1916–17. And this tradition of open hostility between upper and lower class had apparently been the same for at least a century past. A typical joke in *Punch* in the sixties is a picture of a small, nervous-looking gentleman riding through a slum street and a crowd of street-boys closing in on him with shouts ' 'Ere comes a swell! Let's frighten 'is 'oss!' Just fancy the street boys trying to frighten his horse now! They would be much likelier to hang round him in vague hopes of a tip. During the past dozen years the English working class have grown servile with a rather horrifying rapidity. It was bound to happen, for the frightful weapon of unemployment has cowed them. Before the war their economic position was comparatively strong, for though there was no dole to fall back upon, there was not much unemployment, and the power of the boss class was not so obvious as it is now. A man did not see ruin staring him in the face every time he cheeked a 'toff', and naturally he did cheek a 'toff' whenever it seemed safe to do so. G.J. Renier, in his book on Oscar Wilde, points out that the strange, obscene burst of popular fury which followed the Wilde trial was essentially social in character. The London mob had caught a member of the upper classes on the hop, and they took care to keep him hopping. All this was natural and even proper. If you treat people as the English working class have been treated during the past two centuries, you must expect them to resent it. On the other hand the children of shabby-genteel families could not be blamed if they grew up with a hatred of the working class, typified for them by prowling gangs of 'cads'.

But there was another and more serious difficulty. Here you come to the real secret of class distinctions in the West – the real reason why a European of bourgeois upbringing, even when he calls himself a Communist, cannot without a hard effort think of a working man as his equal. It is summed up in four frightful words which people nowadays are chary of uttering, but which were bandied about quite freely in my childhood. The words were: *The lower classes smell.*

That was what we were taught – *the lower classes smell.* And here, obviously, you are at an impassable barrier. For no feeling of like or dislike is quite so fundamental as a *physical* feeling. Race-hatred, religious hatred, differences of education, of temperament, of intellect, even differences of moral code, can be got over; but physical repulsion cannot. You can have an affection for a murderer or a sodomite, but you cannot have an affection for a man whose breath stinks – habitually stinks, I mean. However well you may wish him, however much you may admire his mind and character, if his breath stinks he is horrible and in your heart of hearts you will hate him. It may not greatly matter if the average middle-class person is brought up to believe that the working classes are ignorant, lazy, drunken, boorish, and dishonest; it is when he is brought up to believe that they are dirty that the harm is done. And in my childhood we *were* brought up to believe that they were dirty. Very early in life you acquired the idea that there was something subtly repulsive about a working-class body; you would not get nearer to it than you could help. You watched a great sweaty navvy walking down the road with his pick over his shoulder; you looked at his discoloured shirt and his corduroy trousers stiff with the dirt of a decade; you thought of those nests and layers of greasy rags below, and, under all, the unwashed body, brown all over (that was how I used to imagine it), with its strong, bacon-like reek. You watched a tramp taking off his boots in a ditch – ugh! It did not seriously occur to you that the tramp might not enjoy having black feet. And even 'lower-class' people whom you knew to be quite clean – servants for instance – were faintly unappetizing. The smell of their sweat, the very texture of their skins, were mysteriously different from yours.

Everyone who has grown up pronouncing his aitches and in a house with a bathroom and one servant is likely to have grown up with these feelings; hence the chasmic, impassable quality of class-distinctions in the West. It is queer how seldom this is admitted. At the moment I can think of only one book where it is set forth without humbug, and that is Mr Somerset Maugham's *On a Chinese Screen*. Mr Maugham describes a high Chinese official arriving at a wayside inn and blustering and calling everybody names in order to impress upon them that he is a supreme dignitary and they are only worms. Five minutes later, having asserted his dignity in the way he thinks proper, he is eating his dinner in perfect amity with the baggage coolies. As an official he feels that he has got to make his presence felt, but he has no feeling that the coolies are of different clay from himself. I have observed countless similar scenes in Burma. Among Mongolians – among all Asiatics, for all I know – there is a sort of natural equality, an easy intimacy between man and man, which is simply unthinkable in the West. Mr Maugham adds:

In the West we are divided from our fellows by our sense of smell. The working man is our master, inclined to rule us with an iron hand, but it cannot be denied that he stinks: none can wonder at it, for a bath in the dawn when you have to hurry to your work before the factory bell rings is no pleasant thing, nor does heavy labour tend to sweetness; and you do not change your linen more than you can help when the week's washing must be done by a sharp-tongued wife. I do not blame the working man because he stinks, but stink he does. It makes social intercourse difficult to persons of sensitive nostril. The matutinal tub divides the classes more effectually than birth, wealth, or education.

Meanwhile, *do* the 'lower classes' smell? Of course, as a whole, they are dirtier than the upper classes. They are bound to be, considering the circumstances in which they live, for even at this late date less than half the houses in England have bathrooms. Besides, the habit of washing yourself all over every day is a very recent one in Europe, and the working classes are generally more conservative than the bourgeoisie. But the English are growing visibly cleaner, and we may hope that in a hundred years they will be almost as clean as the Japanese. It is a pity that those who idealize the working class so often think it necessary to praise every working-class characteristic and therefore to pretend that dirtiness is somehow meritorious in itself. Here, curiously enough, the Socialist and the sentimental democratic Catholic of the type of Chesterton sometimes join hands; both will tell you that dirtiness is healthy and 'natural' and cleanliness is a mere fad or at best a luxury.* They seem not to see that they are merely giving colour to the notion that working-class people are dirty from choice and not from necessity. Actually, people who have access to a bath will generally use it. But the essential thing is that middle-class people *believe* that the working class are dirty – you see from the passage quoted above that Mr Maugham himself believes it – and, what is worse, that they are somehow *inherently* dirty. As a child, one of the most dreadful things I could imagine was to drink out of a bottle after a navvy. Once when I was thirteen, I was in a train coming from a market town, and the third-class carriage was packed full of shepherds and pig-men who had been selling their beasts. Somebody produced a quart bottle of beer and passed it round; it travelled from mouth to mouth to mouth, everyone taking a swig. I cannot describe the horror I felt as that bottle worked its way towards me. If I drank from it after all those lower-class male mouths I felt certain I should vomit; on the other hand, if they offered it to me I dared not refuse for fear of offending them – you see here how the middle-class squeamishness works both ways. Nowadays, thank God, I have no feelings of that kind. A working man's body, as such, is no more repulsive to me than a millionaire's. I still don't like drinking out of a cup or bottle after another person – another man, I mean; with women I don't mind – but at least the question of class does not enter. It was rubbing shoulders with the tramps that cured me of it. Tramps are not really very dirty as English people go, but they have the name for being dirty, and when you have shared a bed with a tramp and drunk tea out of the same snuff-tin, you feel that you have seen the worst and the worst has no terrors for you.

I have dwelt on these subjects because they are vitally important. To get rid of class-distinctions you have got to start by understanding how one class appears when seen through the eyes of another. It is useless to say that the middle classes are 'snobbish' and leave it at that. You get no

* According to Chesterton, dirtiness is merely a kind of 'discomfort' and therefore ranks as self-mortification. Unfortunately, the discomfort of dirtiness is chiefly suffered by other people. It is not really very uncomfortable to be dirty – not nearly so uncomfortable as having a cold bath on a winter morning.

further if you do not realize that snobbishness is bound up with a species of idealism. It derives from the early training in which a middle-class child is taught almost simultaneously to wash his neck, to be ready to die for his country, and to despise the 'lower classes'.

Here I shall be accused of being behind the times, for I was a child before and during the war and it may be claimed that children nowadays are brought up with more enlightened notions. It is probably true that class-feeling is for the moment a very little less bitter than it was. The working class are submissive where they used to be openly hostile, and the post-war manufacture of cheap clothes and the general softening of manners have toned down the surface differences between class and class. But undoubtedly the essential feeling is still there. Every middle-class person has a dormant class-prejudice which needs only a small thing to arouse it; and if he is over forty he probably has a firm conviction that his own class has been sacrificed to the class below. Suggest to the average unthinking person of gentle birth who is struggling to keep up appearances on four or five hundred a year that he is a member of an exploiting parasite class, and he will think you are mad. In perfect sincerity he will point out to you a dozen ways in which he is worse-off than a working man. In his eyes the workers are not a submerged race of slaves, they are a sinister flood creeping upwards to engulf himself and his friends and his family and to sweep all culture and all decency out of existence. Hence that queer watchful anxiety lest the working class shall grow too prosperous. In a number of *Punch* soon after the war, when coal was still fetching high prices, there is a picture of four or five miners with grim, sinister faces riding in a cheap motor-car. A friend they are passing calls out and asks them where they have borrowed it. They answer, 'We've bought the thing!' This, you see, is 'good enough for *Punch*'; for miners to buy a motor-car, even one car between four or five of them, is a monstrosity, a sort of crime against nature. That was the attitude of a dozen years ago, and I see no evidence of any fundamental change. The notion that the working class have been absurdly pampered, hopelessly demoralized by doles, old age pensions, free education, etc., is still widely held; it has merely been a little shaken, perhaps, by the recent recognition that unemployment does exist. For quantities of middle-class people, probably for a large majority of those over fifty, the typical working man still rides to the Labour Exchange on a motor-bike and keeps coal in his bath-tub: 'And, if you'll believe it, my dear, they actually *get married* on the dole!'

The reason why class-hatred seems to be diminishing is that nowadays it tends not to get into print, partly owing to the mealy-mouthed habits

of our time, partly because newspapers and even books now have to appeal
to a working-class public. As a rule you can best study it in private
conversations. But if you want some printed examples, it is worth having
a look at the *obiter dicta* of the late Professor Saintsbury. Saintsbury was
a very learned man and along certain lines a judicious literary critic, but
when he talked of political or economic matters he only differed from the
rest of his class by the fact that he was too thick-skinned and had been
born too early to see any reason for pretending to common decency.
According to Saintsbury, unemployment insurance was simply 'contri-
buting to the support of lazy ne'er-do-wells', and the whole trade union
movement was no more than a kind of organized mendicancy:

'Pauper' is almost actionable now, is it not, when used as a word? though to *be*
paupers, in the sense of being wholly or partly supported at the expense of other
people, is the ardent, and to a considerable extent achieved, aspiration of a large
proportion of our population, and of an entire political party.

(Second Scrap Book)

It is to be noticed, however, that Saintsbury recognizes that unemployment is bound to exist, and, in fact, thinks that it ought to exist, so long
as the unemployed are made to suffer as much as possible:

Is not 'casual' labour the very secret and safety-valve of a safe and sound labour-
system generally?
. . . In a complicated industrial and commercial state constant employment at
regular wages is impossible; while dole-supported unemployment, at anything like
the wages of employment, is demoralizing to begin with and ruinous at its more
or less quickly arriving end.

(Last Scrap Book)

What exactly is to happen to the 'casual labourers' when no casual
labour happens to be available is not made clear. Presumably (Saintsbury
speaks approvingly of 'good Poor Laws') they are to go into the workhouse or sleep in the streets. As to the notion that every human being
ought as a matter of course to have the chance of earning at least a
tolerable livelihood, Saintsbury dismisses it with contempt:

Even the 'right to live'. . . extends no further than the right to protection against
murder. Charity certainly will, morality possibly may, and public utility perhaps
ought to add to this protection supererogatory provision for continuance of life;
but it is questionable whether strict justice demands it.
As for the insane doctrine that being born in a country gives some right to the
possession of the soil of that country, it hardly requires notice.

(Last Scrap Book)

It is worth reflecting for a moment upon the beautiful implications of this last passage. The interest of passages like these (and they are scattered all through Saintsbury's work) lies in their having been printed at all. Most people are a little shy of putting that kind of thing on paper. But what Saintsbury is saying here is what any little worm with a fairly safe five hundred a year *thinks*, and therefore in a way one must admire him for saying it. It takes a lot of guts to be *openly* such a skunk as that.

This is the outlook of a confessed reactionary. But how about the middle-class person whose views are not reactionary but 'advanced'? Beneath his revolutionary mask, is he really so different from the other?

A middle-class person embraces Socialism and perhaps even joins the Communist Party. How much real difference does it make? Obviously, living within the framework of capitalist society, he has got to go on earning his living, and one cannot blame him if he clings to his bourgeois economic status. But is there any change in his tastes, his habits, his manners, his imaginative background – his 'ideology', in Communist jargon? Is there *any* change in him except that he now votes Labour, or, when possible, Communist at the elections? It is noticeable that he still habitually associates with his own class; he is vastly more at home with a member of his own class, who thinks him a dangerous Bolshie, than with a member of the working class who supposedly agrees with him; his tastes in food, wine, clothes, books, pictures, music, ballet, are still recognizably bourgeois tastes; most significant of all, he invariably marries into his own class. Look at any bourgeois Socialist. Look at Comrade X, member of the C.P.G.B. and author of *Marxism for Infants*. Comrade X, it so happens, is an old Etonian. He would be ready to die on the barricades, in theory anyway, but you notice that he still leaves his bottom waistcoat button undone. He idealizes the proletariat, but it is remarkable how little his habits resemble theirs. Perhaps once, out of sheer bravado, he has smoked a cigar with the band on, but it would be almost physically impossible for him to put pieces of cheese into his mouth on the point of his knife, or to sit indoors with his cap on, or even to drink his tea out of the saucer. I have known numbers of bourgeois Socialists, I have listened by the hour to their tirades against their own class, and yet never, not even once, have I met one who had picked up proletarian table-manners. Yet, after all, why not? Why should a man who thinks all virtue resides in the proletariat still take such pains to drink his soup silently? It can only be because in his heart he feels that proletarian manners are disgusting. So you see he is still responding to the training of his childhood, when he was taught to hate, fear, and despise the working class.

9

WHEN I was fourteen or fifteen I was an odious little snob, but no worse than other boys of my own age and class. I suppose there is no place in the world where snobbery is quite so ever-present or where it is cultivated in such refined and subtle forms as in an English public school. Here at least one cannot say that English 'education' fails to do its job. You forget your Latin and Greek within a few months of leaving school – I studied Greek for eight or ten years, and now, at thirty-three, I cannot even repeat the Greek alphabet – but your snobbishness, unless you persistently root it out like the bindweed it is, sticks by you till your grave.

At school I was in a difficult position, for I was among boys who, for the most part, were much richer than myself, and I only went to an expensive public school because I happened to win a scholarship. This is the common experience of boys of the lower-upper-middle class, the sons of clergymen, Anglo-Indian officials, etc., and the effects it had on me were probably the usual ones. On the one hand it made me cling tighter than ever to my gentility; on the other hand it filled me with resentment against the boys whose parents were richer than mine and who took care to let me know it. I despised anyone who was not describable as a 'gentleman', but also I hated the hoggishly rich, especially those who had grown rich too recently. The correct and elegant thing, I felt, was to be of gentle birth but to have no money. This is part of the *credo* of the lower-upper-middle class. It has a romantic, Jacobite-in-exile feeling about it which is very comforting.

But those years, during and just after the war, were a queer time to be at school, for England was nearer revolution than she has been since or had been for a century earlier. Throughout almost the whole nation there was running a wave of revolutionary feeling which has since been reversed and forgotten, but which has left various deposits of sediment behind. Essentially, though of course one could not then see it in perspective, it was a revolt of youth against age, resulting directly from the war. In the war the young had been sacrificed and the old had behaved in a way which, even at this distance of time, is horrible to contemplate; they had been sternly patriotic in safe places while their sons went down like swathes of hay before the German machine guns. Moreover, the war had been conducted mainly by old men and had been conducted with supreme incompetence. By 1918 everyone under forty was in a bad temper with his elders, and the mood of anti-militarism which followed naturally upon the fighting was extended into a general revolt against orthodoxy and authority. At that time there was, among the young, a curious cult of hatred of 'old men'. The dominance of 'old men' was held to be responsible for every evil known to humanity, and every accepted institution from Scott's novels to the House of Lords was derided merely because 'old men' were in favour of it. For several years it was all the fashion to be a 'Bolshie', as people then called it. England was full of half-baked antinomian opinions. Pacifism, internationalism, humanitarianism of all kinds, feminism, free love, divorce-reform, atheism, birth-control – things like these were getting a better hearing than they would get in normal times. And of course the revolutionary mood extended to those who had been too young to fight, even to public schoolboys. At that time we all thought of ourselves as enlightened creatures of a new age, casting off the orthodoxy that had been forced upon us by those detested 'old men'. We retained, basically, the snobbish outlook of our class, we took it for granted that we could continue to draw our dividends or tumble into soft jobs, but also it seemed natural to us to be 'agin the Government'. We derided the O.T.C., the Christian religion, and perhaps even compulsory games and the Royal Family, and we did not realize that we were merely taking part in a worldwide gesture of distaste for war. Two incidents stick in my mind as examples of the queer revolutionary feeling of that time. One day the master who taught us English set us a kind of general knowledge paper of which one of the questions was, 'Whom do you consider the ten greatest men now living?' Of sixteen boys in the class (our average age was about seventeen) fifteen included Lenin in their list. This was at a snobbish expensive public school, and the date was 1920, when the horrors of the Russian Revolution was still fresh in everyone's mind. Also there were the so-called peace celebrations in 1919. Our elders had decided for us that we should celebrate peace in the traditional manner by whooping over the fallen foe. We were to march into the school-yard, carrying torches, and sing jingo songs of the type of 'Rule Britannia'. The boys – to their honour, I think – guyed the whole proceeding and sang blasphemous and seditious words to the tunes provided. I doubt whether things would happen in quite that manner now. Certainly the public schoolboys I meet nowadays, even the intelligent ones, are much more right-wing in their opinions than I and my contemporaries were fifteen years ago.

Hence, at the age of seventeen or eighteen, I was both a snob and a revolutionary. I was against all authority. I had read and re-read the entire published works of Shaw, Wells, and Galsworthy (at that time still regarded as dangerously 'advanced' writers), and I loosely described myself as a Socialist. But I had not much grasp of what Socialism meant, and no notion that the working class were human beings. At a distance, and through the medium of books – Jack London's *The People of the Abyss*, for instance – I could agonize over their sufferings, but I still hated them and despised them when I came anywhere near them. I was still revolted by their accents and infuriated by their habitual rudeness. One must remember that just then, immediately after the war, the English working class were in a fighting mood. That was the period of the great coal strikes, when a miner was thought of as a fiend incarnate and old ladies looked under their beds every night lest Robert Smillie should be concealed there. All through the war and for a little time afterwards there had been high wages and abundant employment; things were now returning to something worse than normal, and naturally the working class resisted. The men who had fought had been lured into the army by gaudy promises, and now they were coming home to a world where there were no jobs and not even any houses. Moreover, they had been at war and were coming home with the soldier's attitude to life, which is fundamentally, in spite of discipline, a lawless attitude. There was a turbulent feeling in the air. To that time belongs the song with the memorable refrain:

> There's nothing sure but
> The rich get richer and the poor get children;
> In the mean time,
> In between time,
> Ain't we got fun?

People had not yet settled down to a lifetime of unemployment mitigated by endless cups of tea. They still vaguely expected the Utopia for which they had fought, and even more than before they were openly hostile to the aitch-pronouncing class. So to the shock-absorbers of the bourgeoisie, such as myself, 'common people' still appeared brutal and repulsive. Looking back upon that period, I seem to have spent half the time in denouncing the capitalist system and the other half in raging over the insolence of bus-conductors.

When I was not yet twenty I went to Burma, in the Indian Imperial

Police. In an 'outpost of Empire' like Burma the class-question appeared at first sight to have been shelved. There was no obvious class-friction here, because the all-important thing was not whether you had been to one of the right schools but whether your skin was technically white. As a matter of fact most of the white men in Burma were not of the type who in England would be called 'gentlemen', but except for the common soldiers and a few nondescripts they lived lives appropriate to 'gentlemen' – had servants, that is, and called their evening meal 'dinner' – and officially they were regarded as being all of the same class. They were 'white men', in contra-distinction to the other and inferior class, the 'natives'. But one did not feel towards the 'natives' as one felt towards the 'lower classes' at home. The essential point was that the 'natives', at any rate the Burmese, were not felt to be physically repulsive. One looked down on them as 'natives', but one was quite ready to be physically intimate with them; and this, I noticed, was the case even with white men who had the most vicious colour prejudice. When you have a lot of servants you soon get into lazy habits, and I habitually allowed myself, for instance, to be dressed and undressed by my Burmese boy. This was because he was a Burman and undisgusting; I could not have endured to let an English manservant handle me in that intimate manner. I felt towards a Burman almost as I felt towards a woman. Like most other races, the Burmese have a distinctive smell – I cannot describe it: it is a smell that makes one's teeth tingle – but this smell never disgusted me. (Incidentally, Orientals say that *we* smell. The Chinese, I believe, say that a white man smells like a corpse. The Burmese say the same – though no Burman was ever rude enough to say so to me.) And in a way my attitude was defensible, for if one faces the fact one must admit that most Mongolians have much nicer bodies than most white men. Compare the firm-knit silken skin of the Burman, which does not wrinkle at all till he is past forty, and then merely withers up like a piece of dry leather, with the coarse-grained, flabby, sagging skin of the white man. The white man has lank ugly hair growing down his legs and the backs of his arms and in an ugly patch on his chest. The Burman has only a tuft or two of stiff black hair at the appropriate places; for the rest he is quite hairless and is usually beardless as well. The white man almost always goes bald, the Burman seldom or never. The Burman's teeth are perfect, though generally discoloured by betel juice, the white man's teeth invariably decay. The white man is generally ill-shaped, and when he grows fat he bulges in improbable places; the Mongol has beautiful bones and in old age he is almost as shapely as in youth. Admittedly the white races throw up a few individuals who for a few years are supremely beautiful; but on the whole, say what you will, they are far less comely than Orientals. But it was not of this that I was thinking when I found the English 'lower classes' so much more repellant than Burmese 'natives'. I was still thinking in terms of my early-acquired class-prejudice. When I was not much past twenty I was attached for a short time to a British regiment. Of course I admired and liked the private soldiers as any youth of twenty would admire and like hefty, cheery youths five years older than himself with the medals of the Great War on their chests. And yet, after all, they faintly repelled me; they were 'common people' and I did not care to be too close to them. In the hot mornings when the company marched down the road, myself in the rear with one of the junior subalterns, the steam of those hundred sweating bodies in front made my stomach turn. And this, you observe, was pure prejudice. For a soldier is probably as inoffensive, physically, as it is possible for a male white person to be. He is generally young, he is nearly always healthy from fresh air and exercise, and a rigorous discipline compels him to be clean. But I could not see it like that. All I knew was that it was *lower-class* sweat that I was smelling, and the thought of it made me sick.

When later on I got rid of my class-prejudice, or part of it, it was in a roundabout way and by a process that took several years. The thing that changed my attitude to the class-issue was something only indirectly connected with it – something almost irrelevant.

I was in the Indian Police five years, and by the end of that time I hated the imperialism I was serving with a bitterness which I probably cannot make clear. In the free air of England that kind of thing is not fully intelligible. In order to hate imperialism you have got to be part of it. Seen from the outside the British rule in India appears – indeed, it *is* – benevolent and even necessary; and so no doubt are the French rule in Morocco and the Dutch rule in Borneo, for people usually govern foreigners better than they govern themselves. But it is not possible to be a part of such a system without recognizing it as an unjustifiable tyranny. Even the thickest-skinned Anglo-Indian is aware of this. Every 'native' face he sees in the street brings home to him his monstrous intrusion. And the majority of Anglo-Indians, intermittently at least, are not nearly so complacent about their position as people in England believe. From the most unexpected people, from gin-pickled old scoundrels high up in the Government service, I have heard some such remark as: 'Of course we've no right in this blasted country at all. Only now we're here for God's sake let's stay here.' The truth is that no modern man, in his heart of hearts, believes that it is right to invade a foreign country and hold the population down by force. Foreign oppression is a much more obvious, understandable evil than economic oppression. Thus in England we tamely admit to being robbed in order to keep half a million worthless idlers in luxury, but we would fight to the last man sooner than be ruled by Chinamen; similarly, people who live on unearned dividends without a single qualm of conscience, see clearly enough that it is wrong to go and lord it in a foreign country where you are not wanted. The result is that every Anglo-Indian is haunted by a sense of guilt which he usually conceals as best he can, because there is no freedom of speech, and merely to be overheard making a seditious remark may damage his career. All over India there are Englishmen who secretly loathe the system of which they are part; and just occasionally, when they are quite certain of being in the right company, their hidden bitterness overflows. I remember a night I spent on the train with a man in the Educational Service, a stranger to myself whose name I never discovered. It was too hot to sleep and we spent the night in talking. Half an hour's cautious questioning decided each of us that the other was 'safe'; and then for hours, while the train jolted slowly through the pitch-black night, sitting up in our bunks with bottles of beer handy, we damned the British Empire – damned it from the inside, intelligently and intimately. It did us both good. But we had been speaking forbidden things, and in the haggard morning light when the train crawled into Mandalay, we parted as guiltily as any adulterous couple.

So far as my observation goes nearly all Anglo-Indian officials have moments when their conscience troubles them. The exceptions are men who are doing something which is demonstrably useful and would still have to be done whether the British were in India or not: forest officers, for instance, and doctors and engineers. But I was in the police, which is to say that I was part of the actual machinery of despotism. Moreover, in the police you see the dirty work of Empire at close quarters, and there is an appreciable difference between doing dirty work and merely profiting by it. Most people approve of capital punishment, but most people wouldn't do the hangman's job. Even the other Europeans in Burma slightly looked down on the police because of the brutal work they had to do. I remember once when I was inspecting a police station, an American missionary whom I knew fairly well came in for some purpose or other. Like most Nonconformist missionaries he was a complete ass but quite a good fellow. One of my native sub-inspectors was bullying a suspect (I described this scene in *Burmese Days*). The American watched it, and then turning to me said thoughtfully, 'I wouldn't care to have your job.' It made me horribly ashamed. So *that* was the kind of job I had! Even an ass of an

American missionary, a teetotal cock-virgin from the Middle West, had the right to look down on me and pity me! But I should have felt the same shame even if there had been no one to bring it home to me. I had begun to have an indescribable loathing of the whole machinery of so-called justice. Say what you will, our criminal law (far more humane, by the way, in India than in England) is a horrible thing. It needs very insensitive people to administer it. The wretched prisoners squatting in the reeking cages of the lock-ups, the grey cowed faces of the long-term convicts, the , scarred buttocks of the men who had been flogged with bamboos, the women and children howling when their menfolk were led away under arrest – things like these are beyond bearing when you are in any way directly responsible for them. I watched a man hanged once; it seemed to me worse than a thousand murders. I never went into a jail without feeling (most visitors to jails feel the same) that my place was on the other side of the bars. I thought then – I think now, for that matter – that the worst criminal who ever walked is morally superior to a hanging judge. But of course I had to keep these notions to myself, because of the almost utter silence that is imposed on every Englishman in the East. In the end I worked out an anarchistic theory that all government is evil, that the punishment always does more harm than the crime and that people can be trusted to behave decently if only you will let them alone. This of course was sentimental nonsense. I see now as I did not see then, that it is always necessary to protect peaceful people from violence. In any state of society where crime can be profitable you have got to have a harsh criminal law and administer it ruthlessly; the alternative is Al Capone. But the feeling that punishment is evil arises inescapably in those who have to administer it. I should expect to find that even in England many policemen, judges, prison warders, and the like are haunted by a secret horror of what they do. But in Burma it was a double oppression that we were committing. Not only were we hanging people and putting them in jail and so forth; we were doing it in the capacity of unwanted foreign invaders. The Burmese themselves never really recognized our jurisdiction. The thief whom we put in prison did not think of himself as a criminal justly punished, he thought of himself as the victim of a foreign conqueror. The thing that was done to him was merely a wanton meaningless cruelty. His face, behind the stout teak bars of the lock-up and the iron bars of the jail, said so clearly. And unfortunately I had not trained myself to be indifferent to the expression of the human face.

When I came home on leave in 1927 I was already half determined to throw up my job, and one sniff of English air decided me. I was not going back to be a part of that evil despotism. But I wanted much more than merely to escape from my job. For five years I had been part of an oppressive system, and it had left me with a bad conscience. Innumerable remembered faces – faces of prisoners in the dock, of men waiting in the condemned cells, of subordinates I had bullied and aged peasants I had snubbed, of servants and coolies I had hit with my fist in moments of rage (nearly everyone does these things in the East, at any rate occasionally: Orientals can be very provoking) – haunted me intolerably. I was conscious of an immense weight of guilt that I had got to expiate. I suppose that sounds exaggerated; but if you do for five years a job that you thoroughly disapprove of, you will probably feel the same. I had reduced everything to the simple theory that the oppressed are always right and the oppressors are always wrong: a mistaken theory, but the natural result of being one of the oppressors yourself. I felt that I had got to escape not merely from imperialism but from every form of man's dominion over man. I wanted to submerge myself, to get right down among the oppressed, to be one of them and on their side against their tyrants. And, chiefly because I had had to think everything out in solitude, I had carried my hatred of oppression to extraordinary lengths. At that time failure seemed to me to be the only virtue. Every suspicion of self-advancement, even to 'succeed' in life to the extent of making a few hundreds a year, seemed to me spiritually ugly, a species of bullying.

It was in this way that my thoughts turned towards the English working class. It was the first time that I had ever been really aware of the working class, and to begin with it was only because they supplied an analogy. They were the symbolic victims of injustice, playing the same part in England as the Burmese played in Burma. In Burma the issue had been quite simple. The whites were up and the blacks were down, and therefore as a matter of course one's sympathy was with the blacks. I now realized that there was no need to go as far as Burma to find tyranny and exploitation. Here in England, down under one's feet, were the submerged working class, suffering miseries which in their different way were as bad as any an Oriental ever knows. The word 'unemployment' was on everyone's lips. That was more or less new to me, after Burma, but the drivel which the middle classes were still talking ('These unemployed are all unemployables', etc., etc.) failed to deceive me. I often wonder whether that kind of stuff deceives even the fools who utter it. On the other hand I had at that time no interest in Socialism or any other economic theory. It seemed to me then – it sometimes seems to me now, for that matter – that economic injustice will stop the moment we want it to stop, and no sooner, and if we genuinely want it to stop the method adopted hardly matters.

But I knew nothing about working-class conditions. I had read the unemployment figures but I had no notion of what they implied; above all, I did not know the essential fact that 'respectable' poverty is always the worst. The frightful doom of a decent working man suddenly thrown on the streets after a lifetime of steady work, his agonized struggles against economic laws which he does not understand, the disintegration of families, the corroding sense of shame – all this was outside the range of my experience. When I thought of poverty I thought of it in terms of brute starvation. Therefore my mind turned immediately towards the extreme cases, the social outcasts: tramps, beggars, criminals, prostitutes. These were 'the lowest of the low', and these were the people with whom I wanted to get in contact. What I profoundly wanted, at that time, was to find some way of getting out of the respectable world altogether. I meditated upon it a great deal, I even planned parts of it in detail; how one could sell everything, give everything away, change one's name and start out with no money and nothing but the clothes one stood up in. But in real life nobody ever does that kind of thing; apart from the relatives and friends who have to be considered, it is doubtful whether an educated man *could* do it if there were any other course open to him. But at least I could go among these people, see what their lives were like and feel myself temporarily part of their world. Once I had been among them and accepted by them, I should have touched bottom, and – this is what I felt: I was aware even then that it was irrational – part of my guilt would drop from me.

I thought it over and decided what I would do. I would go suitably disguised to Limehouse and Whitechapel and such places and sleep in common lodging-houses and pal up with dock labourers, street hawkers, derelict people, beggars, and, if possible, criminals. And I would find out about tramps and how you got in touch with them and what was the proper procedure for entering the casual ward; and then, when I felt that I knew the ropes well enough, I would go on the road myself.

At the start it was not easy. It meant masquerading and I have no talent for acting. I cannot, for instance, disguise my accent, at any rate not for more than a very few minutes. I imagined – notice the frightful class-consciousness of the Englishman – that I should be spotted as a 'gentleman' the moment I opened my mouth; so I had a hard luck story ready in case I should be questioned. I got hold of the right kind of clothes and dirtied them in appropriate places. I am a difficult person to disguise, being abnormally tall, but I did at least know what a tramp looks like. (How few people do know this, by the way! Look at any picture of a tramp in *Punch*. They are always twenty years out of date.) One evening, having made ready at a friend's house, I set out and wandered eastward till I landed up at a common lodging-house in Limehouse Causeway. It was a dark, dirty-looking place. I knew it was a common lodging-house by the sign 'Good Beds for Single Men' in the window. Heavens, how I had to screw up my courage before I went in! It seems ridiculous now. But you see I was still half afraid of the working class. I wanted to get in touch with them, I even wanted to become one of them, but I still thought of them as alien and dangerous; going into the dark doorway of that common lodging-house seemed to me like going down into some dreadful subterranean place – a sewer full of rats, for instance. I went in fully expecting a fight. The people would spot that I was not one of themselves and immediately infer that I had come to spy on them; and then they would set upon me and throw me out – that was what I expected. I felt that I had got to do it, but I did not enjoy the prospect.

Inside the door a man in shirt-sleeves appeared from somewhere or other. This was the 'deputy', and I told him that I wanted a bed for the night. My accent did not make him stare, I noticed; he merely demanded ninepence and then showed me the way to a frowsy firelit kitchen underground. There were stevedores and navvies and a few sailors sitting about and playing draughts and drinking tea. They barely glanced at me as I entered. But this was Saturday night and a hefty young stevedore was drunk and was reeling about the room. He turned, saw me, and lurched towards me with broad red face thrust out and a dangerous-looking fishy gleam in his eyes. I stiffened myself. So the fight was coming already! The next moment the stevedore collapsed on my chest and flung his arms round my neck. ' 'Ave a cup of tea, chum!' he cried tearfully; ' 'ave a cup of tea!'

I had a cup of tea. It was a kind of baptism. After that my fears vanished. Nobody questioned me, nobody showed offensive curiosity; everybody was polite and gentle and took me utterly for granted. I stayed two or three days in that common lodging-house, and a few weeks later, having picked up a certain amount of information about the habits of destitute people, I went on the road for the first time.

I have described all this in *Down and Out in Paris and London* (nearly all the incidents described there actually happened, though they have been rearranged) and I do not want to repeat it. Later I went on the road for much longer periods, sometimes from choice, sometimes from necessity. I have lived in common lodging-houses for months together. But it is that first expedition that sticks most vividly in my mind, because of the strangeness of it – the strangeness of being at last down there among 'the lowest of the low', and on terms of utter equality with working-class people. A tramp, it is true, is not a typical working-class person; still, when you are among tramps you are at any rate merged in one section – one sub-caste – of the working class, a thing which so far as I know can happen to you in no other way. For several days I wandered through the northern outskirts of London with an Irish tramp. I was his mate, temporarily. We shared the same cell at night, and he told me the history of his life and I told him a fictitious history of mine, and we took it in turns to beg at likely-looking houses and divided up the proceeds. I was very happy. Here I was, among 'the lowest of the low', at the bedrock of the Western world! The class-bar was down, or seemed to be down. And down there in the squalid and, as a matter of fact, horribly boring sub-world of the tramp I had a feeling of release, of adventure, which seems absurd when I look back, but which was sufficiently vivid at the time.

10

BUT unfortunately you do not solve the class problem by making friends with tramps. At most you get rid of some of your own class-prejudice by doing so.

Tramps, beggars, criminals, and social outcasts generally are very exceptional beings and no more typical of the working class as a whole than, say, the literary intelligentsia are typical of the bourgeoisie. It is quite easy to be on terms of intimacy with a foreign 'intellectual', but it is not at all easy to be on terms of intimacy with an ordinary respectable foreigner of the middle class. How many Englishmen have seen the inside of an ordinary French bourgeois family, for instance? Probably it would be quite impossible to do so, short of marrying into it. And it is rather similar with the English working class. Nothing is easier than to be bosom pals with a pickpocket, if you know where to look for him; but it is very difficult to be bosom pals with a bricklayer.

But why is it so easy to be on equal terms with social outcasts? People have often said to me, 'Surely when you are with the tramps they don't really accept you as one of themselves? Surely they notice that you are different – notice the difference of accent?' etc., etc. As a matter of fact, a fair proportion of tramps, well over a quarter I should say, notice nothing of the kind. To begin with, many people have no ear for accent and judge you entirely by your clothes. I was often struck by this fact when I was begging at back doors. Some people were obviously surprised by my 'educated' accent, others completely failed to notice it; I was dirty and ragged and that was all they saw. Again, tramps come from all parts of the British Isles and the variation in English accents is enormous. A tramp is used to hearing all kinds of accents among his mates, some of them so strange to him that he can hardly understand them, and a man from, say, Cardiff or Durham or Dublin does not necessarily know which of the south English accents is an 'educated' one. In any case men with 'educated' accents, though rare among tramps, are not unknown. But even when tramps are aware that you are of different origin from themselves, it does not necessarily alter their attitude. From their point of view all that matters is that you, like themselves, are 'on the bum'. And in that world it is not done to ask too many questions. You can tell people the history of your life if you choose, and most tramps do so on the smallest provocation, but you are under no compulsion to tell it and whatever story you tell will be accepted without question. Even a bishop could be at home among tramps if he wore the right clothes; and even if they knew he was a bishop it might not make any difference, provided that they also knew or believed that he was genuinely destitute. Once you are in that world and seemingly *of* it, it hardly matters what you have been in the past. It is a sort of world-within-a-world where everyone is equal, a small squalid democracy – perhaps the nearest thing to a democracy that exists in England.

But when you come to the normal working class the position is totally different. To begin with, there is no short cut into their midst. You can become a tramp simply by putting on the right clothes and going to the nearest casual ward, but you can't become a navvy or a coal-miner. You couldn't get a job as a navvy or a coal-miner even if you were equal to the work. Via Socialist politics you can get in touch with the working-class intelligentsia, but they are hardly more typical than tramps or burglars. For the rest you can only mingle with the working class by staying in their houses as a lodger, which always has a dangerous resemblance to 'slumming'. For some months I lived entirely in coal-miners' houses. I ate my meals with the family, I washed at the kitchen sink, I shared bedrooms with miners, drank beer with them, played darts with them, talked to them by the hour together. But though I was among them, and I hope and trust they did not find me a nuisance, I was not one of them, and they knew it even better than I did. However much you like them, however interesting you find their conversation, there is always that accursed itch of class-difference, like the pea under the princess's mattress. It is not a question of dislike or distaste, only of *difference*, but it is enough to make real intimacy impossible. Even with miners who described themselves as Communists I found that it needed tactful manoeuvrings to prevent them from calling me 'sir'; and all of them, except in moments of great animation, softened their northern accents for my benefit. I liked them and hoped they liked me; but I went among them as a foreigner, and both of us were aware of it. Whichever way you turn this curse of class-difference confronts you like a wall of stone. Or rather it is not so much like a stone wall as the plate-glass pane of an aquarium; it is so easy to pretend that it isn't there, and so impossible to get through it.

Unfortunately it is nowadays the fashion to pretend that the glass is penetrable. Of course everyone knows that class-prejudice exists, but at the same time everyone claims that *he*, in some mysterious way, is exempt from it. Snobbishness is one of those vices which we can discern in everyone else but never in ourselves. Not only the *croyant et pratiquant* Socialist, but every 'intellectual' takes it as a matter of course that *he* at least is outside the class-racket; *he*, unlike his neighbours, can see through the absurdity of wealth, ranks, titles, etc., etc. 'I'm not a snob' is nowadays a kind of universal *credo*. Who is there who has not jeered at the House of Lords, the military caste, the Royal Family, the public schools, the huntin' and shootin' people, the old ladies in Cheltenham boarding-houses, the horrors of 'county' society, and the social hierarchy generally? To do so has become an automatic gesture. You notice this particularly in novels. Every novelist of serious pretensions adopts an ironic attitude towards his upper-class characters. Indeed when a novelist has to put a definitely upper-class person – a duke or a baronet or whatnot – into one of his stories he guys him more or less instinctively. There is an important subsidiary cause of this in the poverty of the modern upper-class dialect. The speech of 'educated' people is now so lifeless and characterless that a novelist can do nothing with it. By far the easiest way of making it amusing is to burlesque it, which means pretending that every upper-class person is an ineffectual ass. The trick is imitated from novelist to novelist, and in the end becomes almost a reflex action.

And yet all the while, at the bottom of his heart, everyone knows that this is humbug. We all rail against class-distinctions, but very few people seriously want to abolish them. Here you come upon the important fact that every revolutionary opinion draws part of its strength from a secret conviction that nothing can be changed.

If you want a good illustration of this, it is worth studying the novels and plays of John Galsworthy, keeping one eye on their chronology. Galsworthy is a very fine specimen of the thin-skinned, tear-in-the-eye, pre-war humanitarian. He starts out with a morbid pity-complex which extends even to thinking that every married woman is an angel chained to a satyr. He is in a perpetual quiver of indignation over the sufferings of overworked clerks, of under-paid farm hands, of fallen women, of criminals, of prostitutes, of animals. The world, as he sees it in his earlier books (*The Man of Property, Justice*, etc.), is divided into oppressors and oppressed, with the oppressors sitting on top like some monstrous stone idol which all the dynamite in the world cannot overthrow. But is it so certain that he really wants it overthrown? On the contrary, in his fight against an immovable tyranny he is upheld by the consciousness that it *is* immovable. When things happen unexpectedly and the world-order which he has known begins to crumble, he feels somewhat differently about it. So, having set out to be the champion of the underdog against tyranny and injustice, he ends by advocating (*vide The Silver Spoon*) that the English working class, to cure their economic ills, shall be deported to the colonies like batches of cattle. If he had lived ten years longer he would quite probably have arrived at some genteel version of Fascism. This is the inevitable fate of the sentimentalist. All his opinions change into their opposites at the first brush of reality.

The same streak of soggy half-baked insincerity runs through all 'advanced' opinion. Take the question of imperialism, for instance. Every left-wing 'intellectual' is, as a matter of course, an anti-imperialist. He claims to be outside the empire-racket as automatically and self-righteously as he claims to be outside the class-racket. Even the right-wing 'intellectual', who is not definitely in revolt against British imperialism, pretends to regard it with a sort of amused detachment. It is so easy to be witty about the British Empire. The White Man's Burden and 'Rule, Britannia' and Kipling's novels and Anglo-Indian bores – who could even mention such things without a snigger? And is there any cultured person who has not at least once in his life made a joke about that old Indian havildar who said that if the British left India there would not be a rupee or a virgin left between Peshawar and Delhi (or wherever it was)? That is the attitude of the typical left-winger towards imperialism, and a thoroughly flabby, boneless attitude it is. For in the last resort, the only important question is, Do you want the British Empire to hold together or do you want it to disintegrate? And at the bottom of his heart no Englishman, least of all the kind of person who is witty about Anglo-Indian colonels, does want it to disintegrate. For, apart from any other consideration, the high standard of life we enjoy in England depends upon our keeping a tight hold on the Empire, particularly the tropical portions of it such as India and Africa. Under the capitalist system, in order that England may live in comparative comfort, a hundred million Indians must live on the verge of starvation – an evil state of affairs, but you acquiesce in it every time you step into a taxi or eat a plate of strawberries and cream. The alternative is to throw the Empire overboard and reduce England to a cold and unimportant little island where we should all have to work very hard and live mainly on herrings and potatoes. That is the very last thing that any left-winger wants. Yet the left-winger continues to feel that he has no moral responsibility for imperialism. He is perfectly ready to accept the products of Empire and to save his soul by sneering at the people who hold the Empire together.

It is at this point that one begins to grasp the unreality of most people's attitude towards the class question. So long as it is merely a question of ameliorating the worker's lot, every decent person is agreed. Take a coal-miner, for example. Everyone, barring fools and scoundrels, would *like* to see the miner better off. If, for instance, the miner could ride to the coal face in a comfortable trolley instead of crawling on his hands and knees, if he could work a three-hour shift instead of seven and a half hours, if he could live in a decent house with five bedrooms and a bathroom and have ten pounds a week wages – splendid! Moreover, anyone who uses his brain knows perfectly well that this is within the range of possibility. The world, potentially at least, is immensely rich; develop it as it might be developed, and we could all live like princes, supposing that we wanted to. And to a very superficial glance the social side of the question looks equally simple. In a sense it is true that almost everyone would like to see class-distinctions abolished. Obviously this perpetual uneasiness between man and man, from which we suffer in modern England, is a curse and a nuisance. Hence the temptation to believe that it can be shouted out of existence with a few scoutmasterish bellows of good-will. Stop calling me 'sir', you chaps! Surely we're all men? Let's pal up and get our shoulders to the wheel and remember that we're all equal, and what the devil does it matter if I know what kind of ties to wear and you don't, and I drink my soup comparatively quietly and you drink yours with the noise of water going down a waste-pipe – and so on and so on and so on; all of it the most pernicious rubbish, but quite alluring when it is suitably expressed.

But unfortunately you get no further by merely wishing class-distinctions away. More exactly, it *is* necessary to wish them away, but your wish has no efficacy unless you grasp what it involves. The fact that has got to be faced is that to abolish class-distinctions means abolishing a part of yourself. Here am I, a typical member of the middle class. It is easy for me to say that I want to get rid of class-distinctions, but nearly everything I think and do is a result of class-distinctions. All my notions – notions of good and evil, of pleasant and unpleasant, of funny and serious, of ugly and beautiful – are essentially *middle-class* notions; my taste in books and food and clothes, my sense of honour, my table manners, my turns of speech, my accent, even the characteristic movements of my body, are the products of a special kind of upbringing and a special niche about half-way up the social hierarchy. When I grasp this I grasp that it is no use clapping a proletarian on the back and telling him that he is as good a man as I am; if I want real contact with him, I have got to make an effort for which very likely I am unprepared. For to get outside the class-racket I have got to suppress not merely my private snobbishness, but most of my other tastes and prejudices as well. I have got to alter myself so completely that at the end I should hardly be recognizable as the same person. What is involved is not merely the amelioration of working-class conditions, nor an avoidance of the more stupid forms of snobbery, but a complete abandonment of the upper-class and middle-class attitude to life. And whether I say Yes or No probably depends upon the extent to which I grasp what is demanded of me.

Many people, however, imagine that they can abolish class-distinctions without making any uncomfortable change in their own habits and 'ideology'. Hence the eager class-breaking activities which one can see in progress on all sides. Everywhere there are people of goodwill who quite honestly believe that they are working for the overthrow of class-distinctions. The middle-class Socialist enthuses over the proletariat and runs 'summer schools' where the proletarian and the repentant bourgeois are supposed to fall upon one another's necks and be brothers for ever; and the bourgeois visitors come away saying how wonderful and inspiring it has all been (the proletarian ones come away saying something different). And then there is the outer-suburban creeping Jesus, a hangover from the William Morris period, but still surprisingly common, who goes about saying 'Why must we level *down*? Why not level *up*?' and proposes to level the working class 'up' (up to his own standard) by means of hygiene, fruit juice, birth-control, poetry, etc. Even the Duke of York (now King George VI) runs a yearly camp where public-school boys and boys from the slums are supposed to mix on exactly equal terms, and *do* mix for the time being, rather like the animals in one of those 'Happy Family' cages where a dog, a cat, two ferrets, a rabbit, and three canaries preserve an armed truce while the showman's eye is on them.

All such deliberate, conscious efforts at class-breaking are, I am convinced, a very serious mistake. Sometimes they are merely futile, but where they do show a definite result it is usually to *intensify* class-prejudice. This, if you come to think of it, is only what might be expected. You have forced the pace and set up an uneasy, unnatural equality between class and class; the resultant friction brings to the surface all kinds of feelings that might otherwise have remained buried, perhaps for ever. As I said apropos of Galsworthy, the opinions of the sentimentalist change into their opposites at the first touch of reality. Scratch the average pacifist and you find a jingo. The middle-class I.L.P.'er and the bearded fruit-juice drinker are all for a classless society so long as they see the proletariat through the wrong end of the telescope; force them into any *real* contact with a proletarian – let them get into a fight with a drunken fish-porter on Saturday night, for instance – and they are capable of swinging back to the most ordinary middle-class snobbishness. Most middle-class Socialists, however, are very unlikely to get into fights with drunken fish-porters; when they do make a genuine contact with the working class, it is usually with the working-class intelligentsia. But the working-class intelligentsia is sharply divisible into two different types. There is the type who remains working-class – who goes on working as a mechanic or a dock-labourer or whatever it may be and does not bother to change his working-class accent and habits, but who 'improves his mind' in his spare time and works for the I.L.P. or the Communist Party; and there is the type who does alter his way of life, at least externally, and who by means of State scholarships succeeds in climbing into the middle class. The first is one of the finest types of man we have. I can think of some I have met whom not even the most hidebound Tory could help liking and admiring. The other type, with exceptions – D. H. Lawrence, for example – is less admirable.

To begin with, it is a pity, though it is a natural result of the scholarship system, that the proletariat should tend to interpenetrate the middle class via the literary intelligentsia. For it is not easy to crash your way into the literary intelligentsia if you happen to be a decent human being. The modern English literary world, at any rate the high-brow section of it, is a sort of poisonous jungle where only weeds can flourish. It is just possible to be a literary gent and to keep your decency if you are a definitely *popular* writer – a writer of detective stories, for instance; but to be a highbrow, with a footing in the snootier magazines, means delivering yourself over to horrible campaigns of wire-pulling and backstairs-crawling. In the highbrow world you 'get on', if you 'get on' at all, not so much by your literary ability as by being the life and soul of cocktail parties and kissing the bums of verminous little lions. This, then, is the world that most readily opens its doors to the proletarian who is climbing out of his own class. The 'clever' boy of a working-class family, the sort of boy who wins scholarships and is obviously not fitted for a life of manual labour, may find other ways of rising into the class above – a slightly different type, for instance, rises via Labour Party politics – but the literary way is by far the most usual. Literary London now teems with young men who are of proletarian origin and have been educated by means of scholarships. Many of them are very disagreeable people, quite unrepresentative of their class, and it is most unfortunate that when a person of bourgeois origin does succeed in meeting a proletarian face to face on equal terms, this is the type he most commonly meets. For the result is to drive the bourgeois, who has idealized the proletariat so long as he knew nothing about them, back into frenzies of snobbishness. The process is sometimes very comic to watch, if you happen to be watching it from the outside. The poor well-meaning bourgeois, eager to embrace his proletarian brother, leaps forward with open arms; and only a little while later he is in retreat, minus a borrowed five pounds and exclaiming dolefully, 'But, dash it, the fellow's not a gentleman!'

The thing that disconcerts the bourgeois in a contact of this kind is to find certain of his own professions being taken seriously. I have pointed out that the left-wing opinions of the average 'intellectual' are mainly spurious. From pure imitativeness he jeers at things which in fact he believes in. As one example out of many, take the public-school code of honour, with its 'team spirit' and 'Don't hit a man when he's down', and all the rest of that familiar bunkum. Who has not laughed at it? Who, calling himself an 'intellectual', would dare *not* to laugh at it? But it is a bit different when you meet somebody who laughs at it *from the outside*; just as we spend our lives in abusing England but grow very angry when we hear a foreigner saying exactly the same things. No one has been more amusing about the public schools than 'Beachcomber' of the *Express*. He laughs, quite rightly, at the ridiculous code which makes cheating at cards the worst of all sins. But would 'Beachcomber' like it if one of his own friends was caught cheating at cards? I doubt it. It is only when you meet someone of a different culture from yourself that you begin to realize what your own beliefs really are. If you are a bourgeois 'intellectual' you too readily imagine that you have somehow become unbourgeois because you find it easy to laugh at patriotism and the C. of E. and the Old School Tie and Colonel Blimp and all the rest of it. But from the point of view of the proletarian 'intellectual', who at least by origin is genuinely outside the bourgeois culture, your resemblances to Colonel Blimp may be more important than your differences. Very likely he looks upon you and Colonel Blimp as practically equivalent persons; and in a way he is right, though neither you nor Colonel Blimp would admit it. So that the meeting of proletarian and bourgeois, when they do succeed in meeting, is not always the embrace of long-lost brothers; too often it is the clash of alien cultures which can only meet in war.

I have been looking at this from the point of view of the bourgeois who finds his secret beliefs challenged and is driven back to a frightened conservatism. But one has also got to consider the antagonism that is aroused in the proletarian 'intellectual'. By his own efforts and sometimes with frightful agonies he has struggled out of his own class into another where he expects to find a wider freedom and a greater intellectual refinement; and all he finds, very often, is a sort of hollowness, a deadness, a lack of any warm human feeling – of any real life whatever. Sometimes the bourgeoisie seem to him just dummies with money and water in their veins instead of blood. This at any rate is what he *says*, and almost any young highbrow of proletarian origin will spin you this line of talk. Hence the 'proletarian' cant from which we now suffer. Everyone knows, or ought to know by this time, how it runs: the bourgeoisie are 'dead' (a favourite word of abuse nowadays and very effective because meaningless), bourgeois culture is bankrupt, bourgeois 'values' are despicable, and so on and so forth; if you want examples, see any number of the *Left Review* or any of the younger Communist writers such as Alec Brown, Philip Henderson, etc. The sincerity of much of this is suspect, but D. H. Lawrence, who was sincere, whatever else he may not have been, expresses the same thought over and over again. It is curious how he harps upon that idea that the English bourgeoisie are all *dead*, or at least gelded. Mellors, the gamekeeper in *Lady Chatterley's Lover* (really Lawrence himself), has had the opportunity to get out of his own class and does not particularly want to return to it, because English working people have various 'disagreeable habits'; on the other hand the bourgeoisie, with whom he has also mixed to some extent, seem to him half dead, a race of eunuchs. Lady Chatterley's husband, symbolically, is impotent in the actual physical sense. And then there is the poem about the young man (once again Lawrence himself) who 'got up to the top of the tree' but came down saying:

> Oh you've got to be like a monkey
> if you climb up the tree!
> You've no more use for the solid earth
> and the lad you used to be.
> You sit in the boughs and gibber
> with superiority.
>
> They all gibber and gibber and chatter,
> and never a word they say
> comes really out of their guts, lad,
> they make it up half-way . . .
>
> I tell you something's been done to 'em,
> to the pullets up above;
> there's not a cock bird among 'em, etc., etc.

You could hardly have it in plainer terms than that. Possibly by the people at 'the top of the tree' Lawrence only means the real bourgeoisie, those in the £2000 a year class and over, but I doubt it. More probably he means everyone who is more or less within the bourgeois culture – everyone who was brought up with a mincing accent and in a house where there were one or two servants. And at this point you realize the danger of the 'proletarian' cant – realize, I mean, the terrible antagonism that it is capable of arousing. For when you come to such an accusation as this, you are up against a blank wall. Lawrence tells me that because I have been to a public school I am a eunuch. Well, what about it? I can produce medical evidence to the contrary, but what good will that do? Lawrence's condemnation remains. If you tell me I am a scoundrel I may mend my ways, but if you tell me I am a eunuch you are tempting me to hit back in any way that seems feasible. If you want to make an enemy of a man, tell him that his ills are incurable.

This then is the net result of most meetings between proletarian and bourgeois: they lay bare a real antagonism which is intensified by the 'proletarian' cant, itself the product of forced contacts between class and class. The only sensible procedure is to go slow and not force the pace. If you secretly think of yourself as a gentleman and as such the superior of the greengrocer's errand boy, it is far better to say so than to tell lies about it. Ultimately you have got to drop your snobbishness, but it is fatal to pretend to drop it before you are really ready to do so.

Meanwhile one can observe on every side that dreary phenomenon, the middle-class person who is an ardent Socialist at twenty-five and a sniffish Conservative at thirty-five. In a way his recoil is natural enough – at any rate, one can see how his thoughts run. Perhaps a classless society *doesn't* mean a beatific state of affairs in which we shall all go on behaving exactly as before except that there will be no class-hatred and no snobbishness; perhaps it means a bleak world in which all our ideals, our codes, our tastes – our 'ideology', in fact – will have no meaning. Perhaps this class-breaking business isn't so simple as it looked! On the contrary, it is a wild ride into the darkness, and it may be that at the end of it the smile will be on the face of the tiger. With loving though slightly patronizing smiles we set out to greet our proletarian brothers, and behold! our proletarian brothers – in so far as we understand them – are not asking for our greetings, they are asking us to commit suicide. When the bourgeois sees it in *that* form he takes to flight, and if his flight is rapid enough it may carry him to Fascism.

11

MEANWHILE what about Socialism?

It hardly needs pointing out that at this moment we are in a very serious mess, so serious that even the dullest-witted people find it difficult to remain unaware of it. We are living in a world in which nobody is free, in which hardly anybody is secure, in which it is almost impossible to be honest and to remain alive. For enormous blocks of the working class the conditions of life are such as I have described in the opening chapters of this book, and there is no chance of those conditions showing any fundamental improvement. The very best the English working class can hope for is an occasional temporary decrease in unemployment when this or that industry is artificially stimulated by, for instance, rearmament. Even the middle classes, for the first time in their history, are feeling the pinch. They have not known actual hunger yet, but more and more of them find themselves floundering in a sort of deadly net of frustration in which it is harder and harder to persuade yourself that you are either happy, active, or useful. Even the lucky ones at the top, the real bourgeoisie, are haunted periodically by a consciousness of the miseries below, and still more by fears of the menacing future. And this is merely a preliminary stage, in a country still rich with the loot of a hundred years. Presently there may be coming God knows what horrors – horrors of which, in this sheltered island, we have not even a traditional knowledge.

And all the while everyone who uses his brain knows that Socialism, as a world-system and wholeheartedly applied, is a way out. It would at least ensure our getting enough to eat even if it deprived us of everything else. Indeed, from one point of view, Socialism is such elementary common sense that I am sometimes amazed that it has not established itself already. The world is a raft sailing through space with, potentially, plenty of provisions for everybody; the idea that we must all cooperate and see to it that everyone does his fair share of the work and gets his fair share of the provisions seems so blatantly obvious that one would say that no one could possibly fail to accept it unless he had some corrupt motive for clinging to the present system. Yet the fact that we have got to face is that Socialism is *not* establishing itself. Instead of going forward, the cause of Socialism is visibly going back. At this moment Socialists almost everywhere are in retreat before the onslaught of Fascism, and events are moving at terrible speed. As I write this the Spanish Fascist forces are bombarding Madrid, and it is quite likely that before the book is printed we shall have another Fascist country to add to the list, not to mention a Fascist control of the Mediterranean which may have the effect of delivering British foreign policy into the hands of Mussolini. I do not, however, want here to discuss the wider political issues. What I am concerned with is the fact that Socialism is losing ground exactly where it ought to be gaining it. With so much in its favour – for every empty belly is an argument for Socialism – the *idea* of Socialism is less widely accepted than it was ten years ago. The average thinking person nowadays is not merely not a Socialist, he is actively hostile to Socialism. This must be due chiefly to mistaken methods of propaganda. It means that Socialism, in the form of which it is now presented to us, has about it something inherently distasteful – something that drives away the very people who ought to be flocking to its support.

A few years ago this might have seemed unimportant. It seems only yesterday that Socialists, especially orthodox Marxists, were telling me with superior smiles that Socialism was going to arrive of its own accord by some mysterious process called 'historic necessity'. Possibly that belief still lingers, but it has been shaken, to say the least of it. Hence the sudden attempts of Communists in various countries to ally themselves with democratic forces which they have been sabotaging for years past. At a

moment like this it is desperately necessary to discover just *why* Socialism
has failed in its appeal. And it is no use writing off the current distaste
for Socialism as the product of stupidity or corrupt motives. If you want
to remove that distaste you have got to understand it, which means getting
inside the mind of the ordinary objector to Socialism, or at least regarding
his viewpoint sympathetically. No case is really answered until it has had
a fair hearing. Therefore, rather paradoxically, in order to defend Socialism
it is necessary to start by attacking it.

In the last three chapters I tried to analyse the difficulties that are raised
by our anachronistic class-system; I shall have to touch on that subject
again, because I believe that the present intensely stupid handling of the
class-issue may stampede quantities of potential Socialists into Fascism.
In the chapter following this one I want to discuss certain underlying
assumptions that alienate sensitive minds from Socialism. But in the
present chapter I am merely dealing with the obvious, preliminary objections – the kind of thing that the person who is not a Socialist (I don't
mean the 'Where's the money to come from?' type) always starts by
saying when you tax him on the subject. Some of these objections may
appear frivolous or self-contradictory, but that is beside the point; I am
merely discussing symptoms. Anything is relevant which helps to make
clear why Socialism is not accepted. And please notice that I am arguing
for Socialism, not *against* it. But for the moment I am *advocatus diaboli*.
I am making out a case for the sort of person who is in sympathy with
the fundamental aims of Socialism, who has the brains to see that Socialism
would 'work', but who in practice always takes to flight when Socialism
is mentioned.

Question a person of this type, and you will often get the semi-frivolous
answer: 'I don't object to Socialism, but I do object to Socialists.' Logically
it is a poor argument, but it carries weight with many people. As with the
Christian religion, the worst advertisement for Socialism is its adherents.

The first thing that must strike any outside observer is that Socialism
in its developed form is a theory confined entirely to the middle classes.
The typical Socialist is not, as tremulous old ladies imagine, a ferocious-
looking working man with greasy overalls and a raucous voice. He is either
a youthful snob-Bolshevik who in five years' time will quite probably have
made a wealthy marriage and been converted to Roman Catholicism; or,
still more typically, a prim little man with a white-collar job, usually a
secret teetotaller and often with vegetarian leanings, with a history of
Nonconformity behind him, and, above all, with a social position which
he has no intention of forfeiting. This last type is surprisingly common in

Socialist parties of every shade; it has perhaps been taken over *en bloc* from the old Liberal Party. In addition to this there is the horrible – the really disquieting – prevalence of cranks wherever Socialists are gathered together. One sometimes gets the impression that the mere words 'Socialism' and 'Communism' draw towards them with magnetic force every fruit-juice drinker, nudist, sandal-wearer, sex-maniac, Quaker, 'Nature Cure' quack, pacifist, and feminist in England. One day this summer I was riding through Letchworth when the bus stopped and two dreadful-looking old men got on to it. They were both about sixty, both very short, pink, and chubby, and both hatless. One of them was obscenely bald, the other had long grey hair bobbed in the Lloyd George style. They were dressed in pistachio-coloured shirts and khaki shorts into which their huge bottoms were crammed so tightly that you could study every dimple. Their appearance created a mild stir of horror on top of the bus. The man next to me, a commercial traveller I should say, glanced at me, at them, and back again at me' and murmured 'Socialists', as who should say, 'Red Indians'. He was probably right – the I.L.P. were holding their summer school at Letchworth. But the point is that to him, as an ordinary man, a crank meant a Socialist and a Socialist meant a crank. Any Socialist, he probably felt, could be counted on to have *something* eccentric about him. And some such notion seems to exist even among Socialists themselves. For instance, I have here a prospectus from another summer school which states its terms per week and then asks me to say 'whether my diet is ordinary or vegetarian'. They take it for granted, you see, that it is necessary to ask this question. This kind of thing is by itself sufficient to alienate plenty of decent people. And their instinct is perfectly sound, for the food-crank is by definition a person willing to cut himself off from human society in hopes of adding five years on to the life of his carcase; that is, a person out of touch with common humanity.

To this you have got to add the ugly fact that most middle-class Socialists, while theoretically pining for a classless society, cling like glue to their miserable fragments of social prestige. I remember my sensations of horror on first attending an I.L.P. branch meeting in London. (It might have been rather different in the North, where the bourgeoisie are less thickly scattered.) Are *these* mingy little beasts, I thought, the champions of the working class? For every person there, male and female, bore the worst stigmata of sniffish middle-class superiority. If a real working man, a miner dirty from the pit, for instance, had suddenly walked into their midst, they would have been embarrassed, angry, and disgusted; some, I should think, would have fled holding their noses. You can see the same tendency in Socialist literature, which, even when it is not openly written *de haut en bas*, is always completely removed from the working class in idiom and manner of thought. The Coles, Webbs, Stracheys, etc., are not *exactly* proletarian writers. It is doubtful whether anything describable as proletarian literature now exists – even the *Daily Worker* is written in standard South English – but a good music-hall comedian comes nearer to producing it than any Socialist writer I can think of. As for the technical jargon of the Communists, it is as far removed from the common speech as the language of a mathematical textbook. I remember hearing a professional Communist speaker address a working-class audience. His speech was the usual bookish stuff, full of long sentences and parentheses and 'Notwithstanding' and 'Be that as it may', besides the usual jargon of 'ideology' and 'class-consciousness' and 'proletarian solidarity' and all the rest of it. After him a Lancashire working man got up and spoke to the crowd in their own broad lingo. There was not much doubt which of the two was nearer to his audience, but I do not suppose for a moment that the Lancashire working man was an orthodox Communist.

For it must be remembered that a working man, so long as he remains a genuine working man, is seldom or never a Socialist in the complete, logically consistent sense. Very likely he votes Labour, or even Communist if he gets the chance, but his conception of Socialism is quite different from that of the book-trained Socialist higher up. To the ordinary working man, the sort you would meet in any pub on Saturday night, Socialism does not mean much more than better wages and shorter hours and nobody bossing you about. To the more revolutionary type, the type who is a hunger-marcher and is blacklisted by employers, the word is a sort of rallying-cry against the forces of oppression, a vague threat of future violence. But, so far as my experience goes, no genuine working man grasps the deeper implications of Socialism. Often, in my opinion, he is a truer Socialist than the orthodox Marxist, because he does remember what the other so often forgets, that Socialism means justice and common decency. But what he does not grasp is that Socialism cannot be narrowed down to mere economic justice and that a reform of that magnitude is bound to work immense changes in our civilization and his own way of life. His vision of the Socialist future is a vision of present society with the worst abuses left out, and with interest centring round the same things as at present – family life, the pub, football, and local politics. As for the philosophic side of Marxism, the pea-and-thimble trick with those three mysterious entities, thesis, antithesis, and synthesis, I have never met a working man who had the faintest interest in it. It is of course true that plenty of people of working-class *origin* are Socialists of the theoretical bookish type. But they are never people who have *remained* working men; they don't work with their hands, that is. They belong either to the type I mentioned in the last chapter, the type who squirms into the middle class via the literary intelligentsia, or the type who becomes a Labour M.P. or a high-up trade union official. This last type is one of the most desolating spectacles the world contains. He has been picked out to fight for his mates, and all it means to him is a soft job and the chance of 'bettering' himself. Not merely while but *by* fighting the bourgeoisie he becomes a bourgeois himself. And meanwhile it is quite possible that he has remained an orthodox Marxist. But I have yet to meet a *working* miner, steel-worker, cotton-weaver, docker, navvy, or whatnot who was 'ideologically' sound.

One of the analogies between Communism and Roman Catholicism is that only the 'educated' are completely orthodox. The most immediately striking thing about the English Roman Catholics – I don't mean the real Catholics, I mean the converts: Ronald Knox, Arnold Lunn *et hoc genus* – is their intense self-consciousness. Apparently they never think, certainly they never write, about anything but the fact that they *are* Roman Catholics; this single fact and the self-praise resulting from it form the entire stock-in-trade of the Catholic literary man. But the really interesting thing about these people is the way in which they have worked out the supposed implications of orthodoxy until the tiniest details of life are involved. Even the liquids you drink, apparently, can be orthodox or heretical; hence the campaigns of Chesterton, 'Beachcomber', etc., against tea and in favour of beer. According to Chesterton, tea-drinking is 'pagan', while beer-drinking is 'Christian', and coffee is 'the puritan's opium'. It is unfortunate for this theory that Catholics abound in the 'Temperance' movement and the greatest tea-boozers in the world are the Catholic Irish; but what I am interested in here is the attitude of mind that can make even food and drink an occasion for religious intolerance. A working-class Catholic would never be so absurdly consistent as that. He does not spend his time in brooding on the fact that he is a Roman Catholic, and he is not particularly conscious of being different from his non-Catholic neighbours. Tell an Irish dock-labourer in the slums of Liverpool that his cup of tea is 'pagan', and he will call you a fool. And even in more serious matters he does not always grasp the implications of his faith. In the Roman Catholic homes of Lancashire you see the crucifix on the wall and the *Daily Worker* on the table. It is only the 'educated' man, especially the literary man, who knows how to be a bigot. And, *mutatis mutandis*, it is the same with Communism. The creed is never found in its pure form in a genuine proletarian.

It may be said, however, that even if the theoretical book-trained Socialist is not a working man himself, at least he is actuated by a love of the working class. He is endeavouring to shed his bourgeois status and fight on the side of the proletariat – that, obviously, must be his motive.

But is it? Sometimes I look at a Socialist – the intellectual, tract-writing type of Socialist, with his pullover, his fuzzy hair, and his Marxian quotation – and wonder what the devil his motive really *is*. It is often difficult to believe that it is a love of anybody, especially of the working class, from whom he is of all people the furthest removed. The underlying motive of many Socialists, I believe, is simply a hypertrophied sense of order. The present state of affairs offends them not because it causes misery, still less because it makes freedom impossible, but because it is untidy; what they desire, basically, is to reduce the world to something resembling a chessboard. Take the plays of a lifelong Socialist like Shaw. How much understanding or even awareness of working-class life do they display? Shaw himself declares that you can only bring a working man on the stage 'as an object of compassion'; in practice he doesn't bring him on even as that, but merely as a sort of W. W. Jacobs figure of fun – the ready-made comic East Ender, like those in *Major Barbara* and *Captain Brassbound's Conversion*. At best his attitude to the working class is the sniggering *Punch* attitude, in more serious moments (consider, for instance, the young man who symbolizes the dispossessed classes in *Misalliance*) he finds them merely contemptible and disgusting. Poverty and, what is more, the habits of mind created by poverty, are something to be abolished *from above*, by violence if necessary; perhaps even preferably by violence. Hence his worship of 'great' men and appetite for dictatorships, Fascist or Communist; for to him, apparently (*vide* his remarks apropos of the Italo-Abyssinian war and the Stalin-Wells conversations), Stalin and Mussolini are almost equivalent persons. You get the same thing in a more mealy-mouthed form in Mrs Sidney Webb's autobiography, which gives, unconsciously, a most revealing picture of the high-minded Socialist slum-visitor. The truth is that, to many people calling themselves Socialists, revolution does not mean a movement of the masses with which they hope to associate themselves; it means a set of reforms which 'we', the clever ones, are going to impose upon 'them', the Lower Orders. On the other hand, it would be a mistake to regard the book-trained Socialist as a bloodless creature entirely incapable of emotion. Though seldom giving much evidence of affection for the exploited, he is perfectly capable of displaying hatred – a sort of queer, theoretical, *in vacuo* hatred – against the exploiters. Hence the grand old Socialist sport of denouncing the bourgeoisie. It is strange how easily almost any Socialist writer can lash himself into frenzies of rage against the class to which, by birth or by adoption, he himself invariably belongs. Sometimes the hatred of bourgeois habits and 'ideology' is so far-reaching that it extends even to bourgeois characters in books. According to Henri Barbusse, the characters in the novels of Proust, Gide, etc., are 'characters whom one would dearly love to have at the other side of a barricade'. 'A barricade', you observe. Judging from *Le Feu*, I should have thought Barbusse's experience of barricades had left him with a distaste for them. But the imaginary bayoneting of 'bourgeois', who presumably don't hit back, is a bit different from the real article.

The best example of bourgeois-baiting literature that I have yet come across is Mirsky's *Intelligentsia of Great Britain*. This is a very interesting and ably-written book, and it should be read by everyone who wants to understand the rise of Fascism. Mirsky (formerly Prince Mirsky) was a White Russian *émigré* who came to England and was for some years a lecturer in Russian literature at London University. Later he was converted to Communism, returned to Russia, and produced his book as a sort of 'show-up' of the British intelligentsia from a Marxist standpoint. It is a viciously malignant book, with an unmistakable note of 'Now I'm out of your reach I can say what I like about you' running all through it, and apart from a general distortion it contains some quite definite and probably intentional misrepresentation: as, for instance, when Conrad is declared to be 'no less imperialist than Kipling', and D. H. Lawrence is described as writing 'bare-bodied pornography' and as having 'succeeded in erasing all clues to his proletarian origin' – as though Lawrence had been a pork-butcher climbing into the House of Lords! This kind of thing is very disquieting when one remembers that it is addressed to a Russian audience who have no means of checking its accuracy. But what I am thinking of at the moment is the effect of such a book on the English public. Here you have a literary man of aristocratic extraction, a man who had probably never in his life spoken to a working man on anything approaching equal terms, uttering venomous screams of libel against his 'bourgeois' colleagues. Why? So far as appearances go, from pure malignity. He is battling *against* the British intelligentsia, but what is he battling *for*? Within the book itself there is no indication. Hence the net effect of books like this is to give outsiders the impression that there is nothing in Communism except *hatred*. And here once again you come upon that queer resemblance between Communism and (convert) Roman Catholicism. If you want to find a book as evil-spirited as *The Intelligentsia of Great Britain*, the likeliest place to look is among the popular Roman Catholic apologists. You will find there the same venom and the same dishonesty, though, to do the Catholic justice, you will not usually find the same bad manners. Queer that Comrade Mirsky's spiritual brother should be Father — —! The Communist and the Catholic are not saying the same thing, in a sense they are even saying opposite things, and each would gladly boil the other in oil if circumstances permitted; but from the point of view of an outsider they are very much alike.

The fact is that Socialism, *in the form in which it is now presented*, appeals chiefly to unsatisfactory or even inhuman types. On the one hand you have the warm-hearted, unthinking Socialist, the typical working-class Socialist, who only wants to abolish poverty and does not always grasp what this implies. On the other hand, you have the intellectual, book-trained Socialist, who understands that it is necessary to throw our present civilization down the sink and is quite willing to do so. And this type is drawn, to begin with, entirely from the middle class, and from a rootless town-bred section of the middle class at that. Still more unfortunately, it includes – so much so that to an outsider it even appears to be composed of – the kind of people I have been discussing; the foaming denouncers of the bourgeoisie, and the more-water-in-your-beer reformers of whom Shaw is the prototype, and the astute young social-literary climbers who are Communists now, as they will be Fascists five years hence, because it is all the go, and all that dreary tribe of high-minded women and sandal-wearers and bearded fruit-juice drinkers who come flocking towards the smell of 'progress' like bluebottles to a dead cat. The ordinary decent person, who is in sympathy with the *essential* aims of Socialism, is given the impression that there is no room for his kind in any Socialist party that means business. Worse, he is driven to the cynical conclusion that Socialism is a kind of doom which is probably coming but must be staved off as long as possible. Of course, as I have suggested already, it is not strictly fair to judge a movement by its adherents; but the point is that people invariably do so, and that the popular conception of Socialism is coloured by the conception of a Socialist as a dull or disagreeable person. 'Socialism' is pictured as a state of affairs in which our more vocal Socialists would feel thoroughly at home. This does great harm to the cause. The ordinary man may not flinch from a dictatorship of the proletariat, if you offer it tactfully; offer him a dictatorship of the prigs, and he gets ready to fight.

There is a widespread feeling that any civilization in which Socialism was a reality would bear the same relation to our own as a brand-new bottle of colonial burgundy bears to a few spoonfuls of first-class Beaujolais. We live, admittedly, amid the wreck of a civilization, but it has been a great civilization in its day, and in patches it still flourishes almost undisturbed. It still has its bouquet, so to speak; whereas the imagined Socialist future, like the colonial burgundy, tastes only of iron and water. Hence the fact, which is really a disastrous one, that artists of any consequence can never be persuaded into the Socialist fold. This is particularly the case with the writer whose political opinions are more directly and obviously connected with his work than those of, say, a painter. If one faces facts one must admit that nearly everything describable as Socialist literature is dull, tasteless, and bad. Consider the situation in England at the present moment. A whole generation has grown up more or less in familiarity with the idea of Socialism; and yet the higher-water mark, so to speak, of Socialist literature is W. H. Auden, a sort of gutless Kipling,* and the even feebler poets who are associated with him. Every writer of consequence and every book worth reading is on the other side. I am willing to believe that it is otherwise in Russia – about which I know nothing, however – for presumably in post-revolutionary Russia the mere violence of events would tend to throw up a vigorous literature of sorts. But it is certain that in Western Europe Socialism has produced no literature worth having. A little while ago, when the issues were less clear, there were writers of some vitality who called themselves Socialists, but they were using the word as a vague label. Thus, if Ibsen and Zola described themselves as Socialists, it did not mean much more than that they were 'progressives', while in the case of Anatole France it meant merely that he was an anticlerical. The real Socialist writers, the propagandist writers, have always been dull, empty windbags – Shaw, Barbusse, Upton Sinclair, William Morris, Waldo Frank, etc., etc. I am not, of course, suggesting that Socialism is to be condemned because literary gents don't like it; I am not even suggesting that it ought necessarily to produce literature on its own account, though I do think it a bad sign that it has produced no songs worth singing. I am merely pointing to the fact that writers of genuine talent are usually indifferent to Socialism, and sometimes actively and mischievously hostile. And this is a disaster, not only for the writers themselves, but for the cause of Socialism, which has great need of them.

* Orwell somewhat retracted this remark later. See 'Inside the Whale', *England Your England*, p. 120 (Secker & Warburg Collected Edition).

This, then, is the superficial aspect of the ordinary man's recoil from
Socialism. I know the whole dreary argument very thoroughly, because I
know it from both sides. Everything that I say here I have both said to
ardent Socialists who were trying to convert me, and had said to me by
bored non-Socialists whom I was trying to convert. The whole thing
amounts to a kind of *malaise* produced by dislike of individual Socialists,
especially of the cocksure Marx-quoting type. Is it childish to be influenced
by that kind of thing? Is it silly? Is it even contemptible? It is all that,
but the point is that *it happens*, and therefore it is important to keep it in
mind.

12

HOWEVER there is a much more serious difficulty than the local and
temporary objections which I discussed in the last chapter.

Faced by the fact that intelligent people are so often on the other side,
the Socialist is apt to set it down to corrupt motives (conscious or
unconscious), or to an ignorant belief that Socialism would not 'work', or
to a mere dread of the horrors and discomforts of the revolutionary period
before Socialism is established. Undoubtedly all these are important, but
there are plenty of people who are influenced by none of them and are
nevertheless hostile to Socialism. Their reason for recoiling from Socialism
is spiritual, or 'ideological'. They object to it not on the ground that it
would not 'work', but precisely because it would 'work' too well. What
they are afraid of is not the things that are going to happen in their own
lifetime, but the things that are going to happen in a remote future when
Socialism is a reality.

I have very seldom met a convinced Socialist who could grasp that
thinking people may be repelled by the *objective* towards which Socialism
appears to be moving. The Marxist, especially, dismisses this kind of thing
as bourgeois sentimentality. Marxists as a rule are not very good at reading
the minds of their adversaries; if they were, the situation in Europe might
be less desperate than it is at present. Possessing a technique which seems
to explain everything, they do not often bother to discover what is going
on inside other people's heads. Here, for instance, is an illustration of the

kind of thing I mean. Discussing the widely held theory – which in one sense is certainly true – that Fascism is a product of Communism, Mr N. A. Holdaway, one of the ablest Marxist writers we possess, writes as follows:

The hoary legend of Communism leading to Fascism ... The element of truth in it is this: that the appearance of Communist activity warns the ruling class that democratic Labour Parties are no longer capable of holding the working class in check, and that capitalist dictatorship must assume another form if it is to survive.

You see here the defects of the method. Because he has detected the underlying economic cause of Fascism, he tacitly assumes that the spiritual side of it is of no importance. Fascism is written off as a manoeuvre of the 'ruling class', which at bottom it is. But this in itself would only explain why Fascism appeals to capitalists. What about the millions who are not capitalists, who in a material sense have nothing to gain from Fascism and are often aware of it, and who, nevertheless, are Fascists? Obviously their approach has been purely along the ideological line. They could only be stampeded into Fascism because Communism attacked or seemed to attack certain things (patriotism, religion, etc.) which lay deeper than the economic motive; and in *that* sense it is perfectly true that Communism leads to Fascism. It is a pity that Marxists nearly always concentrate on letting economic cats out of ideological bags; it does in one sense reveal the truth, but with this penalty, that most of their propaganda misses its mark. It is the spiritual recoil from Socialism, especially as it manifests itself in sensitive people, that I want to discuss in this chapter. I shall have to analyse it at some length, because it is very widespread, very powerful, and, among Socialists, almost completely ignored.

The first thing to notice is that the idea of Socialism is bound up, more or less inextricably, with the idea of machine-production. Socialism is essentially an *urban* creed. It grew up more or less concurrently with industrialism, it has always had its roots in the town proletariat and the town intellectual, and it is doubtful whether it could ever have arisen in any but an industrial society. Granted industrialism, the idea of Socialism presents itself naturally, because private ownership is only tolerable when every individual (or family or other unit) is at least moderately self-supporting; but the effect of industrialism is to make it impossible for anyone to be self-supporting even for a moment. Industrialism, once it rises above a fairly low level, *must* lead to some form of collectivism. Not necessarily to Socialism, of course; conceivably it might lead to the Slave-State of which Fascism is a kind of prophecy. And the converse is also true. Machine-production suggests Socialism, but Socialism as a world-system implies machine-production, because it demands certain things not compatible with a primitive way of life. It demands, for instance, constant intercommunication and exchange of goods between all parts of the earth; it demands some degree of centralized control; it demands an approximately equal standard of life for all human beings and probably a certain uniformity of education. We may take it, therefore, that any world in which Socialism was a reality would be at least as highly mechanized as the United States at this moment, probably much more so. In any case, no Socialist would think of denying this. The Socialist world is always pictured as a completely mechanized, immensely organized world, depending on the machine as the civilizations of antiquity depend on the slave.

So far so good, or so bad. Many, perhaps a majority, of thinking people are not in love with machine-civilization, but everyone who is not a fool knows that it is nonsense to talk at this moment about scrapping the machine. But the unfortunate thing is that Socialism, as usually presented, is bound up with the idea of mechanical progress, not merely as a necessary development but as an end in itself, almost as a kind of religion. This idea is implicit in, for instance, most of the propagandist stuff that is written about the rapid mechanical advance in Soviet Russia (the Dneiper dam, tractors, etc., etc.). Karel Capek hits it off well enough in the horrible ending of *R.U.R.*, when the Robots, having slaughtered the last human being, announce their intention to 'build many houses' (just for the sake of building houses, you see). The kind of person who most readily accepts Socialism is also the kind of person who views mechanical progress, *as such*, with enthusiasm. And this is so much the case that Socialists are often unable to grasp that the opposite opinion exists. As a rule the most persuasive argument they can think of is to tell you that the present mechanization of the world is as nothing to what we shall see when Socialism is established. Where there is one aeroplane now, in those days there will be fifty! All the work that is now done by hand will then be done by machinery: everything that is now made of leather, wood, or stone will be made of rubber, glass, or steel; there will be no disorder, no loose ends, no wildernesses, no wild animals, no weeds, no disease, no poverty, no pain – and so on and so forth. The Socialist world is to be above all things an *ordered* world, an *efficient* world. But it is precisely from that vision of the future as a sort of glittering Wells-world that sensitive minds recoil. Please notice that this essentially fat-bellied version of 'progress' is not an integral part of Socialist doctrine; but it has come to be thought of as one, with the result that the temperamental conservatism which is latent in all kinds of people is easily mobilized against Socialism.

Every sensitive person has moments when he is suspicious of machinery and to some extent of physical science. But it is important to sort out the various motives, which have differed greatly at different times, for hostility to science and machinery, and to disregard the jealousy of the modern literary gent who hates science because science has stolen literature's thunder. The earliest full-length attack on science and machinery that I am acquainted with is in the third part of *Gulliver's Travels*. But Swift's attack, though brilliant as a *tour de force*, is irrelevant and even silly, because it is written from the standpoint – perhaps this seems a queer thing to say of the author of *Gulliver's Travels* – of a man who lacked imagination. To Swift, science was merely a kind of futile muckraking and the machines were nonsensical contraptions that would never work. His standard was that of practical usefulness, and he lacked the vision to see that an experiment which is not demonstrably useful at the moment may yield results in the future. Elsewhere in the book he names it as the best of all achievements 'to make two blades of grass grow where one grew before'; not seeing, apparently, that this is just what the machine can do. A little later the despised machines began working, physical science increased its scope, and there came the celebrated conflict between religion and science which agitated our grandfathers. That conflict is over and both sides have retreated and claimed a victory, but an anti-scientific bias still lingers in the minds of most religious believers. All through the nineteenth century protesting voices were raised against science and machinery (see Dickens's *Hard Times*, for instance), but usually for the rather shallow reason that industrialism in its first stages was cruel and ugly. Samuel Butler's attack on the machine in the well-known chapter of *Erewhon* is a different matter. But Butler himself lived in a less desperate age than our own, an age in which it was still possible for a first-rate man to be a dilettante part of the time, and therefore the whole thing appeared to him as a kind of intellectual exercise. He saw clearly enough our abject dependence on the machine, but instead of bothering to work out its consequences he preferred to exaggerate it for the sake of what was not much more than a joke. It is only in our own age, when mechanization has finally triumphed, that we can actually *feel* the tendency of the machine to make a fully human life impossible. There is probably no one capable of thinking and feeling who has not occasionally looked at a gas-pipe chair and reflected that the machine is the enemy of life. As a rule, however, this feeling is instinctive rather than reasoned. People know that in some way or another 'progress' is a swindle, but they reach this conclusion by a kind of mental shorthand; my job here is to supply the logical steps that are usually left out. But first one must ask, what is the function of the machine? Obviously its primary function is to save work, and the type of person to whom machine-civilization is entirely acceptable seldom sees any reason for looking further. Here for instance is a person who claims, or rather screams, that he is thoroughly at home in the modern mechanized world. I am quoting from *World Without Faith*, by Mr John Beevers. This is what he says:

It is plain lunacy to say that the average £2 10s. to £4 a week man of today is a lower type than an eighteenth-century farm labourer. Or than the labourer or peasant of any exclusively agricultural community now or in the past. It just isn't true. It is so damn silly to cry out about the civilizing effects of work in the fields and farmyards as against that done in a big locomotive works or an automobile factory. Work is a nuisance. We work because we have to and all work is done to provide us with leisure and the means of spending that leisure as enjoyably as possible.

And again:

Man is going to have time enough and power enough to hunt for his own heaven on earth without worrying about the supernatural one. The earth will be so pleasant a place that the priest and the parson won't be left with much of a tale to tell. Half the stuffing is knocked out of them by one neat blow. Etc., etc., etc.

There is a whole chapter to this effect (Chapter 4 of Mr Beevers's book), and it is of some interest as an exhibition of machine-worship in its most completely vulgar, ignorant, and half-baked form. It is the authentic voice of a large section of the modern world. Every aspirin-eater in the outer suburbs would echo it fervently. Notice the shrill wail of anger ('It just isn't troo-o-o!', etc.) with which Mr Beevers meets the suggestion that his grandfather may have been a better man than himself; and the still more horrible suggestion that if we returned to a simpler way of life he might have to toughen his muscles with a job of work. Work, you see, is done 'to provide us with leisure'. Leisure for what? Leisure to become more like Mr Beevers, presumably. Though as a matter of fact, from that line of talk about 'heaven on earth', you can make a fairly good guess at what he would like civilization to be; a sort of Lyons Corner House lasting *in saecula saeculorum* and getting bigger and noisier all the time. And in any book by anyone who feels at home in the machine-world – in any book by H. G. Wells, for instance – you will find passages of the same kind. How often have we not heard it, that glutinously uplifting stuff about 'the machines, our new race of slaves, which will set humanity free', etc., etc., etc. To these people, apparently, the only danger of the machine is its possible use for destructive purposes; as, for instance, aeroplanes are used in war. Barring wars and unforeseen disasters, the future is envisaged as an ever more rapid march of mechanical progress; machines to save work, machines to save thought, machines to save pain, hygiene, efficiency, organization, more hygiene, more efficiency, more organization, more machines – until finally you land up in the by now familiar Wellsian Utopia, aptly caricatured by Huxley in *Brave New World*, the paradise of little fat men. Of course in their day-dreams of the future the little fat men are neither fat nor little; they are Men Like Gods. But why should they be? All mechanical progress is towards greater and greater efficiency; ultimately, therefore, towards a world in which *nothing goes wrong*. But in a world in which nothing went wrong, many of the qualities which Mr Wells regards as 'godlike' would be no more valuable than the animal faculty of moving the ears. The beings in *Men Like Gods* and *The Dream* are represented, for example, as brave, generous, and physically strong. But in a world from which physical danger had been banished – and obviously mechanical progress tends to eliminate danger – would physical courage be likely to survive? *Could* it survive? And why should physical strength survive in a world where there was never the need for physical labour? As for such qualities as loyalty, generosity, etc., in a world where nothing went wrong, they would be not only irrelevant but probably unimaginable. The truth is that many of the qualities we admire in human beings can only function in opposition to some kind of disaster, pain, or difficulty; but the tendency of mechanical progress is to eliminate disaster, pain, and difficulty. In books like *The Dream* and *Men Like Gods* it is assumed that such qualities as strength, courage, generosity, etc., will be kept alive because they are comely qualities and necessary attributes of a full human being. Presumably, for instance, the inhabitants of Utopia would create artificial dangers in order to exercise their courage, and do dumb-bell exercises to harden muscles which they would never be obliged to use. And here you observe the huge contradiction which is usually present in the idea of progress. The tendency of mechanical progress is to make your environment safe and soft; and yet you are striving to keep yourself brave and hard. You are at the same moment furiously pressing forward and desperately holding back. It is as though a London stockbroker should go to his office in a suit of chain mail and insist on talking medieval Latin. So in the last analysis the champion of progress is also the champion of anachronisms.

Meanwhile I am assuming that the tendency of mechanical progress *is* to make life safe and soft. This may be disputed, because at any given moment the effect of some recent mechanical invention may appear to be the opposite. Take for instance the transition from horses to motor vehicles. At a first glance one might say, considering the enormous toll of road deaths, that the motor-car does not exactly tend to make life safer. Moreover it probably needs as much toughness to be a first-rate dirt-track rider as to be a broncho-buster or to ride in the Grand National. Nevertheless the *tendency* of all machinery is to become safer and easier to handle. The danger of accidents would disappear if we chose to tackle our road-planning problem seriously, as we shall do sooner or later; and meanwhile the motor-car has evolved to a point at which anyone who is not blind or paralytic can drive it after a few lessons. Even now it needs far less nerve and skill to drive a car ordinarily well than to ride a horse ordinarily well; in twenty years' time it may need no nerve or skill at all. Therefore, one must say that, taking society as a whole, the result of the transition from horses to cars has been an increase in human softness. Presently somebody comes along with another invention, the aeroplane for instance, which does not at first sight appear to make life safer. The first men who went up in aeroplanes were superlatively brave, and even today it must need an exceptionally good nerve to be a pilot. But the same tendency as before is at work. The aeroplane, like the motor-car, will be made foolproof; a million engineers are working, almost unconsciously, in that direction. Finally – this is the objective, though it may never quite be reached – you will get an aeroplane whose pilot needs no more skill or courage than a baby needs in its perambulator. And all mechanical progress is and must be in this direction. A machine evolves by becoming more efficient, that is, more foolproof; hence the objective of mechanical progress is a foolproof world – which may or may not mean a world inhabited by fools. Mr Wells would probably retort that the world can never become foolproof, because, however high a standard of efficiency you have reached, there is always some greater difficulty ahead. For example (this is Mr Wells's favourite idea – he has used it in goodness knows how many perorations), when you have got this planet of ours perfectly into trim, you start upon the enormous task of reaching and colonizing another. But this is merely to push the objective further into the future; the objective itself remains the same. Colonize another planet, and the game of mechanical progress begins anew; for the foolproof world you have substituted the foolproof solar system – the foolproof universe. In tying yourself to the ideal of mechanical efficiency, you tie yourself to the ideal of softness. But softness is repulsive; and thus all progress is seen to be a frantic struggle towards an objective which you hope and pray will never be reached. Now and again, but not often, you meet somebody who grasps that what is usually called progress also entails what is usually called degeneracy, and who is nevertheless in favour of progress. Hence the fact that in Mr Shaw's Utopia a statue was erected to Falstaff, as the first man who ever made a speech in favour of cowardice.

But the trouble goes immensely deeper than this. Hitherto I have only pointed out the absurdity of aiming at mechanical progress and also at the preservation of qualities which mechanical progress makes unnecessary. The question one has got to consider is whether there is *any* human activity which would not be maimed by the dominance of the machine.

The function of the machine is to save work. In a fully mechanized world all the dull drudgery will be done by machinery, leaving us free for more interesting pursuits. So expressed, this sounds splendid. It makes one sick to see half a dozen men sweating their guts out to dig a trench for a water-pipe, when some easily devised machine would scoop the earth out in a couple of minutes. Why not let the machine do the work and the men go and do something else. But presently the question arises, what else are they to do? Supposedly they are set free from 'work' in order that they may do something which is not 'work'. But what is work and what is not work? Is it work to dig, to carpenter, to plant trees, to fell trees, to ride, to fish, to hunt, to feed chickens, to play the piano, to take photographs, to build a house, to cook, to sew, to trim hats, to mend motor bicycles? All of these things are work to somebody, and all of them are play to somebody. There are in fact very few activities which cannot be classed either as work or play according as you choose to regard them. The labourer set free from digging may want to spend his leisure, or part of it, in playing the piano, while the professional pianist may be only too glad to get out and dig at the potato patch. Hence the antithesis between work, as something intolerably tedious, and not-work, as something desirable, is false. The truth is that when a human being is not eating, drinking, sleeping, making love, talking, playing games, or merely lounging about – and these things will not fill up a lifetime – he needs work and usually looks for it, though he may not call it work. Above the level of a third- or fourth-grade moron, life has got to be lived largely in terms of effort. For man is not, as the vulgarer hedonists seem to suppose, a kind of walking stomach; he has also got a hand, an eye, and a brain. Cease to use your hands, and you have lopped off a huge chunk of your consciousness. And now consider again those half-dozen men who were digging the trench for the water-pipe. A machine has set them free from digging, and they are going to amuse themselves with something else – carpentering, for instance. But whatever they want to do, they will find that another machine has set them free from *that*. For in a fully mechanized world there would be no more need to carpenter, to cook, to mend motor bicycles, etc., than there would be to dig. There is scarcely anything, from catching a whale to carving a cherry stone, that could not conceivably be done by machinery. The machine would even encroach upon the activities we now class as 'art'; it is doing so already, via the camera and the radio. Mechanize the world as fully as it might be mechanized, and whichever way you turn there will be some machine cutting you off from the chance of working – that is, of living.

At a first glance this might not seem to matter. Why should you not get on with your 'creative work' and disregard the machines that would do it for you? But it is not so simple as it sounds. Here am I, working eight hours a day in an insurance office; in my spare time I want to do something 'creative', so I choose to do a bit of carpentering – to make myself a table, for instance. Notice that from the very start there is a touch of artificiality about the whole business, for the factories can turn me out a far better table than I can make for myself. But even when I get to work on my table, it is not possible for me to feel towards it as the cabinet-maker of a hundred years ago felt towards his table, still less as Robinson Crusoe felt towards his. For before I start, most of the work has already been done for me by machinery. The tools I use demand the minimum of skill. I can get, for instance, planes which will cut out any moulding; the cabinet-maker of a hundred years ago would have had to do the work with chisel and gouge, which demanded real skill of eye and hand. The boards I buy are ready planed and the legs are ready turned by the lathe. I can even go to the wood-shop and buy all the parts of the table ready-made and only needing to be fitted together; my work being reduced to driving in a few pegs and using a piece of sandpaper. And if this is so at present, in the mechanized future it will be enormously more so. With the tools and materials available *then*, there will be no possibility of mistake, hence no room for skill. Making a table will be easier and duller than peeling a potato. In such circumstances it is nonsense to talk of 'creative work'. In any case the arts of the hand (which have got to be transmitted by apprenticeship) would long since have disappeared. Some of them have disappeared already, under the competition of the machine. Look round any country churchyard and see whether you can find a decently-cut tombstone later than 1820. The art, or rather the craft, of stonework has died out so completely that it would take centuries to revive it.

But it may be said, why not retain the machine *and* retain 'creative work'? Why not cultivate anachronisms as a spare-time hobby? Many people have played with this idea; it seems to solve with such beautiful ease the problems set by the machine. The citizen of Utopia, we are told, coming home from his daily two hours of turning a handle in the tomato-canning factory, will deliberately revert to a more primitive way of life and solace his creative instincts with a bit of fretwork, pottery-glazing, or handloom-weaving. And why is this picture an absurdity – as it is, of course? Because of a principle that is not always recognized, though always acted upon: that so long as the machine is *there*, one is under an obligation to use it. No one draws water from the well when he can turn on the tap. One sees a good illustration of this in the matter of travel. Everyone who has travelled by primitive methods in an undeveloped country knows that the difference between that kind of travel and modern travel in trains, cars, etc., is the difference between life and death. The nomad who walks or rides, with his baggage stowed on a camel or an ox-cart, may suffer every kind of discomfort, but at least he is living while he is travelling; whereas for the passenger in an express train or a luxury liner his journey is an interregnum, a kind of temporary death. And yet so long as the railways exist, one has got to travel by train – or by car or aeroplane. Here am I, forty miles from London. When I want to go up to London why do I not pack my luggage on to a mule and set out on foot, making a two days of it? Because, with the Green Line buses whizzing past me every ten minutes, such a journey would be intolerably irksome. In order that one may enjoy primitive methods of travel, it is necessary that no other method should be available. No human being ever wants to do anything in a more cumbrous way than is necessary. Hence the absurdity of that picture of Utopians saving their souls with fretwork. In a world where everything could be done by machinery, everything would be done by machinery. Deliberately to revert to primitive methods to use archaic tools, to put silly little difficulties in your own way, would be a piece of dilettantism, of pretty-pretty arty and craftiness. It would be like solemnly sitting down to eat your dinner with stone implements. Revert to handwork in a machine age, and you are back in Ye Olde Tea Shoppe or the Tudor villa with the sham beams tacked to the wall.

The tendency of mechanical progress, then, is to frustrate the human need for effort and creation. It makes unnecessary and even impossible

the activities of the eye and the hand. The apostle of 'progress' will
sometimes declare that this does not matter, but you can usually drive
him into a corner by pointing out the horrible lengths to which the process
can be carried. Why, for instance, use your hands at all – why use them
even for blowing your nose or sharpening a pencil? Surely you could fix
some kind of steel and rubber contraption to your shoulders and let your
arm wither into stumps of skin and bone? And so with every organ and
every faculty. There is really no reason why a human being should do
more than eat, drink, sleep, breathe, and procreate; *everything* else could
be done for him by machinery. Therefore the logical end of mechanical
progress is to reduce the human being to something resembling a brain in
a bottle. That is the goal towards which we are already moving, though,
of course, we have no intention of getting there; just as a man who drinks
a bottle of whisky a day does not actually intend to get cirrhosis of the
liver. The implied objective of 'progress' is – not *exactly*, perhaps, the
brain in the bottle, but at any rate some frightful subhuman depth of
softness and helplessness. And the unfortunate thing is that at present the
word 'progress' and the word 'Socialism' are linked inseparably in almost
everyone's mind. The kind of person who hates machinery also takes
it for granted to hate Socialism; the Socialist is always in favour of
mechanization, rationalization, modernization – or at least thinks that he
ought to be in favour of them. Quite recently, for instance, a prominent
I.L.P.'er confessed to me with a sort of wistful shame – as though it were
something faintly improper – that he was 'fond of horses'. Horses, you
see, belong to the vanished agricultural past, and all sentiment for the
past carries with it a vague smell of heresy. I do not believe that this need
necessarily be so, but undoubtedly it is so. And in itself it is quite enough
to explain the alienation of decent minds from Socialism.

A generation ago every intelligent person was in some sense a revolutionary; nowadays it would be nearer the mark to say that every intelligent
person is a reactionary. In this connexion it is worth comparing H. G.
Wells's *The Sleeper Awakes* with Aldous Huxley's *Brave New World*,
written thirty years later. Each is a pessimistic Utopia, a vision of a sort
of prig's paradise in which all the dreams of the 'progressive' person come
true. Considered merely as a piece of imaginative construction *The Sleeper
Awakes* is, I think, much superior, but it suffers from vast contradictions
because of the fact that Wells, as the arch-priest of 'progress', cannot
write with any conviction *against* 'progress'. He draws a picture of a
glittering, strangely sinister world in which the privileged classes live a
life of shallow gutless hedonism, and the workers, reduced to a state of

THE ROAD TO WIGAN PIER   281

utter slavery and sub-human ignorance, toil like troglodytes in caverns underground. As soon as one examines this idea – it is further developed in a splendid short story in *Stories of Space and Time* – one sees its inconsistency. For in the immensely mechanized world that Wells is imagining, why should the workers have to work harder than at present? Obviously the tendency of the machine is to eliminate work, not to increase it. In the machine-world the workers might be enslaved, ill-treated, and even underfed, but they certainly would not be condemned to ceaseless manual toil; because in that case what would be the function of the machine? You can have machines doing all the work or human beings doing all the work, but you can't have both. Those armies of underground workers, with their blue uniform and their debased, half-human language, are only put in 'to make your flesh creep'. Wells wants to suggest that 'progress' might take a wrong turning; but the only evil he cares to imagine is inequality – one class grabbing all the wealth and power and oppressing the others, apparently out of pure spite. Give it quite a small twist, he seems to suggest, overthrow the privileged class – change over from world-capitalism to Socialism, in fact – and all will be well. The machine-civilization is to continue, but its products are to be shared out equally. The thought he dare not face is that the machine itself may be the enemy. So in his more characteristic Utopias (*The Dream, Men Like Gods*, etc.), he returns to optimism and to a vision of humanity, 'liberated' by the machine, as a race of enlightened sunbathers whose sole topic of conversation is their own superiority to their ancestors. *Brave New World* belongs to a later time and to a generation which has seen through the swindle of 'progress'. It contains its own contradictions (the most important of them is pointed out in Mr John Strachey's *The Coming Struggle for Power*), but it is at least a memorable assault on the more fat-bellied type of perfectionism. Allowing for the exaggerations of caricature, it probably expresses what a majority of thinking people feel about machine-civilization.

The sensitive person's hostility to the machine is in one sense unrealistic, because of the obvious fact that the machine has come to stay. But as an attitude of mind there is a great deal to be said for it. The machine has got to be accepted, but it is probably better to accept it rather as one accepts a drug – that is, grudgingly and suspiciously. Like a drug, the machine is useful, dangerous, and habit-forming. The oftener one surrenders to it the tighter its grip becomes. You have only to look about you at this moment to realize with what sinister speed the machine is getting us into its power. To begin with, there is the frightful debauchery of taste that has already been effected by a century of mechanization. This is almost too obvious and too generally admitted to need pointing out. But as a single instance, take taste in its narrowest sense – the taste for decent food. In the highly mechanized countries, thanks to tinned food, cold storage, synthetic flavouring matters, etc., the palate is almost a dead organ. As you can see by looking at any greengrocer's shop, what the majority of English people mean by an apple is a lump of highly-coloured cotton wool from America or Australia; they will devour these things, apparently with pleasure, and let the English apples rot under the trees. It is the shiny, standardized, machine-made look of the American apple that appeals to them; the superior taste of the English apple is something they simply do not notice. Or look at the factory-made, foil-wrapped cheese and 'blended' butter in any grocer's; look at the hideous rows of tins which usurp more and more of the space in any food-shop, even a dairy; look at a sixpenny Swiss roll or a twopenny ice-cream; look at the filthy chemical by-product that people will pour down their throats under the name of beer. Wherever you look you will see some slick machine-made article triumphing over the old-fashioned article that still tastes of something other than sawdust. And what applies to food applies also to furniture, houses, clothes, books, amusements, and everything else that makes up our environment. There are now millions of people, and they are increasing every year, to whom the blaring of a radio is not only a more acceptable but a more *normal* background to their thoughts than the lowing of cattle or the song of birds. The mechanization of the world could never proceed very far while taste, even the taste-buds of the tongue, remained uncorrupted, because in that case most of the products of the machine would be simply unwanted. In a healthy world there would be no demand for tinned foods, aspirins, gramophones, gaspipe chairs, machine guns, daily newspapers, telephones, motor-cars, etc. etc.; and on the other hand there would be a constant demand for the things the machine cannot produce. But meanwhile the machine is here, and its corrupting effects are almost irresistible. One inveighs against it, but one goes on using it. Even a bare-arse savage, given the chance, will learn the vices of civilization within a few months. Mechanization leads to the decay of taste, the decay of taste leads to the demand for machine-made articles and hence to more mechanization, and so a vicious circle is established.

But in addition to this there is a tendency for the mechanization of the world to proceed as it were automatically, whether we want it or not. This is due to the fact that in modern Western man the faculty of mechanical invention has been fed and stimulated till it has reached almost the status of an instinct. People invent new machines and improve existing ones almost unconsciously, rather as a somnambulist will go on working in his sleep. In the past, when it was taken for granted that life on this planet is harsh or at any rate laborious, it seemed the natural fate to go on using the clumsy implements of your forefathers, and only a few eccentric persons, centuries apart, proposed innovations; hence throughout enormous ages such things as the ox-cart, the plough, the sickle, etc., remained radically unchanged. It is on record that screws have been in use since remote antiquity and yet that it was not till the middle of the nineteenth century that anyone thought of making screws with points on them; for several thousand years they remained flat-ended and holes had to be drilled for them before they could be inserted. In our own epoch such a thing would be unthinkable. For almost every modern Western man has his inventive faculty to some extent developed; the Western man invents machines as naturally as the Polynesian islander swims. Give a Western man a job of work and he immediately begins devising a machine that would do it for him; give him a machine and he thinks of ways of improving it. I understand this tendency well enough, for in an ineffectual sort of way I have that type of mind myself. I have not either the patience or the mechanical skill to devise any machine that would work, but I am perpetually seeing, as it were, the ghosts of possible machines that might save me the trouble of using my brain or muscles. A person with a more definite mechanical turn would probably construct some of them and put them into operation. But under our present economic system, whether he constructed them – or rather, whether anyone else had the benefit of them – would depend upon whether they were commercially valuable. The Socialists are right, therefore, when they claim that the rate of mechanical progress will be much more rapid once Socialism is established. Given a mechanical civilization the process of invention and improvement will always continue, but the tendency of capitalism is to slow it down, because under capitalism any invention which does not promise fairly immediate profits is neglected; some, indeed, which threaten to reduce profits are suppressed almost as ruthlessly as the flexible glass mentioned by Petronius.* Establish Socialism – remove the profit principle – and the inventor will have a free hand. The mechanization of the world, already rapid enough, would be or at any rate could be enormously accelerated.

And this prospect is a slightly sinister one, because it is obvious even

* For example: Some years ago someone invented a gramophone needle that would last for decades. One of the big gramophone companies bought up the patent rights, and that was the last that was ever heard of it.

now that the process of mechanization is out of control. It is happening merely because humanity has got the habit. A chemist perfects a new method of synthesizing rubber, or a mechanic devises a new pattern of gudgeon-pin. Why? Not for any clearly understood purpose, but simply from the impulse to invent and improve, which has now become instinctive. Put a pacifist to work in a bomb-factory and in two months he will be devising a new type of bomb. Hence the appearance of such diabolical things as poison gases, which are not expected even by their inventors to be beneficial to humanity. Our attitude towards such things as poison gases *ought* to be the attitude of the king of Brobdingnag towards gunpowder; but because we live in a mechanical and scientific age we are infected with the notion that, whatever else happens, 'progress' must continue and knowledge must never be suppressed. Verbally, no doubt, we would agree that machinery is made for man and not man for machinery; in practice any attempt to check the development of the machine appears to us an attack on knowledge and therefore a kind of blasphemy. And even if the whole of humanity suddenly revolted against the machine and decided to escape to a simpler way of life, the escape would still be immensely difficult. It would not do, as in Butler's *Erewhon*, to smash every machine invented after a certain date; we should also have to smash the habit of mind that would, almost involuntarily, devise fresh machines as soon as the old ones were smashed. And in all of us there is at least a tinge of that habit of mind. In every country in the world the large army of scientists and technicians, with the rest of us panting at their heels, are marching along the road of 'progress' with the blind persistence of a column of ants. Comparatively few people want it to happen, plenty of people actively want it *not* to happen, and yet it is happening. The process of mechanization has itself become a machine, a huge glittering vehicle whirling us we are not certain where, but probably towards the padded Wells-world and the brain in the bottle.

This, then, is the case against the machine. Whether it is a sound or unsound case hardly matters. The point is that these or very similar arguments would be echoed by every person who is hostile to machine-civilization. And unfortunately, because of that nexus of thought, 'Social-ism - progress - machinery - Russia - tractor - hygiene - machinery - progress', which exists in almost everyone's mind, it is usually the *same* person who is hostile to Socialism. The kind of person who hates central heating and gaspipe chairs is also the kind of person who, when you mention Socialism, murmurs something about 'beehive state' and moves away with a pained expression. So far as my observation goes, very few

Socialists grasp why this is so, or even that it *is* so. Get the more vocal type of Socialist into a corner, repeat to him the substance of what I have said in this chapter, and see what kind of answer you get. As a matter of fact you will get several answers; I am so familiar with them that I know them almost by heart.

In the first place he will tell you that it is impossible to 'go back' (or to 'put back the hand of progress' – as though the hand of progress hadn't been pretty violently put back several times in human history!), and will then accuse you of being a medievalist and begin to descant upon the horrors of the Middle Ages, leprosy, the Inquisition, etc. As a matter of fact, most attacks upon the Middle Ages and the past generally by apologists of modernity are beside the point, because their essential trick is to project a modern man, with his squeamishness and his high standards of comfort, into an age when such things were unheard of. But notice that in any case this is not an answer. For a dislike of the mechanized future does not imply the smallest reverence for any period of the past. D. H. Lawrence, wiser than the medievalist, chose to idealize the Etruscans about whom we know conveniently little. But there is no need to idealize even the Etruscans or the Pelasgians, or the Aztecs, or the Sumerians, or any other vanished and romantic people. When one pictures a desirable civilization, one pictures it merely as an objective; there is no need to pretend that it has ever existed in space and time. Press this point home, explain that you wish to aim at making life simpler and harder instead of softer and more complex, and the Socialist will usually assume that you want to revert to a 'state of nature' – meaning some stinking palaeolithic cave: as though there were nothing between a flint scraper and the steel mills of Sheffield, or between a skin coracle and the *Queen Mary*!

Finally, however, you will get an answer which is rather more to the point and which runs roughly as follows: 'Yes, what you are saying is all very well in its way. No doubt it would be very noble to harden ourselves and do without aspirins and central heating and so forth. But the point is, you see, that nobody seriously wants it. It would mean going back to an agricultural way of life, which means beastly hard work and isn't at all the same thing as playing at gardening. I don't want hard work, you don't want hard work – nobody wants it who knows what it means. You only talk as you do because you've never done a day's work in your life,' etc., etc.

Now this in a sense is true. It amounts to saying, 'We're soft – for God's sake let's stay soft!' which at least is realistic. As I have pointed out already, the machine has got us in its grip and to escape will be immensely difficult. Nevertheless this answer is really an evasion, because it fails to make clear what we mean when we say that we 'want' this or that. I am a degenerate modern semi-intellectual who would die if I did not get my early morning cup of tea and my *New Statesman* every Friday. Clearly I do not, in a sense, 'want' to return to a simpler, harder, probably agricultural way of life. In the same sense I don't 'want' to cut down my drinking, to pay my debts, to take enough exercise, to be faithful to my wife, etc., etc. But in another and more permanent sense I do want these things, and perhaps in the same sense I want a civilization in which 'progress' is not definable as making the world safe for little fat men. These that I have outlined are practically the only arguments that I have been able to get from Socialists – thinking, book-trained Socialists – when I have tried to explain to them just *how* they are driving away possible adherents. Of course there is also the old argument that Socialism is going to arrive anyway, whether people like it or not, because of that trouble-saving thing, 'historic necessity'. But 'historic necessity', or rather the belief in it, has failed to survive Hitler.

Meanwhile the thinking person, by intellect usually left-wing but by temperament often right-wing, hovers at the gate of the Socialist fold. He is no doubt aware that he *ought* to be a Socialist. But he observes first the dullness of individual Socialists, then the apparent flabbiness of Socialist ideals, and veers away. Till quite recently it was natural to veer towards indifferentism. Ten years ago, even five years ago, the typical literary gent wrote books on baroque architecture and had a soul above politics. But that attitude is becoming difficult and even unfashionable. The times are growing harsher, the issues are clearer, the belief that nothing will ever change (i.e. that your dividends will always be safe) is less prevalent. The fence on which the literary gent sits, once as comfortable as the plush cushion of a cathedral stall, is now pinching his bottom intolerably; more and more he shows a disposition to drop off on one side or the other. It is interesting to notice how many of our leading writers, who a dozen years ago were art for art's saking for all they were worth and would have considered it too vulgar for words even to vote at a general election, are now taking a definite political standpoint; while most of the younger writers, at least those of them who are not mere footlers, have been 'political' from the start. I believe that when the pinch comes there is a terrible danger that the main movement of the intelligentsia will be towards Fascism. Just how soon the pinch will come it is difficult to say; it depends, probably, upon events in Europe; but it may be that within two years or even a year we shall have reached the decisive moment. That will also be the moment when every person with any brains or any decency will know in his bones that he ought to be on the Socialist side. But he will not necessarily come there of his own accord; there are too many ancient prejudices standing in the way. He will have to be persuaded, and by methods that imply an understanding of his viewpoint. Socialists cannot afford to waste any more time in preaching to the converted. Their job now is to make Socialists as rapidly as possible; instead of which, all too often, they are making Fascists.

When I speak of Fascism in England, I am not necessarily thinking of Mosley and his pimpled followers. English Fascism, when it arrives, is likely to be of a sedate and subtle kind (presumably, at any rate at first, it won't be *called* Fascism), and it is doubtful whether a Gilbert and Sullivan heavy dragoon of Mosley's stamp would ever be much more than a joke to the majority of English people; though even Mosley will bear watching, for experience shows (*vide* the careers of Hitler, Napoleon III) that to a political climber it is sometimes an advantage not to be taken too seriously at the beginning of his career. But what I am thinking of at this moment is the Fascist attitude of mind, which beyond any doubt is gaining ground among people who ought to know better. Fascism as it appears in the intellectual is a sort of mirror-image – not actually of Socialism but of a plausible travesty of Socialism. It boils down to a determination to do the *opposite* of whatever the mythical Socialist does. If you present Socialism in a bad and misleading light – if you let people imagine that it does not mean much more than pouring European civilization down the sink at the command of Marxist prigs – you risk driving the intellectual into Fascism. You frighten him into a sort of angry defensive attitude in which he simply refuses to listen to the Socialist case. Some such attitude is already quite clearly discernible in writers like Pound, Wyndham Lewis, Roy Campbell, etc., in most of the Roman Catholic writers and many of the Douglas Credit group, in certain popular novelists, and even, if one looks below the surface, in so-superior conservative highbrows like Eliot and his countless followers. If you want some unmistakable illustrations of the growth of Fascist feeling in England, have a look at some of the innumerable letters that were written to the Press during the Abyssinian war, approving the Italian action, and also the howl of glee that went up from both Catholic and Anglican pulpits (see the *Daily Mail* of 17 August 1936) over the Fascist rising in Spain.

In order to combat Fascism it is necessary to understand it, which involves admitting that it contains some good as well as much evil. In practice, of course, it is merely an infamous tyranny, and its methods of

288 THE ROAD TO WIGAN PIER

attaining and holding power are such that even its most ardent apologists prefer to talk about something else. But the underlying feeling of Fascism, the feeling that first draws people into the Fascist camp, may be less contemptible. It is not *always*, as the *Saturday Review* would lead one to suppose, a squealing terror of the Bolshevik bogey-man. Everyone who has given the movement so much as a glance knows that the rank-and-file Fascist is often quite a well-meaning person – quite genuinely anxious, for instance, to better the lot of the unemployed. But more important than this is the fact that Fascism draws its strength from the good as well as the bad varieties of conservatism. To anyone with a feeling for tradition and for discipline it comes with its appeal ready-made. Probably it is very easy, when you have had a bellyful of the more tactless kind of Socialist propaganda, to see Fascism as the last line defence of all that is good in European civilization. Even the Fascist bully at his symbolic worst, with rubber truncheon in one hand and castor oil bottle in the other, does not necessarily feel himself a bully; more probably he feels like Roland in the pass at Roncevaux, defending Christendom against the barbarian. We have got to admit that if Fascism is everywhere advancing, this is largely the fault of Socialists themselves. Partly it is due to the mistaken Communist tactic of sabotaging democracy, i.e. sawing off the branch you are sitting on; but still more to the fact that Socialists have, so to speak, presented their case wrong side foremost. They have never made it sufficiently clear that the essential aims of Socialism are justice and liberty. With their eyes glued to economic facts, they have proceeded on the assumption that man has no soul, and explicitly or implicitly they have set up the goal of a materialistic Utopia. As a result Fascism has been able to play upon every instinct that revolts against hedonism and a cheap conception of 'progress'. It has been able to pose as the upholder of the European tradition, and to appeal to Christian belief, to patriotism, and to the military virtues. It is far worse than useless to write Fascism off as 'mass sadism', or some easy phrase of that kind. If you pretend that it is merely an aberration which will presently pass off of its own accord, you are dreaming a dream from which you will awake when somebody coshes you with a rubber truncheon. The only possible course is to examine the Fascist case, grasp that there is something to be said for it, and then make it clear to the world that whatever good Fascism contains is also implicit in Socialism.

At present the situation is desperate. Even if nothing worse befalls us, there are the conditions which I described in the earlier part of this book and which are not going to improve under our present economic system.

Still more urgent is the danger of Fascist domination in Europe. And unless Socialist doctrine, in an effective form, can be diffused widely and very quickly, there is no certainty that Fascism will ever be overthrown. For Socialism is the only real enemy that Fascism has to face. The capitalist-imperialist governments, even though they themselves are about to be plundered, will not fight with any conviction against Fascism as such. Our rulers, those of them who understand the issue, would probably prefer to hand over every square inch of the British Empire to Italy, Germany, and Japan than to see Socialism triumphant. It was easy to laugh at Fascism when we imagined that it was based on hysterical nationalism, because it seemed obvious that the Fascist states, each regarding itself as the chosen people and patriotic *contra mundum*, would clash with one another. But nothing of the kind is happening. Fascism is now an international movement, which means not only that the Fascist nations can combine for purposes of loot, but that they are groping, perhaps only half consciously as yet, towards a world-system. For the vision of the totalitarian state there is being substituted the vision of the totalitarian world. As I pointed out earlier, the advance of machine-technique must lead ultimately to some form of collectivism, but that form need not necessarily be equalitarian; that is, it need not be Socialism. *Pace* the economists, it is quite easy to imagine a world-society, economically collectivist – that is, with the profit principle eliminated – but with all political, military, and educational power in the hands of a small caste of rulers and their bravos. That or something like it is the objective of Fascism. And that, of course, is the slave-state, or rather the slave-world; it would probably be a stable form of society, and the chances are, considering the enormous wealth of the world if scientifically exploited, that the slaves would be well-fed and contented. It is usual to speak of the Fascist objective as the 'beehive state', which does a grave injustice to bees. A world of rabbits ruled by stoats would be nearer the mark. It is against this beastly possibility that we have got to combine.

The only thing *for* which we can combine is the underlying ideal of Socialism; justice and liberty. But it is hardly strong enough to call this ideal 'underlying'. It is almost completely forgotten. It has been buried beneath layer after layer of doctrinaire priggishness, party squabbles, and half-baked 'progressivism' until it is like a diamond hidden under a mountain of dung. The job of the Socialist is to get it out again. Justice and liberty! *Those* are the words that have got to ring like a bugle across the world. For a long time past, certainly for the last ten years, the devil has had all the best tunes. We have reached a stage when the very word

'Socialism' calls up, on the one hand, a picture of aeroplanes, tractors, and huge glittering factories of glass and concrete; on the other, a picture of vegetarians with wilting beards, of Bolshevik commissars (half gangster, half gramophone), of earnest ladies in sandals, shock-headed Marxists chewing polysyllables, escaped Quakers, birth-control fanatics, and Labour Party backstairs-crawlers. Socialism, at least in this island, does not smell any longer of revolution and the overthrow of tyrants; it smells of crankishness, machine-worship, and the stupid cult of Russia. Unless you can remove that smell, and very rapidly, Fascism may win.

13

AND finally, is there anything one can do about it?

In the first part of this book I illustrated, by a few brief sidelights, the kind of mess we are in; in this second part I have been trying to explain why, in my opinion, so many normal decent people are repelled by the only remedy, namely by Socialism. Obviously the most urgent need of the next few years is to capture those normal decent ones before Fascism plays its trump card. I do not want to raise here the question of parties and political expedients. More important than any party label (though doubtless the mere menace of Fascism will presently bring some kind of Popular Front into existence) is the diffusion of Socialist doctrine in an effective form. People have got to be made ready to *act* as Socialists. There are, I believe, countless people who, without being aware of it, are in sympathy with the essential aims of Socialism, and who could be won over almost without a struggle if only one could find the word that would move them. Everyone who knows the meaning of poverty, everyone who has a genuine hatred of tyranny and war, is on the Socialist side, potentially. My job here, therefore, is to suggest – necessarily in very general terms – how a reconciliation might be effected between Socialism and its more intelligent enemies.

First, as to the enemies themselves – I mean all those people who grasp that capitalism is evil but who are conscious of a sort of queasy, shuddering sensation when Socialism is mentioned. As I have pointed out, this is trace-able to two main causes. One is the personal inferiority of many individual Socialists; the other is the fact that Socialism is too often coupled with a fat-bellied, godless conception of 'progress' which revolts anyone with a feeling for tradition or the rudiments of an aesthetic sense. Let me take the second point first.

The distaste for 'progress' and machine-civilization which is so common among sensitive people is only defensible as an attitude of mind. It is not valid as a reason for rejecting Socialism, because it presupposes an alternative which does not exist. When you say, 'I object to mechanization and standardization – therefore I object to Socialism', you are saying in effect, 'I am free to do without the machine if I choose', which is nonsense. We are all dependent upon the machine, and if the machines stopped working most of us would die. You may hate the machine-civilization, probably you are right to hate it, but for the present there can be no question of accepting or rejecting it. The machine-civilization *is here*, and it can only be criticized from the inside, because all of us are inside it. It is only romantic fools who flatter themselves that they have escaped, like the literary gent in his Tudor cottage with bathroom h. and c., and the he-man who goes off to live a 'primitive' life in the jungle with a Mannlicher rifle and four wagon-loads of tinned food. And almost certainly the machine-civilization will continue to triumph. There is no reason to think that it will destroy itself or stop functioning of its own accord. For some time past it has been fashionable to say that war is presently going to 'wreck civilization' altogether; but, though the next full-sized war will certainly be horrible enough to make all previous ones seem a joke, it is immensely unlikely that it will put a stop to mechanical progress. It is true that a very vulnerable country like England, and perhaps the whole of western Europe, could be reduced to chaos by a few thousand well-placed bombs, but no war is at present thinkable which could wipe out industrialization in all countries simultaneously. We may take it that the return to a simpler, free, less mechanized way of life, however desirable it may be, is not going to happen. This is not fatalism, it is merely acceptance of facts. It is meaningless to oppose Socialism on the ground that you object to the beehive State, for the beehive State *is here*. The choice is not, as yet, between a human and an inhuman world. It is simply between Socialism and Fascism, which at its very best is Socialism with the virtues left out.

The job of the thinking person, therefore, is not to reject Socialism but to make up his mind to humanize it. Once Socialism is in a way to being established, those who can see through the swindle of 'progress' will probably find themselves resisting. In fact, it is their special function to do so. In the machine-world they have got to be a sort of permanent opposition, which is not the same thing as being an obstructionist or a traitor. But in this I am speaking of the future. For the moment the only possible course for any

decent person, however much of a Tory or an anarchist by temperament, is
to work for the establishment of Socialism. Nothing else can save us from
the misery of the present or the nightmare of the future. To oppose Socialism
now, when twenty million Englishmen are underfed and Fascism has conquered half Europe, is suicidal. It is like starting a civil war when the Goths
are crossing the frontier.

Therefore it is all the more important to get rid of that mere nervous
prejudice against Socialism which is not founded on any serious objection.
As I have pointed out already, many people who are not repelled by Socialism
are repelled by Socialists. Socialism, as now presented, is unattractive largely
because it appears, at any rate from the outside, to be the plaything of cranks,
doctrinaires, parlour Bolsheviks, and so forth. But it is worth remembering
that this is only so because the cranks, doctrinaires, etc., have been allowed
to get there first; if the movement were invaded by better brains and more
common decency, the objectionable types would cease to dominate it. For
the present one must just set one's teeth and ignore them; they will loom
much smaller when the movement has been humanized. Besides, they are
irrelevant. We have got to fight for justice and liberty, and Socialism does
mean justice and liberty when the nonsense is stripped off it. It is only the
essentials that are worth remembering. To recoil from Socialism because so
many individual Socialists are inferior people is as absurd as refusing to
travel by train because you dislike the ticket-collector's face.

And secondly, as to the Socialist himself – more especially the vocal, tract-
writing type of Socialist.

We are at a moment when it is desperately necessary for left-wingers of
all complexions to drop their differences and hang together. Indeed this is
already happening to a small extent. Obviously, then, the more intransigent
kind of Socialist has now got to ally himself with people who are not in
perfect agreement with him. As a rule he is rightly unwilling to do so, because
he sees the very real danger of watering the whole Socialist movement
down to some kind of pale-pink humbug even more ineffectual than the
parliamentary Labour Party. At the moment, for instance, there is great
danger that the Popular Front which Fascism will presumably bring into
existence will not be genuinely Socialist in character, but will simply be a
manoeuvre against German and Italian (not English) Fascism. Thus the
need to unite against Fascism might draw the Socialist into alliance with his
very worst enemies. But the principle to go upon is this: that you are never
in danger of allying yourself with the wrong people provided that you keep
the essentials of your movement in the foreground. And what are the essentials of Socialism? What is the mark of a real Socialist? I suggest that the

real Socialist is one who wishes – not merely conceives it as desirable, but actively wishes – to see tyranny overthrown. But I fancy that the majority of orthodox Marxists would not accept that definition, or would only accept it very grudgingly. Sometimes, when I listen to these people talking, and still more when I read their books, I get the impression that, to them, the whole Socialist movement is no more than a kind of exciting heresy-hunt – a leaping to and fro of frenzied witch-doctors to the beat of tom-toms and the tune of 'Fee fi, fo, fum, I smell the blood of a right-wing deviationist!' It is because of this kind of thing that it is so much easier to feel yourself a Socialist when you are among working-class people. The working-class Socialist, like the working-class Catholic, is weak on doctrine and can hardly open his mouth without uttering a heresy, but he has the heart of the matter in him. He does grasp the central fact that Socialism means the overthrow of tyranny, and the 'Marseillaise', if it were translated for his benefit, would appeal to him more deeply than any learned treatise on dialectical materialism. At this moment it is waste of time to insist that acceptance of Socialism means acceptance of the philosophic side of Marxism, plus adulation of Russia. The Socialist movement has not time to be a league of dialectical materialists; it has got to be a league of the oppressed against the oppressors. You have got to attract the man who means business, and you have got to drive away the mealy-mouthed Liberal who wants foreign Fascism destroyed in order that he may go on drawing his dividends peacefully – the type of humbug who passes resolutions 'against Fascism and Communism', i.e. against rats and rat-poison. Socialism means the overthrow of tyranny, at home as well as abroad. So long as you keep *that* fact well to the front, you will never be in much doubt as to who are your real supporters. As for minor differences – and the profoundest philosophical difference is unimportant compared with saving the twenty million Englishmen whose bones are rotting from malnutrition – the time to argue about them is afterwards.

I do not think the Socialist need make any sacrifice of essentials, but certainly he will have to make a great sacrifice of externals. It would help enormously, for instance, if the smell of crankishness which still clings to the Socialist movement could be dispelled. If only the sandals and the pistachio-coloured shirts could be put in a pile and burnt, and every vegetarian, teetotaller, and creeping Jesus sent home to Welwyn Garden City to do his yoga exercises quietly! But that, I am afraid, is not going to happen. What *is* possible, however, is for the more intelligent kind of Socialist to stop alienating possible supporters in silly and quite irrelevant ways. There are so many minor priggishnesses which could so easily be dropped. Take for instance the dreary attitude of the typical Marxist towards literature. Out of the many that come into my mind, I will give just one example. It sounds trivial, but it isn't. In the old *Worker's Weekly* (one of the forerunners of the *Daily Worker*) there used to be a column of literary chat of the 'Books on the Editor's Table' type. For several weeks running there had been a certain amount of talk about Shakespeare; whereupon an incensed reader wrote to say, 'Dear Comrade, we don't want to hear about these bourgeois writers like Shakespeare. Can't you give us something a bit more proletarian?' etc., etc. The editor's reply was simple. 'If you will turn to the index of Marx's *Capital*,' he wrote, 'you will find that Shakespeare is mentioned several times.' And please notice that this was enough to silence the objector. Once Shakespeare had received the benediction of Marx, he became respectable. *That* is the mentality that drives ordinary sensible people away from the Socialist movement. You do not need to care about Shakespeare to be repelled by that kind of thing. Again, there is the horrible jargon that nearly all Socialists think it necessary to employ. When the ordinary person hears phrases like 'bourgeois ideology' and 'proletarian solidarity' and 'expropriation of the expropriators', he is not inspired by them, he is merely disgusted. Even the single word 'Comrade' has done its dirty little bit towards discrediting the Socialist movement. How many a waverer has halted on the brink, gone perhaps to some public meeting and watched self-conscious Socialists dutifully addressing one another as 'Comrade', and then slid away, disillusioned, into the nearest four-ale bar! And his instinct is sound; for where is the sense of sticking on to yourself a ridiculous label which even after long practice can hardly be mentioned without a gulp of shame? It is fatal to let the ordinary inquirer get away with the idea that being a Socialist means wearing sandals and burbling about dialectical materialism. You have got to make it clear that there is room in the Socialist movement for human beings, or the game is up.

And this raises a great difficulty. It means that the issue of class, as distinct from mere economic status, has got to be faced more realistically than it is being faced at present.

I devoted three chapters to discussing the class-difficulty. The principal fact that will have emerged, I think, is that though the English class-system has outlived its usefulness, it *has* outlived it and shows no signs of dying. It greatly confuses the issue to assume, as the orthodox Marxist so often does (see for instance Mr Alec Brown's in some ways interesting book, *The Fate of the Middle Classes*), that social status is determined solely by income. Economically, no doubt, there are only two classes, the rich and the poor, but socially there is a whole hierarchy of classes, and the manners and traditions learned by each class in childhood are not only very different but

– this is the essential point – generally persist from birth to death. Hence the anomalous individuals that you find in every class of society. You find writers like Wells and Bennett who have grown immensely rich and have yet preserved intact their lower-middle-class Nonconformist prejudices; you find millionaires who cannot pronounce their aitches; you find petty shopkeepers whose income is far lower than that of the bricklayer and who, nevertheless, consider themselves (and are considered) the bricklayer's social superiors; you find board-school boys ruling Indian provinces and public-school men touting vacuum cleaners. If social stratification corresponded precisely to economic stratification, the public-school man would assume a cockney accent the day his income dropped below £200 a year. But does he? On the contrary, he immediately becomes twenty times more Public School than before. He clings to the Old School Tie as to a lifeline. And even the aitchless millionaire, though sometimes he goes to an elocutionist and learns a B.B.C. accent, seldom succeeds in disguising himself as completely as he would like to. It is in fact very difficult to escape, culturally, from the class into which you have been born.

As prosperity declines, social anomalies grow commoner. You don't get more aitchless millionaires, but you do get more and more public-school men touting vacuum cleaners and more and more small shopkeepers driven into the workhouse. Large sections of the middle class are being gradually proletarianized; but the important point is that they do not, at any rate in the first generation, adopt a proletarian outlook. Here am I, for instance, with a bourgeois upbringing and a working-class income. Which class do I belong to? Economically I belong to the working class, but it is almost impossible for me to think of myself as anything but a member of the bourgeoisie. And supposing I had to take sides, whom should I side with, the upper class which is trying to squeeze me out of existence, or the working class whose manners are not my manners? It is probable that I personally, in any important issue, would side with the working class. But what about the tens or hundreds of thousands of others who are in approximately the same position? And what about that far larger class, running into millions this time – the office-workers and black-coated employees of all kinds – whose traditions are less definitely middle class but who would certainly not thank you if you called them proletarians? All of these people have the same interests and the same enemies as the working class. All are being robbed and bullied by the same system. Yet how many of them realize it? When the pinch came nearly all of them would side with their oppressors and against those who ought to be their allies. It is quite easy to imagine a middle class crushed down to the worst depths of poverty and still remaining bitterly anti-working-class in sentiment; this being, of course, a ready-made Fascist Party.

Obviously the Socialist movement has got to capture the exploited middle class before it is too late; above all it must capture the office-workers, who are so numerous and, if they knew how to combine, so powerful. Equally obviously it has so far failed to do so. The very last person in whom you can hope to find revolutionary opinions is a clerk or a commercial traveller. Why? Very largely, I think, because of the 'proletarian' cant with which Socialist propaganda is mixed up. In order to symbolize the class war, there has been set up the more or less mythical figure of a 'proletarian', a muscular but downtrodden man in greasy overalls, in contradistinction to a 'capitalist', a fat, wicked man in a top hat and fur coat. It is tacitly assumed that there is no one in between; the truth being, of course, that in a country like England about a quarter of the population is in between. If you are going to harp on the 'dictatorship of the proletariat', it is an elementary precaution to start by explaining who the proletariat *are*. But because of the Socialist tendency to idealize the manual worker as such, this has never been made sufficiently clear. How many of the wretched shivering army of clerks and shopwalkers, who in some ways are actually worse off than a miner or a dock-hand, think of themselves as proletarians? A proletarian – so they have been taught to think – means a man without a collar. So that when you try to move them by talking about 'class war', you only succeed in scaring them; they forget their incomes and remember their accents, and fly to the defence of the class that is exploiting them.

Socialists have a big job ahead of them here. They have got to demonstrate, beyond possibility of doubt, just where the line of cleavage between exploiter and exploited comes. Once again it is a question of sticking to essentials; and the essential point here is that all people with small, insecure incomes are in the same boat and ought to be fighting on the same side. Probably we could do with a little less talk about 'capitalist' and 'proletarian' and a little more about the robbers and the robbed. But at any rate we must drop that misleading habit of pretending that the only proletarians are manual labourers. It has got to be brought home to the clerk, the engineer, the commercial traveller, the middle-class man who has 'come down in the world', the village grocer, the lower-grade civil servant, and all other doubtful cases that they *are* the proletariat, and that Socialism means a fair deal for them as well as for the navvy and the factory-hand. They must not be allowed to think that the battle is between those who pronounce their aitches and those who don't; for if they think that, they will join in on the side of the aitches.

I am implying that different classes must be persuaded to act together without, for the moment, being asked to drop their class-differences. And that sounds dangerous. It sounds rather too like the Duke of York's summer camp and that dismal line of talk about class-cooperation and putting our shoulders to the wheel, which is eyewash or Fascism, or both. There can be no cooperation between classes whose real interests are opposed. The capitalist cannot cooperate with the proletarian. The cat cannot cooperate with the mouse; and if the cat does suggest cooperation and the mouse is fool enough to agree, in a very little while the mouse will be disappearing down the cat's throat. But it is always possible to cooperate so long as it is upon a basis of common interests. The people who have got to act together are all those who cringe to the boss and all those who shudder when they think of the rent. This means that the small-holder has got to ally himself with the factory-hand, the typist with the coal-miner, the schoolmaster with the garage mechanic. There is some hope of getting them to do so if they can be made to understand where their interest lies. But this will not happen if their social prejudices, which in some of them are at least as strong as any economic consideration, are needlessly irritated. There is, after all, a real difference of manners and traditions between a bank clerk and a dock labourer, and the bank clerk's feeling of superiority is very deeply rooted. Later on he will have to get rid of it, but this is not a good moment for asking him to do so. Therefore it would be a very great advantage if that rather meaningless and mechanical bourgeois-baiting, which is a part of nearly all Socialist propaganda, could be dropped for the time being. Throughout left-wing thought and writing – and the whole way through it, from the leading articles in the *Daily Worker* to the comic columns in the *News Chronicle* – there runs an anti-genteel tradition, a persistent and often very stupid gibing at genteel mannerisms and genteel loyalties (or, in Communist jargon, 'bourgeois values'). It is largely humbug, coming as it does from bourgeois-baiters who are bourgeois themselves, but it does great harm, because it allows a minor issue to block a major one. It directs attention away from the central fact that poverty is poverty, whether the tool you work with is a pick-axe or a fountain-pen.

Once again, here am I, with my middle-class origins and my income of about three pounds a week from all sources. For what I am worth it would be better to get me in on the Socialist side than to turn me into a Fascist. But if you are constantly bullying me about my 'bourgeois ideology', if you give me to understand that in some subtle way I am an inferior person because I have never worked with my hands, you will only succeed in antagonizing me. For you are telling me either that I am inherently useless or that I ought to alter myself in some way that is beyond my power. I cannot proletarianize my accent or certain of my tastes and beliefs, and I would not if I could. Why should I? I don't ask anybody else to speak my dialect; why should anybody else ask me to speak his? It would be far better to take those miserable class-stigmata for granted and emphasize them as little as possible. They are comparable to a race-difference, and experience shows that one *can* coop-erate with foreigners, even with foreigners whom one dislikes, when it is really necessary. Economically, I am in the same boat with the miner, the navvy, and the farm-hand; remind me of that and I will fight at their side. But culturally I am different from the miner, the navvy, and the farm-hand: lay the emphasis on that and you may arm me against them. If I were a solitary anomaly I should not matter, but what is true of myself is true of countless others. Every bank clerk dreaming of the sack, every shopkeeper teetering on the brink of bankruptcy, is in essentially the same position. These are the sinking middle class, and most of them are clinging to their gentility under the impression that it keeps them afloat. It is not good policy to *start* by telling them to throw away the life-belt. There is a quite obvious danger that in the next few years large sections of the middle class will make a sudden and violent swing to the Right. In doing so they may become formidable. The weakness of the middle class hitherto has lain in the fact that they have never learned to combine; but if you frighten them into combining *against* you, you may find that you have raised up a devil. We had a brief glimpse of this possibility in the General Strike.

To sum up: There is no chance of righting the conditions I described in the earlier chapters of this book, or of saving England from Fascism, unless we can bring an effective Socialist party into existence. It will have to be a party with genuinely revolutionary intentions, and it will have to be numeri-cally strong enough to act. We can only get it if we offer an objective which fairly ordinary people will recognize as desirable. Beyond all else, therefore, we need intelligent propaganda. Less about 'class consciousness', 'expropri-ation of the expropriators', 'bourgeois ideology', and 'proletarian solidarity', not to mention the sacred sisters, thesis, antithesis, and synthesis; and more about justice, liberty, and the plight of the unemployed. And less about mechanical progress, tractors, the Dnieper dam, and the latest salmon-canning factory in Moscow; that kind of thing is not an integral part of Socialist doctrine, and it drives away many people whom the Socialist cause needs, including most of those who can hold a pen. All that is needed is to hammer two facts home into the public consciousness. One, that the interests of all exploited people are the same; the other, that Socialism is compatible with common decency.

As for the terribly difficult issue of class-distinctions, the only possible policy for the moment is to go easy and not frighten more people than can be helped. And above all, no more of those muscular-curate efforts at class-breaking. If you belong to the bourgeoisie, don't be too eager to bound forward and embrace your proletarian brothers; they may not like it, and if they show that they don't like it you will probably find that your class-prejudices are not so dead as you imagined. And if you belong to the proletariat, by birth or in the sight of God, don't sneer too automatically at the Old School Tie; it covers loyalties which can be useful to you if you know how to handle them.

Yet I believe there is some hope that when Socialism is a living issue, a thing that large numbers of Englishmen genuinely care about, the class-difficulty may solve itself more rapidly than now seems thinkable. In the next few years we shall either get that effective Socialist party that we need, or we shall not get it. If we do not get it, then Fascism is coming; probably a slimy Anglicized form of Fascism, with cultured policemen instead of Nazi gorillas and the lion and the unicorn instead of the swastika. But if we do get it there will be a struggle, conceivably a physical one, for our plutocracy will not sit quiet under a genuinely revolutionary government. And when the widely separate classes who, necessarily, would form any real Socialist party have fought side by side, they may feel differently about one another. And then perhaps this misery of class-prejudice will fade away, and we of the sinking middle class – the private schoolmaster, the half-starved free-lance journalist, the colonel's spinster daughter with £75 a year, the jobless Cambridge graduate, the ship's officer without a ship, the clerks, the civil servants, the commercial travellers, and the thrice-bankrupt drapers in the country towns – may sink without further struggles into the working class where we belong, and probably when we get there it will not be so dreadful as we feared, for, after all, we have nothing to lose but our aitches.

HOMAGE
TO
CATALONIA

Answer not a fool according to his folly, lest thou be like unto him.
Answer a fool according to his folly, lest he be wise in his own conceit.

PROVERBS XXVI, 5–6

1

In the Lenin Barracks in Barcelona, the day before I joined the militia, I saw an Italian militiaman standing in front of the officers' table.

He was a tough-looking youth of twenty-five or six, with reddish-yellow hair and powerful shoulders. His peaked leather cap was pulled fiercely over one eye. He was standing in profile to me, his chin on his breast, gazing with a puzzled frown at a map which one of the officers had open on the table. Something in his face deeply moved me. It was the face of a man who would commit murder and throw away his life for a friend – the kind of face you would expect in an Anarchist, though as likely as not he was a Communist. There were both candour and ferocity in it; also the pathetic reverence that illiterate people have for their supposed superiors. Obviously he could not make head or tail of the map; obviously he regarded map-reading as a stupendous intellectual feat. I hardly know why, but I have seldom seen anyone – any man, I mean – to whom I have taken such an immediate liking. While they were talking round the table some remark brought it out that I was a foreigner. The Italian raised his head and said quickly:

'*Italiano?*'

I answered in my bad Spanish: '*No, Inglés. Y tú?*'

'*Italiano.*'

As we went out he stepped across the room and gripped my hand very hard. Queer, the affection you can feel for a stranger! It was as though his spirit and mine had momentarily succeeded in bridging the gulf of language and tradition and meeting in utter intimacy. I hoped he liked me as well as I liked him. But I also knew that to retain my first impression of him I must not see him again; and needless to say I never did see him again. One was always making contacts of that kind in Spain.

I mention this Italian militiaman because he has stuck vividly in my memory. With his shabby uniform and fierce pathetic face he typifies for me the special atmosphere of that time. He is bound up with all my memories of that period of the war – the red flags in Barcelona, the gaunt trains full of shabby soldiers creeping to the front, the grey war-stricken towns farther up the line, the muddy, ice-cold trenches in the mountains.

This was in late December 1936, less than seven months ago as I write, and yet it is a period that has already receded into enormous distance. Later events have obliterated it much more completely than they have obliterated 1935, or 1905, for that matter. I had come to Spain with some notion of writing newspaper articles, but I had joined the militia almost immediately, because at that time and in that atmosphere it seemed the only conceivable thing to do. The Anarchists were still in virtual control of Catalonia and the revolution was still in full swing. To anyone who had been there since the beginning it probably seemed even in December or January that the revolutionary period was ending; but when one came straight from England the aspect of Barcelona was something startling and overwhelming. It was the first time that I had ever been in a town where the working class was in the saddle. Practically every building of any size had been seized by the workers and was draped with red flags or with the red and black flag of the Anarchists; every wall was scrawled with the hammer and sickle and with the initials of the revolutionary parties; almost every church had been gutted and its images burnt. Churches here and there were being systematically demolished by gangs of workmen. Every shop and café had an inscription saying that it had been collectivized; even the bootblacks had been collectivized and their boxes painted red and black. Waiters and shop-walkers looked you in the face and treated you as an equal. Servile and even ceremonial forms of speech had temporarily disappeared. Nobody said 'Señor' or 'Don' or even 'Usted'; everyone called everyone else 'Comrade' and 'Thou', and said 'Salud!' instead of 'Buenos días'. Tipping was forbidden by law; almost my first experience was receiving a lecture from a hotel manager for trying to tip a lift-boy. There were no private motor-cars, they had all been commandeered, and all the trams and taxis and much of the other transport were painted red and black. The revolutionary posters were everywhere, flaming from the walls in clean reds and blues that made the few remaining advertisements look like daubs of mud. Down the Ramblas, the wide central artery of the town where crowds of people streamed constantly to and fro, the loudspeakers were bellowing revolutionary songs all day and far into the night. And it was the aspect of the crowds that was the queerest thing of all. In outward appearance it was a town in which the wealthy classes had practically ceased to exist. Except for a small number of women and foreigners there were no 'well-dressed' people at all. Practically everyone wore rough working-class clothes, or blue overalls; or some variant of the militia uniform. All this was queer and moving. There was much in it that I did not understand, in some ways I did not even like it, but I recognized it immediately as a state of affairs worth fighting for. Also I believed that things were as they appeared, that this was really a workers' State and that the entire bourgeoisie had either fled, been killed, or voluntarily come over to the workers' side; I did not realize that great numbers of well-to-do bourgeois were simply lying low and disguising themselves as proletarians for the time being.

Together with all this there was something of the evil atmosphere of war. The town had a gaunt untidy look, roads and buildings were in poor repair, the streets at night were dimly lit for fear of air-raids, the shops were mostly shabby and half-empty. Meat was scarce and milk practically unobtainable, there was a shortage of coal, sugar, and petrol, and a really serious shortage of bread. Even at this period the bread-queues were often hundreds of yards long. Yet so far as one could judge the people were contented and hopeful. There was no unemployment, and the price of living was still extremely low; you saw very few conspicuously destitute people, and no beggars except the gipsies. Above all, there was a belief in the revolution and the future, a feeling of having suddenly emerged into an era of equality and freedom. Human beings were trying to behave as human beings and not as cogs in the capitalist machine. In the barbers' shops were Anarchist notices (the barbers were mostly Anarchists) solemnly explaining that barbers were no longer slaves. In the streets were coloured posters appealing to prostitutes to stop being prostitutes. To anyone from the hard-boiled, sneering civilization of the English-speaking races there was something rather pathetic in the literalness with which these idealistic Spaniards took the hackneyed phrases of revolution. At that time revolutionary ballads of the naivest kind, all about proletarian brotherhood and the wickedness of Mussolini, were being sold on the streets for a few centimes each. I have often seen an illiterate militiaman buy one of these ballads, laboriously spell out the words, and then, when he had got the hang of it, begin singing it to an appropriate tune.

All this time I was at the Lenin Barracks, ostensibly in training for the front. When I joined the militia I had been told that I should be sent to the front the next day, but in fact I had to wait while a fresh *centuria* was got ready. The workers' militias, hurriedly raised by the trade unions at the beginning of the war, had not yet been organized on an ordinary army basis. The units of command were the 'section', of about thirty men, the *centuria*, of about a hundred men, and the 'column', which in practice meant any large number of men. The Lenin Barracks was a block of splendid stone buildings with a riding-school and enormous cobbled courtyards; it had been a cavalry barracks and had been captured during the July fighting. My *centuria* slept in one of the stables, under the stone mangers where the names of the cavalry chargers were still inscribed. All the horses had been seized and sent to the front, but the whole place still smelt of horse-piss and rotten oats. I was at the barracks about a week. Chiefly I remember the horsy smells, the quavering bugle-calls (all our buglers were amateurs – I first learned the Spanish bugle-calls by listening to them outside the Fascist lines), the tramp-tramp of hobnailed boots in the barrack yard, the long morning parades in the wintry sunshine, the wild games of football, fifty a side, in the gravelled riding-school. There were perhaps a thousand men at the barracks, and a score or so of women, apart from the militiamen's wives who did the cooking. There were still women serving in the militias, though not very many. In the early battles they had fought side by side with the men as a matter of course. It is a thing that seems natural in time of revolution. Ideas were changing already, however. The militiamen had to be kept out of the riding-school while the women were drilling there because they laughed at the women and put them off. A few months earlier no one would have seen anything comic in a woman handling a gun.

The whole barracks was in the state of filth and chaos to which the militia reduced every building they occupied and which seems to be one of the by-products of revolution. In every corner you came upon piles of smashed furniture, broken saddles, brass cavalry-helmets, empty sabre-scabbards, and decaying food. There was frightful wastage of food, especially bread. From my barrack-room alone a basketful of bread was thrown away at every meal – a disgraceful thing when the civilian population was short of it. We ate at long trestle-tables out of permanently greasy tin pannikins, and drank out of a dreadful thing called a *porrón*. A *porrón* is a sort of glass bottle with a pointed spout from which a thin jet of wine spurts out whenever you tip it up; you can thus drink from a distance, without touching it with your lips, and it can be passed from hand to hand. I went on strike and demanded a drinking-cup as soon as I saw a *porrón* in use. To my eye the things were altogether too like bed-bottles, especially when they were filled with white wine.

By degrees they were issuing the recruits with uniforms, and because this was Spain everything was issued piecemeal, so that it was never quite certain who had received what, and various of the things we most needed, such as belts and cartridge-boxes, were not issued till the last moment, when the train was actually waiting to take us to the front. I have spoken of the militia 'uniform', which probably gives a wrong impression. It was not exactly a uniform. Perhaps a 'multiform' would be the proper name for it. Everyone's clothes followed the same general plan, but they were never quite the same in any two cases. Practically everyone in the army wore corduroy knee-breeches, but there the uniformity ended. Some wore puttees, others corduroy gaiters, others leather leggings or high boots. Everyone wore a zipper jacket, but some of the jackets were of leather, others of wool and of every conceivable colour. The kinds of cap were about as numerous as their wearers. It was usual to adorn the front of your cap with a party badge, and in addition nearly every man wore a red or red and black handkerchief round his throat. A militia column at that time was an extraordinary-looking rabble. But the clothes had to be issued as this or that factory rushed them out, and they were not bad clothes considering the circumstances. The shirts and socks were wretched cotton things, however, quite useless against cold. I hate to think of what the militiamen must have gone through in the earlier months before anything was organized. I remember coming upon a newspaper of only about two months earlier in which one of the P.O.U.M. leaders, after a visit to the front, said that he would try to see to it that 'every militiaman had a blanket'. A phrase to make you shudder if you have ever slept in a trench.

On my second day at the barracks there began what was comically called 'instruction'. At the beginning there were frightful scenes of chaos. The recruits were mostly boys of sixteen or seventeen from the back streets of Barcelona, full of revolutionary ardour but completely ignorant of the meaning of war. It was impossible even to get them to stand in line. Discipline did not exist; if a man disliked an order he would step out of the ranks and argue fiercely with the officer. The lieutenant who instructed us was a stout, fresh-faced, pleasant young man who had previously been a Regular Army officer, and still looked like one, with his smart carriage and spick-and-span uniform. Curiously enough he was a sincere and ardent Socialist. Even more than the men themselves he insisted upon complete social equality between all ranks. I remember his pained surprise when an ignorant recruit addressed him as 'Señor'. 'What! Señor? Who is that calling me Señor? Are we not all comrades?' I doubt whether it made his job any easier. Meanwhile the raw recruits were getting no military training that could be of the slightest use to them. I had been told that foreigners were not obliged to attend 'instruction' (the Spaniards, I noticed, had a pathetic belief that all foreigners knew more of military matters than themselves), but naturally I turned out with the others. I was very anxious to learn how to use a machine-gun; it was a weapon I had never had a chance to handle. To my dismay I found that we were taught nothing about the use of weapons. The so-called instruction was simply parade-ground drill of the most antiquated, stupid kind; right turn, left turn, about turn, marching at attention in column of threes and all the rest of that useless nonsense which I had learned when I was fifteen years old. It was an extraordinary form for the training of a guerilla army to take. Obviously if you have only a few days in which to train a soldier, you must teach him the things he will most need; how to take cover, how to advance across open ground, how to mount guards and build a parapet – above all, how to use his weapons. Yet this mob of eager children, who were going to be thrown into the front line in a few days' time, were not even taught how to fire a rifle or pull the pin out of a bomb. At the time I did not grasp that this was because there were no weapons to be had. In the P.O.U.M. militia the shortage of rifles was so desperate that fresh troops reaching the front always had to take their rifles from the troops they relieved in the line. In the whole of the Lenin Barracks there were, I believe, no rifles except those used by the sentries.

After a few days, though still a complete rabble by any ordinary standard, we were considered fit to be seen in public, and in the mornings we were marched out to the public gardens on the hill beyond the Plaza de España. This was the common drill-ground of all the party militias, besides the Carabineros and the first contingents of the newly formed Popular Army. Up in the public gardens it was a strange and heartening sight. Down every path and alley-way, amid the formal flower-beds, squads and companies of men marched stiffly to and fro, throwing out their chests and trying desperately to look like soldiers. All of them were unarmed and none completely in uniform, though on most of them the militia uniform was breaking out in patches here and there. The procedure was always very much the same. For three hours we strutted to and fro (the Spanish marching step is very short and rapid), then we halted, broke the ranks, and flocked thirstily to a little grocer's shop which was half-way down the hill and was doing a roaring trade in cheap wine. Everyone was very friendly to me. As an Englishman I was something of a curiosity, and the Carabinero officers made much of me and stood me drinks. Meanwhile, whenever I could get our lieutenant into a corner, I was clamouring to be instructed in the use of a machine-gun. I used to drag my Hugo's dictionary out of my pocket and start on him in my villainous Spanish:

'Yo sé manejar fusil. No sé manejar ametralladora. Quiero apprender ametralladora. Quándo vamos apprender ametralladora?'

The answer was always a harassed smile and a promise that there should be machine-gun instruction mañana. Needless to say mañana never came. Several days passed and the recruits learned to march in step and spring to attention almost smartly, but if they knew which end of a rifle the bullet came out of, that was all they knew. One day an armed Carabinero strolled up to us when we were halting and allowed us to examine his rifle. It turned out that in the whole of my section no one except myself even knew how to load the rifle, much less how to take aim.

All this time I was having the usual struggles with the Spanish language. Apart from myself there was only one Englishman at the barracks, and nobody even among the officers spoke a word of French. Things were not made easier for me by the fact that when my companions spoke to one another they generally spoke in Catalan. The only way I could get along was to carry everywhere a small dictionary which I whipped out of my pocket in moments of crisis. But I would sooner be a foreigner in Spain than in most countries. How easy it is to make friends in Spain! Within a day or two there was a score of militiamen who called me by my Christian name, showed me the ropes, and overwhelmed me with hospitality. I am not writing a book of propaganda and I do not want to idealize the P.O.U.M. militia. The whole militia-system had serious faults, and the men themselves were a mixed lot, for by this time voluntary recruitment was falling off and many of the best men were already at the front or dead. There was always among us a certain percentage who were completely useless. Boys of fifteen were being brought up for enlistment by their parents, quite openly for the sake of the ten pesetas a day which was the militiaman's wage; also for the sake of the bread which the militia received in plenty and could smuggle home to their parents. But I defy anyone to be thrown as I was among the Spanish working class – I ought perhaps to say the Catalan working class, for apart from a few Aragonese and Andalusians I mixed only with Catalans – and not be struck by their essential decency; above all, their straightforwardness and generosity. A Spaniard's generosity, in the ordinary sense of the word, is at times almost embarrassing. If you ask him for a cigarette he will force the whole packet upon you. And beyond this there is generosity in a deeper sense, a real largeness of spirit, which I have met with again and again in the most unpromising circumstances. Some of the journalists and other foreigners who travelled in Spain during the war have declared that in secret the Spaniards were bitterly jealous of foreign aid. All I can say is that I never observed anything of the kind. I remember that a few days before I left the barracks a group of men returned on leave from the front. They were talking excitedly about their experiences and were full of enthusiasm for some French troops who had been next to them at Huesca. The French were very brave, they said; adding enthusiastically: '*Más valientes que nosotros*' – 'Braver than we are!' Of course I demurred, whereupon they explained that the French knew more of the art of war – were more expert with bombs, machine-guns, and so forth. Yet the remark was significant. An Englishman would cut his hand off sooner than say a thing like that.

Every foreigner who served in the militia spent his first few weeks in learning to love the Spaniards and in being exasperated by certain of their characteristics. In the front line my own exasperation sometimes reached the pitch of fury. The Spaniards are good at many things, but not at making war. All foreigners alike are appalled by their inefficiency, above all their maddening unpunctuality. The one Spanish word that no foreigner can avoid learning is *mañana* – 'tomorrow' (literally, 'the morning'). Whenever it is conceivably possible, the business of today is put off until *mañana*. This is so notorious that even the Spaniards themselves make jokes about it. In Spain nothing, from a meal to a battle, ever happens at the appointed time. As a general rule things happen too late, but just occasionally – just so that you shan't even be able to depend on their happening late – they happen too early. A train which is due to leave at eight will normally leave at any time between nine and ten, but perhaps once a week, thanks to some private whim of the engine-driver, it leaves at half past seven. Such things can be a little trying. In theory I rather admire the Spaniards for not sharing our Northern time-neurosis; but unfortunately I share it myself.

After endless rumours, *mañanas*, and delays we were suddenly ordered to the front at two hours' notice, when much of our equipment was still unissued. There were terrible tumults in the quartermaster's store; in the end numbers of men had to leave without their full equipment. The barracks had promptly filled with women who seemed to have sprung up from the ground and were helping their men-folk to roll their blankets and pack their kit-bags. It was rather humiliating that I had to be shown how to put on my new leather cartridge-boxes by a Spanish girl, the wife of Williams, the other English militiaman. She was a gentle, dark-eyed, intensely feminine creature who looked as though her life-work was to rock a cradle, but who as a matter of fact had fought bravely in the street-battles of July. At this time she was carrying a baby which was born just ten months after the outbreak of war and had perhaps been begotten behind a barricade.

The train was due to leave at eight, and it was about ten past eight when the harassed, sweating officers managed to marshal us in the barrack square. I remember very vividly the torchlit scene – the uproar and excitement, the red flags flapping in the torchlight, the massed ranks of militiamen with their knapsacks on their backs and their rolled blankets worn bandolier-wise across the shoulder; and the shouting and the clatter of boots and tin pannikins, and then a tremendous and finally successful hissing for silence; and then some political commissar standing beneath a huge rolling red banner and making us a speech in Catalan. Finally they marched us to the station, taking the longest route, three or four miles, so as to show us to the whole town. In the Ramblas they halted us while a borrowed band played some revolutionary tune or other. Once again the conquering-hero stuff – shouting and enthusiasm, red flags and red and black flags everywhere, friendly crowds thronging the pavement to have a look at us, women waving from the windows. How natural it all seemed then; how remote and improbable now! The train was packed so tight with men that there was barely room even on the floor, let alone on the seats. At the last moment Williams's wife came rushing down the platform and gave us a bottle of wine and a foot of that bright red sausage which tastes of soap and gives you diarrhoea. The train crawled out of Catalonia and on to the plateau of Aragon at the normal wartime speed of something under twenty kilometres an hour.

2

BARBASTRO, though a long way from the front line, looked bleak and chipped. Swarms of militiamen in shabby uniforms wandered up and down the streets, trying to keep warm. On a ruinous wall I came upon a poster dating from the previous year and announcing that 'six handsome bulls' would be killed in the arena on such and such a date. How forlorn its faded colours looked! Where were the handsome bulls and the handsome bull-fighters now? It appeared that even in Barcelona there were hardly any bullfights nowadays; for some reason all the best matadors were Fascists.

They sent my company by lorry to Sietamo, then westward to Alcubierre, which was just behind the line fronting Zaragoza. Sietamo had been fought over three times before the Anarchists finally took it in October, and parts of it were smashed to pieces by shell-fire and most of the houses pockmarked by rifle-bullets. We were 1500 feet above sea-level now. It was beastly cold, with dense mists that came swirling up from nowhere.

Between Sietamo and Alcubierre the lorry-driver lost his way (this was one of the regular features of the war) and we were wandering for hours in the mist. It was late at night when we reached Alcubierre. Somebody shepherded us through morasses of mud into a mule-stable where we dug ourselves down into the chaff and promptly fell asleep. Chaff is not bad to sleep in when it is clean, not so good as hay but better than straw. It was only in the morning light that I discovered that the chaff was full of breadcrusts, torn newspapers, bones, dead rats, and jagged milk tins.

We were near the front line now, near enough to smell the characteristic smell of war – in my experience a smell of excrement and decaying food. Alcubierre had never been shelled and was in a better state than most of the villages immediately behind the line. Yet I believe that even in peacetime you could not travel in that part of Spain without being struck by the peculiar squalid misery of the Aragonese villages. They are built like fortresses, a mass of mean little houses of mud and stone huddling round the church, and even in spring you see hardly a flower anywhere; the houses have no gardens, only back-yards where ragged fowls skate over the beds of mule-dung. It was vile weather, with alternate mist and rain. The narrow earth roads had been churned into a sea of mud, in places two feet deep, through which the lorries struggled with racing wheels and the peasants led their clumsy carts which were pulled by strings of mules, sometimes as many as six in a string, always pulling tandem. The constant come-and-go of troops had reduced the village to a state of unspeakable filth. It did not possess and never had possessed such a thing as a lavatory or a drain of any kind, and there was not a square yard anywhere where you could tread without watching your step. The church had long been used as a latrine; so had all the fields for a quarter of a mile round. I never think of my first two months at war without thinking of wintry stubble fields whose edges are crusted with dung.

Two days passed and no rifles were issued to us. When you had been to the Comité de Guerra and inspected the row of holes in the wall – holes made by rifle-volleys, various Fascists having been executed there – you had seen all the sights that Alcubierre contained. Up in the front line things were obviously quiet; very few wounded were coming in. The chief excitement was the arrival of Fascist deserters, who were brought under guard from the front line. Many of the troops opposite us on this part of the line were not Fascists at all, merely wretched conscripts who had been doing their military service at the time when war broke out and were only too anxious to escape. Occasionally small batches of them took the risk of slipping across to our lines. No doubt more would have done so if their relatives had not been in Fascist territory. These deserters were the first 'real' Fascists I had ever seen. It struck me that they were indistinguishable from ourselves, except that they wore khaki overalls. They were always ravenously hungry when they arrived – natural enough after a day or two of dodging about in no man's land, but it was always triumphantly pointed to as a proof that the Fascist troops were starving. I watched one of them being fed in a peasant's house. It was somehow rather a pitiful sight. A tall boy of twenty, deeply windburnt, with his clothes in rags, crouched over the fire shovelling a pannikinful of stew into himself at desperate speed; and all the while his eyes flitted nervously round the ring of militiamen who stood watching him. I think he still half-believed that we were bloodthirsty 'Reds' and were going to shoot him as soon as he had finished his meal; the armed man who guarded him kept stroking his shoulder and making reassuring noises. On one memorable day fifteen deserters arrived in a single batch. They were led through the village in triumph with a man riding in front of them on a white horse. I managed to take a rather blurry photograph which was stolen from me later.

On our third morning in Alcubierre the rifles arrived. A sergeant with a coarse dark-yellow face was handing them out in the mule-stable. I got a shock of dismay when I saw the thing they gave me. It was a German Mauser dated 1896 – more than forty years old! It was rusty, the bolt was stiff, the wooden barrel-guard was split; one glance down the muzzle showed that it was corroded and past praying for. Most of the rifles were equally bad, some of them even worse, and no attempt was made to give the best weapons to the men who knew how to use them. The best rifle of the lot, only ten years old, was given to a half-witted little beast of fifteen, known to everyone as the *maricón* (Nancy-boy). The sergeant gave us five minutes' 'instruction', which consisted in explaining how you loaded a rifle and how you took the bolt to pieces. Many of the militiamen had never had a gun in their hands before, and very few, I imagine, knew what the sights were for. Cartridges were handed out, fifty to a man, and then the ranks were formed and we strapped our kits on our backs and set out for the front line, about three miles away.

The *centuria*, eighty men and several dogs, wound raggedly up the road. Every militia column had at least one dog attached to it as a mascot. One wretched brute that marched with us had had P.O.U.M. branded on it in huge letters and slunk along as though conscious that there was something wrong with its appearance. At the head of the column, beside the red flag, Georges Kopp, the stout Belgian commandante, was riding a black horse; a little way ahead a youth from the brigand-like militia cavalry pranced

to and fro, galloping up every piece of rising ground and posing himself
in picturesque attitudes at the summit. The splendid horses of the Spanish
cavalry had been captured in large numbers during the revolution and
handed over to the militia, who, of course, were busy riding them to death.

The road wound between yellow infertile fields, untouched since last
year's harvest. Ahead of us was the low sierra that lies between Alcubierre
and Zaragoza. We were getting near the front line now, near the bombs,
the machine-guns, and the mud. In secret I was frightened. I knew the
line was quiet at present, but unlike most of the men about me I was old
enough to remember the Great War, though not old enough to have fought
in it. War, to me, meant roaring projectiles and skipping shards of steel;
above all it meant mud, lice, hunger, and cold. It is curious, but I dreaded
the cold much more than I dreaded the enemy. The thought of it had been
haunting me all the time I was in Barcelona; I had even lain awake at
nights thinking of the cold in the trenches, the stand-to's in the grisly
dawns, the long hours on sentry-go with a frosted rifle, the icy mud that
would slop over my boot-tops. I admit, too, that I felt a kind of horror as
I looked at the people I was marching among. You cannot possibly conceive
what a rabble we looked. We straggled along with far less cohesion than
a flock of sheep; before we had gone two miles the rear of the column was
out of sight. And quite half of the so-called men were children – but I
mean literally children, of sixteen years old at the very most. Yet they
were all happy and excited at the prospect of getting to the front at last.
As we neared the line the boys round the red flag in front began to utter
shouts of 'Visca P.O.U.M.!' 'Fascistas-maricones!' and so forth – shouts
which were meant to be war-like and menacing, but which, from those
childish throats, sounded as pathetic as the cries of kittens. It seemed
dreadful that the defenders of the Republic should be this mob of ragged
children carrying worn-out rifles which they did not know how to use. I
remember wondering what would happen if a Fascist aeroplane passed
our way – whether the airman would even bother to dive down and give
us a burst from his machine-gun. Surely even from the air he could see
that we were not real soldiers?

As the road struck into the sierra we branched off to the right and
climbed a narrow mule-track that wound round the mountain-side. The
hills in that part of Spain are of a queer formation, horseshoe-shaped with
flattish tops and very steep sides running down into immense ravines. On
the higher slopes nothing grows except stunted shrubs and heath, with the
white bones of the limestone sticking out everywhere. The front line here
was not a continuous line of trenches, which would have been impossible

in such mountainous country; it was simply a chain of fortified posts, always known as 'positions', perched on each hill-top. In the distance you could see our 'position' at the crown of the horseshoe; a ragged barricade of sand-bags, a red flag fluttering, the smoke of dug-out fires. A little nearer, and you could smell a sickening sweetish stink that lived in my nostrils for weeks afterwards. Into the cleft immediately behind the position all the refuse of months had been tipped – a deep festering bed of breadcrusts, excrement, and rusty tins.

The company we were relieving were getting their kits together. They had been three months in the line; their uniforms were caked with mud, their boots falling to pieces, their faces mostly bearded. The captain commanding the position, Levinski by name, but known to everyone as Benjamin, and by birth a Polish Jew, but speaking French as his native language, crawled out of his dug-out and greeted us. He was a short youth of about twenty-five, with stiff black hair and a pale eager face which at this period of the war was always very dirty. A few stray bullets were cracking high overhead. The position was a semi-circular enclosure about fifty yards across, with a parapet that was partly sand-bags and partly lumps of limestone. There were thirty or forty dug-outs running into the ground like rat-holes. Williams, myself, and Williams's Spanish brother-in-law made a swift dive for the nearest unoccupied dug-out that looked habitable. Somewhere in front an occasional rifle banged, making queer rolling echoes among the stony hills. We had just dumped our kits and were crawling out of the dug-out when there was another bang and one of the children of our company rushed back from the parapet with his face pouring blood. He had fired his rifle and had somehow managed to blow out the bolt; his scalp was torn to ribbons by the splinters of the burst cartridge-case. It was our first casualty, and, characteristically, self-inflicted.

In the afternoon we did our first guard and Benjamin showed us round the position. In front of the parapet there ran a system of narrow trenches hewn out of the rock, with extremely primitive loopholes made of piles of limestone. There were twelve sentries, placed at various points in the trench and behind the inner parapet. In front of the trench was the barbed wire, and then the hillside slid down into a seemingly bottomless ravine; opposite were naked hills, in places mere cliffs of rock, all grey and wintry, with no life anywhere, not even a bird. I peered cautiously through a loophole, trying to find the Fascist trench.

'Where are the enemy?'

Benjamin waved his hand expansively. 'Over zere.' (Benjamin spoke English – terrible English.)

'But *where*?'

According to my ideas of trench warfare the Fascists would be fifty or a hundred yards away. I could see nothing – seemingly their trenches were very well concealed. Then with a shock of dismay I saw where Benjamin was pointing; on the opposite hill-top, beyond the ravine, seven hundred metres away at the very least, the tiny outline of a parapet and a red-and-yellow flag – the Fascist position. I was indescribably disappointed. We were nowhere near them! At that range our rifles were completely useless. But at this moment there was a shout of excitement. Two Fascists, greyish figurines in the distance, were scrambling up the naked hill-side opposite. Benjamin grabbed the nearest man's rifle, took aim, and pulled the trigger. Click! A dud cartridge; I thought it a bad omen. The new sentries were no sooner in the trench than they began firing a terrific fusillade at nothing in particular. I could see the Fascists, tiny as ants, dodging to and fro behind their parapet, and sometimes a black dot which was a head would pause for a moment, impudently exposed. It was obviously no use firing. But presently the sentry on my left, leaving his post in the typical Spanish fashion, sidled up to me and began urging me to fire. I tried to explain that at that range and with these rifles you could not hit a man except by accident. But he was only a child, and he kept motioning with his rifle towards one of the dots, grinning as eagerly as a dog that expects a pebble to be thrown. Finally I put my sights up to seven hundred and let fly. The dot disappeared. I hope it went near enough to make him jump. It was the first time in my life that I had fired a gun at a human being.

Now that I had seen the front I was profoundly disgusted. They called this war! And we were hardly even in touch with the enemy! I made no attempt to keep my head below the level of the trench. A little while later, however, a bullet shot past my ear with a vicious crack and banged into the parados behind. Alas! I ducked. All my life I had sworn that I would not duck the first time a bullet passed over me; but the movement appears to be instinctive, and almost everybody does it at least once.

3

In trench warfare five things are important: firewood, food, tobacco, candles, and the enemy. In winter on the Zaragoza front they were important in that order, with the enemy a bad last. Except at night, when a surprise-attack was always conceivable, nobody bothered about the enemy. They were simply remote black insects whom one occasionally saw hopping to and fro. The real preoccupation of both armies was trying to keep warm.

I ought to say in passing that all the time I was in Spain I saw very little fighting. I was on the Aragon front from January to May, and between January and late March little or nothing happened on that front, except at Teruel. In March there was heavy fighting round Huesca, but I personally played only a minor part in it. Later, in June, there was the disastrous attack on Huesca in which several thousand men were killed in a single day, but I had been wounded and disabled before that happened. The things that one normally thinks of as the horrors of war seldom happened to me. No aeroplane ever dropped a bomb anywhere near me, I do not think a shell ever exploded within fifty yards of me, and I was only in hand-to-hand fighting once (once is once too often, I may say). Of course I was often under heavy machine-gun fire, but usually at longish ranges. Even at Huesca you were generally safe enough if you took reasonable precautions.

Up here, in the hills round Zaragoza, it was simply the mingled boredom and discomfort of stationary warfare. A life as uneventful as a city clerk's, and almost as regular. Sentry-go, patrols, digging; digging, patrols, sentry-go. On every hill-top, Fascist or Loyalist, a knot of ragged, dirty men shivering round their flag and trying to keep warm. And all day and night the meaningless bullets wandering across the empty valleys and only by some rare improbable chance getting home on a human body.

Often I used to gaze round the wintry landscape and marvel at the futility of it all. The inconclusiveness of such a kind of war! Earlier, about October, there had been savage fighting for all these hills; then, because the lack of men and arms, especially artillery, made any large-scale operation impossible, each army had dug itself in and settled down on the

hill-tops it had won. Over to our right there was a small outpost, also
P.O.U.M., and on the spur to our left, at seven o'clock of us, a P.S.U.C. position
faced a taller spur with several small Fascist posts dotted on its peaks.
The so-called line zigzagged to and fro in a pattern that would have been
quite unintelligible if every position had not flown a flag. The P.O.U.M. and
P.S.U.C. flags were red, those of the Anarchists red and black; the Fascists
generally flew the monarchist flag (red-yellow-red), but occasionally they
flew the flag of the Republic (red-yellow-purple). The scenery was stupendous, if you could forget that every mountain-top was occupied by troops
and was therefore littered with tin cans and crusted with dung. To the
right of us the sierra bent south-eastwards and made way for the wide,
veined valley that stretched across to Huesca. In the middle of the plain
a few tiny cubes sprawled like a throw of dice; this was the town of Robres,
which was in Loyalist possession. Often in the mornings the valley was
hidden under seas of cloud, out of which the hills rose flat and blue, giving
the landscape a strange resemblance to a photographic negative. Beyond
Huesca there were more hills of the same formation as our own, streaked
with a pattern of snow which altered day by day. In the far distance the
monstrous peaks of the Pyrenees, where the snow never melts, seemed to
float upon nothing. Even down in the plain everything looked dead and
bare. The hills opposite us were grey and wrinkled like the skins of
elephants. Almost always the sky was empty of birds. I do not think I
have ever seen a country where there were so few birds. The only birds
one saw at any time were a kind of magpie, and the coveys of partridges
that startled one at night with their sudden whirring, and, very rarely, the
flights of eagles that drifted slowly over, generally followed by rifle-shots
which they did not deign to notice.

At night and in misty weather, patrols were sent out in the valley
between ourselves and the Fascists. The job was not popular, it was too
cold and too easy to get lost, and I soon found that I could get leave to
go out on patrol as often as I wished. In the huge jagged ravines there
were no paths or tracks of any kind; you could only find your way about
by making successive journeys and noting fresh landmarks each time. As
the bullet flies the nearest Fascist post was seven hundred metres from
our own, but it was a mile and a half by the only practicable route. It was
rather fun wandering about the dark valleys with the stray bullets flying
high overhead like redshanks whistling. Better than night-time were the
heavy mists, which often lasted all day and which had a habit of clinging
round the hill-tops and leaving the valleys clear. When you were anywhere
near the Fascist lines you had to creep at a snail's pace; it was very difficult

to move quietly on those hill-sides, among the crackling shrubs and tinkling limestones. It was only at the third or fourth attempt that I managed to find my way to the Fascist lines. The mist was very thick, and I crept up to the barbed wire to listen. I could hear the Fascists talking and singing inside. Then to my alarm I heard several of them coming down the hill towards me. I cowered behind a bush that suddenly seemed very small, and tried to cock my rifle without noise. However, they branched off and did not come within sight of me. Behind the bush where I was hiding I came upon various relics of the earlier fighting – a pile of empty cartridge-cases, a leather cap with a bullet-hole in it, and a red flag, obviously one of our own. I took it back to the position, where it was unsentimentally torn up for cleaning-rags.

I had been made a corporal, or *cabo*, as it was called, as soon as we reached the front, and was in command of a guard of twelve men. It was no sinecure, especially at first. The *centuria* was an untrained mob composed mostly of boys in their teens. Here and there in the militia you came across children as young as eleven or twelve, usually refugees from Fascist territory who had been enlisted as militiamen as the easiest way of providing for them. As a rule they were employed on light work in the rear, but sometimes they managed to worm their way to the front line, where they were a public menace. I remember one little brute throwing a hand-grenade into the dug-out fire 'for a joke'. At Monte Pocero I do not think there was anyone younger than fifteen, but the average age must have been well under twenty. Boys of this age ought never to be used in the front line, because they cannot stand the lack of sleep which is inseparable from trench warfare. At the beginning it was almost impossible to keep our position properly guarded at night. The wretched children of my section could only be roused by dragging them out of their dug-outs feet foremost, and as soon as your back was turned they left their posts and slipped into shelter; or they would even, in spite of the frightful cold, lean up against the wall of the trench and fall fast asleep. Luckily the enemy were very unenterprising. There were nights when it seemed to me that our position could be stormed by twenty Boy Scouts armed with airguns, or twenty Girl Guides armed with battledores, for that matter.

At this time and until much later the Catalan militias were still on the same basis as they had been at the beginning of the war. In the early days of Franco's revolt the militias had been hurriedly raised by the various trade unions and political parties; each was essentially a political organiza-tion, owing allegiance to its party as much as to the central Government. When the Popular Army, which was a 'non-political' army organized on more or less ordinary lines, was raised at the beginning of 1937, the party militias were theoretically incorporated in it. But for a long time the only changes that occurred were on paper; the new Popular Army troops did not reach the Aragon front in any numbers till June, and until that time the militia-system remained unchanged. The essential point of the system was social equality between officers and men. Everyone from general to private drew the same pay, ate the same food, wore the same clothes, and mingled on terms of complete equality. If you wanted to slap the general commanding the division on the back and ask him for a cigarette, you could do so, and no one thought it curious. In theory at any rate each militia was a democracy and not a hierarchy. It was understood that orders had to be obeyed, but it was also understood that when you gave an order you gave it as comrade to comrade and not as superior to inferior. There were officers and N.C.O.s, but there was no military rank in the ordinary sense; no titles, no badges, no heel-clicking and saluting. They had attempted to produce within the militias a sort of temporary working model of the classless society. Of course there was no perfect equality, but there was a nearer approach to it than I had ever seen or than I would have thought conceivable in time of war.

But I admit that at first sight the state of affairs at the front horrified me. How on earth could the war be won by an army of this type? It was what everyone was saying at the time, and though it was true it was also unreasonable. For in the circumstances the militias could not have been much better than they were. A modern mechanized army does not spring up out of the ground, and if the Government had waited until it had trained troops at its disposal, Franco would never have been resisted. Later it became the fashion to decry the militias, and therefore to pretend that the faults which were due to lack of training and weapons were the result of the equalitarian system. Actually, a newly raised draft of militia was an undisciplined mob not because the officers called the private 'Comrade' but because raw troops are *always* an undisciplined mob. In practice the democratic 'revolutionary' type of discipline is more reliable than might be expected. In a workers' army discipline is theoretically voluntary. It is based on class-loyalty, whereas the discipline of a bourgeois conscript army is based ultimately on fear. (The Popular Army that replaced the militias was midway between the two types.) In the militias the bullying and abuse that go on in an ordinary army would never have been tolerated for a moment. The normal military punishments existed, but they were only invoked for very serious offences. When a man refused to obey an order you did not immediately get him punished; you first appealed to him in the name of comradeship. Cynical people with no experience of handling men will say instantly that this would never 'work', but as a matter of fact it does 'work' in the long run. The discipline of even the worst drafts of militia visibly improved as time went on. In January the job of keeping a dozen raw recruits up to the mark almost turned my hair grey. In May for a short while I was acting-lieutenant in command of about thirty men, English and Spanish. We had all been under fire for months, and I never had the slightest difficulty in getting an order obeyed or in getting men to volunteer for a dangerous job. 'Revolutionary' discipline depends on political consciousness – on an understanding of *why* orders must be obeyed; it takes time to diffuse this, but it also takes time to drill a man into an automaton on the barrack-square. The journalists who sneered at the militia-system seldom remembered that the militias had to hold the line while the Popular Army was training in the rear. And it is a tribute to the strength of 'revolutionary' discipline that the militias stayed in the field at all. For until about June 1937 there was nothing to keep them there, except class loyalty. Individual deserters could be shot – were shot, occasionally – but if a thousand men had decided to walk out of the line together there was no force to stop them. A conscript army in the same circumstances – with its battle-police removed – would have melted away. Yet the militias held the line, though God knows they won very few victories, and even individual desertions were not common. In four or five months in the P.O.U.M. militia I only heard of four men deserting, and two of those were fairly certainly spies who had enlisted to obtain information. At the beginning the apparent chaos, the general lack of training, the fact that you often had to argue for five minutes before you could get an order obeyed, appalled and infuriated me. I had British Army ideas, and certainly the Spanish militias were very unlike the British Army. But considering the circumstances they were better troops than one had any right to expect.

Meanwhile, firewood – always firewood. Throughout that period there is probably no entry in my diary that does not mention firewood, or rather the lack of it. We were between two and three thousand feet above sea-level, it was mid winter and the cold was unspeakable. The temperature was not exceptionally low, on many nights it did not even freeze, and the wintry sun often shone for an hour in the middle of the day; but even if it was not really cold, I assure you that it seemed so. Sometimes there were shrieking winds that tore your cap off and twisted your hair in all directions, sometimes there were mists that poured into the trench like a liquid and seemed to penetrate your bones; frequently it rained, and even a quarter of an hour's rain was enough to make conditions intolerable. The thin skin of earth over the limestone turned promptly into a slippery grease, and as you were always walking on a slope it was impossible to keep your footing. On dark nights I have often fallen half a dozen times in twenty yards; and this was dangerous, because it meant that the lock of one's rifle became jammed with mud. For days together clothes, boots, blankets, and rifles were more or less coated with mud. I had brought as many thick clothes as I could carry, but many of the men were terribly underclad. For the whole garrison, about a hundred men, there were only twelve great-coats, which had to be handed from sentry to sentry, and most of the men had only one blanket. One icy night I made a list in my diary of the clothes I was wearing. It is of some interest as showing the amount of clothes the human body can carry. I was wearing a thick vest and pants, a flannel shirt, two pull-overs, a woollen jacket, a pigskin jacket, corduroy breeches, puttees, thick socks, boots, a stout trench-coat, a muffler, lined leather gloves, and a woollen cap. Nevertheless I was shivering like a jelly. But I admit I am unusually sensitive to cold.

Firewood was the one thing that really mattered. The point about the firewood was that there was practically no firewood to be had. Our miserable mountain had not even at its best much vegetation, and for months it had been ranged over by freezing militiamen, with the result that everything thicker than one's finger had long since been burnt. When we were not eating, sleeping, on guard, or on fatigue-duty we were in the valley behind the position, scrounging for fuel. All my memories of that time are memories of scrambling up and down the almost perpendicular slopes, over the jagged limestone that knocked one's boots to pieces, pouncing eagerly on tiny twigs of wood. Three people searching for a couple of hours could collect enough fuel to keep the dug-out fire alight for about an hour. The eagerness of our search for firewood turned us all into botanists. We classified according to their burning qualities every plant that grew on the mountain-side; the various heaths and grasses that were good to start a fire with but burnt out in a few minutes, the wild rosemary and the tiny whin bushes that would burn when the fire was well alight, the stunted oak tree, smaller than a gooseberry bush, that was practically unburnable. There was a kind of dried-up reed that was very good for starting fires with, but these grew only on the hill-top to the left of the position, and you had to go under fire to get them. If the Fascist machine-gunners saw you they gave you a drum of ammunition all to yourself. Generally their aim was high and the bullets sang overhead like birds, but sometimes they crackled and chipped the limestone uncomfortably close, whereupon you flung yourself on your face. You went on gathering reeds, however; nothing mattered in comparison with firewood.

Beside the cold the other discomforts seemed petty. Of course all of us were permanently dirty. Our water, like our food, came on mule-back from Alcubierre, and each man's share worked out at about a quart a day. It was beastly water, hardly more transparent than milk. Theoretically it was for drinking only, but I always stole a pannikinful for washing in the mornings. I used to wash one day and shave the next; there was never enough water for both. The position stank abominably, and outside the little enclosure of the barricade there was excrement everywhere. Some of the militiamen habitually defecated in the trench, a disgusting thing when one had to walk round it in the darkness. But the dirt never worried me. Dirt is a thing people make too much fuss about. It is astonishing how quickly you get used to doing without a handkerchief and to eating out of the tin pannikin in which you also wash. Nor was sleeping in one's clothes any hardship after a day or two. It was of course impossible to take one's clothes and especially one's boots off at night; one had to be ready to turn out instantly in case of an attack. In eighty nights I only took my clothes off three times, though I did occasionally manage to get them off in the daytime. It was too cold for lice as yet, but rats and mice abounded. It is often said that you don't find rats and mice in the same place, but you do when there is enough food for them.

In other ways we were not badly off. The food was good enough and there was plenty of wine. Cigarettes were still being issued at the rate of a packet a day, matches were issued every other day, and there was even an issue of candles. They were very thin candles, like those on a Christmas cake, and were popularly supposed to have been looted from churches. Every dug-out was issued daily with three inches of candle, which would burn for about twenty minutes. At that time it was still possible to buy candles, and I had brought several pounds of them with me. Later on the famine of matches and candles made life a misery. You do not realize the importance of these things until you lack them. In a night-alarm, for instance, when everyone in the dug-out is scrambling for his rifle and treading on everybody else's face, being able to strike a light may make the difference between life and death. Every militiaman possessed a tinder-lighter and several yards of yellow wick. Next to his rifle it was his most important possession. The tinder-lighters had the great advantage that they could be struck in a wind, but they would only smoulder, so that they were no use for lighting a fire. When the match famine was at its worst our only way of producing a flame was to pull the bullet out of a cartridge and touch the cordite off with a tinder-lighter.

It was an extraordinary life that we were living – an extraordinary way to be at war, if you could call it war. The whole militia chafed against the inaction and clamoured constantly to know why we were not allowed to attack. But it was perfectly obvious that there would be no battle for a long while yet, unless the enemy started it. Georges Kopp, on his periodical tours of inspection, was quite frank with us. 'This is not a war,' he used to say, 'it is a comic opera with an occasional death.' As a matter of fact the stagnation on the Aragon front had political causes of which I knew nothing at that time; but the purely military difficulties – quite apart from the lack of reserves of men – were obvious to anybody.

To begin with, there was the nature of the country. The front line, ours and the Fascists', lay in positions of immense natural strength, which as a rule could only be approached from one side. Provided a few trenches have been dug, such places cannot be taken by infantry, except in overwhelming numbers. In our own position or most of those round us a dozen men with two machine-guns could have held off a battalion. Perched on the hill-tops as we were, we should have made lovely marks for artillery; but there was no artillery. Sometimes I used to gaze round the landscape and long – oh, how passionately! – for a couple of batteries of guns. One could have destroyed the enemy positions one after another as easily as smashing nuts with a hammer. But on our side the guns simply did not exist. The Fascists did occasionally manage to bring a gun or two from Zaragoza and fire a very few shells, so few that they never even found the range and the shells plunged harmlessly into the empty ravines. Against machine-guns and without artillery there are only three things you can do: dig yourself in at a safe distance – four hundred yards, say – advance across the open and be massacred, or make small-scale night-attacks that will not alter the general situation. Practically the alternatives are stagnation or suicide.

And beyond this there was the complete lack of war materials of every description. It needs an effort to realize how badly the militias were armed at this time. Any public school O.T.C. in England is far more like a modern army than we were. The badness of our weapons was so astonishing that it is worth recording in detail.

For this sector of the front the entire artillery consisted of four trench-mortars with *fifteen rounds* for each gun. Of course they were far too precious to be fired and the mortars were kept in Alcubierre. There were machine-guns at the rate of approximately one to fifty men; they were oldish guns, but fairly accurate up to three or four hundred yards. Beyond this we had only rifles, and the majority of the rifles were scrap-iron. There were three types of rifle in use. The first was the long Mauser. These were seldom less than twenty years old, their sights were about as much use as a broken speedometer, and in most of them the rifling was hopelessly corroded; about one rifle in ten was not bad, however. Then there was the short Mauser, or *mousqueton*, really a cavalry weapon. These were more popular than the others because they were lighter to carry and less nuisance in a trench, also because they were comparatively new and looked efficient. Actually they were almost useless. They were made out of reassembled parts, no bolt belonged to its rifle, and three-quarters of them could be counted on to jam after five shots. There were also a few Winchester rifles. These were nice to shoot with, but they were wildly inaccurate, and as their cartridges had no clips they could only be fired one shot at a time. Ammunition was so scarce that each man entering the line was only issued with fifty rounds, and most of it was exceedingly bad. The Spanish-made cartridges were all refills and would jam even the best rifles. The Mexican cartridges were better and were therefore reserved for the machine-guns. Best of all was the German-made ammunition, but as this came only from prisoners and deserters there was not much of it. I always kept a clip of German or Mexican ammunition in my pocket for use in an emergency. But in practice when the emergency came I seldom fired my rifle; I was too frightened of the beastly thing jamming and too anxious to reserve at any rate one round that would go off.

We had no tin hats, no bayonets, hardly any revolvers or pistols, and not more than one bomb between five or ten men. The bomb in use at this time was a frightful object known as the 'F.A.I. bomb', it having been produced by the Anarchists in the early days of the war. It was on the principle of a Mills bomb, but the lever was held down not by a pin but a piece of tape. You broke the tape and then got rid of the bomb with the utmost possible speed. It was said of these bombs that they were 'impartial'; they killed the man they were thrown at and the man who threw them. There were several other types, even more primitive but probably a little less dangerous – to the thrower, I mean. It was not till late March that I saw a bomb worth throwing.

And apart from weapons there was a shortage of all the minor necessities of war. We had no maps or charts, for instance. Spain has never been fully surveyed, and the only detailed maps of this area were the old military ones, which were almost all in the possession of the Fascists. We had no range-finders, no telescopes, no periscopes, no field-glasses except for a few privately-owned pairs, no flares or Very lights, no wire-cutters, no armourers' tools, hardly even any cleaning materials. The Spaniards seemed never to have heard of a pull-through and looked on in surprise when I constructed one. When you wanted your rifle cleaned you took it to the sergeant, who possessed a long brass ramrod which was invariably bent and therefore scratched the rifling. There was not even any gun oil. You greased your rifle with olive oil, when you could get hold of it; at different times I have greased mine with vaseline, with cold cream, and even with bacon-fat. Moreover, there were no lanterns or electric torches – at this time there was not, I believe, such a thing as an electric torch throughout the whole of our sector of the front, and you could not buy one nearer than Barcelona, and only with difficulty even there.

As time went on, and the desultory rifle-fire rattled among the hills, I began to wonder with increasing scepticism whether anything would ever happen to bring a bit of life, or rather a bit of death, into this cock-eyed war. It was pneumonia that we were fighting against, not against men. When the trenches are more than five hundred yards apart no one gets hit except by accident. Of course there were casualties, but the majority of them were self-inflicted. If I remember rightly, the first five men I saw wounded in Spain were all wounded by our own weapons – I don't mean intentionally, but owing to accident or carelessness. Our worn-out rifles were a danger in themselves. Some of them had a nasty trick of going off if the butt was tapped on the ground; I saw a man shoot himself through the hand owing to this. And in the darkness the raw recruits were always firing at one another. One evening when it was barely even dusk a sentry let fly at me from a distance of twenty yards; but he missed me by a yard – goodness knows how many times the Spanish standard of marksmanship has saved my life. Another time I had gone out on patrol in the mist and had carefully warned the guard commander beforehand. But in coming back I stumbled against a bush, the startled sentry called out that the Fascists were coming, and I had the pleasure of hearing the guard commander order everyone to open rapid fire in my direction. Of course I lay down and the bullets went harmlessly over me. Nothing will convince a Spaniard, at least a young Spaniard, that fire-arms are dangerous. Once, rather later than this, I was photographing some machine-gunners with their gun, which was pointed directly towards me.

'Don't fire,' I said half-jokingly as I focused the camera.

'Oh no, we won't fire.'

The next moment there was a frightful roar and a stream of bullets tore past my face so close that my cheek was stung by grains of cordite. It was unintentional, but the machine-gunners considered it a great joke. Yet only a few days earlier they had seen a mule-driver accidentally shot by a political delegate who was playing the fool with an automatic pistol and had put five bullets in the mule-driver's lungs.

The difficult passwords which the army was using at this time were a minor source of danger. They were those tiresome double passwords in which one word has to be answered by another. Usually they were of an elevating and revolutionary nature, such as *Cultura – progreso*, or *Seremos – invencibles*, and it was often impossible to get illiterate sentries to remember these highfalutin' words. One night, I remember, the password was *Cataluña – eroica*, and a moon-faced peasant lad named Jaime Domenech approached me, greatly puzzled, and asked me to explain.

'*Eroica* – what does *eroica* mean?'

I told him that it meant the same as *valiente*. A little while later he was stumbling up the trench in the darkness, and the sentry challenged him:

'*Alto! Cataluña!*'

'*Valiente!*' yelled Jaime, certain that he was saying the right thing.

Bang!

However, the sentry missed him. In this war everyone always did miss everyone else, when it was humanly possible.

4

WHEN I had been about three weeks in the line a contingent of twenty or thirty men, sent out from England by the I.L.P., arrived at Alcubierre, and in order to keep the English on this front together Williams and I were sent to join them. Our new position was at Monte Oscuro, several miles farther west and within sight of Zaragoza.

The position was perched on a sort of razor-back of limestone with dug-outs driven horizontally into the cliff like sand-martins' nests. They went into the ground for prodigious distances, and inside they were pitch dark and so low that you could not even kneel in them, let alone stand. On the peaks to the left of us there were two more P.O.U.M. positions, one of them an object of fascination to every man in the line, because there were three militiawomen there who did the cooking. These women were not exactly beautiful, but it was found necessary to put the position out of bounds to

men of other companies. Five hundred yards to our right there was a
P.S.U.C. post at the bend of the Alcubierre road. It was just here that the
road changed hands. At night you could watch the lamps of our supply-
lorries winding out from Alcubierre and, simultaneously, those of the
Fascists coming from Zaragoza. You could see Zaragoza itself, a thin
string of lights like the lighted portholes of a ship, twelve miles south-
westward. The Government troops had gazed at it from that distance since
August 1936, and they are gazing at it still.

There were about thirty of ourselves, including one Spaniard (Ramón,
Williams's brother-in-law), and there were a dozen Spanish machine-
gunners. Apart from the one or two inevitable nuisances – for, as everyone
knows, war attracts riff-raff – the English were an exceptionally good
crowd, both physically and mentally. Perhaps the best of the bunch was
Bob Smillie – the grandson of the famous miners' leader – who afterwards
died such an evil and meaningless death in Valencia. It says a lot for the
Spanish character that the English and the Spaniards always got on well
together, in spite of the language difficulty. All Spaniards, we discovered,
knew two English expressions. One was 'O.K., baby', the other was a word
used by the Barcelona whores in their dealings with English sailors, and
I am afraid the compositors would not print it.

Once again there was nothing happening all along the line: only the
random crack of bullets and, very rarely, the crash of a Fascist mortar
that sent everyone running to the top trench to see which hill the shells
were bursting on. The enemy was somewhat closer to us here, perhaps
three or four hundred yards away.Their nearest position was exactly
opposite ours, with a machine-gun nest whose loopholes constantly tempted
one to waste cartridges. The Fascists seldom bothered with rifle-shots, but
sent bursts of accurate machine-gun fire at anyone who exposed himself.
Nevertheless it was ten days or more before we had our first casualty. The
troops opposite us were Spaniards, but according to the deserters there
were a few German N.C.O.s among them. At some time in the past there
had also been Moors there – poor devils, how they must have felt the cold!
– for out in no man's land there was a dead Moor who was one of the
sights of the locality. A mile or two to the left of us the line ceased to be
continuous and there was a tract of country, lower-lying and thickly
wooded, which belonged neither to the Fascists nor ourselves. Both we
and they used to make daylight patrols there. It was not bad fun in a Boy
Scoutish way, though I never saw a Fascist patrol nearer than several
hundred yards. By a lot of crawling on your belly you could work your
way partly through the Fascist lines and could even see the farm-house

flying the monarchist flag, which was the local Fascist headquarters. Occasionally we gave it a rifle-volley and then slipped into cover before the machine-guns could locate us. I hope we broke a few windows, but it was a good eight hundred metres away, and with our rifles you could not make sure of hitting even a house at that range.

The weather was mostly clear and cold; sometimes sunny at midday, but always cold. Here and there in the soil of the hill-sides you found the green beaks of wild crocuses or irises poking through; evidently spring was coming, but coming very slowly. The nights were colder than ever. Coming off guard in the small hours we used to rake together what was left of the cook-house fire and then stand in the red-hot embers. It was bad for your boots, but it was very good for your feet. But there were mornings when the sight of the dawn among the mountain-tops made it almost worth while to be out of bed at godless hours. I hate mountains, even from a spectacular point of view. But sometimes the dawn breaking behind the hill-tops in our rear, the first narrow streaks of gold, like swords slitting the darkness, and then the growing light and the seas of carmine cloud stretching away into inconceivable distances, were worth watching even when you had been up all night, when your legs were numb from the knees down, and you were sullenly reflecting that there was no hope of food for another three hours. I saw the dawn oftener during this campaign than during the rest of my life put together – or during the part that is to come, I hope.

We were short-handed here, which meant longer guards and more fatigues. I was beginning to suffer a little from the lack of sleep which is inevitable even in the quietest kind of war. Apart from guard-duties and patrols there were constant night-alarms and stand-to's, and in any case you can't sleep properly in a beastly hole in the ground with your feet aching with the cold. In my first three or four months in the line I do not suppose I had more than a dozen periods of twenty-four hours that were completely without sleep; on the other hand I certainly did not have a dozen nights of full sleep. Twenty or thirty hours' sleep in a week was quite a normal amount. The effects of this were not so bad as might be expected; one grew very stupid, and the job of climbing up and down the hills grew harder instead of easier, but one felt well and one was constantly hungry – heavens, how hungry! All food seemed good, even the eternal haricot beans which everyone in Spain finally learned to hate the sight of. Our water, what there was of it, came from miles away, on the backs of mules or little persecuted donkeys. For some reason the Aragon peasants treated their mules well but their donkeys abominably. If a donkey refused

to go it was quite usual to kick him in the testicles. The issue of candles
had ceased, and matches were running short. The Spaniards taught us
how to make olive oil lamps out of a condensed milk tin, a cartridge-clip,
and a bit of rag. When you had any olive oil, which was not often, these
things would burn with a smoky flicker, about a quarter candle power,
just enough to find your rifle by.

There seemed no hope of any real fighting. When we left Monte Pocero
I had counted my cartridges and found that in nearly three weeks I had
fired just three shots at the enemy. They say it takes a thousand bullets
to kill a man, and at this rate it would be twenty years before I killed my
first Fascist. At Monte Oscuro the lines were closer and one fired oftener,
but I am reasonably certain that I never hit anyone. As a matter of fact,
on this front and at this period of the war the real weapon was not the
rifle but the megaphone. Being unable to kill your enemy you shouted at
him instead. This method of warfare is so extraordinary that it needs
explaining.

Wherever the lines were within hailing distance of one another there
was always a good deal of shouting from trench to trench. From ourselves:
'Fascistas – maricones!' From the Fascists: 'Viva España! Viva Franco!'
– or, when they knew that there were English opposite them: 'Go home,
you English! We don't want foreigners here!' On the Government side, in
the party militias, the shouting of propaganda to undermine the enemy
morale had been developed into a regular technique. In every suitable
position men, usually machine-gunners, were told off for shouting-duty
and provided with megaphones. Generally they shouted a set-piece, full
of revolutionary sentiments which explained to the Fascist soldiers that
they were merely the hirelings of international capitalism, that they were
fighting against their own class, etc., etc., and urged them to come over
to our side. This was repeated over and over by relays of men; sometimes
it continued almost the whole night. There is very little doubt that it had
its effect; everyone agreed that the trickle of Fascist deserters was partly
caused by it. If one comes to think of it, when some poor devil of a sentry
– very likely a Socialist or Anarchist trade union member who has been
conscripted against his will – is freezing at his post, the slogan 'Don't fight
against your own class!' ringing again and again through the darkness is
bound to make an impression on him. It might make just the difference
between deserting and not deserting. Of course such a proceeding does
not fit in with the English conception of war. I admit I was amazed and
scandalized when I first saw it done. The idea of trying to convert your
enemy instead of shooting him! I now think that from any point of view

it was a legitimate manoeuvre. In ordinary trench warfare, when there is no artillery, it is extremely difficult to inflict casualties on the enemy without receiving an equal number yourself. If you can immobilize a certain number of men by making them desert, so much the better; deserters are actually more useful to you than corpses, because they can give information. But at the beginning it dismayed all of us; it made us feel that the Spaniards were not taking this war of theirs sufficiently seriously. The man who did the shouting at the P.S.U.C. post down on our right was an artist at the job. Sometimes, instead of shouting revolutionary slogans he simply told the Fascists how much better we were fed than they were. His account of the Government rations was apt to be a little imaginative. 'Buttered toast!' – you could hear his voice echoing across the lonely valley – 'We're just sitting down to buttered toast over here! Lovely slices of buttered toast!' I do not doubt that, like the rest of us, he had not seen butter for weeks or months past, but in the icy night the news of buttered toast probably set many a Fascist mouth watering. It even made mine water, though I knew he was lying.

One day in February we saw a Fascist aeroplane approaching. As usual, a machine-gun was dragged into the open and its barrel cocked up, and everyone lay on his back to get a good aim. Our isolated positions were not worth bombing, and as a rule the few Fascist aeroplanes that passed our way circled round to avoid machine-gun fire. This time the aeroplane came straight over, too high up to be worth shooting at, and out of it came tumbling not bombs but white glittering things that turned over and over in the air. A few fluttered down into the position. They were copies of a Fascist newspaper, the *Heraldo de Aragón*, announcing the fall of Malaga.

That night the Fascists made a sort of abortive attack. I was just getting down into kip, half dead with sleep, when there was a heavy stream of bullets overhead and someone shouted into the dug-out: 'They're attacking!' I grabbed my rifle and slithered up to my post, which was at the top of the position, beside the machine-gun. There was utter darkness and diabolical noise. The fire of, I think five machine-guns was pouring upon us, and there was a series of heavy crashes caused by the Fascists flinging bombs over their own parapet in the most idiotic manner. It was intensely dark. Down in the valley to the left of us I could see the greenish flash of rifles where a small party of Fascists, probably a patrol, were chipping in. The bullets were flying round us in the darkness, crack-zip-crack. A few shells came whistling over, but they fell nowhere near us and (as usual in this war) most of them failed to explode. I had a bad moment when yet another machine-gun opened fire from the hill-top in our rear –

actually a gun that had been brought up to support us, but at the time it looked as though we were surrounded. Presently our own machine-gun jammed, as it always did jam with those vile cartridges, and the ramrod was lost in the impenetrable darkness. Apparently there was nothing that one could do except stand still and be shot at. The Spanish machine-gunners disdained to take cover, in fact exposed themselves deliberately, so I had to do likewise. Petty though it was, the whole experience was very interesting. It was the first time that I had been properly speaking under fire, and to my humiliation I found that I was horribly frightened. You always, I notice, feel the same when you are under heavy fire – not so much afraid of being hit as afraid because you don't know *where* you will be hit. You are wondering all the while just where the bullet will nip you, and it gives your whole body a most unpleasant sensitiveness.

After an hour or two the firing slowed down and died away. Meanwhile we had had only one casualty. The Fascists had advanced a couple of machine-guns into no man's land, but they had kept a safe distance and made no attempt to storm our parapet. They were in fact not attacking, merely wasting cartridges and making a cheerful noise to celebrate the fall of Malaga. The chief importance of the affair was that it taught me to read the war news in the papers with a more disbelieving eye. A day or two later the newspapers and the radio published reports of a tremendous attack with cavalry and tanks (up a perpendicular hill-side!) which had been beaten off by the heroic English. When the Fascists told us that Malaga had fallen we set it down as a lie, but next day there were more convincing rumours, and it must have been a day or two later that it was admitted officially. By degrees the whole disgraceful story leaked out – how the town had been evacuated without firing a shot, and how the fury of the Italians had fallen not upon the troops, who were gone, but upon the wretched civilian population, some of whom were pursued and machine-gunned for a hundred miles. The news sent a sort of chill all along the line, for, whatever the truth may have been, every man in the militia believed that the loss of Malaga was due to treachery. It was the first talk I had heard of treachery or divided aims. It set up in my mind the first vague doubts about this war in which, hitherto, the rights and wrongs had seemed so beautifully simple.

In mid February we left Monte Oscuro and were sent, together with all the P.O.U.M. troops in this sector, to make a part of the army besieging Huesca. It was a fifty-mile lorry journey across the wintry plain, where the clipped vines were not yet budding and the blades of the winter barley were just poking through the lumpy soil. Four kilometres from our new trenches Huesca glittered small and clear like a city of dolls' houses. Months earlier, when Sietamo was taken, the general commanding the Government troops had said gaily: 'Tomorrow we'll have coffee in Huesca.' It turned out that he was mistaken. There had been bloody attacks, but the town did not fall, and 'Tomorrow we'll have coffee in Huesca' had become a standing joke throughout the army. If I ever go back to Spain I shall make a point of having a cup of coffee in Huesca.

5

ON the eastern side of Huesca, until late March, nothing happened – almost literally nothing. We were twelve hundred metres from the enemy. When the Fascists were driven back into Huesca the Republican Army troops who held this part of the line had not been over-zealous in their advance, so that the line formed a kind of pocket. Later it would have to be advanced – a ticklish job under fire – but for the present the enemy might as well have been non-existent; our sole preoccupation was keeping warm and getting enough to eat. As a matter of fact there were things in this period that interested me greatly, and I will describe some of them later. But I shall be keeping nearer to the order of events if I try here to give some account of the internal political situation on the Government side.

At the beginning I had ignored the political side of the war, and it was only about this time that it began to force itself upon my attention. If you are not interested in the horrors of party politics, please skip; I am trying to keep the political parts of this narrative in separate chapters for precisely that purpose. But at the same time it would be quite impossible to write about the Spanish war from a purely military angle. It was above all things a political war. No event in it, at any rate during the first year, is intelligible unless one has some grasp of the inter-party struggle that was going on behind the Government lines.

When I came to Spain, and for some time afterwards, I was not only uninterested in the political situation but unaware of it. I knew there was a war on, but I had no notion what kind of a war. If you had asked me why I had joined the militia I should have answered: 'To fight against Fascism,' and if you had asked me what I was fighting *for*, I should have answered: 'Common decency.' I had accepted the *News Chronicle – New Statesman*

version of the war as the defence of civilization against a maniacal outbreak
by an army of Colonel Blimps in the pay of Hitler. The revolutionary atmosphere of Barcelona had attracted me deeply, but I had made no attempt to
understand it. As for the kaleidoscope of political parties and trade unions,
with their tiresome names – P.S.U.C., P.O.U.M., F.A.I., C.N.T., U.G.T., J.C.I., J.S.U.,
A.I.T. – they merely exasperated me. It looked at first sight as though Spain
were suffering from a plague of initials. I knew that I was serving in something called the P.O.U.M. (I had only joined the P.O.U.M. militia rather than any
other because I happened to arrive in Barcelona with I.L.P. papers), but I did
not realize that there were serious differences between the political parties.
At Monte Pocero, when they pointed to the position on our left and said:
'Those are the Socialists' (meaning the P.S.U.C.), I was puzzled and said:
'Aren't we all Socialists?' I thought it idiotic that people fighting for their
lives should *have* separate parties; my attitude always was, 'Why can't we
drop all this political nonsense and get on with the war?' This of course was
the correct 'anti-Fascist' attitude which had been carefully disseminated by
the English newspapers, largely in order to prevent people from grasping the
real nature of the struggle. But in Spain, especially in Catalonia, it was an
attitude that no one could or did keep up indefinitely. Everyone, however
unwillingly, took sides sooner or later. For even if one cared nothing for the
political parties and their conflicting 'lines', it was too obvious that one's
own destiny was involved. As a militiaman one was a soldier against Franco,
but one was also a pawn in an enormous struggle that was being fought
out between two political theories. When I scrounged for firewood on the
mountain-side and wondered whether this was really a war or whether the
News Chronicle had made it up, when I dodged the Communist machine-
guns in the Barcelona riots, when I finally fled from Spain with the police
one jump behind me – all these things happened to me in that particular
way because I was serving in the P.O.U.M. militia and not in the P.S.U.C. So
great is the difference between two sets of initials!

To understand the alignment on the Government side one has got to
remember how the war started. When the fighting broke out on 18 July it is
probable that every anti-Fascist in Europe felt a thrill of hope. For here at
last, apparently, was democracy standing up to Fascism. For years past the
so-called democratic countries had been surrendering to Fascism at every
step. The Japanese had been allowed to do as they liked in Manchuria. Hitler
had walked into power and proceeded to massacre political opponents of all
shades. Mussolini had bombed the Abyssinians while fifty-three nations (I
think it was fifty-three) made pious noises 'off'. But when Franco tried to
overthrow a mildly Left-wing Government the Spanish people, against all

expectation, had risen against him. It seemed – possibly it was – the turning of the tide.

But there were several points that escaped general notice. To begin with, Franco was not strictly comparable with Hitler or Mussolini. His rising was a military mutiny backed up by the aristocracy and the Church, and in the main, especially at the beginning, it was an attempt not so much to impose Fascism as to restore feudalism. This meant that Franco had against him not only the working class but also various sections of the liberal bourgeoisie – the very people who are the supporters of Fascism when it appears in a more modern form. More important than this was the fact that the Spanish working class did not, as we might conceivably do in England, resist Franco in the name of 'democracy' and the *status quo*; their resistance was accompanied by – one might almost say it consisted of – a definite revolutionary outbreak. Land was seized by the peasants; many factories and most of the transport were seized by the trade unions; churches were wrecked and the priests driven out or killed. The *Daily Mail*, amid the cheers of the Catholic clergy, was able to represent Franco as a patriot delivering his country from hordes of fiendish 'Reds'.

For the first few months of the war Franco's real opponent was not so much the Government as the trade unions. As soon as the rising broke out the organized town workers replied by calling a general strike and then by demanding – and, after a struggle, getting – arms from the public arsenals. If they had not acted spontaneously and more or less independently it is quite conceivable that Franco would never have been resisted. There can, of course, be no certainty about this, but there is at least reason for thinking it. The Government had made little or no attempt to forestall the rising, which had been foreseen for a long time past, and when the trouble started its attitude was weak and hesitant, so much so, indeed, that Spain had three premiers in a single day.* Moreover, the one step that could save the immediate situation, the arming of the workers, was only taken unwillingly and in response to violent popular clamour. However, the arms were distributed, and in the big towns of eastern Spain the Fascists were defeated by a huge effort, mainly of the working class, aided by some of the armed forces (Assault Guards, etc.) who had remained loyal. It was the kind of effort that could probably only be made by people who were fighting with a revolutionary intention – i.e. believed that they were fighting for something better than the *status quo*. In the various centres of revolt it is thought that three thousand people died in the streets in a single day. Men and women armed

---

* Quiroga, Barrios, and Giral. The first two refused to distribute arms to the trade unions.

only with sticks of dynamite rushed across the open squares and stormed stone buildings held by trained soldiers with machine-guns. Machine-gun nests that the Fascists had placed at strategic spots were smashed by rushing taxis at them at sixty miles an hour. Even if one had heard nothing of the seizure of the land by the peasants, the setting up of local soviets, etc., it would be hard to believe that the Anarchists and Socialists who were the backbone of the resistance were doing this kind of thing for the preservation of capitalist democracy, which especially in the Anarchist view was no more than a centralized swindling machine.

Meanwhile the workers had weapons in their hands, and at this stage they refrained from giving them up. (Even a year later it was computed that the Anarcho-Syndicalists in Catalonia possessed 30,000 rifles.) The estates of the big pro-Fascist landlords were in many places seized by the peasants. Along with the collectivization of industry and transport there was an attempt to set up the rough beginnings of a workers' government by means of local committees, workers' patrols to replace the old pro-capitalist police forces, workers' militias based on the trade unions, and so forth. Of course the process was not uniform, and it went further in Catalonia than elsewhere. There were areas where the institutions of local government remained almost untouched, and others where they existed side by side with revolutionary committees. In a few places independent Anarchist communes were set up, and some of them remained in being till about a year later, when they were forcibly suppressed by the Government. In Catalonia, for the first few months, most of the actual power was in the hands of the Anarcho-Syndicalists, who controlled most of the key industries. The thing that had happened in Spain was, in fact, not merely a civil war, but the beginning of a revolution. It is this fact that the anti-Fascist press outside Spain has made it its special business to obscure. The issue has been narrowed down to 'Fascism versus democracy' and the revolutionary aspect concealed as much as possible. In England, where the Press is more centralized and the public more easily deceived than elsewhere, only two versions of the Spanish war have had any publicity to speak of: the Right-wing version of Christian patriots versus Bolsheviks dripping with blood, and the Left-wing version of gentlemanly republicans quelling a military revolt. The central issue has been successfully covered up.

There were several reasons for this. To begin with, appalling lies about atrocities were being circulated by the pro-Fascist press, and well-meaning propagandists undoubtedly thought that they were aiding the Spanish Government by denying that Spain had 'gone Red'. But the main reason was this: that, except for the small revolutionary groups which exist in all countries, the whole world was determined upon preventing revolution in Spain. In particular the Communist Party, with Soviet Russia behind it, had thrown its whole weight against the revolution. It was the Communist thesis that revolution at this stage would be fatal and that what was to be aimed at in Spain was not workers' control, but bourgeois democracy. It hardly needs pointing out why 'liberal' capitalist opinion took the same line. Foreign capital was heavily invested in Spain. The Barcelona Traction Company, for instance, represented ten millions of British capital; and meanwhile the trade unions had seized all the transport in Catalonia. If the revolution went forward there would be no compensation, or very little; if the capitalist republic prevailed, foreign investments would be safe. And since the revolution had got to be crushed, it greatly simplified things to pretend that no revolution had happened. In this way the real significance of every event could be covered up; every shift of power from the trade unions to the central Government could be represented as a necessary step in military reorganization. The situation produced was curious in the extreme. Outside Spain few people grasped that there was a revolution; inside Spain nobody doubted it. Even the P.S.U.C. newspapers, Communist-controlled and more or less committed to an anti-revolutionary policy, talked about 'our glorious revolution'. And meanwhile the Communist press in foreign countries was shouting that there was no sign of revolution anywhere; the seizure of factories, setting up of workers' committees, etc., had not happened – or, alternatively, had happened, but 'had no political significance'. According to the *Daily Worker* (6 August 1936) those who said that the Spanish people were fighting for social revolution, or for anything other than bourgeois democracy, were 'downright lying scoundrels'. On the other hand, Juan López, a member of the Valencia Government, declared in February 1937 that 'the Spanish people are shedding their blood, not for the democratic Republic and its paper Constitution, but for . . . a revolution'. So it would appear that the downright lying scoundrels included members of the Government for which we were bidden to fight. Some of the foreign anti-Fascist papers even descended to the pitiful lie of pretending that churches were only attacked when they were used as Fascist fortresses. Actually churches were pillaged everywhere and as a matter of course, because it was perfectly well understood that the Spanish Church was part of the capitalist racket. In six months in Spain I only saw two undamaged churches, and until about July 1937 no churches were allowed to reopen and hold services, except for one or two Protestant churches in Madrid.

But, after all, it was only the beginning of a revolution, not the complete thing. Even when the workers, certainly in Catalonia and possibly elsewhere, had the power to do so, they did not overthrow or completely replace the Government. Obviously they could not do so when Franco was hammering at the gate and sections of the middle class were on their side. The country was in a transitional state that was capable either of developing in the direction of Socialism or of reverting to an ordinary capitalist republic. The peasants had most of the land, and they were likely to keep it, unless Franco won; all large industries had been collectivized, but whether they remained collectivized, or whether capitalism was reintroduced, would depend finally upon which group gained control. At the beginning both the Central Government and the Generalite de Cataluña (the semi-autonomous Catalan Government) could definitely be said to represent the working class. The Government was headed by Caballero, a Left-wing Socialist, and contained ministers representing the U.G.T. (Socialist trade unions) and the C.N.T. (Syndicalist unions controlled by the Anarchists). The Catalan Generalite was for a while virtually superseded by an anti-Fascist Defence Committee* consisting mainly of delegates from the trade unions. Later the Defence Committee was dissolved and the Generalite was reconstituted so as to represent the unions and the various Left-wing parties. But every subsequent reshuffling of the Government was a move towards the Right. First the P.O.U.M. was expelled from the Generalite; six months later Caballero was replaced by the Right-wing Socialist Negrín; shortly afterwards the C.N.T. was eliminated from the Government; then the U.G.T.; then the C.N.T. was turned out of the Generalite; finally, a year after the outbreak of war and revolution, there remained a Government composed entirely of Right-wing Socialists, Liberals, and Communists.

The general swing to the Right dates from about October – November 1936, when the U.S.S.R. began to supply arms to the Government and power began to pass from the Anarchists to the Communists. Except Russia and Mexico no country had had the decency to come to the rescue of the Government, and Mexico, for obvious reasons, could not supply arms in large quantities. Consequently the Russians were in a position to dictate terms. There is very little doubt that these terms were, in substance, 'Prevent revolution or you get no weapons', and that the first move against the revolutionary elements, the expulsion of the P.O.U.M. from the Catalan Generalite, was done under orders from the U.S.S.R. It has been denied that any direct pressure was exerted by the Russian Government, but the point is not of great importance, for the Communist parties of all countries can be taken

* Comité Central de Milicias Antifascistas. Delegates were chosen in proportion to the membership of their organizations. Nine delegates represented the trade unions, three the Catalan Liberal parties, and two the various Marxist parties (P.O.U.M., Communists, and others).

as carrying out Russian policy, and it is not denied that the Communist Party
was the chief mover first against the P.O.U.M., later against the Anarchists
and against Caballero's section of the Socialists, and, in general, against a
revolutionary policy. Once the U.S.S.R. had intervened the triumph of the
Communist Party was assured. To begin with, gratitude to Russia for the
arms and the fact that the Communist Party, especially since the arrival of
the International Brigades, looked capable of winning the war, immensely
raised the Communist prestige. Secondly, the Russian arms were supplied
via the Communist Party and the parties allied to them, who saw to it that
as few as possible got to their political opponents.* Thirdly, by proclaiming
a non-revolutionary policy the Communists were able to gather in all those
whom the extremists had scared. It was easy, for instance, to rally the
wealthier peasants against the collectivization policy of the Anarchists.
There was an enormous growth in the membership of the party, and the
influx was largely from the middle class – shop-keepers, officials, army
officers, well-to-do peasants, etc., etc. The war was essentially a triangular
struggle. The fight against Franco had to continue, but the simultaneous
aim of the Government was to recover such power as remained in the hands
of the trade unions. It was done by a series of small moves – a policy of pin-
pricks, as somebody called it – and on the whole very cleverly. There was no
general and obvious counter-revolutionary move, and until May 1937 it was
scarcely necessary to use force. The workers could always be brought to heel
by an argument that is almost too obvious to need stating: 'Unless you do
this, that, and the other we shall lose the war.' In every case, needless to say,
it appeared that the thing demanded by military necessity was the surrender
of something that the workers had won for themselves in 1936. But the
argument could hardly fail, because to lose the war was the last thing that the
revolutionary parties wanted; if the war was lost democracy and revolution,
Socialism and Anarchism, became meaningless words. The Anarchists, the
only revolutionary party that was big enough to matter, were obliged to give
way on point after point. The process of collectivization was checked, the
local committees were got rid of, the workers' patrols were abolished and
the pre-war police forces, largely reinforced and very heavily armed, were
restored, and various key industries which had been under the control of the
trade unions were taken over by the Government (the seizure of the Barcelona Telephone Exchange, which led to the May fighting, was one incident

* This was why there were so few Russian arms on the Aragon front, where the troops were
predominantly Anarchist. Until April 1937 the only Russian weapon I saw – with the exception
of some aeroplanes which may or may not have been Russian – was a solitary sub-machine-
gun.

in this process); finally, most important of all, the workers' militias, based on the trade unions, were gradually broken up and redistributed among the new Popular Army, a 'non-political' army on semi-bourgeois lines, with a differential pay rate, a privileged officer-caste, etc., etc. In the special circumstances this was the really decisive step; it happened later in Catalonia than elsewhere because it was there that the revolutionary parties were strongest. Obviously the only guarantee that the workers could have of retaining their winnings was to keep some of the armed forces under their own control. As usual, the breaking-up of the militias was done in the name of military efficiency; and no one denied that a thorough military reorganization was needed. It would, however, have been quite possible to reorganize the militias and make them more efficient while keeping them under direct control of the trade unions; the main purpose of the change was to make sure that the Anarchists did not possess an army of their own. Moreover, the democratic spirit of the militias made them breeding-grounds for revolutionary ideas. The Communists were well aware of this, and inveighed ceaselessly and bitterly against the P.O.U.M. and Anarchist principle of equal pay for all ranks. A general 'bourgeoisification', a deliberate destruction of the equalitarian spirit of the first few months of the revolution, was taking place. All happened so swiftly that people making successive visits to Spain at intervals of a few months have declared that they seemed scarcely to be visiting the same country; what had seemed on the surface and for a brief instant to be a workers' State was changing before one's eyes into an ordinary bourgeois republic with the normal division into rich and poor. By the autumn of 1937 the 'Socialist' Negrín was declaring in public speeches that 'we respect private property', and members of the Cortes who at the beginning of the war had had to fly the country because of their suspected Fascist sympathies were returning to Spain.

The whole process is easy to understand if one remembers that it proceeds from the temporary alliance that Fascism, in certain forms, forces upon the bourgeois and the worker. This alliance, known as the Popular Front, is in essential an alliance of enemies, and it seems probable that it must always end by one partner swallowing the other. The only unexpected feature in the Spanish situation – and outside Spain it has caused an immense amount of misunderstanding – is that among the parties on the Government side the Communists stood not upon the extreme Left, but upon the extreme Right. In reality this should cause no surprise, because the tactics of the Communist Party elsewhere, especially in France, have made it clear that Official Communism must be regarded, at any rate for the time being, as an anti-revolutionary force. The whole of Comintern policy is now subordinated (excusably, considering the world situation) to the defence of U.S.S.R., which depends upon a system of military alliances. In particular, the U.S.S.R. is in alliance with France, a capitalist-imperialist country. The alliance is of little use to Russia unless French capitalism is strong, therefore Communist policy in France has got to be anti-revolutionary. This means not only that French Communists now march behind the tricolour and sing the Marseillaise, but, what is more important, that they have had to drop all effective agitation in the French colonies. It is less than three years since Thorez, the Secretary of the French Communist Party, was declaring that the French workers would never be bamboozled into fighting against their German comrades;* he is now one of the loudest-lunged patriots in France. The clue to the behaviour of the Communist Party in any country is the military relation of that country, actual or potential, towards the U.S.S.R. In England, for instance, the position is still uncertain, hence the English Communist Party is still hostile to the National Government, and, ostensibly, opposed to rearmament. If, however, Great Britain enters into an alliance or military understanding with the U.S.S.R., the English Communist, like the French Communist, will have no choice but to become a good patriot and imperialist; there are premonitory signs of this already. In Spain the Communist 'line' was undoubtedly influenced by the fact that France, Russia's ally, would strongly object to a revolutionary neighbour and would raise heaven and earth to prevent the liberation of Spanish Morocco. The *Daily Mail*, with its tales of red revolution financed by Moscow, was even more wildly wrong than usual. In reality it was the Communists above all others who prevented revolution in Spain. Later, when the Right-wing forces were in full control, the Communists showed themselves willing to go a great deal further than the Liberals in hunting down the revolutionary leaders.†

I have tried to sketch the general course of the Spanish revolution during its first year, because this makes it easier to understand the situation at any given moment. But I do not want to suggest that in February I held all of the opinions that are implied in what I have said above. To begin with, the things that most enlightened me had not yet happened, and in any case my sympathies were in some ways different from what they are now. This was partly because the political side of the war bored me and I naturally reacted against the viewpoint of which I heard most – i.e. the P.O.U.M. – I.L.P. viewpoint. The Englishmen I was among were mostly I.L.P. members, with a few C.P.

---

* In the Chamber of Deputies, March 1935
† For the best account of the interplay between the parties on the Government side, see Franz Borkenau's *The Spanish Cockpit*. This is by a long way the ablest book that has yet appeared on the Spanish war.

members among them, and most of them were much better educated politically than myself. For weeks on end, during the dull period when nothing
was happening round Huesca, I found myself in the middle of a political
discussion that practically never ended. In the draughty evil-smelling barn
of the farm-house where we were billeted, in the stuffy blackness of dug-
outs, behind the parapet in the freezing midnight hours, the conflicting party
'lines' were debated over and over. Among the Spaniards it was the same,
and most of the newspapers we saw made the inter-party feud their chief
feature. One would have had to be deaf or an imbecile not to pick up some
idea of what the various parties stood for.

From the point of view of political theory there were only three parties
that mattered, the P.S.U.C., the P.O.U.M., and the C.N.T. – F.A.I., loosely described
as the Anarchists. I take the P.S.U.C. first, as being the most important; it was
the party that finally triumphed, and even at this time it was visibly in the
ascendant.

It is necessary to explain that when one speaks of the P.S.U.C. 'line' one
really means the Communist Party 'line'. The P.S.U.C. (Partido Socialista
Unificado de Cataluña) was the Socialist Party of Catalonia; it had been
formed at the beginning of the war by the fusion of various Marxist parties,
including the Catalan Communist Party, but it was now entirely under
Communist control and was affiliated to the Third International. Elsewhere
in Spain no formal unification between Socialists and Communists had taken
place, but the Communist viewpoint and the Right-wing Socialist viewpoint
could everywhere be regarded as identical. Roughly speaking, the P.S.U.C.
was the political organ of the U.G.T. (Unión General de Trabajadores), the
Socialist trade unions. The membership of these unions throughout Spain
now numbered about a million and a half. They contained many sections of
the manual workers, but since the outbreak of war they had also been swollen
by a large influx of middle-class members, for in the early 'revolutionary'
days people of all kinds had found it useful to join either the U.G.T. or the
C.N.T. The two blocks of unions overlapped, but of the two the C.N.T. was more
definitely a working-class organization. The P.S.U.C. was therefore a party
partly of the workers and partly of the small bourgeoisie – the shopkeepers,
the officials, and the wealthier peasants.

The P.S.U.C. 'line' which was preached in the Communist and pro-Communist press throughout the world, was approximately this:

'At present nothing matters except winning the war; without victory in
the war all else is meaningless. Therefore this is not the moment to talk of
pressing forward with the revolution. We can't afford to alienate the peasants
by forcing collectivization upon them, and we can't afford to frighten away

the middle classes who were fighting on our side. Above all for the sake of efficiency we must do away with revolutionary chaos. We must have a strong central government in place of local committees, and we must have a properly trained and fully militarized army under a unified command. Clinging on to fragments of workers' control and parroting revolutionary phrases is worse than useless; it is not merely obstructive, but even counter-revolutionary, because it leads to divisions which can be used against us by the Fascists. At this stage we are not fighting for the dictatorship of the proletariat, we are fighting for parliamentary democracy. Whoever tries to turn the civil war into a social revolution is playing into the hands of the Fascists and is in effect, if not in intention, a traitor.'

The P.O.U.M. 'line' differed from this on every point except, of course, the importance of winning the war. The P.O.U.M. (Partido Obrero de Unificación Marxista) was one of those dissident Communist parties which have appeared in many countries in the last few years as a result of the opposition to 'Stalinism'; i.e. to the change, real or apparent, in Communist policy. It was made up partly of ex-Communists and partly of an earlier party, the Workers' and Peasants' Bloc. Numerically it was a small party,* with not much influence outside Catalonia, and chiefly important because it contained an unusually high proportion of politically conscious members. In Catalonia its chief stronghold was Lerida. It did not represent any block of trade unions. The P.O.U.M. militiamen were mostly C.N.T. members, but the actual party-members generally belonged to the U.G.T. It was, however, only in the C.N.T. that the P.O.U.M. had any influence. The P.O.U.M. 'line' was approximately this:

'It is nonsense to talk of opposing Fascism by bourgeois "democracy". Bourgeois "democracy" is only another name for capitalism, and so is Fascism; to fight against Fascism on behalf of "democracy" is to fight against one form of capitalism on behalf of a second which is liable to turn into the first at any moment. The only real alternative to Fascism is workers' control. If you set up any less goal than this, you will either hand the victory to Franco, or, at best, let in Fascism by the back door. Meanwhile the workers must cling to every scrap of what they have won; if they yield anything to the semi-bourgeois Government they can depend upon being cheated. The workers' militias and police-forces must be preserved in their present form and every effort to "bourgeoisify" them must be resisted. If the workers do

---

* The figures for the P.O.U.M. membership are given as: July 1936, 10,000; December 1936, 70,000; June 1937, 40,000. But these are from P.O.U.M. sources; a hostile estimate would probably divide them by four. The only thing one can say with any certainty about the membership of the Spanish political parties is that every party over-estimates its own numbers.

not control the armed forces, the armed forces will control the workers. The war and the revolution are inseparable.'

The Anarchist viewpoint is less easily defined. In any case the loose term 'Anarchists' is used to cover a multitude of people of very varying opinions. The huge block of unions making up the C.N.T. (Confederación Nacional de Trabajadores), with round about two million members in all, had for its political organ the F.A.I. (Federación Anarquista Ibérica), an actual Anarchist organization. But even the members of the F.A.I., though always tinged, as perhaps most Spaniards are, with the Anarchist philosophy, were not necessarily Anarchists in the purest sense. Especially since the beginning of the war they had moved more in the direction of ordinary Socialism, because circumstances had forced them to take part in centralized administration and even to break all their principles by entering the Government. Nevertheless they differed fundamentally from the Communists in so much that, like the P.O.U.M., they aimed at workers' control and not a parliamentary democracy. They accepted the P.O.U.M. slogan: 'The war and the revolution are inseparable', though they were less dogmatic about it. Roughly speaking, the C.N.T. – F.A.I. stood for: (1) Direct control over industry by the workers engaged in each industry, e.g. transport, the textile factories, etc.; (2) Government by local committees and resistance to all forms of centralized authoritarianism; (3) Uncompromising hostility to the bourgeoisie and the Church. The last point, though the least precise, was the most important. The Anarchists were the opposite of the majority of so-called revolutionaries in so much that though their principles were rather vague their hatred of privilege and injustice was perfectly genuine. Philosophically, Communism and Anarchism are poles apart. Practically – i.e. in the form of society aimed at – the difference is mainly one of emphasis, but it is quite irreconcilable. The Communist's emphasis is always on centralism and efficiency, the Anarchist's on liberty and equality. Anarchism is deeply rooted in Spain and is likely to outlive Communism when the Russian influence is withdrawn. During the first two months of the war it was the Anarchists more than anyone else who had saved the situation, and much later than this the Anarchist militia, in spite of their indiscipline, were notoriously the best fighters among the purely Spanish forces. From about February 1937 onwards the Anarchists and the P.O.U.M. could to some extent be lumped together. If the Anarchists, the P.O.U.M., and the Left wing of the Socialists had had the sense to combine at the start and press a realistic policy, the history of the war might have been different. But in the early period, when the revolutionary parties seemed to have the game in their hands, this was impossible. Between the Anarchists and the Socialists there were ancient jealousies, the P.O.U.M., as Marxists, were sceptical of Anarchism, while from the pure Anarchist standpoint the 'Trotskyism' of the P.O.U.M. was not much preferable to the 'Stalinism' of the Communists. Nevertheless the Communist tactics tended to drive the two parties together. When the P.O.U.M. joined in the disastrous fighting in Barcelona in May, it was mainly from an instinct to stand by the C.N.T., and later, when the P.O.U.M. was suppressed, the Anarchists were the only people who dared to raise a voice in its defence.

So, roughly speaking, the alignment of forces was this. On the one side the C.N.T. − F.A.I., the P.O.U.M., and a section of the Socialists, standing for workers' control: on the other side the Right-wing Socialists, Liberals, and Communists, standing for centralized government and a militarized army.

It is easy to see why, at this time, I preferred the Communist viewpoint to that of the P.O.U.M. The Communists had a definite practical policy, an obviously better policy from the point of view of the common sense which looks only a few months ahead. And certainly the day-to-day policy of the P.O.U.M., their propaganda and so forth, was unspeakably bad; it must have been so, or they would have been able to attract a bigger mass-following. What clinched everything was that the Communists − so it seemed to me − were getting on with the war while we and the Anarchists were standing still. This was the general feeling at the time. The Communists had gained power and a vast increase of membership partly by appealing to the middle classes against the revolutionaries, but partly also because they were the only people who looked capable of winning the war. The Russian arms and the magnificent defence of Madrid by troops mainly under Communist control had made the Communists the heroes of Spain. As someone put it, every Russian aeroplane that flew over our heads was Communist propaganda. The revolutionary purism of the P.O.U.M., though I saw its logic, seemed to me rather futile. After all, the one thing that mattered was to win the war.

Meanwhile there was the diabolical inter-party feud that was going on in the newspapers, in pamphlets, on posters, in books − everywhere. At this time the newspapers I saw most often were the P.O.U.M. papers *La Batalla* and *Adelante*, and their ceaseless carping against the 'counter-revolutionary' P.S.U.C. struck me as priggish and tiresome. Later, when I studied the P.S.U.C. and Communist press more closely, I realized that the P.O.U.M. were almost blameless compared with their adversaries. Apart from anything else, they had much smaller opportunities. Unlike the Communists, they had no footing in any press outside their own country, and inside Spain they were at an immense disadvantage because the press censorship was mainly under Communist control, which meant that the P.O.U.M. papers were liable to be suppressed or fined if they said anything damaging. It is also fair to the

P.O.U.M. to say that though they might preach endless sermons on revolution and quote Lenin *ad nauseam,* they did not usually indulge in personal libel. Also they kept their polemics mainly to newspaper articles. Their large coloured posters, designed for a wider public (posters are important in Spain, with its large illiterate population), did not attack rival parties, but were simply anti-Fascist or abstractedly revolutionary; so were the songs the militiamen sang. The Communist attacks were quite a different matter. I shall have to deal with some of these later in this book. Here I can only give a brief indication of the Communist line of attack.

On the surface the quarrel between the Communists and the P.O.U.M. was one of tactics. The P.O.U.M. was for immediate revolution, the Communists not. So far so good; there was much to be said on both sides. Further, the Communists contended that the P.O.U.M. propaganda divided and weakened the Government forces and thus endangered the war; again, though finally I do not agree, a good case could be made out for this. But here the peculiarity of Communist tactics came in. Tentatively at first, then more loudly, they began to assert that the P.O.U.M. was splitting the Government forces not by bad judgement but by deliberate design. The P.O.U.M. was declared to be no more than a gang of disguised Fascists, in the pay of Franco and Hitler, who were pressing a pseudo-revolutionary policy as a way of aiding the Fascist cause. The P.O.U.M. was a 'Trotskyist' organization and 'Franco's Fifth Column'. This implied that scores of thousands of working-class people, including eight or ten thousand soldiers who were freezing in the front-line trenches and hundreds of foreigners who had come to Spain to fight against Fascism, often sacrificing their livelihood and their nationality by doing so, were simply traitors in the pay of the enemy. And this story was spread all over Spain by means of posters, etc., and repeated over and over in the Communist and pro-Communist press of the whole world. I could fill half a dozen books with quotations if I chose to collect them.

This, then, was what they were saying about us: we were Trotskyists, Fascists, traitors, murderers, cowards, spies, and so forth. I admit it was not pleasant, especially when one thought of some of the people who were responsible for it. It is not a nice thing to see a Spanish boy of fifteen carried down the line on a stretcher, with a dazed white face looking out from among the blankets, and to think of the sleek persons in London and Paris who are writing pamphlets to prove that this boy is a Fascist in disguise. One of the most horrible features of war is that all the war-propaganda, all the screaming and lies and hatred, comes invariably from people who are not fighting. The P.S.U.C. militiamen whom I knew in the line, the Communists from the International Brigade whom I met from time to time, never called me a Trotskyist or a traitor; they left that kind of thing to the journalists in the rear. The people who wrote pamphlets against us and vilified us in the newspapers all remained safe at home, or at worst in the newspaper offices of Valencia, hundreds of miles from the bullets and the mud. And apart from the libels of the inter-party feud, all the usual war-stuff, the tub-thumping, the heroics, the vilification of the enemy – all these were done, as usual, by people who were not fighting and who in many cases would have run a hundred miles sooner than fight. One of the dreariest effects of this war has been to teach me that the Left-wing press is every bit as spurious and dishonest as that of the Right.* I do earnestly feel that on our side – the Government side – this war was different from ordinary, imperialistic wars; but from the nature of the war-propaganda you would never have guessed it. The fighting had barely started when the newspapers of the Right and Left dived simultaneously into the same cesspool of abuse. We all remember the *Daily Mail's* poster: 'REDS CRUCIFY NUNS', while to the *Daily Worker* Franco's Foreign Legion was 'composed of murderers, white-slavers, dope-fiends, and the offal of every European country'. As late as October 1937 the *New Statesman* was treating us to tales of Fascist barricades made of the bodies of living children (a most unhandy thing to make barricades with), and Mr Arthur Bryant was declaring that 'the sawing-off of a Conservative tradesman's legs' was 'a commonplace' in Loyalist Spain. The people who write that kind of stuff never fight; possibly they believe that to write it is a substitute for fighting. It is the same in all wars; the soldiers do the fighting, the journalists do the shouting, and no true patriot ever gets near a front-line trench, except on the briefest of propaganda-tours. Sometimes it is a comfort to me to think that the aeroplane is altering the conditions of war. Perhaps when the next great war comes we may see that sight unprecedented in all history, a jingo with a bullet-hole in him.

As far as the journalistic part of it went, this war was a racket like all other wars. But there was this difference, that whereas the journalists usually reserve their most murderous invective for the enemy, in this case, as time went on, the Communists and the P.O.U.M. came to write more bitterly about one another than about the Fascists. Nevertheless at the time I could not bring myself to take it very seriously. The inter-party feud was annoying and even disgusting, but it appeared to me as a domestic squabble. I did not believe that it would alter anything or that there was any really irreconcilable difference of policy. I grasped that the Communists and Liberals had set

* I should like to make an exception of the *Manchester Guardian*. In connection with this book I have had to go through the files of a good many English papers. Of our larger papers, the *Manchester Guardian* is the only one that leaves me with an increased respect for its honesty.

their faces against allowing the revolution to go forward; I did not grasp that they might be capable of swinging it *back*.

There was a good reason for this. All this time I was at the front, and at the front the social and political atmosphere did not change. I had left Barcelona in early January and I did not go on leave till late April; and all this time – indeed, till later – in the strip of Aragon controlled by Anarchist and P.O.U.M. troops, the same conditions persisted, at least outwardly. The revolutionary atmosphere remained as I had first known it. General and private, peasant and militia-man, still met as equals; everyone drew the same pay, wore the same clothes, ate the same food, and called everyone else 'thou' and 'comrade'; there was no boss-class, no menial-class, no beggars, no prostitutes, no lawyers, no priests, no boot-licking, no cap-touching. I was breathing the air of equality, and I was simple enough to imagine that it existed all over Spain. I did not realize that more or less by chance I was isolated among the most revolutionary section of the Spanish working class.

So, when my more politically educated comrades told me that one could not take a purely military attitude towards the war, and that the choice lay between revolution and Fascism, I was inclined to laugh at them. On the whole I accepted the Communist viewpoint, which boiled down to saying: 'We can't talk of revolution till we've won the war', and not the P.O.U.M. viewpoint, which boiled down to saying: 'We must go forward or we shall go back.' When later on I decided that the P.O.U.M. were right, or at any rate righter than the Communists, it was not altogether upon a point of theory. On paper the Communist case was a good one; the trouble was that their actual behaviour made it difficult to believe that they were advancing it in good faith. The often-repeated slogan: 'The war first and the revolution afterwards', though devoutly believed in by the average P.S.U.C. militiaman, who honestly thought that the revolution could continue when the war had been won, was eyewash. The thing for which the Communists were working was not to postpone the Spanish revolution till a more suitable time, but to make sure that it never happened. This became more and more obvious as time went on, as power was twisted more and more out of working-class hands, and as more and more revolutionaries of every shade were flung into jail. Every move was made in the name of military necessity, because this pretext was, so to speak, ready-made, but the effect was to drive the workers back from an advantageous position and into a position in which, when the war was over, they would find it impossible to resist the reintroduction of capitalism. Please notice that I am saying nothing against the rank-and-file Communists, least of all against the thousands of Communists who died heroically round Madrid. But those were not the men who were directing party policy. As for the people higher up, it is inconceivable that they were not acting with their eyes open.

But, finally, the war was worth winning even if the revolution was lost. And in the end I came to doubt whether, in the long run, the Communist policy made for victory. Very few people seem to have reflected that a different policy might be appropriate at different periods of the war. The Anarchists probably saved the situation in the first two months, but they were incapable of organizing resistance beyond a certain point; the Communists probably saved the situation in October – December, but to win the war outright was a different matter. In England the Communist war-policy has been accepted without question, because very few criticisms of it have been allowed to get into print and because its general line – do away with revolutionary chaos, speed up production, militarize the army – sounds realistic and efficient. It is worth pointing out its inherent weakness.

In order to check every revolutionary tendency and make the war as much like an ordinary war as possible, it became necessary to throw away the strategic opportunities that actually existed. I have described how we were armed, or not armed, on the Aragon front. There is very little doubt that arms were deliberately withheld lest too many of them should get into the hands of the Anarchists, who would afterwards use them for a revolutionary purpose; consequently the big Aragon offensive which would have made Franco draw back from Bilbao, and possibly from Madrid, never happened. But this was comparatively a small matter. What was more important was that once the war had been narrowed down to a 'war for democracy' it became impossible to make any large-scale appeal for working-class aid abroad. If we face facts we must admit that the working class of the world has regarded the Spanish war with detachment. Tens of thousands of individuals came to fight, but the tens of millions behind them remained apathetic. During the first year of the war the entire British public is thought to have subscribed to various 'aid Spain' funds about a quarter of a million pounds – probably less than half of what they spend in a single week on going to the pictures. The way in which the working class in the democratic countries could really have helped her Spanish comrades was by industrial action – strikes and boycotts. No such thing ever even began to happen. The Labour and Communist leaders everywhere declared that it was unthinkable; and no doubt they were right, so long as they were also shouting at the tops of their voices that 'red' Spain was not 'red'. Since 1914–18 'war for democracy' has had a sinister sound. For years past the Communists themselves had been teaching the militant workers in all countries that 'democracy' was a polite name for capitalism. To say first 'Democracy is a swindle', and then 'Fight for democracy!' is not good tactics. If, with the huge prestige of Soviet Russia behind them, they had appealed to the workers of the world in the name not of 'democratic Spain', but of 'revolutionary Spain', it is hard to believe that they would not have got a response.

But what was most important of all, with a non-revolutionary policy it was difficult, if not impossible, to strike at Franco's rear. By the summer of 1937 Franco was controlling a larger population than the Government – much larger, if one counts in the colonies – with about the same number of troops. As everyone knows, with a hostile population at your back it is impossible to keep an army in the field without an equally large army to guard your communications, suppress sabotage, etc. Obviously, therefore, there was no real popular movement in Franco's rear. It was inconceivable that the people in his territory, at any rate the town-workers and the poorer peasants, liked or wanted Franco, but with every swing to the Right the Government's superiority became less apparent. What clinches everything is the case of Morocco. Why was there no rising in Morocco? Franco was trying to set up an infamous dictatorship, and the Moors actually preferred him to the Popular Front Government! The palpable truth is that no attempt was made to foment a rising in Morocco, because to do so would have meant putting a revolutionary construction on the war. The first necessity, to convince the Moors of the Government's good faith, would have been to proclaim Morocco liberated. And we can imagine how pleased the French would have been by that! The best strategic opportunity of the war was flung away in the vain hope of placating French and British capitalism. The whole tendency of the Communist policy was to reduce the war to an ordinary, non-revolutionary war in which the Government was heavily handicapped. For a war of that kind has got to be won by mechanical means, i.e. ultimately, by limitless supplies of weapons; and the Government's chief donor of weapons, the U.S.S.R., was at a great disadvantage, geographically, compared with Italy and Germany. Perhaps the P.O.U.M. and Anarchist slogan: 'The war and the revolution are inseparable', was less visionary than it sounds.

I have given my reasons for thinking that the Communist anti-revolutionary policy was mistaken, but so far as its effect upon the war goes I do not hope that my judgement is right. A thousand times I hope that it is wrong. I would wish to see this war won by any means whatever. And of course we cannot tell yet what may happen. The Government may swing to the Left again, the Moors may revolt of their own accord, England may decide to buy Italy out, the war may be won by straightforward military means – there is no knowing. I let the above opinions stand, and time will show how far I am right or wrong.

But in February 1937 I did not see things quite in this light. I was sick of the inaction on the Aragon front and chiefly conscious that I had not done my fair share of the fighting. I used to think of the recruiting poster in Barcelona which demanded accusingly of passers-by: 'What have *you* done for democracy?' and feel that I could only answer: 'I have drawn my rations.' When I joined the militia I had promised myself to kill one Fascist – after all, if each of us killed one they would soon be extinct – and I had killed nobody yet, had hardly had the chance to do so. And of course I wanted to go to Madrid. Everyone in the army, whatever his political opinions, always wanted to go to Madrid. This would probably mean exchanging into the International Column, for the P.O.U.M. had now very few troops at Madrid and the Anarchists not so many as formerly.

For the present, of course, one had to stay in the line, but I told everyone that when we went on leave I should, if possible, exchange into the International Column, which meant putting myself under Communist control. Various people tried to dissuade me, but no one attempted to interfere. It is fair to say that there was very little heresy-hunting in the P.O.U.M., perhaps not enough, considering their special circumstances; short of being a pro-Fascist no one was penalized for holding the wrong political opinions. I spent much of my time in the militia in bitterly criticizing the P.O.U.M. 'line', but I never got into trouble for it. There was not even any pressure upon one to become a political member of the party, though I think the majority of the militiamen did so. I myself never joined the party – for which afterwards, when the P.O.U.M. was suppressed, I was rather sorry.

6

MEANWHILE the daily – more particularly nightly – round, the common task. Sentry-go, patrols, digging; mud, rain, shrieking winds, and occasional snow. It was not till well into April that the nights grew noticeably warmer. Up here on the plateau the March days were mostly like an English March, with bright blue skies and nagging winds. The winter barley was a foot high, crimson buds were forming on the cherry trees (the line here ran through deserted orchards and vegetable gardens), and if you searched the ditches you could find violets and a kind of wild

hyacinth like a poor specimen of a bluebell. Immediately behind the line
there ran a wonderful, green, bubbling stream, the first transparent water
I had seen since coming to the front. One day I set my teeth and crawled
into the river to have my first bath in six weeks. It was what you might
call a brief bath, for the water was mainly snow-water and not much above
freezing-point.

Meanwhile nothing happened, nothing ever happened. The English had
got into the habit of saying that this wasn't a war, it was a bloody
pantomime. We were hardly under direct fire from the Fascists. The only
danger was from stray bullets, which, as the lines curved forward on either
side, came from several directions. All the casualties at this time were
from strays. Arthur Clinton got a mysterious bullet that smashed his left
shoulder and disabled his arm, permanently, I am afraid. There was a
little shell-fire, but it was extraordinarily ineffectual. The scream and
crash of the shells was actually looked upon as a mild diversion. The
Fascists never dropped their shells on our parapet. A few hundred yards
behind us there was a country house, called La Granja, with big farm-
buildings, which was used as a store, headquarters, and cook-house for
this sector of the line. It was this that the Fascist gunners were trying for,
but they were five or six kilometres away and they never aimed well
enough to do more than smash the windows and chip the walls. You were
only in danger if you happened to be coming up the road when the firing
started, and the shells plunged into the fields on either side of you. One
learned almost immediately the mysterious art of knowing by the sound
of a shell how close it will fall. The shells the Fascists were firing at this
period were wretchedly bad. Although they were 150 mm. they only made
a crater about six feet wide by four deep, and at least one in four failed
to explode. There were the usual romantic tales of sabotage in the Fascist
factories and unexploded shells in which, instead of the charge, there was
found a scrap of paper saying 'Red Front', but I never saw one. The truth
was that the shells were hopelessly old; someone picked up a brass fuse-
cap stamped with the date, and it was 1917. The Fascist guns were of the
same make and calibre as our own, and the unexploded shells were often
reconditioned and fired back. There was said to be one old shell with a
nickname of its own which travelled daily to and fro, never exploding.

At night small patrols used to be sent into no man's land to lie in ditches
near the Fascist lines and listen for sounds (bugle-calls, motor-horns, and
so forth) that indicated activity in Huesca. There was a constant come-
and-go of Fascist troops, and the numbers could be checked to some extent
from listeners' reports. We always had special orders to report the ringing

of church bells. It seemed that the Fascists always heard mass before going into action. In among the fields and orchards there were deserted mud-walled huts which it was safe to explore with a lighted match when you had plugged up the windows. Sometimes You came on valuable pieces of loot such as a hatchet or a Fascist water-bottle (better than ours and greatly sought after). You could explore in the daytime as well, but mostly it had to be done crawling on all fours. It was queer to creep about in those empty, fertile fields where everything had been arrested just at the harvest-moment. Last year's crops had never been touched. The unpruned vines were snaking across the ground, the cobs on the standing maize had gone as hard as stone, the mangels and sugar-beets were hypertrophied into huge woody lumps. How the peasants must have cursed both armies! Sometimes parties of men went spud-gathering in no man's land. About a mile to the right of us, where the lines were closer together, there was a patch of potatoes that was frequented both by the Fascists and ourselves. We went there in the daytime, they only at night, as it was commanded by our machine-guns. One night to our annoyance they turned out *en masse* and cleared up the whole patch. We discovered another patch farther on, where there was practically no cover and you had to lift the potatoes lying on your belly – a fatiguing job. If their machine-gunners spotted you, you had to flatten yourself out like a rat when it squirms under a door, with the bullets cutting up the clods a few yards behind you. It seemed worth it at the time. Potatoes were getting very scarce. If you got a sackful you could take them down to the cook-house and swap them for a water-bottleful of coffee.

And still nothing happened, nothing ever looked like happening. 'When are we going to attack? Why don't we attack?' were the questions you heard night and day from Spaniard and Englishman alike. When you think what fighting means it is queer that soldiers want to fight, and yet undoubtedly they do. In stationary warfare there are three things that all soldiers long for: a battle, more cigarettes, and a week's leave. We were somewhat better armed now than before. Each man had a hundred and fifty rounds of ammunition instead of fifty, and by degrees we were being issued with bayonets, steel helmets, and a few bombs. There were constant rumours of forthcoming battles, which I have since thought were deliberately circulated to keep up the spirits of the troops. It did not need much military knowledge to see that there would be no major action on this side of Huesca, at any rate for the time being. The strategic point was the road to Jaca, over on the other side. Later, when the Anarchists made their

attacks on the Jaca road, our job was to make 'holding attacks' and force
the Fascists to divert troops from the other side.

During all this time, about six weeks, there was only one action on our
part of the front. This was when our Shock Troopers attacked the
Manicomio, a disused lunatic asylum which the Fascists had converted
into a fortress. There were several hundred refugee Germans serving with
the P.O.U.M. They were organized in a special battalion called the Batallón
de Choque, and from a military point of view they were on quite a different
level from the rest of the militia – indeed, were more like soldiers than
anyone I saw in Spain, except the Assault Guards and some of the
International Column. The attack was mucked up, as usual. How many
operations in this war, on the Government side, were *not* mucked up, I
wonder? The Shock Troops took the Manicomio by storm, but the troops,
of I forget which militia, who were to support them by seizing the
neighbouring hill that commanded the Manicomio, were badly let down.
The captain who led them was one of those Regular Army officers of
doubtful loyalty whom the Government persisted in employing. Either
from fright or treachery he warned the Fascists by flinging a bomb when
they were two hundred yards away. I am glad to say his men shot him
dead on the spot. But the surprise-attack was no surprise, and the
militiamen were mown down by heavy fire and driven off the hill, and at
nightfall the Shock Troops had to abandon the Manicomio. Through the
night the ambulances filed down the abominable road to Sietamo, killing
the badly wounded with their joltings. All of us were lousy by this time;
though still cold it was warm enough for that. I have had a big experience
of body vermin of various kinds, and for sheer beastliness the louse beats
everything I have encountered. Other insects, mosquitoes for instance,
make you suffer more, but at least they aren't *resident* vermin. The human
louse somewhat resembles a tiny lobster, and he lives chiefly in your
trousers. Short of burning all your clothes there is no known way of getting
rid of him. Down the seams of your trousers he lays his glittering white
eggs, like tiny grains of rice, which hatch out and breed families of their
own at horrible speed. I think the pacifists might find it helpful to illustrate
their pamphlets with enlarged photographs of lice. Glory of war, indeed!
In war *all* soldiers are lousy, at least when it is warm enough. The men
who fought at Verdun, at Waterloo, at Flodden, at Senlac, at Thermopylae
– every one of them had lice crawling over his testicles. We kept the brutes
down to some extent by burning out the eggs and by bathing as often as
we could face it. Nothing short of lice could have driven me into that ice-
cold river.

Everything was running short – boots, clothes, tobacco, soap, candles, matches, olive oil. Our uniforms were dropping to pieces, and many of the men had no boots, only rope-soled sandals. You came on piles of worn-out boots everywhere. Once we kept a dug-out fire burning for two days mainly with boots, which are not bad fuel. By this time my wife was in Barcelona and used to send me tea, chocolate, and even cigars when such things were procurable; but even in Barcelona everything was running short, especially tobacco. The tea was a godsend, though we had no milk and seldom any sugar. Parcels were constantly being sent from England to men in the contingent but they never arrived; food, clothes, cigarettes – everything was either refused by the Post Office or seized in France. Curiously enough, the only firm that succeeded in sending packets of tea – even, on one memorable occasion, a tin of biscuits – to my wife was the Army and Navy Stores. Poor old Army and Navy! They did their duty nobly, but perhaps they might have felt happier if the stuff had been going to Franco's side of the barricade. The shortage of tobacco was the worst of all. At the beginning we had been issued with a packet of cigarettes a day, then it got down to eight cigarettes a day, then to five. Finally there were ten deadly days when there was no issue of tobacco at all. For the first time, in Spain, I saw something that you see every day in London – people picking up fag-ends.

Towards the end of March I got a poisoned hand that had to be lanced and put in a sling. I had to go into hospital, but it was not worth sending me to Sietamo for such a petty injury, so I stayed in the so-called hospital at Monflorite, which was merely a casualty clearing station. I was there ten days, part of the time in bed. The *practicantes* (hospital assistants) stole practically every valuable object I possessed, including my camera and all my photographs. At the front everyone stole, it was the inevitable effect of shortage, but the hospital people were always the worst. Later, in the hospital at Barcelona, an American who had come to join the International Column on a ship that was torpedoed by an Italian submarine, told me how he was carried ashore wounded, and how, even as they lifted him into the ambulance, the stretcher-bearers pinched his wristwatch.

While my arm was in the sling I spent several blissful days wandering about the country-side. Monflorite was the usual huddle of mud and stone houses, with narrow tortuous alleys that had been churned by lorries till they looked like the craters of the moon. The church had been badly knocked about but was used as a military store. In the whole neighbourhood there were only two farm-houses of any size, Torre Lorenzo and Torre

Fabián, and only two really large buildings, obviously the houses of the landowners who had once lorded it over the countryside; you could see their wealth reflected in the miserable huts of the peasants. Just behind the river, close to the front line, there was an enormous flour-mill with a country-house attached to it. It seemed shameful to see the huge costly machine rusting useless and the wooden flour-chutes torn down for firewood. Later on, to get firewood for the troops farther back, parties of men were sent in lorries to wreck the place systematically. They used to smash the floorboards of a room by bursting a hand-grenade in it. La Granja, our store and cook-house, had possibly at one time been a convent. It had huge courtyards and out-houses, covering an acre or more, with stabling for thirty or forty horses. The country-houses in that part of Spain are of no interest architecturally, but their farm-buildings, of lime-washed stone with round arches and magnificent roof-beams, are noble places, built on a plan that has probably not altered for centuries. Sometimes it gave you a sneaking sympathy with the Fascist ex-owners to see the way the militia treated the buildings they had seized. In La Granja every room that was not in use had been turned into a latrine – a frightful shambles of smashed furniture and excrement. The little church that adjoined it, its walls perforated by shell-holes, had its floor inches deep in dung. In the great courtyard where the cooks ladled out the rations the litter of rusty tins, mud, mule dung, and decaying food was revolting. It gave point to the old army song:

> There are rats, rats,
> Rats as big as cats,
> In the quartermaster's store!

The ones at La Granja itself really were as big as cats, or nearly; great bloated brutes that waddled over the beds of muck, too impudent even to run away unless you shot at them.

Spring was really here at last. The blue in the sky was softer, the air grew suddenly balmy. The frogs were mating noisily in the ditches. Round the drinking-pool that served for the village mules I found exquisite green frogs the size of a penny, so brilliant that the young grass looked dull beside them. Peasant lads went out with buckets hunting for snails, which they roasted alive on sheets of tin. As soon as the weather improved the peasants had turned out for the spring ploughing. It is typical of the utter vagueness in which the Spanish agrarian revolution is wrapped that I could not even discover for certain whether the land here was collectivized or whether the peasants had simply divided it up among themselves. I fancy that in theory it was collectivized, this being P.O.U.M. and Anarchist territory. At any rate the landowners were gone, the fields were being cultivated, and people seemed satisfied. The friendliness of the peasants towards ourselves never ceased to astonish me. To some of the older ones the war must have seemed meaningless, visibly it produced a shortage of everything and a dismal dull life for everybody, and at the best of times peasants hate having troops quartered upon them. Yet they were invariably friendly – I suppose reflecting that, however intolerable we might be in other ways, we did stand between them and their one-time landlords. Civil war is a queer thing. Huesca was not five miles away, it was these people's market town, all of them had relatives there, every week of their lives they had gone there to sell their poultry and vegetables. And now for eight months an impenetrable barrier of barbed wire and machine-guns had lain between. Occasionally it slipped their memory. Once I was talking to an old woman who was carrying one of those tiny iron lamps in which the Spaniards burn olive oil. 'Where can I buy a lamp like that?' I said. 'In Huesca,' she said without thinking, and then we both laughed. The village girls were splendid vivid creatures with coal-black hair, a swinging walk, and a straightforward, man-to-man demeanour which was probably a by-product of the revolution.

Men in ragged blue shirts and black corduroy breeches, with broad-brimmed straw hats, were ploughing the fields behind teams of mules with rhythmically flopping ears. Their ploughs were wretched things, only stirring the soil, not cutting anything we should regard as a furrow. All the agricultural implements were pitifully antiquated, everything being governed by the expensiveness of metal. A broken ploughshare, for instance, was patched, and then patched again, till sometimes it was mainly patches. Rakes and pitchforks were made of wood. Spades, among a people who seldom possessed boots, were unknown; they did their digging with a clumsy hoe like those used in India. There was a kind of harrow that took one straight back to the later Stone Age. It was made of boards joined together, to about the size of a kitchen table; in the boards hundreds of holes were morticed, and into each hole was jammed a piece of flint which had been chipped into shape exactly as men used to chip them ten thousand years ago. I remember my feelings almost of horror when I first came upon one of these things in a derelict hut in no man's land. I had to puzzle over it for a long while before grasping that it was a harrow. It made me sick to think of the work that must go into the making of such a thing, and the poverty that was obliged to use flint in place of steel. I have felt more kindly towards industrialism ever since. But in the village there were two up-to-date farm tractors, no doubt seized from some big landowner's estate.

Once or twice I wandered out to the little walled graveyard that stood a mile or so from the village. The dead from the front were normally sent to Sietamo; these were the village dead. It was queerly different from an English graveyard. No reverence for the dead here! Everything overgrown with bushes and coarse grass, human bones littered everywhere. But the really surprising thing was the almost complete lack of religious inscriptions on the gravestones, though they all dated from before the revolution. Only once, I think, I saw the 'Pray for the Soul of So-and-So' which is usual on Catholic graves. Most of the inscriptions were purely secular, with ludicrous poems about the virtues of the deceased. On perhaps one grave in four or five there was a small cross or a perfunctory reference to Heaven; this had usually been chipped off by some industrious atheist with a chisel.

It struck me that the people in this part of Spain must be genuinely without religious feeling – religious feeling, I mean, in the orthodox sense. It is curious that all the time I was in Spain I never once saw a person cross himself; yet you would think such a movement would become instinctive, revolution or no revolution. Obviously the Spanish Church will come back (as the saying goes, night and the Jesuits always return), but there is no doubt that at the outbreak of the revolution it collapsed and was smashed up to an extent that would be unthinkable even for the moribund C. of E. in like circumstances. To the Spanish people, at any rate in Catalonia and Aragon, the Church was a racket pure and simple. And possibly Christian belief was replaced to some extent by Anarchism, whose influence is widely spread and which undoubtedly has a religious tinge.

It was the day I came back from hospital that we advanced the line to what was really its proper position, about a thousand yards forward, along the little stream that lay a couple of hundred yards in front of the Fascist line. This operation ought to have been carried out months earlier. The point of doing it now was that the Anarchists were attacking on the Jaca road, and to advance on this side made them divert troops to face us.

We were sixty or seventy hours without sleep, and my memories go down into a sort of blue, or rather a series of pictures. Listening-duty in no man's land, a hundred yards from the Casa Francesa, a fortified farmhouse which was part of the Fascist line. Seven hours lying in a horrible marsh, in reedy-smelling water into which one's body subsided gradually deeper and deeper: the reedy smell, the numbing cold, the stars immovable in the black sky, the harsh croaking of the frogs. Though this was April it was the coldest night that I remember in Spain. Only a hundred yards behind us the working-parties were hard at it, but there was utter silence except for the chorus of the frogs. Just once during the night I heard a sound – the familiar noise of a sand-bag being flattened with a spade. It is queer how, just now and again, Spaniards can carry out a brilliant feat of organization. The whole move was beautifully planned. In seven hours six hundred men constructed twelve hundred metres of trench and parapet, at distances of from a hundred and fifty to three hundred yards from the Fascist line, and all so silently that the Fascists heard nothing, and during the night there was only one casualty. There were more next day, of course. Every man had his job assigned to him, even to the cook-house orderlies who suddenly arrived when the work was done with buckets of wine laced with brandy.

And then the dawn coming up and the Fascists suddenly discovering that we were there. The square white block of the Casa Francesa, though it was two hundred yards away, seemed to tower over us, and the machine-guns in its sand-bagged upper windows seemed to be pointing straight down into the trench. We all stood gaping at it, wondering why the Fascists didn't see us. Then a vicious swirl of bullets, and everyone had flung himself on his knees and was frantically digging, deepening the trench and scooping out small shelters in the side. My arm was still in bandages, I could not dig, and I spent most of that day reading a detective story – *The Missing Money-lender* its name was. I don't remember the plot of it, but I remember very clearly the feeling of sitting there reading it; the dampish clay of the trench bottom underneath me, the constant shifting of my legs out of the way as men hurried stopping down the trench, the crack-crack-crack of bullets a foot or two overhead. Thomas Parker got a bullet through the top of his thigh, which, as he said, was nearer to being a D.S.O. than he cared about. Casualties were happening all along the line, but nothing to what there would have been if they had caught us on the move during the night. A deserter told us afterwards that five Fascist sentries were shot for negligence. Even now they could have massacred us if they had had the initiative to bring up a few mortars. It was an awkward job getting the wounded down the narrow, crowded trench. I saw one poor devil, his breeches dark with blood, flung out of his stretcher and gasping in agony. One had to carry wounded men a long distance, a mile or more, for even when a road existed the ambulances never came very near the front line. If they came too near the Fascists had a habit of shelling them – justifiably, for in modern war no one scruples to use an ambulance for carrying ammunition.

And then, next night, waiting at Torre Fabián for an attack that was called off at the last moment by wireless. In the barn where we waited the floor was a thin layer of chaff over deep beds of bones, human bones and cows' bones mixed up, and the place was alive with rats. The filthy brutes came swarming out of the ground on every side. If there is one thing I hate more than another it is a rat running over me in the darkness. However, I had the satisfaction of catching one of them a good punch that sent him flying.

And then waiting fifty or sixty yards from the Fascist parapet for the order to attack. A long line of men crouching in an irrigation ditch with their bayonets peeping over the edge and the whites of their eyes shining through the darkness. Kopp and Benjamin squatting behind us with a man who had a wireless receiving-box strapped to his shoulders. On the western horizon rosy gun-flashes followed at intervals of several seconds by enormous explosions. And then a pip-pip-pip noise from the wireless and the whispered order that we were to get out of it while the going was good. We did so, but not quickly enough. Twelve wretched children of the J.C.I. (the Youth League of the P.O.U.M., corresponding to the J.S.U. of the P.S.U.C.) who had been posted only about forty yards from the Fascist parapet, were caught by the dawn and unable to escape. All day they had to lie there, with only tufts of grass for cover, the Fascists shooting at them every time they moved. By nightfall seven were dead, then the other five managed to creep away in the darkness.

And then, for many mornings to follow, the sound of the Anarchist attacks on the other side of Huesca. Always the same sound. Suddenly, at some time in the small hours, the opening crash of several score bombs bursting simultaneously – even from miles away a diabolical, rending crash – and then the unbroken roar of massed rifles and machine-guns, a heavy rolling sound curiously similar to the roll of drums. By degrees the firing would spread all round the lines that encircled Huesca, and we would stumble out into the trench to lean sleepily against the parapet while a ragged meaningless fire swept overhead.

In the daytime the guns thundered fitfully. Torre Fabián, now our cookhouse, was shelled and partially destroyed. It is curious that when you are watching artillery-fire from a safe distance you always want the gunner to hit his mark, even though the mark contains your dinner and some of your comrades. The Fascists were shooting well that morning; perhaps there were German gunners on the job. They bracketed neatly on Torre Fabián. One shell beyond it, one shell short of it, then whizz-BOOM! Burst rafters leaping upwards and a sheet of uralite skimming down the air like a flicked playing-card. The next shell took off a corner of a building as neatly as a giant might do it with a knife. But the cooks produced dinner on time – a memorable feat.

As the days went on the unseen but audible guns began each to assume a distinct personality. There were the two batteries of Russian 75-mm. guns which fired from close in our rear and which somehow evoked in my mind the picture of a fat man hitting a golf-ball. These were the first Russian guns I had seen – or heard, rather. They had a low trajectory and a very high velocity, so that you heard the cartridge explosion, the whizz, and the shell-burst almost simultaneously. Behind Monflorite were two very heavy guns which fired a few times a day, with a deep, muffled roar that was like the baying of distant chained-up monsters. Up at Mount Aragon, the medieval fortress which the Government troops had stormed last year (the first time in its history, it was said), and which guarded one of the approaches to Huesca, there was a heavy gun which must have dated well back into the nineteenth century. Its great shells whistled over so slowly that you felt certain you could run beside them and keep up with them. A shell from this gun sounded like nothing so much as a man riding along on a bicycle and whistling. The trench-mortars, small though they were, made the most evil sound of all. Their shells are really a kind of winged torpedo, shaped like the darts thrown in public-houses and about the size of a quart bottle; they go off with a devilish metallic crash, as of some monstrous globe of brittle steel being shattered on an anvil. Sometimes our aeroplanes flew over and let loose the aerial torpedoes whose tremendous echoing roar makes the earth tremble even at two miles' distance. The shell-bursts from the Fascist anti-aircraft guns dotted the sky like cloudlets in a bad water-colour, but I never saw them get within a thousand yards of an aeroplane. When an aeroplane swoops down and uses its machine-gun the sound, from below, is like the fluttering of wings.

On our part of the line not much was happening. Two hundred yards to the right of us, where the Fascists were on higher ground, their snipers picked off a few of our comrades. Two hundred yards to the left, at the bridge over the stream, a sort of duel was going on between the Fascist mortars and the men who were building a concrete barricade across the bridge. The evil little shells whizzed over, zwing-crash! zwing-crash!, making a doubly diabolical noise when they landed on the asphalt road. A hundred yards away you could stand in perfect safety and watch the columns of earth and black smoke leaping into the air like magic trees. The poor devils round the bridge spent much of the daytime cowering in the little man-holes they had scooped in the side of the trench. But there

were less casualties than might have been expected, and the barricade rose
steadily, a wall of concrete two feet thick, with embrasures for two
machine-guns and a small field gun. The concrete was being reinforced
with old bedsteads, which apparently was the only iron that could be found
for the purpose.

7

ONE afternoon Benjamin told us that he wanted fifteen volunteers. The
attack on the Fascist redoubt which had been called off on the previous
occasion was to be carried out tonight. I oiled my ten Mexican cartridges,
dirtied my bayonet (the things give your position away if they flash too
much), and packed up a hunk of bread, three inches of red sausage, and
a cigar which my wife had sent from Barcelona and which I had been
hoarding for a long time. Bombs were served out, three to a man. The
Spanish Government had at last succeeded in producing a decent bomb.
It was on the principle of a Mills bomb, but with two pins instead of one.
After you had pulled the pins out there was an interval of seven seconds
before the bomb exploded. Its chief disadvantage was that one pin was
very stiff and the other very loose, so that you had the choice of leaving
both pins in place and being unable to pull the stiff one out in a moment
of emergency, or pulling out the stiff one beforehand and being in a
constant stew lest the thing should explode in your pocket. But it was a
handy little bomb to throw.

A little before midnight Benjamin led the fifteen of us down to Torre
Fabián. Ever since evening the rain had been pelting down. The irrigation
ditches were brimming over, and every time you stumbled into one you
were in water up to your waist. In the pitch darkness and sheeting rain in
the farm-yard a dim mass of men was waiting. Kopp addressed us, first
in Spanish, then in English, and explained the plan of attack. The Fascist
line here made an L-bend and the parapet we were to attack lay on rising
ground at the corner of the L. About thirty of us, half English, and half
Spanish, under the command of Jorge Roca, our battalion commander (a
battalion in the militia was about four hundred men), and Benjamin, were
to creep up and cut the Fascist wire. Jorge would fling the first bomb as
a signal, then the rest of us were to send in a rain of bombs, drive

the Fascists out of the parapet, and seize it before they could rally. Simultaneously seventy Shock Troopers were to assault the next Fascist 'position', which lay two hundred yards to the right of the other, joined to it by a communication-trench. To prevent us from shooting each other in the darkness white armlets would be worn. At this moment a messenger arrived to say that there were no white armlets. Out of the darkness a plaintive voice suggested: 'Couldn't we arrange for the Fascists to wear white armlets instead?'

There was an hour or two to put in. The barn over the mule stable was so wrecked by shell-fire that you could not move about in it without a light. Half the floor had been torn away by a plunging shell and there was a twenty-foot drop on to the stones beneath. Someone found a pick and levered a burst plank out of the floor, and in a few minutes we had got a fire alight and our drenched clothes were steaming. Someone else produced a pack of cards. A rumour – one of those mysterious rumours that are endemic in war – flew round that hot coffee with brandy in it was about to be served out. We filed eagerly down the almost-collapsing staircase and wandered round the dark yard, inquiring where the coffee was to be found. Alas! there was no coffee. Instead, they called us together, ranged us into single file, and then Jorge and Benjamin set off rapidly into the darkness, the rest of us following.

It was still raining and intensely dark, but the wind had dropped. The mud was unspeakable. The paths through the beet-fields were simply a succession of lumps, as slippery as a greasy pole, with huge pools everywhere. Long before we got to the place where we were to leave our own parapet everyone had fallen several times and our rifles were coated with mud. At the parapet a small knot of men, our reserves, were waiting, and the doctor and a row of stretchers. We filed through the gap in the parapet and waded through another irrigation ditch. Splash-gurgle! Once again in water up to your waist, with the filthy, slimy mud oozing over your boot-tops. On the grass outside Jorge waited till we were all through. Then, bent almost double, he began creeping slowly forward. The Fascist parapet was about a hundred and fifty yards away. Our one chance of getting there was to move without noise.

I was in front with Jorge and Benjamin. Bent double, but with faces raised, we crept into the almost utter darkness at a pace that grew slower at every step. The rain beat lightly in our faces. When I glanced back I could see the men who were nearest to me, a bunch of humped shapes like huge black mushrooms gliding slowly forward. But every time I raised my head Benjamin, close beside me, whispered fiercely in my ear: 'To keep ze head down! To keep ze head down!' I could have told him that he needn't worry. I knew by experiment that on a dark night you can never see a man at twenty paces. It was far more important to go quietly. If they once heard us we were done for. They had only to spray the darkness with their machine-gun and there was nothing for it but to run or be massacred.

But on the sodden ground it was almost impossible to move quietly. Do what you would your feet stuck to the mud, and every step you took was slop-slop, slop-slop. And the devil of it was that the wind had dropped, and in spite of the rain it was a very quiet night. Sounds would carry a long way. There was a dreadful moment when I kicked against a tin and thought every Fascist within miles must have heard it. But no, not a sound, no answering shot, no movement in the Fascist lines. We crept onwards, always more slowly. I cannot convey to you the depth of my desire to get there. Just to get within bombing distance before they heard us! At such a time you have not even any fear, only a tremendous hopeless longing to get over the intervening ground. I have felt exactly the same thing when stalking a wild animal; the same agonized desire to get within range, the same dreamlike certainty that it is impossible. And how the distance stretched out! I knew the ground well, it was barely a hundred and fifty yards, and yet it seemed more like a mile. When you are creeping at that pace you are aware as an ant might be of the enormous variations in the ground; the splendid patch of smooth grass here, the evil patch of sticky mud there, the tall rustling reeds that have got to be avoided, the heap of stones that almost makes you give up hope because it seems impossible to get over it without noise.

We had been creeping forward for such an age that I began to think we had gone the wrong way. Then in the darkness thin parallel lines of something blacker were faintly visible. It was the outer wire (the Fascists had two lines of wire). Jorge knelt down, fumbled in his pocket. He had our only pair of wire-cutters. Snip, snip. The trailing stuff was lifted delicately aside. We waited for the men at the back to close up. They seemed to be making a frightful noise. It might be fifty yards to the Fascist parapet now. Still onwards, bent double. A stealthy step, lowering your foot as gently as a cat approaching a mousehole; then a pause to listen; then another step. Once I raised my head; in silence Benjamin put his hand behind my neck and pulled it violently down. I knew that the inner wire was barely twenty yards from the parapet. It seemed to me inconceivable that thirty men could get there unheard. Our breathing was enough to give us away. Yet somehow we did get there. The Fascist parapet was visible now, a dim black mound, looming high above us. Once again Jorge knelt and fumbled. Snip, snip. There was no way of cutting the stuff silently.

So that was the inner wire. We crawled through it on all fours and rather more rapidly. If we had time to deploy now all was well. Jorge and Benjamin crawled across to the right. But the men behind, who were spread out, had to form into single file to get through the narrow gap in the wire, and just as this moment there was a flash and a bang from the Fascist parapet. The sentry had heard us at last. Jorge poised himself on one knee and swung his arm like a bowler. Crash! His bomb burst somewhere over the parapet. At once, far more promptly than one would have thought possible, a roar of fire, ten or twenty rifles, burst out from the Fascist parapet. They had been waiting for us after all. Momentarily you could see every sand-bag in the lurid light. Men too far back were flinging their bombs and some of them were falling short of the parapet. Every loophole seemed to be spouting jets of flame. It is always hateful to be shot at in the dark – every rifle-flash seems to be pointed straight at yourself – but it was the bombs that were the worst. You cannot conceive the horror of these things till you have seen one burst close to you in darkness; in the daytime there is only the crash of the explosion, in the darkness there is the blinding red glare as well. I had flung myself down at the first volley. All this while I was lying on my side in the greasy mud, wrestling savagely with the pin of a bomb. The damned thing *would* not come out. Finally I realized that I was twisting it in the wrong direction. I got the pin out, rose to my knees, hurled the bomb, and threw myself down again. The bomb burst over to the right, outside the parapet; fright had spoiled my aim. Just at this moment another bomb burst right in front of me, so close that I could feel the heat of the explosion. I flattened myself out and dug my face into the mud so hard that I hurt my neck and thought that I was wounded. Through the din I heard an English voice behind me say quietly: 'I'm hit.' The bomb had, in fact, wounded several people round about me without touching myself. I rose to my knees and flung my second bomb. I forget where that one went.

The Fascists were firing, our people behind were firing, and I was very conscious of being in the middle. I felt the blast of a shot and realized that a man was firing from immediately behind me. I stood up and shouted at him: 'Don't shoot at me, you bloody fool!' At this moment I saw that Benjamin, ten or fifteen yards to my right, was motioning to me with his arm. I ran across to him. It meant crossing the line of spouting loop-holes, and as I went I clapped my left hand over my cheek; an idiotic gesture –

as though one's hand could stop a bullet! – but I had a horror of being hit in the face. Benjamin was kneeling on one knee with a pleased, devilish sort of expression on his face and firing carefully at the rifle-flashes with his automatic pistol. Jorge had dropped wounded at the first volley and was somewhere out of sight. I knelt beside Benjamin, pulled the pin out of my third bomb and flung it. Ah! No doubt about it that time. The bomb crashed inside the parapet, at the corner, just by the machine-gun nest.

The Fascist fire seemed to have slackened very suddenly. Benjamin leapt to his feet and shouted: 'Forward! Charge!' We dashed up the short steep slope on which the parapet stood. I say 'dashed'; 'lumbered' would be a better word; the fact is that you can't move fast when you are sodden and mudded from head to foot and weighted down with a heavy rifle and bayonet and a hundred and fifty cartridges. I took it for granted that there would be a Fascist waiting for me at the top. If he fired at that range he could not miss me, and yet somehow I never expected him to fire, only to try for me with his bayonet. I seemed to feel in advance the sensation of our bayonets crossing, and I wondered whether his arm would be stronger than mine. However, there was no Fascist waiting. With a vague feeling of relief I found that it was a low parapet and the sand-bags gave a good foothold. As a rule they are difficult to get over. Everything inside was smashed to pieces, beams flung all over the place, and great shards of uralite littered everywhere. Our bombs had wrecked all the huts and dug-outs. And still there was not a soul visible. I thought they would be lurking somewhere underground, and shouted in English (I could not think of any Spanish at the moment): 'Come on out of it! Surrender!' No answer. Then a man, a shadowy figure in the half-light, skipped over the roof of one of the ruined huts and dashed away to the left. I started after him, prodding my bayonet ineffectually into the darkness. As I rounded the corner of the hut I saw a man – I don't know whether or not it was the same man as I had seen before – fleeing up the communication-trench that led to the other Fascist position. I must have been very close to him, for I could see him clearly. He was bareheaded and seemed to have nothing on except a blanket which he was clutching round his shoulders. If I had fired I could have blown him to pieces. But for fear of shooting one another we had been ordered to use only bayonets once we were inside the parapet, and in any case I never even thought of firing. Instead, my mind leapt backwards twenty years, to our boxing instructor at school, showing me in vivid pantomime how he had bayoneted a Turk at the Dardanelles. I gripped my rifle by the small of the butt and lunged at the man's back.

He was just out of my reach. Another lunge: still out of reach. And for a little distance we proceeded like this, he rushing up the trench and I after him on the ground above, prodding at his shoulder-blades and never quite getting there – a comic memory for me to look back upon, though I suppose it seemed less comic to him.

Of course, he knew the ground better than I and had soon slipped away from me. When I came back the position was full of shouting men. The noise of firing had lessened somewhat. The Fascists were still pouring a heavy fire at us from three sides, but it was coming from a greater distance. We had driven them back for the time being. I remember saying in an oracular manner: 'We can hold this place for half an hour, not more.' I don't know why I picked on half an hour. Looking over the right-hand parapet you could see innumerable greenish rifle-flashes stabbing the darkness; but they were a long way back, a hundred or two hundred yards. Our job now was to search the position and loot anything that was worth looting. Benjamin and some others were already scrabbling among the ruins of a big hut or dug-out in the middle of the position. Benjamin staggered excitedly through the ruined roof, tugging at the rope handle of an ammunition box.

'Comrades! Ammunition! Plenty ammunition here!'

'We don't want ammunition,' said a voice, 'we want rifles.' This was true. Half our rifles were jammed with mud and unusable. They could be cleaned, but it is dangerous to take the bolt out of a rifle in the darkness; you put it down somewhere and then you lose it. I had a tiny electric torch which my wife had managed to buy in Barcelona, otherwise we had no light of any description between us. A few men with good rifles began a desultory fire at the flashes in the distance. No one dared fire too rapidly; even the best of the rifles were liable to jam if they got too hot. There were about sixteen of us inside the parapet, including one or two who were wounded. A number of wounded, English and Spanish, were lying outside. Patrick O'Hara, a Belfast Irishman who had had some training in first-aid, went to and fro with packets of bandages, binding up the wounded men and, of course, being shot at every time he returned to the parapet, in spite of his indignant shouts of 'Poum!'

We began searching the position. There were several dead men lying about, but I did not stop to examine them. The thing I was after was the machine-gun. All the while when we were lying outside I had been wondering vaguely why the gun did not fire. I flashed my torch inside the machine-gun nest. A bitter disappointment! The gun was not there. Its tripod was there, and various boxes of ammunition and spare parts, but the gun was gone. They must have unscrewed it and carried it off at the first alarm. No doubt they were acting under orders, but it was a stupid and cowardly thing to do, for if they had kept the gun in place they could have slaughtered the whole lot of us. We were furious. We had set our hearts on capturing a machine-gun.

We poked here and there but did not find anything of much value. There were quantities of Fascist bombs lying about – a rather inferior type of bomb, which you touched off by pulling a string – and I put a couple of them in my pocket as souvenirs. It was impossible not to be struck by the bare misery of the Fascist dug-outs. The litter of spare clothes, books, food, petty personal belongings that you saw in our own dug-outs was completely absent; these poor unpaid conscripts seemed to own nothing except blankets and a few soggy hunks of bread. Up at the far end there was a small dug-out which was partly above ground and had a tiny window. We flashed the torch through the window and instantly raised a cheer. A cylindrical object in a leather case, four feet high and six inches in diameter, was leaning against the wall. Obviously the machine-gun barrel. We dashed round and got in at the doorway, to find that the thing in the leather case was not a machine-gun but something which, in our weapon-starved army, was even more precious. It was an enormous telescope, probably of at least sixty or seventy magnifications, with a folding tripod. Such telescopes simply did not exist on our side of the line and they were desperately needed. We brought it out in triumph and leaned it against the parapet, to be carried off after.

At this moment someone shouted that the Fascists were closing in. Certainly the din of firing had grown very much louder. But it was obvious that the Fascists would not counter-attack from the right, which meant crossing no man's land and assaulting their own parapet. If they had any sense at all they would come at us from inside the line. I went round to the other side of the dug-outs. The position was roughly horseshoe-shaped, with the dug-outs in the middle, so that we had another parapet covering us on the left. A heavy fire was coming from that direction, but it did not matter greatly. The danger-spot was straight in front, where there was no protection at all. A stream of bullets was passing just overhead. They must be coming from the other Fascist position farther up the line; evidently the Shock Troopers had not captured it after all. But this time the noise was deafening. It was the unbroken, drum-like roar of massed rifles which I was used to hearing from a little distance; this was the first time I had been in the middle of it. And by now, of course, the firing had spread along the line for miles around. Douglas Thompson, with a wounded arm dangling useless at his side, was leaning against the parapet and firing one-handed at the flashes. Someone whose rifle had jammed was loading for him.

There were four or five of us round this side. It was obvious what we must do. We must drag the sand-bags from the front parapet and make a barricade across the unprotected side. And we had got to be quick. The fire was high at present, but they might lower it at any moment; by the flashes all round I could see that we had a hundred or two hundred men against us. We began wrenching the sand-bags loose, carrying them twenty yards forward and dumping them into a rough heap. It was a vile job. They were big sand-bags, weighing a hundredweight each and it took every ounce of your strength to prise them loose; and then the rotten sacking split and the damp earth cascaded all over you, down your neck and up your sleeves. I remember feeling a deep horror at everything: the chaos, the darkness, the frightful din, the slithering to and fro in the mud, the struggles with the bursting sand-bags – all the time encumbered with my rifle, which I dared not put down for fear of losing it. I even shouted to someone as we staggered along with a bag between us: 'This is war! Isn't it bloody?' Suddenly a succession of tall figures came leaping over the front parapet. As they came nearer we saw that they wore the uniform of the Shock Troopers, and we cheered, thinking they were reinforcements. However, there were only four of them, three Germans and a Spaniard. We heard afterwards what had happened to the Shock Troopers. They did not know the ground and in the darkness had been led to the wrong place, where they were caught on the Fascist wire and numbers of them were shot down. These were four who had got lost, luckily for themselves. The Germans did not speak a word of English, French, or Spanish. With difficulty and much gesticulation we explained what we were doing and got them to help us in building the barricade.

The Fascists had brought up a machine-gun now. You could see it spitting like a squib a hundred or two hundred yards away; the bullets came over us with a steady, frosty crackle. Before long we had flung enough sand-bags into place to make a low breastwork behind which the few men who were on this side of the position could lie down and fire. I was kneeling behind them. A mortar-shell whizzed over and crashed somewhere in no man's land. That was another danger, but it would take them some minutes to find our range. Now that we had finished wrestling with those beastly sand-bags it was not bad fun in a way; the noise, the darkness, the flashes approaching, our own men blazing back at the flashes. One even had time to think a little. I remember wondering whether I was frightened, and deciding that I was not. Outside, where I was probably in less danger, I had been half sick with fright. Suddenly there was another shout that the Fascists were closing in. There was no doubt about it this time, the rifle-flashes were much nearer. I saw a flash hardly twenty yards away. Obviously they were working their way up the communication-trench. At twenty yards they were within easy bombing range; there were eight or nine of us bunched together and a single well-placed bomb would blow us all to fragments. Bob Smillie, the blood running down his face from a small wound, sprang to his knee and flung a bomb. We cowered, waiting for the crash. The fuse fizzled red as it sailed through the air, but the bomb failed to explode. (At least a quarter of these bombs were duds). I had no bombs left except the Fascist ones and I was not certain how these worked. I shouted to the others to know if anyone had a bomb to spare. Douglas Moyle felt in his pocket and passed one across. I flung it and threw myself on my face. By one of those strokes of luck that happen about once in a year I had managed to drop the bomb almost exactly where the rifle had flashed. There was the roar of the explosion and then, instantly, a diabolical outcry of screams and groans. We had got one of them, anyway; I don't know whether he was killed, but certainly he was badly hurt. Poor wretch, poor wretch! I felt a vague sorrow as I heard him screaming. But at the same instant, in the dim light of the rifle-flashes, I saw or thought I saw a figure standing near the place where the rifle had flashed. I threw up my rifle and let fly. Another scream, but I think it was still the effect of the bomb. Several more bombs were thrown. The next rifle-flashes we saw were a long way off, a hundred yards or more. So we had driven them back, temporarily at least.

Everyone began cursing and saying why the hell didn't they send us some supports. With a sub-machine-gun or twenty men with clean rifles we could hold this place against a battalion. At this moment Paddy Donovan, who was second-in-command to Benjamin and had been sent back for orders, climbed over the front parapet.

'Hi! Come on out of it! All men to retire at once!'

'What?'

'Retire! Get out of it!'

'Why?'

'Orders. Back to our own lines double-quick.'

People were already climbing over the front parapet. Several of them were struggling with a heavy ammunition box. My mind flew to the telescope which I had left leaning against the parapet on the other side of the position. But at this moment I saw that the four Shock Troopers, acting I suppose on some mysterious orders they had received beforehand, had begun running up the communication-trench. It led to the other Fascist position and – if they got there – to certain death. They were disappearing into the darkness. I ran after them, trying to think of the Spanish for 'retire'; finally I shouted, '*Atrás! Atrás!*' which perhaps conveyed the right meaning. The Spaniard understood it and brought the others back. Paddy was waiting at the parapet.

'Come on, hurry up.'

'But the telescope!'

'B— the telescope! Benjamin's waiting outside.'

We climbed out. Paddy held the wire aside for me. As soon as we got away from the shelter of the Fascist parapet we were under a devilish fire that seemed to be coming at us from every direction. Part of it, I do not doubt, came from our own side, for everyone was firing all along the line. Whichever way we turned a fresh stream of bullets swept past; we were driven this way and that in the darkness like a flock of sheep. It did not make it any easier that we were dragging a captured box of ammunition – one of those boxes that hold 1750 rounds and weigh about a hundred-weight – besides a box of bombs and several Fascist rifles. In a few minutes, although the distance from parapet to parapet was not two hundred yards and most of us knew the ground, we were completely lost. We found ourselves slithering about in a muddy field, knowing nothing except that bullets were coming from both sides. There was no moon to go by, but the sky was growing a little lighter. Our lines lay east of Huesca; I wanted to stay where we were till the first crack of dawn showed us which was east and which was west; but the others were against it. We slithered onwards, changing our direction several times and taking it in turns to haul at the ammunition-box. At last we saw the low flat line of a parapet looming in front of us. It might be ours or it might be the Fascists'; nobody had the dimmest idea which way we were going. Benjamin crawled on his belly through some tall whitish weed till he was about twenty yards from the parapet and tried a challenge. A shout of 'Poum!' answered him. We jumped to our feet, found our way along the parapet, slopped once more through the irrigation ditch – splash-gurgle! – and were in safety.

Kopp was waiting inside the parapet with a few Spaniards. The doctor and the stretchers were gone. It appeared that all the wounded had been got in except Jorge and one of our own men, Hiddlestone by name, who were missing. Kopp was pacing up and down, very pale. Even the fat folds at the back of his neck were pale; he was paying no attention to the bullets that streamed over the low parapet and cracked close to his head. Most of us were squatting behind the parapet for cover. Kopp was muttering. Jorge! *Cogño!* Jorge!' And then in English. 'If Jorge is gone it is terreeble, terreeble!' Jorge was his personal friend and one of his best officers. Suddenly he turned to us and asked for five volunteers, two English and three Spanish, to go and look for the missing men. Moyle and I volunteered with three Spaniards.

As we got outside the Spaniards murmured that it was getting dangerously light. This was true enough; the sky was dimly blue. There was a tremendous noise of excited voices coming from the Fascist redoubt. Evidently they had re-occupied the place in much greater force than before. We were sixty or seventy yards from the parapet when they must have seen or heard us, for they sent over a heavy burst of fire which made us drop on our faces. One of them flung a bomb over the parapet – a sure sign of panic. We were lying in the grass, waiting for an opportunity to move on, when we heard or thought we heard – I have no doubt it was pure imagination, but it seemed real enough at the time – that the Fascist voices were much closer. They had left the parapet and were coming after us. 'Run!' I yelled to Moyle, and jumped to my feet. And heavens, how I ran! I had thought earlier in the night that you can't run when you are sodden from head to foot and weighted down with a rifle and cartridges; I learned now you can *always* run when you think you have fifty or a hundred armed men after you. But if I could run fast, others could run faster. In my flight something that might have been a shower of meteors sped past me. It was the three Spaniards, who had been in front. They were back to our own parapet before they stopped and I could catch up with them. The truth was that our nerves were all to pieces. I knew, however, that in a half light one man is invisible where five are clearly visible, so I went back alone. I managed to get to the outer wire and searched the ground as well as I could, which was not very well, for I had to lie on my belly. There was no sign of Jorge or Hiddlestone, so I crept back. We learned afterwards that both Jorge and Hiddlestone had been taken to the dressing-station earlier. Jorge was lightly wounded through the shoulder. Hiddlestone had received a dreadful wound – a bullet which travelled right up his left arm, breaking the bone in several places; as he lay helpless on the ground a bomb had burst near him and torn various other parts of his body. He recovered, I am glad to say. Later he told me that he had worked his way some distance lying on his back, then had clutched hold of a wounded Spaniard and they had helped one another in.

It was getting light now. Along the line for miles around a ragged meaningless fire was thundering, like the rain that goes on raining after a storm. I remember the desolate look of everything, the morasses of mud, the weeping poplar trees, the yellow water in the trench-bottoms; and men's exhausted faces, unshaven, streaked with mud, and blackened to the eyes with smoke. When I got back to my dug-out the three men I shared it with were already fast sleep. They had flung themselves down with all their equipment on and their muddy rifles clutched against them. Everything was sodden, inside the dug-out as well as outside. By long searching I managed to collect enough chips of dry wood to make a tiny fire. Then I smoked the cigar which I had been hoarding and which, surprisingly enough, had not got broken during the night.

Afterwards we learned that the action had been a success, as such things go. It was merely a raid to make the Fascists divert troops from the other side of Huesca, where the Anarchists were attacking again. I had judged that the Fascists had thrown a hundred or two hundred men into the counter-attack, but a deserter told us later on that it was six hundred. I dare say he was lying – deserters, for obvious reasons, often try to curry favour. It was a great pity about the telescope. The thought of losing that beautiful bit of loot worries me even now.

8

THE days grew hotter and even the nights grew tolerably warm. On a bullet-chipped tree in front of our parapet thick clusters of cherries were forming. Bathing in the river ceased to be an agony and became almost a pleasure. Wild roses with pink blooms the size of saucers straggled over the shell-holes round Torre Fabián. Behind the line you met peasants wearing wild roses over their ears. In the evenings they used to go out with green nets, hunting quails. You spread the net over the tops of the grasses and then lay down and made a noise like a female quail. Any male quail that was within hearing then came running towards you, and when he was underneath the net you threw a stone to scare him, whereupon he sprang into the air and was entangled in the net. Apparently only male quails were caught, which struck me as unfair.

There was a section of Andalusians next to us in the line now. I do not know quite how they got to this front. The current explanation was that they had run away from Malaga so fast that they had forgotten to stop at Valencia; but this, of course, came from the Catalans, who professed to look down on the Andalusians as a race of semi-savages. Certainly the Andalusians were very ignorant. Few if any of them could read, and they seemed not even to know the one thing that everybody knows in Spain – which political party they belonged to. They thought they were Anarchists, but were not quite certain; perhaps they were Communists. They were gnarled, rustic-looking men, shepherds or labourers from the olive groves, perhaps, with faces deeply stained by the ferocious suns of farther south. They were very useful to us, for they had an extraordinary dexterity at rolling the dried-up Spanish tobacco into cigarettes. The issue of cigarettes had ceased, but in Monflorite it was occasionally possible to buy packets of the cheapest kind of tobacco, which in appearance and texture was very like chopped chaff. Its flavour was not bad, but it was so dry that even when you had succeeded in making a cigarette the tobacco promptly fell out and left an empty cylinder. The Andalusians, however, could roll admirable cigarettes and had a special technique for tucking the ends in.

Two Englishmen were laid low by sunstroke. My salient memories of that time are the heat of the midday sun, and working half-naked with sand-bags punishing one's shoulders which were already flayed by the sun; and the lousiness of our clothes and boots, which were literally dropping to pieces; and the struggles with the mule which brought our rations and which did not mind rifle-fire but took to flight when shrapnel burst in the air; and the mosquitoes (just beginning to be active) and the rats, which were a public nuisance and would even devour leather belts and cartridge-pouches. Nothing was happening except an occasional casualty from a sniper's bullet and the sporadic artillery-fire and air-raids on Huesca. Now that the trees were in full leaf we had constructed snipers' platforms, like machans, in the poplar trees that fringed the line. On the other side of Huesca the attacks were petering out. The Anarchists had had heavy losses and had not succeeded in completely cutting the Jaca road. They had managed to establish themselves close enough on either side to bring the road itself under machine-gun fire and make it impassable for traffic; but the gap was a kilometre wide and the Fascists had constructed a sunken road, a sort of enormous trench, along which a certain number of lorries could come and go. Deserters reported that in Huesca there were plenty of munitions and very little food. But the town was evidently not going to fall. Probably it would have been impossible to take it with the fifteen thousand ill-armed men who were available. Later, in June, the Government brought troops from the Madrid front and concentrated thirty thousand men on Huesca, with an enormous quantity of aeroplanes, but still the town did not fall.

When we went on leave I had been a hundred and fifteen days in the line, and at the time this period seemed to me to have been one of the most futile of my whole life. I had joined the militia in order to fight against Fascism, and as yet I had scarcely fought at all, had merely existed as a sort of passive object, doing nothing in return for my rations except to suffer from cold and lack of sleep. Perhaps that is the fate of most soldiers in most wars. But now that I can see this period in perspective I do not altogether regret it. I wish, indeed, that I could have served the Spanish Government a little more effectively; but from a personal point of view – from the point of view of my own development – those first three or four months that I spent in the line were less futile than I then thought. They formed a kind of interregnum in my life, quite different from anything that had gone before and perhaps from anything that is to come, and they taught me things that I could not have learned in any other way.

The essential point is that all this time I had been isolated – for at the front one was almost completely isolated from the outside world: even of what was happening in Barcelona one had only a dim conception – among people who could roughly but not too inaccurately be described as revolutionaries. This was the result of the militia-system, which on the Aragon front was not radically altered till about June 1937. The workers' militias, based on the trade unions and each composed of people of approximately the same political opinions, had the effect of canalizing into one place all the most revolutionary sentiment in the country. I had dropped more or less by chance into the only community of any size in Western Europe where political consciousness and disbelief in capitalism were more normal than their opposites. Up here in Aragon one was among tens of thousands of people, mainly though not entirely of working-class origin, all living at the same level and mingling on term of equality. In theory it was perfect equality, and even in practice it was not far from it. There is a sense in which it would be true to say that one was experiencing a foretaste of Socialism, by which I mean that the prevailing mental atmosphere was that of Socialism. Many of the normal motives of civilized life – snobbishness, money-grubbing, fear of the boss, etc. – had simply ceased to exist. The ordinary class-division of society had disappeared to an extent that is almost unthinkable in the money-tainted air of England; there was no one there except the peasants and ourselves, and no one owned anyone else as his master. Of course such a state of affairs could not last. It was simply a temporary and local phase in an enormous game that is being played over the whole surface of the earth. But it lasted long enough to have its effect upon anyone who experienced it. However much one cursed at the time, one realized afterwards that one had been in contact with something strange and valuable. One had been in a community where hope was more normal than apathy or cynicism, where the word 'comrade' stood for comradeship and not, as in most countries, for humbug. One had breathed the air of equality. I am well aware that it is now the fashion to deny that Socialism has anything to do with equality. In every country in the world a huge tribe of party-hacks and sleek little professors are busy 'proving' that Socialism means no more than a planned state-capitalism with the grab-motive left intact. But fortunately there also exists a vision of Socialism quite different from this. The thing that attracts ordinary men to Socialism and makes them willing to risk their skins for it, the 'mystique' of Socialism, is the idea of equality; to the vast majority of people Socialism means a classless society, or it means nothing at all. And it was here that those few months in the militia were valuable to me. For the Spanish militias, while they lasted, were a sort of microcosm of a classless society. In that community where no one was on the make, where there was a shortage of everything but no privilege and no boot-licking, one got, perhaps, a crude forecast of what the opening stages of Socialism might be like. And, after all, instead of disillusioning me it deeply attracted me. The effect was to make my desire to see Socialism established much more actual than it had been before. Partly, perhaps, this was due to the good luck of being among Spaniards, who, with their innate decency and their ever-present Anarchist tinge, would make even the opening stages of Socialism tolerable if they had the chance.

Of course at the time I was hardly conscious of the changes that were occurring in my own mind. Like everyone about me I was chiefly conscious of boredom, heat, cold, dirt, lice, privation, and occasional danger. It is quite different now. This period which then seemed so futile and eventless is now of great importance to me. It is so different from the rest of my life that already it has taken on the magic quality which, as a rule, belongs only to memories that are years old. It was beastly while it was happening, but it is a good patch for my mind to browse upon. I wish I could convey to you the atmosphere of that time. I hope I have done so, a little, in the earlier chapters of this book. It is all bound up in my mind with the winter cold, the ragged uniforms of militiamen, the oval Spanish faces, the morse-like tapping of machine-guns, the smells of urine and rotting bread, the tinny taste of bean-stews wolfed hurriedly out of unclean pannikins.

The whole period stays by me with curious vividness. In my memory I live over incidents that might seem too petty to be worth recalling. I am in the dug-out at Monte Pocero again, on the ledge of limestone that serves as a bed, and young Ramón is snoring with his nose flattened between my shoulder-blades. I am stumbling up the mucky trench, through the mist that swirls round me like cold steam. I am half-way up a crack in the mountain-side, struggling to keep my balance and to tug a root of wild rosemary out of the ground. High overhead some meaningless bullets are singing.

I am lying hidden among small fir-trees on the low ground west of Monte Oscuro, with Kopp and Bob Edwards and three Spaniards. Up the naked grey hill to the right of us a string of Fascists are climbing like ants. Close in front a bugle-call rings out from the Fascist lines. Kopp catches my eye and, with a schoolboy gesture, thumbs his nose at the sound.

I am in the mucky yard at La Granja, among the mob of men who are struggling with their tin pannikins round the cauldron of stew. The fat and harassed cook is warding them off with the ladle. At a table nearby a bearded man with a huge automatic pistol strapped to his belt is hewing loaves of bread into five pieces. Behind me a Cockney voice (Bill Chambers, with whom I quarrelled bitterly and who was afterwards killed outside Huesca) is singing:

> There are rats, rats,
> Rats as big as cats,
> In the . . .

A shell comes screaming over. Children of fifteen fling themselves on their faces. The cook dodges behind the cauldron. Everyone rises with a sheepish expression as the shell plunges and booms a hundred yards away.

I am walking up and down the line of sentries, under the dark boughs of the poplars. In the flooded ditch outside the rats are paddling about, making as much noise as otters. As the yellow dawn comes up behind us, the Andalusian sentry, muffled in his cloak, begins singing. Across no man's land, a hundred or two hundred yards away, you can hear the Fascist sentry also singing.

On 25 April, after the usual *mañanas*, another section relieved us and we handed over our rifles, packed our kits, and marched back to Monflorite. I was not sorry to leave the line. The lice were multiplying in my trousers far faster than I could massacre them, and for a month past I had had no socks and my boots had very little sole left, so that I was walking more or less barefoot. I wanted a hot bath, clean clothes, and a night between sheets more passionately than it is possible to want anything when one has been living a normal civilized life. We slept a few hours in a barn in Monflorite, jumped a lorry in the small hours, caught the five o'clock train at Barbastro, and – having the luck to connect with a fast train at Lerida – were in Barcelona by three o'clock in the afternoon of the 26th. And after that the trouble began.

9

FROM Mandalay, in Upper Burma, you can travel by train to Maymyo, the principal hill-station of the province, on the edge of the Shan plateau. It is rather a queer experience. You start off in the typical atmosphere of an eastern city – the scorching sunlight, the dusty palms, the smells of fish and spices and garlic, the squashy tropical fruits, the swarming dark-faced human beings – and because you are so used to it you carry this atmosphere intact, so to speak, in your railway carriage. Mentally you are still in Mandalay when the train stops at Maymyo, four thousand feet above sea-level. But in stepping out of the carriage you step into a different hemisphere. Suddenly you are breathing cool sweet air that might be that of England, and all round you are green grass, bracken, fir-trees, and hill-women with pink cheeks selling baskets of strawberries.

Getting back to Barcelona, after three and a half months at the front, reminded me of this. There was the same abrupt and startling change of atmosphere. In the train, all the way to Barcelona, the atmosphere of the front persisted; the dirt, the noise, the discomfort, the ragged clothes the feeling of privation, comradeship, and equality. The train, already full of militiamen when it left Barbastro, was invaded by more and more peasants at every station on the line; peasants with bundles of vegetables, with terrified fowls which they carried head-downwards, with sacks which looped and writhed all over the floor and were discovered to be full of live rabbits – finally with a quite considerable flock of sheep which were driven into the compartments and wedged into every empty space. The militia-men shouted revolutionary songs which drowned the rattle of the train and kissed their hands or waved red and black handkerchiefs to every pretty girl along the line. Bottles of wine and of anis, the filthy Aragonese liqueur, travelled from hand to hand. With the Spanish goat-skin water-bottles you can squirt a jet of wine right across a railway carriage into your friend's mouth, which saves a lot of trouble. Next to me a black-eyed boy of fifteen was recounting sensational and, I do not doubt, completely untrue stories of his own exploits at the front to two old leather-faced peasants who listened open-mouthed. Presently the peasants undid their bundles and gave us some sticky dark-red wine. Everyone was profoundly happy, more happy than I can convey. But when the train had rolled through Sabadell and into Barcelona, we stepped into an atmosphere that was scarcely less alien and hostile to us and our kind than if this had been Paris or London.

Everyone who has made two visits, at intervals of months, to Barcelona during the war has remarked upon the extraordinary changes that took place in it. And curiously enough, whether they went there first in August and again in January, or, like myself, first in December and again in April, the thing they said was always the same: that the revolutionary atmosphere had vanished. No doubt to anyone who had been there in August, when the blood was scarcely dry in the streets and militia were quartered in the smart hotels, Barcelona in December would have seemed bourgeois; to me, fresh from England, it was liker to a workers' city than anything I had conceived possible. Now the tide had rolled back. Once again it was an ordinary city, a little pinched and chipped by war, but with no outward sign of working-class predominance.

The change in the aspect of the crowds was startling. The militia uniform and the blue overalls had almost disappeared; everyone seemed to be wearing the smart summer suits in which Spanish tailors specialize. Fat prosperous men, elegant women, and sleek cars were everywhere. (It appeared that there were still no private cars; nevertheless, anyone who 'was anyone' seemed able to command a car.) The officers of the new Popular Army, a type that had scarcely existed when I left Barcelona, swarmed in surprising numbers. The Popular Army was officered at the rate of one officer to ten men. A certain number of these officers had served in the militia and been brought back from the front for technical instruction, but the majority were young men who had gone to the School of War in preference to joining the militia. Their relation to their men was not quite the same as in a bourgeois army, but there was a definite social difference, expressed by the difference of pay and uniform. The men wore a kind of coarse brown overalls, the officers wore an elegant khaki uniform with a tight waist, like a British Army officer's uniform, only a little more so. I do not suppose that more than one in twenty of them had yet been to the front, but all of them had automatic pistols strapped to their belts; we, at the front, could not get pistols for love or money. As we made our way up the street I noticed that people were staring at our dirty exteriors. Of course, like all men who have been several months in the line, we were a dreadful sight. I was conscious of looking like a scarecrow. My leather jacket was in tatters, my woollen cap had lost its shape and slid perpetually over one eye, my boots consisted of very little beyond splayed-out uppers. All of us were in more or less the same state, and in addition we were dirty and unshaven, so it was no wonder that the people stared. But it dismayed me a little, and brought it home to me that some queer things had been happening in the last three months.

During the next few days I discovered by innumerable signs that my first impression had not been wrong. A deep change had come over the town. There were two facts that were the keynote of all else. One was that the people – the civil population – had lost much of their interest in the war; the other was that the normal division of society into rich and poor, upper class and lower class, was reasserting itself.

The general indifference to the war was surprising and rather disgusting. It horrified people who came to Barcelona from Madrid or even from Valencia. Partly it was due to the remoteness of Barcelona from the actual fighting; I noticed the same thing a month later in Tarragona, where the ordinary life of a smart seaside town was continuing almost undisturbed. But it was significant that all over Spain voluntary enlistment had dwindled from about January onwards. In Catalonia, in February, there had been a wave of enthusiasm over the first big drive for the Popular Army, but it had not led to any great increase in recruiting. The war was only six months old or thereabouts when the Spanish Government had to resort to conscription, which would be natural in a foreign war, but seems anomalous in a civil war. Undoubtedly it was bound up with the disappointment of the revolutionary hopes with which the war had started. The trade union members who formed themselves into militias and chased the Fascists back to Zaragoza in the first few weeks of war had done so largely because they believed themselves to be fighting for working-class control; but it was becoming more and more obvious that working-class control was a lost cause, and the common people, especially the town proletariat, who have to fill the ranks in any war, civil or foreign, could not be blamed for a certain apathy. Nobody wanted to lose the war, but the majority were chiefly anxious for it to be over. You noticed this wherever you went. Everywhere you met with the same perfunctory remark: 'This war – terrible, isn't it? When is it going to end?' Politically conscious people were far more aware of the internecine struggle between Anarchist and

Communist than of the fight against Franco. To the mass of the people
the food shortage was the most important thing. 'The front' had come to
be thought of as a mythical far-off place to which young men disappeared
and either did not return or returned after three or four months with vast
sums of money in their pockets. (A militiaman usually received his back
pay when he went on leave.) Wounded men, even when they were hopping
about on crutches, did not receive any special consideration. To be in the
militia was no longer fashionable. The shops, always the barometers of
public taste, showed this clearly. When I first reached Barcelona the
shops, poor and shabby though they were, had specialized in militiamen's
equipment. Forage-caps, zipper jackets, Sam Browne belts, hunting-knives,
water-bottles, revolver-holsters were displayed in every window. Now the
shops were markedly smarter, but the war had been thrust into the
background. As I discovered later, when buying my kit before going back
to the front, certain things that one badly needed at the front were very
difficult to procure.

Meanwhile there was going on a systematic propaganda against the
party militias and in favour of the Popular Army. The position here was
rather curious. Since February the entire armed forces had theoretically
been incorporated in the Popular Army, and the militias were, on paper,
reconstructed along Popular Army lines, with differential pay-rates,
gazetted rank, etc., etc. The divisions were made up of 'mixed brigades',
which were supposed to consist partly of Popular Army troops and partly
of militia. But the only changes that had actually taken place were changes
of name. The P.O.U.M. troops, for instance, previously called the Lenin
Division, were now known as the 29th Division. Until June very few
Popular Army troops reached the Aragon front, and in consequence the
militias were able to retain their separate structure and their special
character. But on every wall the Government agents had stencilled: 'We
need a Popular Army', and over the radio and in the Communist Press
there was a ceaseless and sometimes very malignant jibing against the
militias, who were described as ill-trained, undisciplined, etc., etc.; the
Popular Army was always described as 'heroic'. From much of this
propaganda you would have derived the impression that there was something disgraceful in having gone to the front voluntarily and something
praiseworthy in waiting to be conscripted. For the time being, however,
the militias were holding the line while the Popular Army was training in
the rear, and this fact had to be advertised as little as possible. Drafts of
militia returning to the front were no longer marched through the streets
with drums beating and flags flying. They were smuggled away by train

or lorry at five o'clock in the morning. A few drafts of the Popular Army were now beginning to leave for the front, and these, as before, were marched ceremoniously through the streets; but even they, owing to the general waning of interest in the war, met with comparatively little enthusiasm. The fact that the militia troops were also, on paper, Popular Army troops, was skilfully used in the Press propaganda. Any credit that happened to be going was automatically handed to the Popular Army, while all blame was reserved for the militias. It sometimes happened that the same troops were praised in one capacity and blamed in the other.

But besides all this there was the startling change in the social atmosphere – a thing difficult to conceive unless you have actually experienced it. When I first reached Barcelona I had thought it a town where class distinctions and great differences of wealth hardly existed. Certainly that was what it looked like. 'Smart' clothes were an abnormality, nobody cringed or took tips, waiters and flower-women and bootblacks looked you in the eye and called you 'comrade'. I had not grasped that this was mainly a mixture of hope and camouflage. The working class believed in a revolution that had been begun but never consolidated, and the bourgeoisie were scared and temporarily disguising themselves as workers. In the first months of revolution there must have been many thousands of people who deliberately put on overalls and shouted revolutionary slogans as a way of saving their skins. Now things were returning to normal. The smart restaurants and hotels were full of rich people wolfing expensive meals, while for the working-class population food-prices had jumped enormously without any corresponding rise in wages. Apart from the expensiveness of everything, there were recurrent shortages of this and that, which, of course, always hit the poor rather than the rich. The restaurants and hotels seemed to have little difficulty in getting whatever they wanted, but in the working-class quarters the queues for bread, olive oil, and other necessaries were hundreds of yards long. Previously in Barcelona I had been struck by the absence of beggars; now there were quantities of them. Outside the delicatessen shops at the top of the Ramblas gangs of barefooted children were always waiting to swarm round anyone who came out and clamour for scraps of food. The 'revolutionary' forms of speech were dropping out of use. Strangers seldom addressed you as *tú* and *camarada* nowadays; it was usually *señor* and *usted*. *Buenos días* was beginning to replace *salud*. The waiters were back in their boiled shirts and the shop-walkers were cringing in the familiar manner. My wife and I went into a hosiery shop on the Ramblas to buy some stockings. The shopman bowed and rubbed his hands as they do not do even in England nowadays, though they used to do it twenty or thirty years ago. In a furtive indirect way the practice of tipping was coming back. The workers' patrols had been ordered to dissolve and the pre-war police forces were back on the streets. One result of this was that the cabaret show and high-class brothels, many of which had been closed by the workers' patrols, had promptly re-opened.* A small but significant instance of the way in which everything was now orientated in favour of the wealthier classes could be seen in the tobacco shortage. For the mass of the people the shortage of tobacco was so desperate that cigarettes filled with sliced liquorice-root were being sold in the streets. I tried some of these once. (A lot of people tried them once.) Franco held the Canaries, where all the Spanish tobacco is grown; consequently the only stocks of tobacco left on the Government side were those that had been in existence before the war. These were running so low that the tobacconists' shops only opened once a week; after waiting for a couple of hours in a queue you might, if you were lucky, get a three-quarter-ounce packet of tobacco. Theoretically the Government would not allow tobacco to be purchased from abroad, because this meant reducing the gold-reserves, which had got to be kept for arms and other necessities. Actually there was a steady supply of smuggled foreign cigarettes of the more expensive kinds, Lucky Strikes and so forth, which gave a grand opportunity for profiteering. You could buy the smuggled cigarettes openly in the smart hotels and hardly less openly in the streets, provided that you could pay ten pesetas (a militiaman's daily wage) for a packet. The smuggling was for the benefit of wealthy people, and was therefore connived at. If you had enough money there was nothing that you could not get in any quantity, with the possible exception of bread, which was rationed fairly strictly. This open contrast of wealth and poverty would have been impossible a few months earlier, when the working class still were or seemed to be in control. But it would not be fair to attribute it solely to the shift of political power. Partly it was a result of the safety of life in Barcelona, where there was little to remind one of the war except an occasional air-raid. Everyone who had been in Madrid said that it was completely different there. In Madrid the common danger forced people of almost all kinds into some sense of comradeship. A fat man eating quails while children are begging for bread is a disgusting sight, but you are less likely to see it when you are within sound of the guns.

A day or two after the street-fighting I remember passing through one of the fashionable streets and coming upon a confectioner's shop with a

---

* The workers' patrols are said to have closed 75 per cent of the brothels.

window full of pastries and bon-bons of the most elegant kinds, at staggering prices. It was the kind of shop you see in Bond Street or the Rue de la Paix. And I remember feeling a vague horror and amazement that money could still be wasted upon such things in a hungry war-stricken country. But God forbid that I should pretend to any personal superiority. After several months of discomfort I had a ravenous desire for decent food and wine, cocktails, American cigarettes, and so forth, and I admit to having wallowed in every luxury that I had money to buy. During that first week, before the street-fighting began, I had several preoccupations which interacted upon one another in a curious way. In the first place, as I have said, I was busy making myself as comfortable as I could. Secondly, thanks to over-eating and over-drinking, I was slightly out of health all that week. I would feel a little unwell, go to bed for half a day, get up and eat another excessive meal, and then feel ill again. At the same time I was making secret negotiations to buy a revolver. I badly wanted a revolver – in trench-fighting much more useful than a rifle – and they were very difficult to get hold of. The Government issued them to policemen and Popular Army officers, but refused to issue them to the militia; you had to buy them, illegally, from the secret stores of the Anarchists. After a lot of fuss and nuisance an Anarchist friend managed to procure me a tiny 26-mm. automatic pistol, a wretched weapon, useless at more than five yards but better than nothing. And besides all this I was making preliminary arrangements to leave the P.O.U.M. militia and enter some other unit that would ensure my being sent to the Madrid front.

I had told everyone for a long time past that I was going to leave the P.O.U.M. As far as my purely personal preferences went I would have liked to join the Anarchists. If one became a member of the C.N.T. it was possible to enter the F.A.I. militia, but I was told that the F.A.I. were likelier to send me to Teruel than to Madrid. If I wanted to go to Madrid I must join the International Column, which meant getting a recommendation from a member of the Communist Party. I sought out a Communist friend, attached to the Spanish Medical Aid, and explained my case to him. He seemed very anxious to recruit me and asked me, if possible, to persuade some of the other I.L.P. Englishmen to come with me. If I had been in better health I should probably have agreed there and then. It is hard to say now what difference this would have made. Quite possibly I should have been sent to Albacete before the Barcelona fighting started; in which case, not having seen the fighting at close quarters, I might have accepted the official version of it as truthful. On the other hand, if I had been in Barcelona during the fighting, under Communist orders but still with a sense of personal loyalty to my comrades in the P.O.U.M., my position would have been impossible. But I had another week's leave due to me and I was very anxious to get my health back before returning to the line. Also – the kind of detail that is always deciding one's destiny – I had to wait while the boot-makers made me a new pair of marching boots. (The entire Spanish army had failed to produce a pair of boots big enough to fit me.) I told my Communist friend that I would make definite arrangements later. Meanwhile I wanted a rest. I even had a notion that we – my wife and I – might go to the seaside for two or three days. What an idea! The political atmosphere ought to have warned me that that was not the kind of thing one could do nowadays.

For under the surface-aspect of the town, under the luxury and growing poverty, under the seeming gaiety of the streets, with their flower-stalls, their many-coloured flags, their propaganda-posters, and thronging crowds, there was an unmistakable and horrible feeling of political rivalry and hatred. People of all shades of opinion were saying forebodingly: 'There's going to be trouble before long.' The danger was quite simple and intelligible. It was the antagonism between those who wished the revolution to go forward and those who wished to check or prevent it – ultimately, between Anarchists and Communists. Politically there was now no power in Catalonia except the P.S.U.C. and their Liberal allies. But over against this there was the uncertain strength of the C.N.T., less well-armed and less sure of what they wanted than their adversaries, but powerful because of their numbers and their predominance in various key industries. Given this alignment of forces there was bound to be trouble. From the point of view of the P.S.U.C.-controlled Generalite, the first necessity, to make their position secure, was to get the weapons out of the C.N.T. workers' hands. As I have pointed out earlier, the move to break up the party militias was at bottom a manoeuvre towards this end. At the same time the pre-war armed police forces, Civil Guards, and so forth, had been brought back into use and were being heavily reinforced and armed. This could mean only one thing. The Civil Guards, in particular, were a gendarmerie of the ordinary continental type, who for nearly a century past had acted as the bodyguards of the possessing class. Meanwhile a decree had been issued that all arms held by private persons were to be surrendered. Naturally this order had not been obeyed; it was clear that the Anarchists' weapons could only be taken from them by force. Throughout this time there were rumours, always vague and contradictory owing to newspaper censorship, of minor clashes that were occurring all over Catalonia. In various places the armed police forces had made attacks on Anarchist strongholds. At

Puigcerdá, on the French frontier, a band of Carabineros were sent to seize the Customs Office, previously controlled by Anarchists, and Antonio Martin, a well-known Anarchist, was killed. Similar incidents had occurred at Figueras and, I think, at Tarragona. In Barcelona there had been a series of more or less unofficial brawls in the working-class suburbs. C.N.T. and U.G.T. members had been murdering one another for some time past; on several occasions the murders were followed by huge, provocative funerals which were quite deliberately intended to stir up political hatred. A short time earlier a C.N.T. member had been murdered, and the C.N.T. had turned out in hundreds of thousands to follow the cortège. At the end of April, just after I got to Barcelona, Roldan, a prominent member of the U.G.T., was murdered, presumably by someone in the C.N.T. The Government ordered all shops to close and staged an enormous funeral procession, largely of Popular Army troops, which took two hours to pass a given point. From the hotel window I watched it without enthusiasm. It was obvious that the so-called funeral was merely a display of strength; a little more of this kind of thing and there might be bloodshed. The same night my wife and I were woken by a fusillade of shots from the Plaza de Cataluña, a hundred or two hundred yards away. We learned next day that it was a C.N.T. man being bumped off, presumably by someone in the U.G.T. It was of course distinctly possible that all these murders were committed by *agents provocateurs*. One can gauge the attitude of the foreign capitalist Press towards the Communist-Anarchist feud by the fact that Roldan's murder was given wide publicity, while the answering murder was carefully unmentioned.

The 1st of May was approaching, and there was talk of a monster demonstration in which both the C.N.T. and the U.G.T. were to take part. The C.N.T. leaders, more moderate than many of their followers, had long been working for a reconciliation with the U.G.T.; indeed the keynote of their policy was to try and form the two blocks of unions into one huge coalition. The idea was that the C.N.T. and U.G.T. should march together and display their solidarity. But at the last moment the demonstration was called off. It was perfectly clear that it would only lead to rioting. So nothing happened on 1 May. It was a queer state of affairs. Barcelona, the so-called revolutionary city, was probably the only city in non-Fascist Europe that had no celebrations that day. But I admit I was rather relieved. The I.L.P. contingent was expected to march in the P.O.U.M. section of the procession, and everyone expected trouble. The last thing I wished for was to be mixed up in some meaningless street-fight. To be marching up the street behind red flags inscribed with elevating slogans, and then to be bumped off from an upper window by some total stranger with a sub-machine-gun – that is not my idea of a useful way to die.

10

ABOUT midday on 3 May a friend crossing the lounge of the hotel said casually: 'There's been some kind of trouble at the Telephone Exchange, I hear.' For some reason I paid no attention to it at the time.

That afternoon, between three and four, I was half-way down the Ramblas when I heard several rifle-shots behind me. I turned round and saw some youths, with rifles in their hands and the red and black handkerchiefs of the Anarchists round their throats, edging up a side-street that ran off the Ramblas northward. They were evidently exchanging shots with someone in a tall octagonal tower – a church, I think – that commanded the side-street. I thought instantly: 'It's started!' But I thought it without any very great feeling of surprise – for days past everyone had been expecting 'it' to start at any moment. I realized that I must get back to the hotel at once and see if my wife was all right. But the knot of Anarchists round the opening of the side-street were motioning the people back and shouting to them not to cross the line of fire. More shots rang out. The bullets from the tower were flying across the street and a crowd of panic-stricken people was rushing down the Ramblas, away from the firing; up and down the street you could hear snap – snap – snap as the shopkeepers slammed the steel shutters over their windows. I saw two Popular Army officers retreating cautiously from tree to tree with their hands on their revolvers. In front of me the crowd was surging into the Metro station in the middle of the Ramblas to take cover. I immediately decided not to follow them. It might mean being trapped underground for hours.

At this moment an American doctor who had been with us at the front ran up to me and grabbed me by the arm. He was greatly excited.

'Come on, we must get down to the Hotel Falcón.' (The Hotel Falcón was a sort of boarding-house maintained by the P.O.U.M. and used chiefly by militiamen on leave.) 'The P.O.U.M. chaps will be meeting there. The trouble's starting. We must hang together.'

'But what the devil is it all about?' I said.

The doctor was hauling me along by the arm. He was too excited to give a very clear statement. It appeared that he had been in the Plaza de Cataluña when several lorry-loads of armed Civil Guards had driven up to the Telephone Exchange, which was operated mainly by C.N.T. workers, and made a sudden assault upon it. Then some Anarchists had arrived and there had been a general affray. I gathered that the 'trouble' earlier in the day had been a demand by the Government to hand over the Telephone Exchange, which, of course, was refused.

As we moved down the street a lorry raced past us from the opposite direction. It was full of Anarchists with rifles in their hands. In front a ragged youth was lying on a pile of mattresses behind a light machine-gun. When we got to the Hotel Falcón, which was at the bottom of the Ramblas, a crowd of people was seething in the entrance-hall; there was a great confusion, nobody seemed to know what we were expected to do, and nobody was armed except the handful of Shock Troopers who usually acted as guards for the building. I went across to the Comité Local of the P.O.U.M., which was almost opposite. Upstairs, in the room where militiamen normally went to draw their pay, another crowd was seething. A tall, pale, rather handsome man of about thirty, in civilian clothes, was trying to restore order and handing out belts and cartridge-boxes from a pile in the corner. There seemed to be no rifles as yet. The doctor had disappeared – I believe there had already been casualties and a call for doctors – but another Englishman had arrived. Presently, from an inner office, the tall man and some others began bringing out armfuls of rifles and handing them round. The other Englishman and myself, as foreigners, were slightly under suspicion and at first nobody would give us a rifle. Then a militiaman whom I had known at the front arrived and recognized me, after which we were given rifles and a few clips of cartridges, somewhat grudgingly.

There was a sound of firing in the distance and the streets were completely empty of people. Everyone said that it was impossible to go up the Ramblas. The Civil Guards had seized buildings in commanding positions and were letting fly at everyone who passed. I would have risked it and gone back to the hotel, but there was a vague idea floating round that the Comité Local was likely to be attacked at any moment and we had better stand by. All over the building, on the stairs, and on the pavement outside, small knots of people were standing and talking excitedly. No one seemed to have a very clear idea of what was happening. All I could gather was that the Civil Guards had attacked the Telephone Exchange and seized various strategic spots that commanded other buildings belonging to the workers. There was a general Impression that the Civil Guards were 'after' the C.N.T. and the working class generally. It was noticeable that, at this stage, no one seemed to put the blame on the Government. The poorer classes in Barcelona looked upon the Civil Guards as something rather resembling the Black and Tans, and it seemed to be taken for granted that they had started this attack on their own initiative. Once I heard how things stood I felt easier in my mind. The issue was clear enough. On one side the C.N.T., on the other side the police. I have no particular love for the idealized 'worker' as he appears in the bourgeois Communist's mind, but when I see an actual flesh-and-blood worker in conflict with his natural enemy, the policeman, I do not have to ask myself which side I am on.

A long time passed and nothing seemed to be happening at our end of the town. It did not occur to me that I could ring up the hotel and find out whether my wife was all right; I took it for granted that the Telephone Exchange would have stopped working – though, as a matter of fact, it was only out of action for a couple of hours. There seemed to be about three hundred people in the two buildings. Predominantly they were people of the poorest class, from the back-streets down by the quays; there was a number of women among them, some of them carrying babies, and a crowd of little ragged boys. I fancy that many of them had no notion what was happening and had simply fled into the P.O.U.M. buildings for protection. There was also a number of militiamen on leave, and a sprinkling of foreigners. As far as I could estimate, there were only about sixty rifles between the lot of us. The office upstairs was ceaselessly besieged by a crowd of people who were demanding rifles and being told that there were none left. The younger militia boys, who seemed to regard the whole affair as a kind of picnic, were prowling round and trying to wheedle or steal rifles from anyone who had them. It was not long before one of them got my rifle away from me by a clever dodge and immediately made himself scarce. So I was unarmed again, except for my tiny automatic pistol, for which I had only one clip of cartridges.

It grew dark, I was getting hungry, and seemingly there was no food in the Falcón. My friend and I slipped out to his hotel, which was not far away, to get some dinner. The streets were utterly dark and silent, not a soul stirring, steel shutters drawn over all the shop windows, but no barricades built yet. There was a great fuss before they would let us into the hotel, which was locked and barred. When we got back I learned that the Telephone Exchange was working and went to the telephone in the office upstairs to ring up my wife. Characteristically, there was no telephone directory in the building, and I did not know the number of the Hotel Continental; after a searching from room to room for about an hour I came upon a guide-book which gave me the number. I could not make contact with my wife, but I managed to get hold of John McNair, the I.L.P. representative in Barcelona. He told me that all was well, nobody had been shot, and asked me if we were all right at the Comité Local. I said that we should be all right if we had some cigarettes. I only meant this as a joke; nevertheless half an hour later McNair appeared with two packets of Lucky Strike. He had braved the pitch-dark streets, roamed by Anarchist patrols who had twice stopped him at the pistol's point and examined his papers. I shall not forget this small act of heroism. We were very glad of the cigarettes.

They had placed armed guards at most of the windows, and in the street below a little group of Shock Troopers were stopping and questioning the few passers-by. An Anarchist patrol car drove up, bristling with weapons. Beside the driver a beautiful dark-haired girl of about eighteen was nursing a sub-machine-gun across her knees. I spent a long time wandering about the building, a great rambling place of which it was impossible to learn the geography. Everywhere was the usual litter, the broken furniture and torn paper that seem to be the inevitable products of revolution. All over the place people were sleeping; on a broken sofa in a passage two poor women from the quayside were peacefully snoring. The place had been a cabaret-theatre before the P.O.U.M. took it over. There were raised stages in several of the rooms; on one of them was a desolate grand piano. Finally I discovered what I was looking for – the armoury. I did not know how this affair was going to turn out, and I badly wanted a weapon. I had heard it said so often that all the rival parties, P.S.U.C., P.O.U.M., and C.N.T. – F.A.I. alike, were hoarding arms in Barcelona, that I could not believe that two of the principal P.O.U.M. buildings contained only the fifty or sixty rifles that I had seen. The room which acted as an armoury was unguarded and had a flimsy door; another Englishman and myself had no difficulty in prising it open. When we got inside we found that what they had told us was true – there *were* no more weapons. All we found there were about two dozen small-bore rifles of an obsolete pattern and a few shot-guns, with no cartridges for any of them. I went up to the office and asked if they had any spare pistol ammunition; they had none. There were a few boxes of bombs, however, which one of the Anarchist patrol cars had brought us. I put a couple in one of my cartridge-boxes. They were a crude type of bomb, ignited by rubbing a sort of match at the top and very liable to go off of their own accord.

People were sprawling asleep all over the floor. In one room a baby was crying, crying ceaselessly. Though this was May the night was getting cold. On one of the cabaret-stages the curtains were still up, so I ripped a curtain down with my knife, rolled myself up in it, and had a few hours' sleep. My sleep was disturbed, I remember, by the thought of those beastly bombs, which might blow me into the air if I rolled on them too vigorously. At three in the morning the tall handsome man who seemed to be in command woke me up, gave me a rifle, and put me on guard at one of the windows. He told me that Salas, the Chief of Police responsible for the attack on the Telephone Exchange, had been placed under arrest. (Actually, as we learned later, he had only been deprived of his post. Nevertheless the news confirmed the general impression that the Civil Guards had acted without orders.) As soon as it was dawn the people downstairs began building two barricades, one outside the Comité Local and the other outside the Hotel Falcón. The Barcelona streets are paved with square cobbles, easily built up into a wall, and under the cobbles is a kind of shingle that is good for filling sand-bags. The building of those barricades was a strange and wonderful sight; I would have given something to be able to photograph it. With the kind of passionate energy that Spaniards display when they have definitely decided to begin upon any job of work, long lines of men, women, and quite small children were tearing up the cobblestones, hauling them along in a hand-cart that had been found somewhere, and staggering to and fro under heavy sacks of sand. In the doorway of the Comité Local a German Jewish girl, in a pair of militia-man's trousers whose knee-buttons just reached her ankles, was watching with a smile. In a couple of hours the barricades were head-high, with riflemen posted at the loopholes, and behind one barricade a fire was burning and men were frying eggs.

They had taken my rifle away again, and there seemed to be nothing that one could usefully do. Another Englishman and myself decided to go back to the Hotel Continental. There was a lot of firing in the distance, but seemingly none in the Ramblas. On the way up we looked in at the food-market. A very few stalls had opened; they were besieged by a crowd of people from the working-class quarters south of the Ramblas. Just as we got there, there was a heavy crash of rifle-fire outside, some panes of glass in the roof were shivered, and the crowd went flying for the back exits. A few stalls remained open, however; we managed to get a cup of coffee each and buy a wedge of goat's-milk cheese which I tucked in beside my bombs. A few days later I was very glad of that cheese.

At the street-corner where I had seen the Anarchists begin firing the day before a barricade was now standing. The man behind it (I was on the other side of the street) shouted to me to be careful. The Civil Guards in the church tower were firing indiscriminately at everyone who passed. I paused and then crossed the opening at a run; sure enough, a bullet cracked past me, uncomfortably close. When I neared the P.O.U.M. Executive Building, still on the other side of the road, there were fresh shouts of warning from some Shock Troopers standing in the doorway – shouts which, at the moment, I did not understand. There were trees and a newspaper kiosk between myself and the building (streets of this type in Spain have a broad walk running down the middle), and I could not see what they were pointing at. I went up to the Continental, made sure that all was well, washed my face, and then went back to the P.O.U.M. Executive Building (it was about a hundred yards down the street) to ask for orders. By this time the roar of rifle and machine-gun fire from various directions was almost comparable to the din of a battle. I had just found Kopp and was asking him what we were supposed to do when there was a series of appalling crashes down below. The din was so loud that I was sure someone must be firing at us with a field-gun. Actually it was only hand-grenades, which make double their usual noise when they burst among stone buildings.

Kopp glanced out of the window, cocked his stick behind his back, said: 'Let us investigate,' and strolled down the stairs in his usual unconcerned manner, I following. Just inside the doorway a group of Shock Troopers were bowling bombs down the pavement as though playing skittles. The bombs were bursting twenty yards away with a frightful, ear-splitting crash which was mixed up with the banging of rifles. Half across the street, from behind the newspaper kiosk, a head – it was the head of an American militiaman whom I knew well – was sticking up, for all the world like a coconut at a fair. It was only afterwards that I grasped what was really happening. Next door to the P.O.U.M. building there was a café with a hotel above it, called the Café Moka. The day before twenty or thirty armed Civil Guards had entered the café and then, when the fighting started, had suddenly seized the building and barricaded themselves in. Presumably they had been ordered to seize the café as a preliminary to attacking the P.O.U.M. offices later. Early in the morning they had attempted to come out, shots had been exchanged, and one Shock Trooper was badly wounded and a Civil Guard killed. The Civil Guards had fled back into the café, but when the American came down the street they had opened fire on him, though he was not armed. The American had flung himself

behind the kiosk for cover, and the Shock Troopers were flinging bombs
at the Civil Guards to drive them indoors again.

Kopp took in the scene at a glance, pushed his way forward and hauled
back a red-haired German Shock Trooper who was just drawing the pin
out of a bomb with his teeth. He shouted to everyone to stand back from
the doorway, and told us in several languages that we had got to avoid
bloodshed. Then he stepped out on to the pavement and, in sight of the
Civil Guards, ostentatiously took off his pistol and laid it on the ground.
Two Spanish militia officers did the same, and the three of them walked
slowly up to the doorway where the Civil Guards were huddling. It was a
thing I would not have done for twenty pounds. They were walking,
unarmed, up to men who were frightened out of their wits and had loaded
guns in their hands. A Civil Guard, in shirt-sleeves and livid with fright,
came out of the door to parley with Kopp. He kept pointing in an agitated
manner at two unexploded bombs that were lying on the pavement. Kopp
came back and told us we had better touch the bombs off. Lying there,
they were a danger to anyone who passed. A Shock Trooper fired his rifle
at one of the bombs and burst it, then fired at the other and missed. I
asked him to give me his rifle, knelt down and let fly at the second bomb.
I also missed it, I am sorry to say. This was the only shot I fired during
the disturbances. The pavement was covered with broken glass from the
sign over the Café Moka, and two cars that were parked outside, one of
them Kopp's official car, had been riddled with bullets and their wind-
screens smashed by bursting bombs.

Kopp took me upstairs again and explained the situation. We had got
to defend the P.O.U.M. buildings if they were attacked, but the P.O.U.M.
leaders had sent instructions that we were to stand on the defensive and
not open fire if we could possibly avoid it. Immediately opposite there was
a cinematograph, called the Poliorama, with a museum above it, and at
the top, high above the general level of the roofs, a small observatory with
twin domes. The domes commanded the street, and a few men posted up
there with rifles could prevent any attack on the P.O.U.M. buildings. The
caretakers at the cinema were C.N.T. members and would let us come and
go. As for the Civil Guards in the Café Moka, there would be no trouble
with them; they did not want to fight and would be only too glad to live
and let live. Kopp repeated that our orders were not to fire unless we were
fired on ourselves or our buildings attacked. I gathered, though he did not
say so, that the P.O.U.M. leaders were furious at being dragged into this
affair, but felt that they had got to stand by the C.N.T.

They had already placed guards in the observatory. The next three days and nights I spent continuously on the roof of the Poliorama, except for brief intervals when I slipped across to the hotel for meals. I was in no danger, I suffered from nothing worse than hunger and boredom, yet it was one of the most unbearable periods of my whole life. I think few experiences could be more sickening, more disillusioning, or, finally, more nerve-racking than those evil days of street warfare.

I used to sit on the roof marvelling at the folly of it all. From the little windows in the observatory you could see for miles around – vista after vista of tall slender buildings, glass domes, and fantastic curly roofs with brilliant green and copper tiles; over to eastward the glittering pale blue sea – the first glimpse of the sea that I had had since coming to Spain. And the whole huge town of a million people was locked in a sort of violent inertia, a nightmare of noise without movement. The sunlit streets were quite empty. Nothing was happening except the streaming of bullets from barricades and sand-bagged windows. Not a vehicle was stirring in the streets; here and there along the Ramblas the trams stood motionless where their drivers had jumped out of them when the fighting started. And all the while the devilish noise, echoing from thousands of stone buildings, went on and on and on, like a tropical rainstorm. Crack-crack, rattle-rattle, roar – sometimes it died away to a few shots, sometimes it quickened to a deafening fusillade, but it never stopped while daylight lasted, and punctually next dawn it started again.

What the devil was happening, who was fighting whom, and who was winning, was at first very difficult to discover. The people of Barcelona are so used to street-fighting and so familiar with the local geography that they knew by a kind of instinct which political party will hold which streets and which buildings. A foreigner is at a hopeless disadvantage. Looking out from the observatory, I could grasp that the Ramblas, which is one of the principal streets of the town, formed a dividing line. To the right of the Ramblas the working-class quarters were solidly Anarchist; to the left a confused fight was going on among the tortuous by-streets, but on that side the P.S.U.C. and the Civil Guards were more or less in control. Up at our end of the Ramblas, round the Plaza de Cataluña, the position was so complicated that it would have been quite unintelligible if every building had not flown a party flag. The principal landmark here was the Hotel Colón, the headquarters of the P.S.U.C., dominating the Plaza de Cataluña. In a window near the last O but one in the huge 'Hotel Colón' that sprawled across its face they had a machine-gun that could sweep the square with deadly effect. A hundred yards to the right of us, down the Ramblas, the J.S.U., the youth league of the P.S.U.C. (corresponding to the

Young Communist League in England), were holding a big department store whose sand-bagged side-windows fronted our observatory. They had hauled down their red flag and hoisted the Catalan national flag. On the Telephone Exchange, the starting-point of all the trouble, the Catalan national flag and the Anarchist flag were flying side by side. Some kind of temporary compromise had been arrived at there, the exchange was working uninterruptedly and there was no firing from the building.

In our position it was strangely peaceful. The Civil Guards in the Café Moka had drawn down the steel curtains and piled up the café furniture to make a barricade. Later half a dozen of them came on to the roof, opposite to ourselves, and built another barricade of mattresses, over which they hung a Catalan national flag. But it was obvious that they had no wish to start a fight. Kopp had made a definite agreement with them: if they did not fire at us we would not fire at them. He had grown quite friendly with the Civil Guards by this time, and had been to visit them several times in the Café Moka. Naturally they had looted everything drinkable the café possessed, and they made Kopp a present of fifteen bottles of beer. In return Kopp had actually given them one of our rifles to make up for one they had somehow lost on the previous day. Nevertheless, it was a queer feeling sitting on that roof. Sometimes I was merely bored with the whole affair, paid no attention to the hellish noise, and spent hours reading a succession of Penguin Library books which, luckily, I had bought a few days earlier; sometimes I was very conscious of the armed men watching me fifty yards away. It was a little like being in the trenches again; several times I caught myself, from force of habit, speaking of the Civil Guards as 'the Fascists'. There were generally about six of us up there. We placed a man on guard in each of the observatory towers, and the rest of us sat on the lead roof below, where there was no cover except a stone palisade. I was well aware that at any moment the Civil Guards might receive telephone orders to open fire. They had agreed to give us warning before doing so, but there was no certainty that they would keep to their agreement. Only once, however, did trouble look like starting. One of the Civil Guards opposite knelt down and began firing across the barricade. I was on guard in the observatory at the time. I trained my rifle on him and shouted across:

'Hi! Don't you shoot at us!'

'What?'

'Don't you fire at us or we'll fire back!'

'No, no! I wasn't firing at you. Look – down there!'

He motioned with his rifle towards the side-street that ran past the bottom of our building. Sure enough, a youth in blue overalls, with a rifle in his hand, was dodging round the corner. Evidently he had just taken a shot at the Civil Guards on the roof.

'I was firing at him. He fired first.' (I believe this was true.) 'We don't want to shoot you. We're only workers, the same as you are.'

He made the anti-Fascist salute, which I returned. I shouted across:

'Have you got any more beer left?'

'No, it's all gone.'

The same day, for no apparent reason, a man in the J.S.U. building farther down the street suddenly raised his rifle and let fly at me when I was leaning out of the window. Perhaps I made a tempting mark. I did not fire back. Though he was only a hundred yards away the bullet went so wide that it did not even hit the roof of the observatory. As usual, Spanish standards of marksmanship had saved me. I was fired at several times from this building.

The devilish racket of firing went on and on. But so far as I could see, and from all I heard, the fighting was defensive on both sides. People simply remained in their buildings or behind their barricades and blazed away at the people opposite. About half a mile away from us there was a street where some of the main offices of the C.N.T. and the U.G.T. were almost exactly facing one another; from that direction the volume of noise was terrific. I passed down that street the day after the fighting was over and the panes of the shop-windows were like sieves. (Most of the shopkeepers in Barcelona had their windows criss-crossed with strips of paper, so that when a bullet hit a pane it did not shiver to pieces.) Sometimes the rattle of rifle and machine-gun fire was punctuated by the crash of hand-grenades. And at long intervals, perhaps a dozen times in all, there were tremendously heavy explosions which at the time I could not account for; they sounded like aerial bombs, but that was impossible, for there were no aeroplanes about. I was told afterwards – quite possibly it was true – that *agents provocateurs* were touching off masses of explosive in order to increase the general noise and panic. There was, however, no artillery-fire. I was listening for this, for if the guns began to fire it would mean that the affair was becoming serious (artillery is the determining factor in street warfare). Afterwards there were wild tales in the newspapers about batteries of guns firing in the streets, but no one was able to point to a building that had been hit by a shell. In any case the sound of gunfire is unmistakable if one is used to it.

Almost from the start food was running short. With difficulty and under cover of darkness (for the Civil Guards were constantly sniping into the

Ramblas) food was brought from the Hotel Falcón for the fifteen or twenty militiamen who were in the P.O.U.M. Executive Building, but there was barely enough to go round, and as many of us as possible went to the Hotel Continental for our meals. The Continental had been 'collectivized' by the Generalite and not, like most of the hotels, by the C.N.T. or U.G.T., and it was regarded as neutral ground. No sooner had the fighting started than the hotel filled to the brim with a most extraordinary collection of people. There were foreign journalists, political suspects of every shade, an American airman in the service of the Government, various Communist agents, including a fat, sinister-looking Russian, said to be an agent of the Ogpu, who was nicknamed Charlie Chan and wore attached to his waist-band a revolver and a neat little bomb, some families of well-to-do Spaniards who looked like Fascist sympathizers, two or three wounded men from the International Column, a gang of lorry drivers from some huge French lorries which had been carrying a load of oranges back to France and had been held up by the fighting, and a number of Popular Army officers. The Popular Army, as a body, remained neutral throughout the fighting, though a few soldiers slipped away from the barracks and took part as individuals; on the Tuesday morning I had seen a couple of them at the P.O.U.M. barricades. At the beginning, before the food-shortage became acute and the newspapers began stirring up hatred, there was a tendency to regard the whole affair as a joke. This was the kind of thing that happened every year in Barcelona, people were saying. George Tioli, an Italian journalist, a great friend of ours, came in with his trousers drenched with blood. He had gone out to see what was happening and had been binding up a wounded man on the pavement when someone playfully tossed a hand-grenade at him, fortunately not wounding him seriously. I remember his remarking that the Barcelona paving-stones ought to be numbered; it would save such a lot of trouble in building and demolishing barricades. And I remember a couple of men from the International Column sitting in my room at the hotel when I came in tired, hungry, and dirty after a night on guard. Their attitude was completely neutral. If they had been good party-men they would, I suppose, have urged me to change sides, or even have pinioned me and taken away the bombs of which my pockets were full; instead they merely commiserated with me for having to spend my leave in doing guard-duty on a roof. The general attitude was: 'This is only a dust-up between the Anarchists and the police – it doesn't mean anything.' In spite of the extent of the fighting and the number of casualties I believe this was nearer the truth than the official version which represented the affair as a planned rising.

It was about Wednesday (5 May) that a change seemed to come over things. The shuttered streets looked ghastly. A very few pedestrians, forced abroad for one reason or another, crept to and fro, flourishing white handkerchiefs, and at a spot in the middle of the Ramblas that was safe from bullets some men were crying newspapers to the empty street. On Tuesday *Solidaridad Obrera*, the Anarchist paper, had described the attack on the Telephone Exchange as a 'monstrous provocation' (or words to that effect), but on Wednesday it changed its tune and began imploring everyone to go back to work. The Anarchist leaders were broadcasting the same message. The office of *La Batalla*, the P.O.U.M. paper, which was not defended, had been raided and seized by the Civil Guards at about the same time as the Telephone Exchange, but the paper was being printed, and a few copies distributed, from another address. It urged everyone to remain at the barricades. People were divided in their minds and wondering uneasily how the devil this was going to end. I doubt whether anyone left the barricades as yet, but everyone was sick of the meaningless fighting, which could obviously lead to no real decision, because no one wanted this to develop into a full-sized civil war which might mean losing the war against Franco. I heard this fear expressed on all sides. So far as one could gather from what people were saying at the time the C.N.T. rank and file wanted, and had wanted from the beginning, only two things: the handing back of the Telephone Exchange and the disarming of the hated Civil Guards. If the Generalite had promised to do these two things, and also promised to put an end to the food profiteering, there is little doubt that the barricades would have been down in two hours. But it was obvious that the Generalite was not going to give in. Ugly rumours were flying round. It was said that the Valencia Government was sending six thousand men to occupy Barcelona, and that five thousand Anarchist and P.O.U.M. troops had left the Aragon front to oppose them. Only the first of these rumours was true. Watching from the observatory tower we saw the low grey shapes of warships closing in upon the harbour. Douglas Moyle, who had been a sailor, said that they looked like British destroyers. As a matter of fact they *were* British destroyers, though we did not learn this till afterwards.

That evening we heard that on the Plaza de España four hundred Civil Guards had surrendered and handed their arms to the Anarchists; also the news was vaguely filtering through that in the suburbs (mainly working-class quarters) the C.N.T. were in control. It looked as though we were winning. But the same evening Kopp sent for me and, with a grave face, told me that according to information he had just received the Government was about to outlaw the P.O.U.M. and declare a state of war upon it. The news gave me a shock. It was the first glimpse I had had of the interpretation that was likely to be put upon this affair later on. I dimly foresaw that when the fighting ended the entire blame would be laid upon the P.O.U.M., which was the weakest party and therefore the most suitable scapegoat. And meanwhile our local neutrality was at an end. If the Government declared war upon us we had no choice but to defend ourselves, and here at the Executive building we could be certain that the Civil Guards next door would get orders to attack us. Our only chance was to attack them first. Kopp was waiting for orders on the telephone; if we heard definitely that the P.O.U.M. was outlawed we must make preparations at once to seize the Café Moka.

I remember the long, nightmarish evening that we spent in fortifying the building. We locked the steel curtains across the front entrance and behind them built a barricade of slabs of stone left behind by the workmen who had been making some alterations. We went over our stock of weapons. Counting the six rifles that were on the roof of the Poliorama opposite, we had twenty-one rifles, one of them defective, about fifty rounds of ammunition for each rifle, and a few dozen bombs; otherwise nothing except a few pistols and revolvers. About a dozen men, mostly Germans, had volunteered for the attack on the Café Moka, if it came off. We should attack from the roof, of course, some time in the small hours, and take them by surprise; they were more numerous, but our morale was better, and no doubt we could storm the place, though people were bound to be killed in doing so. We had no food in the building except a few slabs of chocolate, and the rumour had gone round that 'they' were going to cut off the water supply. (Nobody knew who 'they' were. It might be the Government that controlled the waterworks, or it might be the C.N.T. – nobody knew.) We spent a long time filling up every basin in the lavatories, every bucket we could lay hands on, and, finally, the fifteen beer bottles, now empty, which the Civil Guards had given to Kopp.

I was in a ghastly frame of mind and dog-tired after about sixty hours without much sleep. It was now late into the night. People were sleeping all over the floor behind the barricade downstairs. Upstairs there was a small room, with a sofa in it, which we intended to use as a dressing-station, though, needless to say, we discovered that there was neither iodine nor bandages in the building. My wife had come down from the hotel in case a nurse should be needed. I lay down on the sofa, feeling that I would like half an hour's rest before the attack on the Moka, in which I should presumably be killed. I remember the intolerable discomfort caused by my pistol, which was strapped to my belt and sticking into the small of my back. And the next thing I remember is waking up with a jerk to find my wife standing beside me. It was broad daylight, nothing had happened, the Government had not declared war on the P.O.U.M., the water had not been cut off, and except for the sporadic firing in the streets everything was normal. My wife said that she had not had the heart to wake me and had slept in an arm-chair in one of the front rooms.

That afternoon there was a kind of armistice. The firing died away and with surprising suddenness the streets filled with people. A few shops began to pull up their shutters, and the market was packed with a huge crowd clamouring for food, though the stalls were almost empty. It was noticeable, however, that the trams did not start running. The Civil Guards were still behind their barricades in the Moka; on neither side were the fortified buildings evacuated. Everyone was rushing round and trying to buy food. And on every side you heard the same anxious questions: 'Do you think it's stopped? Do you think it's going to start again?' 'It' – the fighting – was now thought of as some kind of natural calamity, like a hurricane or an earthquake, which was happening to us all alike and which we had no power of stopping. And sure enough, almost immediately – I suppose there must really have been several hours' truce, but they seemed more like minutes than hours – a sudden crash of rifle-fire, like a June cloud-burst, sent everyone scurrying; the steel shutters snapped into place, the streets emptied like magic, the barricades were manned, and 'it' had started again.

I went back to my post on the roof with a feeling of concentrated disgust and fury. When you are taking part in events like these you are, I suppose, in a small way, making history, and you ought by rights to feel like a historical character. But you never do, because at such times the physical details always outweigh everything else. Throughout the fighting I never made the correct 'analysis' of the situation that was so glibly made by journalists hundreds of miles away. What I was chiefly thinking about was not the rights and wrongs of this miserable internecine scrap, but simply the discomfort and boredom of sitting day and night on that intolerable roof, and the hunger which was growing worse and worse – for none of us had had a proper meal since Monday. It was in my mind all the while that I should have to go back to the front as soon as this business was over. It was infuriating. I had been a hundred and fifteen days in the line and had come back to Barcelona ravenous for a bit of rest and comfort; and instead I had to spend my time sitting on a roof opposite Civil Guards as bored as myself, who periodically waved to me and assured me that they were 'workers' (meaning that they hoped I would not shoot them), but who would certainly open fire if they got the order to do so. If this was history it did not feel like it. It was more like a bad period at the front, when men were short and we had to do abnormal hours of guard-duty; instead of being heroic one just had to stay at one's post, bored, dropping with sleep, and completely uninterested as to what it was all about.

Inside the hotel, among the heterogeneous mob who for the most part had not dared to put their noses out of doors, a horrible atmosphere of suspicion had grown up. Various people were infected with spy mania and were creeping round whispering that everyone else was a spy of the Communists, or the Trotskyists, or the Anarchists, or whatnot. The fat Russian agent was cornering all the foreign refugees in turn and explaining plausibly that this whole affair was an Anarchist plot. I watched him with some interest, for it was the first time that I had seen a person whose profession was telling lies – unless one counts journalists. There was something repulsive in the parody of smart hotel life that was still going on behind shuttered windows amid the rattle of rifle-fire. The front dining-room had been abandoned after a bullet came through the window and chipped a pillar, and the guests were crowded into a darkish room at the back, where there were never quite enough tables to go round. The waiters were reduced in numbers – some of them were C.N.T. members and had joined in the general strike – and had dropped their boiled shirts for the time being, but meals were still being served with a pretence of ceremony. There was, however, practically nothing to eat. On that Thursday night the principal dish at dinner was *one* sardine each. The hotel had had no bread for days, and even the wine was running so low that we were drinking older and older wines at higher and higher prices. This shortage of food went on for several days after the fighting was over. Three days running, I remember, my wife and I breakfasted off a little piece of goat's-milk cheese with no bread and nothing to drink. The only thing that was plentiful was oranges. The French lorry drivers brought quantities of their oranges into the hotel. They were a tough-looking bunch; they had with them some flashy Spanish girls and a huge porter in a black blouse. At any other time the little snob of a hotel manager would have done his best to make them uncomfortable, in fact would have refused to have them on the premises, but at present they were popular because, unlike the rest of us, they had a private store of bread which everyone was trying to cadge from them.

I spent that final night on the roof, and the next day it did really look

as though the fighting was coming to an end. I do not think there was
much firing that day – the Friday. No one seemed to know for certain
whether the troops from Valencia were really coming; they arrived that
evening, as a matter of fact. The Government was broadcasting half-
soothing, half-threatening messages, asking everyone to go home and
saying that after a certain hour anyone found carrying arms would be
arrested. Not much attention was paid to the Government's broadcasts,
but everywhere the people were fading away from the barricades. I have
no doubt that it was mainly the food shortage that was responsible. From
every side you heard the same remark: 'We have no more food, we must
go back to work.' On the other hand the Civil Guards, who could count
on getting their rations so long as there was any food in the town, were
able to stay at their posts. By the afternoon the streets were almost normal,
though the deserted barricades were still standing; the Ramblas were
thronged with people, the shops nearly all open, and – most reassuring of
all – the trams that had stood so long in frozen blocks jerked into motion
and began running. The Civil Guards were still holding the Café Moka
and had not taken down their barricades, but some of them brought chairs
out and sat on the pavement with their rifles across their knees. I winked
at one of them as I went past and got a not unfriendly grin; he recognized
me, of course. Over the Telephone Exchange the Anarchist flag had been
hauled down and only the Catalan flag was flying. That meant that the
workers were definitely beaten; I realized – though, owing to my political
ignorance, not so clearly as I ought to have done – that when the
Government felt more sure of itself there would be reprisals. But at the
time I was not interested in that aspect of things. All I felt was a profound
relief that the devilish din of firing was over, and that one could buy some
food and have a bit of rest and peace before going back to the front.

It must have been late that evening that the troops from Valencia first
appeared in the streets. They were the Assault Guards, another formation
similar to the Civil Guards and the Carabineros (i.e. a formation intended
primarily for police work), and the picked troops of the Republic. Quite
suddenly they seemed to spring up out of the ground; you saw them
everywhere patrolling the streets in groups of ten – tall men in grey or
blue uniforms, with long rifles slung over their shoulders, and a sub-
machine-gun to each group. Meanwhile there was a delicate job to be
done. The six rifles which we had used for the guard in the observatory
towers were still lying there, and by hook or by crook we had got to get
them back to the P.O.U.M. building. It was only a question of getting them
across the street. They were part of the regular armoury of the building,

but to bring them into the street was to contravene the Government's order, and if we were caught with them in our hands we should certainly be arrested – worse, the rifles would be confiscated. With only twenty-one rifles in the building we could not afford to lose six of them. After a lot of discussion as to the best method, a red-haired Spanish boy and myself began to smuggle them out. It was easy enough to dodge the Assault Guard patrols; the danger was the Civil Guards in the Moka, who were well aware that we had rifles in the observatory and might give the show away if they saw us carrying them across. Each of us partially undressed and slung a rifle over the left shoulder, the butt under the armpit, the barrel down the trouser-leg. It was unfortunate that they were long Mausers. Even a man as tall as I am cannot wear a long Mauser down his trouser-leg without discomfort. It was an intolerable job getting down the corkscrew staircase of the observatory with a completely rigid left leg. Once in the street, we found that the only way to move was with extreme slowness, so slowly that you did not have to bend your knees. Outside the picture-house I saw a group of people staring at me with great interest as I crept along at tortoise-speed. I have often wondered what they thought was the matter with me. Wounded in the war, perhaps. However, all the rifles were smuggled across without incident.

Next day the Assault Guards were everywhere, walking the streets like conquerors. There was no doubt that the Government was simply making a display of force in order to overawe a population which it already knew would not resist; if there had been any real fear of further outbreaks the Assault Guards would have been kept in barracks and not scattered through the streets in small bands. They were splendid troops, much the best I had seen in Spain, and, though I suppose they were in a sense 'the enemy', I could not help liking the look of them. But it was with a sort of amazement that I watched them strolling to and fro. I was used to the ragged, scarcely-armed militia on the Aragon front, and I had not known that the Republic possessed troops like these. It was not only that they were picked men physically, it was their weapons that most astonished me. All of them were armed with brand-new rifles of the type known as 'the Russian rifle' (these rifles were sent to Spain by the U.S.S.R., but were, I believe, manufactured in America). I examined one of them. It was a far from perfect rifle, but vastly better than the dreadful old blunderbusses we had at the front. The Assault Guards had one sub-machine-gun between ten men and an automatic pistol each; we at the front had approximately one machine-gun between fifty men, and as for pistols and revolvers, you could only procure them illegally. As a matter of fact, though I had not

noticed it till now, it was the same everywhere. The Civil Guards and
Carabineros, who were not intended for the front at all, were better armed
and far better clad than ourselves. I suspect it is the same in all wars –
always the same contrast between the sleek police in the rear and the
ragged soldiers in the line. On the whole the Assault Guards got on very
well with the population after the first day or two. On the first day there
was a certain amount of trouble because some of the Assault Guards –
acting on instructions, I suppose – began behaving in a provocative manner.
Bands of them boarded trams, searched the passengers, and, if they had
C.N.T. membership cards in their pockets, tore them up and stamped on
them. This led to scuffles with armed Anarchists, and one or two people
were killed. Very soon, however, the Assault Guards dropped their con-
quering air and relations became more friendly. It was noticeable that
most of them had picked up a girl after a day or two.

The Barcelona fighting had given the Valencia Government the long-
wanted excuse to assume fuller control of Catalonia. The workers' militias
were to be broken up and redistributed among the Popular Army. The
Spanish Republican flag was flying all over Barcelona – the first time I
had seen it, I think, except over a Fascist trench. In the working-class
quarters the barricades were being pulled down, rather fragmentarily, for
it is a lot easier to build a barricade than to put the stones back. Outside
the P.S.U.C. buildings the barricades were allowed to remain standing, and
indeed many were standing as late as June. The Civil Guards were still
occupying strategic points. Huge seizures of arms were being made from
C.N.T. strongholds, though I have no doubt a good many escaped seizure.
La Batalla was still appearing, but it was censored until the front page
was almost completely blank. The P.S.U.C. papers were uncensored and
were publishing inflamatory articles demanding the suppression of the
P.O.U.M. The P.O.U.M. was declared to be a disguised Fascist organization,
and a cartoon representing the P.O.U.M. as a figure slipping off a mask
marked with the hammer and sickle and revealing a hideous, maniacal
face marked with the swastika, was being circulated all over the town by
P.S.U.C. agents. Evidently the official version of the Barcelona fighting was
already fixed upon: it was to be represented as a 'fifth column' Fascist
rising engineered solely by the P.O.U.M.

In the hotel the horrible atmosphere of suspicion and hostility had grown
worse now that the fighting was over. In the face of the accusations that
were being flung about it was impossible to remain neutral. The posts were
working again, the foreign Communist papers were beginning to arrive,
and their accounts of the fighting were not only violently partisan but, of

course, wildly inaccurate as to facts. I think some of the Communists on the spot, who had seen what was actually happening, were dismayed by the interpretation that was being put upon events, but naturally they had to stick to their own side. Our Communist friend approached me once again and asked me whether I would not transfer into the International Column.

I was rather surprised. 'Your papers are saying I'm a Fascist,' I said. 'Surely I should be politically suspect, coming from the P.O.U.M.'

'Oh, that doesn't matter. After all, you were only acting under orders.'

I had to tell him that after this affair I could not join any Communist-controlled unit. Sooner or later it might mean being used against the Spanish working class. One could not tell when this kind of thing would break out again, and if I had to use my rifle at all in such an affair I would use it on the side of the working class and not against them. He was very decent about it. But from now on the whole atmosphere was changed. You could not, as before, 'agree to differ' and have drinks with a man who was supposedly your political opponent. There were some ugly wrangles in the hotel lounge. Meanwhile the jails were already full and overflowing. After the fighting was over the Anarchists had, of course, released their prisoners, but the Civil Guards had not released theirs, and most of them were thrown into prison and kept there without trial, in many cases for months on end. As usual, completely innocent people were being arrested owing to police bungling. I mentioned earlier that Douglas Thompson was wounded about the beginning of April. Afterwards we had lost touch with him, as usually happened when a man was wounded, for wounded men were frequently moved from one hospital to another. Actually he was at Tarragona hospital and was sent back to Barcelona about the time when the fighting started. On the Tuesday morning I met him in the street, considerably bewildered by the firing that was going on all round. He asked the question everyone was asking:

'What the devil is this all about?'

I explained as well as I could. Thompson said promptly:

'I'm going to keep out of this. My arm's still bad. I shall go back to my hotel and stay there.'

He went back to his hotel, but unfortunately (how important it is in street-fighting to understand the local geography!) it was a hotel in a part of the town controlled by the Civil Guards. The place was raided and Thompson was arrested, flung into jail, and kept for eight days in a cell so full of people that nobody had room to lie down. There were many similar cases. Numerous foreigners with doubtful political records were on the run, with the police on their track and in constant fear of denunciation. It was worst for the Italians and Germans, who had no passports and were generally wanted by the secret police in their own countries. If they were arrested they were liable to be deported to France, which might mean being sent back to Italy or Germany, where God knew what horrors were awaiting them. One or two foreign women hurriedly regularized their position by 'marrying' Spaniards. A German girl who had no papers at all dodged the police by posing for several days as a man's mistress. I remember the look of shame and misery on the poor girl's face when I accidentally bumped into her coming out of the man's bedroom. Of course she was not his mistress, but no doubt she thought I thought she was. You had all the while a hateful feeling that someone hitherto your friend might be denouncing you to the secret police. The long nightmare of the fighting, the noise, the lack of food and sleep, the mingled strain and boredom of sitting on the roof and wondering whether in another minute I should be shot myself or be obliged to shoot somebody else had put my nerves on edge. I had got to the point when every time a door banged I grabbed for my pistol. On the Saturday morning there was an uproar of shots outside and everyone cried out: 'It's starting again!' I ran into the street to find that it was only some Assault Guards shooting a mad dog. No one who was in Barcelona then, or for months later, will forget the horrible atmosphere produced by fear, suspicion, hatred, censored newspapers, crammed jails, enormous food queues, and prowling gangs of armed men.

I have tried to give some idea of what it felt like to be in the middle of the Barcelona fighting; yet I do not suppose I have succeeded in conveying much of the strangeness of that time. One of the things that stick in my mind when I look back is the casual contacts one made at the time, the sudden glimpses of non-combatants to whom the whole thing was simply a meaningless uproar. I remember the fashionably-dressed woman I saw strolling down the Ramblas, with a shopping-basket over her arm and leading a white poodle, while the rifles cracked and roared a street or two away. It is conceivable that she was deaf. And the man I saw rushing across the completely empty Plaza de Cataluña, brandishing a white handkerchief in each hand. And the large party of people all dressed in black who kept trying for about an hour to cross the Plaza de Cataluña and always failing. Every time they emerged from the side-street at the corner the P.S.U.C. machine-gunners in the Hotel Colón opened fire and drove them back – I don't know why, for they were obviously unarmed. I have since thought that they may have been a funeral party. And the little man who acted as caretaker at the museum over the Poliorama and who seemed to regard the whole affair as a social occasion. He was so pleased to have the English visiting him – the English were so *simpático*, he said. He hoped we would all come and see him again when the trouble was over; as a matter of fact I did go and see him. And the other little man, sheltering in a doorway, who jerked his head in a pleased manner towards the hell of firing on the Plaza de Cataluña and said (as though remarking that it was a fine morning): 'So we've got the nineteenth of July back again!' And the people in the shoe-shop who were making my marching-boots. I went there before the fighting, after it was over, and, for a very few minutes, during the brief armistice on 5 May. It was an expensive shop, and the shop-people were U.G.T. and may have been P.S.U.C. members – at any rate they were politically on the other side and they knew that I was serving with the P.O.U.M. Yet their attitude was completely indifferent. 'Such a pity, this kind of thing, isn't it? And so bad for business. What a pity it doesn't stop! As though there wasn't enough of that kind of thing at the front!' etc., etc. There must have been quantities of people, perhaps a majority of the inhabitants of Barcelona, who regarded the whole affair without a flicker of interest, or with no more interest than they would have felt in an air-raid.

In this chapter I have described only my personal experiences. In the next chapter I must discuss as best I can the larger issues – what actually happened and with what results, what were the rights and wrongs of the affair, and who if anyone was responsible. So much political capital has been made out of the Barcelona fighting that it is important to try and get a balanced view of it. An immense amount, enough to fill many books, has already been written on the subject, and I do not suppose I should exaggerate if I said that nine-tenths of it is untruthful. Nearly all the newspaper accounts published at the time were manufactured by journalists at a distance, and were not only inaccurate in their facts but intentionally misleading. As usual, only one side of the question has been allowed to get to the wider public. Like everyone who was in Barcelona at the time, I saw only what was happening in my immediate neighbourhood, but I saw and heard quite enough to be able to contradict many of the lies that have been circulated. As before, if you are not interested in political controversy and the mob of parties and sub-parties with their confusing names (rather like the names of the generals in a Chinese war), please skip. It is a horrible thing to have to enter into the details of inter-party polemics; it is like diving into a cesspool. But it is necessary to try

and establish the truth, so far as it is possible. This squalid brawl in a
distant city is more important than might appear at first sight.

11

IT will never be possible to get a completely accurate and unbiased account
of the Barcelona fighting, because the necessary records do not exist. Future
historians will have nothing to go upon except a mass of accusations and
party propaganda. I myself have little data beyond what I saw with my own
eyes and what I have learned from other eye-witnesses whom I believe to be
reliable. I can, however, contradict some of the more flagrant lies and help
to get the affair into some kind of perspective.

First of all, what actually happened?

For some time past there had been tension throughout Catalonia. In
earlier chapters of this book I have given some account of the struggle
between Communists and Anarchists. By May 1937 things had reached a
point at which some kind of violent outbreak could be regarded as inevitable.
The immediate cause of friction was the Government's order to surrender
all private weapons, coinciding with the decision to build up a heavily-armed
'non-political' police-force from which trade union members were to be
excluded. The meaning of this was obvious to everyone; and it was also
obvious that the next move would be the taking over of some of the key
industries controlled by the C.N.T. In addition there was a certain amount of
resentment among the working classes because of the growing contrast of
wealth and poverty and a general vague feeling that the revolution had been
sabotaged. Many people were agreeably surprised when there was no rioting
on 1 May. On 3 May the Government decided to take over the Telephone
Exchange, which had been operated since the beginning of the war mainly
by C.N.T. workers; it was alleged that it was badly run and that official calls
were being tapped. Salas, the Chief of Police (who may or may not have
been exceeding his orders), sent three lorry-loads of armed Civil Guards to
seize the building, while the streets outside were cleared by armed police in
civilian clothes. At about the same time bands of Civil Guards seized various
other buildings in strategic spots. Whatever the real intention may have
been, there was a widespread belief that this was the signal for a general
attack on the C.N.T. by the Civil Guards and the P.S.U.C. (Communists and

Socialists). The word flew round the town that the workers' buildings were being attacked, armed Anarchists appeared on the streets, work ceased, and fighting broke out immediately. That night and the next morning barricades were built all over the town, and there was no break in the fighting until the morning of 6 May. The fighting was, however, mainly defensive on both sides. Buildings were besieged, but, so far as I know, none were stormed, and there was no use of artillery. Roughly speaking, the C.N.T. – F.A.I. – P.O.U.M. forces held the working-class suburbs, and the armed police-forces and the P.S.U.C. held the central and official portion of the town. On 6 May there was an armistice, but fighting soon broke out again, probably because of premature attempts by Civil Guards to disarm C.N.T. workers. Next morning, however, the people began to leave the barricades of their own accord. Up till, roughly, the night of 5 May the C.N.T. had had the better of it, and large numbers of Civil Guards had surrendered. But there was no generally accepted leadership and no fixed plan – indeed, so far as one could judge, no plan at all except a vague determination to resist the Civil Guards. The official leaders of the C.N.T. had joined with those of the U.G.T. in imploring everyone to go back to work; above all, food was running short. In such circumstances nobody was sure enough of the issue to go on fighting. By the afternoon of 7 May conditions were almost normal. That evening six thousand Assault Guards, sent by sea from Valencia, arrived and took control of the town. The Government issued an order for the surrender of all arms except those held by the regular forces, and during the next few days large numbers of arms were seized. The casualties during the fighting were officially given out as four hundred killed and about a thousand wounded. Four hundred killed is possibly an exaggeration, but as there is no way of verifying this we must accept it as accurate.

Secondly, as to the after-effects of the fighting. Obviously it is impossible to say with any certainty what these were. There is no evidence that the outbreak had any direct effect upon the course of the war, though obviously it must have had if it continued even a few days longer. It was made the excuse for bringing Catalonia under the direct control of Valencia, for hastening the break-up of the militias, and for the suppression of the P.O.U.M., and no doubt it also had its share in bringing down the Caballero Government. But we may take it as certain that these things would have happened in any case. The real question is whether the C.N.T. workers who came into the street gained or lost by showing fight on this occasion. It is pure guesswork, but my own opinion is that they gained more than they lost. The seizure of the Barcelona Telephone Exchange was simply one incident in a long process. Since the previous year direct power had been gradually manoeuvred out of the hands of the syndicates, and the general movement was away from working-class control and towards centralized control, leading on to State capitalism or, possibly, towards the reintroduction of private capitalism. The fact that at this point there was resistance probably slowed the process down. A year after the outbreak of war the Catalan workers had lost much of their power, but their position was still comparatively favourable. It might have been much less so if they had made it clear that they would lie down under no matter what provocation. There are occasions when it pays better to fight and be beaten than not to fight at all.

Thirdly, what purpose, if any, lay behind the outbreak? Was it any kind of *coup d'état* or revolutionary attempt? Did it definitely aim at over-throwing the Government? Was it preconcerted at all?

My own opinion is that the fighting was only preconcerted in the sense that everyone expected it. There were no signs of any very definite plan on either side. On the Anarchist side the action was almost certainly spontaneous, for it was an affair mainly of the rank and file. The people came into the streets and their political leaders followed reluctantly, or did not follow at all. The only people who even *talked* in a revolutionary strain were the Friends of Durruti, a small extremist group within the F.A.I., and the P.O.U.M. But once again they were following and not leading. The Friends of Durruti distributed some kind of revolutionary leaflet, but this did not appear until 5 May and cannot be said to have started the fighting, which had started of its own accord two days earlier. The official leaders of the C.N.T. disowned the whole affair from the start. There were a number of reasons for this. To begin with, the fact that the C.N.T. was still represented in the Government and the Generalite ensured that its leaders would be more conservative than their followers. Secondly, the main object of the C.N.T. leaders was to form an alliance with the U.G.T., and the fighting was bound to widen the split between C.N.T. and U.G.T., at any rate for the time being. Thirdly – though this was not generally known at the time – the Anarchist leaders feared that if things went beyond a certain point and the workers took possession of the town, as they were perhaps in a position to do on 5 May, there would be foreign intervention. A British cruiser and two British destroyers had closed in upon the harbour, and no doubt there were other warships not far away. The English newspapers gave it out that these ships were proceeding to Barcelona 'to protect British interests', but in fact they made no move to do so; that is, they did not land any men or take off any refugees. There can be no certainty about this, but it was at least inherently likely that the British Government, which had not raised a finger to save the Spanish Government from Franco, would intervene quickly enough to save it from its own working class.

The P.O.U.M. leaders did not disown the affair, in fact they encouraged their followers to remain at the barricades and even gave their approval (in *La Batalla*, 6 May) to the extremist leaflet issued by the Friends of Durruti. (There is great uncertainty about this leaflet, of which no one now seems able to produce a copy.) In some of the foreign papers it was described as an 'inflammatory poster' which was 'plastered' all over the town. There was certainly no such poster. From comparison of various reports I should say that the leaflet called for (i) The formation of a revolutionary council (junta). (ii) The shooting of those responsible for the attack on the Telephone Exchange. (iii) The disarming of the Civil Guards. There is also some uncertainty as to how far *La Batalla* expressed agreement with the leaflet. I myself did not see the leaflet or *La Batalla* of that date. The only handbill I saw during the fighting was one issued by the tiny group of Trotskyists ('Bolshevik-Leninists') on 4 May. This merely said: 'Everyone to the barricades – general strike of all industries except war industries.' (In other words, it merely demanded what was happening already.) But in reality the attitude of the P.O.U.M. leaders was hesitating. They had never been in favour of insurrection until the war against Franco was won; on the other hand the workers had come into the streets, and the P.O.U.M. leaders took the rather pedantic Marxist line that when the workers are on the streets it is the duty of the revolutionary parties to be with them. Hence, in spite of uttering revolutionary slogans about the 'reawakening of the spirit of 19 July', and so forth, they did their best to limit the workers' action to the defensive. They never, for instance, ordered an attack on any building; they merely ordered their followers to remain on guard and, as I mentioned in the last chapter, not to fire when it could be avoided. *La Batalla* also issued instructions that no troops were to leave the front.* As far as one can estimate it, I should say that the responsibility of the P.O.U.M. amounts to having urged everyone to remain at the barricades, and probably to having persuaded a certain number to remain there longer than they would otherwise have done. Those who were in personal touch with the P.O.U.M. leaders at the time (I myself was not) have told me that they were in reality dismayed by the whole business, but felt that they had got to associate themselves with it. Afterwards, of course, political capital was made out of it in the usual manner. Gorkin, one of the P.O.U.M. leaders, even spoke later of 'the glorious days of May'. From the

* A recent number of *Inprecor* states the exact opposite – that *La Batalla* orders the P.O.U.M. troops to leave the front! The point can easily be settled by referring to *La Batalla* of the date named.

HOMAGE TO CATALONIA

propaganda point of view this may have been the right line; certainly the P.O.U.M. rose somewhat in numbers during the brief period before its suppression. Tactically it was probably a mistake to give countenance to the leaflet of the Friends of Durruti, which was a very small organization and normally hostile to the P.O.U.M. Considering the general excitement and the things that were being said on both sides, the leaflet did not in effect mean much more than 'Stay at the barricades', but by seeming to approve of it while *Solidaridad Obrera*, the Anarchist paper, repudiated it, the P.O.U.M. leaders made it easy for the Communist press to say afterwards that the fighting was a kind of insurrection engineered solely by the P.O.U.M. However, we may be certain that the Communist press would have said this in any case. It was nothing compared with the accusations that were made both before and afterwards on less evidence. The C.N.T. leaders did not gain much by their more cautious attitude; they were praised for their loyalty but were levered out of both the Government and the Generalite as soon as the opportunity arose.

So far as one could judge from what people were saying at the time, there was no real revolutionary intention anywhere. The people behind the barricades were ordinary C.N.T. workers, probably with a sprinkling of U.G.T. workers among them, and what they were attempting was not to overthrow the Government but to resist what they regarded, rightly or wrongly, as an attack by the police. Their action was essentially defensive, and I doubt whether it should be described, as it was in nearly all the foreign newspapers, as a 'rising'. A rising implies aggressive action and a definite plan. More exactly it was a riot – a very bloody riot, because both sides had fire-arms in their hands and were willing to use them.

But what about the intentions on the other side? If it was not an Anarchist *coup d'état*, was it perhaps a Communist *coup d'état* – a planned effort to smash the power of the C.N.T. at one blow?

I do not believe it was, though certain things might lead one to suspect it. It is significant that something very similar (seizure of the Telephone Exchange by armed police acting under orders from Barcelona) happened in Tarragona two days later. And in Barcelona the raid on the Telephone Exchange was not an isolated act. In various parts of the town bands of Civil Guards and P.S.U.C. adherents seized buildings in strategic spots, if not actually before the fighting started, at any rate with surprising promptitude. But what one has got to remember is that these things were happening in Spain and not in England. Barcelona is a town with a long history of street-fighting. In such places things happen quickly, the factions are ready-made, everyone knows the local geography, and when the guns begin to shoot people take their places almost as in a fire-drill. Presumably those responsible for the seizure of the Telephone Exchange expected trouble – though not on the scale that actually happened – and had made ready to meet it. But it does not follow that they were planning a general attack on the C.N.T. There are two reasons why I do not believe that either side had made preparations for large-scale fighting:

(i) Neither side had brought troops to Barcelona beforehand. The fighting was only between those who were in Barcelona already, mainly civilians and police.

(ii) The food ran short almost immediately. Anyone who has served in Spain knows that the one operation of war that Spaniards perform really well is that of feeding their troops. It is most unlikely that if either side had contemplated a week or two of street-fighting and a general strike they would not have stored food beforehand.

Finally, as to the rights and wrongs of the affair.

A tremendous dust was kicked up in the foreign anti-Fascist press, but, as usual, only one side of the case has had anything like a hearing. As a result the Barcelona fighting has been represented as an insurrection by disloyal Anarchists and Trotskyists who were 'stabbing the Spanish Government in the back', and so forth. The issue was not quite so simple as that. Undoubtedly when you are at war with a deadly enemy it is better not to begin fighting among yourselves; but it is worth remembering that it takes two to make a quarrel and that people do not begin building barricades unless they have received something that they regard as a provocation.

The trouble sprang naturally out of the Government's order to the Anarchists to surrender their arms. In the English press this was translated into English terms and took this form: that arms were desperately needed on the Aragon front and could not be sent there because the unpatriotic Anarchists were holding them back. To put it like this is to ignore the conditions actually existing in Spain. Everyone knew that both the Anarchists and the P.S.U.C. were hoarding arms, and when the fighting broke out in Barcelona this was made clearer still; both sides produced arms in abundance. The Anarchists were well aware that even if they surrendered their arms, the P.S.U.C., politically the main power in Catalonia, would still retain theirs; and this in fact was what happened after the fighting was over. Meanwhile actually visible on the streets, there were quantities of arms which would have been very welcome at the front, but which were being retained for the 'non-political' police forces in the rear. And underneath this there was the irreconcilable difference between Communists and Anarchists, which was bound to lead to some kind of struggle sooner or later. Since the beginning of the war the Spanish Communist Party had grown enormously in numbers and captured most of the political power, and there had come into Spain thousands of foreign Communists, many of whom were openly expressing their intention of 'liquidating' Anarchism as soon as the war against Franco was won. In the circumstances one could hardly expect the Anarchists to hand over the weapons which they had got possession of in the summer of 1936.

The seizure of the Telephone Exchange was simply the match that fired an already existing bomb. It is perhaps just conceivable that those responsible imagined that it would not lead to trouble. Companys, the Catalan President, is said to have declared laughingly a few days earlier that the Anarchists would put up with anything.* But certainly it was not a wise action. For months past there had been a long series of armed clashes between Communists and Anarchists in various parts of Spain. Catalonia and especially Barcelona was in a state of tension that had already led to street affrays, assassinations, and so forth. Suddenly the news ran round the city that armed men were attacking the buildings that the workers had captured in the July fighting and to which they attached great sentimental importance. One must remember that the Civil Guards were not loved by the working-class population. For generations past *la guardia* had been simply an appendage of the landlord and the boss, and the Civil Guards were doubly hated because they were suspected, quite justly, of being of very doubtful loyalty against the Fascists.† It is probable that the emotion that brought people into the streets in the first few hours was much the same emotion as had led them to resist the rebel generals at the beginning of the war. Of course it is arguable that the C.N.T. workers ought to have handed over the Telephone Exchange without protest. One's opinion here will be governed by one's attitude on the question of centralized government and working-class control. More relevantly it may be said: 'Yes, very likely the C.N.T. had a case. But, after all, there was a war on, and they had no business to start a fight behind the lines.' Here I agree entirely. Any internal disorder was likely to aid Franco. But what actually precipitated the fighting? The Government may or may not have had the right to seize the Telephone Exchange; the point is that in the actual circumstances it was bound to lead to a fight. It was a provocative action, a gesture which said in effect, and presumably was meant to say: 'Your power is at an end – we are taking over.' It was not common sense to expect anything but resistance. If one keeps a sense of proportion one must realize that the fault was not – could not be, in a matter of this kind – entirely

* *New Statesman* (14 May).
† At the outbreak of war the Civil Guards had everywhere sided with the stronger party. On several occasions later in the war, e.g. at Santander, the local Civil Guards went over to the Fascists in a body.

on one side. The reason why a one-sided version has been accepted is simply that the Spanish revolutionary parties have no footing in the foreign press. In the English press, in particular, you would have to search for a long time before finding any favourable reference, at any period of the war, to the Spanish Anarchists. They have been systematically denigrated, and, as I know by my own experience, it is almost impossible to get anyone to print anything in their defence.

I have tried to write objectively about the Barcelona fighting, though, obviously, no one can be completely objective on a question of this kind. One is practically obliged to take sides, and it must be clear enough which side I am on. Again, I must inevitably have made mistakes of fact, not only here but in other parts of this narrative. It is very difficult to write accurately about the Spanish war, because of the lack of non-propagandist documents. I warn everyone against my bias, and I warn everyone against my mistakes. Still, I have done my best to be honest. But it will be seen that the account I have given is completely different from that which appeared in the foreign and especially the Communist press. It is necessary to examine the Communist version, because it was published all over the world, has been supplemented at short intervals ever since, and is probably the most widely accepted one.

In the Communist and pro-Communist press the entire blame for the Barcelona fighting was laid upon the P.O.U.M. The affair was represented not as a spontaneous outbreak, but as a deliberate, planned insurrection against the Government, engineered solely by the P.O.U.M. with the aid of a few misguided 'uncontrollables'. More than this, it was definitely a Fascist plot, carried out under Fascist orders with the idea of starting civil war in the rear and thus paralysing the Government. The P.O.U.M. was 'Franco's Fifth Column' – a 'Trotskyist' organization working in league with the Fascists. According to the *Daily Worker* (11 May):

The German and Italian agents, who poured into Barcelona ostensibly to 'prepare' the notorious 'Congress of the Fourth International', had one big task. It was this:

They were – in cooperation with the local Trotskyists – to prepare a situation of disorder and bloodshed, in which it would be possible for the Germans and Italians to declare that they were 'unable to exercise naval control of the Catalan coasts effectively because of the disorder prevailing in Barcelona' and were, therefore, 'unable to do otherwise than land forces in Barcelona'.

In other words, what was being prepared was a situation in which the German and Italian Governments could land troops or marines quite openly on the Catalan coasts, declaring that they were doing so 'in order to preserve order' . . .

The instrument for all this lay ready to hand for the Germans and Italians in the shape of the Trotskyist organization known as the P.O.U.M.

The P.O.U.M., acting in cooperation with well-known criminal elements, and with certain other deluded persons in the Anarchist organizations planned, organized, and led the attack in the rearguard, accurately timed to coincide with the attack on the front at Bilbao, etc., etc.

Later in the article the Barcelona fighting becomes 'the P.O.U.M. attack', and in another article in the same issue it is stated that there is 'no doubt that it is at the door of the P.O.U.M. that the responsibility for the bloodshed in Catalonia must be laid'. *Inprecor* (29 May) states that those who erected the barricades in Barcelona were 'only members of the P.O.U.M. organized from that party for this purpose'.

I could quote a great deal more, but this is clear enough. The P.O.U.M. was wholly responsible and the P.O.U.M. was acting under Fascist orders. In a moment I will give some more extracts from the accounts that appeared in the Communist press; it will be seen that they are so self-contradictory as to be completely worthless. But before doing so it is worth pointing to several *a priori* reasons why this version of the May fighting as a Fascist rising engineered by the P.O.U.M. is next door to incredible.

(i) The P.O.U.M. had not the numbers or influence to provoke disorders of this magnitude. Still less had it the power to call a general strike. It was a political organization with no very definite footing in the trade unions, and it would have been hardly more capable of producing a strike throughout Barcelona than (say) the English Communist Party would be of producing a general strike throughout Glasgow. As I said earlier, the attitude of the P.O.U.M. leaders may have helped to prolong the fighting to some extent; but they could not have originated it even if they had wanted to.

(ii) The alleged Fascist plot rests on bare assertion and all the evidence points in the other direction. We are told that the plan was for the German and Italian Governments to land troops in Catalonia; but no German or Italian troopships approached the coast. As to the 'Congress of the Fourth International' and the 'German and Italian agents', they are pure myth. So far as I know there had not even been any talk of a Congress of the Fourth International. There were vague plans for a Congress of the P.O.U.M. and its brother-parties (English I.L.P., German S.A.P., etc., etc.); this had been tentatively fixed for some time in July – two months later – and not a single delegate had yet arrived. The 'German and Italian agents' have no existence outside the pages of the *Daily Worker*. Anyone who crossed the frontier at that time knows that it was not so easy to 'pour' into Spain, or out of it, for that matter.

(iii) Nothing happened either at Lerida, the chief stronghold of the P.O.U.M., or at the front. It is obvious that if the P.O.U.M. leaders had wanted to aid the Fascists they would have ordered their militia to walk out of the line and let the Fascists through. But nothing of the kind was done or suggested. Nor were any extra men brought out of the line beforehand, though it would have been easy enough to smuggle, say, a thousand or two thousand men back to Barcelona on various pretexts. And there was no attempt even at indirect sabotage of the front. The transport of food, munitions, and so forth continued as usual; I verified this by inquiry afterwards. Above all, a planned rising of the kind suggested would have needed months of preparation, subversive propaganda among the militia, and so forth. But there was no sign or rumour of any such thing. The fact that the militia at the front played no part in the 'rising' should be conclusive. If the P.O.U.M. were really planning a *coup d'état* it is inconceivable that they would not have used the ten thousand or so armed men who were the only striking force they had.

It will be clear enough from this that the Communist thesis of a P.O.U.M. 'rising' under Fascist orders rests on less than no evidence. I will add a few more extracts from the Communist press. The Communist accounts of the opening incident, the raid on the Telephone Exchange, are illuminating; they agree in nothing except in putting the blame on the other side. It is noticeable that in the English Communist papers the blame is put first upon the Anarchists and only later upon the P.O.U.M. There is a fairly obvious reason for this. Not everyone in England has heard of 'Trotskyism', whereas every English-speaking person shudders at the name of 'Anarchist'. Let it once be known that 'Anarchists' are implicated, and the right atmosphere of prejudice is established; after that the blame can safely be transferred to the 'Trotskyists'. The *Daily Worker* begins thus (6 May):

A minority gang of Anarchists on Monday and Tuesday seized and attempted to hold the telephone and telegram buildings, and started firing into the street.

There is nothing like starting off with a reversal of roles. The Civil Guards attack a building held by the C.N.T.; so the C.N.T. are represented as attacking their own building – attacking themselves, in fact. On the other hand, the *Daily Worker* of 11 May states:

The Left Catalan Minister of Public Security, Aiguade, and the United Socialist General Commissar of Public Order, Rodrigue Salas, sent the armed republican police into the Telefónica building to disarm the employees there, most of them members of C.N.T. unions.

This does not seem to agree very well with the first statement; nevertheless the *Daily Worker* contains no admission that the first statement was wrong. The *Daily Worker* of 11 May states that the leaflets of the Friends of Durruti, which were disowned by the C.N.T., appeared on 4 May and 5 May, during the fighting. *Inprecor* (22 May) states that they appeared on 3 May, *before* the fighting, and adds that 'in view of these facts' (the appearance of various leaflets):

The police, led by the Prefect of Police in person, occupied the central telephone exchange in the afternoon of 3 May. The police were shot at while discharging their duty. This was the signal for the provocateurs to begin shooting affrays all over the city.

And here is *Inprecor* for 29 May:

At three o'clock in the afternoon the Commissar for Public Security, Comrade Salas, went to the Telephone Exchange, which on the previous night had been occupied by 50 members of the P.O.U.M. and various uncontrollable elements.

This seems rather curious. The occupation of the Telephone Exchange by 50 P.O.U.M. members is what one might call a picturesque circumstance, and one would have expected somebody to notice it at the time. Yet it appears that it was discovered only three or four weeks later. In another issue of *Inprecor* the 50 P.O.U.M. members become 50 P.O.U.M. militiamen. It would be difficult to pack together more contradictions than are contained in these few short passages. At one moment the C.N.T. are attacking the Telephone Exchange, the next they are being attacked there; a leaflet appears before the seizure of the Telephone Exchange and is the cause of it, or, alternatively, appears afterwards and is the result of it; the people in the Telephone Exchange are alternatively C.N.T. members and P.O.U.M. members – and so on. And in a still later issue of the *Daily Worker* (3 June) Mr J. R. Campbell informs us that the Government only seized the Telephone Exchange because the barricades were already erected!

For reasons of space I have taken only the reports of one incident, but the same discrepancies run all through the accounts in the Communist press. In addition there are various statements which are obviously pure fabrication. Here for instance is something quoted by the *Daily Worker* (7 May) and said to have been issued by the Spanish Embassy in Paris:

A significant feature of the uprising has been that the old monarchist flag was flown from the balcony of various houses in Barcelona, doubtless in the belief that those who took part in the rising had become masters of the situation.

The *Daily Worker* very probably reprinted this statement in good faith, but those responsible for it at the Spanish Embassy must have been quite deliberately lying. Any Spaniard would understand the internal situation better than that. A monarchist flag in Barcelona! It was the one thing that could have united the warring factions in a moment. Even the Communists on the spot were obliged to smile when they read about it. It is the same with the reports in the various Communist papers upon the arms supposed to have been used by the P.O.U.M. during the 'rising'. They would be credible only if one knew nothing whatever of the facts. In the *Daily Worker* of 17 May Mr Frank Pitcairn states:

> There were actually all sorts of arms used by them in the outrage. There were the arms which they have been stealing for months past, and hidden, and there were arms such as tanks, which they stole from the barracks just at the beginning of the rising. It is clear that scores of machine-guns and several thousand rifles are still in their possession.

Inprecor (29 May) also states:

> On 3 May the P.O.U.M. had at its disposal some dozens of machine-guns and several thousand rifles ... On the Plaza de España the Trotskyists brought into action batteries of '75' guns which were destined for the front in Aragon and which the militia had carefully concealed on their premises.

Mr Pitcairn does not tell us how and when it became clear that the P.O.U.M. possessed scores of machine-guns and several thousand rifles. I have given an estimate of the arms which were at three of the principal P.O.U.M. buildings – about eighty rifles, a few bombs, and no machine-guns; i.e. about sufficient for the armed guards which, at that time, all the political parties placed on their buildings. It seems strange that afterwards, when the P.O.U.M. was suppressed and all its buildings seized, these thousands of weapons never came to light; especially the tanks and field-guns, which are not the kind of thing that can be hidden up the chimney. But what is revealing in the two statements above is the complete ignorance they display of the local circumstances. According to Mr Pitcairn the P.O.U.M. stole tanks 'from the barracks'. He does not tell us which barracks. The P.O.U.M. militiamen who were in Barcelona (now comparatively few, as direct recruitment to the party militias had ceased) shared the Lenin Barracks with a considerably larger number of Popular Army troops. Mr Pitcairn is asking us to believe, therefore, that the P.O.U.M. stole tanks with the connivance of the Popular Army. It is the same with the 'premises' on which the 75-mm. guns were concealed. There is no mention of where these 'premises' were. Those batteries of guns, firing on the Plaza de España, appeared in many newspaper reports, but I think we can say with certainty that they never existed. As I mentioned earlier, I heard no artillery-fire during the fighting, though the Plaza de

España was only a mile or so away. A few days later I examined the Plaza de España and could find no buildings that showed marks of shell-fire. And an eye-witness who was in that neighbourhood throughout the fighting declares that no guns ever appeared there. (Incidentally, the tale of the stolen guns may have originated with Antonov-Ovseenko, the Russian Consul-General. He, at any rate, communicated it to a well-known English journalist, who afterwards repeated it in good faith in a weekly paper. Antonov-Ovseenko has since been 'purged'. How this would affect his credibility I do not know.) The truth is, of course, that these tales about tanks, field-guns, and so forth have only been invented because otherwise it is difficult to reconcile the scale of the Barcelona fighting with the P.O.U.M.'s small numbers. It was necessary to claim that the P.O.U.M. was wholly responsible for the fighting; it was also necessary to claim that it was an insignificant party with no following and 'numbered only a few thousand members', according to *Inprecor*. The only hope of making both statements credible was to pretend that the P.O.U.M. had all the weapons of a modern mechanized army.

It is impossible to read through the reports in the Communist Press without realizing that they are consciously aimed at a public ignorant of the facts and have no other purpose than to work up prejudice. Hence, for instance, such statements as Mr Pitcairn's in the *Daily Worker* of 11 May that the 'rising' was suppressed by the Popular Army. The idea here is to give outsiders the impression that all Catalonia was solid against the 'Trotskyists'. But the Popular Army remained neutral throughout the fighting; everyone in Barcelona knew this, and it is difficult to believe that Mr Pitcairn did not know it too. Or again, the juggling in the Communist Press with the figures for killed and wounded, with the object of exaggerating the scale of the disorders. Díaz, General Secretary of the Spanish Communist Party, widely quoted in the Communist Press, gave the numbers as 900 dead and 2500 wounded. The Catalan Minister of Propaganda, who was hardly likely to under-estimate, gave the numbers as 400 killed and 1000 wounded. The Communist Party doubles the bid and adds a few more hundreds for luck.

The foreign capitalist newspapers, in general, laid the blame for the fighting upon the Anarchists, but there were a few that followed the Communist line. One of these was the English *News Chronicle*, whose correspondent, Mr John Langdon-Davies, was in Barcelona at the time. I quote portions of his article here:

A TROTSKYIST REVOLT

... This has not been an Anarchist uprising. It is a frustrated *putsch* of the 'Trotskyist' P.O.U.M., working through their controlled organizations, 'Friends of Durruti' and Libertarian Youth . . . The tragedy began on Monday afternoon when the Government sent armed police into the Telephone Building, to disarm the workers there, mostly C.N.T. men. Grave irregularities in the service had been a scandal for some time. A large crowd gathered in the Plaza de Cataluña outside, while the C.N.T. men resisted, retreating floor by floor to the top of the building . . . The incident was very obscure, but word went round that the Government was out against the Anarchists. The streets filled with armed men . . . By nightfall every workers' centre and Government building was barricaded, and at ten o'clock the first volleys were fired and the first ambulances began ringing their way through the streets. By dawn all Barcelona was under fire . . . As the day wore on and the dead mounted to over a hundred, one could make a guess at what was happening. The Anarchist C.N.T. and Socialist U.G.T. were not technically 'out in the street'. So long as they remained behind the barricades they were merely watchfully waiting, an attitude which included the right to shoot at anything armed in the open street . . . (the) general bursts were invariably aggravated by *pacos* – hidden solitary men, usually Fascists, shooting from roof-tops at nothing in particular, but doing all they could to add to the general panic . . . By Wednesday evening, however, it began to be clear who was behind the revolt. All the walls had been plastered with an inflammatory poster calling for an immediate revolution and for the shooting of Republican and Socialist leaders. It was signed by the 'Friends of Durruti'. On Thursday morning the Anarchists daily denied all knowledge or sympathy with it, but *La Batalla*, the P.O.U.M. paper, reprinted the document with the highest praise. Barcelona, the first city of Spain, was plunged into bloodshed by *agents provocateurs* using this subversive organization.

This does not agree very completely with the Communist versions I have quoted above, but it will be seen that even as it stands it is self-contradictory. First the affair is described as 'a Trotskyist revolt', then it is shown to have resulted from a raid on the Telephone building and the general belief that the Government was 'out against' the Anarchists. The city is barricaded and both C.N.T. and U.G.T. are behind the barricades; two days afterwards the inflammatory poster (actually a leaflet) appears, and this is declared by implication to have started the whole business – effect preceding cause. But there is a piece of very serious misrepresentation here. Mr Langdon-Davies describes the Friends of Durruti and Libertarian Youth as 'controlled organizations' of the P.O.U.M. Both were Anarchist organizations and had no connection with the P.O.U.M. The Libertarian Youth was the youth league of the Anarchists, corresponding to the J.S.U. of the P.S.U.C., etc. The Friends of Durruti was a small organization within the F.A.I., and was in general bitterly hostile to the P.O.U.M. So far as I can discover, there was no one who was a member of both. It would be about equally true to say that the Socialist League is a 'controlled organization' of the English Liberal Party. Was Mr

Langdon-Davies unaware of this? If he was, he should have written with more caution about this very complex subject.

I am not attacking Mr Langdon-Davies's good faith; but admittedly he left Barcelona as soon as the fighting was over, i.e. at the moment when he could have begun serious inquiries, and throughout his report there are clear signs that he has accepted the official version of a 'Trotskyist revolt' without sufficient verification. This is obvious even in the extract I have quoted. 'By nightfall' the barricades are built, and 'at ten o'clock' the first volleys are fired. These are not the words of an eye-witness. From this you would gather that it is usual to wait for your enemy to build a barricade before beginning to shoot at him. The impression given is that some hours elapsed between the building of the barricades and the firing of the first volleys; whereas – naturally – it was the other way about. I and many others saw the first volleys fired early in the afternoon. Again, there are the solitary men, 'usually Fascists', who are shooting from the roof-tops. Mr Langdon-Davies does not explain how he knew that these men were Fascists. Presumably he did not climb on to the roofs and ask them. He is simply repeating what he has been told and, as it fits in with the official version, is not questioning it. As a matter of fact, he indicates one probable source of much of his information by an incautious reference to the Minister of Propaganda at the beginning of his article. Foreign journalists in Spain were hopelessly at the mercy of the Ministry of Propaganda, though one would think that the very name of this ministry would be a sufficient warning. The Minister of Propaganda was, of course, about as likely to give an objective account of the Barcelona trouble as (say) the late Lord Carson would have been to give an objective account of the Dublin rising of 1916.

I have given reasons for thinking that the Communist version of the Barcelona fighting cannot be taken seriously. In addition I must say something about the general charge that the P.O.U.M. was a secret Fascist organization in the pay of Franco and Hitler.

This charge was repeated over and over in the Communist Press, especially from the beginning of 1937 onwards. It was part of the world-wide drive of the official Communist Party against 'Trotskyism', of which the P.O.U.M. was supposed to be representative in Spain. 'Trotskyism', according to *Frente Rojo* (the Valencia Communist paper) 'is not a political doctrine. Trotskyism is an official capitalist organization, a Fascist terrorist band occupied in crime and sabotage against the people.' The P.O.U.M. was a 'Trotskyist' organization in league with the Fascists and part of 'Franco's Fifth Column'. What was noticeable from the start was that no evidence was produced in support of this accusation; the thing was simply asserted with an air of authority. And the attack was made with the maximum of personal libel and with complete irresponsibility as to any effects it might have upon the war. Compared with the job of libelling the P.O.U.M., many Communist writers appear to have considered the betrayal of military secrets unimportant. In a February number of the *Daily Worker*, for instance, a writer (Winifred Bates) is allowed to state that the P.O.U.M. had only half as many troops on its section of the front as it pretended. This was not true, but presumably the writer believed it to be true. She and the *Daily Worker* were perfectly willing, therefore, to hand to the enemy one of the most important pieces of information that can be handed through the columns of a newspaper. In the *New Republic* Mr Ralph Bates stated that the P.O.U.M. troops were 'playing football with the Fascists in no man's land' at a time when, as a matter of fact, the P.O.U.M. troops were suffering heavy casualties and a number of my personal friends were killed and wounded. Again, there was the malignant cartoon which was widely circulated, first in Madrid and later in Barcelona, representing the P.O.U.M. as slipping off a mask marked with the hammer and sickle and revealing a face marked with the swastika. Had the Government not been virtually under Communist control it would never have permitted a thing of this kind to be circulated in wartime. It was a deliberate blow at the morale not only of the P.O.U.M. militia, but of any others who happened to be near them; for it is not encouraging to be told that the troops next to you in the line are traitors. As a matter of fact, I doubt whether the abuse that was heaped upon them from the rear actually had the effect of demoralizing the P.O.U.M. militia. But certainly it was calculated to do so, and those responsible for it must be held to have put political spite before anti-Fascist unity.

The accusation against the P.O.U.M. amounted to this: that a body of some scores of thousands of people, almost entirely working class, besides numerous foreign helpers and sympathizers, mostly refugees from Fascist countries, and thousands of militia, was simply a vast spying organization in Fascist pay. The thing was opposed to common sense, and the past history of the P.O.U.M. was enough to make it incredible. All the P.O.U.M. leaders had revolutionary histories behind them. Some of them had been mixed up in the 1934 revolt, and most of them had been imprisoned for Socialist activities under the Lerroux Government or the monarchy. In 1936 its then leader, Joaquín Maurín, was one of the deputies who gave warning in the Cortes of Franco's impending revolt. Some time after the outbreak of war he was taken prisoner by the Fascists while trying to organize resistance in Franco's rear. When the revolt broke out the P.O.U.M. played a conspicuous part in resisting it, and in Madrid, in particular, many of its members were killed in the street-fighting. It was one of the the first bodies to form columns of militia in Catalonia and Madrid. It seems almost impossible to explain these as the actions of a party in Fascist pay. A party in Fascist pay would simply have joined in on the other side.

Nor was there any sign of pro-Fascist activities during the war. It was arguable – though finally I do not agree – that by pressing for a more revolutionary policy the P.O.U.M. divided the Government forces and thus aided the Fascists; I think any Government of reformist type would be justified in regarding a party like the P.O.U.M. as a nuisance. But this is a very different matter from direct treachery. There is no way of explaining why, if the P.O.U.M. was really a Fascist body, its militia remained loyal. Here were eight or ten thousand men holding important parts of the line during the intolerable conditions of the winter of 1936–7. Many of them were in the trenches four or five months at a stretch. It is difficult to see why they did not simply walk out of the line or go over to the enemy. It was always in their power to do so, and at times the effect might have been decisive. Yet they continued to fight, and it was shortly after the P.O.U.M. was suppressed as a political party, when the event was fresh in everyone's mind, that the militia – not yet redistributed among the Popular Army – took part in the murderous attack to the east of Huesca when several thousand men were killed in one or two days. At the very least one would have expected fraternization with the enemy and a constant trickle of deserters. But, as I have pointed out earlier, the number of desertions was exceptionally small. Again, one would have expected pro-Fascist propaganda, 'defeatism', and so forth. Yet there was no sign of any such thing. Obviously there must have been Fascist spies and *agents provocateurs* in the P.O.U.M.; they exist in all Left-wing parties; but there is no evidence that there were more of them there than elsewhere.

It is true that some of the attacks in the Communist Press said, rather grudgingly, that only the P.O.U.M. leaders were in Fascist pay, and not the rank and file. But this was merely an attempt to detach the rank and file from their leaders. The nature of the accusation implied that ordinary members, militiamen, and so forth, were all in the plot together; for it was obvious that if Nin, Gorkin, and the others were really in Fascist pay, it was more likely to be known to their followers, who were in contact with them, than to journalists in London, Paris, and New York. And in any case, when the P.O.U.M. was suppressed the Communist-controlled secret police acted on the assumption that all were guilty alike, and arrested everyone connected with the P.O.U.M. whom they could lay hands on, including even wounded men, hospital nurses, wives of P.O.U.M. members, and in some cases, even children.

Finally, on 15–16 June, the P.O.U.M. was suppressed and declared an illegal organization. This was one of the first acts of the Negrín Government which came into office in May. When the Executive Committee of the P.O.U.M. had been thrown into jail, the Communist Press produced what purported to be the discovery of an enormous Fascist plot. For a while the Communist Press of the whole world was flaming with this kind of thing (*Daily Worker*, 21 June, summarizing various Spanish Communist papers):

SPANISH TROTSKYISTS PLOT WITH FRANCO

Following the arrest of a large number of leading Trotskyists in Barcelona and elsewhere . . . there became known, over the weekend, details of one of the most ghastly pieces of espionage ever known in wartime, and the ugliest revelation of Trotskyist treachery to date . . . Documents in the possession of the police, together with the full confession of no less than 200 persons under arrest, prove, etc. etc.

What these revelations 'proved' was that the P.O.U.M. leaders were transmitting military secrets to General Franco by radio, were in touch with Berlin, and were acting in collaboration with the secret Fascist organization in Madrid. In addition there were sensational details about secret messages in invisible ink, a mysterious document signed with the letter N. (standing for Nin), and so on and so forth.

But the final upshot was this: six months after the event, as I write, most of the P.O.U.M. leaders are still in jail, but they have never been brought to trial, and the charges of communicating with Franco by radio, etc., have never even been formulated. Had they really been guilty of espionage they would have been tried and shot in a week, as so many Fascist spies had been previously. But not a scrap of evidence was ever produced except the unsupported statements in the Communist Press. As for the two hundred 'full confessions', which, if they had existed, would have been enough to convict anybody, they have never been heard of again. They were, in fact, two hundred efforts of somebody's imagination.

More than this, most of the members of the Spanish Government have disclaimed all belief in the charges against the P.O.U.M. Recently the cabinet decided by five to two in favour of releasing anti-Fascist political prisoners; the two dissentients being the Communist ministers. In August an international delegation headed by James Maxton M.P., went to Spain to inquire into the charges against the P.O.U.M. and the disappearance of Andrés Nin. Prieto, the Minister of National Defence, Irujo, the Minister of Justice, Zugazagoitia, Minister of the Interior, Ortega y Gasset, the Procureur-General, Prat Garcia, and others all repudiated any belief in the P.O.U.M. leaders being guilty of espionage. Irujo added that he had been through the dossier of the case, that none of the so-called pieces of evidence would bear examination, and that the document supposed to have been signed by Nin was 'valueless' – i.e. a forgery. Prieto considered the P.O.U.M. leaders to be responsible for the May fighting in Barcelona, but dismissed the idea of their being Fascist spies. 'What is most grave,' he added, 'is that the arrest of the P.O.U.M. leaders was not decided upon by the Government, and the police carried out these arrests on their own authority. Those responsible are not the heads of the police, but their entourage, which has been infiltrated by the Communists according to their usual custom.' He cited other cases of illegal arrests by the police. Irujo likewise declared that the police had become 'quasi-independent' and were in reality under the control of foreign Communist elements. Prieto hinted fairly broadly to the delegation that the Government could not afford to offend the Communist Party while the Russians were supplying arms. When another delegation, headed by John McGovern M.P., went to Spain in December, they got much the same answers as before, and Zugazagoitia, the Minister of the Interior, repeated Prieto's hint in even plainer terms. 'We have received aid from Russia and have had to permit certain actions which we did not like.' As an illustration of the autonomy of the police, it is interesting to learn that even with a signed order from the Director of Prisons and the Minister of Justice, McGovern and the others could not obtain admission to one of the 'secret prisons' maintained by the Communist Party in Barcelona.*

I think this should be enough to make the matter clear. The accusation of espionage against the P.O.U.M. rested solely upon articles in the Communist press and the activities of the Communist-controlled secret police. The P.O.U.M. leaders, and hundreds or thousands of their followers, are still in prison, and for six months past the Communist press has continued to clamour for the execution of the 'traitors'. But Negrín and the others have kept their heads and refused to stage a wholesale massacre of 'Trotskyists'. Considering the pressure that has been put upon them, it is greatly to their credit that they have done so. Meanwhile, in face of what I have quoted above, it becomes very difficult to believe that the P.O.U.M. was really a Fascist spying organization, unless one also believes that Maxton, McGovern, Prieto, Irujo, Zugazagoitia, and the rest are all in Fascist pay together.

Finally, as to the charge that the P.O.U.M. was 'Trotskyist'. This word is now flung about with greater and greater freedom, and it is used in a way that is extremely misleading and is often intended to mislead. It is worth

---

* For reports on the two delegations see *Le Populaire* (7 September), *La Flèche* (18 September), Report on the Maxton delegation published by *Independent News* (219 Rue Saint-Denis, Paris), and McGovern's pamphlet *Terror in Spain*.

stopping to define it. The word Trotskyist is used to mean three distinct things:

(i) One who, like Trotsky, advocates 'world revolution' as against 'Socialism in a single country'. More loosely, a revolutionary extremist.

(ii) A member of the actual organization of which Trotsky is head.

(iii) A disguised Fascist posing as a revolutionary who acts especially by sabotage in the U.S.S.R., but, in general, by splitting and undermining the Left-wing forces.

In sense (i) the P.O.U.M. could probably be described as Trotskyist. So can the English I.L.P., the German S.A.P., the Left Socialists in France, and so on. But the P.O.U.M. had no connection with Trotsky or the Trotskyist ('Bolshevik-Leninist') organization. When the war broke out the foreign Trotskyists who came to Spain (fifteen or twenty in number) worked at first for the P.O.U.M., as the party nearest to their own viewpoint, but without becoming party-members; later Trotsky ordered his followers to attack the P.O.U.M. policy, and the Trotskyists were purged from the party offices, though a few remained in the militia. Nin, the P.O.U.M. leader after Maurin's capture by the Fascists, was at one time Trotsky's secretary, but had left him some years earlier and formed the P.O.U.M. by the amalgamation of various Opposition Communists with an earlier party, the Workers' and Peasants' Bloc. Nin's one-time association with Trotsky has been used in the Communist press to show that the P.O.U.M. was really Trotskyist. By the same line of argument it could be shown that the English Communist Party is really a Fascist organization, because of Mr John Strachey's one-time association with Sir Oswald Mosley.

In sense (ii), the only exactly defined sense of the word, the P.O.U.M. was certainly not Trotskyist. It is important to make this distinction, because it is taken for granted by the majority of Communists that a Trotskyist in sense (ii) is invariably a Trotskyist in sense (iii) – i.e. that the whole Trotskyist organization is simply a Fascist spying-machine. 'Trotskyism' only came into public notice in the time of the Russian sabotage trials, and to call a man a Trotskyist is practically equivalent to calling him a murderer, *agent provocateur*, etc. But at the same time anyone who criticizes Communist policy from a Left-wing standpoint is liable to be denounced as a Trotskyist. Is it then asserted that everyone professing revolutionary extremism is in Fascist pay?

In practice it is or is not, according to local convenience. When Maxton went to Spain with the delegation I have mentioned above, *Verdad, Frente Rojo*, and other Spanish Communist papers instantly denounced him as a

'Trotsky-Fascist', spy of the Gestapo, and so forth. Yet the English Communists were careful not to repeat this accusation. In the English Communist press Maxton becomes merely a 'reactionary enemy of the working class', which is conveniently vague. The reason, of course, is simply that several sharp lessons have given the English Communist press a wholesome dread of the law of libel. The fact that the accusation was not repeated in a country where it might have to be proved is sufficient confession that it is a lie.

It may seem that I have discussed the accusations against the P.O.U.M. at greater length than was necessary. Compared with the huge miseries of a civil war, this kind of internecine squabble between parties, with its inevitable injustices and false accusations, may appear trivial. It is not really so. I believe that libels and press-campaigns of this kind, and the habits of mind they indicate, are capable of doing the most deadly damage to the anti-Fascist cause.

Anyone who has given the subject a glance knows that the Communist tactic of dealing with political opponents by means of trumped-up accusations is nothing new. Today the key-word is 'Trotsky-Fascist'; yesterday it was 'Social-Fascist'. It is only six or seven years since the Russian State trials 'proved' that the leaders of the Second International, including, for instance, Léon Blum and prominent members of the British Labour Party, were hatching a huge plot for the military invasion of the U.S.S.R. Yet today the French Communists are glad enough to accept Blum as a leader, and the English Communists are raising heaven and earth to get inside the Labour Party. I doubt whether this kind of thing pays, even from a sectarian point of view. And meanwhile there is no possible doubt about the hatred and dissension that the 'Trotsky-Fascist' accusation is causing. Rank-and-file Communists everywhere are led away on a senseless witch-hunt after 'Trotskyists', and parties of the type of the P.O.U.M. are driven back into the terribly sterile position of being mere anti-Communist parties. There is already the beginning of a dangerous split in the world working-class movement. A few more libels against life-long Socialists, a few more frame-ups like the charges against the P.O.U.M., and the split may become irreconcilable. The only hope is to keep political controversy on a plane where exhaustive discussion is possible. Between the Communists and those who stand or claim to stand to the Left of them there is a real difference. The Communists hold that Fascism can be beaten by alliance with sections of the capitalist class (the Popular Front); their opponents hold that this manoeuvre simply gives Fascism new breeding-grounds. The question has got to be settled; to make the wrong decision may be to land ourselves in for centuries of semi-slavery. But so long as no argument is produced except a scream of 'Trotsky-Fascist!' the discussion cannot even begin. It would be impossible for me, for instance, to debate the rights and wrongs of the Barcelona fighting with a Communist Party member, because no Communist – that is to say, no 'good' Communist – could admit that I have given a truthful account of the facts. If he followed his party 'line' dutifully he would have to declare that I am lying or, at best, that I am hopelessly misled and that anyone who glanced at the *Daily Worker* headlines a thousand miles from the scene of events knows more of what was happening in Barcelona than I do. In such circumstances there can be no argument; the necessary minimum of agreement cannot be reached. What purpose is served by saying that men like Maxton are in Fascist pay? Only the purpose of making serious discussion impossible. It is as though in the middle of a chess tournament one competitor should suddenly begin screaming that the other is guilty of arson or bigamy. The point that is really at issue remains untouched. Libel settles nothing.

12

IT must have been three days after the Barcelona fighting ended that we returned to the front. After the fighting – more particularly after the slanging-match in the newspapers – it was difficult to think about this war in quite the same naively idealistic manner as before. I suppose there is no one who spent more than a few weeks in Spain without being in some degree disillusioned. My mind went back to the newspaper correspondent whom I had met my first day in Barcelona, and who said to me: 'This war is a racket the same as any other.' The remark had shocked me deeply, and at that time (December) I do not believe it was true; it was not true even now, in May; but it was becoming truer. The fact is that every war suffers a kind of progressive degradation with every month that it continues, because such things as individual liberty and a truthful press are simply not compatible with military efficiency.

One could begin now to make some kind of guess at what was likely to happen. It was easy to see that the Caballero Government would fall and be replaced by a more Right-wing Government with a stronger Communist influence (this happened a week or two later), which would set itself to break the power of the trade unions once and for all. And afterwards, when Franco was beaten – and putting aside the huge problems raised by the reorganization of Spain – the prospect was not rosy. As for the newspaper talk about this being a 'war for democracy', it was plain eyewash. No one in his senses supposed that there was any hope of democracy, even as we understand it in England or France, in a country so divided and exhausted as Spain would be when the war was over. It would have to be a dictatorship, and it was clear that the chance of a working-class dictatorship had passed. That meant that the general movement would be in the direction of some kind of Fascism. Fascism called, no doubt, by some politer name, and – because this was Spain – more human and less efficient than the German or Italian varieties. The only alternatives were an infinitely worse dictatorship by Franco, or (always a possibility) that the war would end with Spain divided up, either by actual frontiers or into economic zones.

Whichever way you took it it was a depressing outlook. But it did not follow that the Government was not worth fighting for as against the more naked and developed Fascism of Franco and Hitler. Whatever faults the post-war Government might have, Franco's régime would certainly be worse. To the workers – the town proletariat – it might in the end make very little difference who won, but Spain is primarily an agricultural country and the peasants would almost certainly benefit by a Government victory. Some at least of the seized lands would remain in their possession, in which case there would also be a distribution of land in the territory that had been Franco's, and the virtual serfdom that had existed in some parts of Spain was not likely to be restored. The Government in control at the end of the war would at any rate be anti-clerical and anti-feudal. It would keep the Church in check, at least for the time being, and would modernize the country – build roads, for instance, and promote education and public health; a certain amount had been done in this direction even during the war. Franco, on the other hand, in so far as he was not merely the puppet of Italy and Germany, was tied to the big feudal landlords and stood for a stuffy clerico-military reaction. The Popular Front might be a swindle, but Franco was an anachronism. Only millionaires or romantics could want him to win.

Moreover, there was the question of the international prestige of Fascism, which for a year or two past had been haunting me like a nightmare. Since 1930 the Fascists had won all the victories; it was time they got a beating, it hardly mattered from whom. If we could drive Franco and his foreign mercenaries into the sea it might make an immense improvement in the world situation, even if Spain itself emerged with a stifling dictatorship and all its best men in jail. For that alone the war would have been worth winning.

This was how I saw things at the time. I may say that I now think much more highly of the Negrín Government than I did when it came into office. It has kept up the difficult fight with splendid courage, and it has shown more political tolerance than anyone expected. But I still believe that – unless Spain splits up, with unpredictable consequences – the tendency of the post-war Government is bound to be Fascistic. Once again I let this opinion stand, and take the chance that time will do to me what it does to most prophets.

We had just reached the front when we heard that Bob Smillie, on his way back to England, had been arrested at the frontier, taken down to Valencia, and thrown into jail. Smillie had been in Spain since the previous October. He had worked for several months at the P.O.U.M. office and had then joined the militia when the other I.L.P. members arrived, on the understanding that he was to do three months at the front before going back to England to take part in a propaganda tour. It was some time before we could discover what he had been arrested for. He was being kept *incommunicado*, so that not even a lawyer could see him. In Spain there is – at any rate in practice – no habeas corpus, and you can be kept in jail for months at a stretch without even being charged, let alone tried. Finally we learned from a released prisoner that Smillie had been arrested for 'carrying arms'. The 'arms', as I happened to know, were two hand-grenades of the primitive type used at the beginning of the war, which he had been taking home to show off at his lectures, along with shell splinters and other souvenirs. The charges and fuses had been removed from them – they were mere cylinders of steel and completely harmless. It was obvious that this was only a pretext and that he had been arrested because of his known connection with the P.O.U.M. The Barcelona fighting had only just ended and the authorities were, at that moment, extremely anxious not to let anyone out of Spain who was in a position to contradict the official version. As a result people were liable to be arrested at the frontier on more or less frivolous pretexts. Very possibly the intention, at the beginning, was only to detain Smillie for a few days. But the trouble is that, in Spain, once you are in jail you generally stay there, with or without trial.

We were still at Huesca, but they had placed us further to the right, opposite the Fascist redoubt which we had temporarily captured a few weeks earlier. I was now acting as *teniente* – corresponding to second-lieutenant in the British Army, I suppose – in command of about thirty men, English and Spanish. They had sent my name in for a regular commission; whether I should get it was uncertain. Previously the militia officers had refused to accept regular commissions, which meant extra pay and conflicted with the equalitarian ideas of the militia, but they were now obliged to do so. Benjamin had already been gazetted captain and Kopp was in process of being gazetted major. The Government could not, of course, dispense with the militia officers, but it was not confirming any of them in a higher rank than major, presumably in order to keep the higher commands for Regular Army officers and the new officers from the School of War. As a result, in our division, the 29th, and no doubt in many others, you had the queer temporary situation of the divisional commander, the brigade commanders, and the battalion commanders all being majors.

There was not much happening at the front. The battle round the Jaca road had died away and did not begin again till mid June. In our position the chief trouble was the snipers. The Fascist trenches were more than a hundred and fifty yards away, but they were on higher ground and were on two sides of us, our line forming a right-angle salient. The corner of the salient was a dangerous spot; there had always been a toll of sniper casualties there. From time to time the Fascists let fly at us with a rifle-grenade or some similar weapon. It made a ghastly crash – unnerving, because you could not hear it coming in time to dodge – but was not really dangerous; the hole it blew in the ground was no bigger than a wash-tub. The nights were pleasantly warm, the days blazing hot, the mosquitoes were becoming a nuisance, and in spite of the clean clothes we had brought from Barcelona we were almost immediately lousy. Out in the deserted orchards in no man's land the cherries were whitening on the trees. For two days there were torrential rains, the dug-outs flooded, and the parapet sank a foot; after that there were more days of digging out the sticky clay with the wretched Spanish spades which have no handles and bend like tin spoons.

They had promised us a trench-mortar for the company; I was looking forward to it greatly. At nights we patrolled as usual – more dangerous than it used to be, because the Fascist trenches were better manned and they had grown more alert; they had scattered tin cans just outside their wire and used to open up with the machine-guns when they heard a clank. In the daytime we sniped from no man's land. By crawling a hundred yards you could get to a ditch, hidden by tall grasses, which commanded a gap in the Fascist parapet. We had set up a rifle-rest in the ditch. If you waited long enough you generally saw a khaki-clad figure slip hurriedly across the gap. I had several shots. I don't know whether I hit anyone –

it is most unlikely; I am a very poor shot with a rifle. But it was rather fun, the Fascists did not know where the shots were coming from, and I made sure I would get one of them sooner or later. However, the dog it was that died – a Fascist sniper got me instead. I had been about ten days at the front when it happened. The whole experience of being hit by a bullet is very interesting and I think it is worth describing in detail.

It was at the corner of the parapet, at five o'clock in the morning. This was always a dangerous time, because we had the dawn at our backs, and if you stuck your head above the parapet it was clearly outlined against the sky. I was talking to the sentries preparatory to changing the guard. Suddenly, in the very middle of saying something, I felt – it is very hard to describe what I felt, though I remember it with the utmost vividness.

Roughly speaking it was the sensation of being *at the centre* of an explosion. There seemed to be a loud bang and a blinding flash of light all round me, and I felt a tremendous shock – no pain, only a violent shock, such as you get from an electric terminal; with it a sense of utter weakness, a feeling of being stricken and shrivelled up to nothing. The sand-bags in front of me receded into immense distance. I fancy you would feel much the same if you were struck by lightning. I knew immediately that I was hit, but because of the seeming bang and flash I thought it was a rifle nearby that had gone off accidentally and shot me. All this happened in a space of time much less than a second. The next moment my knees crumpled up and I was falling, my head hitting the ground with a violent bang which, to my relief, did not hurt. I had a numb, dazed feeling, a consciousness of being very badly hurt, but no pain in the ordinary sense.

The American sentry I had been talking to had started forward. 'Gosh! Are you hit?' People gathered round. There was the usual fuss – 'Lift him up! Where's he hit? Get his shirt open!' etc., etc. The American called for a knife to cut my shirt open. I knew that there was one in my pocket and tried to get it out, but discovered that my right arm was paralysed. Not being in pain, I felt a vague satisfaction. This ought to please my wife, I thought; she had always wanted me to be wounded, which would save me from being killed when the great battle came. It was only now that it occurred to me to wonder where I was hit, and how badly; I could feel nothing, but I was conscious that the bullet had struck me somewhere in the front of the body. When I tried to speak I found that I had no voice, only a faint squeak, but at the second attempt I managed to ask where I was hit. In the throat, they said. Harry Webb, our stretcher-bearer, had brought a bandage and one of the little bottles of alcohol they gave us for field-dressings. As they lifted me up a lot of blood poured out of my mouth, and I heard a Spaniard behind me say that the bullet had gone clean through my neck. I felt the alcohol, which at ordinary times would sting like the devil, splash on to the wound as a pleasant coolness.

They laid me down again while somebody fetched a stretcher. As soon as I knew that the bullet had gone clean through my neck I took it for granted that I was done for. I had never heard of a man or an animal getting a bullet through the middle of the neck and surviving it. The blood was dribbling out of the corner of my mouth. 'The artery's gone,' I thought. I wondered how long you last when your carotid artery is cut; not many minutes, presumably. Everything was very blurry. There must have been about two minutes during which I assumed that I was killed. And that too was interesting – I mean it is interesting to know what your thoughts would be at such a time. My first thought, conventionally enough, was for my wife. My second was a violent resentment at having to leave this world which, when all is said and done, suits me so well. I had time to feel this very vividly. The stupid mischance infuriated me. The meaninglessness of it! To be bumped off, not even in battle, but in this stale corner of the trenches, thanks to a moment's carelessness! I thought, too, of the man who had shot me – wondered what he was like, whether he was a Spaniard or a foreigner, whether he knew he had got me, and so forth. I could not feel any resentment against him. I reflected that as he was a Fascist I would have killed him if I could, but that if he had been taken prisoner and brought before me at this moment I would merely have congratulated him on his good shooting. It may be, though, that if you were really dying your thoughts would be quite different.

They had just got me on to the stretcher when my paralysed right arm came to life and began hurting damnably. At the time I imagined that I must have broken it in falling; but the pain reassured me, for I knew that your sensations do not become more acute when you are dying. I began to feel more normal and to be sorry for the four poor devils who were sweating and slithering with the stretcher on their shoulders. It was a mile and a half to the ambulance, and vile going, over lumpy, slippery tracks. I knew what a sweat it was, having helped to carry a wounded man down a day or two earlier. The leaves of the silver poplars which, in places, fringed our trenches brushed against my face; I thought what a good thing it was to be alive in a world where silver poplars grow. But all the while the pain in my arm was diabolical, making me swear and then try not to swear, because every time I breathed too hard the blood bubbled out of my mouth.

The doctor re-bandaged the wound, gave me a shot of morphia, and sent me off to Sietamo. The hospitals at Sietamo were hurriedly constructed wooden huts where the wounded were, as a rule, only kept for a few hours before being sent on to Barbastro or Lerida. I was dopey from morphia but still in great pain, practically unable to move and swallowing blood constantly. It was typical of Spanish hospital methods that while I was in this state the untrained nurse tried to force the regulation hospital meal – a huge meal of soup, eggs, greasy stew, and so forth – down my throat and seemed surprised when I would not take it. I asked for a cigarette, but this was one of the periods of tobacco famine and there was not a cigarette in the place. Presently two comrades who had got permission to leave the line for a few hours appeared at my bedside.

'Hullo! You're alive, are you? Good. We want your watch and your revolver and your electric torch. And your knife, if you've got one.'

They made off with all my portable possessions. This always happened when a man was wounded – everything he possessed was promptly divided up; quite rightly, for watches, revolvers, and so forth were precious at the front and if they went down the line in a wounded man's kit they were certain to be stolen somewhere on the way.

By the evening enough sick and wounded had trickled in to make up a few ambulance-loads, and they sent us on to Barbastro. What a journey! It used to be said that in this war you got well if you were wounded in the extremities, but always died of a wound in the abdomen. I now realized why. No one who was liable to bleed internally could have survived those miles of jolting over metal roads that had been smashed to pieces by heavy lorries and never repaired since the war began. Bang, bump, wallop! It took me back to my early childhood and a dreadful thing called the Wiggle-Woggle at the White City Exhibition. They had forgotten to tie us into the stretchers. I had enough strength in my left arm to hang on, but one poor wretch was spilt on to the floor and suffered God knows what agonies. Another, a walking case who was sitting in the corner of the ambulance, vomited all over the place. The hospital in Barbastro was very crowded, the beds so close together that they were almost touching. Next morning they loaded a number of us on to the hospital train and sent us down to Lerida.

I was five or six days in Lerida. It was a big hospital, with sick, wounded, and ordinary civilian patients more or less jumbled up together. Some of the men in my ward had frightful wounds. In the next bed to me there was a youth with black hair who was suffering from some disease or other and was being given medicine that made his urine as green as emerald. His bed-bottle was one of the sights of the ward. An English-speaking

Dutch Communist, having heard that there was an Englishman in the hospital, befriended me and brought me English newspapers. He had been terribly wounded in the October fighting, and had somehow managed to settle down at Lerida hospital and had married one of the nurses. Thanks to his wound, one of his legs had shrivelled till it was no thicker than my arm. Two militiamen on leave, whom I had met my first week at the front, came in to see a wounded friend and recognized me. They were kids of about eighteen. They stood awkwardly beside my bed, trying to think of something to say, and then, as a way of demonstrating that they were sorry I was wounded, suddenly took all the tobacco out of their pockets, gave it to me, and fled before I could give it back. How typically Spanish! I discovered afterwards that you could not buy tobacco anywhere in the town and what they had given me was a week's ration.

After a few days I was able to get up and walk about with my arm in a sling. For some reason it hurt much more when it hung down. I also had, for the time being, a good deal of internal pain from the damage I had done myself in falling, and my voice had disappeared almost completely, but I never had a moment's pain from the bullet wound itself. It seems this is usually the case. The tremendous shock of a bullet prevents sensation locally; a splinter of shell or bomb, which is jagged and usually hits you less hard, would probably hurt like the devil. There was a pleasant garden in the hospital grounds, and in it was a pool with gold-fishes and some small dark grey fish – bleak, I think. I used to sit watching them for hours. The way things were done at Lerida gave me an insight into the hospital system on the Aragon front – whether it was the same on other fronts I do not know. In some ways the hospitals were very good. The doctors were able men and there seemed to be no shortage of drugs and equipment. But there were two bad faults on account of which, I have no doubt, hundreds or thousands of men have died who might have been saved.

One was the fact that all the hospitals anywhere near the front line were used more or less as casualty clearing-stations. The result was that you got no treatment there unless you were too badly wounded to be moved. In theory most of the wounded were sent straight to Barcelona or Tarragona, but owing to the lack of transport they were often a week or ten days in getting there. They were kept hanging about at Sietamo, Barbastro, Monzon, Lerida, and other places, and meanwhile they were getting no treatment except an occasional clean bandage, sometimes not even that. Men with dreadful shell wounds, smashed bones, and so forth, were swathed in a sort of casing made of bandages and plaster of Paris;

a description of the wound was written in pencil on the outside, and as a rule the casing was not removed till the man reached Barcelona or Tarragona ten days later. It was almost impossible to get one's wound examined on the way; the few doctors could not cope with the work, and they simply walked hurriedly past your bed, saying: 'Yes, yes, they'll attend to you at Barcelona.' There were always rumours that the hospital train was leaving for Barcelona *mañana*. The other fault was the lack of competent nurses. Apparently there was no supply of trained nurses in Spain, perhaps because before the war this work was done chiefly by nuns. I have no complaint against the Spanish nurses, they always treated me with the greatest kindness, but there is no doubt that they were terribly ignorant. All of them knew how to take a temperature, and some of them knew how to tie a bandage, but that was about all. The result was that men who were too ill to fend for themselves were often shamefully neglected. The nurses would let a man remain constipated for a week on end, and they seldom washed those who were too weak to wash themselves. I remember one poor devil with a smashed arm telling me that he had been three weeks without having his face washed. Even beds were left unmade for days together. The food in all the hospitals was very good – too good, indeed. Even more in Spain than elsewhere it seemed to be the tradition to stuff sick people with heavy food. At Lerida the meals were terrific. Breakfast, at about six in the morning, consisted of soup, an omelette, stew, bread, white wine, and coffee, and lunch was even larger – this at a time when most of the civil population was seriously underfed. Spaniards seem not to recognize such a thing as a light diet. They give the same food to sick people as to well ones – always the same rich, greasy cookery, with everything sodden in olive oil.

One morning it was announced that the men in my ward were to be sent down to Barcelona today. I managed to send a wire to my wife, telling her that I was coming, and presently they packed us into buses and took us down to the station. It was only when the train was actually starting that the hospital orderly who travelled with us casually let fall that we were not going to Barcelona after all, but to Tarragona. I suppose the engine-driver had changed his mind. 'Just like Spain!' I thought. But it was very Spanish, too, that they agreed to hold up the train while I sent another wire, and more Spanish still that the wire never got there.

They had put us into ordinary third-class carriages with wooden seats, and many of the men were badly wounded and had only got out of bed for the first time that morning. Before long, what with the heat and the jolting, half of them were in a state of collapse and several vomited on the floor. The hospital orderly threaded his way among the corpse-like forms that sprawled everywhere, carrying a large goatskin bottle full of water which he squirted into this mouth or that. It was beastly water; I remember the taste of it still. We got into Tarragona as the sun was getting low. The line runs along the shore a stone's throw from the sea. As our train drew into the station a troop-train full of men from the International Column was drawing out, and a knot of people on the bridge were waving to them. It was a very long train, packed to bursting-point with men, with field-guns lashed on the open trucks and more men clustering round the guns. I remember with peculiar vividness the spectacle of that train passing in the yellow evening light; window after window full of dark, smiling faces, the long tilted barrels of the guns, the scarlet scarves fluttering – all this gliding slowly past us against a turquoise-coloured sea.

'*Extranjeros* – foreigners,' said someone. 'They're Italians.'

Obviously they were Italians. No other people could have grouped themselves so picturesquely or returned the salutes of the crowd with so much grace – a grace that was none the less because about half the men on the train were drinking out of up-ended wine bottles. We heard afterwards that these were some of the troops who won the great victory at Guadalajara in March; they had been on leave and were being transferred to the Aragon front. Most of them, I am afraid, were killed at Huesca only a few weeks later. The men who were well enough to stand had moved across the carriage to cheer the Italians as they went past. A crutch waved out of the window; bandaged forearms made the Red Salute. It was like an allegorical picture of war; the trainload of fresh men gliding proudly up the line, the maimed men sliding slowly down, and all the while the guns on the open trucks making one's heart leap as guns always do, and reviving that pernicious feeling, so difficult to get rid of, that war *is* glorious after all.

The hospital at Tarragona was a very big one and full of wounded from all fronts. What wounds one saw there! They had a way of treating certain wounds which I suppose was in accordance with the latest medical practice, but which was peculiarly horrible to look at. This was to leave the wound completely open and unbandaged, but protected from flies by a net of butter-muslin, stretched over wires. Under the muslin you would see the red jelly of a half-healed wound. There was one man wounded in the face and throat who had his head inside a sort of spherical helmet of butter-muslin; his mouth was closed up and he breathed through a little tube that was fixed between his lips. Poor devil, he looked so lonely, wandering to and fro, looking at you through his muslin cage and unable to speak. I was three or four days at Tarragona. My strength was coming back, and one day, by going slowly, I managed to walk down as far as the beach. It was queer to see the seaside life going on almost as usual; the smart cafés along the promenade and the plump local bourgeoisie bathing and sunning themselves in deck-chairs as though there had not been a war within a thousand miles. Nevertheless, as it happened, I saw a bather drowned, which one would have thought impossible in that shallow and tepid sea.

Finally, eight or nine days after leaving the front, I had my wound examined. In the surgery where newly-arrived cases were examined, doctors with huge pairs of shears were hacking away the breast-plates of plaster in which men with smashed ribs, collar-bones, and so forth had been cased at the dressing-stations behind the line; out of the neck-hole of the huge clumsy breast-plate you would see protruding an anxious, dirty face, scrubby with a week's beard. The doctor, a brisk, handsome man of about thirty, sat me down in a chair, grasped my tongue with a piece of rough gauze, pulled it out as far as it would go, thrust a dentist's mirror down my throat, and told me to say 'Eh!' After doing this till my tongue was bleeding and my eyes running with water, he told me that one vocal cord was paralysed.

'When shall I get my voice back?' I said.

'Your voice? Oh, you'll never get your voice back,' he said cheerfully.

However, he was wrong, as it turned out. For about two months I could not speak much above a whisper, but after that my voice became normal rather suddenly, the other vocal cord having 'compensated'. The pain in my arm was due to the bullet having pierced a bunch of nerves at the back of the neck. It was a shooting pain like neuralgia, and it went on hurting continuously for about a month, especially at night, so that I did not get much sleep. The fingers of my right hand were also semi-paralysed. Even now, five months afterwards, my forefinger is still numb – a queer effect for a neck wound to have.

The wound was a curiosity in a small way and various doctors examined it with much clicking of tongues and '*Que suerte! Que suerte!*' One of them told me with an air of authority that the bullet had missed the artery by 'about a millimetre'. I don't know how he knew. No one I met at this time – doctors, nurses, *practicantes*, or fellow-patients – failed to assure me that a man who is hit through the neck and survives it is the luckiest creature alive. I could not help thinking that it would be even luckier not to be hit at all.

13

IN Barcelona, during all those last weeks I spent there, there was a peculiar evil feeling in the air – an atmosphere of suspicion, fear, uncertainty, and veiled hatred. The May fighting had left ineradicable after-effects behind it. With the fall of the Caballero Government the Communists had come definitely into power, the charge of internal order had been handed over to Communist ministers, and no one doubted that they would smash their political rivals as soon as they got a quarter of a chance. Nothing was happening as yet, I myself had not even any mental picture of what was going to happen; and yet there was a perpetual vague sense of danger, a consciousness of some evil thing that was impending. However little you were actually conspiring, the atmosphere forced you to feel like a conspirator. You seemed to spend all your time holding whispered conversations in corners of cafés and wondering whether that person at the next table was a police spy.

Sinister rumours of all kinds were flying round, thanks to the Press censorship. One was that the Negrín–Prieto Government was planning to compromise the war. At the time I was inclined to believe this, for the Fascists were closing in on Bilbao and the Government was visibly doing nothing to save it. Basque flags were displayed all over the town, girls rattled collecting-boxes in the cafés, and there were the usual broadcasts about 'heroic defenders', but the Basques were getting no real assistance. It was tempting to believe that the Government was playing a double game. Later events have proved that I was quite wrong here, but it seems probable that Bilbao could have been saved if a little more energy had been shown. An offensive on the Aragon front, even an unsuccessful one, would have forced Franco to divert part of his army; as it was the Government did not begin any offensive action till it was far too late – indeed, till about the time when Bilbao fell. The C.N.T. was distributing in huge numbers a leaflet saying: 'Be on your guard!' and hinting that 'a certain Party' (meaning the Communists) was plotting a *coup d'état*. There was also a widespread fear that Catalonia was going to be invaded. Earlier, when we went back to the front, I had seen the powerful defences that were being constructed scores of miles behind the front line, and fresh bomb-proof shelters were being dug all over Barcelona. There were frequent scares of air-raids and sea-raids; more often than not these were false alarms, but every time the sirens blew the lights all over the town blacked out for hours on end and timid people dived for the cellars. Police spies were everywhere. The jails were still crammed with prisoners left over from the May fighting, and others – always, of course, Anarchist and P.O.U.M. adherents – were disappearing into jail by ones and twos. So far as one could discover, no one was ever tried or even charged – not even charged with anything so definite as 'Trotskyism'; you were simply flung into jail and kept there, usually *incommunicado*. Bob Smillie was still in jail in Valencia. We could discover nothing except that neither the I.L.P. representative on the spot nor the lawyer who had been engaged was permitted to see him. Foreigners from the International Column and other militias were getting into jail in larger and larger numbers. Usually they were arrested as deserters. It was typical of the general situation that nobody now knew for certain whether a militiaman was a volunteer or a regular soldier. A few months earlier anyone enlisting in the militia had been told that he was a volunteer and could, if he wished, get his discharge papers at any time when he was due for leave. Now it appeared that the Government had changed its mind, a militiaman was a regular soldier and counted as a deserter if he tried to go home. But even about this no one seemed certain. At some parts of the front the authorities were still issuing discharges. At the frontier these were sometimes recognized, sometimes not; if not, you were promptly thrown into jail. Later the number of foreign 'deserters' in jail swelled into hundreds, but most of them were repatriated when a fuss was made in their own countries.

Bands of armed Assault Guards roamed everywhere in the streets, the Civil Guards were still holding cafés and other buildings in strategic spots, and many of the P.S.U.C. buildings were still sandbagged and barricaded. At various points in the town there were posts manned by Civil Guards or Carabineros who stopped passers-by and demanded their papers. Everyone warned me not to show my P.O.U.M. militiaman's card but merely to show my passport and my hospital ticket. Even to be known to have served in the P.O.U.M. militia was vaguely dangerous. P.O.U.M. militiamen who were wounded or on leave were penalized in petty ways – it was made difficult for them to draw their pay, for instance. *La Batalla* was still appearing, but it was censored almost out of existence, and *Solidaridad* and the other Anarchist papers were also heavily censored. There was a new rule that censored portions of a newspaper must not be left blank but filled up with

other matter; as a result it was often impossible to tell when something
had been cut out.

The food shortage, which had fluctuated throughout the war, was in
one of its bad stages. Bread was scarce and the cheaper sorts were being
adulterated with rice; the bread the soldiers were getting in the barracks
was dreadful stuff like putty. Milk and sugar were very scarce and tobacco
almost non-existent, except for the expensive smuggled cigarettes. There
was an acute shortage of olive oil, which Spaniards use for half a dozen
different purposes. The queues of women waiting to buy olive oil were
controlled by mounted Civil Guards who sometimes amused themselves
by backing their horses into the queue and trying to make them tread on
the women's toes. A minor annoyance of the time was the lack of small
change. The silver had been withdrawn and as yet no new coinage had
been issued, so that there was nothing between the ten-centime piece and
the note for two and a half pesetas, and all notes below ten pesetas were
very scarce.* For the poorest people this meant an aggravation of the food
shortage. A woman with only a ten-peseta note in her possession might
wait for hours in a queue outside the grocery and then be unable to buy
anything after all because the grocer had no change and she could not
afford to spend the whole note.

It is not easy to convey the nightmare atmosphere of that time – the
peculiar uneasiness produced by rumours that were always changing, by
censored newspapers, and the constant presence of armed men. It is not
easy to convey it because, at the moment, the thing essential to such an
atmosphere does not exist in England. In England political intolerance is
not yet taken for granted. There is political persecution in a petty way; if
I were a coal-miner I would not care to be known to the boss as
a Communist; but the 'good party man', the gangster-gramophone of
continental politics, is still a rarity, and the notion of 'liquidating' or
'eliminating' everyone who happens to disagree with you does not yet seem
natural. It seemed only too natural in Barcelona. The 'Stalinists' were in
the saddle, and therefore it was a matter of course that every 'Trotskyist'
was in danger. The thing everyone feared was a thing which, after all, did
not happen – a fresh outbreak of street-fighting, which, as before, would
be blamed on the P.O.U.M. and the Anarchists. There were times when I
caught my ears listening for the first shots. It was as though some huge
evil intelligence were brooding over the town. Everyone noticed it and
remarked upon it. And it was queer how everyone expressed it in almost

* The purchasing value of the peseta was about fourpence.

the same words: 'The atmosphere of this place – it's horrible. Like being in a lunatic asylum.' But perhaps I ought not to say *everyone*. Some of the English visitors who flitted briefly through Spain, from hotel to hotel, seem not to have noticed that there was anything wrong with the general atmosphere. The Duchess of Atholl writes, I notice (*Sunday Express*, 17 October 1937):

I was in Valencia, Madrid, and Barcelona . . . perfect order prevailed in all three towns without any display of force. All the hotels in which I stayed were not only 'normal' and 'decent', but extremely comfortable, in spite of the shortage of butter and coffee.

It is a peculiarity of English travellers that they do not really believe in the existence of anything outside the smart hotels. I hope they found some butter for the Duchess of Atholl.

I was at the Sanatorium Maurín, one of the sanatoria run by the P.O.U.M. It was in the suburbs near Tibidabo, the queer-shaped mountain that rises abruptly behind Barcelona and is traditionally supposed to have been the hill from which Satan showed Jesus the countries of the earth (hence its name). The house had previously belonged to some wealthy bourgeois and had been seized at the time of the revolution. Most of the men there had either been invalided out of the line or had some wound that had permanently disabled them – amputated limbs, and so forth. There were several other Englishmen there: Williams, with a damaged leg, and Stafford Cottman, a boy of eighteen, who had been sent back from the trenches with suspected tuberculosis, and Arthur Clinton, whose smashed left arm was still strapped on to one of those huge wire contraptions, nicknamed aeroplanes, which the Spanish hospitals were using. My wife was still staying at the Hotel Continental, and I generally came into Barcelona in the daytime. In the morning I used to attend the General Hospital for electrical treatment of my arm. It was a queer business – a series of prickly electric shocks that made the various sets of muscles jerk up and down – but it seemed to do some good; the use of my fingers came back and the pain grew somewhat less. Both of us had decided that the best thing we could do was to go back to England as soon as possible. I was extremely weak, my voice was gone, seemingly for good, and the doctors told me that at best it would be several months before I was fit to fight. I had got to start earning some money sooner or later, and there did not seem much sense in staying in Spain and eating food that was needed for other people. But my motives were mainly selfish. I had an overwhelming desire to get away from it all; away from the horrible atmosphere of political suspicion and hatred, from streets thronged by armed men, from air-raids, trenches, machine-guns, screaming trams, milkless tea, oil cookery, and shortage of cigarettes – from almost everything that I had learnt to associate with Spain.

The doctors at the General Hospital had certified me medically unfit, but to get my discharge I had to see a medical board at one of the hospitals near the front and then go to Sietamo to get my papers stamped at the P.O.U.M. militia headquarters. Kopp had just come back from the front, full of jubilation. He had just been in action and said that Huesca was going to be taken at last. The Government had brought troops from the Madrid front and were concentrating thirty thousand men, with aeroplanes in huge numbers. The Italians I had seen going up the line from Tarragona had attacked on the Jaca road but had had heavy casualties and lost two tanks. However, the town was bound to fall, Kopp said. (Alas! It didn't. The attack was a frightful mess-up and led to nothing except an orgy of lying in the newspapers.) Meanwhile Kopp had to go down to Valencia for an interview at the Ministry of War. He had a letter from General Pozas, now commanding the Army of the East – the usual letter, describing Kopp as a 'person of all confidence' and recommending him for a special appointment in the engineering section (Kopp had been an engineer in civil life). He left for Valencia the same day as I left for Sietamo – 15 June.

It was five days before I got back to Barcelona. A lorry-load of us reached Sietamo about midnight, and as soon as we got to the P.O.U.M. headquarters they lined us up and began handling out rifles and cartridges, before even taking our names. It seemed that the attack was beginning and they were likely to call for reserves at any moment. I had my hospital ticket in my pocket, but I could not very well refuse to go with the others. I kipped down on the ground, with a cartridge-box for a pillow, in a mood of deep dismay. Being wounded had spoiled my nerve for the time being – I believe this usually happens – and the prospect of being under fire frightened me horribly. However, there was a bit of *mañana*, as usual, we were not called out after all, and next morning I produced my hospital ticket and went in search of my discharge. It meant a series of confused, tiresome journeys. As usual they bandied one to and fro from hospital to hospital – Sietamo, Barbastro, Monzon, then back to Sietamo to get my discharge stamped, then down the line again via Barbastro and Lerida – and the convergence of troops on Huesca had monopolized all the transport and disorganized everything. I remember sleeping in queer places – once in a hospital bed, but once in a ditch, once on a very narrow bench which

I fell off in the middle of the night, and once in a sort of municipal lodging-house in Barbastro. As soon as you got away from the railroad there was no way of travelling except by jumping chance lorries. You had to wait by the roadside for hours, sometimes three or four hours at a stretch, with knots of disconsolate peasants who carried bundles full of ducks and rabbits, waving to lorry after lorry. When finally you struck a lorry that was not chock full of men, loaves of bread, or ammunition-boxes the bumping over the vile roads wallowed you to pulp. No horse has ever thrown me so high as those lorries used to throw me. The only way of travelling was to crowd all together and cling to one another. To my humiliation I found that I was still too weak to climb on to a lorry without being helped.

I slept a night at Monzon Hospital, where I went to see my medical board. In the next bed to me there was an Assault Guard, wounded over the left eye. He was friendly and gave me cigarettes. I said: 'In Barcelona we should have been shooting one another,' and we laughed over this. It was queer how the general spirit seemed to change when you got anywhere near the front line. All or nearly all of the vicious hatred of the political parties evaporated. During all the time I was at the front I never once remember any P.S.U.C. adherent showing me hostility because I was P.O.U.M. That kind of thing belonged in Barcelona or in places even remoter from the war. There were a lot of Assault Guards in Sietamo. They had been sent on from Barcelona to take part in the attack on Huesca. The Assault Guards were a corps not intended primarily for the front, and many of them had not been under fire before. Down in Barcelona they were lords of the street, but up here they were *quintos* (rookies) and palled up with militia children of fifteen who had been in the line for months.

At Monzon Hospital the doctor did the usual tongue-pulling and mirror-thrusting business, assured me in the same cheerful manner as the others that I should never have a voice again, and signed my certificate. While I waited to be examined there was going on inside the surgery some dreadful operation without anaesthetics – why without anaesthetics I do not know. It went on and on, scream after scream, and when I went in there were chairs flung about and on the floor were pools of blood and urine.

The details of that final journey stand out in my mind with strange clarity. I was in a different mood, a more observing mood, than I had been in for months past. I had got my discharge, stamped with the seal of the 29th Division, and the doctor's certificate in which I was 'declared useless'. I was free to go back to England; consequently I felt able, almost for the

first time, to look at Spain. I had a day to put in to Barbastro, for there
was only one train a day. Previously I had seen Barbastro in brief glimpses,
and it had seemed to me simply a part of the war – a grey, muddy, cold
place, full of roaring lorries and shabby troops. It seemed queerly different
now. Wandering through it I became aware of pleasant tortuous streets,
old stone bridges, wine shops with great oozy barrels as tall as a man, and
intriguing semi-subterranean shops where men were making cartwheels,
daggers, wooden spoons, and goatskin water-bottles. I watched a man
making a skin bottle and discovered with great interest, what I had never
known before, that they are made with the fur inside and the fur is not
removed, so that you are really drinking distilled goat's hair. I had drunk
out of them for months without knowing this. And at the back of the town
there was a shallow jade-green river, and rising out of it a perpendicular
cliff of rock, with houses built into the rock, so that from your bedroom
window you could spit straight into the water a hundred feet below.
Innumerable doves lived in the holes in the cliff. And in Lerida there were
old crumbling buildings upon whose cornices thousands upon thousands
of swallows had built their nests, so that at a little distance the crusted
pattern of nests was like some florid moulding of the rococo period. It was
queer how for nearly six months past I had had no eyes for such things.
With my discharge papers in my pocket I felt like a human being again,
and also a little like a tourist. For almost the first time I felt that I was
really in Spain, in a country that I had longed all my life to visit. In the
quiet back streets of Lerida and Barbastro I seemed to catch a momentary
glimpse, a sort of far-off rumour of the Spain that dwells in everyone's
imagination. White sierras, goatherds, dungeons of the Inquisition,
Moorish palaces, black winding trains of mules, grey olive trees and groves
of lemons, girls in black mantillas, the wines of Malaga and Alicante,
cathedrals, cardinals, bull-fights, gypsies, serenades – in short, Spain. Of
all Europe it was the country that had had most hold upon my imagination.
It seemed a pity that when at last I had managed to come here I had seen
only this north-eastern corner, in the middle of a confused war and for
the most part in winter.

It was late when I got back to Barcelona, and there were no taxis. It
was no use trying to get to the Sanatorium Maurín, which was right
outside the town, so I made for the Hotel Continental, stopping for dinner
on the way. I remember the conversation I had with a very fatherly waiter
about the oak jugs, bound with copper, in which they served the wine. I
said I would like to buy a set of them to take back to England. The waiter
was sympathetic. 'Yes, beautiful, were they not? But impossible to buy

nowadays. Nobody was manufacturing them any longer – nobody was manufacturing anything. This war – such a pity!' We agreed that the war was a pity. Once again I felt like a tourist. The waiter asked me gently, had I liked Spain; would I come back to Spain? Oh, yes, I should come back to Spain. The peaceful quality of this conversation sticks in my memory, because of what happened immediately afterwards.

When I got to the hotel my wife was sitting in the lounge. She got up and came towards me in what struck me as a very unconcerned manner; then she put an arm round my neck and, with a sweet smile for the benefit of the other people in the lounge, hissed in my ear:

'*Get out!*'

'What?'

'Get out of here *at once!*'

'What?'

'Don't keep standing here! You must get outside quickly!'

'What? Why? What do you mean?'

She had me by the arm and was already leading me towards the stairs. Half-way down we met a Frenchman – I am not going to give his name, for though he had no connection with the P.O.U.M. he was a good friend to us all during the trouble. He looked at me with a concerned face.

'Listen! You mustn't come in here. Get out quickly and hide yourself before they ring up the police.'

And behold! at the bottom of the stairs one of the hotel staff, who was a P.O.U.M. member (unknown to the management, I fancy), slipped furtively out of the lift and told me in broken English to get out. Even now I did not grasp what had happened.

'What the devil is all this about?' I said as soon as we were on the pavement.

'Haven't you *heard?*'

'No. Heard what? I've heard nothing.'

'The P.O.U.M.'s been suppressed. They've seized all the buildings. Practically everyone's in prison. And they say they're shooting people already.'

So that was it. We had to have somewhere to talk. All the big cafés on the Ramblas were thronged with police, but we found a quiet café in a side street. My wife explained to me what had happened while I was away.

On 15 June the police had suddenly arrested Andrés Nin in his office, and the same evening had raided the Hotel Falcón and arrested all the people in it, mostly militiamen on leave. The place was converted immediately into a prison, and in a very little while it was filled to the brim with prisoners of all kinds. Next day the P.O.U.M. was declared an illegal organization and all its offices, bookstalls, sanatoria, Red Aid centres, and so forth were seized. Meanwhile the police were arresting everyone they could lay hands on who was known to have any connection with the P.O.U.M. Within a day or two all or almost all of the forty members of the Executive Committee were in prison. Possibly one or two had escaped into hiding, but the police were adopting the trick (extensively used on both sides in this war) of seizing a man's wife as a hostage if he disappeared. There was no way of discovering how many people had been arrested. My wife had heard that it was about four hundred in Barcelona alone. I have since thought that even at that time the numbers must have been greater. And the most fantastic people had been arrested. In some cases the police had even gone to the length of dragging wounded militiamen out of the hospitals.

It was all profoundly dismaying. What the devil was it all about? I could understand their suppressing the P.O.U.M., but what were they arresting people for? For nothing, so far as one could discover. Apparently the suppression of the P.O.U.M. had a retrospective effect; the P.O.U.M. was now illegal, and therefore one was breaking the law by having previously belonged to it. As usual, none of the arrested people had been charged. Meanwhile, however, the Valencia Communist papers were flaming with the story of a huge 'Fascist plot', radio communication with the enemy, documents signed in invisible ink, etc., etc. I have dealt with this story earlier. The significant thing was that it was appearing only in the Valencia papers; I think I am right in saying that there was not a single word about it, or about the suppression of the P.O.U.M., in any Barcelona papers, Communist, Anarchist, or Republican. We first learned the precise nature of the charges against the P.O.U.M. leaders not from any Spanish paper but from the English papers that reached Barcelona a day or two later. What we could not know at this time was that the Government was not responsible for the charge of treachery and espionage, and that members of the Government were later to repudiate it. We only vaguely knew that the P.O.U.M. leaders, and presumably all the rest of us, were accused of being in Fascist pay. And already the rumours were flying round that people were being secretly shot in jail. There was a lot of exaggeration about this, but it certainly happened in some cases, and there is not much doubt that it happened in the case of Nin. After his arrest Nin was transferred to Valencia and thence to Madrid, and as early as 21 June the rumour reached Barcelona that he had been shot. Later the rumour took a more definite shape: Nin had been shot in prison by the secret police and his body dumped into the street. This story came from several sources, including Federico Montsenys, an ex-member of the Government. From that day to this Nin has never been heard of alive again. When, later, the Government were questioned by delegates from various countries, they shilly-shallied and would say only that Nin had disappeared and they knew nothing of his whereabouts. Some of the newspapers produced a tale that he had escaped to Fascist territory. No evidence was given in support of it, and Irujo, the Minister of Justice, later declared that the Espagne news-agency had falsified his official *communiqué*.* In any case it is most unlikely that a political prisoner of Nin's importance would be allowed to escape. Unless at some future time he is produced alive, I think we must take it that he was murdered in prison.

The tale of arrests went on and on, extending over months, until the number of political prisoners, not counting Fascists, swelled into thousands. One noticeable thing was the autonomy of the lower ranks of the police. Many of the arrests were admittedly illegal, and various people whose release had been ordered by the Chief of Police were re-arrested at the jail gate and carried off to 'secret prisons'. A typical case is that of Kurt Landau and his wife. They were arrested about 17 June, and Landau immediately 'disappeared'. Five months later his wife was still in jail, untried and without news of her husband. She declared a hunger-strike, after which the Minister of Justice sent word to assure her that her husband was dead. Shortly afterwards she was released, to be almost immediately re-arrested and flung into prison again. And it was noticeable that the police, at any rate at first, seemed completely indifferent as to any effect their actions might have upon the war. They were quite ready to arrest military officers in important posts without getting permission beforehand. About the end of June José Rovira, the general commanding the 29th Division, was arrested somewhere near the front line by a party of police who had been sent from Barcelona. His men sent a delegation to protest at the Ministry of War. It was found that neither the Ministry of War, nor Ortega, the chief of Police, had even been informed of Rovira's arrest. In the whole business the detail that most sticks in my throat, though perhaps it is not of great importance, is that all news of what was happening was kept from the troops at the front. As you will have seen, neither I nor anyone else at the front had heard anything about the suppression of the P.O.U.M. All the P.O.U.M. militia headquarters, Red Aid centres, and so forth were functioning as usual, and as late as 20 June and as far down the line as Lerida, only about 100 miles from Barcelona,

---

* See the reports of the Maxton delegation which I referred to in Chapter 11.

no one had heard what was happening. All word of it was kept out of the Barcelona papers (the Valencia papers, which were running the spy stories, did not reach the Aragon front), and no doubt one reason for arresting all the P.O.U.M. militiamen on leave in Barcelona was to prevent them from getting back to the front with the news. The draft with which I had gone up the line on 15 June must have been about the last to go. I am still puzzled to know how the thing was kept secret, for the supply lorries and so forth were still passing to and fro; but there is no doubt that it *was* kept secret, and, as I have since learned from a number of others, the men in the front line heard nothing till several days later. The motive for all this is clear enough. The attack on Huesca was beginning, the P.O.U.M. militia was still a separate unit, and it was probably feared that if the men knew what was happening they would refuse to fight. Actually nothing of the kind happened when the news arrived. In the intervening days there must have been numbers of men who were killed without ever learning that the newspapers in the rear were calling them Fascists. This kind of thing is a little difficult to forgive. I know it was the usual policy to keep bad news from the troops, and perhaps as a rule that is justified. But it is a different matter to send men into battle and not even tell them that behind their backs their party is being suppressed, their leaders accused of treachery, and their friends and relatives thrown into prison.

My wife began telling me what had happened to our various friends. Some of the English and other foreigners had got across the frontier. Williams and Stafford Cottman had not been arrested when the Sanatorium Maurín was raided, and were in hiding somewhere. So was John McNair, who had been in France and had re-entered Spain after the P.O.U.M. was declared illegal – a rash thing to do, but he had not cared to stay in safety while his comrades were in danger. For the rest it was simply a chronicle of 'They've got so and so' and 'They've got so and so'. They seemed to have 'got' nearly everyone. It took me aback to hear that they had also 'got' George Kopp.

'What! Kopp? I thought he was in Valencia.'

It appeared that Kopp had come back to Barcelona; he had a letter from the Ministry of War to the colonel commanding the engineering operations on the eastern front. He knew that the P.O.U.M. had been suppressed, of course, but probably it did not occur to him that the police could be such fools as to arrest him when he was on his way to the front on an urgent military mission. He had come round to the Hotel Continental to fetch his kit-bags; my wife had been out at the time, and the hotel people had managed to detain him with some lying story while they rang up the police. I admit I was angry when I heard of Kopp's arrest. He was my personal friend, I had served under him for months, I had been under fire with him, and I knew his history. He was a man who had sacrificed everything – family, nationality, livelihood – simply to come to Spain and fight against Fascism. By leaving Belgium without permission and joining a foreign army while he was on the Belgian Army reserve, and, earlier, by helping to manufacture munitions illegally for the Spanish Government, he had piled up years of imprisonment for himself if he should ever return to his own country. He had been in the line since October 1936, had worked his way up from militiaman to major, had been in action I do not know how many times, and had been wounded once. During the May trouble, as I had seen for myself, he had prevented fighting locally and probably saved ten or twenty lives. And all they could do in return was to fling him into jail. It is waste of time to be angry, but the stupid malignity of this kind of thing does try one's patience.

Meanwhile they had not 'got' my wife. Although she had remained at the Continental the police had made no move to arrest her. It was fairly obvious that she was being used as a decoy duck. A couple of nights earlier, however, in the small hours of the morning, six of the plain-clothes police had invaded our room at the hotel and searched it. They had seized every scrap of paper we possessed, except, fortunately, our passports and cheque-book. They had taken my diaries, all our books, all the press-cuttings that had been piling up for months past (I have often wondered what use those press-cuttings were to them), all my war souvenirs, and all our letters. (Incidentally, they took away a number of letters I had received from readers. Some of them had not been answered, and of course I have not the addresses. If anyone who wrote to me about my last book, and did not get an answer, happens to read these lines, will he please accept this as an apology?) I learned afterwards that the police had also seized various belongings that I had left at the Sanatorium Maurín. They even carried off a bundle of my dirty linen. Perhaps they thought it had messages written on it in invisible ink.

It was obvious that it would be safer for my wife to stay at the hotel, at any rate for the time being. If she tried to disappear they would be after her immediately. As for myself, I should have to go straight into hiding. The prospect revolted me. In spite of the innumerable arrests it was almost impossible for me to believe that I was in any danger. The whole thing seemed too meaningless. It was the same refusal to take this idiotic onslaught seriously that had led Kopp into jail. I kept saying, but why should anyone want to arrest me? What had I done? I was not even

a party member of the P.O.U.M. Certainly I had carried arms during the
May fighting, but so had (at a guess) forty or fifty thousand people.
Besides, I was badly in need of a proper night's sleep. I wanted to risk it
and go back to the hotel. My wife would not hear of it. Patiently she
explained the state of affairs. It did not matter what I had done or not
done. This was not a round-up of criminals; it was merely a reign of terror.
I was not guilty of any definite act, but I was guilty of 'Trotskyism'. The
fact that I had served in the P.O.U.M. militia was quite enough to get me
into prison. It was no use hanging on to the English notion that you are
safe so long as you keep the law. Practically the law was what the police
chose to make it. The only thing to do was to lie low and conceal the fact
that I had anything to do with the P.O.U.M. We went through the papers
in my pockets. My wife made me tear up my militiaman's card, which
had P.O.U.M. on it in big letters, also a photo of a group of militiamen with
a P.O.U.M. flag in the background; that was the kind of thing that got you
arrested nowadays. I had to keep my discharge papers, however. Even
these were a danger, for they bore the seal of the 29th Division, and the
police would probably know that the 29th Division was the P.O.U.M.; but
without them I could be arrested as a deserter.

The thing we had got to think of now was getting out of Spain. There
was no sense in staying here with the certainty of imprisonment sooner or
later. As a matter of fact both of us would greatly have liked to stay, just
to see what happened. But I foresaw that Spanish prisons would be lousy
places (actually they were a lot worse than I imagined), once in prison
you never knew when you would get out, and I was in wretched health,
apart from the pain in my arm. We arranged to meet next day at the
British Consulate, where Cottman and McNair were also coming. It would
probably take a couple of days to get our passports in order. Before leaving
Spain you had to have your passport stamped in three separate places –
by the Chief of Police, by the French Consul, and by the Catalan
immigration authorities. The Chief of Police was the danger, of course.
But perhaps the British Consul could fix things up without letting it be
known that we had anything to do with the P.O.U.M. Obviously there must
be a list of foreign 'Trotskyist' suspects, and very likely our names were
on it, but with luck we might get to the frontier before the list. There was
sure to be a lot of muddle and *mañana*. Fortunately this was Spain and
not Germany. The Spanish secret police had some of the spirit of the
Gestapo, but not much of its competence.

So we parted. My wife went back to the hotel and I wandered off into
the darkness to find somewhere to sleep. I remember feeling sulky and

bored. I had so wanted a night in bed! There was nowhere I could go, no house where I could take refuge. The P.O.U.M. had practically no underground organization. No doubt the leaders had always realized that the party was likely to be suppressed, but they had never expected a wholesale witch-hunt of this description. They had expected it so little, indeed, that they were actually continuing the alterations to the P.O.U.M. buildings (among other things they were constructing a cinema in the Executive Building, which had previously been a bank) up to the very day when the P.O.U.M. was suppressed. Consequently the rendezvous and hiding-places which every revolutionary party ought to possess as a matter of course did not exist. Goodness knows how many people – people whose homes had been raided by the police – were sleeping in the streets that night. I had had five days of tiresome journeys, sleeping in impossible places, my arm was hurting damnably, and now these fools were chasing me to and fro and I had got to sleep on the ground again. That was about as far as my thoughts went. I did not make any of the correct political reflections. I never do when things are happening. It seems to be always the case when I get mixed up in war or politics – I am conscious of nothing save physical discomfort and a deep desire for this damned nonsense to be over. Afterwards I can see the significance of events, but while they are happening I merely want to be out of them – an ignoble trait, perhaps.

I walked a long way and fetched up somewhere near the General Hospital. I wanted a place where I could lie down without some nosing policeman finding me and demanding my papers. I tried an air-raid shelter, but it was newly dug and dripping with damp. Then I came upon the ruins of a church that had been gutted and burnt in the revolution. It was a mere shell, four roofless walls surrounding piles of rubble. In the half-darkness I poked about and found a kind of hollow where I could lie down. Lumps of broken masonry are not good to lie on, but fortunately it was a warm night and I managed to get several hours' sleep.

14

THE worst of being wanted by the police in a town like Barcelona is that everything opens so late. When you sleep out of doors you always wake about dawn, and none of the Barcelona cafés opens much before nine. It was hours before I could get a cup of coffee or a shave. It seemed queer, in the barber's shop, to see the Anarchist notice still on the wall, explaining that tips were prohibited. 'The Revolution has struck off our chains,' the notice said. I felt like telling the barbers that their chains would soon be back again if they didn't look out.

I wandered back to the centre of the town. Over the P.O.U.M. buildings the red flags had been torn down, Republican flags were floating in their place, and knots of armed Civil Guards were lounging in the doorways. At the Red Aid centre on the corner of the Plaza de Cataluña the police had amused themselves by smashing most of the windows. The P.O.U.M. book-stalls had been emptied of books and the notice-board farther down the Ramblas had been plastered with an anti-P.O.U.M. cartoon – the one representing the mask and the Fascist face beneath. Down at the bottom of the Ramblas, near the quay, I came upon a queer sight; a row of militiamen, still ragged and muddy from the front, sprawling exhaustedly on the chairs placed there for the bootblacks. I knew who they were – indeed, I recognized one of them. They were P.O.U.M. militiamen who had come down the line on the previous day to find that the P.O.U.M. had been suppressed, and had had to spend the night in the streets because their homes had been raided. Any P.O.U.M. militiaman who returned to Barcelona at this time had the choice of going straight into hiding or into jail – not a pleasant reception after three or four months in the line.

It was a queer situation that we were in. At night one was a hunted fugitive, but in the daytime one could live an almost normal life. Every house known to harbour P.O.U.M. supporters was – or at any rate was likely to be – under observation, and it was impossible to go to a hotel or boarding-house, because it had been decreed that on the arrival of a stranger the hotel-keeper must inform the police immediately. Practically this meant spending the night out of doors. In the daytime, on the other hand, in a town the size of Barcelona, you were fairly safe. The streets were thronged by Civil Guards, Assault Guards, Carabineros, and ordinary police, besides God knows how many spies in plain clothes; still, they could not stop everyone who passed, and if you looked normal you might escape notice. The thing to do was to avoid hanging round P.O.U.M. buildings and going to cafés and restaurants where the waiters knew you by sight. I spent a long time that day, and the next, in having a bath at one of the public baths. This struck me as a good way of putting in the time and keeping out of sight. Unfortunately the same idea occurred to a lot of people, and a few days later – after I left Barcelona – the police raided one of the public baths and arrested a number of 'Trotskyists' in a state of nature.

Half-way up the Ramblas I ran into one of the wounded men from the Sanatorium Maurín. We exchanged the sort of invisible wink that people were exchanging at that time, and managed in an unobtrusive way to meet in a café farther up the street. He had escaped arrest when the Maurín was raided, but, like the others, had been driven into the street. He was in shirt-sleeves – had had to flee without his jacket – and had no money. He described to me how one of the Civil Guards had torn the large coloured portrait of Maurín from the wall and kicked it to pieces. Maurín (one of the founders of the P.O.U.M.) was a prisoner in the hands of the Fascists and at that time was believed to have been shot by them.

I met my wife at the British Consulate at ten o'clock. McNair and Cottman turned up shortly afterwards. The first thing they told me was that Bob Smillie was dead. He had died in prison at Valencia – of what, nobody knew for certain. He had been buried immediately, and the I.L.P. representative on the spot, David Murray, had been refused permission to see his body.

Of course I assumed at once that Smillie had been shot. It was what everyone believed at the time, but I have since thought that I may have been wrong. Later the cause of his death was given out as appendicitis, and we heard afterwards from another prisoner who had been released that Smillie had certainly been ill in prison. So perhaps the appendicitis story was true. The refusal to let Murray see his body may have been due to pure spite. I must say this, however. Bob Smillie was only twenty-two years old and physically he was one of the toughest people I have met. He was, I think, the only person I knew, English or Spanish, who went three months in the trenches without a day's illness. People so tough as that do not usually die of appendicitis if they are properly looked after. But when you saw what the Spanish jails were like – the makeshift jails used for political prisoners – you realized how much chance there was of a sick man getting proper attention. The jails were places that could only be described as dungeons. In England you would have to go back to the eighteenth century to find anything comparable. People were penned together in small rooms where there was barely space for them to lie down, and often they were kept in cellars and other dark places. This was not as a temporary measure – there were cases of people being kept four and five months almost without sight of daylight. And they were fed on a filthy and insufficient diet of two plates of soup and two pieces of bread a day. (Some months later, however, the food seems to have improved a little.) I am not exaggerating; ask any political suspect who was imprisoned in Spain. I have had accounts of the Spanish jails from a number of separate sources, and they agree with one another too well to be disbelieved; besides, I had a few glimpses into one Spanish jail myself. Another English friend who was imprisoned later writes that his experiences in jail 'make Smillie's case easier to understand'. Smillie's death is not a thing I can easily forgive. Here was this brave and gifted boy, who had thrown up his career at Glasgow University in order to come and fight against Fascism, and who, as I saw for myself, had done his job at the front with faultless courage and willingness; and all they could find to do with him was to fling him into jail and let him die like a neglected animal. I know that in the middle of a huge and bloody war it is no use making too much fuss over an individual death. One aeroplane bomb in a crowded street causes more suffering than quite a lot of political persecution. But what angers one about a death like this is its utter pointlessness. To be killed in battle – yes, that is what one expects; but to be flung into jail, not even for any imaginary offence, but simply owing to dull blind spite, and then left to die in solitude – that is a different matter. I fail to see how this kind of thing – and it is not as though Smillie's case were exceptional – brought victory any nearer.

My wife and I visited Kopp that afternoon. You were allowed to visit prisoners who were not *incommunicado*, though it was not safe to do so more than once or twice. The police watched the people who came and went, and if you visited the jails too often you stamped yourself as a friend of 'Trotskyists' and probably ended in jail yourself. This had already happened to a number of people.

Kopp was not *incommunicado* and we got a permit to see him without difficulty. As they led us through the steel doors into the jail, a Spanish militiaman whom I had known at the front was being led out between two Civil Guards. His eye met mine; again the ghostly wink. And the first person we saw inside was an American militiaman who had left for home a few days earlier; his papers were in good order, but they had arrested him at the frontier all the same, probably because he was still wearing corduroy breeches and was therefore identifiable as a militiaman. We walked past one another as though we had been total strangers. That was dreadful. I had known him for months, had shared a dug-out with him, he had helped to carry me down the line when I was wounded; but it was the only thing one could do. The blue-clad guards were snooping everywhere. It would be fatal to recognize too many people.

The so-called jail was really the ground floor of a shop. Into two rooms each measuring about twenty feet square, close on a hundred people were penned. The place had the real eighteenth-century Newgate Calendar appearance, with its frowsy dirt, its huddle of human bodies, its lack of furniture – just the bare stone floor, one bench, and a few ragged blankets – and its murky light, for the corrugated steel shutters had been drawn over the windows. On the grimy walls revolutionary slogans – *'Visca* P.O.U.M.!' *'Viva la Revolución!'* and so forth – had been scrawled. The place had been used as a dump for political prisoners for months past. There was a deafening racket of voices. This was the visiting hour, and the place was so packed with people that it was difficult to move. Nearly all of them were of the poorest of the working-class population. You saw women undoing pitiful packets of food which they had brought for their imprisoned men-folk. There were several of the wounded men from the Sanatorium Maurín among the prisoners. Two of them had amputated legs; one of them had been brought to prison without his crutch and was hopping about on one foot. There was also a boy of not more than twelve; they were even arresting children, apparently. The place had the beastly stench that you always get when crowds of people are penned together without proper sanitary arrangements.

Kopp elbowed his way through the crowd to meet us. His plump fresh-coloured face looked much as usual, and in that filthy place he had kept his uniform neat and had even contrived to shave. There was another officer in the uniform of the Popular Army among the prisoners. He and Kopp saluted as they struggled past one another; the gesture was pathetic, somehow. Kopp seemed in excellent spirits. 'Well, I suppose we shall all be shot,' he said cheerfully. The word 'shot' gave me a sort of inward shudder. A bullet had entered my own body recently and the feeling of it was fresh in my memory; it is not nice to think of that happening to anyone you know well. At that time I took it for granted that all the principal people in the P.O.U.M., and Kopp among them, *would* be shot. The first rumour of Nin's death had just filtered through, and we knew that the P.O.U.M. were being accused of treachery and espionage. Everything pointed to a huge frame-up trial followed by a massacre of leading 'Trotskyists.' It is a terrible thing to see your friend in jail and to know yourself impotent to help him. For there was nothing that one could do; useless even to appeal to the Belgian authorities, for Kopp had broken the law of his own country by coming here. I had to leave most of the talking to my wife; with my squeaking voice I could not make myself heard in the din. Kopp was telling us about the friends he had made among the other prisoners, about the guards, some of whom were good fellows, but some of whom abused and beat the more timid prisoners, and about the food, which was 'pig-wash'. Fortunately we had thought to bring a packet of food, also cigarettes. Then Kopp began telling us about the papers that had been taken from him when he was arrested. Among them was his letter from the Ministry of War, addressed to the colonel commanding engineering operations in the Army of the East. The police had seized it and refused to give it back; it was said to be lying in the Chief of Police's office. It might make a very great difference if it were recovered.

I saw instantly how important this might be. An official letter of that kind, bearing the recommendation of the Ministry of War and of General Pozas, would establish Kopp's bona fides. But the trouble was to prove that the letter existed; if it were opened in the Chief of Police's office one could be sure that some nark or other would destroy it. There was only one person who might possibly be able to get it back, and that was the officer to whom it was addressed. Kopp had already thought of this, and he had written a letter which he wanted me to smuggle out of the jail and post. But it was obviously quicker and surer to go in person. I left my wife with Kopp, rushed out, and, after a long search, found a taxi. I knew that time was everything. It was now about half past five, the colonel would probably leave his office at six, and by tomorrow the letter might be God knew where – destroyed, perhaps, or lost somewhere in the chaos of documents that was presumably piling up as suspect after suspect was arrested. The colonel's office was at the War Department down by the quay. As I hurried up the steps the Assault Guard on duty at the door barred the way with his long bayonet and demanded 'papers'. I waved my discharge ticket at him; evidently he could not read, and he let me pass, impressed by the vague mystery of 'papers'. Inside, the place was a huge complicated warren running round a central courtyard, with hundreds of offices on each floor; and, as this was Spain, nobody had the vaguest idea where the office I was looking for was. I kept repeating: '*El coronel* – , *jefe de ingenieros, Ejército de Este!*' People smiled and shrugged their shoulders gracefully. Everyone who had an opinion sent me in a different direction; up these stairs, down those, along interminable passages which turned out to be blind alleys. And time was slipping away. I had the strangest sensation of being in a nightmare: the rushing up and down flights of stairs, the mysterious people coming and going, the glimpses through open doors of chaotic offices with papers strewn everywhere and typewriters clicking; and time slipping away and a life perhaps in the balance.

However, I got there in time, and slightly to my surprise I was granted a hearing. I did not see Colonel —, but his aide-de-camp or secretary, a little slip of an officer in smart uniform, with large and squinting eyes, came out to interview me in the ante-room. I began to pour forth my story. I had come on behalf of my superior officer, Major Jorge Kopp, who was on an urgent mission to the front and had been arrested by mistake. The letter to Colonel — was of a confidential nature and should be recovered without delay. I had served with Kopp for months, he was an officer of the highest character, obviously his arrest was a mistake, the police had confused him with someone else, etc., etc., etc. I kept piling it on about the urgency of Kopp's mission to the front, knowing that this was the strongest point. But it must have sounded a strange tale, in my villainous Spanish which lapsed into French at every crisis. The worst was that my voice gave out almost at once and it was only by violent straining that I could produce a sort of croak. I was in dread that it would disappear altogether and the little officer would grow tired of trying to listen to me. I have often wondered what he thought was wrong with my voice – whether he thought I was drunk or merely suffering from a guilty conscience.

However, he heard me patiently, nodded his head a great number of times, and gave a guarded assent to what I said. Yes, it sounded as though there might have been a mistake. Clearly the matter should be looked into. *Mañana* – I protested. Not *mañana*! The matter was urgent; Kopp was due at the front already. Again the officer seemed to agree. Then came the question I was dreading:

'This Major Kopp – what force was he serving in?'

The terrible word had to come out: 'In the P.O.U.M. militia.'

'P.O.U.M.!'

I wish I could convey to you the shocked alarm in his voice. You have got to remember how the P.O.U.M. was regarded at that moment. The spy-scare was at its height; probably all good Republicans did believe for a day or two that the P.O.U.M. was a huge spying organization in German pay. To have to say such a thing to an officer in the Popular Army was

like going into the Cavalry Club immediately after the Red Letter scare
and announcing yourself a Communist. His dark eyes moved obliquely
across my face. Another long pause, then he said slowly:

'And you say you were with him at the front. Then you were serving in
the P.O.U.M. militia yourself?'

'Yes.'

He turned and dived into the colonel's room. I could hear an agitated
conversation. 'It's all up,' I thought. We should never get Kopp's letter
back. Moreover I had had to confess that I was in the P.O.U.M. myself, and
no doubt they would ring up the police and get me arrested, just to add
another Trotskyist to the bag. Presently, however, the officer reappeared,
fitting on his cap, and sternly signed to me to follow. We were going to
the Chief of Police's office. It was a long way, twenty minutes' walk. The
little officer marched stiffly in front with a military step. We did not
exchange a single word the whole way. When we got to the Chief of
Police's office a crowd of the most dreadful-looking scoundrels, Obviously
police narks, informers, and spies of every kind, were hanging about
outside the door. The little officer went in; there was a long, heated
conversation. You could hear voices furiously raised; you pictured violent
gestures, shrugging of the shoulders, bangings on the table. Evidently the
police were refusing to give the letter up. At last, however, the officer
emerged, flushed, but carrying a large official envelope. It was Kopp's
letter. We had won a tiny victory – which, as it turned out, made not the
slightest difference. The letter was duly delivered, but Kopp's military
superiors were quite unable to get him out of jail.

The officer promised me that the letter should be delivered. But what
about Kopp? I said. Could we not get him released? He shrugged his
shoulders. That was another matter. They did not know what Kopp had
been arrested for. He would only tell me that the proper inquiries would
be made. There was no more to be said; it was time to part. Both of us
bowed slightly. And then there happened a strange and moving thing. The
little officer hesitated a moment, then stepped across, and shook hands
with me.

I do not know if I can bring home to you how deeply that action touched
me. It sounds a small thing, but it was not. You have got to realize what
was the feeling of the time – the horrible atmosphere of suspicion and
hatred, the lies and rumours circulating everywhere, the posters screaming
from the hoardings that I and everyone like me was a Fascist spy. And
you have got to remember that we were standing outside the Chief of
Police's office, in front of that filthy gang of tale-bearers and *agents*

provocateurs, any one of whom might know that I was 'wanted' by the police. It was like publicly shaking hands with a German during the Great War. I suppose he had decided in some way that I was not really a Fascist spy; still, it was good of him to shake hands.

I record this, trivial though it may sound, because it is somehow typical of Spain – of the flashes of magnanimity that you get from Spaniards in the worst of circumstances. I have the most evil memories of Spain, but I have very few bad memories of Spaniards. I only twice remember even being seriously angry with a Spaniard, and on each occasion, when I look back, I believe I was in the wrong myself. They have, there is no doubt, a generosity, a species of nobility, that do not really belong to the twentieth century. It is this that makes one hope that in Spain even Fascism may take a comparatively loose and bearable form. Few Spaniards possess the damnable efficiency and consistency that a modern totalitarian state needs. There had been a queer little illustration of this fact a few nights earlier, when the police had searched my wife's room. As a matter of fact that search was a very interesting business, and I wish I had seen it, though perhaps it is as well that I did not, for I might not have kept my temper.

The police conducted the search in the recognized Ogpu or Gestapo style. In the small hours of the morning there was a pounding on the door, and six men marched in, switched on the light, and immediately took up various positions about the room, obviously agreed upon beforehand. They then searched both rooms (there was a bathroom attached) with inconceivable thoroughness. They sounded the walls, took up the mats, examined the floor, felt the curtains, probed under the bath and the radiator, emptied every drawer and suitcase and felt every garment and held it up to the light. They impounded all papers, including the contents of the waste-paper basket, and all our books into the bargain. They were thrown into ecstasies of suspicion by finding that we possessed a French translation of Hitler's *Mein Kampf*. If that had been the only book they found our doom would have been sealed. It is obvious that a person who reads *Mein Kampf* must be a Fascist. The next moment, however, they came upon a copy of Stalin's pamphlet, *Ways of Liquidating Trotskyists and other Double Dealers*, which reassured them somewhat. In one drawer there was a number of packets of cigarette papers. They picked each packet to pieces and examined each paper separately, in case there should be messages written on them. Altogether they were on the job for nearly two hours. Yet all this time they *never searched the bed*. My wife was lying in bed all the while; obviously there might have been half a dozen sub-machine-guns under the mattress, not to mention a library of

462   HOMAGE TO CATALONIA

Trotskyist documents under the pillow. Yet the detectives made no move to touch the bed, never even looked underneath it. I cannot believe that this is a regular feature of the Ogpu routine. One must remember that the police were almost entirely under Communist control, and these men were probably Communist Party members themselves. But they were also Spaniards, and to turn a woman out of bed was a little too much for them. This part of the job was silently dropped, making the whole search meaningless.

That night McNair, Cottman, and I slept in some long grass at the edge of a derelict building-lot. It was a cold night for the time of year and no one slept much. I remember the long dismal hours of loitering about before one could get a cup of coffee. For the first time since I had been in Barcelona I went to have a look at the cathedral – a modern cathedral, and one of the most hideous buildings in the world. It has four crenellated spires exactly the shape of hock bottles. Unlike most of the churches in Barcelona it was not damaged during the revolution – it was spared because of its 'artistic value', people said. I think the Anarchists showed bad taste in not blowing it up when they had the chance, though they did hang a red and black banner between its spires. That afternoon my wife and I went to see Kopp for the last time. There was nothing that we could do for him, absolutely nothing, except to say good-bye and leave money with Spanish friends who would take him food and cigarettes. A little while later, however, after we had left Barcelona, he was placed *incommunicado* and not even food could be sent to him. That night, walking down the Ramblas, we passed the Café Moka, which the Civil Guards were still holding in force. On an impulse I went in and spoke to two of them who were leaning against the counter with their rifles slung over their shoulders. I asked them if they knew which of their comrades had been on duty here at the time of the May fighting. They did not know, and, with the usual Spanish vagueness, did not know how one could find out. I said that my friend Jorge Kopp was in prison and would perhaps be put on trial for something in connection with the May fighting; that the men who were on duty here would know that he had stopped the fighting and saved some of their lives; they ought to come forward and give evidence to that effect. One of the men I was talking to was a dull, heavy-looking man who kept shaking his head because he could not hear my voice in the din of the traffic. But the other was different. He said he had heard of Kopp's action from some of his comrades; Kopp was *buen chico* (a good fellow). But even at the time I knew that it was all useless. If Kopp were ever tried, it would be, as in all such trials, with faked evidence. If he has been shot (and I am afraid it is quite likely), that will be his epitaph: the *buen chico* of the poor Civil Guard who was part of a dirty system but had remained enough of a human being to know a decent action when he saw one.

It was an extraordinary, insane existence that we were leading. By night we were criminals, but by day we were prosperous English visitors – that was our pose, anyway. Even after a night in the open, a shave, a bath, and a shoe-shine do wonders with your appearance. The safest thing at present was to look as bourgeois as possible. We frequented the fashionable residential quarter of the town, where our faces were not known, went to expensive restaurants, and were very English with the waiters. For the first time in my life I took to writing things on walls. The passage-ways of several smart restaurants had '*Visca* P.O.U.M.!' scrawled on them as large as I could write it. All the while, though I was technically in hiding, I could not feel myself in danger. The whole thing seemed too absurd. I had the ineradicable English belief that 'they' cannot arrest you unless you have broken the law. It is a most dangerous belief to have during a political pogrom. There was a warrant out for McNair's arrest, and the chances were that the rest of us were on the list as well. The arrests, raids, searchings were continuing without pause; practically everyone we knew, except those who were still at the front, was in jail by this time. The police were even boarding the French ships that periodically took off refugees and seizing suspected 'Trotskyists'.

Thanks to the kindness of the British consul, who must have had a very trying time during that week, we had managed to get our passports into order. The sooner we left the better. There was a train that was due to leave for Port Bou at half past seven in the evening and might normally be expected to leave at about half past eight. We arranged that my wife should order a taxi beforehand and then pack her bags, pay her bill, and leave the hotel at the last possible moment. If she gave the hotel people too much notice they would be sure to send for the police. I got down to the station at about seven to find that the train had already gone – it had left at ten to seven. The engine-driver had changed his mind, as usual. Fortunately we managed to warn my wife in time. There was another train early the following morning. McNair, Cottman, and I had dinner at a little restaurant near the station and by cautious questioning discovered that the restaurant-keeper was a C.N.T. member and friendly. He let us a three-bedded room and forgot to warn the police. It was the first time in five nights that I had been able to sleep with my clothes off. Next morning my wife slipped out of the hotel successfully. The train was about an hour late in starting. I filled in the time by writing a long letter to the Ministry

of War, telling them about Kopp's case – that without a doubt he had
been arrested by mistake, that he was urgently needed at the front, that
countless people would testify that he was innocent of any offence, etc.,
etc., etc. I wonder if anyone read that letter, written on pages torn out of
a note-book in wobbly handwriting (my fingers were still partly paralysed)
and still more wobbly Spanish. At any rate, neither this letter nor anything
else took effect. As I write, six months after the event, Kopp (if he has
not been shot) is still in jail, untried and uncharged. At the beginning we
had two or three letters from him, smuggled out by released prisoners and
posted in France. They all told the same story – imprisonment in filthy
dark dens, bad and insufficient food, serious illness due to the conditions
of imprisonment, and refusal of medical attention. I have had all this
confirmed from several other sources, English and French. More recently
he disappeared into one of the 'secret prisons' with which it seems
impossible to make any kind of communication. His case is the case of
scores or hundreds of foreigners and no one knows how many thousands
of Spaniards.

In the end we crossed the frontier without incident. The train had a
first class and a dining-car, the first I had seen in Spain. Until recently
there had been only one class on the trains in Catalonia. Two detectives
came round the train taking the names of foreigners, but when they saw
us in the dining-car they seemed satisfied that we were respectable. It was
queer how everything had changed. Only six months ago, when the
Anarchists still reigned, it was looking like a proletarian that made you
respectable. On the way down from Perpignan to Cerbères a French
commercial traveller in my carriage had said to me in all solemnity: 'You
mustn't go into Spain looking like that. Take off that collar and tie. They'll
tear them off you in Barcelona.' He was exaggerating, but it showed how
Catalonia was regarded. And at the frontier the Anarchist guards had
turned back a smartly dressed Frenchman and his wife, solely – I think –
because they looked too bourgeois. Now it was the other way about; to
look bourgeois was the one salvation. At the passport office they looked
us up in the card-index of suspects, but thanks to the inefficiency of the
police our names were not listed, not even McNair's. We were searched
from head to foot, but we possessed nothing incriminating, except my
discharge-papers, and the carabineros who searched me did not know that
the 29th Division was the P.O.U.M. So we slipped through the barrier, and
after just six months I was on French soil again. My only souvenirs of
Spain were a goatskin water-bottle and one of those tiny iron lamps in
which the Aragon peasants burn olive oil – lamps almost exactly the shape

of the terra-cotta lamps that the Romans used two thousand years ago – which I had picked up in some ruined hut, and which had somehow got stuck in my luggage.

After all, it turned out that we had come away none too soon. The very first newspaper we saw announced McNair's arrest for espionage. The Spanish authorities had been a little premature in announcing this. Fortunately, 'Trotskyism' is not extraditable.

I wonder what is the appropriate first action when you come from a country at war and set foot on peaceful soil. Mine was to rush to the tobacco-kiosk and buy as many cigars and cigarettes as I could stuff into my pockets. Then we all went to the buffet and had a cup of tea, the first tea with fresh milk in it that we had had for many months. It was several days before I could get used to the idea that you could buy cigarettes whenever you wanted them. I always half-expected to see the tobacconists' doors barred and the forbidding notice '*No hay tabaco*' in the window.

McNair and Cottman were going on to Paris. My wife and I got off the train at Banyuls, the first station up the line, feeling that we would like a rest. We were not too well received in Banyuls when they discovered that we had come from Barcelona. Quite a number of times I was involved in the same conversation: 'You come from Spain? Which side were you fighting on? The Government? Oh!' – and then a marked coolness. The little town seemed solidly pro-Franco, no doubt because of the various Spanish Fascist refugees who had arrived there from time to time. The waiter at the café I frequented was a pro-Franco Spaniard and used to give me lowering glances as he served me with an aperitif. It was otherwise in Perpignan, which was stiff with Government partisans and where all the different factions were caballing against one another almost as in Barcelona. There was one café where the word 'P.O.U.M.' immediately procured you French friends and smiles from the waiter.

I think we stayed three days in Banyuls. It was a strangely restless time. In this quiet fishing-town, remote from bombs, machine-guns, food-queues, propaganda, and intrigue, we ought to have felt profoundly relieved and thankful. We felt nothing of the kind. The things we had seen in Spain did not recede and fall into proportion now that we were away from them; instead they rushed back upon us and were far more vivid than before. We thought, talked, dreamed incessantly of Spain. For months past we had been telling ourselves that 'when we get out of Spain' we would go somewhere beside the Mediterranean and be quiet for a little while and perhaps do a little fishing; but now that we were here it was merely a bore and a disappointment. It was chilly weather, a persistent wind blew off the sea, the water was dull and choppy, round the harbour's edge a scum of ashes, corks, and fish-guts bobbed against the stones. It sounds like lunacy, but the thing that both of us wanted was to be back in Spain. Though it could have done no good to anybody, might indeed have done serious harm, both of us wished that we had stayed to be imprisoned along with the others. I suppose I have failed to convey more than a little of what those months in Spain meant to me. I have recorded some of the outward events, but I cannot record the feeling they have left me with. It is all mixed up with sights, smells, and sounds that cannot be conveyed in writing: the smell of the trenches, the mountain dawns stretching away into inconceivable distances, the frosty crackle of bullets, the roar and glare of bombs; the clear cold light of the Barcelona mornings, and the stamp of boots in the barrack yard, back in December when people still believed in the revolution; and the food-queues and the red and black flags and the faces of Spanish militiamen; above all the faces of militiamen — men whom I knew in the line and who are now scattered Lord knows where, some killed in battle, some maimed, some in prison — most of them, I hope, still safe and sound. Good luck to them all; I hope they win their war and drive all the foreigners out of Spain, Germans, Russians, and Italians alike. This war, in which I played so ineffectual a part, has left me with memories that are mostly evil, and yet I do not wish that I had missed it. When you have had a glimpse of such a disaster as this — and however it ends the Spanish war will turn out to have been an appalling disaster, quite apart from the slaughter and physical suffering — the result is not necessarily disillusionment and cynicism. Curiously enough the whole experience has left me with not less but more belief in the decency of human beings. And I hope the account I have given is not too misleading. I believe that on such an issue as this no one is or can be completely truthful. It is difficult to be certain about anything except what you have seen with your own eyes, and consciously or unconsciously everyone writes as a partisan. In case I have not said this somewhere earlier in the book I will say it now: beware of my partisanship, my mistakes of fact, and the distortion inevitably caused by my having seen only one corner of events. And beware of exactly the same things when you read any other book on this period of the Spanish war.

Because of the feeling that we ought to be doing something, though actually there was nothing we could do, we left Banyuls earlier than we had intended. With every mile that you went northward France grew greener and softer. Away from the mountain and the vine, back to the meadow and the elm. When I had passed through Paris on my way to

Spain it had seemed to me decayed and gloomy, very different from the Paris I had known eight years earlier, when living was cheap and Hitler was not heard of. Half the cafés I used to know were shut for lack of custom, and everyone was obsessed with the high cost of living and the fear of war. Now, after poor Spain, even Paris seemed gay and prosperous. And the Exhibition was in full swing, though we managed to avoid visiting it.

And then England – southern England, probably the sleekest landscape in the world. It is difficult when you pass that way, especially when you are peacefully recovering from sea-sickness with the plush cushions of a boat-train carriage under your bum, to believe that anything is really happening anywhere. Earthquakes in Japan, famines in China, revolutions in Mexico? Don't worry, the milk will be on the doorstep tomorrow morning, the *New Statesman* will come out on Friday. The industrial towns were far away, a smudge of smoke and misery hidden by the curve of the earth's surface. Down here it was still the England I had known in my childhood: the railway-cuttings smothered in wild flowers, the deep meadows where the great shining horses browse and meditate, the slow-moving streams bordered by willows, the green bosoms of the elms, the larkspurs in the cottage gardens; and then the huge peaceful wilderness of outer London, the barges on the miry river, the familiar streets, the posters telling of cricket matches and Royal weddings, the men in bowler hats, the pigeons in Trafalgar Square, the red buses, the blue policemen – all sleeping the deep, deep sleep of England, from which I sometimes fear that we shall never wake till we are jerked out of it by the roar of bombs.

LOOKING BACK
ON THE
SPANISH WAR

1

FIRST of all the physical memories, the sounds, the smells and the surfaces of things.

It is curious that more vividly than anything that came afterwards in the Spanish war I remember the week of so-called training that we received before being sent to the front – the huge cavalry barracks in Barcelona with its draughty stables and cobbled yards, the icy cold of the pump where one washed, the filthy meals made tolerable by pannikins of wine, the trousered militia-women chopping firewood, and the roll-call in the early mornings where my prosaic English name made a sort of comic interlude among the resounding Spanish ones, Manuel Gonzalez, Pedro Aguilar, Ramon Fenellosa, Roque Ballaster, Jaime Domenech, Sebastian Viltron, Ramon Nuvo Bosch. I name those particular men because I remember the faces of all of them. Except for two who were mere riff-raff and have doubtless become good Falangists by this time, it is probable that all of them are dead. Two of them I know to be dead. The eldest would have been about twenty-five, the youngest sixteen.

One of the essential experiences of war is never being able to escape from disgusting smells of human origin. Latrines are an overworked subject in war literature, and I would not mention them if it were not that the latrine in our barracks did its necessary bit towards puncturing my own illusions about the Spanish civil war. The Latin type of latrine, at which you have to squat, is bad enough at its best, but these were made of some kind of polished stone so slippery that it was all you could do to keep on your feet. In addition they were always blocked. Now I have plenty of other disgusting things in my memory, but I believe it was these latrines that first brought home to me the thought, so often to recur: 'Here we are, soldiers of a revolutionary army, defending Democracy against Fascism, fighting a war which is *about* something, and the detail of our lives is just as sordid and degrading as it could be in prison, let alone in a bourgeois army.' Many other things reinforced this impression later; for instance, the boredom and animal hunger of trench life, the squalid intrigues over scraps of food, the mean, nagging quarrels which people exhausted by lack of sleep indulge in.

The essential horror of army life (whoever has been a soldier will know what I mean by the essential horror of army life) is barely affected by the nature of the war you happen to be fighting in. Discipline, for instance, is ultimately the same in all armies. Orders have to be obeyed and enforced by punishment if necessary, the relationship of officer and man has to be the relationship of superior and inferior. The picture of war set forth in books like *All Quiet on the Western Front* is substantially true. Bullets hurt, corpses stink, men under fire are often so frightened that they wet their trousers. It is true that the social background from which an army springs will colour its training, tactics and general efficiency, and also that the consciousness of being in the right can bolster up morale, though this affects the civilian population more than the troops. (People forget that a soldier anywhere near the front line is usually too hungry, or frightened, or cold, or, above all, too tired to bother about the political origins of the war.) But the laws of nature are not suspended for a 'red' army any more than for a 'white' one. A louse is a louse and a bomb is a bomb, even though the cause you are fighting for happens to be just.

Why is it worth while to point out anything so obvious? Because the bulk of the British and American intelligentsia were manifestly unaware of it then, and are now. Our memories are short nowadays, but look back a bit, dig out the files of *New Masses* or the *Daily Worker*, and just have a look at the romantic warmongering muck that our left-wingers were spilling at that time. All the stale old phrases! And the unimaginative callousness of it! The sang-froid with which London faced the bombing of Madrid! Here I am not bothering about the counter-propagandists of the Right, the Lunns; Garvins *et hoc genus*; they go without saying. But here were the very people who for twenty years had hooted and jeered at the 'glory' of war, at atrocity stories, at patriotism, even at physical courage, coming out with stuff that with the alteration of a few names would have fitted into the *Daily Mail* of 1918. If there was one thing that the British intelligentsia were committed to, it was the debunking version of war, the theory that war is all corpses and latrines and never leads to any good result. Well, the same people who in 1933 sniggered pityingly if you said that in certain circumstances you would fight for your country, in 1937 were denouncing you as a Trotsky–Fascist if you suggested that the stories in *New Masses* about freshly wounded men clamouring to get back into the fighting might be exaggerated. And the Left intelligentsia made their swing-over from 'War is hell' to 'War is glorious' not only with no sense of incongruity but almost without any intervening stage. Later the bulk of them were to make other transitions equally violent. There must be a quite large number of people, a sort of central core of the intelligentsia, who approved the 'King and Country' declaration in 1935, shouted for a 'firm line against Germany' in 1937, supported the People's Convention in 1940, and are demanding a Second Front now.

As far as the mass Of the people go, the extraordinary swings of opinion which occur nowadays, the emotions which can be turned on and off like a tap, are the result of newspaper and radio hypnosis. In the intelligentsia I should say they result rather from money and mere physical safety. At a given moment they may be 'pro-war' or 'anti-war', but in either case they have no realistic picture of war in their minds. When they enthused over the Spanish war they knew, of course, that people were being killed and that to be killed is unpleasant, but they did feel that for a soldier in the Spanish Republican army the experience of war was somehow not degrading. Somehow the latrines stank less, discipline was less irksome. You have only to glance at the *New Statesman* to see that they believed that; exactly similar blah is being written about the Red Army at this moment. We have become too civilized to grasp the obvious. For the truth is very simple. To survive you often have to fight, and to fight you have to dirty yourself. War is evil, and it is often the lesser evil. Those who take the sword perish by the sword, and those who don't take the sword perish by smelly diseases. The fact that such a platitude is worth writing down shows what the years of rentier capitalism have done to us.

2

IN connection with what I have just said, a footnote on atrocities.

I have little direct evidence about the atrocities in the Spanish civil war. I know that some were committed by the Republicans, and far more (they are still continuing) by the Fascists. But what impressed me then, and has impressed me ever since, is that atrocities are believed in or disbelieved in solely on grounds of political predilection. Everyone believes in the atrocities of the enemy and disbelieves in those of his own side, without ever bothering to examine the evidence. Recently I drew up a table of atrocities during the period between 1918 and the present; there was never a year when atrocities were not occurring somewhere or other, and there was hardly a single case when the Left and the Right believed in the same stories simultaneously. And stranger yet, at any moment the situation can suddenly reverse itself and yesterday's proved-to-the-hilt atrocity story can become a ridiculous lie, merely because the political landscape has changed.

In the present war we are in the curious situation that our 'atrocity campaign' was done largely before the war started, and done mostly by the Left, the people who normally pride themselves on their incredulity. In the same period the Right, the atrocity-mongers of 1914–18, were gazing at Nazi Germany and flatly refusing to see any evil in it. Then as soon as war broke out it was the pro-Nazis of yesterday who were repeating horror stories, while the anti-Nazis suddenly found themselves doubting whether the Gestapo really existed. Nor was this solely the result of the Russo–German Pact. It was partly because before the war the Left had wrongly believed that Britain and Germany would never fight and were therefore able to be anti-German and anti-British simultaneously; partly also because official war-propaganda, with its disgusting hypocrisy and self-righteousness, always tends to make thinking people sympathize with the enemy. Part of the price we paid for the systematic lying of 1914–17 was the exaggerated pro-German reaction which followed. During the years 1918–33 you were hooted at in left-wing circles if you suggested that Germany bore even a fraction of responsibility for the war. In all the denunciations of Versailles I listened to during those years I don't think I ever once heard the question, 'What would have happened if Germany had won?' even mentioned, let alone discussed. So also with atrocities. The truth, it is felt, becomes untruth when your enemy utters it. Recently I noticed that the very people who swallowed any and every horror story about the Japanese in Nanking in 1937 refused to believe exactly the same stories about Hong Kong in 1942. There was even a tendency to feel that the Nanking atrocities had become, as it were, retrospectively untrue because the British Government now drew attention to them.

But unfortunately the truth about atrocities is far worse than that they are lied about and made into propaganda. The truth is that they happen. The fact often adduced as a reason for scepticism – that the same horror stories come up in war after war – merely makes it rather more likely that these stories are true. Evidently they are widespread fantasies, and war provides an opportunity of putting them into practice. Also, although it has ceased to be fashionable to say so, there is little question that what one may roughly call the 'whites' commit fur more and worse atrocities than the 'reds'. There is not the slightest doubt, for instance, about the behaviour of the Japanese in China. Nor is there much doubt about the long tale of Fascist outrages during the last ten years in Europe. The volume of testimony is enormous, and a respectable proportion of it comes from the German press and radio. These things really happened, that is the thing to keep one's eye on. They happened even though Lord Halifax said they happened. The raping and butchering in Chinese cities, the tortures in the cellars of the Gestapo, the elderly Jewish professors flung into cesspools, the machine-gunning of refugees along the Spanish roads – they all happened, and they did not happen any the less because the *Daily Telegraph* has suddenly found out about them when it is five years too late.

3

TWO memories, the first not proving anything in particular, the second, I think, giving one a certain insight into the atmosphere of a revolutionary period:

Early one morning another man and I had gone out to snipe at the Fascists in the trenches outside Huesca. Their line and ours here lay three hundred yards apart, at which range our aged rifles would not shoot accurately, but by sneaking out to a spot about a hundred yards from the Fascist trench you might, if you were lucky, get a shot at someone through a gap in the parapet. Unfortunately the ground between was a flat beet field with no cover except a few ditches, and it was necessary to go out while it was still dark and return soon after dawn, before the light became too good. This time no Fascists appeared, and we stayed too long and were caught by the dawn. We were in a ditch, but behind us were two hundred yards of flat ground with hardly enough cover for a rabbit. We were still trying to nerve ourselves to make a dash for it when there was an uproar and a blowing of whistles in the Fascist trench. Some of our aeroplanes were coming over. At this moment, a man presumably carrying a message to an officer, jumped out of the trench and ran along the top of the parapet in full view. He was half-dressed and was holding up his trousers with both hands as he ran. I refrained from shooting at him. It is true that I am a poor shot and unlikely to hit a running man at a hundred yards, and also that I was thinking chiefly about getting back to our trench while the Fascists had their attention fixed on the aeroplanes. Still, I did not shoot partly because of that detail about the trousers. I had come here to shoot at 'Fascists'; but a man who is holding up his trousers isn't a 'Fascist', he is visibly a fellow-creature, similar to yourself, and you don't feel like shooting at him.

What does this incident demonstrate? Nothing very much, because it is the kind of thing that happens all the time in all wars. The other is different. I don't suppose that in telling it I can make it moving to you who read it, but I ask you to believe that it is moving to me, as an incident characteristic of the moral atmosphere of a particular moment in time.

One of the recruits who joined us while I was at the barracks was a wild-looking boy from the back streets of Barcelona. He was ragged and barefooted. He was also extremely dark (Arab blood, I dare say), and made gestures you do not usually see a European make; one in particular – the arm outstretched, the palm vertical – was a gesture characteristic of Indians. One day a bundle of cigars, which you could still buy dirt cheap at that time, was stolen out of my bunk. Rather foolishly I reported this to the officer, and one of the scallywags I have already mentioned promptly came forward and said quite untruly that twenty-five pesetas had been stolen from his bunk. For some reason the officer instantly decided that the brown-faced boy must be the thief. They were very hard on stealing in the militia, and in theory people could be shot for it. The wretched boy allowed himself to be led off to the guardroom to be searched. What most struck me was that he barely attempted to protest his innocence. In the fatalism of his attitude you could see the desperate poverty in which he had been bred. The officer ordered him to take his clothes off. With a humility which was horrible to me he stripped himself naked, and his clothes were searched. Of course neither the cigars nor the money were there; in fact he had not stolen them. What was most painful of all was that he seemed no less ashamed after his innocence had been established. That night I took him to the pictures and gave him brandy and chocolate. But that too was horrible – I mean the attempt to wipe out an injury with money. For a few minutes I had half believed him to be a thief, and that could not be wiped out.

Well, a few weeks later at the front I had trouble with one of the men in my section. By this time I was a 'cabo', or corporal, in command of twelve men. It was static warfare, horribly cold, and the chief job was getting sentries to stay awake at their posts. One day a man suddenly refused to go to a certain post, which he said quite truly was exposed to enemy fire. He was a feeble creature, and I seized hold of him and began to drag him towards his post. This roused the feelings of the others against me, for Spaniards, I think, resent being touched more than we do. Instantly

I was surrounded by a ring of shouting men: 'Fascist! Fascist! Let that man go! This isn't a bourgeois army. Fascist!' etc., etc. As best I could in my bad Spanish I shouted back that orders had got to be obeyed, and the row developed into one of those enormous arguments by means of which discipline is gradually hammered out in revolutionary armies. Some said I was right, others said I was wrong. But the point is that the one who took my side the most warmly of all was the brown-faced boy. As soon as he saw what was happening he sprang into the ring and began passionately defending me. With his strange, wild, Indian gesture he kept exclaiming, 'He's the best corporal we've got!'(*No hay cabo como el.*) Later on he applied for leave to exchange into my section.

Why is this incident touching to me? Because in any normal circumstances it would have been impossible for good feelings ever to be re-established between this boy and myself. The implied accusation of theft would not have been made any better, probably somewhat worse, by my efforts to make amends. One of the effects of safe and civilized life is an immense oversensitiveness which makes all the primary emotions seem somewhat disgusting. Generosity is as painful as meanness, gratitude as hateful as ingratitude. But in Spain in 1936 we were not living in a normal time. It was a time when generous feelings and gestures were easier than they ordinarily are. I could relate a dozen similar incidents, not really communicable but bound up in my own mind with the special atmosphere of the time, the shabby clothes and the gay-coloured revolutionary posters, the universal use of the word 'comrade', the anti-Fascist ballads printed on flimsy paper and sold for a penny, the phrases like 'international proletarian solidarity', pathetically repeated by ignorant men who believed them to mean something. Could you feel friendly towards somebody, and stick up for him in a quarrel, after you had been ignominiously searched in his presence for property you were supposed to have stolen from him? No, you couldn't; but you might if you had both been through some emotionally widening experience. That is one of the by-products of revolution, though in this case it was only the beginnings of a revolution, and obviously foredoomed to failure.

4

THE struggle for power between the Spanish Republican parties is an unhappy, far-off thing which I have no wish to revive at this date. I only mention it in order to say: believe nothing, or next to nothing, of what you read about internal affairs on the Government side. It is all, from whatever source, party propaganda – that is to say, lies. The broad truth about the war is simple enough. The Spanish bourgeoisie saw their chance of crushing the labour movement, and took it, aided by the Nazis and by the forces of reaction all over the world. It is doubtful whether more than that will ever be established.

I remember saying once to Arthur Koestler, 'History stopped in 1936', at which he nodded in immediate understanding. We were both thinking of totalitarianism in general, but more particularly of the Spanish civil war. Early in life I have noticed that no event is ever correctly reported in a newspaper, but in Spain, for the first time, I saw newspaper reports which did not bear any relation to the facts, not even the relationship which is implied in an ordinary lie. I saw great battles reported where there had been no fighting, and complete silence where hundreds of men had been killed. I saw troops who had fought bravely denounced as cowards and traitors, and others who had never seen a shot fired hailed as the heroes of imaginary victories; and I saw newspapers in London retailing these lies and eager intellectuals building emotional superstructures over events that had never happened. I saw, in fact, history being written not in terms of what happened but of what ought to have happened according to various 'party lines'. Yet in a way, horrible as all this was, it was unimportant. It concerned secondary issues – namely, the struggle for power between the Comintern and the Spanish left-wing parties, and the efforts of the Russian Government to prevent revolution in Spain. But the broad picture of the war which the Spanish Government presented to the world was not untruthful. The main issues were what it said they were. But as for the Fascists and their backers, how could they come even as near to the truth as that? How could they possibly mention their real aims? Their version of the war was pure fantasy, and in the circumstances it could not have been otherwise.

The only propaganda line open to the Nazis and Fascists was to represent themselves as Christian patriots saving Spain from a Russian dictatorship. This involved pretending that life in Government Spain was just one long massacre (*vide* the *Catholic Herald* or the *Daily Mail* – but these were child's play compared with the Continental Fascist press), and it involved immensely exaggerating the scale of Russian intervention. Out of the huge pyramid of lies which the Catholic and reactionary press all over the world built up, let me take just one point – the presence in Spain of a Russian army. Devout Franco partisans all believed in this; estimates of its strength went as high as half a million. Now, there was no Russian army in Spain. There may have been a handful of airmen and other technicians, a few hundred at the most, but an army there was not. Some thousands of foreigners who fought in Spain, not to mention millions of Spaniards, were witnesses of this. Well, their testimony made no impression at all upon the Franco propagandists, not one of whom had set foot in Government Spain. Simultaneously these people refused utterly to admit the fact of German or Italian intervention at the same time as the Germany and Italian press were openly boasting about the exploits of their 'legionaries'. I have chosen to mention only one point, but in fact the whole of Fascist propaganda about the war was on this level.

This kind of thing is frightening to me, because it often gives me the feeling that the very concept of objective truth is fading out of the world. After all, the chances are that those lies, or at any rate similar lies, will pass into history. How will the history of the Spanish war be written? If Franco remains in power his nominees will write the history books, and (to stick to my chosen point) that Russian army which never existed will become historical fact, and schoolchildren will learn about it generations hence. But suppose Fascism is finally defeated and some kind of democratic government restored in Spain in the fairly near future; even then, how is the history of the war to be written? What kind of records will Franco have left behind him? Suppose even that the records kept on the Government side are recoverable – even so, how is a true history of the war to be written? For, as I have pointed out already, the Government also dealt extensively in lies. From the anti-Fascist angle one could write a broadly truthful history of the war, but it would be a partisan history, unreliable on every minor point. Yet, after all, *some* kind of history will be written, and after those who actually remember the war are dead, it will be universally accepted. So for all practical purposes the lie will have become truth.

I know it is the fashion to say that most of recorded history is lies anyway. I am willing to believe that history is for the most part inaccurate and biased, but what is peculiar to our own age is the abandonment of the idea that history *could* be truthfully written. In the past people deliberately lied, or they unconsciously coloured what they wrote, or they struggled after the truth, well knowing that they must make many mistakes; but in each case they believed that 'facts' existed and were more or less discoverable. And in practice there was always a considerable body of fact which would have been agreed to by almost everyone. If you look up the history of the last war in, for instance, the *Encyclopaedia Britannica*, you will find that a respectable amount of the material is drawn from German sources. A British and a German historian would disagree deeply on many things, even on fundamentals, but there would still be that body of, as it were, neutral fact on which neither would seriously challenge the other. It is just this common basis of agreement, with its implication that human beings are all one species of animal, that totalitarianism destroys. Nazi theory indeed specifically denies that such a thing as 'the truth' exists. There is, for instance, no such thing as 'Science'. There is only 'German Science', 'Jewish Science', etc. The implied objective of this line of thought is a nightmare world in which the Leader, or some ruling clique, controls not only the future but *the past*. If the Leader says of such and such an event, 'It never happened' – well, it never happened. If he says that two and two are five – well, two and two are five. This prospect frightens me much more than bombs – and after our experiences of the last few years that is not a frivolous statement.

But is it perhaps childish or morbid to terrify oneself with visions of a totalitarian future? Before writing off the totalitarian world as a nightmare that can't come true, just remember that in 1925 the world of today would have seemed a nightmare that couldn't come true. Against that shifting phantasmagoric world in which black may be white tomorrow and yesterday's weather can be changed by decree; there are in reality only two safeguards. One is that however much you deny the truth, the truth goes on existing, as it were, behind your back, and you consequently can't violate it in ways that impair military efficiency. The other is that so long as some parts of the earth remain unconquered, the liberal tradition can be kept alive. Let Fascism, or possibly even a combination of several Fascisms, conquer the whole world, and those two conditions no longer exist. We in England underrate the danger of this kind of thing, because our traditions and our past security have given us a sentimental belief that it all comes right in the end and the thing you most fear never really happens. Nourished for hundreds of years on a literature in which Right invariably triumphs in the last chapter, we believe half-instinctively that evil always defeats itself in the long run. Pacifism, for instance, is founded largely on this belief. Don't resist evil, and it will somehow destroy itself. But why should it? What evidence is there that it does? And what instance is there of a modern industrialized state collapsing unless conquered from the outside by military force?

Consider for instance the re-institution of slavery. Who could have imagined twenty years ago that slavery would return to Europe? Well, slavery has been restored under our noses. The forced-labour camps all over Europe and North Africa where Poles, Russians, Jews and political prisoners of every race toil at road-making or swamp-draining for their bare rations, are simple chattel slavery. The most one can say is that the buying and selling of slaves by individuals is not yet permitted. In other ways – the breaking-up of families, for instance – the conditions are probably worse than they were on the American cotton plantations. There is no reason for thinking that this state of affairs will change while any totalitarian domination endures. We don't grasp its full implications, because in our mystical way we feel that a régime founded on slavery *must* collapse. But it is worth comparing the duration of the slave empires of antiquity with that of any modern state. Civilizations founded on slavery have lasted for such periods as four thousand years.

When I think of antiquity, the detail that frightens me is that those hundreds of millions of slaves on whose backs civilization rested generation after generation have left behind them no record whatever. We do not even know their names. In the whole of Greek and Roman history, how many slaves' names are known to you? I can think of two, or possibly three. One is Spartacus and the other is Epictetus. Also, in the Roman room at the British Museum there is a glass jar with the maker's name inscribed on the bottom, 'Felix fecit'. I have a mental picture of poor Felix (a Gaul with red hair and a metal collar round his neck), but in fact he may not have been a slave; so there are only two slaves whose names I definitely know, and probably few people can remember more. The rest have gone down into utter silence.

5

THE backbone of the resistance against Franco was the Spanish working class, especially the urban trade union members. In the long run – it is important to remember that it is only in the long run – the working class remains the most reliable enemy of Fascism, simply because the working class stands to gain most by a decent reconstruction of society. Unlike other classes or categories, it can't be permanently bribed.

To say this is not to idealize the working class. In the long struggle that has followed the Russian Revolution it is the manual workers who have been defeated, and it is impossible not to feel that it was their own fault. Time after time, in country after country, the organized working-class movements have been crushed by open, illegal violence, and their comrades abroad, linked to them in theoretical solidarity, have simply looked on and done nothing; and underneath this, secret cause of many betrayals, has lain the fact that between white and coloured workers there is not even lip-service to solidarity. Who can believe in the class-conscious international proletariat after the events of the past ten years? To the British working class the massacre of their comrades in Vienna, Berlin, Madrid, or wherever it might be seemed less interesting and less important than yesterday's football match. Yet this does not alter the fact that the working class will go on struggling against Fascism after the others have caved in. One feature of the Nazi conquest of France was the astonishing defections among the intelligentsia, including some of the left-wing political intelligentsia. The intelligentsia are the people who squeal loudest against Fascism, and yet a respectable proportion of them collapse into defeatism when the pinch comes. They are far-sighted enough to see the odds against them, and moroeover they can be bribed – for it is evident that the Nazis think it worth while to bribe intellectuals. With the working class it is the other way about. Too ignorant to see through the trick that is being played on them, they easily swallow the promises of Fascism, yet sooner or later they always take up the struggle again. They must do so, because in their own bodies they always discover that the promises of Fascism cannot be fulfilled. To win over the working class permanently, the Fascists would have to raise the general standard of living, which they are unable and probably unwilling to do. The struggle of the working class is like the growth of a plant. The plant is blind and stupid, but it knows enough to keep pushing upwards towards the light, and it will do this in the face of endless discouragements. What are the workers struggling for? Simply for the decent life which they are more and more aware is now technically possible. Their consciousness of this aim ebbs and flows. In Spain, for a while, people were acting consciously, moving towards a goal which they wanted to reach and believed they could reach. It accounted for the curiously buoyant feeling that life in Government Spain had during the early months of the war. The common people knew in their bones that the Republic was their friend and Franco was their enemy. They knew that they were in the right, because they were fighting for something which the world owed them and was able to give them.

One has to remember this to see the Spanish war in its true perspective. When one thinks of the cruelty, squalor, and futility of war – and in this particular case of the intrigues, the persecutions, the lies and the misunderstandings – there is always the temptation to say: 'One side is as bad as the other. I am neutral.' In practice, however, one cannot be neutral, and there is hardly such a thing as a war in which it makes no difference who wins. Nearly always one stands more or less for progress, the other side more or less for reaction. The hatred which the Spanish Republic excited in millionaires, dukes, cardinals, play-boys, Blimps, and whatnot would in itself be enough to show one how the land lay. In essence it was a class war. If it had been won, the cause of the common people everywhere would have been strengthened. It was lost, and the dividend-drawers all over the world rubbed their hands. That was the real issue; all else was froth on its surface.

6

THE outcome of the Spanish war was settled in London, Paris, Rome, Berlin – at any rate not in Spain. After the summer of 1937 those with eyes in their heads realized that the Government could not win the war unless there were some profound change in the international set-up, and in deciding to fight on Negrín and the others may have been partly influenced by the expectation that the world war which actually broke out in 1939 was coming in 1938. The much-publicized disunity on the Government side was not a main cause of defeat. The Government militias were hurriedly raised, ill-armed and unimaginative in their military outlook, but they would have been the same if complete political agreement had existed from the start. At the outbreak of war the average Spanish factory-worker did not even know how to fire a rifle (there had never been universal conscription in Spain), and the traditional pacifism of the Left was a great handicap. The thousands of foreigners who served in Spain made good infantry, but there were very few experts of any kind among them. The Trotskyist thesis that the war could have been won if the revolution had not been sabotaged was probably false. To nationalize factories, demolish churches, and issue revolutionary manifestoes would not have made the armies more efficient. The Fascists won because they were the stronger; they had modern arms and the others hadn't. No political strategy could offset that.

The most baffling thing in the Spanish war was the behaviour of the great powers. The war was actually won for Franco by the Germans and Italians, whose motives were obvious enough. The motives of France and Britain are less easy to understand. In 1936 it was clear to everyone that if Britain would only help the Spanish Government, even to the extent of a few million pounds' worth of arms, Franco would collapse and German strategy would be severely dislocated. By that time one did not need to be a clairvoyant to foresee that war between Britain and Germany was coming; one could even foretell within a year or two when it would come. Yet in the most mean, cowardly, hypocritical way the British ruling class did all they could to hand Spain over to Franco and the Nazis. Why? Because they were pro-Fascist, was the obvious answer. Undoubtedly they were, and yet when it came to the final showdown they chose to stand up to Germany. It is still very uncertain what plan they acted on in backing Franco, and they may have had no clear plan at all. Whether the British ruling class are wicked or merely stupid is one of the most difficult questions of our time, and at certain moments a very important question. As to the Russians, their motives in the Spanish war are completely inscrutable. Did they, as the pinks believed, intervene in Spain in order to defend Democracy and thwart the Nazis? Then why did they intervene on such a niggardly scale and finally leave Spain in the lurch? Or did they, as the Catholics maintained, intervene in order to foster revolution in Spain? Then why did they do all in their power to crush the Spanish revolutionary movements, defend private property and hand power to the middle class as against the working class? Or did they, as the Trotskyists suggested, intervene simply in order to *prevent* a Spanish revolution? Then why not have backed Franco? Indeed, their actions are most easily explained if one assumes that they were acting on several contradictory motives. I believe that in the future we shall come to feel that Stalin's foreign policy, instead of being so diabolically clever as it is claimed to be, has been merely opportunistic and stupid. But at any rate, the Spanish civil war demonstrated that the Nazis knew what they were doing and their opponents did not. The war was fought at a low technical level and its major strategy was very simple. That side which had arms would win. The Nazis and the Italians gave arms to the Spanish Fascist friends, and the western democracies and the Russians didn't give arms to those who should have been their friends. So the Spanish Republic perished, having 'gained what no republic missed'.

Whether it was right, as all left-wingers in other countries undoubtedly did, to encourage the Spaniards to go on fighting when they could not win is a question hard to answer. I myself think it was right, because I believe that it is better even from the point of view of survival to fight and be conquered than to surrender without fighting. The effects on the grand strategy of the struggle against Fascism cannot be assessed yet. The ragged, weaponless armies of the Republic held out for two and a half years, which was undoubtedly longer than their enemies expected. But whether that dislocated the Fascist timetable, or whether, on the other hand, it merely postponed the major war and gave the Nazis extra time to get their war machine into trim, is still uncertain.

7

I NEVER think of the Spanish war without two memories coming into my mind. One is of the hospital ward at Lerida and the rather sad voices of the wounded militiamen singing some song with a refrain that ended –

Una resolucion,
Luchar hast' al fin!

Well, they fought to the end all right. For the last eighteen months of the war the Republican armies must have been fighting almost without cigarettes, and with precious little food. Even when I left Spain in the middle of 1937, meat and bread were scarce, tobacco a rarity, coffee and sugar almost unobtainable.

The other memory is of the Italian militiaman who shook my hand in the guardroom, the day I joined the militia. I wrote about this man at the beginning of my book on the Spanish war,* and do not want to repeat what I said there. When I remember – oh, how vividly! – his shabby uniform and fierce, pathetic, innocent face, the complex side-issues of the war seem to fade away and I see clearly that there was at any rate no doubt as to who was in the right. In spite of power politics and journalistic lying, the central issue of the war was the attempt of people like this to win the decent life which they knew to be their birthright. It is difficult to think of this particular man's probable end without several kinds of bitterness. Since I met him in the Lenin Barracks he was probably a Trotskyist or an Anarchist, and in the peculiar conditions of our time, when people of that sort are not killed by the Gestapo they are usually killed by the G.P.U. But that does not affect the long-term issues. This man's face, which I saw only for a minute or two, remains with me as a sort of visual reminder of what the war was really about. He symbolizes for me the flower of the European working class, harried by the police of all countries, the people who fill the mass graves of the Spanish battlefields and are now, to the tune of several millions, rotting in forced-labour camps.

When one thinks of all the people who support or have supported Fascism, one stands amazed at their diversity. What a crew! Think of a programme which at any rate for a while could bring Hitler, Pétain, Montagu Norman, Pavelitch, William Randolph Hearst, Streicher, Buchman, Ezra Pound, Juan March, Cocteau, Thyssen, Father Coughlin, the Mufti of Jerusalem, Arnold Lunn, Antonescu, Spengler, Beverley Nichols, Lady Houston, and Marinetti all into the same boat! But the clue is really very simple. They are all people with something to lose, or people who long for a hierarchical society and dread the prospect of a world of free and equal human beings. Behind all the ballyhoo that is talked about 'godless' Russia and the 'materialism' of the working class lies the simple intention of those with money or privileges to cling to them. Ditto, though it contains a partial truth, with all the talk about the worthlessness of social reconstruction not accompanied by a 'change of heart'. The pious ones, from the Pope to the yogis of California, are great on the 'change of heart', much more reassuring from their point of view than a change in the economic system. Pétain attributes the fall of France to the common people's 'love of pleasure'. One sees this in its right

* *Homage to Catalonia*

perspective if one stops to wonder how much pleasure the ordinary French peasant's or working man's life would contain compared with Pétain's own. The damned impertinence of these politicians, priests, literary men, and whatnot who lecture the working-class socialist for his 'materialism'! All that the working man demands is what these others would consider the indispensable minimum without which human life cannot be lived at all. Enough to eat, freedom from the haunting terror of unemployment, the knowledge that your children will get a fair chance, a bath once a day, clean linen reasonably often, a roof that doesn't leak, and short enough working hours to leave you with a little energy when the day is done. Not one of those who preach against 'materialism' would consider life livable without these things. And how easily that minimum could be attained if we chose to set our minds to it for only twenty years! To raise the standard of living of the whole world to that of Britain would not be a greater undertaking than the war we have just fought. I don't claim, and I don't know who does, that that wouldn't solve anything in itself. It is merely that privation and brute labour have to be abolished before the real problems of humanity can be tackled. The major problem of our time is the decay of the belief in personal immortality, and it cannot be dealt with while the average human being is either drudging like an ox or shivering in fear of the secret police. How right the working classes are in their 'materialism'! How right they are to realize that the belly comes before the soul, not in the scale of values but in point of time! Understand that, and the long horror that we are enduring becomes at least intelligible. All the considerations are likely to make one falter – the siren voices of a Pétain or of a Gandhi, the inescapable fact that in order to fight one has to degrade oneself, the equivocal moral position of Britain, with its democratic phrases and its coolie empire, the sinister development of Soviet Russia, the squalid farce of left-wing politics – all this fades away and one sees only the struggle of the gradually awakening common people against the lords of property and their hired liars and bumsuckers. The question is very simple. Shall people like that Italian soldier be allowed to live the decent, fully human life which is now technically achievable, or shan't they? Shall the common man be pushed back into the mud, or shall he not? I myself believe, perhaps on insufficient grounds, that the common man will win his fight sooner or later, but I want it to be sooner and not later – some time within the next hundred years, say, and not some time within the next ten thousand years. That was the real issue of the Spanish war, and of the last war, and perhaps of other wars yet to come.

I never saw the Italian militiaman again, nor did I ever learn his name.

It can be taken as quite certain that he is dead. Nearly two years later, when the war was visibly lost, I wrote these verses in his memory:

> The Italian soldier shook my hand
> Beside the guard-room table;
> The strong hand and the subtle hand
> Whose palm are only able
>
> To meet within the sound of guns,
> But oh! what peace I knew then
> In gazing on his battered face
> Purer than any woman's!
>
> For the flyblown words that make me spew
> Still in his ears were holy,
> And he was born knowing what I had learned
> Out of books and slowly.
>
> The treacherous guns had told their tale
> And we both had bought it,
> But my gold brick was made of gold –
> Oh! who ever would have thought it?
>
> Good luck go with you, Italian soldier!
> But luck is not for the brave;
> What would the world give back to you?
> Always less than you gave.
>
> Between the shadow and the ghost,
> Between the white and the red,
> Between the bullet and the lie,
> Where would you hide your head?
>
> For where is Manuel Gonzalez,
> And where is Pedro Aguilar,
> And where is Ramon Fenellosa?
> The earthworms know where they are.
>
> Your name and your deeds were forgotten
> Before your bones were dry,
> And the lie that slew you is buried
> Under a deeper lie;
>
> But the thing I saw in your face
> No power can disinherit:
> No bomb that ever burst
> Shatters the crystal spirit.

1943